Debating the Earth

Debating the Earth

The Environmental Politics Reader

Edited by John S. Dryzek and David Schlosberg

OXFORD UNIVERSITY PRESS
1998

Oxford University Press, Great Clarendon Street, Oxford OX2 6DP

Oxford New York

Athens Auckland Bangkok Bogota Bombay Buenos Aires
Calcutta Cape Town Dar es Salaam Delhi Florence Hong Kong Istanbul
Karachi Kuala Lumpur Madras Madrid Melbourne Mexico City
Nairobi Paris Singapore Taipei Tokyo Toronto Warsaw
and associated companies in
Berlin Ibadan

Oxford is a registered trade mark of Oxford University Press

Published in the United States
by Oxford University Press Inc., New York

Introduction and selection © Oxford University Press 1998

First published 1998

British Library Cataloguing in Publication Data
Data available

Library of Congress Cataloging in Publication Data

Debating the earth : the environmental politics reader / edited by
  John S. Dryzek and David Schlosberg.
    Includes bibliographical references.
    1. Environmental policy.   I. Dryzek, John S., 1953–   .
  II. Schlosberg, David.
  GE170.D43   1998 363.7′05—dc21   98-6477 CIP
ISBN 0–19–878228–4
ISBN 0–19–878227–6 (Pbk.)

Typeset by Best-set Typesetter Ltd., Hong Kong
Printed in Great Britain
on acid-free paper by Bookcraft (Bath) Ltd
Midsomer Norton, Somerset

Acknowledgements

This reader represents our conception of what a core set of readings in environmental politics should look like. Our judgements have been informed by many people who shared with us their ideas, suggestions, and syllabi: notably, Jane Bennett, David Carruthers, Robert Garner, Adolf Gundersen, Robert Goodin, Tim Hayward, Andrew Light, Albert Matheny, Michael McGinnis, James O'Connor, Daniel Press, Bob Taylor, Bron Taylor, and Leslie Thiele. Tim Barton of Oxford University Press helped to guide this project from conception to fruition. Graduate Assistant Paul Vaughn is to be commended for his editorial assistance. Finally we thank our students at the University of Oregon, Northern Arizona University, and the University of Melbourne, upon whom many of these readings have been field tested.

J.S.D. and D.S.

Contents

PART THREE
ENVIRONMENT AND ECONOMICS

PART FOUR
GREEN SOCIAL CRITIQUES

PART FIVE
SOCIETY, THE STATE, AND THE ENVIRONMENT

List of Figures

List of Tables

Introduction

John S. Dryzek and David Schlosberg

The Emergence of Environmental Politics

Environmental politics is about how humanity organizes itself to relate to the nature that sustains it. Thus it encompasses matters of how people deal with the planet and its life, and how they relate to each other through the medium of the environment. It impinges on other areas of political concern such as those related to poverty, education, race, the economy, international relations, and human rights inasmuch as what happens in these areas affects our environment (and vice versa). Environmental politics has in the past 30 years come from nowhere to constitute what is now a large, lively, burgeoning and diverse field, which we survey in this reader.

The issues which we now group under the environmental heading emerged sporadically in the first six decades of the twentieth century. Early German ideas about conservation biology crossed the Atlantic to inform the development of a doctrine of resource conservation, which developed alongside a very different American tradition of reverence for wilderness. Meanwhile concern grew over health and cleanliness in cities and workplaces. Europeans too concerned themselves with issues of public health, and tended to emphasize access to open space rather than wilderness, of which they had none.

'The environment' as a collective name for all these concerns arrived in the 1960s, which dates the beginning of environmental politics as such. Since then, the growth of environmental literature has matched the growth of environmental concern, which has spread to the Third World and the global system itself. Particular concerns have featured energy shortages, toxic wastes, air and water pollution, the hazards of nuclear power, biotechnology, species extinction, pesticides, animal rights, wilderness protection, climate change, and inequality in the distribution of environmental risks and benefits. Environmental politics today encompasses discussions of the various political, social, and economic causes of ecological problems and crises; the ethics of our relationship with the natural systems that sustain us; our environmental relationships with our fellow-humans; environmental movements; and designs for alternative, more sustainable forms of political organization.

We present here a text that highlights the diversity of political responses to environmental crisis. We look at the various definitions of environmental crisis (including its denial), its causes and effects, and institutional, policy, lifestyle, and community organizing responses to environmental problems.

Environmental politics has a broad scope. For the purposes of this reader, we delimit it a bit more precisely. This is not a reader on environmental policy as such, though numerous policy issues—including land and river basin management, pollution control, environmental impact assessment, wilderness protection, hazardous waste management, and corporate accountabil-ity—will enter the discussion. Nor is this a reader on environmental philosophy or ethics, though discussions of ecocentric values, deep ecology, social ecology, and ecofeminism are included, with a view to their political ramifications. And this is not a reader on environmental economics, though issues of economic sustainability, resource privatization, and the en-vironmental implications of capitalism will be discussed—again with an eye to their political aspects. Thus the realms of environmental policy, ethics, and economics are integral parts of our coverage, though mainly in their political dimensions and consequences.

Organization of this Collection

Our readings are organized in a way that highlights the differences and debates between the various schools of thought on environmental affairs. The reader is divided into five parts, representing five key axes of environmental debate. Each part is then broken down further into sections.

We begin in Part One with the debate over the reality and severity of the environmental crisis itself, which has now raged for three decades. Obviously the kind of environmental politics we do or should get depends a lot on the nature and severity of this crisis. In Section I we visit some classic and contemporary claims about the severity of global ecological limits to human activity, which have catastrophic consequences should we hit them. Section II covers counter-arguments to the effect that there are no limits which human ingenuity cannot overcome, such that in truth there is no environmental crisis, only a few environmental problems that can be dealt with quite easily.

Part Two covers two kinds of reformist responses to environmental issues. Section III focuses on the administrative management of the environment; while a less spectacular debate than that over global limits, this sort of management represents much if not most of what has actually been done by governments in the recent decades of environmental concern. Section IV focuses on attempts to expand public participation in environmental politics and management within the liberal democratic framework that characterizes most developed nations.

Part Three moves to the links between the environment and the economy, and how politics mediates and affects this link. Section V covers arguments to the effect that the free market is in truth the best protector of the environment, provided only that governments can arrange an appropriate specification of private property rights in natural resources and other environmen-tal goods. Section VI represents recent claims about the compatibility of economic growth, envi-ronmental protection, and social justice, provided that these values are subsumed under the concept of sustainable development. Adding precision to such claims, Section VII looks at the idea of ecological modernization, under which a re-tooling of the economy along ecologically sound lines proves beneficial to business and the economy as a whole.

In Part Four we look at some more radical interpretations of environmental crisis and what might be done about it. Section VIII covers deep ecology and bioregionalism, which trace the cause of environmental crisis to human alienation from nature, and offer solutions in the form of a deeper environmental consciousness, which will in turn require political change in the form of new kinds of human community. Section IX covers social and socialist ecology, which are inclined to see both causes and solutions in the realm of social, economic, and political structure, rather than contenting themselves with questions of deep consciousness. Section X on environmental justice looks at the fastest-growing part of the environmental movement in North America, examining its political critiques, principles, and practices, which turn on the unequal distribution of environmental risks.

Finally, Part Five addresses the possibilities for environmental action beyond the boundaries of the liberal state. Section XI looks at examples of green movement activities in civil society, a realm of political action that keeps its distance from state structures. We conclude in Section XII with an examination of the radical democratic potential of ecological politics.

In keeping with our emphasis on the debates in the field of environmental politics, we have in most of the sections included a critique of the line of argument represented therein. So in Section II Paul Ehrlich claims the Promethean denial of environmental crisis rests on bad science; in Section III Douglas Torgerson points to the limits of administrative rationalism; in Section IV William Ophuls offers a scathing critique of liberal democracy; in Section V Robert Goodin equates market instruments with selling indulgences to sin; in Section VI Herman Daly highlights problems with the idea of sustainable development in particular, and Vandana Shiva takes issue with development in general; and in Section VIII Martin Lewis claims that radical ecology rests on delusions. But debates rage across the sections as well as within them. Thus the liberal democratic proposals of Section IV emerge as correctives to perceived deficiencies in the administrative rationalism of Section III. The more radical democracy of Section XII and its associated movements discussed in Section XI expose the deficiencies of administrative rationalism and liberal democracy alike. The radical ecologies of Sections VIII and IX share this critique, and also have little time for the economic orientation of Sections VI and VII.

The way we have chosen to carve up the field corresponds to what we believe are the key faultlines in environmental politics. But we do not claim this is the only way to organize these debates. For example, we decided that ecofeminism does not fit neatly into one box, and indeed there are good reasons not to make a ghetto of it. Thus our ecofeminist selections are spread across four debates to which ecofeminist writings have contributed, rather than gathered under a single heading. Additionally, some of our authors might make a case for different company than that we have assigned to them. For example, Andrew Dobson's discussion of green strategies which we have put in Section XI on green movements also speaks to green action in liberal democracy as discussed in Section IV. Ulrich Beck's article can be located in the modernization debate, which is why we include it in Section VII, but Beck himself is quite critical of the kinds of proposals that are often made under the heading of ecological modernization, and his own political sympathies lie more with the ecological democrats of Section XII.

Finally, while we have aspired to a degree of comprehensiveness in our coverage, the sheer size and diversity of the environmental politics field means that we have had to leave out many valuable contributions to the literature. Such is the nature of a reader of this sort. To compensate for these exclusions, in the introduction to each section we have included suggestions for further reading that extends or responds to the themes of the section.

PART ONE

FEAST OR FAMINE? THE SEVERITY OF ENVIRONMENTAL PROBLEMS

Environmental issues have long histories. But the atmosphere of general environmental crisis first perceived in the 1960s and its associated social movements precipitated an avalanche of environmental writing. From Rachel Carson's *Silent Spring* in 1962 to Lois Gibbs's recent *Dying from Dioxin* (1995), many writers have addressed the ways in which the modern industrial world has encountered environmental crises, ranging from resource exhaustion to species extinction to endangered human health. But one thing is constant in the realm of environmental politics: where there are critiques and doomsayers, there are sure to be counter-arguments and cornucopians. Part One offers both some classic and contemporary arguments in this long debate about the severity of environmental problems—the necessary precursor to arguments about political responses to environmental crisis.

Section I: Limits and Survivalism

The 1970s are known to both supporters and critics of environmentalism as 'The Doomsday Decade'. With a growing interest in the effects of growth and industrialization, a number of gloomy publications came out during this period—books with titles such as *The Last Days of Mankind* (1974), *The Death of Tomorrow* (1972), *Terracide* (1970), *The Doomsday Syndrome* (1972), *The Doomsday Book* (1970), *The Coming Dark Age* (1973), *This Endangered Planet* (1972), etc. A quote from *Blueprint for Survival* (1972) gives an example of the mood of the time: 'If current trends are allowed to persist, the breakdown of society and the irreversible disruption of the life-support systems on this planet, possibly by the end of the century, certainly within the lifetimes of our children, are inevitable.'

Most of these works are full of serious, full-scale attacks on the various practices of modern economic life in the advanced industrialized countries, especially land and resource use, pollution, and various types of waste. The basic argument is simple: modern economic life assumes that growth and expansion can go on without limits, while the planet is made up of systems of finite resources that are threatened and carrying capacities that we are in danger of overshooting. All three of our selections in this section argue that, unless changed, modern patterns of growth and development will lead to ecological collapse.

The first of the selections here, from the Club of Rome's classic *Limits to Growth* (1972), is not a product of the stereotypical environmental activists of the late 1960s; rather, the research was conducted by an international research team at MIT, using complex computer modelling techniques. The piece we have chosen focuses on the concept of *exponential* growth, in order to demonstrate the quickly increasing nature of environmental problems—including the growth of population and the depletion of natural resources. The argument here is that limits are looming: either the continuation of existing patterns of industrialization and growth will lead to ecosystem collapse, or we need to develop self-imposed restraints on our actions to avoid such a catastrophe.

Like the Club of Rome, Garrett Hardin's essay on 'The Tragedy of the Commons', also argues that business as usual in regard to natural resources and the environment will lead to a collapse of ecosystems. But rather than focus on the nature of growth, Hardin's critique centres on how the rational self-interested actions of individuals lead to devastating collective consequences. While many have criticized Hardin's lack of understanding of the communitarian nature of true commons management, his argument holds true to the ways natural resources are currently treated in the market economy. Hardin is well-known not only for this commons analysis, but also for his suggested solution: 'mutual coercion mutually agreed upon'. His authoritarian prescriptions are a precursor to some later critiques of democratic management of environmental problems.

Finally, to demonstrate that concern with catastrophic ecological collapse is not something left behind in the Doomsday Decade, we offer a piece, co-authored by prominent economists and ecologists, that reiterates some of the same concerns with growth and carrying capacity two decades later. Kenneth Arrow and his co-authors represent the emerging field of ecological economics (not to be confused with the more conventional field of environmental economics, which makes an appearance in Section V). They argue that all economic activity ultimately depends on the health of the environment in which it is embedded. In order to avoid the collapse of both economy and ecology, institutions must be designed to protect the latter.

Further Reading

In addition to the original *Limits To Growth* (and its 1992 update, *Beyond the Limits*), the *Blueprint for Survival* (1972), by Edward Goldsmith and the other editors of Britain's *The Ecologist* magazine, is one of the classic doomsday critiques of the modern industrial order's effects on ecological stability. It is also one of the few works in the limits literature that proposes a decentralized political approach to the crisis. In the USA, the 1981 *Global 2000 Report to the President* (at that time the equally gloomy Jimmy Carter), finished the doomsday decade with a prediction of ecological collapse 'if present trends continue . . .'. William Catton's *Overshoot* (1980) also stands out as one of the classics of the era. Finally, the annual *State of the World* volumes put out by Lester Brown and the Worldwatch Institute continue to remind us of perennial indicators of ecological catastrophe. The *Limits to Growth* thesis met an early trenchant critique in H. S. D. Cole et al., *Models of Doom: A Critique of the Limits to Growth* (1973). Unrepentant survivalists writing in the 1990s include Robert Heilbroner, *An Inquiry into the Human Prospect: Looked at Again for the 1990s* (1991) and Garrett Hardin, *Living Within Limits: Ecology, Economics, and Population* (1993).

The origins of ecological economics may be found in Nicholas Georgescu-Roegen's *Energy and Economic Myths* (1976) and Herman Daly's *Toward a Steady-State Economy* (1973), which is updated in his *Valuing the Earth* (1993).

While touched on here briefly by both the Club of Rome and the Hardin selections, population growth is one of the key issues of the limits literature. The classic work is Paul Ehrlich's *Population Bomb* (1968). That book, and the response by Francis Moore Lappé and Joseph Collins in *Food First* (1977) spawned the continuing argument (which we return to in Part Four) over whether it is population per se, or the social organization and condition of that population, that leads to the threat of ecological collapse. Many have criticized Hardin's understanding of the management of the commons; the most thorough is Elinor Ostrom's *Governing the Commons* (1990), which lays out more cooperative and discursive methods of commons management, in contrast to Hardin's focus on the need for central power to squash individual interest.

The most forceful criticisms of the literature of limits, however, are to be found in the writings of the Prometheans and Cornucopians, who deny the reality of ecological limits. We turn to these authors in the following section.

1   The Nature of Exponential Growth

Donella H. Meadows, Dennis L. Meadows, Jørgen Randers, and William H. Behrens III

People at present think that five sons are not too many and each son has five sons also, and before the death of the grandfather there are already 25 descendants. Therefore people are more and wealth is less; they work hard and receive little.

(Han Fei-Tzu, *c.*500 BC)

All five elements basic to the study reported here—population, food production, industrialization, pollution, and consumption of nonrenewable natural resources—are increasing. The amount of their increase each year follows a pattern that mathematicians call exponential growth. Nearly all of mankind's current activities, from use of fertilizer to expansion of cities, can be represented by exponential growth curves (see Figures 1.1 and 1.2). Since much of this book deals with the causes and implications of exponential growth curves, it is important to begin with an understanding of their general characteristics.

The Mathematics of Exponential Growth

Most people are accustomed to thinking of growth as a *linear* process. A quantity is growing linearly when it increases by a constant amount in a constant time period. For example, a child who becomes one inch taller each year is growing linearly. If a miser hides $10 each year under his mattress, his horde of money is also increasing in a linear way. The amount of increase each year is obviously not affected by the size of the child nor the amount of money already under the mattress.

A quantity exhibits *exponential* growth when it increases by a constant percentage of the whole in a constant time period. A colony of yeast cells in which each cell divides into two cells every 10 minutes is growing exponentially. For each single cell, after 10 minutes there will be two cells, an increase of 100 percent . After the next 10 minutes there will be four cells, then eight, then sixteen. If a miser takes $100 from his mattress and invests it at 7 percent (so that the total amount accumulated increases by 7 percent each year), the invested money will grow much faster than the linearly increasing stock under the mattress (see Figure 1.3). The amount added each year to a bank account or each 10 minutes to a yeast colony is not constant. It contin-

From Donella H. Meadows, Dennis L. Meadows, Jørgen Randers, William H. Behrens III, *The Limits to Growth* (New York: Universe Books, 1972), 25–44. Reprinted with permission of Universe Publishing.

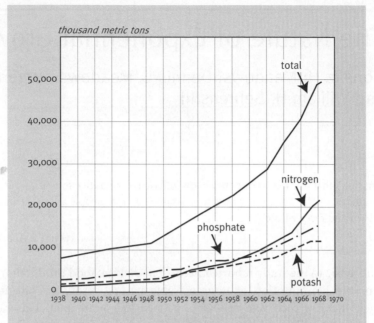

Fig. 1.1 **World fertilizer consumption. World fertilizer consumption is increasing exponentially, with a doubling time of about 10 years. Total use is now five times greater than it was during World War II.**

Note: Figures do not include the USSR or the People's Republic of China.
Source: UN Department of Economic and Social Affairs, *Statistical Yearbook 1955*, *Statistical Yearbook 1960*, and *Statistical Yearbook 1970* (New York: United Nations, 1956, 1961, and 1971).

ually increases, as the total accumulated amount increases. Such exponential growth is a common process in biological, financial, and many other systems of the world.

Common as it is, exponential growth can yield surprising results—results that have fascinated mankind for centuries. There is an old Persian legend about a clever courtier who presented a beautiful chessboard to his king and requested that the king give him in return 1 grain of rice for the first square on the board, 2 grains for the second square, 4 grains for the third, and so forth. The king readily agreed and ordered rice to be brought from his stores. The fourth square of the chessboard required 8 grains, the tenth square took 512 grains, the fifteenth required 16,384, and the twenty-first square gave the courtier more than a million grains of rice. By the fortieth square a million million rice grains had to be brought from the storerooms. The king's entire rice

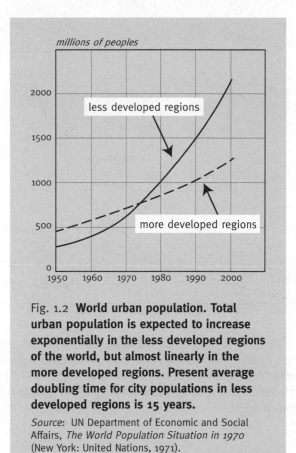

Fig. 1.2 **World urban population. Total urban population is expected to increase exponentially in the less developed regions of the world, but almost linearly in the more developed regions. Present average doubling time for city populations in less developed regions is 15 years.**

Source: UN Department of Economic and Social Affairs, *The World Population Situation in 1970* (New York: United Nations, 1971).

supply was exhausted long before he reached the sixty-fourth square. Exponential increase is deceptive because it generates immense numbers very quickly.

A French riddle for children illustrates another aspect of exponential growth—the apparent suddenness with which it approaches a fixed limit. Suppose you own a pond on which a water lily is growing. The lily plant doubles in size each day. If the lily were allowed to grow unchecked, it would completely cover the pond in 30 days, choking off the other forms of life in the water. For a long time the lily plant seems small, and so you decide not to worry about cutting it back until it covers half the pond. On what day will that be? On the twenty-ninth day, of course. You have one day to save your pond.[1]

It is useful to think of exponential growth in terms of *doubling time*, or the time it takes a growing quantity to double in size. In the case of the lily plant described above, the doubling time is 1 day. A sum of money left in a bank at 7 percent interest will double in 10 years. There is a simple mathematical relationship between the interest rate, or rate of growth, and the time it

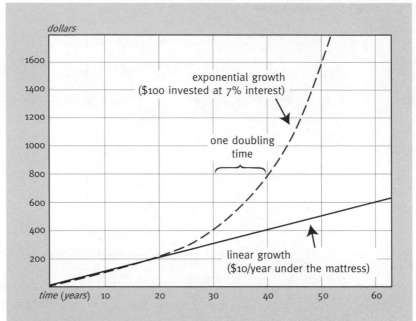

Fig. 1.3 The growth of savings. If a miser hides $10 each year under his mattress, his savings will grow linearly, as shown by the lower curve. If, after 10 years, he invests his $100 at 7 percent interest, that $100 will grow exponentially, with a doubling time of 10 years.

will take a quantity to double in size. The doubling time is approximately equal to 70 divided by the growth rate, as illustrated in Table 1.1.

Models and Exponential Growth

Exponential growth is a dynamic phenomenon, which means that it involves elements that change over time. In simple systems, like the bank account or the lily pond, the cause of exponential growth and its future course are relatively easy to understand. When many different quantities are growing simultaneously in a system, however, and when all the quantities are interrelated in a complicated way, analysis of the causes of growth and of the future behavior of the system becomes very difficult indeed. Does population growth cause industrialization or does industrialization cause population growth? Is either one singly responsible for increasing pollution, or are they both responsible? Will more food production result in more population? If any one of these elements grows slower or faster, what will happen to the growth rates of all the others? These very questions are being debated in many parts of the world today. The answers

Table 1.1 **Doubling time**

Growth rate (% per year)	Doubling time (years)
0.1	700
0.5	140
1.0	70
2.0	35
4.0	18
5.0	14
7.0	10
10.0	7

can be found through a better understanding of the entire complex system that unites all of these important elements.

Over the course of the last 30 years there has evolved at the Massachusetts Institute of Technology a new method for understanding the dynamic behavior of complex systems. The method is called System Dynamics.[2] The basis of the method is the recognition that the *structure* of any system—the many circular, interlocking, sometimes time-delayed relationships among its components—is often just as important in determining its behavior as the individual components themselves. The world model described in this book is a System Dynamics model.

Dynamic modeling theory indicates that any exponentially growing quantity is somehow involved with a *positive feedback loop*. A positive feedback loop is sometimes called a "vicious circle." An example is the familiar wage-price spiral—wages increase, which causes prices to increase, which leads to demands for higher wages, and so forth. In a positive feedback loop a chain of cause-and-effect relationships closes on itself, so that increasing any one element in the loop will start a sequence of changes that will result in the originally changed element being increased even more.

The positive feedback loop that accounts for exponential increase of money in a bank account is represented in Figure 1.4.

Suppose $100 is deposited in the account. The first year's interest is 7 percent of $100, or $7, which is added to the account, making the total $107. The next year's interest is 7 percent of $107, or $7.49, which makes a new total of $114.49. One year later the interest on that amount will be more than $8.00. The more money there is in the account, the more money will be added each year in interest. The more is added, the more there will be in the account the next year causing even more to be added in interest. And so on. As we go around and around the loop, the accumulated money in the account grows exponentially. The rate of interest (constant at 7 percent) determines the gain around the loop, or the rate at which the bank account grows.

We can begin our dynamic analysis of the long-term world situation by looking for the positive feedback loops underlying the exponential growth in the five physical quantities we have already mentioned. In particular, the growth rates of two of these elements—population and

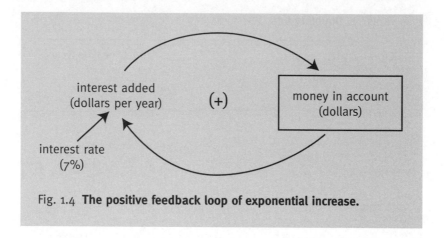

Fig. 1.4 **The positive feedback loop of exponential increase.**

industrialization—are of interest, since the goal of many development policies is to encourage the growth of the latter relative to the former. The two basic positive feedback loops that account for exponential population and industrial growth are simple in principle. We will describe their basic structures in the next few pages. The many interconnections between these two positive feedback loops act to amplify or to diminish the action of the loops, to couple or uncouple the growth rates of population and of industry. These interconnections constitute the rest of the world model and their description will occupy much of the rest of this book.

World Population Growth

The exponential growth curve of world population is shown in Figure 1.5. In 1650 the population numbered about 0.5 billion,[3] and it was growing at a rate of approximately 0.3 percent per year.[4] That corresponds to a doubling time of nearly 250 years. In 1970 the population totaled 3.6 billion and the rate of growth was 2.1 percent per year.[5] The doubling time at this growth rate is 33 years. Thus, not only has the population been growing exponentially, but the rate of growth has also been growing. We might say that population growth has been "super"-exponential; the population curve is rising even faster than it would if growth were strictly exponential.

The feedback loop structure that represents the dynamic behavior of population growth is shown in Figure 1.6. On the left is the positive feedback loop that accounts for the observed exponential growth. In a population with constant average fertility, the larger the population, the more babies will be born each year. The more babies, the larger the population will be the following year. After a delay to allow those babies to grow up and become parents, even more babies will be born, swelling the population still further. Steady growth will continue as long as average fertility remains constant. If, in addition to sons, each woman has on the average two female children, for example, and each of them grows up to have two more female children, the population will double each generation. The growth rate will depend on both the average fertility and the length of the delay between generations. Fertility is not necessarily constant, of course.

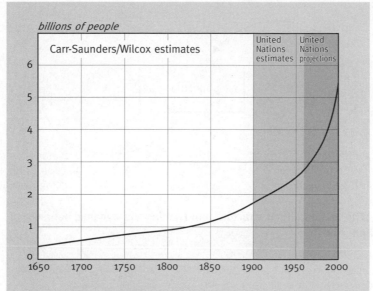

billions of people

Carr-Saunders/Wilcox estimates

United Nations estimates

United Nations projections

Fig. 1.5 **World population. World population since 1650 has been growing exponentially at an increasing rate. Estimated population in 1970 is already slightly higher than the projection illustrated here (which was made in 1958). The present world population growth rate is about 2.1 percent per year, corresponding to a doubling time of 33 years.**

Source: Donald J. Bogue, *Principles of Demography* (New York: John Wiley and Sons, 1969).

There is another feedback loop governing population growth, shown on the right side of the diagram in Figure 1.6. It is a *negative feedback loop*. Whereas positive feedback loops generate runaway growth, negative feedback loops tend to regulate growth and to hold a system in some stable state. They behave much as a thermostat does in controlling the temperature of a room. If the temperature falls, the thermostat activates the heating system, which causes the temperature to rise again. When the temperature reaches its limit, the thermostat cuts off the heating system, and the temperature begins to fall again. In a negative feedback loop a change in one element is propagated around the circle until it comes back to change that element in a direction *opposite* to the initial change.

The negative feedback loop controlling population is based upon average mortality, a reflection of the general health of the population. The number of deaths each year is equal to the total population times the average mortality (which we might think of as the average probability of death at any age). An increase in the size of a population with constant average mortality will result in more deaths per year. More deaths will leave fewer people in the population, and so

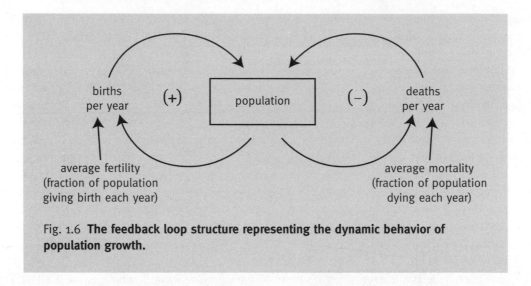

Fig. 1.6 **The feedback loop structure representing the dynamic behavior of population growth.**

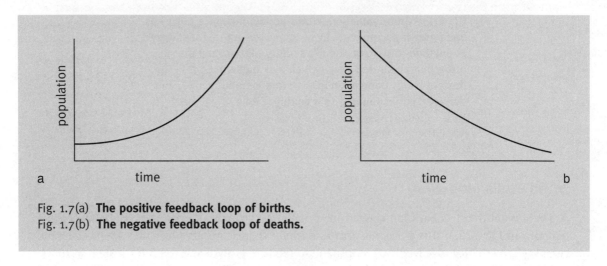

Fig. 1.7(a) **The positive feedback loop of births.**
Fig. 1.7(b) **The negative feedback loop of deaths.**

there will be fewer deaths the next year. If on the average 5 percent of the population dies each year, there will be 500 deaths in a population of 10,000 in one year. Assuming no births for the moment, that would leave 9,500 people the next year. If the probability of death is still 5 percent, there will be only 475 deaths in this smaller population, leaving 9,025 people. The next year there will be only 452 deaths. Again, there is a delay in this feedback loop because the mortality rate is a function of the average age of the population. Also, of course, mortality even at a given age is not necessarily constant.

If there were no deaths in a population, it would grow exponentially by the positive feedback loop of births, as shown in Figure 1.7(a). If there were no births, the population would decline to zero because of the negative feedback loop of deaths, also as shown in Figure 1.7(b). Since every real population experiences both births and deaths, as well as varying fertility and mortality, the dynamic behavior of populations governed by these two interlocking feedback loops can become fairly complicated.

What has caused the recent super-exponential rise in world population? Before the Industrial Revolution both fertility and mortality were comparatively high and irregular. The birth rate generally exceeded the death rate only slightly, and population grew exponentially, but at a very slow and uneven rate. In 1650 the average lifetime of most populations in the world was only about 30 years. Since then, mankind has developed many practices that have had profound effects on the population growth system, especially on mortality rates. With the spread of modern medicine, public health techniques, and new methods of growing and distributing foods, death rates have fallen around the world. World average life expectancy is currently about 53 years[6] and still rising. On a world average the gain around the positive feedback loop (fertility) has decreased only slightly while the gain around the negative feedback loop (mortality) is decreasing. The result is an increasing dominance of the positive feedback loop and the sharp exponential rise in population pictured in Figure 1.5.

What about the population of the future? How might we extend the population curve of Figure 1.5 into the twenty-first century? For the moment we can safely conclude that because of the delays in the controlling feedback loops, especially the positive loop of births, there is no possibility of leveling off the population growth curve before the year 2000, even with the most optimistic assumption of decreasing fertility. Most of the prospective parents of the year 2000 have already been born. Unless there is a sharp rise in mortality, which mankind will certainly strive mightily to avoid, we can look forward to a world population of around 7 billion persons in 30 more years. And if we continue to succeed in lowering mortality with no better success in lowering fertility than we have accomplished in the past, in 60 years there will be four people in the world for every one person living today.

World Economic Growth

A second quantity that has been increasing in the world even faster than human population is industrial output. Figure 1.8 shows the expansion of world industrial production since 1930, with 1963 production as the base of reference. The average growth rate from 1963 to 1968 was 7 percent per year, or 5 percent per year on a per capita basis.

What is the positive feedback loop that accounts for exponential growth of industrial output? The dynamic structure, in Figure 1.9, is actually very similar to the one we have already described for the population system.

With a given amount of industrial capital (factories, trucks, tools, machines, etc.), a certain amount of manufactured output each year is possible. The output actually produced is also dependent on labor, raw materials, and other inputs. For the moment we will assume that these other inputs are sufficient, so that capital is the limiting factor in production. (The world model does include these other inputs.) Much of each year's output is consumable goods, such as textiles, automobiles, and houses, that leave the industrial system. But some fraction of the production is more capital—looms, steel mills, lathes—which is an investment to increase the capital

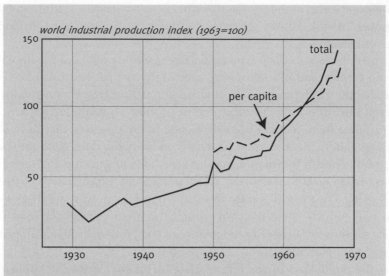

Fig. 1.8 **World industrial production. World industrial production, relative to the base year 1963, also shows a clear exponential increase despite small fluctuations. The 1963–8 average growth rate of total production is 7 percent per year. The per capita growth rate is 5 percent per year.**

Sources: UN Department of Economic and Social Affairs, *Statistical Yearbook 1956* and *Statistical Yearbook 1969* (New York: United Nations, 1957 and 1970).

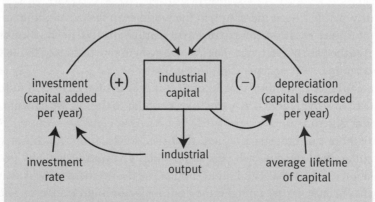

Fig. 1.9 **Positive feedback loop accounting for exponential growth of industrial output.**

stock. Here we have another positive feedback loop. More capital creates more output, some variable fraction of the output is investment, and more investment means more capital. The new, larger capital stock generates even more output, and so on. There are also delays in this feedback loop, since the production of a major piece of industrial capital, such as an electrical generating plant or a refinery, can take several years.

Capital stock is not permanent. As capital wears out or becomes obsolete, it is discarded. To model this situation we must introduce into the capital system a negative feedback loop accounting for capital depreciation. The more capital there is, the more wears out on the average each year; and the more that wears out, the less there will be the next year. This negative feedback loop is exactly analogous to the death rate loop in the population system. As in the population system, the positive loop is strongly dominant in the world today, and the world's industrial capital stock is growing exponentially.

Since industrial output is growing at 7 percent per year and population only at 2 percent per year, it might appear that dominant positive feedback loops are a cause for rejoicing. Simple extrapolation of those growth rates would suggest that the material standard of living of the world's people will double within the next 14 years. Such a conclusion, however, often includes the implicit assumption that the world's growing industrial output is evenly distributed among the world's citizens. The fallacy of this assumption can be appreciated when the per capita economic growth rates of some individual nations are examined (see Figure 1.10).

Most of the world's industrial growth plotted in Figure 1.8 is actually taking place in the already industrialized countries, where the rate of population growth is comparatively low. The most revealing possible illustration of that fact is a simple table listing the economic and population growth rates of the ten most populous nations of the world, where 64 percent of the world's population currently lives. Table 1.2 makes very clear the basis for the saying, "The rich get richer and the poor get children."

It is unlikely that the rates of growth listed in Table 1.2 will continue unchanged even until the end of this century. Many factors will change in the next 30 years. The end of civil disturbance in Nigeria, for example, will probably increase the economic growth rate there, while the onset of civil disturbance and then war in Pakistan has already interfered with economic growth there. Let us recognize, however, that the growth rates listed above are the products of a complicated social and economic system that is essentially stable and that is likely to change slowly rather than quickly, except in cases of severe social disruption.

It is a simple matter of arithmetic to calculate extrapolated values for gross national product (GNP) per capita from now until the year 2000 on the assumption that relative growth rates of population and GNP will remain roughly the same in these ten countries. The result of such a calculation appears in Table 1.3. The values shown there will almost certainly *not* actually be realized. They are not predictions. The values merely indicate the general direction our system, as it is currently structured, is taking us. *They demonstrate that the process of economic growth, as it is occurring today, is inexorably widening the absolute gap between the rich and the poor nations of the world.*

Most people intuitively and correctly reject extrapolations like those shown in Table 1.3, because the results appear ridiculous. It must be recognized, however, that in rejecting

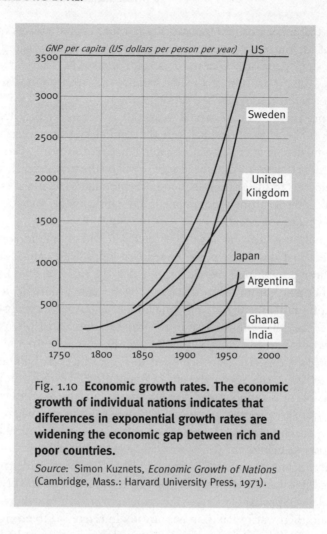

Fig. 1.10 **Economic growth rates. The economic growth of individual nations indicates that differences in exponential growth rates are widening the economic gap between rich and poor countries.**

Source: Simon Kuznets, *Economic Growth of Nations* (Cambridge, Mass.: Harvard University Press, 1971).

extrapolated values, one is also rejecting the assumption that there will be *no change* in the system. If the extrapolations in Table 1.3 do not actually come to pass, it will be because the balance between the positive and negative feedback loops determining the growth rates of population and capital in each nation has been altered. Fertility, mortality, the capital investment rate, the capital depreciation rate—any or all may change. In postulating any different outcome from the one shown in Table 1.3, one must specify which of these factors is likely to change, by how much, and when. These are exactly the questions we are addressing with our model, not on a national basis, but on an aggregated global one.

   To speculate with any degree of realism on future growth rates of population and industrial capital, we must know something more about the other factors in the world that interact with the population-capital system. We shall begin by asking a very basic set of questions.

Table 1.2 **Economic and population growth rates**

Country	Population (1968) (million)	Average annual growth rate of population (1961–8) (% per year)	GNP per capita (1968) (US dollars)	Average annual growth rate of GNP per capita (1961–8) (% per year)
People's Republic of China[a]	730	1.5	90	0.3
India	524	2.5	100	1.0
USSR[a]	238	1.3	1,100	5.8
United States	201	1.4	3,980	3.4
Pakistan	123	2.6	100	3.1
Indonesia	113	2.4	100	0.8
Japan	101	1.0	1,190	9.9
Brazil	88	3.0	250	1.6
Nigeria	63	2.4	70	−0.3
Federal Republic of Germany	60	1.0	1,970	3.4

[a] The International Bank for Reconstruction and Development qualifies its estimates for China and the USSR with the following statement: 'Estimates of GNP per capita and its growth rate have a wide margin of error mainly because of the problems in deriving the GNP at factor cost from net material product and in converting the GNP estimate into US dollars.' United Nations estimates are in general agreement with those of the IBRD.

Source: *World Bank Atlas* (Washington, DC: Internatonal Bank for Reconstruction and Development, 1970).

Table 1.3 **Extrapolated GNP for the year 2000**

Country	GNP per capita (in US dollars[a])
People's Republic of China	100
India	140
USSR	6,330
United States	11,000
Pakistan	250
Indonesia	130
Japan	23,200
Brazil	440
Nigeria	60
Federal Republic of Germany	5,850

[a] Based on the 1968 dollar with no allowance for inflation.

Can the growth rates of population and capital presented in Table 1.3 be physically sustained in the world? How many people can be provided for on this earth, at what level of wealth, and for how long? To answer these questions, we must look in detail at those systems in the world which provide the physical support for population and economic growth.

Notes

1. We are indebted to M. Robert Lattes for telling us this riddle.
2. A detailed description of the method of System Dynamics analysis is presented in J. W. Forrester's *Industrial Dynamics* (Cambridge, Mass.: MIT Press, 1961) and *Principles of Systems* (Cambridge, Mass.: Wright-Allen Press, 1968).
3. The word "billion" in this book will be used to mean 1,000 million, i.e. the European "milliard."
4. A. M. Carr-Saunders, *World Population: Past Growth and Present Trends* (Oxford: Clarendon Press, 1936), 42.
5. US Agency for International Development, *Population Program Assistance* (Washington, DC: Government Printing Office, 1970), 172.
6. *World Population Data Sheet 1968* (Washington, DC: Population Reference Bureau, 1968).

2 The Tragedy of the Commons

Garrett Hardin

At the end of a thoughtful article on the future of nuclear war, Wiesner and York concluded that:

Both sides in the arms race are . . . confronted by the dilemma of steadily increasing military power and steadily decreasing national security. It *is our considered professional judgment that this dilemma has no technical solution*. If the great powers continue to look for solutions in the area of science and technology only, the result will be to worsen the situation.[1]

I would like to focus your attention not on the subject of the article (national security in a nuclear world) but on the kind of conclusion they reached, namely that there is no technical solution to the problem. An implicit and almost universal assumption of discussions published in professional and semipopular scientific journals is that the problem under discussion has a technical solution. A technical solution may be defined as one that requires a change only in the techniques of the natural sciences, demanding little or nothing in the way of change in human values or ideas of morality.

In our day (though not in earlier times) technical solutions are always welcome. Because of previous failures in prophecy, it takes courage to assert that a desired technical solution is not possible. Wiesner and York exhibited this courage; publishing in a science journal, they insisted that the solution to the problem was not to be found in the natural sciences. They cautiously qualified their statement with the phrase "It is our considered professional judgment." Whether they were right or not is not the concern of the present article. Rather, the concern here is with the important concept of a class of human problems which can be called "no technical solution problems," and, more specifically, with the identification and discussion of one of these.

It is easy to show that the class is not a null class. Recall the game of tick-tack-toe. Consider the problem "How can I win the game of tick-tack-toe?" It is well known that I cannot, if I assume (in keeping with the conventions of game theory) that my opponent understands the game perfectly. Put another way, there is no "technical solution" to the problem. I can win only by giving a radical meaning to the word "win." I can hit my opponent over the head; or I can drug him; or I can falsify the records. Every way in which I "win" involves, in some sense, an abandonment of the game, as we intuitively understand it. (I can also, of course, openly abandon the game— refuse to play it. This is what most adults do.)

The class of "no technical solution problems" has members. My thesis is that the "population problem," as conventionally conceived, is a member of this class. How it is conventionally conceived needs some comment. It is fair to say that most people who anguish over the population problem are trying to find a way to avoid the evils of overpopulation without relinquishing any of the privileges they now enjoy. They think that farming the seas or developing new strains of wheat will solve the problem—technologically. I try to show here that the solution they seek cannot be found. The population problem cannot be solved in a technical way, any more than can the problem of winning the game of tick-tack-toe.

What Shall We Maximize?

Population, as Malthus said, naturally tends to grow "geometrically," or, as we would now say, exponentially. In a finite world this means that the per capita share of the world's goods must steadily decrease. Is ours a finite world?

A fair defense can be put forward for the view that the world is infinite; or that we do not know that it is not. But, in terms of the practical problems that we must face in the next few generations with the foreseeable technology, it is clear that we will greatly increase human misery if we do not, during the immediate future, assume that the world available to the terrestrial human population is finite. "Space" is no escape.[2]

A finite world can support only a finite population; therefore, population growth must eventually equal zero. (The case of perpetual wide fluctuations above and below zero is a trivial variant that need not be discussed.) When this condition is met, what will be the situation of mankind? Specifically, can Bentham's goal of "the greatest good for the greatest number" be realized?

No—for two reasons, each sufficient by itself. The first is a theoretical one. It is not mathematically possible to maximize for two (or more) variables at the same time. This was clearly stated by von Neumann and Morgenstern,[3] but the principle is implicit in the theory of partial differential equations, dating back at least to D'Alembert (1717–1783).

The second reason springs directly from biological facts. To live, any organism must have a source of energy (for example, food). This energy is utilized for two purposes: mere maintenance and work. For man, maintenance of life requires about 1,600 kilocalories a day ("maintenance calories"). Anything that he does over and above merely staying alive will be defined as work, and is supported by "work calories" which he takes in. Work calories are used not only for what we call work in common speech; they are also required for all forms of enjoyment, from swimming and automobile racing to playing music and writing poetry. If our goal is to maximize population it is obvious what we must do: We must make the work calories per person approach as close to zero as possible. No gourmet meals, no vacations, no sports, no music, no literature, no art. . . . I think that everyone will grant, without argument or proof, that maximizing population does not maximize goods. Bentham's goal is impossible.

In reaching this conclusion I have made the usual assumption that it is the acquisition of energy that is the problem. The appearance of atomic energy has led some to question this assumption. However, given an infinite source of energy, population growth still produces an inescapable problem. The problem of the acquisition of energy is replaced by the problem of its dissipation, as J. H. Fremlin has so wittily shown.[4] The arithmetic signs in the analysis are, as it were, reversed; but Bentham's goal is still unobtainable.

The optimum population is, then, less than the maximum. The difficulty of defining the optimum is enormous; so far as I know, no one has seriously tackled this problem. Reaching an acceptable and stable solution will surely require more than one generation of hard analytical work—and much persuasion.

We want the maximum good per person; but what is good? To one person it is wilderness, to another it is ski lodges for thousands. To one it is estuaries to nourish ducks for hunters to shoot; to another it is factory land. Comparing one good with another is, we usually say, impossible because goods are incommensurable. Incommensurables cannot be compared.

Theoretically this may be true; but in real life incommensurables *are* commensurable. Only a criterion of judgment and a system of weighting are needed. In nature the criterion is survival. Is it better for a species to be small and hidable, or large and powerful? Natural selection commensurates the incommensurables. The compromise achieved depends on a natural weighting of the values of the variables.

Man must imitate this process. There is no doubt that in fact he already does, but unconsciously. It is when the hidden decisions are made explicit that the arguments begin. The problem for the years ahead is to work out an acceptable theory of weighting. Synergistic effects, nonlinear variation, and difficulties in discounting the future make the intellectual problem difficult, but not (in principle) insoluble.

Has any cultural group solved this practical problem at the present time, even on an intuitive level? One simple fact proves that none has: there is no prosperous population in the world today that has, and has had for some time, a growth rate of zero. Any people that has intuitively identified its optimum point will soon reach it, after which its growth rate becomes and remains zero.

Of course, a positive growth rate might be taken as evidence that a population is below its optimum. However, by any reasonable standards, the most rapidly growing populations on earth today are (in general) the most miserable. This association (which need not be invariable) casts doubt on the optimistic assumption that the positive growth rate of a population is evidence that it has yet to reach its optimum.

We can make little progress in working toward optimum population size until we explicitly exorcize the spirit of Adam Smith in the field of practical demography. In economic affairs, *The Wealth of Nations* (1776) popularized the "invisible hand," the idea that an individual who "intends only his own gain" is, as it were, "led by an invisible hand to promote . . . the public interest."[5] Adam Smith did not assert that this was invariably true, and perhaps neither did any of his followers. But he contributed to a dominant tendency of thought that has ever since interfered with positive action based on rational analysis, namely, the tendency to assume that decisions reached individually will, in fact, be the best decisions for an entire society. If this assumption is correct it justifies the continuance of our present policy of laissez-faire in reproduction. If it is correct we can assume that men will control their individual fecundity so as to produce the optimum population. If the assumption is not correct, we need to reexamine our individual freedoms to see which ones are defensible.

The Tragedy of Freedom in a Commons

The rebuttal to the invisible hand in population control is to be found in a scenario first sketched in a little-known pamphlet in 1833 by a mathematical amateur named William Forster Lloyd (1794–1852).[6] We may well call it "the tragedy of the commons," using the word "tragedy" as the philosopher Whitehead used it: "The essence of dramatic tragedy is not unhappiness. It resides in the solemnity of the remorseless working of things." He then goes on to say, "This inevitableness of destiny can only be illustrated in terms of human life by incidents which in fact involve unhappiness. For it is only by them that the futility of escape can be made evident in the drama."[7]

The tragedy of the commons develops in this way. Picture a pasture open to all. It is to be expected that each herdsman will try to keep as many cattle as possible on the commons. Such an arrangement may work reasonably satisfactorily for centuries because tribal wars, poaching, and disease keep the numbers of both man and beast well below the carrying capacity of the land. Finally, however, comes the day of reckoning, that is, the day when the long-desired goal of social stability becomes a reality. At this point, the inherent logic of the commons remorselessly generates tragedy.

As a rational being, each herdsman seeks to maximize his gain. Explicitly or implicitly, more or less consciously, he asks, "What is the utility to me of adding one more animal to my herd?" This utility has one negative and one positive component.

1. The positive component is a function of the increment of one animal. Since the herdsman receives all the proceeds from the sale of the additional animal, the positive utility is nearly $+1$.

2. The negative component is a function of the additional overgrazing created by one more animal. Since, however, the effects of overgrazing are shared by all the herdsmen, the negative utility for any particular decision-making herdsman is only a fraction of -1.

Adding together the component partial utilities, the rational herdsman concludes that the only sensible course for him to pursue is to add another animal to his herd. And another; and another. . . . But this is the conclusion reached by each and every rational herdsman sharing a commons. Therein is the tragedy. Each man is locked into a system that compels him to increase his herd without limit—in a world that is limited. Ruin is the destination toward which all men rush, each pursuing his own best interest in a society that believes in the freedom of the commons. Freedom in a commons brings ruin to all.

Some would say that this is a platitude. Would that it were! In a sense, it was learned thousands of years ago, but natural selection favors the forces of psychological denial.[8] The individual benefits as an individual from his ability to deny the truth even though society as a whole, of which he is a part, suffers. Education can counteract the natural tendency to do the wrong thing, but the inexorable succession of generations requires that the basis for this knowledge be constantly refreshed.

A simple incident that occurred a few years ago in Leominster, Massachusetts, shows how perishable the knowledge is. During the Christmas shopping season the parking meters downtown were covered with plastic bags that bore tags reading: "Do not open until after Christmas. Free parking courtesy of the mayor and city council." In other words, facing the prospect of an increased demand for already scarce space, the city fathers reinstituted the system of the commons. (Cynically, we suspect that they gained more votes than they lost by this retrogressive act.)

In an approximate way, the logic of the commons has been understood for a long time, perhaps since the discovery of agriculture or the invention of private property in real estate. But it is understood mostly only in special cases which are not sufficiently generalized. Even at this late date, cattlemen leasing national land on the western ranges demonstrate no more than an ambivalent understanding, in constantly pressuring federal authorities to increase the head count to the point where overgrazing produces erosion and weed dominance. Likewise, the oceans of the world continue to suffer from the survival of the philosophy of the commons. Maritime nations still respond automatically to the shibboleth of the "freedom of the seas." Professing to believe in the "inexhaustible resources of the oceans," they bring species after species of fish and whales closer to extinction.[9]

The national parks present another instance of the working out of the tragedy of the commons. At present, they are open to all, without limit. The parks themselves are limited in extent—there is only one Yosemite Valley—whereas population seems to grow without limit. The values that visitors seek in the parks are steadily eroded. Plainly, we must soon cease to treat the parks as commons or they will be of no value to anyone.

What shall we do? We have several options. We might sell them off as private property. We might keep them as public property, but allocate the right to enter them. The allocation might be on the basis of wealth by the use of an auction system. It might be on the basis of merit, as defined by some agreed-upon standards. It might be by lottery. Or it might be on a first-come, first-served basis, administered to long queues. These, I think, are all the reasonable possibilities. They are all objectionable. But we must choose—or acquiesce in the destruction of the commons that we call our national parks.

Pollution

In a reverse way, the tragedy of the commons reappears in problems of pollution. Here it is not a question of taking something out of the commons, but of putting something in—sewage, or chemical, radioactive, and heat wastes into water; noxious and dangerous fumes into the air; and distracting and unpleasant advertising signs into the light of sight. The calculations of utility are much the same as before. The rational man finds that his share of the cost of the wastes he discharges into the commons is less than the cost of purifying his wastes before releasing them. Since this is true for everyone, we are locked into a system of "fouling our own nest," so long as we behave only as independent, rational, free enterprisers.

The tragedy of the commons as a food basket is averted by private property, or something formally like it. But the air and waters surrounding us cannot readily be fenced, and so the tragedy of the commons as a cesspool must be prevented by different means, by coercive laws or taxing devices that make it cheaper for the polluter to treat his pollutants than to discharge them untreated. We have not progressed as far with the solution of this problem as we have with the first. Indeed, our particular concept of private property, which deters us from exhausting the positive resources of the earth, favors pollution. The owner of a factory on the bank of a stream—whose property extends to the middle of the stream—often has difficulty seeing why it is not his natural right to muddy the waters flowing past his door. The law, always behind the times, requires elaborate stitching and fitting to adapt it to this newly perceived aspect of the commons.

The pollution problem is a consequence of population. It did not much matter how a lonely American frontiersman disposed of his waste. "Flowing water purifies itself every ten miles," my grandfather used to say, and the myth was near enough to the truth when he was a boy, for there were not too many people. But as population became denser, the natural chemical and biological recycling processes became overloaded, calling for a redefinition of property rights.

How to Legislate Temperance?

Analysis of the pollution problem as a function of population density uncovers a not generally recognized principle of morality, namely: *the morality of an act is a function of the state of the system at the time it is performed*.[10] Using the commons as a cesspool does not harm the general public under frontier conditions, because there is no public; the same behavior in a metropolis is unbearable. A hundred and fifty years ago a plainsman could kill an American bison, cut out only the tongue for his dinner, and discard the rest of the animal. He was not in any important sense being wasteful. Today, with only a few thousand bison left, we would be appalled at such behavior.

In passing, it is worth noting that the morality of an act cannot be determined from a photograph. One does not know whether a man killing an elephant or setting fire to the grassland is harming others until one knows the total system in which his act appears. "One picture is worth a thousand words," said an ancient Chinese; but it may take 10,000 words to validate it. It is as tempting to ecologists as it is to reformers in general to try to persuade others by way of the photographic shortcut. But the essence of an argument cannot be photographed: it must be presented rationally—in words.

That morality is system-sensitive escaped the attention of most codifiers of ethics in the past. "Thou shalt not . . ." is the form of traditional ethical directives which make no allowance for particular circumstances. The laws of our society follow the pattern of ancient ethics, and therefore are poorly suited to governing a complex, crowded, changeable world. Our epicyclic solution is to augment statutory law with administrative law. Since it is practically impossible to spell out all the conditions under which it is safe to burn trash in the back yard or to run an automobile without smog control, by law we delegate the details to bureaus. The result is administrative law, which is rightly feared for an ancient reason—*Quis custodiet ipsos custodes?*—"Who shall watch the watchers themselves?" John Adams said that we must have "a government of laws and not men." Bureau administrators, trying to evaluate the morality of acts in the total system, are singularly liable to corruption, producing a government by men, not laws.

Prohibition is easy to legislate (though not necessarily to enforce); but how do we legislate temperance? Experience indicates that it can be accomplished best through the mediation of administrative law. We limit possibilities unnecessarily if we suppose that the sentiment of *Quis custodiet* denies us the use of administrative law. We should rather retain the phrase as a perpetual reminder of fearful dangers we cannot avoid. The great challenge facing us now is to invent the corrective feedbacks that are needed to keep custodians honest. We must find ways to legitimate the needed authority of both the custodians and the corrective feedbacks.

Freedom to Breed Is Intolerable

The tragedy of the commons is involved in population problems in another way. In a world governed solely by the principle of "dog eat dog"—if indeed there ever was such a world—how many children a family had would not be a matter of public concern. Parents who bred too exuberantly would leave fewer descendants, not more, because they would be unable to care adequately for their children. David Lack and others have found that such a negative feedback demonstrably controls the fecundity of birds.[11] But men are not birds, and have not acted like them for millenniums, at least.

If each human family were dependent only on its own resources; *if* the children of improvident parents starved to death; *if*, thus, overbreeding brought its own "punishment" to the germ line—*then* there would be no public interest in controlling the breeding of families. But our society is deeply committed to the welfare state,[12] and hence is confronted with another aspect of the tragedy of the commons.

In a welfare state, how shall we deal with the family, the religion, the race, or the class (or indeed any distinguishable and cohesive group) that adopts overbreeding as a policy to secure its own aggrandizement?[13] To couple the concept of freedom to breed with the belief that everyone born has an equal right to the commons is to lock the world into a tragic course of action.

Unfortunately this is just the course of action that is being pursued by the United Nations. In late 1967, some thirty nations agreed to the following:

The Universal Declaration of Human Rights describes the family as the natural and fundamental unit of society. It follows that any choice and decision with regard to the size of the family must irrevocably rest with the family itself, and cannot be made by someone else.[14]

It is painful to have to deny categorically the validity of this right; denying it, one feels as uncomfortable as a resident of Salem, Massachusetts, who denied the reality of witches in the seventeenth century. At the present time, in liberal quarters, something like a taboo acts to inhibit criticism of the United Nations. There is a feeling that the United Nations is "our last and best hope," that we shouldn't find fault with it; we shouldn't play into the hands of the archconservatives. However, let us not forget what Robert Louis Stevenson said: "The truth that is suppressed by friends is the readiest weapon of the enemy." If we love the truth we must openly deny the validity of the Universal Declaration of Human Rights, even though it is promoted by the United Nations. We should also join with Kingsley Davis[15] in attempting to get Planned Parenthood–World Population to see the error of its ways in embracing the same tragic ideal.

Conscience Is Self-Eliminating

It is a mistake to think that we can control the breeding of mankind in the long run by an appeal to conscience. Charles Galton Darwin made this point when he spoke on the centennial of the publication of his grandfather's great book. The argument is straightforward and Darwinian.

People vary. Confronted with appeals to limit breeding, some people will undoubtedly respond to the plea more than others. Those who have more children will produce a larger fraction of the next generation than those with more susceptible consciences. The difference will be accentuated, generation by generation.

In C. G. Darwin's words: "It may well be that it would take hundreds of generations for the progenitive instinct to develop in this way, but if it should do so, nature would have taken her revenge, and the variety *Homo contracipiens* would become extinct and would be replaced by the variety *Homo progenitivus*."[16]

The argument assumes that conscience or the desire for children (no matter which) is hereditary—but hereditary only in the most general formal sense. The result will be the same whether the attitude is transmitted through germ cells, or exosomatically, to use A. J. Lotka's term. (If one denies the latter possibility as well as the former, then what's the point of education?) The argument has here been stated in the context of the population problem, but it applies equally well to any instance in which society appeals to an individual exploiting a commons to restrain himself for the general good—by means of his conscience. To make such an appeal is to set up a selective system that works toward the elimination of conscience from the race.

Pathogenic Effects of Conscience

The long-term disadvantage of an appeal to conscience should be enough to condemn it; but it has serious short-term disadvantages as well. If we ask a man who is exploiting a commons to desist "in the name of conscience," what are we saying to him? What does he hear?—not only at the moment but also in the wee small hours of the night when, half asleep, he remembers not merely the words we used but also the nonverbal communication cues we gave him unawares? Sooner or later, consciously or subconsciously, he senses that he has received two communications, and that they are contradictory: (1, the intended communication) "If you don't do as we ask, we will openly condemn you for not acting like a responsible citizen"; (2, the unintended communication) "If you *do* behave as we ask, we will secretly condemn you for a simpleton who can be shamed into standing aside while the rest of us exploit the commons."

Everyman then is caught in what Bateson has called a "double bind." Bateson and his coworkers have made a plausible case for viewing the double bind as an important causative factor in the genesis of schizophrenia.[17] The double bind may not always be so damaging, but it always endangers the mental health of anyone to whom it is applied. "A bad conscience," said Nietzsche, "is a kind of illness."

To conjure up a conscience in others is tempting to anyone who wishes to extend his control beyond the legal limits. Leaders at the highest level succumb to this temptation. Has any President during the past generation failed to call on labor unions to moderate voluntarily their demands for higher wages, or to steel companies to honor voluntary guidelines on prices? I can recall none. The rhetoric used on such occasions is designed to produce feelings of guilt in noncooperators.

For centuries it was assumed without proof that guilt was a valuable, perhaps even an indispensable, ingredient of the civilized life. Now, in this post-Freudian world, we doubt it. Paul Goodman speaks from the modern point of view when he says: "No good has ever come from feeling guilty, neither intelligence, policy, nor compassion. The guilty do not pay attention to the object but only to themselves, and not even to their own interests, which might make sense, but to their anxieties."[18]

One does not have to be a professional psychiatrist to see the consequences of anxiety. We in the Western world are just emerging from a dreadful two-centuries-long Dark Ages of Eros that was sustained partly by prohibition laws, but perhaps more effectively by the anxiety-generating mechanisms of education. Alex Comfort has told the story well in *The Anxiety Makers*;[19] it is not a pretty one.

Since proof is difficult, we may even concede that the results of anxiety may sometimes, from certain points of view, be desirable. The larger question we should ask is whether, as a matter of policy, we should ever encourage the use of a technique the tendency (if not the intention) of which is psychologically pathogenic. We hear much talk these days of responsible parenthood; the coupled words are incorporated into the titles of some organizations devoted to birth control. Some people have proposed massive propaganda campaigns to instill responsibility into the nation's (or the world's) breeders. But what is the meaning of the word responsibility in this context? Is it not merely a synonym for the word conscience? When we use the word responsibility in the absence of substantial sanctions are we not trying to browbeat a free man in a commons into acting against his own interest? Responsibility is a verbal counterfeit for a substantial *quid pro quo*. It is an attempt to get something for nothing.

If the word responsibility is to be used at all, I suggest that it be in the sense Charles Frankel uses it.[20] "Responsibility," says this philosopher, "is the product of definite social arrangements." Notice that Frankel calls for social arrangements—not propaganda.

Mutual Coercion Mutually Agreed Upon

The social arrangements that produce responsibility are arrangements that create coercion, of some sort. Consider bank robbing. The man who takes money from a bank acts as if the bank were a commons. How do we prevent such action? Certainly not by trying to control his behavior solely by a verbal appeal to his sense of responsibility. Rather than rely on propaganda we follow Frankel's lead and insist that a bank is not a commons; we seek the definite social arrangements that will keep it from becoming a commons. That we thereby infringe on the freedom of would-be robbers we neither deny nor regret.

The morality of bank robbing is particularly easy to understand because we accept complete prohibition of this activity. We are willing to say "Thou shalt not rob banks," without providing for exceptions. But temperance also can be created by coercion. Taxing is a good coercive device. To keep downtown shoppers temperate in their use of parking space we introduce parking meters for short periods, and traffic fines for longer ones. We need not actually forbid a citizen to park as long as he wants to; we need merely make it increasingly expensive for him to do so. Not prohibition, but carefully biased options are what we offer him. A Madison Avenue man might call this persuasion; I prefer the greater candor of the word coercion.

Coercion is a dirty word to most liberals now, but it need not forever be so. As with the four-letter words, its dirtiness can be cleansed away by exposure to the light, by saying it over and over without apology or embarrassment. To many, the word coercion implies arbitrary decisions of distant and irresponsible bureaucrats; but this is not a necessary part of its meaning. The only kind of coercion I recommend is mutual coercion, mutually agreed upon by the majority of the people affected.

To say that we mutually agree to coercion is not to say that we are required to enjoy it, or even to pretend we enjoy it. Who enjoys taxes? We all grumble about them. But we accept compulsory taxes because we recognize that voluntary taxes would favor the conscienceless. We institute and (grumblingly) support taxes and other coercive devices to escape the horror of the commons.

An alternative to the commons need not be perfectly just to be preferable. With real estate and other material goods, the alternative we have chosen is the institution of private property coupled with legal inheritance. Is this system perfectly just? As a genetically trained biologist I deny that it is. It seems to me that, if there are to be differences in individual inheritance, legal possession should be perfectly correlated with biological inheritance—that those who are biologically more fit to be the custodians of property and power should legally inherit more. But genetic recombination continually makes a mockery of the doctrine of "like father, like son" implicit in our laws of legal inheritance. An idiot can inherit millions, and a trust fund can keep his estate intact. We must admit that our legal system of private property plus inheritance is unjust—but we put up with it because we are not convinced, at the moment, that anyone has invented a better system. The alternative of the commons is too horrifying to contemplate. Injustice is preferable to total ruin.

It is one of the peculiarities of the warfare between reform and the status quo that it is thoughtlessly governed by a double standard. Whenever a reform measure is proposed it is often defeated when its opponents triumphantly discover a flaw in it. As Kingsley Davis has pointed out, worshippers of the status quo sometimes imply that no reform is possible without unanimous agreement, an implication contrary to historical fact.[21] As nearly as I can make out, automatic rejection of proposed reforms is based on one of two unconscious assumptions: (1) that the status quo is perfect; or (2) that the choice we face is between reform and no action; if the proposed reform is imperfect, we presumably should take no action at all, while we wait for a perfect proposal.

But we can never do nothing. That which we have done for thousands of years is also action. It also produces evils. Once we are aware that the status quo is action, we can then compare its discoverable advantages and disadvantages with the predicted advantages and disadvantages of the proposed reform, discounting as best we can for our lack of experience. On the basis of such a comparison, we can make a rational decision which will not involve the unworkable assumption that only perfect systems are tolerable.

Recognition of Necessity

Perhaps the simplest summary of this analysis of man's population problems is this: the commons, if justifiable at all, is justifiable only under conditions of low population density. As the human population has increased, the commons has had to be abandoned in one aspect after another.

First we abandoned the commons in food gathering, enclosing farm land and restricting pastures and hunting and fishing areas. These restrictions are still not complete throughout the world.

Somewhat later we saw that the commons as a place for waste disposal would also have to be abandoned. Restrictions on the disposal of domestic sewage are widely accepted in the Western world; we are still struggling to close the commons to pollution by automobiles, factories, insecticide sprayers, fertilizing operations, and atomic energy installations.

In a still more embryonic state is our recognition of the evils of the commons in matters of pleasure. There is almost no restriction on the propagation of sound waves in the public medium. The shopping public is assaulted with mindless music, without its consent. Our government is paying out billions of dollars to create supersonic transport which will disturb 50,000 people for every one person who is whisked from coast to coast three hours faster. Advertisers muddy the airwaves of radio and television and pollute the view of travelers. We are a long way from outlawing the commons in matters of pleasure. Is this because our Puritan inheritance makes us view pleasure as something of a sin, and pain (that is, the pollution of advertising) as the sign of virtue?

Every new enclosure of the commons involves the infringement of somebody's personal liberty. Infringements made in the distant past are accepted because no contemporary complains of a loss. It is the newly proposed infringements that we vigorously oppose; cries of "rights" and "freedom" fill the air. But what does "freedom" mean? When men mutually agreed to pass laws against robbing, mankind became more free, not less so. Individuals locked into the logic of the commons are free only to bring on universal ruin; once they see the necessity of mutual coercion, they become free to pursue other goals. I believe it was Hegel who said, "Freedom is the recognition of necessity."

The most important aspect of necessity that we must now recognize is the necessity of abandoning the commons in breeding. No technical solution can rescue us from the misery of overpopulation. Freedom to breed will bring ruin to all. At the moment, to avoid hard decisions many of us are tempted to propagandize for conscience and responsible parenthood. The temptation must be resisted, because an appeal to independently acting consciences selects for the disappearance of all conscience in the long run, and an increase in anxiety in the short.

The only way we can preserve and nurture other and more precious freedoms is by relinquishing the freedom to breed, and that very soon. "Freedom is the recognition of necessity"—

and it is the role of education to reveal to all the necessity of abandoning the freedom to breed. Only so can we put an end to this aspect of the tragedy of the commons.

Notes

1. J. B. Wiesner and H. F. York, *Scientific American*, 211: 4 (1964), 27. Offprint 319.
2. G. Hardin, *Journal of Heredity*, 50 (1959), 68; S. von Hoernor, *Science*, 137 (1962), 18.
3. J. von Neumann and O. Morgenstern, *Theory of Games and Economic Behavior* (Princeton: Princeton University Press, 1947), 11.
4. J. H. Fremlin, *New Science*, 415 (1964), 285.
5. A. Smith, *The Wealth of Nations* (New York: Modern Library, 1937), 423.
6. W. F. Lloyd, *Two Lectures on the Checks to Population* (Oxford: Oxford University Press, 1833), reprinted (in part) in G. Hardin (ed.), *Population, Evolution, and Birth Control*, 2nd edn. (San Francisco: W. H. Freeman and Company, 1969), 28.
7. A. N. Whitehead, *Science and the Modern World* (New York: Mentor, 1948), p. 17.
8. Hardin, *Population, Evolution, and Birth Control*, 46.
9. S. McVay, *Scientific American*, 216: 8 (1966), 13. Offprint 1046.
10. J. Fletcher, *Situation Ethics* (Philadelphia: Westminster, 1966).
11. D. Lack, *The Natural Regulation of Animal Numbers* (Oxford: Clarendon Press, 1954).
12. H. Girvetz, *From Wealth to Welfare* (Stanford, Calif.: Stanford University Press, 1950).
13. G. Hardin, *Perspectives in Biology and Medicine*, 6 (1963), 366.
14. U. Thant, *International Planned Parenthood News*, 168 (February 1968), 3.
15. K. Davis, *Science*, 158 (1967), 730.
16. S. Tax (ed.), *Evolution after Darwin* (Chicago: University of Chicago Press, 1960), ii. 469.
17. G. Bateson, D. D. Jackson, J. Haley, J. Weakland, *Behavioral Science*, 1 (1956), 251.
18. P. Goodman, *New York Review of Books*, 10: 8 (23 May 1968), 22.
19. A. Comfort, *The Anxiety Makers* (London: Nelson, 1967).
20. C. Frankel, *The Case for Modern Man* (New York: Harper, 1955), 203.
21. J. D. Roslansky, *Genetics and the Future of Man* (New York: Appleton-Century-Crofts, 1966), 177.

3 Economic Growth, Carrying Capacity, and the Environment

Kenneth Arrow, Bert Bolin, Robert Costanza,
Partha Dasgupta, Carl Folke, C. S. Holling,
Bengt-Owe Jansson, Simon Levin, Karl-Göran Mäler,
Charles Perrings, and David Pimentel

National and international economic policy has usually ignored the environment. In areas where the environment is beginning to impinge on policy, as in the General Agreement on Tariffs and Trade (GATT) and the North American Free Trade Agreement (NAFTA), it remains a tangential concern, and the presumption is often made that economic growth and economic liberalization (including the liberalization of international trade) are, in some sense, good for the environment. This notion has meant that economy-wide policy reforms designed to promote growth and liberalization have been encouraged with little regard to their environmental consequences, presumably on the assumption that these consequences would either take care of themselves or could be dealt with separately.

In this article we discuss the relation between economic growth and environmental quality, and the link between economic activity and the carrying capacity and resilience of the environment.[1]

Economic Growth, Institutions, and the Environment

The general proposition that economic growth is good for the environment has been justified by the claim that there exists an empirical relation between per capita income and some measures of environmental quality. It has been observed that as income goes up there is increasing environmental degradation up to a point, after which environmental quality improves. (The relation has an "inverted-U" shape.)

One explanation of this finding is that people in poor countries cannot afford to emphasize amenities over material well-being. Consequently, in the earlier stages of economic development, increased pollution is regarded as an acceptable side effect of economic growth. However, when a country has attained a sufficiently high standard of living, people give attention to environmental amenities. This leads to environmental legislation, new institutions for the protection of the environment, and so forth.

The above argument does not, however, pertain to the environmental resource basis of material well-being, a matter we shall return to subsequently.

So far the inverted U-shaped curve has been shown to apply to a selected set of pollutants only.[2] However, because it is consistent with the notion that people spend proportionately more on environmental quality as their income rises, economists have conjectured that the curve applies to environmental quality generally.[3] But it is important to be clear about the conclusions that can be drawn from these empirical findings. While they do indicate that economic growth may be associated with improvements in some environmental indicators, they imply neither that economic growth is sufficient to induce environmental improvement in general, nor that the environmental effects of growth may be ignored, nor, indeed, that the Earth's resource base is capable of supporting indefinite economic growth. In fact, if this base were to be irreversibly degraded, economic activity itself could be at risk.[4]

There are other reasons for caution in interpreting these inverted U-shaped curves. First, the relation has been shown to be valid for pollutants involving local short-term costs (for example sulfur, particulates, and fecal coliforms), not for the accumulation of stocks of waste or for pollutants involving long-term and more dispersed costs (such as CO_2), which are often increasing functions of income.[5]

Second, the inverted-U relations have been uncovered for emissions of pollutants, not resource stocks. The relation is less likely to hold wherever the feedback effects of resource stocks are significant, such as those involving soil and its cover, forests, and other ecosystems.

Third, the inverted-U curves, as they have been estimated, say nothing about the system-wide consequences of emission reductions. For example, reductions in one pollutant in one country may involve increases in other pollutants in the same country or transfers of pollutants to other countries.[6]

And fourth, in most cases where emissions have declined with rising income, the reductions have been due to local institutional reforms, such as environmental legislation and market-based incentives to reduce environmental impacts. But such reforms often ignore international and intergenerational consequences. Where the environmental costs of economic activity are borne by the poor, by future generations, or by other countries, the incentives to correct the problem are likely to be weak. The environmental consequences of growing economic activity may, accordingly, be very mixed.

The solution to environmental degradation lies in such institutional reforms as would compel private users of environmental resources to take account of the social costs of their actions.[7] The inverted-U relation is evidence that this has happened in some cases. It does not constitute evidence that it will happen in all cases or that it will happen in time to avert the important and irreversible global consequences of growth.

Carrying Capacity and Ecosystem Resilience

The environmental resource base upon which all economic activity ultimately depends includes ecological systems that produce a wide variety of services. This resource base is finite. Furthermore, imprudent use of the environmental resource base may irreversibly reduce the capacity for generating material production in the future. All of this implies that there are limits to the carrying capacity of the planet. It is, of course, possible that improvements in the management of resource systems, accompanied by resource-conserving structural changes in the economy, would enable economic and population growth to take place despite the finiteness of the environmental resource base, at least for some period of time. However, for that to be even conceivable, signals that effectively reflect increasing scarcities of the resource base need to be generated within the economic system.

Carrying capacities in nature are not fixed, static, or simple relations. They are contingent on technology, preferences, and the structure of production and consumption. They are also contingent on the ever-changing state of interactions between the physical and biotic environment. A single number for human carrying capacity would be meaningless because the consequences of both human innovation and biological evolution are inherently unknowable. Nevertheless, a general index of the current scale or intensity of the human economy in relation to that of the biosphere is still useful. For example, Vitousek et al.[8] calculated that the total net terrestrial primary production of the biosphere currently being appropriated for human consumption is around 40%. This does put the scale of the human presence on the planet in perspective.

A more useful index of environmental sustainability is ecosystem resilience. One way of thinking about resilience is to focus on ecosystem dynamics where there are multiple (locally) stable equilibria.[9] Resilience in this sense is a measure of the magnitude of disturbances that can be absorbed before a system centered on one locally stable equilibrium flips to another.[10] Economic activities are sustainable only if the life-support ecosystems on which they depend are resilient. Even though ecological resilience is difficult to measure and even though it varies from system to system and from one kind of disturbance to another, it may be possible to identify indicators and early-warning signals of environmental stress. For example, the diversity of organisms or the heterogeneity of ecological functions have been suggested as signals of ecosystem resilience. But ultimately, the resilience of systems may only be tested by intelligently perturbing them and observing the response with what has been called "adaptive management".[11]

The loss of ecosystem resilience is potentially important for at least three reasons. First, the discontinuous change in ecosystem functions at the system flips from one equilibrium to another could be associated with a sudden loss of biological productivity, and so to a reduced capacity to support human life. Second, it may imply an irreversible change in the set of options open both to present and future generations (examples include soil erosion, depletion of groundwater reservoirs, desertification, and loss of biodiversity). Third, discontinuous and irreversible changes from familiar to unfamiliar states increase the uncertainties associated with the environmental effects of economic activities.

If human activities are to be sustainable, we need to ensure that the ecological systems on which our economies depend are resilient. The problem involved in devising environmental policies is to ensure that resilience is maintained, even though the limits on the nature and scale of economic activities thus required are necessarily uncertain.

Economic Growth and Environmental Policy

We conclude that economic liberalization and other policies that promote gross national product growth are not substitutes for environmental policy. On the contrary, it may well be desirable that they are accompanied by stricter policy reforms. Of particular importance is the need for reforms that would improve the signals that are received by resource users. Environmental damages, including loss of ecological resilience, often occur abruptly. They are frequently not reversible. But abrupt changes can seldom be anticipated from systems of signals that are typically received by decision-makers in the world today. Moreover, the signals that do exist are often not observed, or are wrongly interpreted, or are not part of the incentive structure of societies. This is due to ignorance about the dynamic effects of changes in ecosystem variables (for example, thresholds, buffering capacity, and loss of resilience) and to the presence of institutional impediments, such as lack of well-defined property rights. The development of appropriate institutions depends, among other things, on understanding ecosystem dynamics and on relying on appropriate indicators of change. Above all, given the fundamental uncertainties about the nature of ecosystem dynamics and the dramatic consequences we would face if we were to guess wrong, it is necessary that we act in a precautionary way so as to maintain the diversity and resilience of ecosystems.

Economic growth is not a panacea for environmental quality, indeed, it is not even the main issue. What matters is the content of growth—the composition of inputs (including environmental resources) and outputs (including waste products). This content is determined by, among other things, the economic institutions within which human activities are conducted. These institutions need to be designed so that they provide the right incentives for protecting the resilience of ecological systems. Such measures will not only promote greater efficiency in the allocation of environmental resources at all income levels, but they would also assure a sustainable scale of economic activity within the ecological life-support system. Protecting the capacity of ecological systems to sustain welfare is of as much importance to poor countries as it is to those that are rich.[12]

Notes

1. This is a report of the Second Askö Meeting, held 31 August to 2 September 1994, in the archipelago outside Stockholm, Sweden. The meeting was organized by the Beijer International Institute of Ecological Economics, Royal Swedish Academy of Sciences, Box 50005, S10405 Stockholm, Sweden, The aim of the meeting was to establish a substantive dialogue among a small group of ecologists and economists to gauge whether an interdisciplinary consensus exists on the issues of economic growth, carrying capacity, and the environment and to determine what could be said about the joint development of economic and environmental policy.

2. Phenomena for which the relation holds most clearly, include poor sanitation, impure water

supplies, suspended particulates, SO_2, NO_2, and CO_2 (G. M. Grossman and A. B. Krueger, in P. Garber (ed.), *The U.S., Mexico Free Trade Agreement* (Cambridge, Mass.: MIT Press, 1993), 165–77). N. Shafik and S. Bandyopadhay, "Economic Growth and Environmental Quality: Time Series and Gross Country Evidence," background paper for the World Development Report, World Bank, Washington, DC, 1992.

3. W. Beckerman, *World Dev.* 20 (1992), 481.

4. A. M. Jansson, M. Hammer, C. Folke, R. Costanza (eds), *Investing in Natural Capital: The Ecological Economics Approach to Sustainability* (Washington, DC: Island Press, 1994).

5. Shafik and Bandyopadhay find that CO_2 emissions are an increasing function of per capita income. W. Moomaw and M. Tullis (in R. Socolow, C. Andrews, F. Berkhout, V. Thomas (eds), *Industrial Ecology and Global Change* (Cambridge: Cambridge University Press, 1994), 157–72) show that while cross-sectionally CO_2 emissions per capita rise with income per capita, the experience in individual countries over time is highly variable, depending on the structure of individual economies. They conclude that there are many different development paths, some of which can de-link economic growth from CO_2 emissions, but adequate institutions are required and it is by no means an automatic consequence of growth.

6. R. Lopez, *J. Enivron. Econ. Manage.* 27 (1994), 163; T. M. Selden and D. Song, ibid 147; K. Anderson and R. Blackhurst (eds), *The Greening of World Trade Issues* (Hemel Hempstead: Harvester Wheatsheaf, 1992).

7. A related issue is the measurement of economic growth at the macro level. The conventional measure, GNP, is far from adequate as a measure of true economic performance. We need a more comprehensive index that includes the flow of environmental services as well as the value of net changes in the stocks of natural capital so that the true social costs of growth can be internalized. With this improved index, many of the apparent conflicts between "growth" and the environment would disappear because environmental degradation would be subtracted from the index. (See e.g. P. Dasgupta and K. G. Maler, *The Environment and Emerging Development Issues*, Proceedings of the Annual Bank Conference on Development Economics, 1990 (Supplement to the World Bank Economic Review, 1991).

8. P. M. Vitousek, P. R. Ehrlich, A. H. Ehrlich, P. A. Matson, *BioScience*, 36 (1986), 368.

9. Another way is to focus on ecosystem dynamics in the neighborhood of an equilibrium. The object here is to measure the resistance of a system of disturbances and to determine the speed with which it returns to equilibrium (See S. L. Pimm, *Nature*, 307 (1984), 321).

10. C. S. Holling, *Annu. Rev. Ecol. System*, 4 (1973) 123.

11. Adaptive management views regional development policy and management as "experiments," where interventions at several scales are made to achieve understanding, to produce a social or economic product, and to identify options. See e.g. C. S. Holling (ed.), *Adaptive Environmental Assessment and Management* (London: Wiley, 1978); C. J. Walters, *Adaptive Management of Renewable Resources* (New York: Macmillan. 1986); K. Lee, *Compass and the Gyroscope* (Washington, DC: Island Press, 1993).

12. We thank the two anonymous referees for helpful comments.

Section II: The Promethean Response

One response to the doomsaying of Section I is a literature that denies that there is an environmental crisis either present or looming. This literature is often categorized as cornucopian or Promethean, and embodies two main arguments. First, this school argues that environmental conditions and indicators are much better than documents such as *Limits to Growth* and the *Global 2000 Report* claim. Secondly, it has unlimited confidence in the ability of humans—especially in their technologies and their social organization in markets—to overcome any obstacles they encounter, including supposed limits. Approaching scarcities serve only to inspire human minds to devise innovations and solutions. These minds are to Julian Simon *The Ultimate Resource* (1981). Simon and others in this camp believe that there is an infinite supply of the natural resources we need—and if we start to run out, we'll find something else to use. Thus continued innovation, growth, and technology is the solution to any problem that may be produced by *past* innovation, growth, and technology.

We include here two representations of the Promethean/Cornucopian literature. The introduction to Julian Simon and Herman Kahn's *The Resourceful Earth: A Response to Global 2000* makes the point quite radically and forcefully. Simon and Kahn take on the limits arguments point by point, arguing generally that either the problems laid out by *Global 2000* and others simply do not exist or that all relevant environmental indicators are improving. It remains the best representation of the Promethean position. Greg Easterbrook's 'Ecorealist Manifesto' is from his mammoth work, *A Moment on the Earth: The Coming Age of Environmental Optimism*. Here, Easterbrook argues that, from the perspective of nature, all the problems the doomsayers point out are short-lived and ephemeral—minor annoyances in the great journey of the natural world. Optimism, he argues, flows from his more 'rational' reading of environmental history. Easterbrook claims that all pollution problems will be solved in our lifetimes, and that nature's 'adjustment' to the human presence is almost complete.

While most Prometheans—Simon, Kahn, and Easterbrook included—assert the *scientific* basis of their optimism as fact, their science is often assailed. Simon attacks what he sees as the faulty science of *Global 2000* and other limits literature, though his critics note that he offers evidence selectively in order to minimize problems. The final selection of this section is an excerpt from Paul and Anne Ehrlich's *Betrayal of Science and Reason*, which criticizes the Prometheans' science. The Ehrlichs argue that the politics of the 'brownlash' movement pollutes its science, and vice versa.

Further Reading

Julian Simon is the dean of the Prometheans. His works include *The Resourceful Earth* (1984), *The Ultimate Resource* (1981), and *The State of Humanity* (1995). He debates the survivalist Norman

Myers in Myers and Simon, *Scarcity or Abundance: A Debate on the Environment* (1994). Economists appear prominently in the Promethean literature, beginning with Harold Barnett and Chandler Morse's *Scarcity and Growth* (1963). Oxford economist Wilfred Beckerman makes an early argument *In Defence of Economic Growth* (1974) which he revisits in the bluntly titled *Small is Stupid: Blowing the Whistle on the Greens* (1995). A less academic (and, unintentionally, more humorous) cornucopian treatise is Dixy Lee Ray's *Environmental Overkill* (1993). Aaron Wildavsky's *But Is It True? A Citizen's Guide to Environmental Health and Safety Issues* (1995) argues that the risks which energize environmentalists are revealed by a close examination of the underlying science to be in truth non-existent. Finally, while the scientific critique of the Prometheans is represented by the Ehrlichs, the political fallout in the USA is discussed by Representative George E. Brown (a frustrated member of the House Committee on Science in the notoriously anti-environmental 104th Congress) in *Environmental Science under Siege: Fringe Science and the 104th Congress* (1996).

4 Introduction to *The Resourceful Earth*

Julian L. Simon and Herman Kahn

Executive Summary

The original 1980 *Global 2000 Report to the President* (*Global 2000* hereafter) is frightening. It received extraordinarily wide circulation, and it has influenced crucial governmental policies. But it is dead wrong. Now *The Resourceful Earth*, a response to *Global 2000*, presents the relevant reliable trend evidence which mainly reassures rather than frightens.

Two paragraphs summarize the "Major Findings and Conclusions" of *Global 2000* on its page 1:

If present trends continue, the world in 2000 will be more crowded, more polluted, less stable ecologically, and more vulnerable to disruption than the world we live in now. Serious stresses involving population, resources, and environment are clearly visible ahead. Despite greater material output, the world's people will be poorer in many ways than they are today.

For hundreds of millions of the desperately poor, the outlook for food and other necessities of life will be no better. For many it will be worse. Barring revolutionary advances in technology, life for most people on earth will be more precarious in 2000 than it is now—unless the nations of the world act decisively to alter current trends.

To highlight our differences as vividly as possible, we restate the above summary with our substitutions in italics:

If present trends continue, the world in 2000 will be *less crowded* (though more populated), *less polluted*, *more stable ecologically*, and *less vulnerable to resource-supply disruption* than the world we live in now. Stresses involving population, resources, and environment *will be less in the future than now* ... The world's people will be *richer* in most ways than they are today ... The outlook for food and other necessities of life will be *better* ... life for most people on earth will be *less precarious* economically than it is now.

The high points of our findings are as follows:

(1) Life expectancy has been rising rapidly throughout the world, a sign of demographic, scientific, and economic success. This fact—at least as dramatic and heartening as any other in human history—must be fundamental in any informed discussion of pollution and nutrition.

From Julian L. Simon and Herman Kahn, *The Resourceful Earth* (New York: Basil Blackwell, 1984), 1–27. Reprinted with permission.

(2) The birth rate in less developed countries has been falling substantially during the past two decades, from 2.2 percent yearly in 1964–5 to 1.75 percent in 1982–3, probably a result of modernization and of decreasing child mortality, and a sign of increased control by people over their family lives.

(3) Many people are still hungry, but the food supply has been improving since at least World War II, as measured by grain prices, production per consumer, and the famine death rate.

(4) Trends in world forests are not worrying, though in some places deforestation is troubling.

(5) There is no statistical evidence for rapid loss of species in the next two decades. An increased rate of extinction cannot be ruled out if tropical deforestation is severe, but no evidence about linkage has yet been demonstrated.

(6) The fish catch, after a pause, has resumed its long upward trend.

(7) Land availability will not increasingly constrain world agriculture in coming decades.

(8) In the US, the trend is toward higher-quality cropland, suffering less from erosion than in the past.

(9) The widely-published report of increasingly rapid urbanization of US farmland was based on faulty data.

(10) Water does not pose a problem of physical scarcity or disappearance, although the world and US situations do call for better institutional management through more rational systems of property rights.

(11) The climate does not show signs of unusual and threatening changes.

(12) Mineral resources are becoming less scarce rather than more scarce, affront to common sense though that may be.

(13) There is no persuasive reason to believe that the world oil price will rise in coming decades. The price may fall well below what it has been.

(14) Compared to coal, nuclear power is no more expensive, and is probably much cheaper, under most circumstances. It is also much cheaper than oil.

(15) Nuclear power gives every evidence of costing fewer lives per unit of energy produced than does coal or oil.

(16) Solar energy sources (including wind and wave power) are too dilute to compete economically for much of humankind's energy needs, though for specialized uses and certain climates they can make a valuable contribution.

(17) Threats of air and water pollution have been vastly overblown; these processes were not well analyzed in *Global 2000*.

We do not say that all is well everywhere, and we do not predict that all will be rosy in the future. Children are hungry and sick; people live out lives of physical or intellectual poverty, and lack of opportunity; war or some new pollution may do us in. *The Resourceful Earth does* show that for most relevant matters we have examined, aggregate global and US *trends* are improving rather than deteriorating.

In addition we do not say that a better future happens *automatically* or *without effort*. It will happen because men and women—sometimes as individuals, sometimes as enterprises working for profit, sometimes as voluntary non-profit making groups, and sometimes as governmental agencies—will address problems with muscle and mind, and will *probably* overcome, as has been usual throughout history.

We are confident that the nature of the physical world permits continued improvement in humankind's economic lot in the long run, indefinitely. Of course there are always newly arising local problems, shortages and pollutions, due to climate or to increased population and income. Sometimes temporary large-scale problems arise. But the nature of the world's physical conditions and the resilience in a well-functioning economic and social system enable us to overcome such problems, and the solutions usually leave us better off than if the problem had never arisen; that is the great lesson to be learned from human history.

We are less optimistic, however, about the constraints currently imposed upon material progress by political and institutional forces, in conjunction with popularly-held beliefs and attitudes about natural resources and the environment, such as those urged upon us by *Global 2000*. These constraints include the view that resource and environmental trends point towards deterioration rather than towards improvement, that there are physical limits that will increasingly act as a brake upon progress, and that nuclear energy is more dangerous than energy from other sources. These views lead to calls for subsidies and price controls, as well as government ownership and management of resource production, and government allocation of the resources that are produced. To a considerable extent the US and the rest of the world already suffer from such policies (for example, on agriculture in Africa), and continuation and intensification could seriously damage resource production and choke economic progress. In particular, refusal to use nuclear power could hamper the US in its economic competition with other nations, as well as cause unnecessary deaths in coal mining and other types of conventional energy production. We wish that there were grounds to believe that a shift in thinking will take place on these matters, but we do not find basis for firm hope. So in this respect we are hardly optimistic.

We also wish to emphasize that though the global situation may be reasonably satisfactory or improving in some given respect, there are likely to be areas in which there are severe difficulties which may be on the increase. Such local problems may be due to local mismanagement, or they may be due to natural catastrophe which the larger community may not yet have been able to help mitigate. Such local problems should not be glossed over in any global assessment.

Background

More than one million copies of the original *Global 2000 Report to the President of the United States* have been distributed. It has been translated into five major languages. Other countries such as Germany have commissioned studies imitating *Global 2000*.

Global 2000 also underlies important US policy pronouncements. For example, the following paragraphs, and the rest of the full speech at the Alpbach European Forum in 1980, which was an official "American perspective on the world economy in the 1980s," were founded squarely on *Global 2000*:

Defying the generally buoyant mood, Richard Cooper, U.S. under secretary of state for economic affairs, delivered a grim message. If present trends continue, he said, the world population will swell to five billion by 1990 from four billion at present, leading to "open conflict, greater terrorism and possibly localized anarchy," as well as "congestion, famine, deforestation."

The decade's population growth would equal "nearly half the total world population when I was born," he said. Even then, he added ominously, "some political leaders were calling for more lebensraum" (or living space). (*The Wall Street Journal*, 15 September 1980, 32)

Before *Global 2000* was even completed, President Carter had discussed its conclusions with other world leaders at an economic summit held in Italy. Immediately upon receiving the Report, the President established a task force to ensure that *Global 2000* received priority attention. The task force included the Secretary of State, the director of the Office of Management and Budget, the President's Assistant for Domestic Affairs, and the director of the Office of Science and Technology Policy. Secretary of State Edmund Muskie used *Global 2000* as the centrepiece for an address to the UN General Assembly. The Joint Economic Committee of Congress launched a series of hearings on the Report. The President instructed the State Department to arrange an international meeting of environmental and economic experts to discuss population, natural resources, environment, and economic development, the subjects of *Global 2000*. Finally, in his farewell address to the nation, President Carter referred to the subject of *Global 2000* as one of the three most important problems facing the American people (the other two being arms control and human rights). And *Global 2000*'s effect did not disappear with the change of administration. It continues to be cited as support for a wide variety of forecasts by governmental agencies.[1]

The press received *Global 2000* with great respect and enormous attention. *Time* and *Newsweek* ran full-page stories, and *Global 2000* made front-page newspaper headlines across the country as an "official" government study forecasting global disaster. Though the Report included some qualifications, it was interpreted by all as a prediction of gloom-and-doom. For example, *Science*'s story title was: "Global 2000 Report: Vision of a Gloomy World."[2] *Time*'s title was "Toward a Troubled 21st Century: A Presidential Panel Finds the Global Outlook Extremely Bleak."[3] *Newsweek*'s title was "A Grim Year 2000."[4] The typical local paper in central Illinois had this banner across the top of the front page: "U.S. Report Says World Faces Ecological Disaster."[5] And its story began:

Mass poverty, malnutrition and deterioration of the planet's water and atmosphere resources—that's a bleak government prediction that says civilization has perhaps 20 years to act to head off such a worldwide disaster.

A full-page advertisement for the volume in *The New York Review of Books* was headed:

Government Report as follows: Poisoned seas, acid rain, water running out, atmosphere dying.

However—and seldom can there have been a bigger "however" in the history of such reports—the original *Global 2000* is totally wrong in its specific assertions and its general conclusion. It is replete with major factual errors, not just minor blemishes.[6] Its language is vague at key points, and features many loaded terms. Many of its arguments are illogical or misleading. It paints an overall picture of global trends that is fundamentally wrong, partly because it relies on non-facts and partly because it misinterprets the facts it does present. (In partial defense of the writers who prepared the *Global 2000* work, the summary Volume I—which was the main basis for the news stories—egregiously mis-stated, for reasons which we can only surmise,[7] many analyses and conclusions in the working-paper Volume II, thereby turning optimistic projections into pessimistic ones.)

Our statements about the future in *The Resourceful Earth* are intended as unconditional predictions in the absence of an unforeseeable catastrophe such as nuclear war or total social breakdown. We feel no need to qualify these predictions upon the continuation of current policies, as *Global 2000* claimed to do, and in fact we believe that such a qualification is not meaningful. Throughout history, individuals and communities have responded to actual and expected shortages of raw materials in such fashion that eventually the materials have become more readily available than if the shortages had never arisen. These responses are embodied in the observed long-run trends in supply and cost, and therefore extrapolation of such trends (together with appropriate theoretical attention) takes into account the likely future responses.

Aside from this Introduction and one section in most of the chapters, *The Resourceful Earth* is not primarily an evaluation or criticism of *Global 2000*. (For evaluation and criticism, see Clawson 1981; Dubos 1981; Kahn and Schneider 1981; Simon 1981.) It is a compendium of careful, authoritative, independent studies of many of the topics dealt with by *Global 2000* plus some others, by writers selected by the editors because their claim to the label "expert" is as strong as any such claim can be. Taken together, the chapters are intended to be a fair assessment of the trends together with an analysis of what the trends portend for the future. We hope that *The Resourceful Earth* will also serve as a reference volume of first resort for persons seeking knowledge on these topics. This introduction summarizes the findings of the technical chapters. It also offers some general observations about *Global 2000*, global modeling, and policy recommendations. The findings express the views of the authors of the individual chapters. The editors are responsible for the general observations, though the individual chapter authors have commented upon these general observations. We have also included a section at the end of the volume where individual authors may express their disagreements with any of these general views.

The Resourceful Earth chapters were produced without a penny's added cost to the public. The chapters are presented here exactly as written, with the authors having final authority over their chapters without bureaucratic tampering. This process is in contrast to the largely staff-written and politically edited *Global 2000*; more details are given below about the process of financing, writing, and editing *Global 2000* and *The Resourceful Earth*.

The Specific Conclusions

We now briefly summarize the main issues raised by *Global 2000* as covered by our topical chapters. For convenience, the order will be the same as in the *Global 2000* summary quoted above for the topics mentioned there, followed by the other central issues raised in their summary volume.

"MORE CROWDED"

There surely will be more people on earth in the year 2000 than there are now, barring a calamity. But a growing population does not imply that human living on the globe will be more

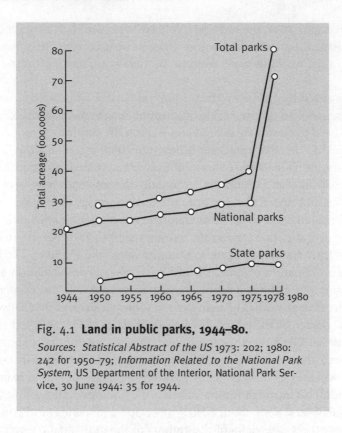

Fig. 4.1 **Land in public parks, 1944–80.**

Sources: Statistical Abstract of the US 1973: 202; 1980: 242 for 1950–79; *Information Related to the National Park System*, US Department of the Interior, National Park Service, 30 June 1944: 35 for 1944.

"crowded" in any meaningful fashion. As the world's people have increasingly higher incomes, they purchase better housing and mobility. The homes of the world's people progressively have more floorspace, which means people dwell in less-crowded space with more privacy. The United States, for which data are readily available, illustrates the trends in developed countries. In 1940, fully 20.2 percent of households had 1.01 or more persons per room, whereas in 1974 only 4.5 percent were that crowded (US Department of Commerce 1977: 90). (Also relevant: in 1940 44.6 percent of housing units lacked some or all plumbing facilities; but in 1974 only 3.2 percent were lacking. In 1940, 55.4 percent had all plumbing facilities, whereas in 1974, 96.8 percent had all plumbing; US Department of Commerce, 1977: 91). The world's people are getting better roads and more vehicles; therefore they can move around more freely, and have the benefits of a wider span of area. In the US, paved highways have increased from zero to over 3 million miles since the turn of the century. Natural park areas have been expanding (Figure 4.1). And trips to parks have increased to an extraordinary degree (Figure 4.2). These trends mean that people increasingly have much more space available and accessible for their use, despite the increase in total population, even in the poorer countries. All this suggests to us that the world is getting less crowded by reasonable tests relevant to human life.

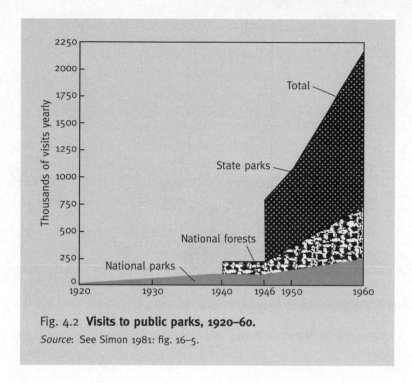

Fig. 4.2 **Visits to public parks, 1920–60.**
Source: See Simon 1981: fig. 16–5.

"MORE POLLUTED"

Global 2000 asserts that the world is getting more polluted. But it cites no systematic data for the world or even for regions. It is certainly reasonable to *assume* that man-made industrial pollutions increase as the most backward countries begin to modernize, get somewhat less poor, and purchase pollution-creating industrial plants. The same is true of consumer pollution—junked cars, plastic bags, and pop tops of beverage cans. But it is misleading to suggest that there are *data* showing that such pollution is a major problem.

In the early stages of industrialization, countries and people are not yet ready to pay for clean-up operations. But further increases in income almost as surely will bring about pollution abatement. (At the same time, biological disease pollution has been declining, even in the poor countries, at a rate far outweighing any hazardous effect of man-made pollution, as seen in increased life-expectancy.)

In the richer countries there is solid evidence that hazardous air pollution has been declining. Figure 4.3 shows the Council on Environmental Quality's new Pollutant Standard Index for the US, and Figure 4.4 shows one key measure of air quality for which data are available since 1960; the benign trend has been under way for quite a while, and does not stem only from the onset of the environmental movement around 1970.

Water quality too, has improved in the richer countries. Figure 4.5 shows the improvements in drinkability of water in the US since 1961. Such alarms of the 1960s and 1970s as the impending "death" of the Great Lakes have turned out totally in error; fishing and swimming conditions

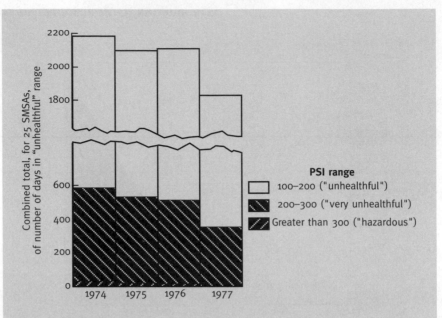

Fig. 4.3 **National trend in urban PSI levels, 1974–7.**

Source: Based on US Environmental Protection Agency data, reproduced from the tenth annual report of the Council on Environmental Quality 1979: 39.

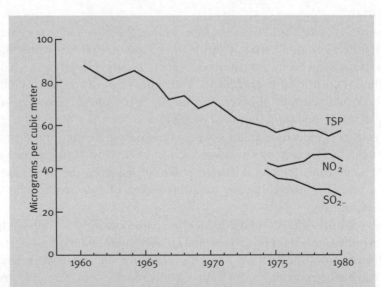

Fig. 4.4 **National ambient concentrations of total suspended particulates, nitrogen dioxide, and sulfur dioxide, 1960–80. Data may not be strictly comparable.**

Source: US Environmental Protection Agency.

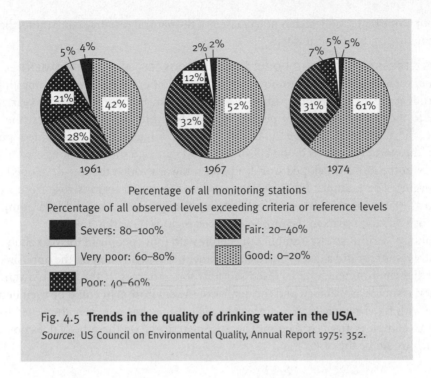

1961   1967   1974

Percentage of all monitoring stations
Percentage of all observed levels exceeding criteria or reference levels

■ Severs: 80–100%   ▨ Fair: 20–40%

□ Very poor: 60–80%   ▨ Good: 0–20%

▨ Poor: 40–60%

Fig. 4.5 **Trends in the quality of drinking water in the USA.**
Source: US Council on Environmental Quality, Annual Report 1975: 352.

there are now excellent. (Ironically, the "death" that was warned of is really a condition of too much organic "life", and is therefore self-curing as soon as people stop adding so much nutrient to the water.) In the developing countries the proportion of the urban population served by a safe water supply rose modestly in the 1970s, and rose markedly among the rural population (but from 14 percent to only 29 percent; Holdgate et al. 1982: 135).

The long-run historical record, to the extent that there are data, offers examples upon which one may seize to argue almost any shade of opinion about pollution. But many of the oft-cited series that purportedly show "deterioration" prove, upon inspection, to be the result of forces other than recent human activities.

"LESS STABLE ECOLOGICALLY, AND MORE VULNERABLE TO DISRUPTION"
These concepts are so diffuse that we have no idea how one would measure them directly. *Global 2000* gives no relevant trend data.

Perhaps *Global 2000* had in mind that there is more danger of disruption as humankind's capacity to alter the ecosystem increases. In itself, this must be true. But at the same time, humankind's ability to restore imbalances in the ecosystem also increases. And the trend data on pollution, food (discussed below), and life expectancy suggest that the life-supporting capacities have been increasing faster than the malign disturbances. Of course some unprecedented catastrophe such as the Black Death may occur, but we can only look into the future as best we can, and conclude that no such catastrophe is in view. The one crucial exception is war, which is outside our scope here, and which is not a matter of the natural resource constraints that depend upon the nature of the physical world.

"SERIOUS STRESSES INVOLVING POPULATION, RESOURCES, AND ENVIRONMENT . . ."

This *Global 2000* phrase sounds ominous, but like many other *Global 2000* warnings it is hard to pin down. If it means that people will have a poorer chance of survival in the year 2000 than now, due to the greater number of people, the trends in life expectancy suggest the contrary. Declining mortality and improving health have accompanied unprecedented population growth in the world (as well as in the US, of course). Figure 4.6 shows the long-run trend of life expectancy in the more-developed world, a pattern toward which the less-developed countries are converging. For example, life expectancy in less-developed regions rose from 43 years in 1950/55 to 53 years in 1970/75 (the rise in Asia being even greater), a much bigger jump than the rise from 65 years to 71 years in the more-developed regions (Gwatkin 1980).

If the phrase "serious stresses" implies that along with more people in the year 2000 will come more costly resources and a deteriorated environment, the trends suggest the opposite, as noted above for the environment, and as discussed next for resources. If the phrase means that life expectancy, resource availability, and the quality of the environment could be even better in the year 2000 with fewer people than are expected, *Global 2000* has not even attempted to demonstrate such a complex causal correction. The existing research on the subject does not suggest to us that such would be the case.

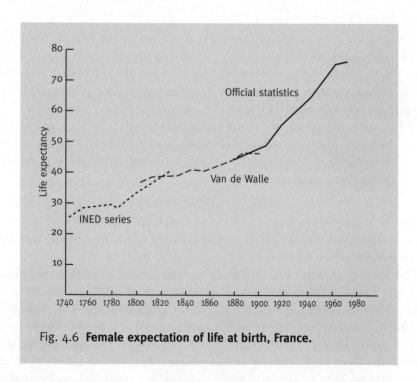

Fig. 4.6 **Female expectation of life at birth, France.**

". . . RESOURCES . . ."

Global 2000 projected a 5 percent yearly increase in the real price of non-fuel minerals until the year 2000. There has always been "serious stress" in the sense that people have to pay a price to get the resources they want. But the relevant economic measures of "stress"—costs and prices—show that the long-run trend is toward less scarcity and lower prices rather than more scarcity and higher prices, hard as that may be for many people to believe. The cost trends of almost every natural resource have been downward over the course of recorded history.

An hour's work in the United States has bought increasingly more of copper, wheat, and oil (which are representative and important raw materials) from 1800 to the present (see, for example, Figure 4.7). The trend is less dramatic in the poorest countries, but the direction of the trend is unmistakable there, too, because per person income has been rising in poor countries as well as rich ones. The same trend has held throughout human history for such minerals as copper and iron (Clark 1957: appendix). Calculations of expenditures for raw materials as a falling proportion of total family budgets make the same point even more strongly.

These trends mean that raw materials have been getting increasingly available and less scarce relative to the most important and most fundamental element of economic life, human work-time. The prices of raw materials have even been falling relative to consumer goods and the Consumer Price Index. All the items in the Consumer Price Index have been produced with increasingly efficient use of labor and capital over the years, but the decrease in cost of raw materials has been even greater than that of other goods. This is a very strong demonstration of progressively decreasing scarcity and increasing availability of raw materials. The trend of raw material prices relative to consumer goods, however, has much less meaning for human welfare than does the trend of resource prices relative to the price of human time—a trend which is decidedly benign, as we have seen. Even if raw materials were rising in price relative to consumer goods, there would be no cause for alarm as long as it takes progressively less effort, and a smaller proportion of our incomes, to obtain the service from raw materials that we need and want.

Moreover, the observed fall in the prices of raw materials understates the positive trend, because as consumers we are interested in the services we get from the raw materials rather than the raw materials themselves. We have learned to use less of given raw materials for given purposes, as well as to substitute cheaper materials to get the same services. Consider a copper pot used long ago for cooking. The consumer is interested in a container that can be put over heat. After iron and aluminium were discovered, quite satisfactory cooking pots—with advantages as well as disadvantages compared with pots of copper—could be made of those materials. The cost that interests us is the cost of providing the cooking service, rather than the cost of the copper.

A single communications satellite in space provides intercontinental telephone connections that would otherwise require thousands of tons of copper. Satellites and microwave transmission and the use of glass fibers in communications are dramatic examples of how a substitute process can supply a service much more cheaply than copper.

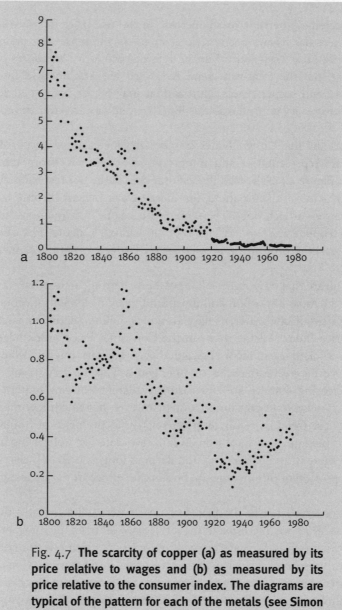

Fig. 4.7 **The scarcity of copper (a) as measured by its price relative to wages and (b) as measured by its price relative to the consumer index. The diagrams are typical of the pattern for each of the metals (see Simon 1981: appendix).**

"THE WORLD'S PEOPLE WILL BE POORER IN MANY WAYS . . ."

The Global 2000 qualifying phrase "in many ways" could imply that a decrease in the number of elephants, or the deaths of some elderly beloved persons, are ways in which the world's people will be poorer in the future than now; if so, the statement is logically correct. But if we consider more general and economically meaningful measures, the world's people have been getting richer rather than poorer, and may be expected to be richer in the future. Measured in conventional terms, average income for the world's population has been rising. Particularly noteworthy, and contrary to common belief, income in the poorer countries has been rising at a percentage rate as great or greater than in the richer countries since World War II (Morawetz 1978). Another vivid proof of the rise in income in poorer countries is the decline in the proportion of the labor force devoted to agriculture—from 68 percent to 58 percent between 1965 and 1981 in the developing countries, consistent with the trend in developed countries where the agricultural labor force has plummeted to, for example, well below 3 percent in the US. The rising average income in poorer countries combined with the rough stability of their internal income-distribution shares suggests that the poorer classes of representative countries have been participating in this income rise along with the richer classes.

"THE OUTLOOK FOR FOOD . . . WILL BE NO BETTER"

Consumption of food per person in the world is up over the last 30 years (Figure 4.8). And data do not show that the bottom of the income scale is faring worse, or even has failed to share in the general improvement, as the average has improved. Africa's food production per capita is down, but no one thinks that has anything to do with physical conditions; it clearly stems from governmental and other social conditions. Famine deaths have decreased in the past century even in absolute terms, let alone relative to population. World food prices have been trending lower for decades and centuries (Figure 4.9), and there is strong reason to believe that this trend will continue. This evidence runs exactly counter to *Global 2000*'s conclusion that "real prices for food are expected to double." If a problem exists for the US, it is a problem caused by abundance. Food production in the US is now so great that farmers are suffering economically. Food stocks in the world are so high that they are causing major problems (Figure 4.10). Agricultural yields per hectare have continued to rise in such countries as China, France, and the US. These gains in production have been accomplished with a decreasing proportion of the labor force—the key input for and constraint upon the economic system.

Careful study of the quantities of actual and potential agricultural land in various countries, plus possibilities for irrigation and multicropping together with yields already routinely reached in the developed countries, suggests that agricultural land will not be a bottleneck in the foreseeable future, even without new technological breakthroughs. And the supply of water for agriculture (which is by far the largest use of water) poses even fewer problems arising from purely physical conditions. Physical measurements of water withdrawal in the world as a whole provide no relevant information. The possibility of the world as a whole running out of water is zero. The supply of water is always a local or regional issue within a country (or occasionally at the border of two countries). The key constraints upon the supply of water arise from institutional

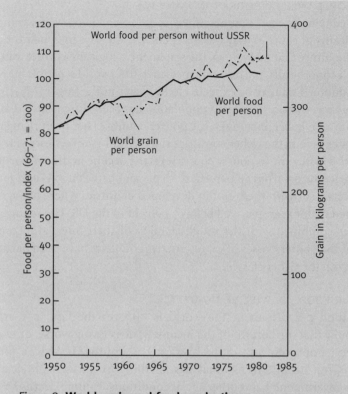

Fig. 4.8 **World grain and food production per person.**

Sources: USDA, FAS, FG-8-82 (3-15-82); Brown, *Building a Sustainable Society* (Norton, 1981), 81 (with authors' extrapolation of 1981 and 1982 population). The Food index includes all food commodities—including grain, pulses, oil-seeds, vegetables, and fruit; it excludes the PRC. Source of index USDA, ERS, Statistical Bulletin No. 669, July 1981; USDA, personal communication, Dr Patrick M. O'Brien (1980, 1981 index).

and political conditions, and especially the structure of property rights to water and the price structure for water, rather than mere physical availability.

The issue of a well-constituted system of property rights—the absence of which often leads to "the tragedy of the commons"—arises sharply with respect to water rights; but appropriate rules for private property are also of fundamental importance in many other natural resource and environmental situations. Drilling rights in oil basins, rights to pollute the air and water, and hunting rights for wild animals, are but three dramatic examples. A sound set of social rules with respect to property can go far to ensure a satisfactory supply of resources and an acceptably clean environment. On this there is ever-growing agreement among naturalists, economists, geologists, and others concerned with these matters.

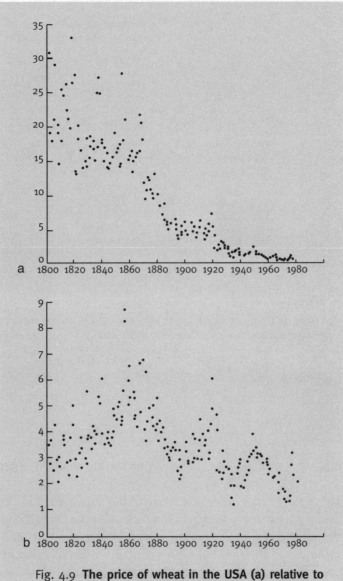

Fig. 4.9 **The price of wheat in the USA (a) relative to wages and (b) relative to the consumer price index.**

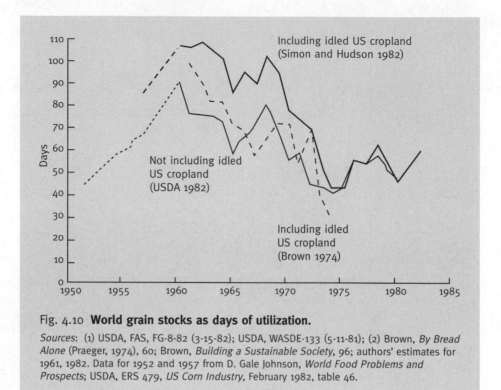

Fig. 4.10 **World grain stocks as days of utilization.**

Sources: (1) USDA, FAS, FG-8-82 (3-15-82); USDA, WASDE-133 (5-11-81); (2) Brown, *By Bread Alone* (Praeger, 1974), 60; Brown, *Building a Sustainable Society*, 96; authors' estimates for 1961, 1982. Data for 1952 and 1957 from D. Gale Johnson, *World Food Problems and Prospects*; USDA, ERS 479, *US Corn Industry*, February 1982, table 46.

"SIGNIFICANT LOSSES OF WORLD FORESTS WILL CONTINUE OVER THE NEXT 20 YEARS"

According to *Global 2000*, "by 2000 some 40 percent of the remaining forest cover in LDCs will be gone." If nonsense is a statement utterly without factual support, this is nonsense. Forests are not declining at all in the temperate regions. In the US, for example, the total quantity of trees has been increasing, and wood production has been increasing rapidly (Figure 4.11). The rate of deforestation in tropical areas has been far slower than suggested by *Global 2000*. The prospects for world wood production to meet demand without grave deforestation are excellent, especially because plantations which require only small land areas have just begun to make the major contribution to total world production of which they are capable.

"ARABLE LAND WILL INCREASE ONLY 4 PERCENT BY 2000. . . . SERIOUS DETERIORATION OF AGRICULTURAL SOILS WILL OCCUR WORLDWIDE, DUE TO EROSION"

Arable land has been increasing at a rate very much faster in recent decades than the rate *Global 2000* projected for coming decades—an increase which we can approximate at fully 16 percent over the 20-year period from 1950 to 1975 for which there are good data (Table 4.1). There is no

uses non-LDC examples to dispute

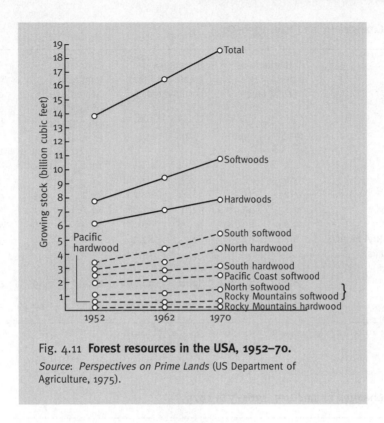

Fig. 4.11 **Forest resources in the USA, 1952–70.**

Source: *Perspectives on Prime Lands* (US Department of Agriculture, 1975).

apparent reason why in the next decades the increase should fall anywhere nearly as low as the 4 percent *Global 2000* suggests. A comprehensive assessment of the earth's land resources for agriculture by an authoritative President's Science Advisory Committee suggested that arable land will not be a key constraint upon food production in the world, and our findings agree. Rather, social and economic conditions are the key constraints on the amount of land brought into production.

In the United States, the conversion of farmland to urbanized land is proceeding at about the same rate as in recent decades, rather than at three times that rate, as was widely reported recently by a now-discredited agency of the US Department of Agriculture (the National Agricultural Lands Study), the source of the *Global 2000* statement on the subject. Furthermore, each year more (and better) new land is being brought into cultivation by irrigation and drainage than is being urbanized and built upon.

Concern about the "loss" of cropland to new housing, and the resulting governmental regulations that have constrained housing starts and raised the price of new homes, especially in California, does not square with contemporary federal policies for reducing planted acreage to meet the problem of "overproduction" of grain. In 1983 perhaps 39 percent of US crop acreage was kept idle by federal subsidy programs, at an unprecedented high cost to US taxpayers of $18.3

Table 4.1(a) **Changes in land use, 1950–60**

	Arable land as a percentage of total area		Percentage of arable land that is cultivated		Cultivated land as a percentage of total land (1×3) and (2×4)		Agricultural land (arable and pasture) as a percentage of total area	
	(1) 1950	(2) 1960	(3) 1950	(4) 1960	1950	1960	1950	1960
Africa	14.27	15.30	36.21	42.72	5.2	6.5	46.50	49.02
Middle East	12.87	13.91	52.11	57.88	6.7	8.1	13.06	17.34
Asia	19.03	20.78	82.06	86.17	15.6	17.9	46.35	49.60
North and South America, USSR, Australia, New Zealand	6.88	7.75	82.75	82.96	5.7	6.4	34.27	38.59
Europe	30.79	30.98	89.02	90.06	27.4	27.9	45.63	46.10
ALL REGIONS	10.73	11.73	82.74	83.99	8.9	9.9	37.35	41.07

Source: Kumar 1973: 107.

Table 4.1(b) **Changes in land use, 1961–5 to 1975**

	Arable land as a percentage of total area				Agriculturl land (arable and pasture) as a percentage of total area			
	1961–5	1966	1970	1975	1961–5	1966	1970	1975
Africa	6.28	6.50	6.76	6.96	32.88	32.96	33.13	33.29
Middle East	6.25	6.38	6.54	6.79	21.91	22.12	22.32	22.62
Far East	28.87	29.37	29.88	30.73	33.08	33.62	33.80	34.56
North America	11.50	11.43	12.17	13.08	26.10	25.85	25.88	25.50
USSR	10.24	10.24	10.39	10.37	26.83	27.34	27.09	26.97
Latin America	5.64	5.97	6.43	6.82	29.56	30.29	31.29	32.41
Western Europe	27.21	26.55	25.97	25.04	46.35	45.08	44.83	43.72
ALL REGIONS	10.41	10.58	10.93	11.25	33.13	33.38	33.71	33.99

Source: UN Food and Agriculture Organization 1976.

billion (compared to an original estimate of $1.8 billion for the year; *New York Times*, 31 January 1983, 5). The argument is sometimes made that governments must act to save cropland for future generations, but this argument lacks support from either economic analysis or technological considerations. The driving motive behind urging government action to "preserve" farmland seems to be more aesthetics than economics.

Soil erosion is not occurring at a dangerous pace in most parts of the United States, contrary to much recent publicity. In most areas top soil is not being lost at a rate that makes broad changes in farming practices economical from either the private or public standpoint, though recent advances in tillage may change the picture somewhat. Regulating or subsidizing particular tillage practices portends greater social cost than benefit in the long run. The largest social cost of soil erosion is not the loss of top soil, but rather the silting-up of drainage ditches in some places, with consequent maintenance expenses. In the aggregate, just the opposite of land ruination has been taking place, as the soil of American farms has been improving rather than deteriorating, and as fewer rather than more crop acres suffer from severe erosion over the decades since the 1930s. The continuing advance in agricultural productivity per acre is consistent with the improvement in the quality of farmland.

"EXTINCTIONS OF PLANT AND ANIMAL SPECIES WILL INCREASE DRAMATICALLY. HUNDREDS OF THOUSANDS OF SPECIES—PERHAPS AS MANY AS 20 PERCENT OF ALL SPECIES ON EARTH—WILL BE IRRETRIEVABLY LOST AS THEIR HABITATS VANISH, ESPECIALLY IN TROPICAL FORESTS"

This assertion by *Global 2000* is remarkably unsupported by statistical evidence. The only scientific observations cited in support of a numerical estimate of future species extinction are (*a*) between 1600 and 1900 perhaps one species every 4 years was extinguished, and (*b*) between 1900 and 1980 perhaps one species every year was extinguished. The leap to *Global 2000*'s estimate of 40,000 species extinguished each year by the year 2000 is based on pure guesswork by the *Global 2000* writers and the source upon which they draw (Myers 1979). We do not neglect the die-off of the passenger pigeon and other species that may be valuable to us. But we note that extinction of species—billions of them, according to Mayr (1982)—has been a biological fact of life throughout the ages, just as has been the development of new species, some or many of which may be more valuable to humans than extinguished species whose niches they fill.

"ATMOSPHERIC CONCENTRATIONS OF CARBON DIOXIDE AND OZONE-DEPLETING CHEMICALS ARE EXPECTED TO INCREASE AT RATES THAT COULD ALTER THE WORLD'S CLIMATE AND UPPER ATMOSPHERE SIGNIFICANTLY BY 2050"

The longest available records of climatic variations reveal very wide temperature swings, much or all of which may be thought of as random. In that context, recent changes in temperature may reasonably be viewed as normal oscillation rather than as a structural change induced by man's activity, including changes in CO_2.

The CO_2 question is subject to major controversy and uncertainty—about the extent of the buildup, about its causes, and especially about its effects. It would not seem prudent to undertake expensive policy alterations at this time because of this lack of knowledge, and because problems that changes in CO_2 concentration might cause would occur far in the future (well beyond the year 2000). Changes in the CO_2 situation may reasonably be seen, however, as an argument for increased use of nuclear power rather than fossil fuel. Continued research and monitoring of the CO_2 situation certainly is called for.

If it is considered desirable to reduce the amount of CO_2 released into the atmosphere by human activity, on the grounds that atmospheric change with unknown effects carries undesired risks, only two possibilities are feasible: reduce total energy consumption, or increase energy production from nuclear power plants. Reduction in total world energy consumption below the level determined by prices reflecting the production cost of energy is clearly unacceptable to most nations of the world because of the negative effects on economic growth, nutrition and health, and consumer satisfaction. This implies an inverse tradeoff relationship between CO_2 and non-fossil (especially nuclear) power.

"ACID RAIN . . ."

There is trend evidence that the pollution of acid rain has been getting more intense, and that it has some ill effects on fresh water lakes and their fish, upon perhaps forests, and hence upon people's ability to enjoy nature. Emissions from combustion of fossil fuels are undoubtedly a partial cause, although natural sources also contribute. There is some evidence of limited local ecological damage, but no proven threat to agriculture or human life. The trend deserves careful monitoring. The consensus of recent official committee reports (with which we agree) questions the use of high-sulfur coal for power production. This squares with our general advocacy of nuclear electricity generation. Whether any tighter pollution controls are warranted, economically or otherwise, has not been established. Fighting acid-rain effects on fish by liming lakes does not generally seem economically feasible. The acid-rain issue increases the comparative advantage of nuclear power plants relative to coal-burning plants. As with CO_2, then, there is an inverse tradeoff relationship between nuclear power and acid rain.

"REGIONAL WATER SHORTAGES WILL BECOME MORE SEVERE"

In the previous decade or so, water experts have concluded that the "likelihood of the world running out of water is zero." The recent UN Report of the World Environment, for example, tells us not to focus upon the ratio between physical water supply and use, as *Global 2000* does nevertheless, and emphasizes making appropriate social and economic as well as technological choices. From this flows "cautious hope from improved methods of management." That is, an appropriate structure of property rights, institutions, and pricing systems, together with some modicum of wisdom in choosing among the technological options open to us, can provide water for our growing needs at reasonable cost indefinitely.

Moreover, *Global 2000*'s statements about the world's future water situation are completely inconsistent with—in fact, are completely opposed to—*Global 2000*'s own analysis of what can reasonably be said about the world's water resources. It develops a sound analysis that finds that no reasonable or useful forecasts can be made about the world's water supply, but then proceeds to offer frightening forecasts totally inconsistent with its analysis. This inconsistency should be more than sufficient grounds to reject *Global 2000*'s gloomy conclusions out of hand.

"ENERGY . . ."

The prospect of running out of energy is purely a bogeyman. The availability of energy has been increasing, and the meaningful cost has been decreasing, over the entire span of humankind's history. We expect this benign trend to continue at least until our sun ceases to shine in perhaps 7 billion years, and until exhaustion of the supply of elemental inputs for fission (and perhaps for fusion).

Barring extraordinary political problems, we expect the price of oil to go down. Even with respect to oil, there is no basis to conclude that the price will rise until the year 2000 and beyond, or that humankind will ever face a greater shortage of oil in economic terms than it does now; rather, decreasing shortage is the more likely, in our view. For the next decade or two, politics—especially the fortunes of the OPEC cartel, and the prevalence of war instability—are likely to be the largest element in influencing oil prices. But no matter what the conditions, the market for oil substitutes probably constitutes a middle-run ceiling price for oil not much above what it is now; there could be a short-run panic run-up, but the world is better protected from that now than in the 1970s. And if free competition prevails, the price will be far below its present level.

Electrical power from nuclear fission plants is available at costs as low or much lower than from coal, depending upon the location, and at lower costs than from oil or gas. Even in the US, where the price of coal is unusually low, existing nuclear plants produce power more cheaply than from coal. Nuclear energy is available in unlimited quantity beyond any conceivable meaningful human horizon. And nuclear power gives every evidence of costing fewer lives per unit of energy produced than does coal or oil. The main constraints are various political interests, public misinformation, and cost-raising counter-productive systems of safety regulation. Nuclear waste disposal with remarkably high levels of safeguards presents no scientific difficulties.

Energy from sources other than fossil fuel and nuclear power, aside from hydropower where it is available, do not hold much promise for supplying the bulk of human energy elements, though solar power can be the cheapest source of power for heating buildings and water in certain geographic locations. The key defect of solar power, as well as with its relatives such as power from waves, is that it is too dilute, requiring very large areas and much capital to collect the energy.

"RAPID GROWTH IN WORLD POPULATION WILL HARDLY HAVE ALTERED BY 2000 . . .
THE RATE OF GROWTH WILL SLOW ONLY MARGINALLY FROM 1.8 PERCENT A YEAR TO
1.7 PERCENT"

Population forecasting involving fertility is notoriously unreliable. The birth rate can go down very rapidly, as numerous countries have demonstrated in the past few decades, including a country as large as China. (The rate can also go up rapidly, as the baby boom in the U.S. following World War II demonstrated.) Therefore, confidence in any such forecast for a matter of decades would be misplaced. The passage of only a handful of years already seems to have knocked the props out from under *Global 2000*'s forecast quoted above. The world's annual growth rate, which was 2.2 percent less than two decades ago in 1964–5, is down to 1.75 percent (US Department of Commerce News, 31 August 1983), a broad decline over the bulk of all the poorer and faster-growth nations. Though the growth rate may have stabilized in the last few years, these data alone seem inconsistent with the *Global 2000* forecast. The author of that forecast acknowledges that we have already moved from their "medium" forecast to their "low" forecast.

Even the apparently sure-fire *Global 2000* forecast that "in terms of sheer numbers, population will be growing faster in 2000 than it is today" might very well turn out to be wrong. Because the total population will be larger in 2000 than now, the fertility rate would have to be considerably smaller than it is now to falsify that forecast. But the drop would have to be only of the magnitude of the drop during the past two decades for that to come about, which would not seem beyond possibility.

More generally, the *Global 2000* forecasts of a larger population are written in language that conveys apprehension. But viewing the long sweep of human history, larger population size has been a clear-cut sign of economic success and has accompanied improvement in the human lot. The growth in numbers over the millennia, from a few thousands or millions living at subsistence to billions living well above subsistence, is proof positive that the problem of sustenance has eased rather than intensified. And the increase in life expectancy, which is the main cause of the increase in population size, is not only a sign of success in agriculture and public health, but also is the fundamental human good.

In the long run, human beings are the only possible source of human progress. Therefore, we consider *Global 2000*'s choice of language to describe population developments to be inappropriate and misleading.

Our positive statements about the recession of the physical constraints upon human progress are based primarily upon presently known progress, not taking into account possible or even likely advancements in technology. If we were to take into account such possibilities as the resources available to us in space and other such advances—even those possibilities which are already solidly worked out scientifically—our assessment would be much more "optimistic" than it is.

Notes

1. Paragraph adapted from Kahn and Schneider (1981). Various other material adapted from Simon (1981).
2. Carter (1980:575–6).
3. *Time*, 4 August 1980, 54.
4. *Newsweek*, 4 August 1980, 38.
5. Champaign-Urbana *News Gazette*, 24 July 1980, 1.
6. For additional material on *Global 2000*'s factual errors and internal inconsistencies, see Simon (1981).
7. Ned Dearborn, one of the three *Global 2000* staff writers, stated in the abstract of a public talk he gave at the 1982 meeting of the American Association for the Advancement of Science:

   By deliberate political choice, only part of the *Global 2000 Report to the President* was featured in the Report's summary volume and press releases—the part containing the Report's projections. The other part, while not suppressed, was barely mentioned in the official material receiving the widest distribution.

References

Ascher, William (1978), *Forecasting* (Baltimore: Johns Hopkins Press).

Barney, Gerald O. (1982), "Improving the Government's Capacity to Analyze and Predict Conditions and Trends of Global Population Resources and Environment," manuscript dated 24 March.

Carter, Luther, J. (1980), "Global 2000 Report: Vision of a Gloomy World," *Science*, 209 (1 August): 575–6.

Champaign-Urbana *News Gazette*, 24 July 1980, 1.

Clark, Colin (1957), *Conditions of Economic Progress*, 3rd edn. (New York: Macmillan).

Clawson, Marion (1981), "Entering the Twenty-First Century—The Global 2000 Report to the President," *Resources*, 66 (Spring): 19.

Council on Environmental Quality, United States Department of State (1981), *Global Future: Time to Act*, January: 1–209.

Dearborn, Ned (1982), Address to American Association for the Advancement of Science, January.

Dubos, Rene (1982), "Half Truths about the Future," *Wall Street Journal*, 8 May, editorial page.

Global 2000 Report to the President, i, ii, and iii (Washington, DC: US Government Printing Office, 1980).

Gwatkin, Davidson R. (1980), "Indications of Change in Developing Country Mortality Trends: The End of an Era?", *Population and Development Review*, 6 (December); 615–44.

Hamilton, C. F. (1982), Memo from Command and Control Technical Center, Defense Communications Agency.

Holdgate, Martin W., Kassas, Mohammed and White, Gilbert F. (1982), *The World Environment, 1971–1982* (Dublin: Tycooly).

Kahn, Herman, and Schneider, Ernest (1981), "Globaloney 2000" *Policy Review*, Spring: 129–47.

Kumar, Joginden (1973), *Population and Land in World Agriculture* (Berkeley: University of California Press).

Mayr, Ernst (1982), *The Growth of Biological Thought: Diversity and Inheritance* (Cambridge, Mass.: Belknap Press of Harvard University Press).

Morawetz, David (1978), *Twenty-Five Years of Economic Development 1950–1975* (Baltimore: Johns Hopkins).

Myers, Norman (1979), *The Sinking Ark* (New York: Pergamon).

Myrdal, Gunnar (1975), *Against the Stream—Critical Essays on Economics* (New York: Vintage Books).

New York Times, 31 January 1983, 5.

Newsweek, 4 August 1980.

Simon, Julian L. (1981), "Global Confusion, 1980: A Hard Look at the Global 2000 Report," *Public Interest*, 62 (Winter): 3–21.

Time, 9 August 1980.

US Department of Commerce, Bureau of the Census (1977), *Social Indicators: 1976* (Washington, DC: US Government Printing Office).

US Department of the Interior, National Park Service (1944), *Information Relating to the National Park System*, 30 June.

Wall Street Journal, 15 September 1980, 32.

Wall Street Journal, 1 April 1983, 13.

Willson, Pete (1982), Memorandum, Alan Guttmacher Institute, 17 September.

5   The Ecorealist Manifesto

Gregg Easterbrook

In the first section of my book, *A Moment on the Earth*, from which this extract is taken the goal was to consider environmental problems from the perspective of nature: a long-term, almost mythic purview of existence, yet one with relevance to daily ecological challenges that confront humanity.

The second section considered environmental problems from the perspective of women and men alive today: a short-term perspective, yet one that can be adjusted to incorporate the wisdom embodied in eons of natural transitions.

The final section looks at how the long-term purview of nature might be combined with the short-term insights of genus *Homo* in ways that allow people, machines, and nature to learn to work together for each other's mutual benefit.

Here I summarize the principles of a new view of ecological thought, the new view called ecorealism. The founding concept of ecorealism is this: Logic, not sentiment, best serves the interests of nature.

If the worthy inclinations of environmentalism are to be transformed from an ephemeral late twentieth-century political fashion to a lasting component of human thought, the ecological impulse must become grounded in rationality. The straightforward, rational case for the environment will prove more durable than the fiercest doomsday emotion. Love nature? Learn science and speak logic. Many lesser creatures will thank you.

And now some principles of ecorealism:

Rationalism

- If ecological rationalism sometimes shows that environmental problems are not as bad as expected, that means warnings will be all the more persuasive when genuine problems are found.
- Graduation from overstatement will make the environmental movement stronger, not weaker.
- The worst thing the environmental movement could become is another absentminded interest group stumbling along toward preconceived ends regardless of what the evidence suggests.
- Skeptical debate is good for the environmental movement. The public need not to be brainwashed into believing in ecological protection, since a clean environment is in everyone's

interest. Thus the environmental movement must learn to entertain skeptical debate in a reasoned manner or will discredit itself, as all close-minded political movements eventually discredit themselves.

- Market forces and cost-benefit thinking aren't perfect but generally will be good for the environment. This is so if only because society may be able to afford several cost-effective conservation initiatives for the price of one poorly conceived program.
- Optimism not only flows from a reasoned reading of natural history, it will be an effective political tool.

Pollution

- In the Western world the Age of Pollution is nearly over. Almost every pollution issue will be solved within the lifetimes of readers of this book.
- In the West many forms of pollution have begun to decline in the very period that environmental doctrine has declared them growing worse.
- Most recoveries from pollution will happen faster than even optimists project.
- Weapons aside, technology is not growing more dangerous and wasteful. It grows cleaner and more resource-efficient.
- Clean technology will be the successor to high technology. Most brute-force systems of material production will be supplanted by production based mainly on knowledge. Nature's creatures make extremely sophisticated "products" with hardly any input of energy or resources. People will learn to do the same.
- Sometimes approximated environmental rules are good ideas even if the result is a less than perfect cleanup. Better to realize 90 percent of an ecological restoration fast than to spend decades conducting lawsuits on how to achieve 100 percent.
- As positive as trends are in the First World, they are negative in the Third. One reason the West must shake off instant-doomsday thinking about the United States and Western Europe is so that resources can be diverted to ecological protection in the developing world.

Change

- It is pointless for men and women to debate what the "correct" reality for nature might have been before people arrived on the scene. There has never been and can never be any fixed, correct environmental reality. There are only moments on the Earth, moments that may be good or bad.
- Every environment and habitat comes into existence fated to end. This is not sad. It should inspire women and men to seek to prolong moments on the Earth, through conservation.
- All environmental errors are reversible save one: extinction. Therefore the prevention of extinctions is a priority.
- Though humanity may today be a cause of species extinction, in a very short time by nature's standards it can become an agent for species preservation.

People

- People may not sit above animals and plants in any metaphysical sense, but clearly are superior in their placement in the natural order. Decent material conditions must be provided for all of the former before there can be long-term assurance of protection for the latter.
- Either humanity was created by a higher power, in which case it is absurd for environmental dogma to consider the human role in nature to be bad; or humanity rose to its position through purely natural processes, in which case it is absurd for environmental dogma to consider the human role in nature to be bad.
- However the deed was done, once genus *Homo* was called forth into being, the wholly spontaneous ordering of the environment ended. And unless there is an extinction of intellect, wholly spontaneous nature will never return. Nature is not diminished by this. A fairly straightforward reading of natural history suggests that evolution spent 3.8 billion years working assiduously to bring about the demise of the wholly spontaneous order, via the creation of intellect.
- In principle the human population is no enemy of nature. Someday that population may be many times larger than at present, without ecological harm. But the world of the present knows more people than current social institutions and technical knowledge can support at an adequate material standard. Thus short-term global population stabilization is desperately required, though the prospect of dramatic long-term expansion of the human population should not be discounted.

Nature

- Nature is not ending, nor is human damage to the environment "unprecedented." Nature has repelled forces of a magnitude many times greater than the worst human malfeasance.
- Nature is not ponderously slow. It's just old. Old and slow are quite different concepts. That the living world can adjust with surprising alacrity is the reason nature has been able to get old. Most natural recoveries from ecological duress happen with amazing speed.
- Significant human tampering with the environment has been in progress for at least ten millennia and perhaps longer. If nature has been interacting with genus *Homo* for thousands of years, then the living things that made it to the present day may be ones whose genetic treasury renders them best suited to resist human mischief. This does not insure any creature will continue to survive any clash with humankind. It does make survival more likely than doomsday orthodoxy asserts.
- If nature's adjustment to the human presence began thousands of years ago, perhaps it will soon be complete. Far from reeling helplessly before a human onslaught, nature may be on the verge of reasserting itself.
- Nature still rules much more of the Earth than does genus *Homo*. To the statistical majority of nature's creatures the arrival of men and women goes unnoticed.
- To people the distinction between artificial and natural means a great deal. To nature it means nothing at all.

- The fundamental force of nature is not amoral struggle between hunter and hunted. Most living things center their existence on cooperation and coexistence, the sort of behavior women and men should emulate. This is one reason nature will soon be viewed again in the way it was by the thinkers of the eighteenth-century Enlightenment—as a trove of wisdom and an exemplar for society.

Where Do We Fit In?

- Nature, limited by spontaneous interactions among elements randomly disturbed, may have an upper-bound limit on its potential to foster life and to evolve. Yet nature appears to enjoy fostering life and evolving. So perhaps nature hoped to acquire new sets of abilities, such as action by design.
- Therefore maybe nature needs us.

6   "Wise Use" and Environmental Anti-Science

Paul R. Ehrlich and Anne H. Ehrlich

Humanity is now facing a sort of slow-motion environmental Dunkirk. It remains to be seen whether civilization can avoid the perilous trap it has set for itself. Unlike the troops crowding the beach at Dunkirk, civilization's fate is in its own hands; no miraculous last-minute rescue is in the cards. Although progress has certainly been made in addressing the human predicament, far more is needed. Even if humanity manages to extricate itself, it is likely that environmental events will be defining ones for our grandchildren's generation—and those events could dwarf World War II in magnitude.

Sadly, much of the progress that has been made in defining, understanding, and seeking solutions to the human predicament over the past thirty years is now being undermined by an environmental backlash, fueled by anti-science ideas and arguments provided by the brownlash. While it assumes a variety of forms, the brownlash appears most clearly as an outpouring of seemingly authoritative opinions in books, articles, and media appearances that greatly distort what is or isn't known by environmental scientists. Taken together, despite the variety of its forms, sources, and issues addressed, the brownlash has produced what amounts to a body of anti-science—a twisting of the findings of empirical science—to bolster a predetermined worldview and to support a political agenda. By virtue of relentless repetition, this flood of anti-environmental sentiment has acquired an unfortunate aura of credibility.

It should be noted that the brownlash is not by any means a coordinated effort. Rather, it seems to be generated by a diversity of individuals and organizations. Some of its promoters have links to right-wing ideology and political groups. And some are well-intentioned individuals, including writers and public figures, who for one reason or another have bought into the notion that environmental regulation has become oppressive and needs to be severely weakened. But the most extreme—and most dangerous—elements are those who, while claiming to represent a scientific viewpoint, misstate scientific findings to support their view that the US government has gone overboard with regulation, especially (but not exclusively) for environmental protection, and that subtle, long-term problems like global warming are nothing to worry about. The words and sentiments of the brownlash are profoundly troubling to us and many of our colleagues. Not only are the underlying agendas seldom revealed, but more important, the confusion and distraction created among the public and policy makers by brownlash

From Paul R. Ehrlich and Anne H. Ehrlich, *The Betrayal of Science and Reason* (Washington, DC: Island Press, 1996), 11–23. Reprinted with permission.

pronouncements interfere with and prolong the already difficult search for realistic and equitable solutions to the human predicament.

Anti-science as promoted by the brownlash is not a unique phenomenon in our society; the largely successful efforts of creationists to keep Americans ignorant of evolution is another example, which is perhaps not entirely unrelated.[1] Both feature a denial of facts and circumstances that don't fit religious or other traditional beliefs; policies built on either could lead our society into serious trouble.

Fortunately, in the case of environmental science, most of the public is fairly well informed about environmental problems and remains committed to environmental protection. When polled, 65 percent of Americans today say they are willing to pay good money for environmental quality.[2] But support for environmental quality is sometimes said to be superficial; while almost everyone is in favor of a sound environment—clean air, clean water, toxic site cleanups, national parks, and so on—many don't feel that environmental deterioration, especially on a regional or global level, is a crucial issue in their own lives. In part this is testimony to the success of environmental protection in the United States. But it is also the case that most people lack an appreciation of the deeper but generally less visible, slowly developing global problems. Thus they don't perceive population growth, global warming, the loss of biodiversity, depletion of groundwater, or exposure to chemicals in plastics and pesticides as a personal threat at the same level as crime in their neighborhood, loss of a job, or a substantial rise in taxes.

So anti-science rhetoric has been particularly effective in promoting a series of erroneous notions, which we will analyze in detail in this book:

- environmental scientists ignore the abundant good news about the environment;
- population growth does not cause environmental damage and may even be beneficial;
- humanity is on the verge of abolishing hunger; food scarcity is a local or regional problem and is not indicative of overpopulation;
- natural resources are superabundant, if not infinite;
- there is no extinction crisis, so most efforts to preserve species are both uneconomic and unnecessary;
- global warming and acid rain are not serious threats to humanity;
- stratospheric ozone depletion is a hoax;
- the risks posed by toxic substances are vastly exaggerated; and
- environmental regulation is wrecking the economy.

How has the brownlash managed to persuade a significant segment of the public that the state of the environment and the directions and rates in which it is changing are not causes for great concern? Even many individuals who are sensitive to local environmental problems have found brownlash distortions of global issues convincing. Part of the answer lies in the overall lack of scientific knowledge among United States citizens. Most Americans readily grasp the issues surrounding something familar and tangible like a local dump site, but they have considerably more difficulty with issues involving genetic variation or the dynamics of the atmosphere. Thus it is relatively easy to rally support against a proposed landfill and infinitely more difficult to impose a carbon tax that might help offset global warming.

Also, individuals not trained to recognize the hallmarks of change have difficulty perceiving and appreciating the gradual deterioration of civilization's life-support systems.[3] This is why record-breaking temperatures and violent storms receive so much attention, while a gradual increase in annual global temperatures—measured in fractions of a degree over decades—is not considered newsworthy. Threatened pandas are featured on television, while the constant and critical losses of insect populations, which are key elements of our life-support systems, pass unnoticed. People who have no meaningful way to grasp regional and global environmental problems cannot easily tell what information is distorted, when, and to what degree.

Decision makers, too, have a tendency to focus mostly on the more obvious and immediate environmental problems—usually described as "pollution"—rather than on the deterioration of natural ecosystems upon whose continued functioning global civilization depends.[4] Indeed, most people still don't realize that humanity has become a truly global force, interfering in a very real and direct way in many of the planet's natural cycles.

For example, human activity puts ten times as much oil into the oceans as comes from natural seeps, has multiplied the natural flow of cadmium into the atmosphere eightfold, has doubled the rate of nitrogen fixation, and is responsible for about half the concentration of methane (a potent greenhouse gas) and nearly a third of the carbon dioxide (also a greenhouse gas) in the atmosphere today—all added since the Industrial Revolution, most notably in the past half-century.[5] Human beings now use or co-opt some 40 percent of the food available to all land animals[6] and about 45 percent of the available freshwater flows.[7]

Another factor that plays into brownlash thinking is the not uncommon belief that environmental quality is improving, not declining. In some ways it is, but the claim of uniform improvement simply does not stand up to close scientific scrutiny. Nor does the claim that the human condition in general is improving everywhere.[8] The degradation of ecosystem services (the conditions and processes through which natural ecosystems support and fulfill human life) is a crucial issue, which is largely ignored by the brownlash and to which we will return. Unfortunately, the superficial progress achieved to date has made it easy to label ecologists doomsayers for continuing to press for change.

At the same time, the public often seems unaware of the success of actions taken at the instigation of the environmental movement. People can easily see the disadvantages of environmental regulations but not the despoliation that would exist without them. Especially resentful are those whose personal or corporate ox is being gored when they are forced to sustain financial losses because of a sensible (or occasionally senseless) application of regulations.

Of course, it is natural for many people to feel personally threatened by efforts to preserve a healthy environment. Consider a car salesman who makes a bigger commission selling a large car than a small one, an executive of a petrochemical company that is liable for damage done by toxic chemicals released into the environment, a logger whose job is jeopardized by enforcement of the Endangered Species Act, a rancher whose way of life may be threatened by higher grazing fees on public lands, a farmer about to lose his farm because of environmentalists' attacks on subsidies for irrigation water, or a developer who wants to continue building subdivisions and is sick and tired of dealing with inconsistent building codes or US Fish and Wildlife Service bureaucrats. In such situations, resentment of some of the rules, regulations, and recommendations designed to enhance human well-being and protect life-support systems is understandable.

Unfortunately, many of these dissatisfied individuals and companies have been recruited into the self-styled "wise-use" movement, which has attracted a surprisingly diverse coalition of people, including representatives of extractive and polluting industries who are motivated by corporate interests as well as private property rights activists and right-wing ideologues. Although some of these individuals simply believe that environmental regulations unfairly distribute the costs of environmental protection, some others are doubtless motivated more by a greedy desire for unrestrained economic expansion.

At a minimum, the wise-use movement firmly opposes most government efforts to maintain environmental quality in the belief that environmental regulation creates unnecessary and burdensome bureaucratic hurdles, which stifle economic growth. Wise-use advocates see little or no need for constraints on the exploitation of resources for short-term economic benefits and argue that such exploitation can be accelerated with no adverse long-term consequences. Thus they espouse unrestricted drilling in the Arctic National Wildlife Refuge, logging in national forests, mining in protected areas or next door to national parks, and full compensation for any loss of actual or potential property value resulting from environmental restrictions.

In promoting the view that immediate economic interests are best served by continuing business as usual, the wise-use movement works to stir up discontent among everyday citizens who, rightly or wrongly, feel abused by environmental regulations. This tactic is described in detail in David Helvarg's book *The War Against the Greens*:

To date the Wise Use/Property Rights backlash has been a bracing if dangerous reminder to environmentalists that power concedes nothing without a demand and that no social movement, be it ethnic, civil, or environmental, can rest on its past laurels. . . . If the anti-enviros' links to the Farm Bureau, Heritage Foundation, NRA, logging companies, resource trade associations, multinational gold-mining companies, [and] ORV manufacturers . . . proves anything, it's that large industrial lobbies and transnational corporations have learned to play the grassroots game.[9]

Wise-use proponents are not always candid about their motivations and intentions. Many of the organizations representing them masquerade as groups seemingly attentive to environmental quality. Adopting a strategy biologists call "aggressive mimicry," they often give themselves names resembling those of genuine environmental or scientific public-interest groups: National Wetland Coalition, Friends of Eagle Mountain, The Sahara Club, the Alliance for Environment and Resources, The Abundant Wildlife Society of North America, The Global Climate Coalition, the National Wilderness Institute,[10] and the American Council on Science and Health.[11] In keeping with aggressive mimicry, these organizations often actively work *against* the interests implied in their names—a practice sometimes called "greenscamming."

One such group, calling itself Northwesterners for More Fish, seeks to limit federal protection of endangered fish species so the activities of utilities, aluminum companies, and timber outfits utilizing the region's rivers are not hindered. Armed with a $2.6 million budget, the group aims to discredit environmentalists who say industry is destroying the fish habitats of the Columbia and other rivers, threatening the Northwest's valuable salmon fishery, among others.[12]

Congressman George Miller, referring to the wise-use movement's support of welfare ranching, overlogging, and government giveaways of mining rights, stated: "What you have . . . is a lot of special interests who are trying to generate some ideological movement to try and disguise what it is individually they want in the name of their own profits, their own greed in terms of the use and abuse of federal lands."[13]

Wise-use sentiments have been adopted by a number of deeply conservative legislators, many of whom have received campaign contributions from these organizations. One member of the House of Representatives recently succeeded in gaining passage of a bill that limited the annual budget for the Mojave National Preserve, the newest addition to the National Park System, to one dollar—thus guaranteeing that the park would have no money for upkeep or for enforcement of park regulations.[14] Fortunately, the bill did not become law.

These same conservative legislators are determined to slash funding for scientific research, especially on such subjects as endangered species, ozone depletion, and global warming, and they have tried to enact severe cutbacks in funds for the National Science Foundation, the US Geological Survey, the National Aeronautics and Space Administration, and the Environmental Protection Agency. Many of them and their supporters see science as self-indulgent, at odds with economic interests, and inextricably linked to regulatory excesses.

The scientific justifications and philosophical underpinnings for the positions of the wise-use movement are largely provided by the brownlash. Prominent promoters of the wise-use viewpoint on a number of issues include such conservative think tanks as the Cato Institute and the Heritage Foundation.[15] Both organizations help generate and disseminate erroneous brownlash ideas and information. Adam Myerson, editor of the Heritage Foundation's journal *Policy Review*, pretty much summed up the brownlash perspective by saying: "Leading scientists have done major work disputing the current henny-pennyism about global warming, acid rain, and other purported environmental catastrophes."[16] In reality, as we will show, most "leading" scientists support what Myerson calls henny-pennyism; the scientists he refers to are a small group largely outside the mainstream of scientific thinking.

In recent years, a flood of books and articles has advanced the notion that all is well with the environment, giving credence to this anti-scientific "What, me worry?" outlook. Brownlash writers often pepper their works with code phrases such as "sound science" and "balance," words that suggest objectivity while in fact having little connection to what is presented. "Sound science" usually means science that is interpreted to support the brownlash view. "Balance" generally means giving undue prominence to the opinions of one or a handful of contrarian scientists who are at odds with the consensus of the scientific community at large.[17]

In this book, we will investigate many examples of what the brownlash calls "sound science" and "balance"; some of the most dramatic ones are in the area of atmospheric anti-science. We'll take a hard look at the claims of the brownlash, mostly using its own words to represent its positions, and will then set the record straight with respect to the underlying science. In our view, not all but the vast majority of brownlash pronouncements are based in either faulty science or the misinterpretation of good science. Our principal sources of brownlash ideas and erroneous information are a series of books that although convincing to some lay readers, are replete with gross scientific errors and severely twisted interpretation, as we will document in considerable detail.

Of course, while pro-environmental organizations and environmental scientists in general may sometimes be dead wrong (as can anybody confronting environmental complexity), they ordinarily are not acting on behalf of narrow economic interests. Yet one of the remarkable triumphs of the wise-use movement and its allies in the past decade has been their ability to define public interest organizations, in the eyes of many legislators, as "special interests"—not different in kind from the American Tobacco Institute, the Western Fuels Association, or other organizations that represent business groups.[18]

But we believe there is a very real difference in kind. Most environmental organizations are funded mainly by membership donations; corporate funding is at most a minor factor for public interest advocacy groups. There are no monetary profits to be gained other than attracting a bigger membership. Environmental scientists have even less to gain; they usually are dependent on university or research institute salaries and research funds from peer-reviewed government grants or sometimes (especially in new or controversial areas where government funds are largely unavailable) from private foundations.

One reason the brownlash messages hold so much appeal to many people, we think, is the fear of further change. Even though the American frontier closed a century ago, many Americans seem to believe they still live in what the great economist Kenneth Boulding once called a "cowboy economy."[19] They still think they can figuratively throw their garbage over the backyard fence with impunity; they regard the environmentally protected public land as "wasted" and think it should be available for their self-beneficial appropriation; they believe that private property rights are absolute (despite a rich economic amd legal literature showing they never have been).[20] They do not understand, as Pace University law professor John Humbach wrote in 1993, that "the Constitution does not guarantee that land speculators will win their bets."[21]

The anti-science brownlash provides a rationalization for the short-term economic interests of these groups: old-growth forests are decadent and should be harvested; extinction is natural, so there's no harm in overharvesting economically important animals; there is abundant undisturbed habitat, so human beings have a right to develop land anywhere and in any way they choose; global warming is a hoax or even will benefit agriculture, so there's no need to limit the burning of fossil fuels; and so on. Anti-science basically claims we can perpetuate the good old days by doing business as usual. But the problem is, we can't.[22]

Thus the brownlash helps create public confusion about the character and magnitude of environmental problems, taking advantage of the lack of consensus among individuals and social groups on the urgency of enhancing environmental protection. A widely shared social consensus, such as the United States last saw during World War II, will be essential if we are to maintain environmental quality while meeting the nation's other needs. By emphasizing dissent, the brownlash works against the formation of any such consensus; instead it has helped thwart the development of a spirit of cooperation mixed with concern for society as a whole. In our opinion, the brownlash fuels conflict by claiming that environmental problems are overblown or nonexistent and that unbridled economic development will propel the world to new levels of prosperity with little or no risk to the natural systems that support society. As a result, environmental groups and wise-use proponents are increasingly polarized.

Unfortunately, some of that polarization has led to ugly confrontations and activities that are not condoned by the brownlash or by most environmentalists, including us. As David Helvarg stated, "Along with the growth of Wise Use/Property Rights, the last six years have seen a startling increase in intimidation, vandalism, and violence directed against grassroots environmental activists."[23] And while confrontations and threats have been generated by both sides—most notably (but by no means exclusively) over the northern spotted owl's protection plan—the level of intimidation engaged in by wise-use proponents is disturbing, to say the least.

One of the most egregious cases involves a US Forest Service officer in central Nevada who has had several attempts made on his life.[24] Why? Because he tried to enforce Forest Service regulations in ways that offended local ranchers. In late 1995, the Forest Service transferred him to another state, literally to save his life. Meanwhile, the rebellious ranchers of Nevada have gone so far as to proclaim that county rights have precedence over the federal management of public lands. In early 1996, however, a federal court rejected their claim and reaffirmed federal jurisdiction over national lands.[25]

For Stanford scientists, of course, it's all too easy to talk about saving old-growth forests, shutting down coal mines, restricting pesticide use, or limiting fish harvests. It's more difficult for us to address the legitimate concerns of those who might pay heavy costs for those actions. Nonetheless, more must be done to address those concerns. After all, the loggers, miners, farmers, and fishers are no more responsible for the human dilemma than those of us who demand and consume their products.

Indeed, most people find it more and more difficult to do what's right environmentally. People are mostly conservative; they don't want to change their ways of life. Furthermore, especially in rich countries, citizens are bombarded by advertising that urges them to consume more and more, while technology, mobility, and an urban lifestyle have largely concealed their dependence on the natural systems and resources that are damaged by overconsumption.

For years, we owned and flew a light aircraft—and loved it. It was extremely convenient for getting to remote field sites or out-of-the-way places for lectures. But we paid a price in some environmental guilt. We worry about driving a car that's too small for safety, and we spend too much time roaring around on airline jets. Like most Americans, we have more gadgets than we need. As Pogo said, "We have met the enemy and he is us."

We have less excuse than most people, since so much of our time is spent trying to figure out how Earth's life-support systems work and how to do what's necessary to keep them working. That's why years ago we decided to have only one child; having a small family was, for us, one very effective way to lessen dramatically our "footprint" on the planet. But like many others, we feel the tension between doing what we think is right for other people, our descendants, and humanity as a whole on one hand and trying to have a pleasant and convenient life for ourselves on the other.

But, of course, timbering, coal mining, and fishing are honorable and useful jobs, and if society suddenly determines that some of those must disappear, society (including Stanford professors) should help bear the costs of easing the transition for those displaced. Sure, nobody helped the employees of horse collar manufacturers when, with the advent of the automobile, the "market" decided they should lose their jobs. But there was no general social decision that horsecollars threatened everyone, and the cooperation of workers who made them was not required for the general good.

Fortunately, despite all the efforts of the brownlash to discourage it, environmental concern in the United States is widespread.[26] Thus a public opinion survey in 1995 indicated that slightly over half of all Americans felt that environmental problems in the United States were "very serious." Indeed, 85 percent were concerned "a fair amount" and 38 percent "a great deal" about the environment. Fifty-eight percent would choose protecting the environment over economic growth, and 65 percent said they would be willing to pay higher prices so that industry could protect the environment better. Responses in other rich nations have been similar, and people in developing nations have shown, if anything, even greater environmental concerns. These responses suggest that the notion that caring about the environment is a luxury of the rich is a myth. Furthermore, our impression is that young people care especially strongly about environmental quality—a good omen if true.

Nor is environmental concern exclusive to Democrats and "liberals." There is a strong Republican and conservative tradition of environmental protection dating back to Teddy Roosevelt and even earlier.[27] Many of our most important environmental laws were passed with bipartisan support during the Nixon and Ford administrations. Recently, some conservative environmentalists have been speaking out against brownlash rhetoric.[28] And public concern is rising about the efforts to cripple environmental laws and regulations posed by right-wing leaders in Congress, thinly disguised as "deregulation" and "necessary budget-cutting." In January 1996, a Republican pollster, Linda Divall, warned that "our party is out of sync with mainstream American opinion when it comes to the environment."[29]

Indeed, some interests that might be expected to sympathize with the wise-use movement have moved beyond such reactionary views. Many leaders in corporations such as paper companies and chemical manufacturers, whose activities are directly harmful to the environment, are concerned about their firms' environmental impacts and are shifting to less damaging practices.[30] Our friends in the ranching community in western Colorado indicate their concern to us every summer. They want to preserve a way of life and a high-quality environment—and are as worried about the progressive suburbanization of the area as are the scientists at the Rocky Mountain Biological Laboratory. Indeed, they have actively participated in discussions with environmentalists and officials of the Department of the Interior to set grazing fees at levels that would not force them out of business but also wouldn't subsidize overgrazing and land abuse.[31]

Loggers, ranchers, miners, petrochemical workers, fishers, and professors all live on the same planet, and all of us must cooperate to preserve a sound environment for our descendants. The environmental problems of the planet can be solved only in a spirit of cooperation, not in one of conflict. Ways must be found to allocate fairly both the benefits and the costs of environmental quality. Environmental scientists have been arguing this for decades,[32] but unhappily, things have not always worked out as those scientists would wish.

In writing this book, we are trying to achieve three goals. The first and most important goal is to counter the erroneous information and misrepresentations put forth by the brownlash, giving a point-by-point rebuttal to the more prominent fables of environmental anti-science. Second, we want to reach out to a broad audience of readers, whether they be interested citizens, journalists, scientists, or policy makers, and provide them with accurate scientific information they can use to evaluate critically and counter the commentary of the brownlash. We hope everyone will learn that environmental conditions and processes are more crucial to human well-being, and more threatened by human activities, than most people realize. To facilitate the process, we have provided important background material and provided references to pertinent scientific literature.

And third, we want to encourage other scientists to speak out and become involved in such issues. To that end, we provide our own insights into how a scientist can become a spokesperson on matters of societal urgency yet retain scientific integrity and the support of the scientific community.

Paul and political scientist Dennis Pirages once wrote: "We are all now caught in a gigantic tragedy of the commons; each person, each family, and each nation is struggling to stay ahead while the whole system is on the verge of collapse. Many people are now coming to realize the predicament, but it remains to be seen if enough people are willing to break the individual patterns of behavior that are leading to social destruction."[33]

Sadly, one consequence of brownlash activities is to stifle any inclination citizens might have to break away from their existing patterns of behavior. Because seeds of doubt and confusion have been sown by the brownlash about the environmental prognosis, Americans hesitate to embark on changes that might entail some sacrifice or inconvenience. Change does not come easily when its necessity and purpose are questioned, when people are told our environment is adequately protected and that reform is promoted only by environmental doomsayers. Americans today are being told that the environmental movement is "the greatest single threat to the American economy"[34] and that environmental reform would make US factories grind to a halt, throwing the nation further down the economic ladder.

If citizens were convinced that some changes in the American way of life were necessary and if attractive options were offered, most would gladly oblige, as they did during World War II. They certainly would be willing to support changes if they understood that those changes could *enhance* their quality of life and that of their children. In our view, the brownlash has achieved some success partly because much of society remains woefully uninformed about environmental science. We hope the ensuing chapters will provide some basic understanding that puts the messages of the brownlash into perspective.

Notes

1. See e.g. C. Holden, "Alabama Schools Disclaim Evolution," *Science*, 270 (1995), 1305.
2. Dunlap, G. Gallup Jr., and A. Gallup, "Of Global Concern: Results of the Health of the Planet Survey," *Environment*, 35: 9 (1993), 7–15, 33–9.
3. R. Ornstein and P. Ehrlich, *New World/New Mind: Moving Toward Conscious Evolution* (New York: Doubleday, 1989).
4. G. Daily (ed.), *Nature's Services* (Washington, DC: Island Press).
5. A. Kinzig and R. Socolow, "Human Impacts on the Nitrogen Cycle," *Physics Today*, 24–31 November 1994; J. Holdren, "The Coming Energy-Environment Train Wreck," lecture, Woods Hole Research Center, Massachusetts, 11 October 1995.
6. P. Vitousek, P. Ehrlich, A. Ehrlich, and P. Matson, "Human Appropriation of the Products of Photosynthesis," *BioScience*, 6 (1986), 368–73.
7. S. Postel, G. Daily, and P. Ehrlich, "Human Appropriation of Renewable Fresh Water," *Science*, 271 (1996), 785–7.

8. R. Douthwaite, *The Growth Illusion* (Tulsa, Okla.: Council Oak Books, 1993). There are also serious issues of increasing maldistribution of wealth that call into doubt the notion that the system is making everyone better off (e.g. S. Pearlstein, "The Winners are Taking all," *Washington Post Weekly*, 11–17 December 1995, 6–8; B. Schwartz, "American Inequality: Its History and Scary Future," *New York Times*, 19 December 1995).

9. D. Helvarg, *The War Against the Greens: The "Wise Use" Movement, the New Right, and Anti-Environmental Violence* (San Francisco: Sierra Club Books, 1994), 458–9.

10. C. Deal, *The Greenpeace Guide to Anti-Environmental Organizations*, (Berkeley: Odonian Press, 1993); J. Fritsch, "Friend or Foe? Nature Groups Say Names Lie," *New York Times*, 25 March 1996. Ironically, as the *Times* pointed out, that these organizations resort to phony environmental names underscores the appeal of the environmental movement.

11. *Consumer Reports*, "The ACSH: Forefront of Science, or Just a Front?," May 1994, 319.

12. Fritsch, "Friend or Foe?".

13. Quoted in Helvarg, *War Against the Greens*, 429.

14. B. Babbit, "Springtime for Polluters," *Washington Post*, 22 October 1995.

15. Deal, *Greenpeace Guide*.

16. Quoted in ibid. 58.

17. M. Hager, "Enter the Contrarians," *Tomorrow*, October–December 1993, 10–19.

18. Helvarg, *War Against the Greens*, 32.

19. K. Boulding, "The Economics of the Coming Spaceship Earth," in H. Jarrett (ed.), *Environmental Quality in a Growing Economy* (Baltimore: Johns Hopkins University Press, 1966).

20. See e.g. D. Bromley, *Environment and Economy: Property Rights and Public Policy* (Oxford: Blackwell 1991).

21. Quoted in Helvarg, *War Against the Greens*, 302.

22. The impossibility of business as usual is most evident in areas of environmental science that the brownlash hasn't discovered yet. The best example of this is the ignoring of the importance of ecosystem services in maintaining civilization. We have yet to find a single brownlash book that even indexes ecosystem services.

23. Helvarg, *War Against the Greens*, 13.

24. T. Williams, "Defense of the Realm," *Sierra*, January–February 1996, 34–9, 121–3.

25. T. Egan, "Court Puts Down Rebellion over Control of Federal Land," *New York Times*, 16 March 1996.

26. Dunlap, Gallup, and Gallup, "Of Global Concern."

27. The late Republican senator John Heinz of Pennsylvania was a member of that tradition, as is Republican Tom Campbell, who represents a California district in the House of Representatives.

28. See e.g. G. Durnil, *The Making of a Conservative Environmentalist* (Bloomington: Indiana University Press, 1995).

29. L. Divall, "The Environmental Counterattack" (editorial), *New York Times*, 5 February 1996.

30. See e.g. B. Allenby and D. Richards (eds.) (National Academy of Engineering), *The Greening of Industrial Systems* (Washington, DC: National Academy of Engineering, 1994).

31. Gary Sprung, High Country Citizens Alliance, Crested Butte, Colorado, personal communication, July 1994.

32. Consider the following from our 1977 environmental science textbook: "As a theoretical example, Steel Company X . . . is pouring filth into [a] lake at a horrendous rate. A study shows it would cost two dollars per share of common stock to build the necessary apparatus for retaining and processing the waste. Should be company be forced to stop polluting and pay the price?

"Certainly it must be forced to stop, but it seems fair that society should pay some of the cost. When Company X located on the lake, everyone knew it would spew pollutants into the lake, but no one objected. The local people wanted to encourage industry. Now, finally, society has changed its mind, and the pollution must stop. But should Company X be forced into bankruptcy by pollution regulations, penalizing stockholders and putting its employees out of work? Should the local politicians who lured the company into locating there and the citizens who encouraged them not pay a cent? Clearly society should order the pollution stopped *and pick up at least part of the bill.* . . . [When jobs are lost in such situations, society] must find mechanisms to compensate people . . . and it must retrain and, if necessary, relocate them" (P. Ehrlich, A. Ehrlich, and J. Holdren,

Ecoscience: Population, Resources, Environment (San Francisco: W. H. Freeman, 1977), 848).

33. D. Pirages and P. Ehrlich, *Ark II: Social Response to Environmental Imperatives* (New York: Viking, 1974), 287.
34. Deal, *Greenpeace Guide*, 58, quoting thirty-nine leading conservatives writing in *Policy Review*.

REFORMIST RESPONSES

The survivalists and Prometheans surveyed in Part One have generated plenty of heat and perhaps some light, but not a great deal in the way of public policy or political reform. In Part Two we turn to less obviously apocalyptic pronouncements that relate more closely to the real world of environmental politics and policy making as it has unfolded in recent decades. That world features attempts to extend the capacities of both the administrative state and liberal democracy in an environmental direction.

Section III: Administrative Rationalism

Environmental problems arise in human dealings with ecological systems. Ecological systems are complex; so are human social systems. One should therefore expect environmental problems to be doubly complex. Complex problems demand the application of expertise, be it in ecology, engineering, economics, biochemistry, climatology, nuclear physics, epidemiology, or hydrology. The most established way to put expertise to use in the service of solving complex problems, concerning the environment no less than elsewhere, is to organize experts into administrative bureaucracies. Aside from specialists with the relevant substantive expertise, such bureaucracies contain experts in management, whose specialization is converting general statements of policy principle (in favour of, say, pollution reduction or wilderness preservation) into specific actions on the ground (say anti-pollution regulations). Along the way these managers will need to harness the appropriate substantive knowledge. Such an arrangement, according to the German sociologist Max Weber (writing in the early twentieth century), constitutes the pinnacle of rationality in collective human problem solving. Today's world is well-populated by Weberian bureaucracies. Until around 1970 these were few and small in the environmental area. But the wave of environmental concern that engulfed the developed world in the late 1960s soon produced a wide range of such bureaucracies: environmental protection agencies, ministries and departments of the environment, expert advisory commissions, and so forth. Indeed, the repertoire of institutional responses to environmental crisis in that era was remarkably similar in different countries. The character of those responses was essentially administrative, and their legacy remains.

Now, very few people actually claim to like bureaucracy, least of all the people who operate it. The fact that there is a lot of it about, notwithstanding this general dislike, is testimony perhaps to the truth of Weber's opinion concerning its problem-solving effectiveness. But what of the effectiveness of such administrative mechanisms in the environmental area? Can bureaucracies be made to operate in environmentally benign fashion? Our selections by Robert Bartlett and Kai Lee suggest that they can, though in quite different ways. Bartlett argues that the main function of one particular landmark piece of legislation—the United States National Environmental Policy Act of 1970—has been to insinuate environmental values into the entire range of agencies of the US federal government and their operations. In so doing, he believes that the Act has advanced the cause of ecological rationality in government, acting as a counterweight to more established economic and political rationality.

While Bartlett believes that environmental laws can change the way bureaucrats think, Lee's emphasis is more structural, entailing the redesign of bureaucracies themselves along ecological lines. To fit ecological specifications, administrative processes need to involve adaptive management, open to learning from both natural processes and political pressures from the people living in or concerned with an ecosystem. Lee's exemplary case of ecosystem management on a large scale is the Columbia River basin in the Northwest United States.

Torgerson is a more thoroughgoing critic of environmental administration, believing that administrative bureaucracies by their very nature cultivate a monolithic view of the world in which experts and administrators do not accept challenge, and are not open to learning. The administrative mind is not easily opened by environmental laws alone. Torgerson would consider that the kind of learning proposed by Lee requires radically participatory and democratic decision-making structures, rather than more enlightened administration.

Further Reading

Herbert Kaufman's *The Forest Ranger* (1960) is an early classic in how individuals working in resource management bureaucracies can assimilate a common set of professional values. Samuel Hays in *Beauty, Health, and Permanence: Environmental Politics in the United States, 1955–1985* (1987) chronicles the subsequent rise of the 'environmental professional'. An elaboration of Kai Lee's work on ecosystem management, social learning, and civic science can be found in his *Compass and Gyroscope: Integrating Science and Politics for the Environment* (1993). Bruce A. Ackerman and William T. Hassler in *Clean Coal, Dirty Air* (1981) offer an entertaining cautionary tale of what can happen when environmental bureaucracies do become overly politicized, and argue for more autonomous expert agencies insulated from direct political control. Steven Yaffee's *The Wisdom of the Spotted Owl* (1994) examines politicization in the US Forest Service, and how it hampered objective evaluations of the state of an endangered species in the Pacific Northwest. Walter Rosenbaum in *Environmental Politics and Policy* (1985) offers another American perspective on the consolidation and strengthening of autonomous administrative agencies in the environmental area. Timothy Doyle and Aynsley Kellow in *Environmental Politics and Policy Making in Australia* (1995) have similar hopes for Australia. A good critical collection on the limits of environmental administration is Robert Paehlke and Douglas Torgerson (eds), *Managing Leviathan: Environmental Politics and the Administrative State* (1990). Many of the limitations of administration as they appear in the 'old' (i.e. 1970s) politics of pollution are exposed in Albert Weale's *The New Politics of Pollution* (1992), which has a more European flavour. Another good comparative study is David Vogel's *National Styles of Regulation: Environmental Policy in Great Britain and the United States* (1986).

7 Rationality and the Logic of the National Environmental Policy Act

Robert V. Bartlett

Ideals pass into great historic forces by embodying themselves in institutions.

(Rashdall 1936)

Science is a multifaceted field of inquiry which in many of its aspects is involved with the procedures that have become known as environmental impact analysis and assessment (EIA). The idea behind the information gathering, analysis, and synthesis activities that constitute EIA originated with the National Environmental Policy Act of 1969 (NEPA).[1] The rationale underlying NEPA has never been easily explained, although many have tried. The legislation was itself influenced by scientific concepts, particularly ecology and systems theory, and reflected the intent of its authors that science be used as an integral tool in developing and administering a national policy for the environment. NEPA, however, is more than a law that uses science in a complex and interesting way. NEPA was a policy Act written in such a manner that its implementation would depend not on establishment of a new agency, nor on the continuing interest of a chief executive, nor on the goodwill of disparate bureaucracies. Implicit in NEPA and its science aspects is a form of rationality relatively new to government and having significance beyond the more obvious features of the Act.

Science and the Legislative Intent of NEPA

Although a casual reading of this brief law would reveal only three instances of the word "science" or its derivatives, science nevertheless is pervasive in nearly every section of NEPA, reflecting the significant influences that the environmental sciences had in the genesis of the Act (Caldwell 1982). Scientific concepts are implicit, for example, in NEPA's statement of purpose:

To declare a national policy which will encourage productive and enjoyable harmony between man and his environment; to promote efforts which will prevent or eliminate damage to the environment and biosphere and stimulate the health and welfare of man; to enrich the understanding of the ecological systems and natural resources important to the Nation; and to establish a Council on Environmental Quality.

From *The Environmental Professional*, 8 (1986), 105–11. Reprinted by permission of Blackwell Science, Inc.

The principal link provided by NEPA between science and administrative decisionmaking is Section 102(2)(C). Unquestionably the best-known provision of NEPA, Section 102(2)(C) institutionalized environmental impact analysis by requiring preparation of environmental impact statements (EISs) for federal agency actions significantly affecting the human environment. The specified content of these "detailed statements" obviously necessitated recourse to science; otherwise, the required discussions of "environmental impact," "irreversible and irretrievable commitments of resources," and "the relationship between local short-term uses of man's environment and the maintenance and enhancement of long-term productivity" could be little more than collections of empty phrases.

Section 102(2)(C) was added to NEPA relatively late in the legislative process, although after much deliberation, expressly to provide an "action-forcing" mechanism for the Act (Finn 1972; Andrews 1976; Liroff 1976; Caldwell 1978; Dreyfus and Ingram 1976). Because of the significant political and economic ramifications of this procedural provision, and the significant bureaucratic reforms that it required, it is not surprising that subsequent attention focused overwhelmingly on the environmental impact statement, to the neglect of the more substantive policies enunciated in the legislation.

The EIS indeed forced action, but the action to be taken was described elsewhere in NEPA, a fact often lost on many who somehow saw the EIS as an end in itself and NEPA as essentially a procedural Act. The EIS requirement could only be understood and appropriately implemented if interpreted within the context of the rest of NEPA, a point officially acknowledged in 1978 with issuance, under presidential executive order, of the first regulations for implementing NEPA.[2] These regulations, promulgated by the Council on Environmental Quality (CEQ), emphasized and reinforced the science-dependent components of the Act.

The influence of scientific ideas can be easily discerned throughout Title I of NEPA, which constitutes the declaration of national policy with provisions for implementation. The impact of human activity on the interrelations of all components of the natural environment is recognized, as is the importance of restoring and maintaining environmental quality for the overall welfare and development of man. Six precepts are provided in Section 101(b) as guides to future action: (1) each generation as trustee of the environment for succeeding generations (drawing from and depending upon the sciences with a distant time horizon); (2) assurance of safe, healthful, productive, and aesthetically and culturally pleasing surroundings (necessitating reliance on a broad range of sciences and technical knowledge, particularly the biological, social, and behavioral sciences and the environmental design arts); (3) attainment of the widest range of beneficial uses of the environment without undesirable and unintended consequences (requiring the capacity to ascertain limits and to adequately predict the consequences of complex actions); (4) preservation of important historic, cultural, and natural aspects of the national heritage and maintenance of an environment supporting diversity and variety of individual choice (using knowledge and methodologies from archeology, cultural anthropology, cultural history, geography, and ecology); (5) achievement of a balance between population and resource use permitting high living standards and wide sharing of life's amenities (possible only with knowledge from ecology, economics, geography, sociology, agronomy, geology, and numerous other sciences); and (6) enhancement of the quality of renewable resources and maximum recycling of depletable resources (requiring application of a developed materials science, resource economics, recycling engineering, and environmental management science). In short, this part of the Act provides goals or directions that derive from the sciences and demand the advancement and application of a broad range of scientific and technical knowledge.

Section 102, which follows, contains more than the EIS requirement. Section 102(2)(A) is pivotal: it directs that all agencies of the federal government shall "utilize a systematic, interdisciplinary approach which will insure the integrated use of the natural and social sciences and the environmental design arts in planning and in decisionmaking which may have an impact on man's environment." In other provisions of significance, federal agencies are directed to: (B) "identify and develop methods and procedures . . . which will insure that presently unquantified environmental amenities and values may be given appropriate consideration in decisionmaking along with economic and technical considerations"; (F) "lend appropriate support to initiatives, resolutions, and programs designed to maximize international cooperation in anticipating and preventing a decline in the quality of mankind's world environment"; and (H) "initiate and utilize ecological information in the planning and development of resource oriented projects."

Title II, establishing the Council on Environmental Quality, reflects the intent of Congress to assure the adequacy of science for the policies it sought to declare and implement through Title I.[3] Clearly, science and science-related concepts were crucial in the development of NEPA and were embodied in the text; moreover, the logic of the Act meant that science would necessarily be indispensable in the implementation of both the substantive policy provisions and the mandated procedural requirements. NEPA unmistakably implies the use of science through its use of such surrogate terms as information, plant and animal systems, studies, surveys, research, and analyses, none of which would have meaning within the context of the Act unless backed by scientific content and methodology. Thus, beyond the explicit statement of intent in Section 102(2)(A), one effect of NEPA has been to revise and extend the ways in which the federal agencies are required to use science in their decision processes.

NEPA and Decisionmaking

Intended by its designers to force action to achieve greater rationality in governmental decisionmaking, NEPA constitutes a far-reaching attempt to influence decisions—and thus to alter the substantive outcomes of government activities—by changing the rules and premises for arriving at legitimate decisions. Federal agencies were henceforth required to undertake a particular kind of analysis, to incorporate this analysis into regular decision processes, and to make public a justiciable document (the EIS) demonstrating compliance. In essence, the EIS requirement was expected to lead to at least partial accomplishment of the general policy goals specified in NEPA by institutionalizing a kind of mandatory, continuing, systematic, integrated, science-based policy analysis, henceforth to be undertaken before a final decision was reached on any proposed action that would significantly affect the quality of the human environment. One of the most deceptively sweeping measures ever passed into law by the Congress of the United States, NEPA represented a far-reaching innovation, not only in environmental policy and management, but also in the design of policy processes and institutions.

NEPA did not employ as a primary strategy either of the two traditional approaches to changing bureaucratic behavior: (1) reorganization and budgetary redistribution, or (2) detailed, administratively enforced rules and standards. Instead, NEPA sought to influence government activities by changing—subtly and yet profoundly—the decision structures and evaluative standards of all federal agencies. Recognizing that decisions do not emerge from a black box, but are shaped and channeled before they are officially "made," NEPA's designers sought to alter the processes and procedures by which decisions that might significantly affect the human environment were actually shaped, channeled, and made. NEPA sought to affect decisionmaking by extending, legitimating, and mandating particular choice criteria and by requiring consideration of a different set of factual premises.

In short, NEPA is quintessential policy legislation—"a set of rules for realizing some outcome"—which has been recognized only belatedly and still inadequately by scholars, administrators, and politicians. NEPA represents an ambitious and idealistic effort at policy design—the formulation, adoption, and implementation of "a decision that governs and affects future decisions" (Boulding 1981). In spite of its brevity and apparent simplicity, NEPA is a complex, elusive, and subtle piece of legislation. Environmental values are typically—as the designers of NEPA knew—precarious values, and the natural bias of most organizations goes "against their realization unless protected by special arrangements" (Taylor 1984).

Serge Taylor points out that there were three other systematic failings of government decision processes that were addressed by NEPA: (1) advantage was not being taken of long planning periods to search for possible impacts and to explore design options, (2) important early choice points in agency decision processes were not visible or accessible to other agencies or the public, and (3) there were only weak norms of analysis underlying the creation, sharing, and criticism of empirical information (Taylor 1984). NEPA addressed these failings by mandating, and requiring the disclosure of, pre-decision analyses emphasizing environmental values and consequences. The justiciable disclosure document was the environmental impact statement—the primary action-forcing mechanism of the Act. Through the EIS requirement, and the emphasis on analysis in other substantive provisions, NEPA's designers sought to institutionalize a kind of policy analysis in the decision processes of the federal bureaucracy.

There have been, of course, other attempts to institutionalize analysis in government—notable examples being cost-benefit analysis, required planning studies, and various budget reforms such as program budgeting and zero-base budgeting (Wildavsky 1983; Andrews 1982). Thus the new policy enacted through NEPA was not without considerable antecedent. But the policy analysis mandated by NEPA had several distinctive features. First and foremost, requiring government agencies to undertake environmental impact analysis involved an attempt to establish a "feedforward" mechanism to inform a particular category of decisions, namely decisions about actions expected to have a significant impact on the human environment (Dryzek 1982). Characteristic of (but not unique to) this category of action are consequences that are often irreversible and impacts that may be geographically or temporally dispersed or may appear at the end of a long causal sequence. Some environmentally important outcomes will only result if a (usually unknown) threshold is exceeded. Sometimes actions have effects that would be unremarkable if the action occurred independently in isolation, but are noteworthy as the product of more than one action (that is, cumulative, interactive, and synergistic effects). The expected presence of these kinds of substantial consequences makes reliance on decomposition, trial-and-error learning, incremental decisionmaking, or system feedback less appropriate.

Such problems, if substantial, necessarily call for a degree of "thinking big" in policy design and analysis. An obvious strategy involves basing decisions upon careful consideration of the future through a sort of strategic feedforward mechanism such as environmental impact analysis (Dryzek 1982; Dryzek 1988$3b$; Simon 1981). NEPA thus attempts to institutionalize a measure of protection against what Alfred E. Kahn has labeled "the tyranny of small decisions" (Kahn 1966).

In essence, NEPA is more than a policy Act; it embodies meta-policy or meta-design—the design of a policy process (Dryzek 1982). NEPA's designers sought to declare and establish a national policy for the environment, but because a coherent environmental policy was necessarily very inclusive, it entailed changing the premises, choice criteria, and procedures under which all sorts of other decisions and policies could in the future be formulated and executed. Not only does NEPA provide a procedural reform—the EIS requirement—to force agencies to undertake environmental impact analyses, but NEPA also amends the statutory mandates of all federal agencies. Section 105 of NEPA states, "The policies and goals set forth in this Act are supplementary to those set forth in existing authorizations of Federal agencies." Thus, in addition to requiring that agencies undertake decision-focused analyses and disclose a summary of these analyses to other agencies and the public, NEPA changed the legislative authorization of each and every federal agency. The EIS is a mechanism to force observance of NEPA's policy goals and to obtain compliance with its other directives, including those pertaining to unquantified environmental amenities and values and the use of science in agency planning and decisionmaking.

Unlike cost-benefit analysis or other analytical approaches that often pretend to be value neutral, environmental impact analysis makes no such pretense; the EIS requirement can only be understood in the context of the rest of NEPA. The EIS requirement was intended to lead toward realization of the general policy goals specified in NEPA by institutionalizing a kind of science-based policy analysis. Implementation of NEPA would be advanced by the availability of judicial enforcement of its substantive and procedural mandate; by the persuasive appeal of NEPA's precepts and declarations; by opening agency decision processes to external influences from Congress, other agencies, and the public; by contributing to a shift in the prevailing values of agency personnel through learning and changes in hiring patterns; and by stimulating the generation of new information that would be incorporated into and focused through a revised approach to planning and decisionmaking.

NEPA and Ecological Rationality

Recourse to science is indispensable to implementation of NEPA; as discussed earlier, science is explicit and implicit throughout both the language and the logic of NEPA. In part, science is important simply because information is important—science, is, after all, a particular approach, perhaps the best we have, to reducing the ambiguity of evidence (Boulding 1981). Also, and more important, a tacit objective of NEPA is the introduction of scientific precepts and canons into the policy process:

We believe that scientists have a more fundamental contribution to make. At their best, scientists bring to impact assessment a process of thought, and habits of inquiry, that stress understanding of changes and consequences rather than touting progress; and that stress honest recognition of preconceived courses of action.

The principal contributions that scientists can make to impact assessment are the scientific method of inquiry, a method which has all too often been sorely lacking, and the concept of probability of occurrence of natural events (Andrews et al. 1977).

Indeed, Serge Taylor has undertaken a detailed analysis of NEPA viewed "as an attempt to import 'scientific' norms and procedures into a political setting of often intense conflict" (Taylor 1984). NEPA, of course, is a great deal more than an attempt to impose science-like norms and procedures on bureaucratic decision processes. To be sure, scientific methods and ways of thinking are often held up as the paradigm of rationality, and it is apparently widely believed by scientists and laymen alike that the world could be vastly improved if only politics were made more like science (Gunnell 1981). Perhaps some of NEPA's designers did subscribe in part to that naive view, but there is no evidence to that effect. NEPA does not preempt the political or administrative roles of government decisionmakers. NEPA was not merely or even primarily an attempt to force bureaucracies to use science-like analysis as a basis for policies and decisions. It was not just any science that NEPA mandated in 1969, but a systematic, interdisciplinary, integrated use of the natural and social sciences, with an emphasis on ecology. NEPA is best understood as an attempt to force greater rationality in government decisionmaking through an experiment in institutional and policy design. But again, it is not just any conception of rationality that underlies NEPA—not some superficial and simplistic view of scientific rationality, nor some warmed over and disguised revisitation of the rational-comprehensive decisionmaking model of classical public administration. Rather, NEPA provides a "constitutional" charter for government use of a particular form of reasoning distinct from other legitimate historical forms: ecological rationality.

The National Environmental Policy Act is best understood and evaluated if it is viewed as an exercise in policy and institutional design—a "natural experiment" in the institutionalization of rationality in government organizations and, indeed, in a whole society. The enactment and implementation of NEPA constitute an effort to structure situations to achieve certain results. Other analysts have perceived that NEPA was intended to force rationality, or to induce rationality (Andrews 1976; Friesema and Culhane, 1976; Fairfax 1978; Culhane et al. 1978). But a narrow conception of rationality can constrain the criteria used to evaluate the natural experiment. Recognition of ecological rationality as a functional and critical kind of reasoning with unique characteristics distinguishing it from other forms of rationality is necessary in order to understand the rationale of, and evaluate the success or failure of, the National Environmental Policy Act (Diesing 1962; Dryzek 1983a; Bartlett 1984a).

The thrust of the declaration of national environmental policy comprising much of Section 101 of NEPA is one of ecological rationality: "to create and maintain conditions under which man and nature can exist in productive harmony." The ultimate test for judging NEPA is whether the society and government to which it applies exhibit functional ecological rationality. Has the nation been able, in the words of NEPA, to "attain the widest range of beneficial uses of the environment without degradation, risk to health or safety, or other undesirable or unintended consequences" and to "enhance the quality of renewable resources and approach the maximum attainable recycling of depletable resources"? Whether achievement of functional ecological rationality is somewhat closer, in part because of NEPA, is the important determination.

With respect to individual actions or decisions, NEPA also presents a standard of ecological rationality. According to NEPA, "it is the continuing responsibility of the Federal Government to use all practicable means . . . to improve and coordinate Federal plans, functions, programs, and resources" consistent with six precepts of Section 101, discussed earlier. Moreover, "to the fullest extent possible," all agencies of the federal government are required by NEPA, before undertaking "action significantly affecting the quality of the human environment," to consider any unavoidable adverse environmental effects, the "relationship between local short-term uses of man's environment and the maintenance and enhancement of long-term productivity," and any "irreversible and irretrievable commitments of resources. All agencies are further required to "recognize the worldwide and long-range character of environmental problems." Thus NEPA specifies several attributes of ecological rationality.

But ecological rationality cannot be achieved by mere declaration; without some attention to processes—whatever the specific mechanisms or resources—no legislation can ever be more than symbolic incantation, the spell of which is likely not to be powerful or lasting. Rather than attempt to achieve ecological rationality through directed reorganization, dictated resources redistribution, or the promulgation of sweeping detailed rules and standards, the designers of NEPA sought to change the procedures used to arrive at and to justify agency choices. Decisions would be affected not only because balances of political influence would be shifted, not only because a different set of incentives would henceforth bear on bureaucratic decisionmakers, but also because a new way of thinking would thereafter be required of bureaucratic agents. Federal agencies were required by NEPA to improve, coordinate, consider, and recognize commitments, relationships, and environmental effects, and they were required to do so in a certain way. That is, agencies were required to "initiate and utilize ecological information," to "utilize a systematic, interdisciplinary approach which will insure the integrated use of the natural and social sciences and the environmental design arts in planning and in decisionmaking," and to "identify and develop methods and procedures . . . which will insure that presently unquantified environmental amenities and values may be given appropriate consideration in decisionmaking." In short, through NEPA, Congress ordered all agencies of the federal government to begin using procedural ecological reasoning in their planning and decisionmaking.

That is not to say that NEPA ignores other, more established realms of rationality. Rather, NEPA emphasizes the integration of other forms of rationality with ecological rationality. Economic as well as social rationality are acknowledged in NEPA's declaration that it is the continuing policy of the federal government "to use all practical means and measures . . . in a manner calculated to . . . fulfill the social, economic, and other requirements of present and future generations of Americans." Economic and social rationality are not ignored or denigrated; rather, their dependence on, and hoped-for consistency with, ecological rationality is emphasized. For example, one of the important six precepts of Section 101 states that it is the continuing responsibility of the federal government to "achieve a balance between population and resource use which will permit high standards of living and a wide sharing of life's amenities." Title II of NEPA, which establishes the Council on Environmental Quality, at several points instructs the CEQ to be conscious of and responsive to social and economic needs, interests, and goals. Section 102(2)(B) directs that methods and procedures be developed to insure that unquantified environmental amenities and values be given appropriate consideration "along with economic and technical considerations." And Section 102(2)(A) requires a systematic, interdisciplinary, integrated use of the social sciences and environmental design arts, along with the natural sciences. Economic cost-benefit analyses are compatible with NEPA-mandated environmental impact analyses, as subsequent CEQ regulations have made clear, and the contemporary techniques collectively known as social impact analysis (SIA) can actually be traced back to NEPA's provisions (Porter et al. 1980; Daneke and Priscoli 1979; Finsterbusch 1980).

Legal rationality is not irrelevant to NEPA either. Section 102(2)(C) of the Act, requiring environmental impact statements, got the attention it did from courts and law journals precisely because it involved modification of a system of rules governing bureaucratic and judicial behavior.

And, except for ecological rationality, it is political rationality that is most important to the logic of NEPA. Diesing writes:

Political decisions are necessary whenever an organization, or society, or person is faced with a political problem; that is, whenever there is a deficiency in its decision structure. The deficiency may be some form of narrowness, in that the structure is not receptive to an adequate range of facts, or that it is not able to break away from well-known formulas in its estimates of problems and suggestions for action, or that it is insufficiently self-critical and slow to admit error, or that its procedures are excessively rigid and thus shut out novelty. (Diesing 1962)

NEPA is, in effect, the result of a political decision that addressed a basic and increasingly critical deficiency in the decision structure of the United States. With respect to various dimensions of environmental quality and ecological life-support, the governmental decision structure had not been receptive to an adequate range of facts, had not been able to break away from well-known formulas, and had been insufficiently critical and excessively rigid. NEPA and environmental impact analysis represent one effort to deal with this political problem, through a process that is overtly and intentionally political, "a process of reasoned deliberation, argument, and criticism rather than a pragmatic calculus" (Anderson 1979).

Ecological rationality as embodied in NEPA has implications for policy formation and implementation well beyond this statute. NEPA provides an important and rich example of an attempt to foster and institutionalize ecological rationality, but by no means is it the only such example. Indeed, the many laws and procedures inspired by NEPA make up a sizable subset of such efforts since 1970—including, among others, federal forest and land management laws and the environmental policy and impact analysis arrangements established by state and local governments and by other nations.

NEPA is, in summary, a manifestation of both ecological and political rationality, which can readily be seen if the Act is analyzed in terms of the "good" achieved by this sort of rationality, namely, practical intelligence. By practical intelligence Diesing is referring not to an intellectual ability to deal with mathematical and linguistic abstractions, but to intelligence which in Dewey's sense is "the ability of the whole society or personality to effecitvely solve the problems confronting it" (Diesing 1962; Dewey 1930).[4] The intent of NEPA—against which judgments about its achievements or lack thereof must ultimately, but even now can only tentatively, be made—is to advance and foster social intelligence with respect to the human environment (Caldwell et al. 1983; Bartlett 1984b).

Notes

1. The general idea of assessing environmental impacts before acting was not new, nor are all assessment techniques and methodologies of recent origin. As early as the 1870s the Army Corps of Engineers had developed techniques for assessing environmental impacts (Rowe 1978). In the 1920s and 1930s, community and natural resource planners often tried to provide for explicit consideration of environmental impacts (Stein 1957; Spreiregen 1971).

2. These regulations replaced guidelines that had previously been issued (40 CFR 1500–1508).

3. The science-related provisions of Title II of NEPA borrowed heavily from the proposed Ecological Research and Survey Act, introduced in 1965 by Senator Gaylord Nelson of Wisconsin. The objective of that bill was to advance development of the science of ecology through federal policy commitment and funding. As enacted, the potential of Title II of NEPA has been largely unrealized—a consequence of lack of significant congressional or presidential support.

4. Diesing continues: "In the hierarchy of values, intelligence (or freedom) is the supreme value. It is supreme, even absolute, because it is instrumental to all other values. . . . No excessive pursuit of intelligence is possible, because intelligence makes all other values achievable" (Diesing 1962). Dewey writes that "our intelligence is bound up . . . with the community of life of which we are a part." Dewey's conception of reason is consistent with and relevant to ecological rationality:

> "Demand for consistency, for 'universality,' far from implying a rejection of all consequences, is a demand to survey consequences broadly, to link effect to effect in a chain of continuity. Whatever force works to this end *is* reason. For reason, let it be repeated is an outcome, a function, not a primitive force. What we need are those habits, dispositions which lead to impartial and consistent foresight of consequences. Then our judgements are reasonable; we are then reasonable creatures" (Dewey 1930).

References

Anderson, C. W. (1979), "The Place of Principles in Policy Analysis," *American Political Science Review*, 73: 722.

Andrews, R. N. L. (1976), *Environmental Policy and Administrative Change: Implementation of the National Environmental Policy Act* (Lexington, Mass.: Lexington Books).

——et al. (1977), *Substantive Guidance for*

Environmental Impact Assessment: An Exploratory Study (Washington, DC: The Institute of Ecology).

Andrews, R. N. L. (1982), "Cost-Benefit Analysis as Regulatory Reform," in D. Swartzman, R. A. Liroff, and K. G. Croke (eds), *Cost-Benefit Analysis and Environmental Regulations: Politics, Ethics, and Methods* (Washington, DC: The Conservation Foundation).

Bartlett, R. V. (1984a), "Institutionalizing Ecological Rationality," presented at Western Social Science Association meeting, San Diego, Calif.

—— (1984b), "Rationality and Science in Public Policy: The National Environmental Policy Act," Ph.D. diss. (Indiana University, Bloomington).

Boulding, K. (1981), *Evolutionary Economics* (Beverly Hills, Calif.: Sage).

Caldwell, L. K. (1978), "The Environmental Impact Statment: A Misused Tool," in R. K. Jain and B. L. Hutchings (eds.), *Environmental Impact Analysis: Emerging Issues in Planning* (Urbana, Ill.: University of Illinois Press).

—— (1982), *Science and the National Environmental Policy Act: Redirecting Policy Through Procedural Reform* (University, Ala.: University of Alabama Press).

—— et al. (1983), *A Study of Ways to Improve the Scientific Content and Methodology of Environmental Impact Analysis* (PB222851; Springfield, Va.: National Technical Information Service).

Culhane, P. J., et al. (1978), "The Effectiveness of NEPA" (letters), *Science*, 202: 1034–1041.

Daneke, G. A., and Priscoli, J. D. (1979), "Social Assessment and Resource Policy: Lessons from Water Planning," *Natural Resources Journal*, 19: 363.

Dewey, J. (1930), *Human Nature and Conduct: An Introduction to Social Psychology* (New York, NY: Modern Library).

Diesing, P. (1962), *Reason in Society: Five Types of Decisions and their Social Conditions* (Urbana, Ill.: University of Illinois Press).

Dreyfus, D. A., and Ingram, H. M. (1976), "The National Environmental Policy Act: A View of Intent and Practice," *Natural Resources Journal*, 16: 243–62.

Dryzek, J. S. (1982), "Policy Design in an Uncertain World," presented at Southern Political Science Association meeting, Atlanta, Ga.

—— (1983a), "Present Choices, Future Consequences: A Case for Thinking Strategically," *World Futures*, 19: 1–19.

—— (1983b), "Don't Toss Coins in Garbage Cans: A Prologue to Policy Design," *Journal of Public Policy*, 3: 345–68.

Fairfax, S. K. (1978), "A Disaster in the Environmental Movement," *Science*, 199: 744–5.

Finn, T. T. (1972), "Conflict and Compromise: Congress Makes a Law—The Passage of the National Environmental Policy Act," Ph.D. diss. (Georgetown University, Washington, DC).

Finsterbusch, K. (1980), *Understanding Social Impacts: Assessing the Effects of Public Projects* (Beverly Hills, Calif.: Sage).

Friesema, H. P., and Culhane, P. J. (1976), "Social Impacts, Politics and the Environmental Impact Statement Process," *Natural Resources Journal*, 16: 339–56.

Gunnell, J. G. (1981), "Encounters of a Third Kind: The Alienation of Theory in American Political Science," *American Journal of Political Science*, 25: 442.

Kahn, A. E. (1966), "The Tyranny of Small Decisions: Market Failures, Imperfections, and the Limits of Economics," *KYKLOS: International Review for Social Secience*, 19: 23–45.

Liroff, R. A. (1976), *A National Policy for the Environment: NEPA and its Aftermath* (Bloomington: Indiana University Press).

Porter, A. L., et al. (1980), *A Guidebook for Technology Assessment and Impact Analysis* (New York: Elsevier North Holland).

Rashdall, H. (1936), *The Universities of Europe in the Middle Ages* (New York: Oxford University Press).

Rowe, P. G., et al. (1978), *Principles for Local Environmental Management* (Cambridge, Mass.: Ballinger).

Simon, H. A. (1981), *The Sciences of the Artificial*, 2nd edn. (Cambridge, Mass.: MIT Press).

Spreiregen, R. D. (1971), "Perspectives on Regional Design," *American Institute of Architects Journal*, 56: 20–2.

Stein, C. S. (1957), *Toward New Towns for America* (New York: Reinhold).

Taylor, S. (1984), *Making Bureaucracies Think: The Environmental Impact Statement Strategy of*

Administrative Reform (Stanford, Calif.: Stanford University Press).

Wildavsky, A. (1983), *The Politics of the Budgetary Process*, 4th edn. (Boston: Little, Brown).

8   The Columbia River Basin: Experimenting with Sustainability

Kai N. Lee

To succeed, sustainable development must be both the product of political choice and the stimulus for institutional transformation. The recent surge of international support for phasing out chlorofluorocarbons and reducing greenhouse-gas emissions suggests that political momentum is building, even if not everywhere or uniformly. There is a lot of hard work beyond politics, however, because choices must be institutionalized if they are to endure; sustainable development will work only as a sustained policy.

How can sustainable development be woven into the institutional fabric? To the scant experience that bears on this question can be added the efforts in the Columbia River basin in the Pacific Northwest region of the United States, where an attempt to rebuild the salmon and steelhead trout runs of the Columbia is now under way.[1]

Rising in the Canadian Rocky Mountains and flowing 1,200 miles through the Pacific Northwest, the Columbia is the fourth largest river in North America and drains an area that includes parts of seven US states and two Canadian provinces (see the map in Figure 8.1). The river's average annual streamflow of 141 million acre-feet is more than 10 times that of the Colorado River.[2] The Columbia's high flows and extensive drainage have made it ideal for colonization, first, by fish and wildlife,[3] as the glaciers retreated at the end of the last ice age and, much later, by dam-building humans.

Not long ago, the Columbia River basin was a wilderness. Because it is a major spawning ground and nursery of Pacific salmon (*Oncorhynchus* spp.) and steelhead trout (*Salmo gairdneri*), the Columbia's biological web reaches far into the North Pacific Ocean, where the fish mature for two to four years before returning to their native streams to reproduce. Before European settlement, this ecosystem supported a population of perhaps 50,000 American Indians,[4] whose world centered on the yearly migrations that brought 10 to 16 million salmon and steelhead back to the river.[5] Harvested by spear, net, and boat, these salmonids provided both food and trade goods for the people of the river basin.[6] The Indian tribes lived in a long-term ecological equilibrium, which fluctuated between bad times and good but endured over many human generations. This original Columbia civilization lasted until about 1850.

From *Environment*, 31:6 (1989), 6–11, 30–33. Reprinted with permission of the Helen Dwight Educational Foundation. Published by Heldref Publications, 1319 Eighteenth St., N. W., Washington, D. C. 20036-1802.

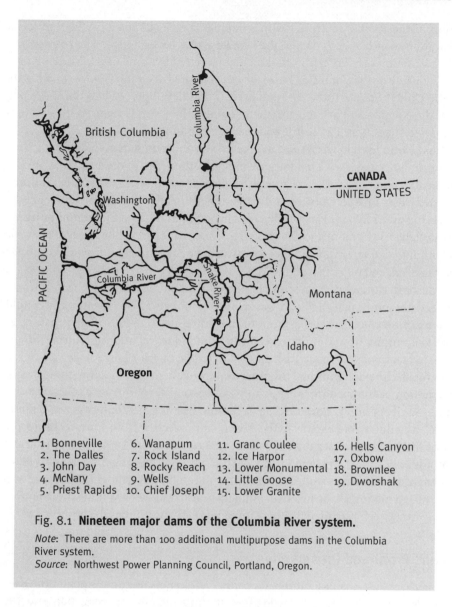

Fig. 8.1 **Nineteen major dams of the Columbia River system.**

1. Bonneville
2. The Dalles
3. John Day
4. McNary
5. Priest Rapids
6. Wanapum
7. Rock Island
8. Rocky Reach
9. Wells
10. Chief Joseph
11. Granc Coulee
12. Ice Harpor
13. Lower Monumental
14. Little Goose
15. Lower Granite
16. Hells Canyon
17. Oxbow
18. Brownlee
19. Dworshak

Note: There are more than 100 additional multipurpose dams in the Columbia River system.
Source: Northwest Power Planning Council, Portland, Oregon.

Industrial Development

The second human civilization to invade the Columbia basin has turned the river into a power plant. The basin's 19 major dams, together with more than five dozen smaller hydro projects, constitute the world's largest hydroelectric power system. Today, dams on the Columbia River and its tributaries generate, on average, about 12,000 megawatts from falling water,[7] which is more than enough power to run New York City.

Largely built by the US government at a time of low labor costs, the dams fostered the industrialization of the Pacific Northwest with cheap electricity marketed by the Bonneville Power Administration, which is now part of the US Department of Energy.[8] The river basin has also become a plantation of more than 3 million acres watered by some of the world's largest irrigation works, including the Columbia Basin Project anchored at Grand Coulee, which is the largest dam in the United States.[9] Industrial and agricultural development have built the population centers of the Northwest: Portland and the Willamette Valley of Oregon, Boise and Spokane in the upper watershed, as well as Seattle and the Puget Sound.

The Indians who lived in wilderness have given way to a population of 8 million,[10] more than 100 times the aboriginal level. That increase in population, by two orders of magnitude, reflects a fundamental change in the relationships between people and the environment. The domesticated river provides power and irrigation while also eliminating its once legendary floods; serving as an inland waterway navigable by tug and barge for 500 miles from Astoria, Oregon, near the river's mouth to Lewiston in central Idaho; affording world-class windsurfing in the Columbia Gorge; and, last but not least, supporting sport and commercial harvests of salmon, steelhead, and other fish and wildlife.

The industrial Columbia is a multiple-purpose marvel, a river, as the historian Donald Worster recently put it, that died and was reborn as money.[11] The governing principle behind the many functions of the river has been to maximize economic return. The river's uses have been ranked accordingly: power first, then urban and industrial uses, agriculture, flood control, navigation, recreation, and, finally, fish and wildlife. The inferior position of fish and wildlife is evident in the decline of the annual fish runs from roughly 10 to 16 million in the pre-industrial era to 2.5 million by the late 1970s.[12]

As these numbers imply, however, the Columbia has not died entirely. Thus, there is hope that, just as the wilderness gave way to the power plant, so a new Columbia may arise, one whose watchword will be *sustainable* multiple use.

This is not only a hope. Since 1969, Indian tribes of the Columbia have reasserted their legal rights to harvest fish, under treaties concluded with the US government in the mid-nineteenth century. Today, $100 million is invested annually in fish and wildlife mitigation, and the river's low-cost electricity is husbanded by innovative and successful efforts to conserve energy.[13]

"Between" Profit and Preservation

This new, perhaps sustainable Columbia is neither wilderness nor power plant but an ecosystem requiring active management. The wilderness the Indians knew is gone. Their world was an integral fabric whose natural time scale was the human generation. That cloth has been cut, and management by preservation, permitting nature to set the terms on which its constituent species will equilibrate, is no longer possible. Some have questioned whether management by preservation is possible today, even in unpeopled parks and biological preserves.[14] Yet following the profit motive to its logical endpoint by increasing energy production as long as its revenues outbid the competing claims of irrigation and other uses is unacceptable. Any management system that optimizes only a single measure of worth is unworkable.

These points have been put negatively. There is a positive side as well: Sustainable development of the Columbia River basin implies a culturally, economically, and ecologically viable relationship between people and the environment they inhabit.

To achieve sustainability, humans must somehow pick a path "between" preservation and profit maximization. "Between" is in quotation marks here to emphasize that preservation and profit maximization are not endpoints of some simple continuum, with sustainability an average or midpoint. Sustainability is a departure in a new direction—one likely to yield less than the maximum achievable short-term profit, but one that involves humans in the landscape more than is contemplated in the popular notion of pristine wilderness.[15]

Picking a path to sustainability is an unlikely job for a political process. Politicians often make decisions in response to perceived crises. When the crisis involves natural resources, the decisions are frequently neither biologically nor economically well informed. Instead, political choices are driven by symbols, whether they be charismatic vertebrates (e.g. marine mammals), waterways (e.g. the Grand Canyon), horror stories (e.g. Prince William Sound), or nightmares (e.g. Chernobyl).

More generally, politics cannot be regarded as an arena in which optimal choices are made. Instead, political decisions set institutional constraints that may either help or hinder the construction of a viable long-term regime. For example, in the statute that authorized the effort to rehabilitate the Columbia,[16] one finds a typically mixed bag.[17] The Northwest Power Act directs that the Columbia and its tributaries be treated "as a system."[18] This language has become the linchpin for an ecosystem-wide planning perspective. However, the Act's language on water rights[19] reaffirms an outmoded legal framework that inhibits the rescue of spawning grounds in headwater streams (some of the best places to rebuild self-sustaining fish populations) even as it fails to address the economic plight of the farmers and ranchers dependent on irrigation.[20]

Indeed, what is likely to emerge from the political process is a mandate that may take a strong stance toward rehabilitation or sustainability but does not reflect a clear strategy for achieving that goal. The combination of noble ends and muddled means is characteristic of democratic governance, in which the political system seeks to accommodate an immiscible set of interests.[21]

The implementation of such mandates is also characteristic: Public organizations usually do not press their powers to the limits allowed by the political stance of their authorizing statutes. As the visible crisis ebbs, opposing forces come into play, some alleged "rule of reason" compromises the plain meaning of political mandates, and the flow toward sustainability peters out in the closed basin called "realism."[22]

At its best, however, the political process can produce substantial improvement, and this fact should not be dismissed. Recently, consensus building among parties exhausted by long wrangling has produced noteworthy agreements in fisheries and forestry management in the Pacific Northwest.[23] When these policies fail, however, sniping continues as it has over toxic waste management throughout the United States.

Sustainable Management

In 1980, the US Congress, calling for the protection and enhancement of the fish and wildlife of the Columbia River basin, passed the Northwest Power Act to mitigate the effects of half a century of hydroelectric power development.[24] Taken at face value, the Act is a mandate for a sustainable balancing of the two uses of the river most directly at odds: electric power and anadromous (migratory) fish.[25]

The executor of the mandate is the Northwest Power Planning Council, an agency created by the Act for three purposes: to formulate a long-range power plan for the Pacific Northwest; to develop a program to rebuild the fish and wildlife populations of the Columbia, based upon suggestions from fish and wildlife agencies and Indian tribes in the basin; and to involve the public in decisions on energy and fish and wildlife.[26] The powers of the council are unusual, if not unique, in US government. The council was formed by an interstate compact, consented to by Congress through the Act, among Idaho, Montana, Oregon, and Washington states. As a result, the gubernatorial appointees who compose the council hold a legal authority that can, in places, bind federal agencies—a rare constitutional power. The Act was stimulated primarily by the region's electric power crisis in the late 1970s, a time when controversy over the role of nuclear power in the region's electricity supply raised the provocative question of public involvement. The prominence during that period of Indian treaty fishing-rights litigation also prompted Congress to include stipulations for fish and wildlife. In response to these congressional concerns, the council adopted an ambitious fish and wildlife program in 1982[27] (subsequently amended in 1984 and 1987) calling for a broad spectrum of mitigating activities, including major changes in river operations[28] to provide "equitable treatment" for fish.

Under the Northwest Power Act, implementation of the council's program is funded from the revenue that the Bonneville Power Administration gathers from its electric power ratepayers. The council has determined that losses of salmon and steelhead from hydropower development amount to between 5 and 11 million adult fish per year.[29] The result is an effort to rehabilitate fish and wildlife on an economic scale unheard of in natural resource management.

Sustainable development of the Columbia River basin requires managing an ecosystem the size of France. If there is to be a sustainable Columbia, it will be a place governed by rules that approach the complexity of ecological interaction. It will be a place where human, economic objectives are deliberately balanced against natural boundaries and biological rhythms.

Ongoing Work

One might think that this is merely utopian, but the work already in progress is quite ambitious. For example, the harvest of Pacific salmon is now being regulated by the states and tribes of the Pacific Northwest and by the Canadian and US governments, both to conserve and rebuild fish stocks and to assure fair apportionment of the catch. The regulations, determined annually, implement the terms of a treaty between the United States and Canada signed in 1985,[30] as well as the treaties governing relations between Indian tribes and the US government.[31]

Enhanced production of fish, by artificial means and by protection and improvement of natural spawning grounds, is under way and will be expanded significantly over the next decade. Several new hatcheries will be built in the basin to supplement the more than 100 existing artificial production facilities operated by state and federal governments with funding from federal appropriations and utilities. The existing hatcheries are mostly in the lower river, below the traditional fishing grounds of the Columbia basin Indian tribes; the new facilities will be upstream. The present intention is to use the hatcheries to raise fish only until they can survive in the wild. Juveniles would then be released into streams where they will imprint the smell of their adopted waters at the time of migration. This way, the fish should return as adults to these streams, rather than to the hatchery, to reproduce. If enough adults do so, a natural spawning run will be re-established, independent of the hatchery.

Natural spawning habitat is being improved primarily by reopening fish passages that were blocked by earlier human usage. For example, in the Wenatchee River of eastern Washington, Dryden and Tumwater Falls Dams, originally built with inadequate fish ladders, have been greatly improved so that migrating adults can now reach the habitat that was once blocked by the dams.[32]

Since adoption of the 1987 program, the council has also identified 40,000 stream miles of "protected areas" where small hydroelectric projects should not be built, to protect the ratepayers' investment in fish and wildlife rehabilitation. The council advises the state and federal agencies responsible for hydroproject licensing, particularly the US Federal Energy Regulatory Commission, which must, by statute, take the council's program "into account at each relevant stage of the decisionmaking processes to the fullest extent practicable."[33]

The upstream and downstream migration of anadromous fish is now under close human supervision. In some years, more than 80 percent of migrants from the upper Snake and Columbia are individually marked before being transported in barges to the estuary. In an effort to protect the fish that are not transported, Congress has appropriated more than $30 million annually to install screens and carve bypass channels in dams to deflect young fish from power turbines. Most ambitious of all, perhaps, the river's flow has been altered to benefit fish migration, at an annual cost of more than $40 million in lost power revenues. The key program, known as the water budget,[34] recreates the spring snowmelt or freshet to flush migrating juveniles to the sea.

Budgeting for Fish

Oddly, it is easier to pay for sustainable management of the Columbia because of the failure of nuclear power in the Pacific Northwest. The wholesale cost of electric power soared more than 700 percent in the early 1980s,[35] largely to pay for nuclear power plants that were never completed. Thus, the revenue stream is much larger than anticipated, and the percentage needed to pay for fisheries has dwindled to near insignificance. The cost of the council's fish and wildlife program alone is scheduled to consume about 1.5 percent of the Bonneville Power Administration's annual budget of $2.7 billion for fiscal year 1990. The total costs for mitigating the effects of hydropower development on fish and wildlife will be somewhat higher because they include debt payments for fish ladders and other facilities engineered into the dams. However, the actual cash outlays are considerably less than the total cost because more than one-third of the economic cost comes from foregone revenues—lost because of changes in river operations that release water when it cannot earn its maximum return, such as during the spring freshet to flush juvenile fish downriver or when water is spilled to channel fish away from dam turbines.

Thus, the Northwest Power Planning Council can search for sustainability under conditions where budgetary limitations are only a secondary consideration. This condition is clearly unrepresentative of attempts to carry out sustainable development generally, so the case of the Columbia basin should be regarded only as a proof-of-principle—a demonstration that sustainability can be achieved (if it indeed is). Conversely, failure in the Pacific Northwest would raise questions about the feasibility of sustainable development anywhere.

The weak budget constraint is not an unmixed blessing, of course, because it encourages choosing expensive alternatives that secure agreement among parties at the table at a cost to ratepayers who may not be well represented. Such logrolling makes a program brittle and fragile, as the US experience with weapons procurement illustrates.

A related problem is the large number of hands on the steering wheel. The Columbia River Basin Fish and Wildlife Program is implemented or significantly influenced by 11 state and federal agencies, 13 Indian tribes, 8 utilities that operate major hydroelectric projects in the Columbia drainage, and numerous organized interests ranging from agricultural groups anxious to protect water rights to flyfishers impatient for the return of wild fish stocks. If the river is to revive in any sustainable sense, it will have to be managed with a stability, durability, and awareness of biology rare in human affairs.

Mindful of the complex institutional repercussions of the changes it was making, the council adopted the concept of adaptive management into its fish and wildlife program in 1984[36] and expanded the idea into a process called "system planning" in 1987.[37] System planning is intended to institute an experimental approach to implementation in the early 1990s. In the meantime, remedial actions are under way and yielding information on what works and what does not before the full-blown adaptive plan is completed.

Adaptive Management

The Columbia River experience highlights two critical elements in the transition to sustainability: biological uncertainty and institutional complexity. In a field containing so many unknowns, learning from experience is the only practical approach. Without signposts, the path to a sustainable economy is easily lost. Consider some of the difficulties on the path to sustainability:[38]

- Data are sparse. It is difficult to observe the state of the ecological system and the human economy interacting with it. Measurements of the natural world, such as the size of migration populations, are inexact at best, and natural systems often yield only one data point per year (e.g. river flow).
- Theory is limited. Reliable observations are few, and theories of natural environments do not permit deductive logic to extrapolate very far from experience. Also, the perturbations caused by humans are frequently both large and unprecedented in natural history, so that it is unclear what theory is applicable.
- Surprise becomes unexceptional. With limited theory comes poor knowledge of the limitations of theory. Predictions are often wrong, expectations unfulfilled, and warnings hollow.

A general strategy has been devised to deal with natural resources under these conditions. The approach is called adaptive management, a term coined by C. S. Holling and his coworkers at the International Institute for Applied Systems Analysis in the late 1970s.[39] Their work is built on a simple, elegant idea: If human understanding of nature is imperfect, then human interactions with nature should be experimental. That is, policies should be designed and implemented as experiments probing the behavior of the natural system. Experiments often surprise and scientists learn from surprises. So, if resource management is considered from the outset as an experiment, surprises are opportunities to learn rather than failures to predict. Adaptive management holds the hope that, by learning from experience, one can reach and maintain a managed equilibrium efficiently and with the resilience to persevere in the face of surprise.[40]

Adaptive management originates in a comprehensive, ecosystem perspective, in which the interactions among the components of the natural environment are highly structured, and the behavior of the system as a whole is consequently rich in surprise.[41] Proceeding from a base of careful observations, experimental interventions into this interacting system provide insights into its dynamic character—insights, like the longstanding belief that diversity reinforces stability, that are helpful, even when they are not universally valid, and useful, even when one cannot rely implicitly on their quantitative implications. The adaptive perspective begins from a scientific viewpoint, and its continuation into the realm of action is informed more by the observational interest of a naturalist or astronomer than by the manipulative tendency of the engineer or entrepreneur.

Adaptive management is ecologically rooted in two more specific ways. First, the adaptive perspective is linked to biological time scales, because effects of experimentation on a population often become visible only when measured over generations. For salmon this implies a time scale of five years or more—a long interval in a governmental world where senior policy officials serve terms shorter than the salmon lifespan. Secondly, the adaptive approach focuses on populations, not individuals. Failures are often fatal for individuals, but rarely for populations. There is, accordingly, a greater willingness to experiment when the unit of concern is the population.

Even if whole populations are being managed, however, the decisions are made by individuals. Put into governmental terms, a policymaker who regards each choice as an opportunity to succeed or fail may be reluctant to venture into the chancy—if realistic—terrain of adaptive management. Though the theory emphasizes the value of learning from failure, it requires individuals with a high tolerance for risk to carry it out. As in economics, where the theory emphasizes the benefits of competition, the risks facing individuals can be imposing.

Although virtually all policy designs take into account feedback from action,[42] the idea of using a deliberately experimental design while paying attention to the choice of controls and the statistical power needed to test hypotheses is one rarely articulated and usually honored in the breach.[43] It is for this reason that the explicit adoption of an adaptive policy in the Columbia River basin is noteworthy.

Negotiating Consensus

Adaptive management responds to biological uncertainty, but it is not clear how the adaptive approach can work in the presence of institutional complexity. That many interests have stakes in the transition to sustainability is hardly surprising, but finding and maintaining a balance among disparate and often non-comparable considerations such as irrigation and tourism is evidently a political task, one that may not be consistent with the rational pursuit of knowledge through adaptive management.

Because control over large ecosystems is fragmented, the search for a sustainable economy requires extensive social interaction: sharing analytical information, such as simulation models and databases; identifying tradeoffs and coalitions for joint action; and learning from surprising outcomes. These interactions are ways to negotiate shared agendas that individual organizations cannot achieve by themselves.

The central role of negotiation emerges from the surprising blend of technocracy and consensus building that has gained visibility and favor among natural resource managers during the 1980s.[44] In cases previously characterized by lengthy litigation and embittered conflict, informal negotiations have produced plans of action acceptable to traditional adversaries: tribes and state governments, environmentalists and developers, and resource managers and harvesters. Although wary of advocacy in the guise of science, the parties have found it possible to use technical analyses and have invented measures to assure the political and scientific credibility of analysts and their findings. The negotiated agreements have included joint oversight mechanisms because unforeseen circumstances are to be expected during implementation. As a social process, the negotiations have sought to achieve and maintain the measure of consensus needed for experiential learning to occur. Thus, consensus building creates the open political environment that is necessary for adaptive management.[45]

Consensus building is central to sustainable development as well, because the natural systems being managed cross the spatial and functional boundaries of existing human institutions. Without this comprehensive perspective, the fragmentation of jurisdictions promotes abuse of the environment, because individual institutions seek to achieve purposes that often turn out to be incompatible with the sustainable use of the whole; this is the tragedy of the commons.[46] Yet implementation of a management plan also requires a decentralized, fragmented perspective, because decisions are carried out by parties whose responsibilities are narrow compared to the breadth of the analytical tools used by planners.[47]

The complexity of both human and natural systems is high enough to outrun anyone's ability to command from a central vantage. Building consensus by negotiation can link central perception to decentralized action. Consensus also may improve long-term plans to rehabilitate ecosystems.

Remedial actions require consensus when they encounter the problems of economic sustainability. Environmental damages from past actions are a sunk cost: The value of the resource has been taken by the exploiter and is no longer available to pay for remediation. The damaged ecosystem also contains hidden opportunities, since the ability of natural systems to recuperate is often uncertain. In that circumstance, strict cost-benefit estimates are likely to undervalue the worth of rehabilitating the ecosystem, especially if it is difficult or impossible to fund rehabilitation from the profits of exploitation.[48] When these conditions occur, a negotiated consensus reflecting a mandate for rehabilitation is needed to justify expenditures. Moreover, past damages may have altered the political environment by driving out a group of resource users (e.g. the Indians of the river basin). In such a case, rebuilding a sustainable suite of uses may require that points of view that were silenced by earlier misuse be actively sought out. Consensus building has been strategically important in the Columbia River basin, where a central agent finances decentralized actions, no one of which meets a narrow cost-benefit test even though their cumulative impact may be economically sound.

A consensus that fosters learning both facilitates and benefits from an open political setting. By lowering the barriers to participation and, in effect, organizing their own political environment, planners can negotiate and sustain a pluralistic, competitive political setting, in which disparate considerations can continue to be weighed as learning goes forward.

Planning and Politics

This consensus-building approach can be seen in the work of the Northwest Power Planning Council.[49] Because important matters are at stake in development projects, a wide spectrum of interests usually is motivated to participate in the planning. Barriers to participation should be low at the outset and can be kept low by the planners. Established relationships are usually weak at the beginning of a development project, and, because there is often substantial uncertainty about how the links among different interests will be changed, it does not require much previous experience to become an effective player. Where external support is important to the implementation of the plan, however, planning must turn to the outside world.

Backed by a legal mandate to keep the public informed and involved, the council lowered barriers to participation and judged its success by its credibility with the public. The council's first chairman, Dan Evans, a popular and well-known figure who had served three terms as governor of Washington State, led the way with an open political style. Evans made a special effort to approach the Indian tribes, whose legal battles on fishing rights began to be fought while he was governor. More generally, the council approached organizational and opinion leaders both in and out of government and consciously developed a constituency for implementation of its energy plan and fish and wildlife program. Support for the council has come almost entirely from organized groups because of the complexity of the council's plans. Despite the wide popularity of efforts to protect and enhance the fish runs, the work of the council is not well known to the public at large. Instead, the council has cultivated a reputation for well-informed, even-handed judgment among organized interests.

The planning now under way illustrates the institutional style of gathering information from sources throughout the basin and subjecting data to public review as a prelude to a public process of priority setting for the 1990s. Building the institutional structure for sustainable development in the Columbia River basin has been based on several conditions:

- commitments in law, reinforced by political support, to preserve and enhance environmentally valued resources;
- explicit recognition of ecological, economic, and social uncertainties;
- a commitment to act on the basis of knowledge;

- adequate funding;
- an institutional process open to experiential learning; and
- a systems orientation.

The Columbia River basin program may be regarded as a proof-of-principle: Sustainable development on a large scale is possible to launch. Given the time necessary to achieve certifiable sustainability, that is as much good news as one can expect in the post-industrial world.

Three Caveats

The challenge of a sustainable Columbia River is no different from the challenge of sustainable development generally. Can humans endure on this planet? Nobody knows. It is clear that continuing the exponential increase in resource use of the past 150 years will have serious effects on the global climate. Stalling the rush toward the inhospitable greenhouse, however, raises the most profound questions of economic justice and strains the ability of the international system to maintain order. Thus, although humans must proceed adaptively in the search for sustainability, learning from experience may be neither sufficient nor feasible in the transition ahead. Three caveats are in order.

First, there is the problem of conceptual tractability. The natural systems to be managed sustainably are inherently complex, and their complexity exceeds both traditional human comprehension and the institutions that have managed portions of them in the past. In a related context, William Ascher and Garry D. Brewer recently argued that a sophisticated cost-benefit framework is politically vulnerable in proportion to its sophistication. Such vulnerability creates a barrier to sustainable development.[50] The hurdle of complexity may prove to be a genetic defect in sustainability.

A second problem is the moral viability of sustainable development. Perhaps only rich, stable nations can afford sustainability and make the transition with some semblance of political consent. The concept of sustainability comes with no guarantee that it is attainable or that, if feasible by some quantitative measure, it will be politically and morally palatable.

Third, adaptive management emphasizes the interest of the population, not that of the individual. Belief systems that value individuals may find little comfort when learning comes at a high cost in suffering. The long delays inherent in many issues of global sustainability also limit the utility of adaptive methods, because the signals of success or failure come back too slowly to inform action. These are the same conditions that one encounters in social welfare policy: slow or incomprehensible feedback combined with urgent, undeniable individual needs. Thus far, social welfare programs have been more anodyne than cure.

The experience of the Columbia River basin points to two unorthodox paths for study and reflection. First, look to the industrial economies for examples of sustainability. Sustainable development may be like the demographic transition: Nations rich and stable enough to be able to experiment with different modes of living may discover the viable alternatives.

Second, the strategic importance of uncertainty in the path to sustainability must be considered. The adaptive approach offers a conceptually sound way to deal with uncertainties in the natural system and with the complexities of institutional structure. Thinking in terms of whole systems while acting through many fragments ("Think globally, act locally") requires an explicit organizational and political strategy. Adaptive management is one such strategy.

Taking sustainability seriously is a question of governance. There are indeed promising leads, but time is short and resources are dwindling. Learning what does not work is a cost of finding ways that will. Minimizing that cost preserves humanity's already limited ability to pursue sustainability with justice and mercy.

Notes

My work is supported in part by the Washington SeaGrant Program. The ideas in this paper draw upon discussions with Danny Sheppard, Jan Carpenter, and Garry D. Brewer. I am grateful for comments and encouragement on earlier versions of this paper from C. S. Holling, William Ascher, William C. Clark, Mohamed El-Ashry, Cindy L. Halbert, Conway B. Leovy, Robert Repetto, and David Stokes.

1. For others cases, see Walter V. C. Reid, James N. Barnes, and Brent Blackwelder, *Bankrolling Successes* (Washington, DC: Environmental Policy Institute, 1988); and Walter V. C. Reid, "Sustainable Development: Lessons from Success," *Environment*, May 1989, 6.

2. William Kahrl (ed.), *California Water Atlas* (Los Altos, Calif.: William Kauffmann, 1978), 3.

3. For a discussion helpful to the non-biologist, see Charles F. Wilkinson and Daniel Keith Conner, "The Law of the Pacific Salmon Fishery," *University of Kansas Law Review*, 32 (1983), 17–109.

4. Randall Schalk, "Estimating Salmon and Steelhead Usage in the Columbia Basin Before 1850: The Anthropological Perspective," *Northwest Environmental Journal*, 2 (1986), 1–30; and Wilkinson and Conner, "Law of the Pacific Salmon Fishery," 27.

5. Northwest Power Planning Council, *Columbia River Basin Fish and Wildlife Program*, appendix E (Portland, Ore.: Northwest Power Planning Council, 1987).

6. Schalk, "Estimating Salmon and Steelhead Usage."

7. Northwest Power Planning Council, *Northwest Conservation and Electric Power Plan*, i and ii (Portland, Ore.: Northwest Power Planning Council, 1986).

8. Gene Tollefson, *BPA and the Struggle for Power at Cost* (Washington, DC: US Government Printing Office, 1987); and Kai N. Lee and Donna L. Klemka, with Marion E. Marts, *Electric Power and the Future of the Pacific Northwest* (Seattle: University of Washington Press, 1980).

9. Donald Worster, *Rivers of Empire: Water, Aridity, and the Growth of the American West* (New York: Pantheon, 1985), 269–72; and Katherine Anne Janeway, "Of Time and the River: The Debate over Completion of the Columbia River Basin Irrigation Project," *Northwest Environmental Journal*, 1 (1985), 97–113.

10. The population figure is that for the area served by the Bonneville Power Administration, the states of Idaho, Oregon, Washington, and Montana west of the continental divide.

11. Worster, commenting on the Colorado River, *Rivers of Empire*, 276.

12. Northwest Power Planning Council, *Columbia River Basin*, 35–9.

13. The energy conservation programs assembled by the Northwest Power Planning Council and implemented by the utilities of the region are described in the council's regional energy plan, *Northwest Conservation*. For an interesting example, see Dulcy Mahar, "The County that Came in from the Cold," *Northwest Energy News* (newsletter of the Northwest Power Planning Council), June/July 1987, 26–9.

14. Alston Chase, *Playing God in Yellowstone* (San Diego: Harvest/Harcourt, Brace, Jovanovich, 1987).

15. Compare with William Ascher and Garry D. Brewer, "Sustainable Development and

Natural Resource Forecasting," in Clark Binkley, G. D. Brewer, and V. Alaric Sample (eds), *Redirecting the RPA*, Bulletin 95 (New Haven: Yale School of Forestry and Environmental Studies, 1988), 216–29. Ascher and Brewer define sustainable development as "the pattern of resources exploitation that maintains the highest possible levels of net social welfare benefits into the future." The difference between this approach and the one taken here is more apparent than real, however, because the question of how to estimate "net social welfare benefits" opens up the issues of value and feasibility that are raised by putting the word "between" in quotation marks.

16. Pacific Northwest Electric Power Planning and Conservation Act of 1980, PL 96–501, 16 US Code §§839–839h; referred to below as the "Northwest Power Act."

17. For a critical appraisal, see Michael C. Blumm, "Reexamining the Parity Promise: More Challenges Than Successes to the Implementation of the Columbia Basin Fish and Wildlife Program," *Environmental Law*, 16 (1986), 461–515.

18. Northwest Power Act, Section 4(h)(1)(A).

19. Ibid., Section 10(h).

20. For a provocative critique of Western water law as both environmental and economic policy, see Charles F. Wilkinson, "Aldo Leopold and Western Water Law: Thinking Perpendicular to the Prior Appropriation Doctrine," *Land and Water Law Review*, 24 (1989), 1–38.

21. For a helpful discussion of why contradictory interests come to be reflected in public policy, see John W. Kingdon, *Agendas, Alternatives, and Public Policies* (Boston: Little, Brown, 1984), chap. 4.

22. John E. Chubb, *Interest Groups and the Bureaucracy: The Politics of Energy* (Stanford, Calif.: Stanford University Press, 1983). Chubb advances a sophisticated analysis of how the interactions between bureaucrats and interest-group leaders blunt and subvert legislative directives.

23. The emergence of joint management of salmon and steelhead harvest by Indian tribes and state agencies, after a prolonged legal struggle over the century-old treaties between the tribes and the US government, is described by Penny H. Harrison, "The Evolution of a New Comprehensive Plan for Managing Columbia River Anadromous Fish," *Environmental Law*, 16 (1986), 705–29. A similar accord on consensual management of timber harvest was concluded in the Timber/Fish/Wildlife agreement in 1987, covering forest management on nonfederal lands in Washington State. See Northwest Renewable Resources Center, *Timber/Fish/Wildlife* (tabloid) (Seattle: Summer 1987) and Cindy L. Halbert, Master's thesis (University of Washington Institute for Marine Studies, 1989).

24. Northewest Power Act, Section 4(h).

25. Michael C. Blumm, "Hydropower vs. Salmon: The Struggle of the Pacific Northwest's Anadromous Fish Resources for a Peaceful Coexistence with the Federal Columbia River Power System," *Environmental Law*, 11 (1981), 211.

26. Northwest Power Act, Section 4.

27. Northwest Power Planning Council, *Columbia River Basin Fish and Wildlife Program* (Portland, Ore.: Northwest Power Planning Council, 1982).

28. Jody Lawrence, "The Water Budget: A step Towards Balancing Power and Fish in the Columbia River Basin," Master's thesis (University of Washington Department of Civil Engineering, 1983).

29. Northwest Power Planning Council, *Columbia River Basin*, 35–9.

30. Treaty between the Government of the United States of America and the Government of Canada Concerning Pacific Salmon, Treaty Document No. 99-2 (entered in force, 18 March 1985).

31. Harrison, "Evolution of a New Plan."

32. Northwest Power Planning Council, *Columbia River Basin*, 237.

33. Northwest Power Act, Section 4(h)(11)(A).

34. Lawrence, "Water Budget."

35. Bonneville Power Administration, *Programs in Perspective*, newsletter, January 1988, 1 (figure 1).

36. Northwest Power Planning Council, *Columbia River Basin Fish and Wildlife Program* (Portland, Ore.: Northwest Power Planning Council, 1984), 108; and Kai N. Lee and Jody Lawrence, "Adaptive Management: Learning from the Columbia River Basin Fish and Wildlife Program," *Environmental Law*, 16 (1986), 431–60.

37. Northwest Power Planning Council, *Columbia River Basin*, Section 200.

38. Ray Hilborn, "Living with Uncertainty in Resource Management," *North American Journal of Fisheries Management*, 7 (1987), 1–5; and Alvin Weinberg, "Science and Trans-Science," *Minerva*, 10 (1972), 209.

39. C. S. Holling (ed.), *Adaptive Environmental Assessment and Management* (New York: John Wiley & Sons, 1978); Peter A. Larkin, "Play It Again Sam—An Essay on Salmon Enhancement," *Journal of the Fisheries Research Board of Canada*, 31 (1974), 1433–56; Environmental and Social Systems Analysts, Ltd., *Review and Evaluation of Adaptive Environmental Assessment and Management* (Ottawa: Environment Canada, 1982); Carl Walters, *Adaptive Management of Renewable Resources* (New York: Macmillan, 1986); National Academy of Sciences, *Ecological Knowledge and Environmental Problem-Solving* (Washington, DC: National Academy Press, 1986); and Gordon H. Orians, "The Place of Science in Environmental Problem-Solving," *Environment*, November 1986, 12–17, 38–41.

40. William C. Clark and R. E. Munn (eds), *Sustainable Development of the Biosphere* (Cambridge: Cambridge University Press, 1986).

41. Holling (ed.), "Adaptive Environmental Assessment," chap. 2.

42. Charles E. Lindblom, "The Science of 'Muddling Through,'" *Public Administration Review*, 19 (1959), 79–88.

43. Alice M. Rivlin, *Systematic Thinking for Social Action* (Washington, DC: Brookings Institution, 1971); and National Academy of Sciences, *Ecological Knowledge*, 104–5.

44. Douglas J. Amy, *The Politics of Environmental Mediation* (New York: Columbia University Press, 1987); Gerald W. Cormick, "The 'Theory' and Practice of Environmental Mediation," *Environmental Professional*, 2 (1980), 24–33; Gail Bingham, *Resolving Environmental Disputes: A Decade of Experience* (Washington, DC: Conservation Foundation, 1986); Allan R. Talbot, *Settling Things: Six Case Studies in Environmental Mediation* (Washington, DC: Conservation Foundation and Ford Foundation, 1983); and Ray Hilborn and Wilf Luedke, "Rationalizing the Irrational: A Case Study of User Group Participation in Chum Salmon Management," *Canadian Journal of Fisheries and Aquatic Science*, 44 (1988), 1796–1805.

45. Negotiated consensus may not be a necessary precondition for adaptive management. The simultaneous emergence of negotiated settlements to natural resource disputes and of adaptive management appears to be a historical accident, though it is clear that both draw upon ideas "in the air," including a bias for consensus as a management style and a commitment to use science in decisionmaking despite conflict.

46. Garrett Hardin, "The Tragedy of the Commons," *Science*, 162: 3859 (1968), 1243–8.

47. G. L. Baskerville, "Redevelopment of a Forest System," paper presented at a symposium on *Ecosystem Redevelopment: Ecological, Economic, and Social Aspects*, Budapest, Hungary, April 1987.

48. H. A. Regier and G. L. Baskerville, "Sustainable Redevelopment of Regional Ecosystems Degraded by Exploitive Development," in Clark and Munn (eds), *Sustainable Development*.

49. Daniel J. Evans and Roy Hemmingway, "Northwest Power Planning: Origins and Strategies," *Northwest Environmental Journal*, 1 (1984), 1–22; and Chubb, *Interest Groups and the Bureaucracy*, 224–7.

50. Ascher and Brewer, "Sustainable Development."

9 Limits of the Administrative Mind: The Problem of Defining Environmental Problems

Douglas Torgerson

To see the environment as an administrative problem means cutting the environment down to size, making it manageable. However, this approach quickly runs into trouble. In grappling with the environment, conventional administration betrays many inadequacies. These shortcomings demonstrate the need for techniques and processes which will deal more sensitively and comprehensively with environmental complexities. Such innovations offer an ambivalent potential either to reinforce or transform the boundaries of administration. This essay probes that potential and offers a critique of the "administrative mind" as an image that, while often only implicit, pervades the administrative world and constrains the definition of environmental problems. From this perspective, conventional administration itself appears as an environmental problem.

Unexpected Problems of the Administrative State

The administrative sphere prides itself on order, but cannot control the consequences it generates. For persistent fragmentation accompanies coherence in this sphere; and the administrative mind is itself limited, especially by its focus on promoting the modern vision of progress. Various disorders arose early with industrialization, indicating the need for a central authority to regulate and promote the steady course of progress. Profound disagreements over the nature and scope of this need did not alter the fact that, whenever problems threatened to thwart the realization of the modern vision, hope was generally placed in the agency of a competent and detached administration[1]—in what has emerged as the *administrative state*.[2] Anticipated in a sense throughout the rise of the industrialization, the administrative state was clearly recognized in the twentieth century when rationalization—the disenchantment of the world—began to permeate economy and society with both industrial technology and bureaucratic organization. The formalized relationships impressed upon social life fell far short of producing overall coherence, and consequent problems of coordination—as they were viewed—placed demands upon the administrative capacity of the state. Problems were generally defined in terms of finding and

Reprinted with permission from Robert Paehlke and Douglas Torgerson (eds), *Managing Leviathan: Environmental Politics and the Administrative State* (Peterborough, Ontario: Broadview Press, 1990), 115–61. The version which appears here has been edited with the cooperation of Douglas Torgerson.

pursuing the most efficient use of human and natural resources. The corresponding tasks of cal-culation, organization, and technological development called for a state administrative appara-tus capable of functioning as regulator and promoter of an increasingly rationalized economy and society. These tasks necessitated a rationalized state able to formulate and implement poli-cies based upon a sound assessment of what was required by the developing industrial order. In effect, this meant not only enhancing the administrative apparatus of the state, but also fostering and coordinating linkages throughout the administrative sphere as a whole.[3] Yet, while the administrative state can thus be regarded as a response to advancing industrialization and the spread of administrative organizations in society, the path for these developments was cleared earlier by state policies which already involved a centralization and expansion of state adminis-trative capacity.

The administrative state, however, should be viewed *not* as a vast apparatus of public admin-istration standing by itself, but in context. The administrative state should be seen as a distinctive historical phenomenon, coming into its own precisely when the state loses its stature as a single, overarching administrative structure. For a historical dynamic of the market mechanism, still largely unacknowledged from a *laissez-faire* perspective, was for that mechanism to undermine itself by promoting a concentration of enterprise and an enormous expansion of bureaucratic administration in the great private corporations. The administrative state thus constitutes a key feature of a more comprehensive administrative sphere, in which the position of the state as a clearly distinct and independent apparatus becomes significantly attenuated.[4] As part of this administrative sphere, indeed, the state proved far less effective in its *laissez-faire* mandate of maintaining competition than in such tasks as facilitating industrial coordination and helping to assess and harness the dormant resources of the earth for efficient use.[5]

Not long after the administrative state had been formed and named—in the mid-twentieth century—the seemingly inevitable advance of rationalization began to encounter unanticipated obstacles. The burgeoning of industrial technology and bureaucratic organization began to gen-erate problems which had been unintended and indeed unimaginable. As certain flaws in tech-nology and bureaucracy became widely apparent, the rationalization of the world became increasingly vulnerable to questions which before could—to the extent they were even possible to ask—be readily deflected. This unsettling development did not, of course, occasion the col-lapse of the administrative state; the result, if anything, was intensified reliance upon it as a coor-dinating mechanism to solve the new problems. The reflex was to expand the scope of measurement and calculation, to devise a comprehensive system of planning and control—a mode of accounting, in short, which would monitor, anticipate, and internalize the disec-onomies of industrial expansion.[6] The emergence of present problems associated with resource constraints and pollution has not yet significantly altered this orientation. Nonetheless, on the fringes of administrative practice and in a thin public sphere[7] the monuments of administration have been called into question; and the emerging array of problems thus appears to contain a significant potential—that of promoting challenges both to the established pattern of develop-ment and to the conventional view of administration.

The administrative state responds by reflex to its emerging problems—and this, perhaps, is its most pressing problem. The celebrated lack of imagination characteristic of the bureaucratic mentality is no doubt part of the difficulty. Indeed, schooled in routines, their attention fixed by rules and conventions, administrative officials are, we have been told, at best predictable. For if deviations from normal procedures are regarded as irresponsible, then little innovation is to be encouraged or expected in the solution or definition of problems.[8] Yet such clichés about bureaucracy do not adequately portray the predicament of the administrative state: a paradox of this tedious institutional form is that it is invested with exalted imagery, the grand vision of order and progress ordained by the administrative mind—a vision which remains potent, even as present problems dramatically violate the expectations it fosters.

Problems of Defining Problems

Far from resting in calm certitude, actual administration is notoriously uncertain and fallible. The imposing image of an administrative mind thus competes with a less exalted, distinctly mundane, process. Yet while in everyday practice no one may fully and explicitly express faith in the administrative mind, the image is nonetheless potent, shaping perceptions, expectations, and viewpoints; while limiting the way problems are defined. The notion of administrative problem-solving as the exclusive domain of a detached and impersonal mind helps to orient a form of life characteristic of the administrative sphere.

UNQUESTIONED JUDGMENT

For problem-solving to be defined as a matter of calculation, all issues of problem definition would have to be thoroughly resolved; and a key issue is the identification of goals. Actual administrative practice of course violates the conventional imagery of unity under an administrative mind where all are committed to a common goal. For a collision and coalescence of particular interests, coming from outside and within, is a salient feature of the administrative sphere. In the very stress upon the necessity of unified authority one can detect an acknowledgement of potential disunity—the worry that internal or external conflicts might disrupt deliberations and thereby undermine the ability of administrators to establish and maintain a coherent order of operations.[9]

To suggest that problems can be solved by calculation is not only to express what might be a genuine conviction; it is also to assert the autonomy, and thus to promote the insularity, of administrative authority. The traditional divide between policy formulation and implementation has supplied a fiction which pays tribute to the inevitable role of judgment in decision; yet this dichotomy has, in effect, served to advance the insularity and unity of administrative authority as the seat of such judgment. Even though calculation may appear partially displaced in this traditional conception, a safe realm of cogitation has been preserved by excluding the troubles of interaction, discussion, disagreement. The judgments are to be unquestionable. If an appeal to reason must here be supplemented by appeals to traditional or charismatic sources of authority, all remains further supported by the mythic and rationalistic imagery of order and progress. In the technocratic conception, there is no longer any requirement for a distinct realm of unquestionable judgment, for what remains of judgment has been narrowed to the vanishing point. The administrative mind constitutes a framework for pure calculation through a management information system which defines problems according to self-evident axioms and uncontroversial postulates.[10] What may be regarded as self-evident or uncontroversial is readily established by the unquestioned presuppositions of the vision of order and progress. While in principle contradictory, these traditional and technocratic approaches readily co-exist in practice; for they are complementary in providing a flexible mechanism for deflecting efforts to question judgments of the administrative mind.

CONCEPTUAL FOCUS

To the extent that problem-solving is influenced by the image of the administrative mind, whether overt or tacit, the effect is to obscure the actual process. Even when a fundamental consensus upon goals can be taken for granted, the search for means generates oppositions and tensions which can provoke a revision of goals. The definition of problems, that is to say, is not simply a matter of choosing goals; there is a complex interplay of means and goals as new difficulties or opportunities become apparent. Consequently, it is possible to speak of solving the wrong problem. The definition of a problem turns upon what concept gains prominence in focusing attention; as long as one concept fixes attention, perhaps because its influence is not noticed, the nature of the problem appears obvious. With an interplay among alternative concepts, however, the definition of the problem is thrown into question. Significant even in contexts of fairly routine administrative matters, such questioning may involve the issue, for example, of whether an organization faces a problem of transportation or of inventory, of attitudes or of structure, of machinery or of people. Similarly, questions may arise concerning the fundamental identity and direction of an organization. Here the emergence and clarification of a leading concept appears as the key breakthrough to a solution—in effect, it appears that the essential step in solving a problem lies in defining it. To say this is to say that problem-solving is primarily concerned with how attention is focused.[11] To reveal an organizing concept which has gone unnoticed serves to refocus attention and to open up the possibility of play and flexibility among concepts.

Much recent innovation in management thought may be interpreted as an attempt—usually remaining marginal in practice—to break free of that fascination with the administrative mind which has guided the understanding of problem-solving in administrative organizations. Particularly in attempts to address the problem of problem definition, the accent has shifted from cogitation to interaction, from the remote operations of an austere mind to a communicative domain of multiple participants.[12] Indeed, it now becomes apparent that the practice of judgment necessary in defining and redefining problems involves an inescapable interplay of opposing ideas and perspectives—of difference, divergence, conflict. Even in the case of a single individual, this process of positing positions and oppositions is not eluded, but internalized. Yet both for individuals and collectivities, the image of the administrative mind can still obscure and inhibit this process.

Concern with the problem of problem definition points to an opening, to a play and flexibility in conceptualization. By drawing attention, in particular, to the administrative mind as a guiding focus of conventional problem definition in administrative organizations, we render explicit what is often implicit; we draw to the forefront a typically ignored background. Such a move, that is, directs attention to context; orientation to context thus becomes something which need not be passively received, but might be consciously developed and refined.[13] As we probe constraints on attention, moreover, we pass beyond the administrative mind to its fundamental rationale: the vision of order and progress. By focusing upon this vision and questioning it, we advance our deliberate project of contextual orientation to the point of a conscious elaboration of developmental constructs.

Defining Environmental Problems

Even to speak of environmental problems reflects some influence of the administrative mind. For the dramatic and widespread expressions of environmental concern, voiced some two decades ago, were animated by an idea which the administrative mind was not prepared to contemplate: that there was a fundamental flaw in the whole pattern of industrial development. Progress, as a quest to dominate nature, was seen to be itself a source of disorder, disrupting the natural systems upon which civilization and human life depended. The concern being voiced was one focused not only on separate problems, but on a whole pattern of problems—the collective consequence of which, it was feared, could be to throw humanity out of the balance of nature. The concern was not just with problems, but with a crisis.

ENVIRONMENTAL CRISIS AND ADMINISTRATIVE VISION

Although environmental concern achieved considerable acceptance and even popularity, the perception of crisis was resisted and rejected by the administrative sphere; indeed, to perceive a fundamental flaw in the whole project of industrialization would be to question the *raison d'être* of this institutional complex. Accordingly, those articulating this sense of crisis were ridiculed—and ridiculed fairly easily since the rationalistic imagery of order and progress was at hand to help in portraying as emotional and irrational those who perceived a crisis. An anomaly in the ideological universe, the perception of crisis was to be explained as an abnormality, as deviance stemming from social or psychological peculiarities, from some corruption of mental faculties. Those who spoke of crisis were the victims and purveyors of irrationalism because—it was charged with no hint of the irony—they lacked *faith* in technology and progress.[14] The exuberant industrial growth and rapid technological innovation of the post-war period encouraged an optimistic atmosphere and gave credence to the notion that the management of government and industry was safely in the hands of experts. During this period, moreover, the increasingly technocratic bent of the administrative mind was reinforced by the widespread adoption of a systems approach.

The perception of an environmental crisis involved seeing various impacts of post-war expansion as an interrelated, emerging whole.[15] Ironically, this very perception gained support not only from the systems-theoretic focus of ecology, but also from systems modelling techniques drawn from the new repertoire of technocratic management itself. With this appeal to rationalistic imagery, the perception of environmental crisis demanded a more measured response than name-calling. While this more considered response may itself have exposed some rather basic limits of technocratic systems management, the controversy became esoteric enough to implicitly encourage renewed reliance upon the administrative mind to resolve the question.[16] At the same time, the challenge which the perception of crisis posed to the administrative sphere—and its animating vision—was too fundamental to be faced directly. Not only the ideology, but also the apparatus of this sphere, rendered irrelevant any perception of a pervasive crisis; for this apparatus had been structured to promote industrialization, not to deal with the aftermath. With a comprehensive vision of order and progress taken for granted, the apparatus was structured so that its various parts would attend to specific, strictly delimited problems one at a time. Even rather routine difficulties were, of course, often complex enough to generate problems of coordination requiring policy adjustments and structural adaptations.[17] However, the structure had no capacity to respond to the perception of a crisis so pervasive and complex as potentially to strike at the foundations of the entire edifice—and to expose it as a house of cards. To be dealt with, the "crisis" had to be viewed and treated not comprehensively, as the product of a basic flaw in the whole project of industrialization, but in a manner which identified *manageable* problems. Although the problems could be regarded as somehow commonly "environmental", they had to be defined, in operational terms, as primarily separate, capable of being solved in a manner which matched the functional differentiation of the administrative apparatus.[18] This approach accorded not only with the established structure of administration, but also with a "commonplace" of the technocratic orientation: "that there is a high measure of certainty that problems have solutions before there is knowledge of how they are to be solved."[19] With this confidence and with environmental concern translated into discrete problems, faith in the established pattern of development could be maintained.

AN ALTERNATIVE VISION

The perception of environmental crisis and continuing confidence in the path of industrialization arose from competing visions of an emerging whole, each necessarily based upon fragmentary evidence. Each viewpoint, in other words, was part of a contextual orientation which contained a particular notion of the pattern of historical development, a notion which—again in each case—was articulated vigorously and lent a sense of future inevitability. Against the dream of an efficient and orderly modern millennium, the perception of environmental crisis posed the nightmare of an apocalypse in which nature would gain retribution for the violations of an arrogant humanity.[20] While continuing confidence in the path of industrialization was reinforced by prevailing cultural norms, the perception of crisis could also draw upon elements of the culture with imagery reviving the romantic reaction against modernity, recalling bucolic myths and old doubts about progress, appealing to populist sentiment, and reverently picturing nature as something essentially harmonious.[21] Humanity, as a matter of both ethics and survival, should seek to live in harmony rather than in conflict with nature. This, it was suggested, was a lesson of ecology. Since this lesson was unlikely to be learned well or quickly enough, catastrophe was in the offing. This accent of environmentalist thought conveyed the idea that nothing short of a total and immediate transformation of the established path would do. Futile gestures or withdrawal were thus the typical consequences.

Nonetheless, there were significant efforts to formulate a possible path of future development which would pose a distinct alternative to the established pattern—one accentuating ecological sensitivity, decentralized initiative, small-scale projects, "appropriate" technology, and community cooperation. This idea of an alternative pattern of development represented, in effect, an effort to promote a contextual reorientation by deliberately elaborating a developmental construct in sharp contrast to the received view. While perhaps promoted as necessary for continued human well-being, an alternative pattern of development was clearly not seen as inevitable; at most, it was a desirable possibility, one which could conceivably be pursued through concerted effort. Since it directly challenged the established administrative artifice and its expectations of order and progress, however, such an alternative could readily be rejected and ridiculed, portrayed as thoroughly unrealistic. Still, by addressing significant, concrete issues of administration and policy within the context of a comprehensively conceived alternative, this approach to development could at least unsettle the complacency of the conventional outlook and provide, by way of dramatic contrast, an intellectual space for questioning a prevailing conceptual framework.[22]

THE ADMINISTRATIVE RESPONSE

Yet these were questions which could not really be taken seriously by the administrative mind. Having defined environmental concern in terms of manageable problems, the administrative sphere responded in a piecemeal fashion—in effect, seeking initially to "clean up" problems left by industrialization. The chief strategy was state promulgation and enforcement of environmental standards which were designed with the announced purpose of keeping specific kinds of "pollution" within tolerable limits, while at the same time achieving a balance with established economic interests. These initiatives sometimes involved the revival or revision of existing regulations, sometimes the development of new ones. Even when effective on its own terms, however, this approach typically employed what—in retrospect—appear obviously to have been expedients and stopgaps: narrowly focused techniques which were insensitive to their own consequences, changing the location and character of emissions and wastes without eliminating them as a problem. Environmental regulation was thus designed with a focus on specific, existing problems.[23]

It was not necessary to admit to a pervasive environmental crisis for the administrative sphere to recognize, however reluctantly, that emerging patterns of technological innovation and economic expansion were bound to generate new problems. A concerted effort to advance an alternative pattern of development would have taken as its central focus the purpose and design of new projects, both individually and collectively; indeed, a chief element of this approach would have been to draw explicit attention to the *pattern* of development and to foster an alternative to it which would anticipate and avoid formerly unanticipated problems. The response of the administrative sphere did not countenance such a decisive change in the existing pattern of development; nonetheless, attempts were made to design more sensitive anticipatory mechanisms while promoting the continuation of the established course. These mechanisms took the shape of innovations in planning techniques—in particular, technology assessment, environmental impact assessment, and social impact assessment. Although generally advanced from a technocratic posture, accentuating the readily calculable while neglecting context, these planning innovations nonetheless implicitly acknowledged that difficulties had arisen with conventional expectations informed by the vision of order and progress. The application of these techniques was generally unenthusiastic; indeed, resistance by particular administrative organizations was often effective in preventing, curtailing, or circumventing anticipatory assessments. Still, this resistance itself suggests that the employment of these new techniques—however technocratically constrained—was worrisome for major interests involved in promoting the established pattern of development. For no matter how marginal the use of these techniques generally has been in the policy processes of the state and of corporations, their application nonetheless created a new factor which somehow had to be reckoned with and which, at important points, could affect the flow of decision-making. Indeed, if not tightly controlled, such assessments could not only direct attention to fundamental problems about specific projects, but could also lead to a questioning of the whole pattern of industrial development—of order and progress itself.[24]

The agencies responsible for environmental management—regulation, impact assessment, and related procedures—were at times developed from already established units with different primary mandates; at other times, new units were created, yet typically with a marginal position within the administrative sphere as a whole. These organizational realignments were in keeping with what would seem a measured response of treating environmental concern in terms of manageable problems.[25] In contrast, many who perceived the advent of a pervasive environmental crisis demanded a far more dramatic response—one which would effectively subordinate the entire administrative sphere and society as a whole under a single head devoted to environmental management.[26] Of course, this proposal was a futile reflex: one which sought simply to change the goal orientation of the administrative mind while ignoring the historical and political processes which, in shaping the apparatus of the administrative sphere, have also promoted ends suited to its form. In any event, both of these approaches shared a view of environmental management as a discrete function, something added on somewhere to an administrative edifice whose basic form was to be taken for granted.

THINKING IN ANOTHER DIRECTION

In conceptions of an alternative pattern of development, environmental management came to be viewed as potentially a characteristic of the whole, rather than a function of a part controlling the whole. Yet this view was itself—given its holistic focus—so sweepingly comprehensive that it seemed to deny itself any place to begin. Conceptually, the approach seemed capable of recommending only a total transformation—a change requiring a scope and magnitude of power which not only would be fantastic, but which would also violate principles of decentralization and participation that were generally seen as necessary features of an alternative path.[27] In practice, however, a focus on particular problems did emerge. In part, this focus tacitly acknowledged the rationale of administrative compartmentalization: that a problematic complex must, whether or not it constituted a "crisis", somehow be reduced to a set of simpler problems, each of which can become an object of separate attention. At the same time, however, the particular way in which the alternative orientation is decomposed into specific problems shows that how one cuts into a problematic complex is decisive for problem definition. What is distinctive about this orientation is that no problem is assumed, in analysis or design, to be entirely discrete; on the contrary, it is a guiding presupposition that efforts to solve a particular problem will affect efforts to solve other problems. Hence problem-solving designs are elaborated with, as it were, an open boundary; attention is permitted and encouraged to remain devoted to a broader context. From this perspective, the definition of one problem partly defines others; there is, indeed, mutual overlapping. Accordingly, administration must, in technique, process and structure, match the complexity of these interrelated problems.[28] Although thought and organizations must somehow be bounded, in other words, this approach to problem definition and administration attempts to test and stretch these limits through deliberate contextual reorientation—and through designs informed by this effort.[29] This distinctive approach to contextual orientation, furthermore, promotes what is in effect a redefinition of conventionally defined environmental problems.

The problem of waste disposal, for example, becomes redefined as a problem of waste reduction and recycling. The problem of controlling pesticide pollution is redefined as a problem of developing agricultural patterns which require less pesticide input while, at the same time, utilizing organic nutrients which otherwise end up as waste. Health care expands its focus from cure to prevention, seeking to reduce pollution both in the workplace and beyond; and trying, moreover, to encourage healthful dietary patterns—which, in turn, are congruent with the agricultural patterns being developed. Air pollution control devices on vehicles are seen (at most) as part of the solution to a problem which also requires vehicle redesign to reduce fuel consumption, perhaps the use of different fuels, and even a reform of the entire transportation network—guided by a reconsideration of settlement patterns and work schedules. The problem of meeting increasing energy demand is redefined so that increases are no longer taken as given: the problem becomes one primarily of meeting energy needs through significantly greater reliance upon conservation and efficiency, an effort which complements and reinforces efforts regarding waste, pollution, health and so on.

What is generally common to environmental problems, as redefined, is that they and their proposed solutions are found by thinking in "another" direction. Such redefinition, indeed, appears risky; for although the new approaches may be insightful, even elegant, they also dispense with guarantees implied by the vision of order and progress, guarantees which depend upon the administrative mind as the coherent locus of comprehension and control. The problem-solving designs—the technical forms—here presuppose an emergent redesign and transformation of the administrative apparatus, anticipating a decentralization and diffusion of responsibility. The principle of design for the administrative form thus abandons the "illusion of final authority"; yet this does not mean that no elements of centralization remain. The point, rather, is that this orientation proceeds by throwing dramatically into question the conventional reflex of relying upon some central, superior authority as the sole agency and ultimate guarantor of direction and coordination. In sum, the guiding outlook is that a new balance needs to be struck between centralization and decentralization, generally favoring the latter. Intrinsic to the problem of defining environmental problems, then, is a problem of organizational design involving the prevailing form of the administrative sphere. But who is to define and undertake this tremendous task of redesign? Merely to pose the question is to suggest an answer, at least in the negative: no *one*.

Beyond the Administrative Mind?

Thinking in a different direction is the goal of various techniques which have been developed to enhance creative problem-solving capacity in administrative organizations. Here the primary focus is upon ways of thinking that will generate new perspectives and insights: that will identify a dominant concept, reverse the terms of a relationship, review a question in relation to an ambiguous image or statement, imagine a different context.[30] Yet the efforts of creative problem-solving have also been extended beyond these various techniques of shifting focus in a thought process. Attention has also been given to processes of interaction, especially in the dynamics of small groups, but also with regard to overcoming the modes of "selective perception"[31] typically generated by differentiation among administrative units. Here organizational designs have been developed to draw differing units and perspectives into closer communication with one another in order to keep organizations attuned to the dynamics and complexities of external contingencies. For planning procedures, indeed, there are designs for encouraging argument and explicitly challenging conventional assumptions.[32] Such innovations—while typically contained within a rather conventional orientation—signal less reliance upon the style of thinking associated with the image of a unified and controlling administrative mind. Indeed, the reliance upon a greater diversity of perspectives points beyond thinking as the analytic activity of an independent mind (cogitation) and draws attention to communication among persons (a form of interaction).[33]

DISCURSIVE DESIGNS: AN AMBIVALENT POTENTIAL

In the administrative techniques and processes employed in environmental management, we witness some parallel movement from cogitation to interaction—from a monological, self-enclosed process to one which is more open, dialogical. Environmental management here involves "discursive designs"[34] such as participatory planning, regulatory negotiation, environmental mediation, and forms of public inquiry. These discursive designs are oriented to principles which implicitly challenge the administrative mind and thus are at least suggestive of different administrative forms. Of course these innovations do not arise in a vacuum, and within their historical and political context, their potential is ambivalent.

Discursive designs point beyond the administrative mind as the organizing principle for environmental management. The prospect is one of moving from a cloistered mode of problem-solving to an institutionalization of discourse which would encourage an interplay of differences in defining and resolving problems. While diverging from a rationalistic preoccupation with cogitation in problem-solving, such an institutionalization of discourse would itself be oriented to a concept of reason which is at once broader and more modest than that of the administrative mind—*viz.*, a "communicative rationality", which becomes manifest in interactive contexts which promote a free creation and exchange of ideas. Such communicative contexts are of course not characteristic of the administrative sphere, for communication here is typically organized to absorb differences and block insights which might support the critical mode of contextual orientation that an institutionalization of discourse presupposes. The result is a distortion of communication.[35]

Distorted communication arises not only because of an uncritical fixation on misleading notions. Such fixation is itself part of a policy process which systematically renders certain priorities central and others marginal, thereby fostering a particular mode of problem recognition: a "mobilization of bias" which, as part of its operation, tends to deflect attention from itself. That is to say, this bias is not simply a particular point of view, but a way of seeing things which is mobilized organizationally to discourage the serious consideration of alternatives. Of the individual, group, and class interests which vie for a hearing in the policy process, those which receive most favored treatment are those which are at once most crucial to the stability of advanced industrial development and most capable of persistently organized expression in an idiom consistent with prevailing presuppositions.[36] These are predominantly interests of institutions in the administrative sphere which possess both the significant incentives and the resources required for advancing their cause effectively. With information a key resource in advancing particular interests, those central to the process have reasons to gain and control information, withholding or releasing it—as it suits their purpose—both from one another and from those on the margins of the process. The effect, as one participant-observer has termed it, is an "*unconscious* conspiracy" to maintain a closed policy process.[37] Broadly based interests, such as that of environmental concern, possess less clearly a potential for effective organization. They have fewer available resources and often speak a language at odds with that of the main idiom. Simply to squeeze in, to gain entry and a measure of legitimacy, they often find it necessary to reformulate, even censor, their message to accord with the established bias.[38]

Discursive designs, in principle, anticipate an institutional form which, with a distinctly more open, decentralized, and participatory orientation, would be conducive to ideas and innovations focused on an alternative pattern of development: an administrative sphere, that is, open to the influence of an active, critical public sphere. Yet as narrow openings in a generally closed world, discursive designs appear precarious, always under the threat of being squeezed shut. What weighs against this prospect is the clear message of environmental concern, voiced by people facing particular threats and by a more or less cohesive network of organizations sharing a broader focus. The administrative apparatus encounters pressure to accommodate these interests, to eliminate their potential for obstruction, to smooth over differences. While troublesome to the administrative mind, discursive designs thus also provide a convenient resource to promote the incorporation of divergent interests into a more stable consensus. At the same time, administrative units responsible for handling environmental problems find environmentalist pressures useful at various junctures in the policy process, so long as these pressures can be contained within acceptable bounds. Accordingly, support for the institutionalization of discursive designs—hence, a more open process—can come from within the administrative apparatus. However, this greater scope for the articulation of environmental concern carries a risk; if institutionalization promotes incorporation, a divergent message can be more or less subtly screened, softened, rendered compatible with the perspective of the administrative mind—or safely ignored. This occurs in an especially subtle—one could say pernicious—manner when the troubling message is translated into a technocratic idiom which deferentially approaches the administrative mind and implicitly presupposes its rationality. In this way, the articulation of environmental concern reenacts an administrative ritual of distorted communication which, if recognized, would be exposed as irrationality masquerading as reason. Those able simultaneously to master and see through the technocratic idiom can, indeed, make it perform their own tricks, with wit and irony exposing the ritual for what it is while propounding a dramatically innovative perspective designed to stretch the administrative mind.[39] Discursive designs thus remain ambivalent.

BETWEEN ADMINISTRATIVE AND PUBLIC SPHERES: SPACE FOR REDEFINING PROBLEMS

The administrative sphere offers little space for open discussion, for questioning—much less changing—problem definition. Under the sway of prevailing priorities, and with these reinforced through the image of the administrative mind, there is little internal impetus to think in a different direction, to break free of clichéd patterns of thought. Contained and organized under this mental framework, the interactive elements of this sphere are typically reduced to modes of interchange which are variously directive and strategic, depersonalized, even anonymous. Pressure for open discussion primarily comes from social movements, groups, and individuals articulating interests which are on the periphery of the administrative sphere—and these include environmental concerns.

The articulation of these interests signals a notable shift from the situation at mid-century when it was possible to portray a cohesive administrative sphere, operating smoothly on the basis of a broad consensus, restricting partisanship to "mutual adjustment" and servicing a quiescent mass society.[40] Subsequent social changes involved the emergence of elements—or, perhaps, fragments—of an active public sphere increasingly capable of monitoring, criticizing, and influencing the operations of the administrative sphere. Demands for openness and participation constitute efforts to overcome a mobilization of bias by pressing peripheral priorities onto and into the administrative sphere—in effect, changing its priorities and creating greater potential for problem redefinition. The administrative sphere, of course, responds by variously repelling, accommodating, and containing these pressures—typically, that is, by changing its mind as little as possible. Discursive designs emerge from the ambivalent pressures of this context, at a point of division and intersection between administration and society: at the boundary, so to speak, of the administrative sphere and the emergent public sphere.[41]

The apparent fragments of a public sphere may ultimately amount to no more than a development within interest group politics, an expansion of pluralist tendencies in society. Yet it remains significant that, as reflected in the case of discursive designs, activity is being focused on the administrative sphere, on the task of gaining access to perceived key centers of decision-making. This is a response to the realization that it would not be adequate to focus effort only on established legislative bodies or on influencing public opinion. In terms of organizational design, the creation of discursive bodies connected to the administrative sphere would tend to match internal and external complexity. To the extent that these bodies were not integrated within the flow of administrative decision-making, however, their tendency would be only to complicate things, proving variously annoying or irrelevant to administration. Integration within the flow of decision-making could, of course, mean absorption—a reduction of the potential complexity.[42] Yet an integration which retained difference would enhance internal complexity in response to the complexity of environmental (and other) problems arising in a wider context. What would be increased, in other words, would be administrative capacity to redefine problems. There would be an increase of "cogitation in interaction"[43] which would challenge the hold of prevailing concepts. The capacity to redefine problems, moreover, would amount to a shift in priorities—hence a decisive change in administrative outlook and practice, together with a move towards realigning the apparatus. Problem definition would step beyond the limits of the administrative mind.

Notes

1. See Karl Polanyi, *The Great Transformation: The Political and Economic Origins of Our Time* (Boston: Beacon Press, 1957), chap. 12; Robert Pinker, *Social Theory and Social Policy* (London: Heinemann Educational Books, 1973), chap. 2, "The Origins of Social Administration"; Edward Chase Kirkland, *Dream and Thought in the Business Community 1860–1900* (Chicago: Quadrangle Books, 1964), chap. 5.

2. Dwight Waldo, *The Administrative State* (New York: Ronald Press, 1948).

3. In addition to Weber, see Samuel Haber, *Uplift and Efficiency: Scientific Management in the Progressive Era, 1890–1920* (Chicago: University of Chicago Press, 1964); Samuel P. Hays, *Conservation and the Gospel of Efficiency: The Progressive Conservation Movement, 1890-1920* (New York: Antheneum, 1969); Robert B. Reich, *The Next American Frontier* (Harmondsworth: Penguin Books, 1984), Part 2, "The Era of Management, 1920–1970"; John Kenneth Galbraith, *The New Industrial State*, rev. edn. (New York: Mentor Books, 1972); Arthur S. Miller, "Legal Foundations of the Corporate State" and Daniel R. Fusfeld, "The Rise of the Corporate State in America," in Warren J. Samuels (ed.), *The Economy as a System of Power*, 2 vols. (New Brunswick, NJ: Transaction Books, 1979), vol. 1.

4. See Gianfranco Poggi, *The Development of the Modern State* (Stanford, Calif.: Stanford University Press, 1978), chap. 6. Cf. Gerhard Lehmbruch, "Liberal Corporatism and Party Government," in Philippe C. Schmitter and Gerhard Lembruch (eds), *Trends Toward Corporatist Intermediation* (Beverly Hills, Calif.: Sage Publications, 1979), esp. 148, 154. I am suggesting that the administrative state should be viewed in this manner because doing so draws attention to relationships which one might neglect by taking the conventional boundary between public and private as an ontological given. I do not deny that the conventional boundary remains an important consideration in analyzing concrete relationships; nor would I rule out in principle other conceptualizations which might reveal further neglected relationships. The problem of conceptualizing the state may, indeed, be viewed as involving the same problem, writ large, as that of defining an organizational boundary. See e.g. Raymond E. Miles et al., "Organization-Environment: Concepts and Issues," *Industrial Relations*, 13: 3 (1974), 244–64; the controversial conception of customers as part of a business organization, seen as a "cooperative system", in Chester I. Barnard, "Concepts of Organization," in his *Organization and Management* (Cambridge, Mass.: Harvard University Press, 1948); and the proposal for a "figure-ground reversal" in Eric Trist, "A Concept of Organizational Ecology," *Australian Journal of Management*, 2: 2 (1977),

161–75. The identity, hence boundary, of the state—the realm of the "political" as distinct from the "economic"—emerged as a significant issue in the exchange between Miliband and Poulantzas. See esp. Ernesto Laclau, "The Specificity of the Political: The Poulantzas–Miliband Debate," *Economy and Society*, 4 (1975), 100–1; Nicos Poulantzas, "The Capitalist State: A Reply to Miliband and Laclau," *New Left Review*, 95 (1976), 81–2.

5. Cf. Hays, *Conservation and the Gospel of Efficiency*, the new preface and chap. 13.

6. See e.g. A. Myrick Freeman III et al., *The Economics of Environmental Policy* (New York: John Wiley and Sons, 1973). On the externalization of costs as "intrinsic" to the market system, see Donella Meadows, "Equity, the Free Market, and the Sustainable State," in Dennis Meadows (ed.), *Alternatives to Growth—I: Toward a Sustainable Future* (Cambridge, Mass.: Ballinger, 1977), 143.

7. Cf. Benjamin R. Barber, *Strong Democracy: Participatory Politics for a New Age* (Berkeley: University of California Press, 1984), chap. 1; Alan Wolfe, "Inauthentic Democracy: A Critique of Public Life in Modern Liberal Society," *Studies in Political Economy*, 21 (1986), 57–81.

8. Cf. Herbert A. Simon, "The Changing Theory and Changing Practice of Public Administration," in Ithiel de Sola Pool (ed.), *Contemporary Political Science* (New York: McGraw-Hill, 1967), 99; Robert K. Merton, "Bureaucratic Structure and Personality," in his *Social Theory and Social Structure*, rev. edn. (New York: The Free Press, 1957).

9. This anxiety is evident in Hobbes. A paradox of the administrative mind, moreover, is that it seeks to unify through a strategy of division; this suggests that only a rather forced unity is possible and that a troubling crack remains in the foundations.

10. The more traditional "decisionistic" model is distinguished from the increasingly salient "technocratic" model in Jürgen Habermas, "The Scientization of Politics and Public Opinion," in his *Toward a Rational Society* (Boston: Beacon Press, 1971), 63 ff. Within this technocratic frame one observes the transition from an earlier focus by technical experts (in scientific management) on achieving efficiency through standardized procedures to a reliance on a more sophisticated systems orientation (in management science). See C. West Churchman, *The Systems Approach*, rev. edn. (New York: Dell Publishing, 1979), chaps. 2–3. For an important effort to refine the concept of technocracy, see Wolf V. Heydebrand, "Technocratic Corporatism," in Richard H. Hall and Robert E. Quinn (eds), *Organizational Theory and Public Policy* (Beverly Hills, Calif.: Sage Publications, 1983). Cf. Laurence H. Tribe, "Policy Science: Analysis or Ideology?," *Philosophy and Public Affairs*, 2 (1972), 66–110; Christopher Nash et al., "Criteria for Evaluating Project Evaluation Techniques," *Journal of the American Institute of Planners*, 41 (1975), 83–90; John Byrne, "Policy Science and the Administrative State: The Political Economy of Cost-Benefit Analysis," in Frank Fischer and John Forester (eds), *Confronting Values in Policy Analysis* (Beverly Hills, Calif.: Sage Publications, 1987)

11. See Donald A. Schon, *Displacement of Concepts* (London: Tavistock Publications, 1963). Also see Ian I. Mitroff, "Systemic Problem-solving," in Morgan W. McCall, Jr. and Michael M. Lombardo (eds), *Leadership* (Durham, NC: Duke University Press, 1978); Edward de Bono, *Lateral Thinking: A Textbook of Creativity* (Harmondsworth: Penguin Books, 1971); Rollo May, *The Courage to Create* (New York: Bantam Books, 1976), esp. chap. 5; James G. March, "The Technology of Foolishness," in James G. March and Johan P. Olsen, *Ambiguity and Choice in Organizations* (Bergen, Norway: Universitetsforlaget, 1976); Jeffrey Pressman and Aaron Wildavsky, *Implementation*, 3rd edn. (Berkeley: University of California Press, 1984); David Dery, *Problem Definition in Policy Analysis* (Lawrence: University Press of Kansas, 1984). For a recent discussion, see Douglas Torgerson, "Power and Insight in Policy Discourse: Post-Positivism and Problem Definition," in Laurent Dobzinskis et al. (eds), *Policy Studies in Canada: The State of the Art* (Toronto: University of Toronto Press, 1995).

12. Much work along these lines is conceived in

explicitly dialectical terms, influenced in particular by Churchman, *Design of Inquiring Systems.* Cf. Ian I. Mitroff and Louis R. Pondy, "On the Organization of Inquiry: A Comparison of Some Radically Different Approaches to Policy Analysis," *Public Administration Review*, 43: 5 (1974), 471–9; Werner Ulrich, *Critical Heuristics of Social Planning: A New Approach to Practical Philosophy* (Bern: Haupt, 1983). Also cf. Jeffrey Pfeffer, *Power in Organizations* (Boston: Pitman Publishing, 1981), chap. 9. Aspects of this orientation were anticipated in the early work of Follett—e.g. "Constructive Conflict" (1925) in *Dynamic Administration*—the very style and texture of which manifests a dialectical play of concepts.

13. See Douglas Torgerson, "Contextual Orientation in Policy Analysis: The Contribution of Harold D. Lasswell," *Policy Sciences*, 18 (1985), 241–61.

14. For further characterization of the dispute, see Gideon Rosenbluth, "Economists and the Growth Controversy," *Canadian Public Policy*, 11: 2 (1976), 225–39. Of course, this controversy had a precursor during the early development of economics as certain doubts were raised about progress. Here the miserable conditions of early capitalist industrialization were viewed against the dismal idea of a natural law in which famine would continually return as food production failed to keep ahead of population growth. Yet this was not to deny progress altogether, for hunger was a "divine sanction": "Malthus . . . had his own version of the gospel of progress . . . Without the stimulus and pressure of surplus numbers of people, progress might end and technology stagnate." Donald Worster, *Nature's Economy: The Roots of Ecology* (Garden City, NY: Anchor Books, 1979), 151. What this suggests is that the vision of progress was not always a happy one; certainly this was the case even with Bentham, the apostle of happiness as "utility". The early dispute divided pessimistic and optimistic doctrines of progress; progress itself was not questioned. See Elie Halévy, *The Growth of Philosophic Radicalism* (Boston: Beacon Press, 1955), 268–76; cf. 492–3.

15. See e.g. Barry Commoner, *The Closing Circle: Man, Nature and Technology* (New York: Alfred A. Knopf, 1971).

16. See Donella H. Meadows et al., *The Limits to Growth* (New York: Universe Books, 1972); also see H. S. D. Cole et al., *Thinking about the Future: A Critique of the "Limits to Growth"* (London: Chatto and Windus Ltd. for the University of Sussex Press, 1973).

17. The formal matrix structure is one device which has been adopted by administrative organizations to balance competing demands from a complex environment. This device violates the principle of unity of command and often elicits resistance; nonetheless, explicit commitment to this traditional principle often coexists with tacit adaptations in the informal structure. See Stanley M. Davis, "Two Models of Organization: Unity of Command versus Balance of Power," *Sloan Management Review*, 16 (1974), 29–40; Ph. G. Herbst, *Alternatives to Hierarchies* (Leiden: Martinus Nijhoff, 1976), chap. 3; Pfeffer, *Power in Organizations*, 356–63.

18. See Geoffry Wandesforde-Smith, "The Bureaucratic Response to Environmental Politics," in Albert E. Dutton and Daniel H. Henning (eds), *Environmental Policy* (New York: Praeger Publishers, 1973); cf. Lynton K. Caldwell, *Man and His Environment: Policy and Administration* (New York: Harper and Row, 1975). Some central environmental agency was often to perform a coordinating role, but this task was made difficult by a marginal position in the administrative apparatus and a restricted definition of what constituted "environmental" problems. See e.g. O. P. Dwivedi, "The Canadian Government Response to Environmental Concern," in O. P. Dwivedi (ed.), *Protecting the Environment* (Vancouver: Copp Clark Publishing, 1974), esp. 176; Michael J. Whittington, "Environmental Policy," in G. Bruce Doern and V. Seymour Wilson (eds), *Issues in Canadian Public Policy* (Toronto: Macmillan of Canada, 1974), esp. 208. For a case study which stresses resulting jurisdictional disputes in the state and discusses the establishment of environmental

units within corporations, see Douglas
Pimlott et al., *Oil under the Ice: Offshore
Drilling in the Canadian Arctic* (Ottawa:
Canadian Arctic Resources Committee, 1976),
chaps. 2, 9, and esp. p. 133. A recent official
document follows the Brundtland Report in
recognizing the typical "Western reaction to
problems: the analysis, sorting, classification
and compartmentalization of 'hard'
information, and then the creation of an
institution to deal with each." William J.
Couch, Federal Environmental Assessment
Review Office (ed.), *Environmental Assessment
in Canada: 1988 Summary of Current Practice*
(Ottawa: Supply and Services Canada, under
the auspices of the Canadian Council of
Resource and Environment Ministers, 1989),
9. Of course, it is an oversimplification to call
the reaction a Western one. Cf. the
Brundtland Report: World Commission on
Environment and Development, *Our
Common Future* (Oxford: Oxford University
Press, 1986), 310 ff.

19. Galbraity, *New Industrial State*, 37. Cf. Thomas
B. Nolan, "The Inexhaustible Resource of
Technology," in Henry Jarrett (ed.),
Perspectives on Conservation (Baltimore: Johns
Hopkins Press for Resources for the Future
Inc., 1961), esp. 66.

20. Cf. David Ehrenfeld, *The Arrogance of
Humanism* (New York: Oxford University
Press, 1978).

21. Cf. Theodore Roszak, *Where the Wasteland
Ends: Politics and Transcendence in
Postindustrial Society* (Garden City, NY:
Anchor Books, 1973).

22. Bookchin's was an early and insightful
contribution. See Murray Bookchin, "Ecology
and Revolutionary Thought" (1965) and
"Toward a Liberatory Technology" (1965) in
his *Post-Scarcity Anarchism* (San Francisco:
Ramparts Press, 1971). Also see E. F.
Schumacher, *Small Is Beautiful: A Study of
Economics as if People Mattered* (London:
Abacus, 1974); David Dickson, *Alternative
Technology and the Politics of Technical Change*
(Glasgow: Fontana, 1974); Victor Ferkiss, *The
Future of Technological Civilization* (New York:
George Braziller, 1974); Herman E. Daly (ed.),

Toward a Steady State Economy (San
Francisco: W. H. Freeman, 1973). For
approaches with a particular focus on energy,
see Amory B. Lovins, *Soft Energy Paths*
(Cambridge, Mass.: Ballinger Publishing,
1977); David B. Brooks, *Zero Energy Growth
for Canada* (Toronto: McClelland and
Stewart, 1981). Thinking along these lines in
Canada came to focus on the concept of a
"conserver society", which was given a quasi-
official formulation in Science Council of
Canada, *Canada as a Conserver Society*
(Ottawa: Science Council of Canada Report
No. 27, 1977).

23. See the discussion of "problem displacement"
in John S. Dryzek, *Rational Ecology:
Environment and Political Economy* (London:
Basil Blackwell, 1987), 16 ff.

24. See Douglas Torgerson, *Industrialization and
Assessment: Social Impact Assessment as a
Social Phenomenon* (Toronto: York University,
1980).

25. See n. 17 above.

26. See e.g. William Ophuls, "Leviathan or
Oblivion?," in Herman E. Daly (ed.), *Toward a
Steady-State Economy* (San Francisco: W. H.
Freeman, 1973); William Ophuls, *Ecology and
the Politics of Scarcity* (San Francisco: W. H.
Freeman, 1977). The idea of an
"environmental dictator" was discussed in
some environmental groups in the 1970s.

27. This tension is evident in Ophuls. Cf. Charles
Taylor, "The Politics of the Steady State," in
Abraham Rotstein (ed.), *Beyond Industrial
Growth* (Toronto: University of Toronto Press,
1976).

28. See Dryzek, *Rational Ecology*, chaps. 3–5; John
S. Dryzek, "Complexity and Rationality in
Public Life," *Political Studies*, 35 (1987), 424–42;
C. A. Hooker and R. Van Hulst, "The Meaning
of Environmental Problems for Public
Political Institutions," in William Leiss (ed.),
Ecology versus Politics in Canada (Toronto:
University of Toronto Press, 1979); Gareth
Morgan, "Cybernetics and Organization
Theory: Epistemology or Technique?," *Human
Relations*, 35 (1982), 521–37.

29. See Eric Trist, "A Concept of Organizational
Ecology," in contrast with Simon's focus on

"bounded rationality"—e.g. Herbert A. Simon, *Administrative Behavior: A Study of Decision-Making Processes in Administrative Organization* 3rd edn. (New York: Free Press, 1976), esp. pp. xxix–xxx, 82; Herbert A. Simon, "The Theory of Problem-solving" (1972) in his *Models of Discovery* (Dordrecht, Holland: D. Reidel Publishing, 1977).

30. See n. 11 above.

31. Cf. Herbert A. Simon and DeWitt C. Dearborne, "Selective Perception," in Simon, *Administrative Behavior*.

32. See e.g. Richard O. Mason and Ian I. Mitroff, *Challenging Strategic Planning Assumptions* (New York: John Wiley and sons, 1981); Ian I. Mitroff and Richard D. Mason, *Creating a Dialectical of Social Science* (Dordrecht, Holland: D. Reidel Publishing, 1981); Churchman, *Systems Approach*, chap. 7; Pfeffer, *Power in Organizations*, chap. 9.

33. The contrast between "interaction" and "cogitation" is made in Aaron Wildavsky, *Speaking Truth to Power: The Art and Craft of Policy Analysis* (Boston: Little, Brown and Company, 1979). For a critique which discriminates between qualitatively different forms of interaction, see John Forester, "The Policy Analysis–Critical Theory Affair: Wildavsky and Habermas as Bedfellows?," in John Forester (ed.), *Critical Theory and Public Life* (Cambridge, Mass.: MIT Press, 1985), esp. 266 ff. The distinctions which Forester makes are crucial to "discursive designs"; see n. 33 below and corresponding text.

34. See John S. Dryzek, "Discursive Designs: Critical Theory and Political Institutions," *American Journal of Political Science*, 31 (1987), 656–79. Discursive designs would be central to what I have called a "third face" of policy analysis. See Douglas Torgerson, "Between Knowledge and Politics: Three Faces of Policy Analysis," *Policy Sciences*, 19 (1986), 33–59.

35. The concept of "communicative rationality" is developed in the work of Habermas. For a convenient and well-informed summary, see Stephen K. White, *The Recent Work of Jürgen Habermas* (Cambridge: Cambridge University Press, 1988), 28 ff. For a discussion of distorted communication influenced by Habermas, see

Douglas Torgerson, "The Communicative Context of Policy Analysis: The Problem of Strategic Interaction in the Policy Process," Ph.D. thesis (University of Toronto, 1984). A brief summary of some key points is contained in Douglas Torgerson, "Interpretive Policy Inquiry: A Response to Its Limitations," *Policy Sciences*, 19 (1986), 397–405. This is not the place to go into the important issues raised by postmodernism and related approaches. Cf. e.g. Michael Ryan, "New French Theory in New German Critique," *New German Critique*, 22 (1981), 145–61.

36. See Claus Offe, "Political Authority and Class Structures: An Analysis of Late Capitalist Societies," *International Journal of Sociology*, 2: 1 (1972), 73–108; Jürgen Habermas, *Legitimation Crisis* (Boston: Beacon Press, 1975), 59–68, 136–8. Also see Robert R. Alford, "Paradigms of Relations between State and Society," in Leon N. Linberg et al. (eds), *Stress and Contradiction in Modern Capitalism: Public Policy and the Theory of the State* (Lexington, Mass.: Lexington Books, 1975). For a discussion of environmental policy framed by the concept of "mobilization of bias", see T. F. Schrecker, *Political Economy of Environmental Hazards* (Ottawa: Law Reform Commission of Canada, 1984). The bias renders some issues "manifest", others "latent", to follow a point developed in William Leiss, "The Political Aspects of Environmental Issues," in Leiss (ed.), *Ecology versus Politics in Canada*, 261 ff. A general discussion of "the logic of a policy system" is presented in Torgerson, "The Communicative Context of Policy Analysis," chap. 7.7.

37. Douglas Hartle, *The Expenditure Budget Process in the Government of Canada* (Toronto: Canadian Tax Foundation, 1978), 122 (original emphasis). For further discussion, see Torgerson, "The Communicative Context of Policy Analysis," esp. 63–5.

38. See Robert H. Socolow, "Failures of Discourse: Obstacles to the Integration of Environmental Values into Natural Resource Policy," in Laurence H. Tribe et al. (eds), *When Values Conflict: Essays on Environmental Analysis,*

Discourse, and Decision (Cambridge, Mass.: Ballinger Publishing, 1976), 4–7, 20–2.

39. See e.g. Amory B. Lovins, "Cost-Risk-Benefit Assessments in Energy Policy," *George Washington Law Review*, 45 (1977), 911–43. Lovins presented this article (still in galleys) as background for his participation in the Debate Stage Hearings, Royal Commission on Electric Power Planning, Toronto, Ontario, 19 October 1977 (RCEPP, Exhibit 233). Later the Commission thanked Lovins for the "insights" which he generated in both closed and open sessions. See Arthur Porter, Chairman, *The Report of the Royal Commission on Electric Power Planning* (Toronto: RCEPP, 1980), i. 210 n. 7. The present article is written in conjunction with research on the historical emergence of the definition of the energy problem in Ontario. The problem of problem definition appears distinctly in this case as part of a problem in organization design. Some relevant background is presented in Douglas Torgerson, "From Dream to Nightmare: The Historical Origins of Canada's Nuclear Electric Future," *Alternatives*, 7: 1 (1977), 8–17.

40. See e.g. Charles E. Lindblom, *The Intelligence of Democracy: Decision Making Through Mutual Adjustment* (New York: Free Press, 1965). The fundamentally settled world presupposed and reflected in that book stands in contrast to the world "headed for catastrophe" invoked in the opening of Charles E. Lindblom, *Politics and Markets* (New York: Basic Books, 1977), 3. His examination of "politico-economic mechanisms" is thus explicitly aimed at finding means of averting an environmental catastrophe. For a further development along these lines, see Dryzek, *Rational Ecology*.

41. The discussion here of the administrative sphere and the public sphere is partly influenced by the treatment of "lifeworld" and "system" in Habermas. See, for a concise discussion, White, *The Recent Work of Jürgen Habermas*, chap. 5; for a brief, pertinent critique, see 140 ff. My view is that elements of the lifeworld "penetrate" the system more fundamentally than Habermas allows—hence the term administrative "sphere" in this article. Moreover, Habermas locates the "administrative system", as he calls it, too readily in the state. See Jürgen Habermas, *The Theory of Communicative Action*, 2 vols. (Boston: Beacon Press, 1984, 1988), esp. ii. 311, 343 f. Cf. Torgerson, "Between Knowledge and Politics," 51.

42. See Socolow, "Failures of Discourse."

13. Dryzek, "Complexity and Rationality," 433.

Section IV: Liberal Democracy

Liberal democracy survived the twentieth century safe, secure, and seemingly triumphant on the global stage. Yet liberal democracy as a system of government has always stood in tension with the administrative state's claims to harness expertise in the interests of rational problem solving. This conflict is played out in the environmental arena no less than elsewhere. Ultimately, do we let the experts or the people decide on what is best for the environment and how to go about it? Here we look at those who argue on behalf of the people—or the people's representatives—having a decisive say not just in formulation of the goals of policy in legislatures, but also in devising the content of particular policy responses to environmental problems.

The liberal democratic approach to environmental affairs is by definition pretty much reconciled to the status quo imposed by the capitalist political economy. As we will see in Part Five, more radical democratic notions challenge this status quo.

Our selection by Mark Sagoff affirms the sovereignty of the democratic public in environmental policy. Sagoff argues that all individuals have preferences as both citizens and consumers, but that their higher citizen preferences can only be expressed through democratic means. Economists err in counting only lower consumer preferences; aside from a defence of liberal democracy, Sagoff's argument can be read as a stinging critique of economic reasoning of the sort that appears in Section V, 'Market Liberalism'. He believes that citizen preferences are far more likely to be conducive to environmental conservation values than are consumer preferences.

Sagoff says little about the detailed institutional implications of his liberal democratic argument. Robert Paehlke has much more to say on this score. He notes that the last three decades of environmental concern have been accompanied not by the centralized authoritarian structures postulated in the discourse of limits and survival, but by the exact opposite. Indeed, over these decades the environmental area has led all others in the scope and extent of democratic innovation, not just in legislative politics, but also in environmental administration and law. Such innovations include public inquiries, right-to-know legislation, alternative dispute resolution, and policy dialogues. For Paehlke, effective environmental problem solving is democratic and open, not administrative or authoritarian.

The issue of how to relate to the status quo of the liberal capitalist state has been a tricky one for the green movement in Germany. The German Green Party, *Die Grünen*, is rightly regarded as the pioneer of effective green politics. But from their founding in 1979 *Die Grünen* were plagued by a split between their "Fundi" and "Realo" factions. The Fundis favoured grass-roots politics and radical action against the system, while the Realos sought to work within the system, especially through legislative politics and coalition-building with other progressive parties. The split was finally resolved with the victory of the Realos in the early 1990s. Helmut Wiesenthal is a leading Green Realo, and presents here his account of how green parties can work effectively to promote their values through liberal democratic means.

William P. Ophuls and A. Stephen Boyan, Jr., in contrast, believe liberal democracy is irredeemable. Focusing on the United States, they believe that liberal democracy does indeed give people what they want. But unlike Sagoff, Ophuls and Boyan believe that people do not express their public-spirited citizen preferences through democratic politics. Instead, they give vent to their selfish material interests. This kind of politics therefore reinforces rather than ameliorates the environmental rapacity of the capitalist economy, and exacerbates rather than resolves the tragedy of the commons. Liberal democracy is just as addicted to permanent economic growth as is capitalism, and so equally unsustainable.

Further Reading

There are many books on how environmental politics and policy proceed in liberal democratic states. One of the best collections (emphasizing the United States) is James P. Lester (ed.), *Environmental Politics and Policy: Theories and Evidence*, 2nd edn. (1995). A defence of liberal democratic deliberation as a way of coping effectively with environmental problems is made by Adolf Gundersen in his *The Environmental Promise of Democratic Deliberation* (1995). The Realo position on green politics receives eloquent expression in an Anglo-American context in Robert Goodin's *Green Political Theory* (1992). Two books which combine sophisticated analysis of the possibility of extending democracy in environmental politics with an awareness of the problems and constraints involved are Bruce A. Williams and Albert R. Matheny, *Democracy, Dialogue, and Environmental Disputes: The Contested Languages of Environmental Disputes* (1995) and Daniel Press, *Democratic Dilemmas in the Age of Ecology: Trees and Toxics in the American West* (1994). The affinities of liberal democratic political systems and ecological systems are highlighted by Gus DiZerega in 'Unexpected Harmonies: Self-Organization in Liberal Modernity and Ecology', *The Trumpeter*, 10 (1993), 25–32. Douglas Amy in *The Politics of Environmental Mediation* (1987) offers a trenchant critique of the kinds of democratic process innovations applauded by Paehlke.

10 The Allocation and Distribution of Resources

Mark Sagoff

In a course I teach on environmental ethics, I ask students to read the opinion of the Supreme Court in *Sierra Club* v. *Morton*.[1] This case involves an environmentalist challenge to a decision by the US Forest Service to lease the Mineral King Valley, a quasi-wilderness area in the middle of Sequoia National Park, to Walt Disney Enterprises, to develop a ski resort. But let the Court describe the facts:

The final Disney plan, approved by the Forest Service in January 1969, outlines a $35 million complex of motels, restaurants, swimming pools, parking lots, and other structures designed to accommodate 14,000 visitors daily. . . . Other facilities, including ski lifts, ski trails, a cog-assisted railway, and utility installations, are to be constructed on the mountain slopes and in other parts of the valley. . . . To provide access to the resort, the State of California proposes to construct a highway 20 miles in length. A section of this road would traverse Sequoia National Park, as would a proposed high-voltage power line.[2]

I asked how many of the students had visited Mineral King or thought they would visit it as long as it remained undeveloped. There were about six hands. Why so few? Too many mosquitoes, someone said. No movies, said another. Another offered to explain in scrupulous detail the difference between chilblain and trench foot. These young people came from Boston, New York, and Philadelphia. They were not eager to subsist, for any length of time, on pemmican and rye biscuits.

Then I asked how many students would like to visit the Mineral King Valley if it were developed in the way Disney planned. A lot more hands went up. Someone wanted to know if he had to ski if he went. No; I told him if he stayed indoors, he need miss nothing. He could get snow blindness from the sour cream. He could meet Ms Right at the après-ski sauna and at encounter sessions. The class got really excited. Two students in back of the room stood on tiptoe, bent their wrists, and leaned forward, as if to ski. I hope I have left no doubt about where the consumer interests of these young people lay.

I brought the students to order by asking if they thought the government was right in giving Disney Enterprises a lease to develop Mineral King. I asked them, in other words, whether they thought that environmental policy, at least in this instance, should be based on the principle of satisfying consumer demand. Was there a connection between what the students as individuals wanted for themselves and what they thought we should do, collectively, as a nation?

From Mark Sagoff, *The Economy of the Earth* (New York: Cambridge University Press, 1988), 50–73. Reprinted with permission.

The response was nearly unanimous. The students believed that the Disney plan was loath-some and despicable, that the Forest Service had violated a public trust by approving it, and that the values for which we stand as a nation compel us to preserve the little wilderness we have for its own sake and as a heritage for future generations. On these ethical and cultural grounds, and in spite of their consumer preferences, the students opposed the Disney plan to develop Mineral King.

Consumer and Citizen Preferences

The consumer interests or preferences of my students are typical of those of Americans in general. Most Americans like a warm bed better than a pile of wet leaves at night. They would rather have their meals prepared in a kitchen than cook them over a camp stove. Disney's market analysts knew all this. They found that the resort would attract more than fourteen thousand tourists a day, in summer and winter alike, which is a lot more people than now hike into Mineral King.[3] The tourists would pay to use the valley, moreover, while the backpackers just walk in.

You might suppose that most Americans approved of the Disney proposal; after all, it would service their consumer demands. You could ride up the mountain and get a martini or watch TV. You could buy a burger and a beer at the gondola stops. The long Kaweah River might be trans-formed into a profitable commercial strip. Every red-blooded American with a camper, an off-road vehicle, a snowmobile, or some snazzy clothes and a taste for a little "action" might visit the Disney playland.

You might think that the public would have enthusiastically supported the Disney plan. Yet the public's response to the Disney project was like that of my students—overwhelming opposi-tion.[4] Public opinion was so unfavorable, indeed, that Congress acted in 1978 to prohibit the pro-ject, by making the Mineral King Valley a part of Sequoia National Park.[5]

Were the rights of the skiers and scenemakers to act freely within a market thwarted by the political action of the preservationists? Perhaps. But perhaps some of the swingers and skiers were themselves preservationists. Like my students, they may themselves condemn the likely consequences of their own consumer interests on cultural or ethical grounds.

I sympathize with my students. Like them and like members of the public generally, I, too, have divided preferences or conflicting "preference maps." Last year, I bribed a judge to fix a cou-ple of traffic tickets, and I was glad to do so because I saved my license. Yet, at election time, I helped to vote the corrupt judge out of office. I speed on the highway; yet I want the police to enforce laws against speeding. I used to buy mixers in returnable bottles—but who can bother to return them? I buy only disposables now, but to soothe my conscience, I urge my state senator to outlaw one-way containers.

I love my car; I hate the bus. Yet I vote for candidates who promise to tax gasoline to pay for public transportation. I send my dues to the Sierra Club to protect areas in Alaska I shall never visit. And I support the work of the American League to Abolish Capital Punishment although, personally, I have nothing to gain one way or the other. (If I hang, I will hang myself.) And of course, I applaud the Endangered Species Act, although I have no earthly use for the Colorado squawfish or the Indiana bat. The political causes I support seem to have little or no basis in my interests as a consumer, because I take different points of view when I vote and when I shop. I have an "Ecology Now" sticker on a car that drips oil everywhere it's parked.

I am not alone in possessing incompatible "consumer" and "citizen" preference orderings. Economists have long been aware of the existence of these conflicting preference schedules in the average individual. Indeed, the distinction between consumer and citizen preferences has long vexed the theory of public finance. R. A. Musgrave, reporting a conversation he had with another economist, Gerhard Colm, states the problem as follows:

He [Colm] holds that the individual voter dealing with political issues has a frame of reference quite distinct from that which underlies his allocation of income as a consumer. In the latter situation the voter acts as a private individual determined by self-interest and deals with his personal wants; in the former, he acts as a political being guided by his image of a good society. The two, Colm holds, are different things.[6]

Are these two different things? Stephen Marglin suggests that they are. He writes:

The preferences that govern one's unilateral market actions no longer govern his actions when the form of reference is shifted from the market to the political arena. The Economic Man and the Citizen are for all intents and purposes two different individuals. It is not a question, therefore, of rejecting individual . . . preference maps; it is, rather, that market and political preference maps are inconsistent.[7]

Marglin observes that if this is true, social choices optimal under one set of preferences will not be optimal under another. What, then, is the meaning of optimality? An efficient policy, let us say, is one that maximizes the satisfaction of preferences weighted by their intensity. If individuals possess conflicting preference-maps, however, how can we say what an efficient policy is?

Marglin jokes that economists, in order to preserve the coherence of the efficiency concept, "might argue on welfare grounds for an authoritarian rejection of individuals' politically-revealed preferences in favor of their market revealed preferences!" One might argue just the reverse as well, namely, that we may reject our market-revealed preferences to pursue politically revealed values!

Very few economists, if any, advocate an authoritarian rejection of either political or consumer preferences. Some would seek a way to combine both sorts of preferences on the same preference map. They might agree with Gordon Tullock, who observes that two assumptions about preferences are essential to modern economic theory.

One of these is simply that the individual orders all alternatives, and the schedule produced is his total preference schedule. The second is that he will be able to make choices among pairs of alternatives, unless he is indifferent between them. . . . From this assumption and a further assumption, that such choices are transitive, it is possible to deduce the preference schedule, and most modern economists have taken this route.[8]

If we make these assumptions, which are essential to the theory of welfare economics, it must be possible to infer, for any individual, a "meta-ordering" of his consumer and political preferences. Markets, to be sure, would *not* reveal this meta-ordering, for it includes politically expressed values. Yet economists, by using interview techniques and the like, might be able, at least in principle, to derive the individual's combined preference schedule and price environmental benefits on that basis.

Attempts to find a "combined" or inclusive preference ordering, however, are bound to fail. They will fail for logical, not merely practical, reasons. Individuals have a variety of often incompatible preference schedules they reveal in the contexts appropriate to each, for example, in markets, family situations, professional contexts, and political circumstances. To try to combine these preference schedules into one is to search for a single comprehensive role the individual plays, it is to ask for the individual to behave *not* as a parent, citizen, consumer, or the like but in all and none of these roles at once. The individual, in effect, must reveal himself or herself as the "rational man" of economic theory simply because economic theory demands it. As one commentator rightly points out, no such social role exists, unless it is the role of a social moron.[9]

In some roles—particularly that of a citizen or a member of a community—the individual states what he or she thinks the group should do; the individual makes a judgment that he or she would expect any member of the community to make insofar as that person reflects on the values of the community, not just on his or her own interests. In that situation, each member of the group judges, as it were, for all, and if they disagree, they must deliberate together to determine who is right and who is wrong. This way of finding the will of the community may require a vote; the vote settles a logical contradiction between beliefs, however, not necessarily a conflict among personal interests. Thus, analysts who attempt to shuffle citizen judgments and personal preferences into the same ordering commit a logical mistake. They confuse judgment with preference, that is to say, beliefs about what *we* should do with expressions of what *I* want or prefer.

Some economic analysts attack the problem of split preference-orderings in another way. They note that efficiency analysis need not take into account the concerns of social equity or justice. Thus, one might rely on an individual's self-regarding market-revealed preferences to determine efficient social policies, for instance, by cost-benefit analysis. Then one could rely upon altruistic or politically revealed preference orderings to organize the redistribution of opportunities and wealth.

This reply may be helpful insofar as consumer preferences reveal a person's interests with regard to his or her own consumption opportunities, while citizen preferences express his or her altruistic concerns about the distribution of consumption opportunities in society generally. Yet citizens advocate many ideal-regarding convictions and beliefs that are not directed to the ways consumption opportunities are distributed. Environmentalists are sensitive to the distributive effects of the policies they favor politically, but they do not necessarily support these policies for the sake of those effects.

One could speculate, indeed, that the distributive effect of environmental protection is often to make the rich richer and the poor poorer.[10] When land is removed from development, housing becomes more expensive; consumer products also cost more when corporations are required to pollute less. The rich can afford to live in environmentally protected areas and, therefore, arguably benefit more than the poor from environmental preservation. It has been very difficult for state governments to site environmentally necessary hazardous-waste treatment and landfill facilities; one often hears, however, that these tend to end up in the neighborhoods of the poor. This would be another example of the way the poor may pay the costs of environmental protection while the rich reap the benefits.

I do not think any systematic relationship exists in fact between the policies environmentalists favor and the relative well-being of the rich and the poor or, for that matter, of present and future generations. The speculations I have offered so far are just that—speculations. I know of no recent empirical study that substantiates them. They suggest, however, that equality or justice is not the only ethical or cultural goal that concerns us as citizens. We may also be concerned as citizens with education, the arts and sciences, safety and health, and the integrity and beauty of the natural environment. These concerns cannot be assimilated to the personal, arbitrary preference-maps of consumers. Nor can they be entirely analyzed in terms of equity or justice.

Allocation and Distribution

I want to approach my thesis in this chapter by way of an important distinction: that between the *allocation* and the *distribution* of resources. The allocation of resources has to do with how they are used; the distribution has to do with who uses them or benefits from their use.[11] The Mineral King Valley, as a matter of *allocation*, could be used as a ski resort, kept as a wilderness, or exploited in some other way. Some individuals or groups would be made better off as a result; some would be made worse off; the decision, in other words, would have *distributive* or *redistributive* effects. The resort, for example, would benefit skiers at the expense of hikers; it would be good for property owners in Tulare County but bad for property owners in Sun Valley. Some might argue in favor of the Disney project because it would produce tax revenues to support social welfare programs for the poor. This would be to argue in favor of an allocation because of a beneficial distributive effect.

Some economic theorists who write about the environment assume that natural resources should be used in the way a perfect market would allocate them: the way that maximizes efficiency, consumer surplus, utility, preference satisfaction, or wealth. For a given allocation, of course, questions of justice, fairness, or equality may arise with respect to the distribution of costs and benefits. Most analysts concede that ethical or political choices may have to be made concerning these distributive effects. They tell us, however, that the best way to produce wealth and the best way to divide it are separate issues best decided separately; they urge us, therefore, not to make an allocative decision on the basis of its distributive consequences.[12] Once the pie is as big as we can make it, we may distribute it in the way we then decide is just or fair.

Analysts who argue along these lines tend to collapse all discussion of regulatory policy into questions concerning efficiency in the allocation of resources and equity or fairness in the distribution of wealth. They argue, for example, that the allocation of fossil fuels should be left to the market, properly regulated for externalities. The inequalities that result may then be remedied, for instance, by a windfall profit tax used to help the poor pay their heating bills.[13]

Not all policy problems allow a neat separation between issues of allocation and issues of distribution; for example, any social transfer of wealth to the poor could increase the cost of labor and thus lead to an inefficient allocation of human resources. Many policy analysts speak, therefore, of a "trade-off" between equality and efficiency. They recommend, however, that policymakers use those two values to justify whatever decisions they make with respect to environmental and regulatory policy. Decisions that cannot be explained as rational attempts to make markets efficient, then, must be explained as attempts to distribute wealth more fairly.

Although some writers like to emphasize a "trade-off" between efficiency and equality, it is useful to recognize that these concepts complement each other and that the conflict between them, insofar as one exists, is largely overstated. Analysts who believe that efficiency is an important social value do so, in general, because they conceive of the social good as the satisfaction of preferences, weighted by their intensity, however arbitrary or contingent these preferences may be. Philosophers who emphasize the claims of justice or equity do not necessarily disagree with this conception of the good, but may in fact rely upon it. When the good is conceived in this way—when it is assimilated to the satisfaction of arbitrary preferences—then it is unsurprising that a conception of the right, that is, a conception of justice, should be prior to it. Some have argued that an adequate philosophy of right has yet to be written: one that shows how we should balance a conception of justice with a more appealing or more persuasive conception of the good than the notions of efficiency and preference-satisfaction imply.[14]

Many well-known writers (Ronald Dworkin is an example) argue that a conception of equality should be the criterion of public policy.[15] Other writers argue that the efficiency criterion should be the principal guideline. Most of the statutes and regulations that govern social policy, particularly for natural resources, public safety, and the environment, however, have fairly specific goals, like improving mine safety or protecting endangered species. These concerns of public policy stand on their own feet, as it were, and do not need to be supported by criteria or guidelines established by a priori philosophical or economic arguments.

What characterizes the debate between the "efficiency" and "equality" positions is not the touted conflict between them but the extent to which each is plausible only in comparison to the other. Both adopt the same vocabulary and conceptual framework; each assimilates all values either to essential human rights or to arbitrary personal preferences. They agree that any claim that is not based on a *right* must, then, simply state a *preference* or reveal a *want*.

Those who advocate the priority of equality find worthy opponents in those who defend the priority of efficiency.[16] They debate at length and without any apparent sense of tedium the extent to which rights "trump" interests because (1) rights go to the essence of free agency and personhood or (2) rights are justified, at a higher level of analysis, in relation to interests.[17] Once discussion takes off on this theoretical path, pitting "deontologists" against "rule utilitarians," it becomes irrelevant to officials and others who need a vocabulary adequate to the moral, aesthetic, historical, scientific, and legal considerations that matter in health, safety, and environmental policy.[18]

Congress, by rescinding the Disney lease, for example, made a decision based on aesthetic and historical considerations such as the argument that a majestic million-year-old wilderness is objectively *better* than a commercial honky-tonk. In this way, Congress responded to the opinions citizens backed up with arguments in public hearings and not to the wants individuals might back up with money in a market or the rights they might assert in court.

To speak bluntly, the problem with efficiency and equality as principles of social policy is that they have the smell of the lamp about them. Each approach assumes that academic economists and philosophers, by practicing deep thinking, discover the fundamental truths about Man, Civil Society, and the State from which the goals of social regulation may be derived. This assumption is false. The goals of social regulation are based in public values and are found in legislation.

Insofar as options are available under the law, policy decisions, often expressed in parts per billion, must be justified, as it were, from the bottom up, not from the top down. To make hard choices, public officials must organize the minute particulars involved in assessing risks, monitoring compliance, and litigating penalties. Discussions of the "trade-off" between efficiency and equality have become a useless academic pastime to which this book seeks to write an epitaph. These discussions have little to contribute to the practical and political concerns of social regulation.

The Rights of Future Generations

Some writers have suggested that the way we use the environment could change if we balanced our consumer interests with those of future generations. Some of these writers have worked hard to define a "social rate of discount"[19] to determine how we should take the interests of future consumers into account.

The rate at which we discount future preferences may make little difference, however, in the way natural resources are used. We can build resorts, highways, shopping centers, tract housing, and power lines to satisfy future as well as present demand. There are few decisions favorable to our wishes that cannot be justified by a likely story about future preferences. Even a nasty strip mine or a hazardous-waste dump produces energy that will strengthen the industrial base left to future generations.

What are future generations likely to want? Will vacationers a hundred years from now want to backpack into Sequoia National Park, or will they prefer to drive their recreational vehicles in? I think the interests of future generations will depend largely on two things. The first is education, or advertising. I suspect that the Disney resort would always be jammed with visitors because Disney knows how to run an effective advertising campaign. Through the use of advertising, corporations typically ensure demand for the goods and services they create so that the product and the market for it are developed at the same time. Since what corporations want to sell is usually a good indicator of what consumers will be trained to buy, perhaps we should let the marketing departments of the top five hundred businesses tell us how to prepare the earth for future generations. The best way to create the bars and pizza palaces and motels and strips tomorrow's consumers will want may be to bring in the bulldozers today.

Second, the tastes of future individuals will depend not only on what is advertised but on what is available. People may come to think that a gondola cruise along an artificial river is a wilderness experience if there is simply nothing to compare it with. When I moved from a rural area to an urban one, I was appalled at the changes: noise, pollution, ugliness, congestion. People said I would get used to it—that I would come to *like* the convenience stores and the fast-food stands. They were right. This is what happens. If individuals in the future have no exposure to anything that we would consider natural or unspoiled, they will not acquire a taste for such things. What they will want will be determined more or less by what we leave to them, however dreary it may be.

Derek Parfit has constructed an argument that supports the point I wish to make. He argues that any policy we adopt today will make people born in the future better off than they would have been had we made some other decision. The reason is that these people would not even exist, and therefore could not be better off, had we made the other choice.

To show this, Parfit describes two policies, which he calls "High Consumption" and "Low Consumption." He then writes:

If we choose High rather than Low Consumption, the standard of living will be higher over the next century. . . . Given the effects of . . . such policies on the details of our lives, different marriages would increasingly be made. More simply, even in the same marriages, the children would increasingly be conceived at different times. . . . this would in fact be enough to make them different children. . . .

Return next to the moral question. If we choose High Consumption, the quality of life will be lower more than a century from now. But the particular people who will then live would never have existed if instead we had chosen Low Consumption. Is our choice of High Consumption worse for these people? Only if it is against their interests to have been born. Even if this makes sense, we can suppose that it would not go as far as this. We can conclude that, if we choose High Consumption, our choice will be worse for no one.[20]

The idea is that whichever policy we choose, future generations will have nothing to complain about, because but for that choice, different marriages would have been made and different children conceived. Whatever policy decision we make, therefore, determines who shall exist, and thus the policy we choose is better for those who will be born than any other policy would have been. Because these people will be all who exist, our choice will make no one worse off. Most people would agree that a policy that is the very best for all those it affects, and that makes no one worse off, is satisfactory from the point of view of distributive justice and efficiency. Thus, whichever policy we choose will be just and efficient with respect to the generations that come after us.

Parfit's argument does not clear us of moral responsibility with respect to future generations; rather, it helps us to understand what our responsibility is. It is not—if I may put it this way—a responsibility *to* the future as much as it is a responsibility *for* the future. If Parfit is correct, the major decisions we make determine the identity of the people who follow us; this, however, is not the only, or the most morally significant, consequence. Our decisions concerning the environment will also determine, to a large extent, what future people are like and what their preferences and tastes will be.

If we leave them an environment that is fit for pigs, they will be like pigs; their tastes will adapt to their conditions as ours might when we move from the country into town. Suppose we destroyed all of our literary, artistic, and musical heritage; suppose we left to future generations only potboiler romances, fluorescent velvet paintings, and disco songs. We would then ensure a race of uncultured near illiterates. Now, suppose we leave an environment dominated by dumps, strip mines, and highways. Again, we will ensure that future individuals will be illiterate, although in another way. Surely, we should strive to make the human race better, not even worse than it already is. Surely, it is morally bad for us to deteriorate into a pack of yahoos who have lost both knowledge of and taste for the things that give value and meaning to life.

Future generations might not complain: A pack of yahoos will *like* a junkyard environment. This is the problem. That kind of future is efficient. It may well be equitable. But it is tragic all the same.

Our obligation to provide future individuals with an environment consistent with ideals we know to be good is an obligation not necessarily to those individuals but to the ideals themselves.[21] It is an obligation to civilization to continue civilization: to pass on to future generations a heritage, natural and cultural, that can be valued and enjoyed without absurdity. These ideals are aesthetic; they have to do not with the utility but with the meaning of things, not with what things are used for but what they express. The programs that preserve them, however, are morally good. The moral good involved is not distributional; for it is not the good *of* individuals we are speaking of, but *good individuals* who appreciate things that are good in themselves. The allocation of resources in environmental law need not always—it sometimes should not—be based on norms of distribution. The way we use resources may also be justified in the context of a reverence we owe to what is wonderful in nature; for in this kind of appreciation, aesthetic and moral theory find a common root.[22]

That political authority should avoid acts of paternalism has been a traditional theme of liberalism. Liberals since John Stuart Mill have argued that the state should restrict the freedom of one individual only to protect the welfare of another—not merely to prevent the individual from harming himself. Although this reluctance to interfere with a person "for his own good" is not absolute in liberalism (or even in Mill himself),[23] it is a consequence of the principle that the state should leave it to individuals to answer the moral questions and thus should not make their mistakes for them.

Yet, to protect a wilderness we may have to prohibit a resort; to provide a resort we may have to destroy a wilderness. So we must make decisions that affect the preferences or values future generations will have, not just the degree to which they can act on their own values or satisfy their preferences. To what extent should the possibility of one lifestyle be restricted to protect the possibility of another? What moral opportunities are worth providing? As we debate public policy for the environment, we must answer questions such as these. We cannot avoid paternalism with respect to future generations.[24]

Yet this paternalism, if that is what it is, is of a peculiar kind. It is not a paternalism about the welfare of future generations; for, as I have argued, whatever policy we choose is likely to be optimal for the individuals and the interests it helps to create. Rather, it is a paternalism about the character of future individuals, their environment, and their values. In short, it is a concern about the character of the future itself. We want individuals to be happier, but we also want them to have surroundings to be happier about. We want them to have what is *worthy of happiness*. We want to be able to respect them and to merit their good opinion. How may we do this except by identifying what is best in our world and trying to preserve it? How may we do this except by determining, as well as we can, what is worth saving, and then by assuming that this is what they will want?

What is worth saving is not merely what can be consumed later; it is what we can take pride in and, indeed, love. To protect wilderness and to restore the environment to meet shared ideals is not merely to show respect and concern for future generations but to show respect for ourselves as well.

To think about our moral responsibilities to future generations is to consider how resources should be used and not merely to consider who should use them. Ethics in allocation, in other words, is not a consequence of ethics in distribution. An environmental ethic cannot be derived entirely from a theory of justice.

The Conflict within Us

If an environmentalist wants to preserve parts of the natural environment for their own sake, he might do well to concede that this is his intention. The environmentalist must then argue that the principles of justice, fairness, and efficiency that may apply to the distribution of income in our society need not apply to the protection or preservation of the natural environment. The reason is that the conflict involved, for example, over Mineral King is not primarily a distributional one. It does not simply pit the skiers against the hikers. The skiers themselves may believe, on aesthetic grounds, that the wilderness should be preserved, even if that belief conflicts with their own consumer preferences. Thus, this conflict pits the consumer against himself as a citizen or as a member of a moral community.

The conflict, in other words, arises not only *among* us but also *within* us. It confronts what I want as an individual with what I believe as a citizen. This is a well-known problem. It is the conflict Pogo describes: "We have met the enemy and he is us."

The conflict is an ethical one. It is not ethical only because it raises a question about the distribution of goods to the rich or the poor, to the present or the future. The ethical question is not simply the distributional question. It concerns, rather, how we satisfy our interests and how we live by our beliefs. This sort of question could never arise in a society that made efficiency and equity in the satisfaction of consumer demand its only goals. That sort of society could deal only with the opposition between the hikers and the skiers. It could never respond to, act upon, or resolve the opposition between the skiers and themselves.

I do not want to comment on the ethical position my students, like many Americans, hold with respect to preserving the natural environment. I merely want to point out that it *is* an ethical position. It is also an opinion that is widely shared, deeply held, and embodied in legislation. I imagine that if the law were changed and the Disney resort were built, more than half the skiers in the lift line would agree, in principle, with my students. They might condemn the resort on ethical grounds. But money is money, and only money talks. The skiers would have paid a lot of money and gone to a lot of trouble to use the facilities. There could be no question—could there?—about what they want.

The problem is a general one. It arises not just because of our high regard for wilderness areas, such as Mineral King, but because of broad values we share about nature, the environment, health, safety, and the quality and meaning of life. Many of us are concerned, for example, that the workplace be safe and free of carcinogens; we may share this conviction even if we are not workers. And so we might favor laws that require very high air-quality standards in petrochemical plants. But as consumers, we may find no way to support the cause of workplace safety. Indeed, if we buy the cheapest products, we may defeat it.

We may be concerned as citizens, or as members of a moral and political community, with all sorts of values—sentimental, historical, ideological, cultural, aesthetic, and ethical—that conflict with the interests we reveal as consumers, buying shoes or choosing tomatoes. The conflict within individuals, rather than between them, may be a very common conflict. The individual as a self-interested consumer opposes himself as a moral agent and concerned citizen.

What kind of society are we? Do we admit into public consideration values of only two kinds: personal interests and distributive norms? Do we insist that the only political decisions we can make are those intended to distribute wealth or welfare, for example, by making markets more equitable and efficient, while every other choice—every allocative decision about the environment—should be left, if possible, for those markets to decide? Should we leave allocative choices to the tourist listening to his John Denver cassette as he pulls his recreational vehicle into the Automobile Reception Center at the Disney resort? Is this fellow the appropriate legislator of our common will?

Suppose *he* opens his mouth to express an ethical opinion—*horribile dictu*—about the use of the environment. Suppose he tells us that we should have kept Mickey Mouse out of the mountains. Must we shut our ears to him? Is that the kind of society we are? Is a perfectly competitive market all we wish to have?

I do not know the answers to these questions. I suspect, however, that most people are resigned, by now, to an affirmative answer to them. How else can one explain the reluctance of environmentalists to argue on openly ethical or political grounds? Why do they prefer to tell stories about the possible economic benefits of the furbish lousewort rather than offer moral reasons for supporting the Endangered Species Act? That law is plainly ethical; it is hardly to be excused on economic grounds. Why do environmentalists look for interests to defend, costs to price, benefits to enter—even if they have to go to the ludicrous extreme of counting the interests of the trees?

Americans, no matter how they shop, generally share the ideology of the environmentalists.[25] Indeed, most Americans might claim that they are environmentalists.[26] Why, then, are they reluctant to confess to themselves that they make environmental law on the basis of shared ideals rather than on the basis of individual utilities? Why do they find it hard to concede that their society is more than a competitive market and that allocative efficiency and distributional equity do not exhaust their repertoire of public values? Why is it so difficult for them to say that one may allocate resources not always as a perfect market would but on substantive, normative, and frankly ethical grounds?

I think the answers have something to do with the insecurity many of us feel when we find ourselves without "neutral" theories and criteria against which to evaluate political, ethical, and aesthetic positions. It's scary to think about problems on their own terms; it's easier to apply a methodology; it's even more tempting to think about the problems raised by the methodology or to investigate the theory itself. Besides, if one side has numbers, the other may need numbers as well. Because developers tell stories about willingness to pay for recreational opportunities at Mineral King, environmentalists tell stories about option values and amenity costs.

As a result, public officials discuss the meaning of magnificent environments using a vocabulary that is appropriate to measure the degree to which consumers may exploit them. A principal purpose of an environmental ethic may be to help policymakers find more appropriate concepts they can use to think about the goals of public policy and to address the obstacles that stand in the way of those goals. The concepts associated with the principles of allocatory efficiency and distributive equity are not especially suitable for this purpose.

Money and Meaning

The things we cherish, admire, or respect are not always the things we are willing to pay for. Indeed, they may be cheapened by being associated with money. It is fair to say that the worth of the things we love is better measured by our *unwillingness* to pay for them. Consider, for example, love itself. A civilized person might climb the highest mountain, swim the deepest river, or cross the hottest desert for love, sweet love. He might do anything, indeed, except be willing to pay for it.

The Church once auctioned off indulgences. It sold future shares in heaven at the margin with a very favorable discount rate. Was it a good idea to establish a market in salvation? Of course it was. How else can you determine how much an infinity of bliss, discounted by the probability that God does not exist, is worth?[27] The Church membership, however, grew a little disillusioned when it saw that the favors of the Lord were auctioned for silver and gold. This disillusionment was one cause of the Reformation.

The things we are unwilling to pay for are not worthless to us. We simply think we ought not to pay for them.[28] Love is not worthless. We would make all kinds of sacrifices for it. Yet a market in love—or in anything we consider "sacred"—is totally inappropriate. These things have a *dignity* rather than a *price.*[29]

The things that have a dignity, I believe, are in general the things that help us to define our relations with one another. The environment we share has such a dignity. The way we use and the way we preserve our common natural heritage help to define our relations or association with one another and with generations in the future and in the past.

Let me return, now, to the example with which I began. My students, as I said, are pulled one way when they are asked to make a consumer choice whether or not to patronize the Disney resort. That question goes to their wants and desires simply as individuals. They are pulled another way when asked to make a political decision whether the United States should turn wilderness areas into ski resorts. That decision calls upon their conception of the values we share or the principles we respect as a nation.

Should we base environmental policy on the interests individuals may act upon as consumers or on the values that they may agree upon as citizens? Our policy may be "rational" either way. We may have a "rational" policy in an economic sense if we limit the role of law to that of protecting rights and correcting market failures. We should then assume that the ends of policymaking are simply "given" in the preferences consumers reveal or would reveal in a market. Alternatively, we might suppose that a "rational" policy advances a certain conception of equality—or meets some other condition or criterion laid down in advance.

We may have a policy that is rational in what we may call a deliberative sense, however, if we strive to base law on principles and ideals that reflect our best conception of what we stand for and respect as a nation. This kind of rationality depends on the virtues of collective problem solving; it considers the reasonableness of ends in relation to the values they embody and the sacrifices we must make to achieve them. This deliberative approach respects the constitutional rights that make it possible for people to contribute as equals to the political process, but it asserts no a priori political theory about the purposes of public policy.

This approach assumes, on the contrary, that the values on which we base social policy are objects of public inquiry. They are not to be derived (as they would be in a market) by aggregating exogenous preferences, or (as they might be in a political philosophy) from metaphysical truths about the nature of persons. Thus, the general goals of public policy are to be determined through a political process in which citizens participate constrained only by rights of the kind protected by the Constitution. These goals are not known beforehand by a vanguard party of political economists or by an elite corps of philosopher-kings.

Compromise and Community

The students in the class I taught had no trouble understanding the difference between the judgments they make as citizens and the preferences they entertain as individuals. They also understood the importance of their "positive" freedom to lobby for their views politically and their "negative" freedom to pursue their personal interests without undue interference from the state.[30] Plainly, these freedoms, like these values and preferences, are bound to come into tension or conflict. If the nation preserves every mountain as a wilderness heritage, there will be no place for these young people to ski.

This tension has been a central problem for political theories of liberalism. As one historian writes: "Liberalism of all sorts [in America] is troubled by the seemingly contrary pulls of responsibility to individual and community, by the divergent demands of absolute adherence to the doctrine of individual integrity and the needs and potentials of the common life."[31]

The students in my class found it fairly easy to resolve the tension between their consumer interests and their public values with respect to the example of Mineral King. They recognized that private ownership, individual freedom of choice, and the profit motive would undoubtedly lead to the construction of the Disney paradise. They reasoned, nevertheless, that we should act on principle to preserve this wilderness, which has an enormous cultural meaning for us, since the resort, though profitable, would not serve important social ends. The students argued that because there are a lot of places for people to party, we do not need to make a ski resort of Sequoia National Park.

But what if the stakes were reversed? What if we should have to make enormous financial sacrifices to protect an environmentally insignificant landscape? Suppose industry would have to pay hundreds of millions of dollars to reduce air pollution by a small, perhaps an insignificant, amount? The students in my class, by and large, answered these questions the way they answered questions about Mineral King. Just as they rejected the dogma of the perfect market, they also rejected the dogma of the perfect environment.

The students recognized that compromise is essential if we are to act as a community to accomplish any goal, however pure or idealistic it may be. To improve air quality, for example, one needs not only a will but a way; one needs to express one's goals in parts per billion or, more generally, to deal with scientific uncertainties and technical constraints. The goal of environmental purity, like the goal of economic efficiency, can become a Holy Grail, in other words, suitable only as the object of an abstract religious quest. To make progress, we need to recognize that God dwells in the details—in parts per billion and in the minute particulars of testing, monitoring, and enforcement.

Although the students thought that social policy usually involves compromise, they kept faith with the ideals they held as citizens. They understood, moreover, that if we are to take these ideals seriously, we must evaluate them in the context of the means available to achieve them. To will the end, in other words, one must also will the means: One must set goals in relation to the obstacles—economic, political, legal, bureaucratic, scientific, technical, and institutional—that stand in the way of carrying them out. We do not become a functioning political community simply by sharing public goals and by celebrating a vision of harmony between nature and society, although ceremonies of this sort are a part of citizenship. To function as a community we must also reach the compromises necessary to move beyond incantation to political and economic achievement.

This is the reason that the Mineral King example—and the difference between citizen and consumer preferences it illustrates—may serve to introduce a course in environmental ethics, but it does not take us very far into the problems of environmental policy. The interesting problems arise when we move, in Winston Churchill's phrase, "from the wonderful cloudland of aspiration to the ugly scaffolding of attempt and achievement."[32] Then we must chasten our goals by adjusting them to economic, legal, scientific, and political realities. How can we do this and still retain the ethical and aspirational nature of our objectives? How do we keep faith with the values of the citizen while recognizing the power of the consumer?

Notes

1 405 US 727 (1972).
2 Ibid. 729.
3 The Council on Environmental Quality wrote: "Mineral King well illustrates the issue of recreational development for the pleasure of tens of thousands of people every year versus the value of an undisturbed naturalness for fewer visitors." *Sixth Annual Report*, 2 (1975), 242. For details relating to the Disney project and its market, see John Harte and Robert Socolow, *Patient Earth* (New York: Holt, Rinehart and Winston, 1971), 168–70; Commentary, "Mineral King Goes Downhill," *Ecology Law Quarterly*, 5 (1976), 555.
4 See Arnold Hano, "Protectionists vs. Recreationists—The Battle of Mineral King,"

New York Times Magazine, 17 August 1969, 24: Peter Browning, "Mickey Mouse in the Mountain," *Harper's*, March 1972, 65–71; "Thar's Gold in Those Hills," *Nation*, 206 (1968), 260.

5 National Parks and Recreation Act of 1978, Pub. L. No. 95–625, sec. 314, 92 Stat. 3467 (codified at 16 USC sec. 45F (supp. III 1979)).

6 Richard A. Musgrave, *The Theory of Public Finance* (New York: McGraw-Hill, 1959), 87–8.

7 Stephen Marglin, "The Social Rate of Discount and the Optimal Rate of Investment," *Quarterly Journal of Economics*, 77 (1963), 98.

8 Gordon Tullock, *Toward a Mathematics of Politics* (Ann Arbor: University of Michigan Press, 1967), 3. Cf. p. 1: "In modern economics and in the political theory which is now developing out of economics, the preference schedule has substituted for the man."

9 A. K. Sen, "Rational Fools: A Critique of the Behavioral Foundations of Economic Theory," *Philosophy and Public Affairs*, 6 (1977), 317–44. Sen writes (pp. 335–6): "A person is given *one* preference ordering, and as and when the need arises this is supposed to reflect his interest, represent his welfare, summarize his idea of what should be done, and describe his actual choices and behavior. Can one preference ordering do all these things? A person thus described may be 'rational' in the limited sense of revealing no inconsistencies in his behavior, but if he has no use for these distinctions . . . , he must be a bit of a fool. The *purely* economic man is close to being a social moron. Economic theory has been much preoccupied with this rational fool decked in the glory of his *one* all-purpose preference ordering."

10 See Martin H. Krieger, "Six Propositions on the Poor and Pollution," *Policy Sciences*, 1 (1970), 311–24; and Henry Peskin, "Environmental Policy and the Distribution of Benefits and Costs," in Paul R. Portney (ed.), *Current Issues in U.S. Environmental Policy* (Baltimore: Resources for the Future, 1978), 144–63.

11 This distinction has been drawn in a somewhat different form by Henry M. Peskin and Eugene Seskin, "Introduction and Overview," in Peskin and Seskin (eds), *Cost Benefit Analysis and Water Pollution Policy*

(Washington, DC: The Urban Institute, 1975), 4–5. These authors use "allocation" to mean the total amount of a resource which should be produced or otherwise made available; they use distribution the way I use the allocation–distribution distinction to mark the difference between resource management and its consequences on income. For a similar treatment, see Burton Weisbrod, "Income Redistribution Effects and Benefit-Cost Analysis," in Samuel B. Chase (ed.), *Problems in Public Expenditure Analysis* (Washington, DC: Brookings Institution, 1968), 177, 178. For the same distinction made in somewhat different language, see Otto Eckstein, *Water-Resource Development* (Cambridge, Mass.: Harvard University Press, 1958), 17.

12 "Allocation programs include measures to affect relative prices and/or the allocation of resources in an economy, motivated by considerations of economic efficiency. Distribution programs consist of efforts to alter the distribution of incomes in society, motivated by considerations of distributive equity." Edward M. Gramlich, *Benefit-Cost Analysis of Government Programs* (Englewood Cliffs, NJ: Prentice-Hall, 1981), 13.

13 See e.g. Thomas C. Schelling, "Economic Reasoning and the Ethics of Policy," *Public Interest*, 63 (1981), 37.

14 For an argument to the effect that the priority of the right to the good is trivial when the good is conceived in terms of preference satisfaction, see Michael J. Sandel, *Liberalism and the Limits of Justice* (Cambridge: Cambridge University Press, 1982). I have reviewed Sandel's arguments in "The Limits of Justice," *Yale Law Journal*, 92: 6 (1983), 1065–1081.

15 Ronald Dworkin, "Liberalism," in Stuart Hampshire (ed.), *Public and Private Morality* (Cambridge: Cambridge University Press, 1978), 112–43.

16 Some critics of liberalism, like Sandel (see n. 14), believe that liberals are doomed to carry on this empty debate. I do not believe that the efficiency-or-equality issue is *necessarily* central to the discussion of public policy within liberalism.

17 Leading examples of this literature include

Ronald Dworkin, *Taking Rights Seriously* (Cambridge, Mass: Harvard University Press, 1977), and Richard Posner, *The Economics of Justice* (Cambridge, Mass: Harvard University Press, 1985).

18 There are some court cases, for example, those involving affirmative action, to which debates of this sort are quite relevant. See e.g. Ronald Dworkin, "Reverse Discrimination," in *Taking Rights Seriously*, 223–39.

19 For discussion relating the social discount rate to environmental ethics, see J. A. Doeleman, "On the Social Rate of Discount: The Case for Macroenvironmental Policy," *Environmental Ethics*, 2 (1980), 45, and sources cited therein.

20 Derek Parfit, "Energy Policy and the Further Future," working paper, Center for Philosophy and Public Policy, University of Maryland, 23 February 1981. A slightly different version of the passage cited appears in Parfit, "Energy Policy and the Further Future: The Identity Problem," in Douglas MacLean and Peter F. Brown (eds), *Energy and the Future* (Totowa, NJ: Rowman & Littlefield, 1983), 167–79, esp. p. 17.

21 William Blackstone summarizes well my view on this point. See Blackstone, "The Search for an Environmental Ethic," in Tom Regan (ed.), *Matters of Life and Death* (Philadelphia: Temple University Press, 1980), 331.

22 Immanuel Kant, *Critique of Judgment*, trans. H. Bernard (New York: Hafner, 1951), sec. 59.

23 Mill argues in several passages that one may be legitimately compelled under certain circumstances to be a "good Samaritan." See "On Liberty," in *Collected Works*, xviii (Toronto: University of Toronto Press, 1977), 224.

24 I have argued this position more fully in "Liberalism and Law," in Douglas MacLean and Claudia Mills (eds), *Liberalism Reconsidered* (Totowa, NJ: Rowman & Littlefield, 1983), 12–24.

25 See Council on Environmental Quality, *Public Opinion on Environmental Issues* (1980).

26 Ibid. 4, 11. For more evidence, see John M. Gilroy and Robert Y. Shapiro, "The Polls: Environmental Protection," *Public Opinion Quarterly*, 50 (1986), 270–9. This excellent survey describes and summarizes many polls.

27 Pascal's wager seems to follow along these lines. "Let us weigh the gain and loss in wagering that God is. Let us estimate the two chances. If you gain, you gain all; if you lose, you lose nothing. Wager, then, without hesitation that He is." B. Pascal, *Pensées*, trans. W. Trotter (1952), sec. 233.

28 Robert Goodin extends this analysis to many goods besides environmental ones. See Goodin, *Political Theory and Public Policy* (Chicago: University of Chicago Press, 1982), chap. 6.

29 "That which is related to general human inclination and needs has a *market price*. . . . But that which constitutes the condition under which alone something can be an end in itself does not have a mere relative worth, *i.e.*, a price, but an intrinsic worth, *i.e.*, *dignity*." Immanuel Kant, *Foundations of the Metaphysics of Morals*, ed. R. Wolff, trans. L. Beck (Indianapolis: Bobbs-Merrill, 1959), 53 (emphasis in original).

30 For a general discussion of the distinction between "positive" and "negative" freedom, see Isaiah Berlin, *Four Essays on Liberty* (London: Oxford University Press, 1969), esp. the third essay and pp. xxxvii–lxiii of the Introduction; and Gerald MacCallum, "Negative and Positive Freedom," *Philosophical Review*, 76 (1967), 312–21.

31 David W. Minar, *Ideas and Politics: The American Experience* (Homewood, Ill.: Dorsey Press, 1964), 416.

32 Quoted in this context by William Ruckelshaus in "Risk, Science, and Society," *Issues in Science and Technology*, 3 (Spring 1985), 24.

11 Environmental Values for a Sustainable Society: The Democratic Challenge

Robert Paehlke

The first Earth Day—20 April 1970—was a more seminal political event than was realized at the time. Since that time, environmental issues have gradually, though sometimes haltingly, become first-order political concerns. By the mid-1980s environmental protection was viewed by many as being as important to our collective well-being as national security, economic prosperity, social justice and—for some—even democracy itself. Some, at that time, would even have argued that if and when trade-offs between first-order values must be made, protecting the environment should be 'first among equals', a transcendent priority. The real challenge is to know what values must and should be traded off, when and to what extent.

In this spirit this chapter will take a hard look at some of the value, and thereby political, implications of the ascendancy of environmental protection as a societal priority. It will emphasize the new relationship between environmental values and the other first-order values: social justice (equity), economic prosperity, national security, and democracy. It will argue that while this ascendancy is welcome, it is probably dangerous to grant any important value a transcendent status. Indeed, it might well be argued that many of our present-day environmental problems have resulted from our having granted such status to economic prosperity and/or national security. In contrast, it could be argued that Marxist theory granted transcendent status to socioeconomic equity and that when this could not be achieved in Marxist practice, few values other than the pursuit of élite power and wealth prevailed.

Perhaps the most fundamental conclusion in this chapter is that important values must be carefully and democratically balanced. Democracy is the guiding value, both as an end and as a means. Environmental protection in particular will be most effectively achieved through the maintenance of, indeed the continuing enhancement of, democratic practice.

The latter assertion flies in the face of the claims and concerns of many environmental and political analysts. Environmentalists frequently asserted in the 1970s that increased scarcity, rooted in resource shortages and ecological limits, would inevitably plague humankind.[1] This scarcity, the result of ecological limits, was viewed by William Ophuls and Robert Heilbroner, for example, as carrying a lamentable threat to political democracy.[2] Some analysts argued that democracy limits society's ability to contend with scarcity and, in effect, redistribute economic decline. Ted Robert Gurr concluded that 'bureaucratic-authoritarian states should be better able than democracies to tolerate the stresses of future ecological crises.'[3]

However, in noting the failings of democratic societies in the face of scarcity, and as pessimistic as he was about the future prospects of democracy, Gurr's analysis also provides an important basis for hope regarding the future. 'The greater the relative increases in scarcity,' he observed, 'and the more rapid its onset, the greater are its negative political consequences.'[4] Therefore, some of these negative political effects could be deflected by early political responses to scarcity. Gurr's view was based, in part, on his pessimism about the ineffectiveness of early responses to environmental problems and resource limitations. The ascendancy of environmental concern in recent years has seen some real gains, real enough at least to buy some time for additional changes, in terms of both technologies and societal value priorities.

Needless to say, all aspects of environmental politics in North America in recent years do not inspire optimism. There were few positive initiatives during the Reagan years, but even then there arose a new momentum for environmental protection, both in terms of public attitudes and in terms of the organizational strength of the environmental movement. Indeed, the Reagan administration provided the movement with more momentum than any 1980s' event save perhaps Chernobyl. In addition, important flaws in the more pessimistic analyses of the relationship between environmental realities and democratic theory have also become more evident in recent years; these will be elaborated on in the conclusion of this chapter. But first let us consider the complex relationships among the first-order political values. The importance of environmental values in the politics of the 1990s and beyond can only be understood through an analysis of the ways in which they intersect with other key societal values such as social justice, economic prosperity and national security. Before turning to that discussion, I will offer a brief summary statement of environmental values themselves.

Environmental Values and Political Decision-Making

Historians, philosophers and opinion-survey analysts have observed that the environmental movement involves a considerable transformation of contemporary social values. Hays noted that new values, rooted in postwar advances in prosperity and educational levels, have emerged in virtually all industrial societies.[5] Others have claimed that recent value shifts run deeper than those which sustained the conservation movement. Sessions has concluded that the ecological 'revolution' involves 'a radical critique of the basic assumptions of modern western society'.[6] Inglehart and other social scientists have measured related shifts in popular attitudes, postulating a 'silent revolution' that entails the spread of 'postmaterialist' values.[7]

But what values comprise the essential core of an environmental perspective? In an earlier work, I set out a list of 13 values; others have developed similar lists.[8] This list, I have come to realize, can be distilled to three core environmental values: (1) the minimization of the negative impacts of human activities on ecosystems, wilderness and habitat, as well as the maximization of biodiversity; (2) the minimization of negative impacts on human health; and (3) the determination of resource allocation and use first and foremost in terms of sustainability in the long term. In three words these values are ecology, health, and sustainability. Values at this level of generality are not sufficient guides to day-to-day policy-making for many reasons. Some of the principles involved in moving from broad general environmental values to specific policies are noted below.

Essentially, environmental values must compete with other values, but they even—some of the time—conflict with each other. For example, high-yield yet sustainable forests may lack the diversity that would otherwise provide habitats for many animal species. Similarly, even the act of protecting human health, and thereby ensuring that human population will rise, virtually guarantees the diminution of non-human habitat. Such dilemmas do not absolve us of the task of sorting out difficult value questions; indeed, the authoritative allocation of values is the primary function of politics. Political analysts and political practitioners alike should be cautious about leaving such questions unanswered in their rush to pursue narrow, technical solutions.

Day-to-day policy-making must avoid a rush to the technical not only because it may result in bad environmental policy but also because a politically and administratively privileged science can pose a threat to democratic decision-making. There are competent scientists on both sides of almost every contentious environmental issue. Their views are crucial to understanding what ought to be done, but science in and of itself is not sufficient to the task. Environmental policy decisions in almost every case involve a value as well as a scientific component. Scientists can usefully contribute to the value discussion as informed citizens, indeed they should do so, but their views are most decidedly not the only views that must be heard. Technocracy and environmentalism are in many ways opposite poles.

The Core Environmental Values: Ecology, Health, and Sustainability

Ecology is at once the most obvious and the most subtle of the three core environmental values. Ecology here is used to represent a complex of related values including non-human habitat, biodiversity and wilderness as well as ecological interconnectedness: the 'web of life'. This value is the only one of the three core environmental values that is nor predominantly anthropocentric. It is thereby the value which especially distinguishes environmentalism and which perhaps carries the most radical potential.[9] As well, the emphasis granted to this value and the particular meanings and interpretations attributed to it are the most reliable measure of the variety of 'shades' of green within Green politics.

Ecological values embody an appreciation of nature in all its varieties and nuances and acknowledge that human beings do not, and cannot, fully understand the myriad ways in which the natural world, including humans, interconnects. Humans are seen as but one species among many, but also as the one species whose dominance could be so thorough going as to threaten many, if not most, other species and thereby itself. The ecological vision is a radical vision as and when it sees the living world as something other than 'resources' and is repelled by a world wherein all the earth is open to, and indeed experiences, human settlement, exploitation and/or management. At the same time it recognizes that this reality may now be not only inevitable but also upon us.

Thus if anything like the present levels of global biodiversity are to be preserved for future ages, some humans must force other humans to back off, to tread lightly and to keep out. As a species we are even capable of loving nature to death, but it is generally less our love than our greed, fear, stupidity, and desperation which are of greatest concern here. In Europe virtually every landscape is a human creation. Even in North America many species, especially large predators, have been reduced to isolated islands of existence and those islands are both inadequate for the long term and threatened in any case. Yet many still imagine, or claim, that replanted forests are ecologically equivalent to the Pacific northwest ancient forests that they replace, while in truth they are much diminished habitat at best. Many species require, for example, standing dead trees—clear-cutting removes such entities from vast segments of land for at least a century and probably for ever. It is common knowledge, of course, that the overexploitation of tropical rain forests threatens thousands of species with extinction or a quasi-existence in zoos and gene banks.[10] From an ecological perspective all the world, save the much-visited 'surviving' islands called parks, will soon become a human farm, an enforced monoculture devoid of variety and complexity and the resilience which only those properties can effectively provide.

Health might be the only environmental value, indeed the only single socio-political value, with the potential seriously to rival capitalist economic concerns in the era after the cold war. The focus on health is perhaps especially pronounced within the already wealthy nations. In the USA in particular health care expenditures threaten to create the largest of all national industries, save perhaps the recent, likely temporary, comeback of the North American auto sector. Moreover, the citizens of all Western nations have become increasingly health-conscious in recent decades. This health-consciousness manifests itself in a variety of ways including dietary change, increased attention to exercise and fitness, and a widespread concern with toxic chemicals in the environment.

The latter of these manifestations is certainly and obviously closely bound up with the rise of the environmental movement, but so too are the other two: diet and fitness. Numerous recent books have combined dietary and environmental concerns focusing variously on food additives and pesticides, on the environmental and health costs of meat-dominated diets (in terms of land, energy, and water use among other things) and the links between the beef industry and the overexploitation of tropical rain forests.[11]

The now widespread concern with fitness is linked to a growing demand for outdoor and wilderness recreational spaces and thereby often (though not inevitably) to a demand for more protected quasi-wilderness habitat as well. But it has also, in combination with environmentalist concern regarding climate warming, created greatly increased demands that bicycles and in-line rollerblades be treated as serious urban transportation options.[12] This latter shift dramatically links environmentalism and fitness as do the health research finding which suggest that jogging in some polluted urban settings may do more harm than good as regards health.

In brief, human physical well-being is not easily separated from environmental well-being. Nonetheless, the minimization of environmental impacts on human health has been a most contentious political issue in recent years, most dramatically in workplace settings. But in the broadest of terms Aaron Wildavsky eloquently argued that in almost any clash between health and wealth values, wealth should be favoured by public policy. Wealth, in his view, largely determines health; the wealthier the nation, the healthier the nation.[13] Wildavsky would thus never expend more public funds on health protection than the calculable value of the lives (statistically) saved, or improved, by the expenditures. A contrasting view is put forward by Mark Sagoff who argues that health and environmental protection have distinctive moral value in themselves and must sometimes come first, economic values notwithstanding.[14]

In the USA and elsewhere in recent years the views of those who would balance health costs and benefits in strictly economic terms have prevailed (in, for example, President Ronald Reagan's executive order 12291 and in several recent US Supreme Court occupational and environmental health decisions). In Sagoff's view this administrative and legal trend runs counter to the historic intent of most environmental health legislation. He would prefer that a balance be sought between all economic costs and benefits, on the one hand, and an ethical assertion of a right to health protection on the other. In his view the latter should not be reduced to the former. As well, Wildavsky might have been asked if additional wealth automatically produces increments of health. And how are any increments so obtained to be distributed? His view does not account for the inferior health performance of some wealthy nations, including the USA. Nor for the enormous health costs associated with the single-minded (if ineffective) drive for economic growth within communist Eastern Europe and the Soviet Union.

Sustainability is perhaps the core environmental value which addresses most directly the long-term viability of industrial societies rather than their desirability. Concern with sustainability is nothing less than an attempt to shift the attention of contemporary societies to the needs of future generations and to reject the assumption that technology will somehow almost automatically resolve all future resource needs. Sustainability implies a radically reduced dependence on non-renewable resources, a commitment to extract renewable resources no more rapidly than they are restored in nature and a minimization of human impacts on the ecosystems upon which we depend.

Those who address sustainability issues have often come to the conclusion that the long-term viability of industrial society is in doubt. Many analysts in the past have underestimated the capacity for adaptability or erred in other ways. Jeavons did not foresee the then-imminent shift from coal to oil and the *Limits to Growth*, nearly a century later, underestimated future resource reserves, especially as regards metals and non-fuel minerals.[15] But what is clear, nonetheless, is that our future will be radically different from our recent and historic past and that resource availability will play a significant role in the adaptations that will be necessary.

For example, present rates of global population growth suggest that *A Diet for a Small Planet* will be the food future for many and present rates of forest and fish extraction are clearly non-sustainable.[16] As well, there remains no obvious substitute for fossil fuels some two decades after the OPEC-induced energy crises of the 1970s. The transformation associated with a shift away from oil, whenever and however it finally comes, will take many decades and will almost certainly in and of itself involve profound changes for industrial society. Present economic assumptions and economic policies are clearly not up to the many sustainability-related tasks that lie ahead or are already upon us.[17]

Politics and Environmental Values

What, then, are the overall political implications of these core environmental values? Environmental values can be seen as new issues, recently thrust on to the political stage—a stage already and for ever too full. They signal the rise of ongoing and potential value/political clashes between environmental objectives and other first-order political values. These clashes, together with possibilities for mutuality, compromise, and coalition-building, portend the future of environmental politics and policy. Such conflicts notwithstanding, there remain substantial opportunities for advancing several, if not all, these important values concurrently.

Each of the other, non-environmental, first-order political values has an attendant political constituency: investors, corporations and trade unions promote economic growth; defence industries and the military make the case for national security; the poor, urban politicians, organized minorities, trade unions, churches and others advance the cause of social justice and equity. Environmental politics, however, is a politics of a different sort in that it is less dominated by economically self-interested individuals and groups.

This is not to say that economic growth, national security or social justice do not have principled adherents. Many who work hard to advance these values have little or nothing to gain materially from variations in outcome. Nor is it to say that those who promote environmental causes do not have economic stakes in environmental protection. For example, Alaskan fishermen clearly have a stake in avoiding another oil spill, such as the one from the *Exxon Valdez*. In addition, many who are involved in environmental siting decisions are there to defend the value of their property. At the same time many, if not most, environmental advocates oppose pollution because they value health over wealth and understand that environmental objectives may imply real personal economic costs. Environmental politics is thereby refreshing evidence that principles still have a place in politics—and is why many more traditional political figures are so obviously uncomfortable in this realm.

This distinctive political character of environmentalism has several important effects. First, an environmental advocate in one setting may become an environmental opponent under different circumstances (for example, fishermen may promote overfishing). Second, regardless of economic status, all human beings must eat, breathe and drink. For these reasons and others, it is more difficult for policy-makers to reject claims to environmental protection than to reject, for example, claims to social justice. Having a less focused constituency, however, can have political costs. Indeed, most political scientists would argue that without an economically interested attentive public, fewer political and organizational resources are available.

But, as well, this diffusion of interest in environmentalism is not without important political advantages. Because environmentalists are advocates on behalf of future generations and other species, not just themselves, they frequently occupy the moral and political high ground. Moreover, many proponents of environmental values have undergone a fundamental revision in worldview; thus they carry a level of conviction that few others can achieve these days. Finally, many environmental objectives may be scientifically understood and defended in a way that few other sociopolitical issues can be. (The role of science in environmentalism also has problematic potentials discussed both above and below.) Thus, if there are political disputes with those who place a more exclusive priority on social justice, national security or economic prosperity, it is far from certain that environmental advocates will lose.

Let us briefly, then, examine each of these three points of potential value conflict.

Environmental Protection and Social Justice

As environmental politics has come to comprise a widening portion of the political agenda, there has been some unease that environmental objectives are sometimes achieved at the expense of socioeconomic equity. In the past, environmentalism was seen as predominantly a white, middle-class concern. In this view, money spent on pollution abatement was money *not* spent on inner-city schools; further, environmental protection cost jobs, especially blue-collar jobs. Environmentalists have also been seen by some as placing an unreasonable importance on wilderness—the seemingly legendary places many cannot afford to visit.

What is perhaps surprising, then, is how small the differences are in the acceptance of environmental values by class, race, or any other demographic measure.[18] In addition, in terms of economic and social realities (rather than perceptions), the advancement of environmental objectives could, I will argue, improve the everyday lives of ordinary people more than many would expect. This is important not only for its own sake but also for the health of democracy as well. Gurr and other critics ground their fears for democracy by positing that in scarcity situations, 'economically advantaged groups are better able to use market forces and political influence to maintain their positions', and therefore social inequalities will increase.[19] This, in turn, implies fundamental risks for democracy.

Environmental objectives intersect with social justice or equity objectives most significantly in two ways: employment opportunities and relative health impacts. While health objectives are very important politically, they are something of a luxury in some circumstances in recent years—the overwhelming priority is employment opportunities, especially for meaningful work that provides for more than bare survival.

Employment opportunities are affected by environmental decisions in at least three ways. First, environmental protection expenditures affect international competitiveness at the level of the manufacturer and the nation. Second, specific environmental protection decisions can directly result in job losses or gains. For example, not cutting a given stand of timber may eliminate jobs which could exist for some additional years; conversely, new abatement regulations may create jobs in the installation and operation of pollution abatement devices. Third, while quantitative employment effects are important, so too are the character, quality, and location of employment gains and losses.

Surprisingly, there are few comprehensive studies of the employment impacts of environmental protection, despite the obvious political significance of the issue. The loss of jobs is frequently raised by industry as an argument against 'too-stringent' environmental protection. Ironically, the opposite may be true: the overall net effect of enhanced environmental protection may be more, rather than fewer, employment opportunities. The threat of environmental job losses may be more bluff and blackmail than reality.[20] Environmental Protection Agency regulations, for example, have probably created more direct jobs than they have cost.[21]

Many types of environmental protection initiatives produce employment. For example, recycling generates large numbers of jobs, whereas the extraction of concentrated virgin (non-recycled) materials is less labour intensive. Bottle bills, which require that containers be refilled, have a net job-creating outcome. The jobs lost in bottle plants are gained in retail stores, trucking, warehouses, and bottle-washing facilities. Energy conservation creates more jobs than would have been created in energy production had the conservation effort not been undertaken.[22] Even increased public transportation use may generate net employment gains.[23]

Another dimension of this debate involves the broader question of total economic mix. Non-manufacturing employment, particularly in services such as health care or education, is labour intensive and imposes only low environmental impacts. Thus when these sectors expand proportionally both unemployment and environmental damage decline.

Environmental protection probably fares less well when the quality and location of employment opportunities are considered. Replacing employment on energy megaprojects with jobs in energy conservation or recycling may replace high-paying, skilled, often unionized jobs with lower-skilled, lower-paying jobs, albeit more of them. This employment increase may well be opposed politically because only existing jobs are defended politically. Environmentalists are sometimes thereby pitted against organized labour, while those who might gain employment from the environmental initiatives are left out of the debate.

However, even these generalizations distort the complexity of socio-economic and political realities. Public transportation jobs are frequently unionized and high paying. The manufacture and installation of pollution abatement equipment requires highly skilled workers. Employment in teaching and health care is not without appeal. As well, from the perspective of the poor, the low-skill and high-skill *urban-centred* jobs that environmental protection generates are urgently needed. Also, full employment, even if achieved through reduced work time at constant hourly wages, would carry social savings partially to offset costs. There would be reduced costs for unemployment insurance and welfare, a broadened income tax base and, possibly, reduced costs for police protection and health care.

What of the distribution of environmental health impacts: are they felt evenly by rich and poor? Everyone eats, breathes and drinks but, for example, some infants now consume 'organic' baby food—at double the cost of ordinary brands. It is well known that hazardous waste sites, incinerators and landfills are disproportionately found in poor and/or black neighbourhoods.[24] Air quality varies by location, often to the disadvantage of the less well-off and health risks vary by occupation though there is evidence that the lowest-paying occupations do not always carry the highest risks. (Nor do the highest-paying professional, sales and managerial jobs). All and all, the better-off are likely at least marginally to be advantaged by lower environmental exposures. The poor, then, would gain disproportionately in any across-the-board environmental clean-up.

There are recently strong indications that environmental advocacy is no longer the exclusive preserve of the white middle class. There are now many organizations that have an active interest in the environmental concerns of the urban and rural poor.[25] There have been several recent environmental issues that have mobilized the poor and helped to build small bridges across racial barriers. Nonetheless, in membership and leadership, the major environmental organizations remain predominantly white.

While environmental protection *can* be implemented at the expense of the poor, it can also be achieved either neutrally or to the relative advantage of the less well-off. The distributional effects of environmental protection depend on which socioeconomic groups are mobilized in defence of the environment. The 1980s saw ground lost on the environmental front, or at least a slowed rate of gain. They also saw an overall decline in political involvement, especially among the less advantaged sectors of society. Apathy and cynicism carry with them real risks for the quality of democracy. Hence an environmental politics of expanding scope should not exclude the concerns of the less advantaged for many good reasons. There are clear limits to the political capabilities of an environmental movement that does not activate and serve all segments of society.

Environmental Values and Economic Growth

Gurr, Ophuls, and Heilbroner all envisioned a linkage between environmental damage and economic scarcity, and between economic scarcity and declining democratic prospects. Ophuls and Heilbroner each carefully reviewed a wide range of sustainability issues and concluded with a lament for democracy. They considered energy availability, agricultural capabilities, resource availability, pollution, population growth and other environmental impacts. 'Once relative abundance and wealth of opportunity are no longer available to mitigate the harsh political dynamics of scarcity,' Ophuls wrote, 'the pressures favoring greater inequality, oppression, and conflict will build up so that the return of scarcity portends the revival of age-old political evils, for our descendants if not for ourselves. In short, the golden age of individualism, liberty, and democracy is all but over.'[26] Heilbroner went further in imagining what would follow: 'a social order that will blend a "religious" orientation and a "military" discipline.'[27]

But there are many possible alternative futures. *Our Common Future* concluded that economic growth must and can continue and that it all but requires enhanced environmental protection.[28] Much earlier, in 1966, economist Kenneth Boulding contrasted economic output with what he called energy and material throughputs.[29] In the perspective this concept opens up, economic activity can increase while the total amount of energy and materials used declines. Both environmental damage and resource shortfalls are a function of energy and materials use, not of economic activity per se.

In other words, it may well be the case that there is not a one-to-one relationship between resource use and economic activity. Most materials in an economy can be used and reused: metals, paper, glass, plastic, wood, chemicals and agricultural wastes are recyclable. Moreover, many high-technology products including computer chips, fibre optics, biotechnologies, calculators, and portable compact-disc players require very little material and energy. The same is true of human services, including education, the arts, and entertainment—all high-growth sectors. In fact, energy and materials used per unit of GNP have been in almost continuous decline for a century or more. As well, the oil-price hikes of the 1970s slowed economic growth, but also induced a further increase in the efficiency of energy and materials use within the total economy.

Why is this important? It means that a widespread sense of extreme stringency can be avoided even if energy and materials use must be curtailed though the changes involved will be neither automatic nor easy. Thus, while our economies will change radically over the coming century, the total value of goods and services will not necessarily shrink. This would be particularly true if societies were deliberately to accelerate the necessary changes by altering production and consumption habits and preferences. These habits are not fixed and immutable. On the contrary, market-based change is always rapid, even if induced by changes in taxation or subsidy policies. As well, the large share of GNP now devoted to military procurement could be scaled down even further, freeing existing economic capacity for other, less environmentally problematic uses.

Environmental Protection, National Security, and World Peace

Our Common Future placed the links between environmental protection and world peace front and centre. This report, descended from the *World Conservation Strategy* (1980), Olaf Palme's *Common Security: A Blueprint for Survival* (1982), and Willy Brandt's *World Armament and World Hunger* (1985) has had a quite wide impact for a document drafted within international diplomatic circles. *Our Common Future* is also, as regards some questions, surprisingly candid. Regarding peace and security, for example, it notes: 'The arms race—in all parts of the world—preempts resources that might be used more productively to diminish the security threats created by environmental conflict and the resentments that are fueled by widespread poverty.'[30]

Our Common Future emphasizes the three-way linkage among peace, development, and environmental damage. 'Environmental stress,' it states, 'is both a cause and an effect of political tension and military conflict. Nations have often fought to assert or resist control over raw materials, energy supplies . . . and other key environmental resources. Such conflicts are likely to increase as these resources become scarcer and competition for them increases.'[31]

Real security, in the view of *Our Common Future* and in the view of many environmentalists who reject this report's view that economic growth is necessary to the achievement of environmental protection, requires a massive transfer of funds from military expenditure to sustainable development. Global military expenditures are equivalent to more than $1,000 per year for each of the world's poorest one billion humans—an amount well beyond their present average income. Simply returning military spending to the proportion of global GNP it represented prior to 1960 could provide $225 annually to each of those persons. Alternatively, investing this amount ($225 billion annually) in sustainable agriculture, reforestation, wetlands restoration, habitat protection and renewable energy could rectify environmental damage *and* transform economic prospects throughout Asia, Africa, and Latin America.

Less grandly, using *Our Common Future's* figures, a 0.1 per cent tax on global military expenditures could provide family planning globally. A 0.3 per cent tax could achieve global literacy and a 0.6 per cent tax would fully fund current proposals to alleviate global desertification and deforestation. What is missing are the political and institutional mechanisms to achieve such historic shifts. What is necessary is the widespread actual achievement of environmentalist Amory Lovins's 1980 phrase 'the demilitarization of the security concept'.[32]

Environmental Protection and Democracy

While democracy may (or may not) be vulnerable to greater scarcity within poorer economies, it may be the most effective means of handling such limitations within wealthier societies. John Passmore, writing around the same time as Ophuls and Heilbroner, noted that 'the view that ecological problems are more likely to be solved in an authoritarian than in a liberal democratic society rests on the implausible assumption that the authoritarian state would be ruled by ecologist-kings. In practice there is more hope of action in democratic societies'.[33] Environmentalists must be ever wary that the real links between science and environmentalism are not over-interpreted. Environmental protection is in the end a value preference, not privileged information rooted in science.

Passmore's perspective is valid for at least three reasons: (1) authoritarian rulers are unlikely to be sensitive to or informed about ecological matters; (2) authoritarian regimes are not necessarily good at inducing positive behaviour, especially in the long term; and (3) democracy provides a good climate for social and economic mobilization and even, if necessary, for developing an acceptance of shared hardship. The changes in the Soviet Union and Eastern Europe in the late 1980s lend contemporary support to these conclusions—pollution is widespread in those regions and it has become increasingly clear that neither environmental protection nor economic growth were maximized in the old authoritarian regimes.

There is also something amiss in Passmore's observation in terms of the contemporary situation. Not all who fear for democracy in a world of scarcity and ecological destruction envision benign (or not so benign) ecologist-kings. Authoritarianism, or quasi-authoritarianism, could be imposed with precisely the opposite intentions. Such regimes might impose environmentally undesirable economic activities on unwilling localities. They might distort or suppress scientific findings (or simply commission 'alternative' findings), or protect the economic or ecological well-being of one locality at the expense of another. Such regimes might well not even intend to solve ecological problems—a frightening vision, but indeed a vision made more plausible the longer global environmental change is delayed.

There are at least five reasons to be more optimistic regarding democracy and the environment than were Gurr, Ophuls, and Heilbroner. First, the environmental movement has consistently helped to strengthen democratic practice in important ways. Second, as previously discussed, enhanced domestic economic equity is in many ways compatible with environmental protection, where population levels have not yet outstripped ecological underpinnings. Third, at higher levels of economic development 'sustainable' becomes as important as 'development'; a reasonable balance between the two may be more easily attained politically. Fourth, as noted earlier, many 'postindustrial' forms of economic activity are probably less damaging to the environment than are basic industrial forms. Fifth, greater technological sophistication results in improved environmental monitoring and in 'decoupling' economic activity and environmental damage by means of 'technical fixes'. I will conclude with a brief elaboration of the first two items in this list.

Conclusion

Most North American environmental legislation in the 1970s and 1980s contained a significant mechanism for public participation. These institutional innovations have strengthened democracy and helped it adapt to new issues. More than that, environmental organizations have consistently worked to open administrative processes and industrial society itself to expanded public scrutiny.[34] Such scrutiny is the essence of democratic practice. In the early days of environmentalism (the 1960s), openness was seen as a means of avoiding the administrative 'capture' to which earlier conservation bureaucracies were prone.[35] More recent legislative initiatives, including workplace and community right-to-know legislation, have gone further.

Rather than merely opening up governmental decision-making, these newer initiatives have taken matters that were once private and opened them to public observation. The movement, use and storage of hazardous materials are now subject to both democratic and market decision-making processes. For example, Title III of the Superfund Amendments and Reauthorization Act 1986 requires that industrial toxic emissions be made a matter of public record. Workplace right-to-know legislation mandates that industrial workers be informed regarding the exposures they encounter. Some Canadian industrial workers have also attained administrative protection of their right to refuse unsafe work. Community right-to-know laws in many US jurisdictions have provided information regarding the use, storage, and transport of hazardous substances.[36] Firemen and other emergency workers, residents and environmentalists alike have learnt from this. The state of California has gone the furthest in requiring notification regarding all carcinogens, be they gasoline additives or supermarket product ingredients. Most such right-to-know measures can help mobilize public opinion and activate people both as consumers and as democratic citizens.

It may well be that in the future environmental decisions will increasingly test the mobilizing capacities of democratic systems. It would appear that several new environmental issues will require solutions that are less 'regulatory' in character, requiring broad behavioural shifts, rather than the regulatory coercion of a small number of economic actors. For example, both recycling and the wider use of public transportation involve such behavioural changes. Behavioural changes involving whole communities are less effectively monitored and enforced than promoted and encouraged. The regulatory mode is inappropriate in altering individual consumer and workplace behaviour (as distinct from workplace equipment).

These newer forms of change require a citizen majority willing to accept and/or participate in such changes. Democracies and democratically managed markets in combination can mobilize educated citizens. So too can authoritarian-bureaucratic systems under some circumstances. But the demise of the Soviet Union suggests that there are limits to the mobilizational capacities of such systems at advanced levels of economic development. Those who are pessimistic about democracy on ecological grounds have not seen this, nor do they allow the possibility that educated populations simply will not be mobilized by regimes they have not chosen.

Just as industry willingness and co-operation is necessary for effective regulatory compliance, citizen willingness is necessary for non-regulatory compliance. But citizens will not change their behaviour unless they perceive that industry and government are also doing what they can. Educated citizens will not participate effectively in collective efforts unless they have been party to decisions regarding priorities. Industry will feel less singled out only if it is not alone in bearing costs.

Thus an effective pluralist democratic system is the best source of balanced, participatory initiatives. Active involvement by individual citizens and private organizations require a sense of mutual effort. Political science research shows that a sense of political efficacy is necessary. It is here that democracy, at its most effective, may prove absolutely essential to the achievement of environmental protection. Cynicism and indifference will undermine any collective ability to protect environmental life-support systems.

Democracy itself must be enhanced effectively to deal with environmental problems. One means of doing this is to expand the environmental powers and roles of municipal and regional governments. A second is to introduce an environmental role within all governmental subdivisions, at all levels. The environmental mandate should not necessarily be concentrated within a single agency. Agencies not traditionally involved with environmental matters, including procurement offices, could be ordering ceramic dishes and organic food for the cafeteria, reducing chemical spray programmes in parks, downsizing the fleet of vehicles and ordering recycled paper. Other divisions should be taking other appropriate initiatives. All should have citizen-based environmental advisory committees. Third, environmentalists must realize that a political democracy will not likely run very far ahead of a nation's commitment to economic equity and social justice. Gurr saw a threat to democracy from the potential inequity of environmental scarcity. While Gurr is accurate in his assessment of the relationship between equity and democracy, this dangerous outcome can be avoided.

In an effective democracy the economic security of the less advantaged cannot be perceived as the price for environmental protection. Environmental activists must be more sensitive to the widespread fear of job loss and displacement. Citizens active in environmental politics must be sensitive to the difference between locally unwanted facilities that are environmentally necessary and carefully sited and those that are not. The fate of environmental protection and the quality of democracy will be very much intertwined in the future.

There is little doubt that human activities pose multiple threats to the habitat of most species on the planet. Doubts remain whether future human numbers are sustainable at present or higher amenity levels in the long term. This is not, however, the same thing as saying that the human species is in grave and immediate danger. Nonetheless environmental dangers have reached such complexity and magnitude that they now intersect with questions of social justice, world peace, and global economic development. The simultaneous handling of all these challenges will require both intelligence and enhanced democratic institutions.

Notes

1. See the work of Thomas R. Malthus, W. Stanley Jeavons, and others discussed in R. C. Paehlke, *Environmentalism and the Future of Progressive Politics* (New Haven: Yale

University Press, 1989), chap. 3. See also D. H. Meadows et al., *The Limits to Growth* (New York: Universe Books, 1972); W. R. Catton, Jr., *Overshoot: The Ecological Basis of Revolutionary Change* (Urbana: University of Illinois Press, 1980).

2. See, in particular, W. Ophuls, *Ecology and the Politics of Scarcity* (San Francisco, W. H. Freeman, 1977); R. L. Heilbroner, *An Inquiry into the Human Prospect* (New York: Norton, 1974); T. R. Gurr, 'On the Political Consequences of Scarcity and Economic Decline', *International Studies Quarterly* 29 (1985), 51–75.

3. Gurr, 'On the Political Consequences of Scarcity', 70.

4. Ibid. 54.

5. S. P. Hayes, 'From Conservation to Environment: Environmental Politics in the United States since World War Two', *Environmental Review* 6 (Fall 1982), 20.

6. G. Sessions, 'The Deep Ecology Movement: A Review', *Environmental Review*, 11 (Summer 1987), 107.

7. R. Inglehart, *The Silent Revolution: Changing Values and Political Styles among Western Publics* (Princeton: Princeton University Press, 1977)

8. See Paehlke, *Environmentalism*, chap. 6.

9. R. Eckersley, *Environmentalism and Political Theory: Toward an Ecocentric Approach* (Albany, NY: SUNY Press, 1992).

10. See N. Myers, 'Biodepletion', in R. Paehlke (ed.), *Encyclopedia of Conservation and Environmentalism* (New York: Garland, 1995); J. A. Livingston, *Rogue Primate* (Toronto: Key Porter Books, 1994); C. Tudge, *Last Animals at the Zoo* (Washington, DC: Island Press, 1992).

11. F. Moore Lappé, *Diet for a Small Planet* (New York: Ballantine Books, 1975); L. Pim, *The Invisible Additive: Environmental Contaminants in Our Food* (Garden City, NY: Doubleday, 1982); J. Robbins, *Diet for a New America* (Walpole, NH: Stillpoint Publishing, 1987).

12. M. Lowe, *The Bicycle: Vehicle for a Small Planet* (Washington, DC: Worldwatch, 1989).

13. A. Wildavsky, *Searching for Safety* (New Brunswick, NJ: Transaction, 1988).

14. M. Sagoff, *The Economy of the Earth* (New York: Cambridge University Press, 1988), 195–6.

15. See the discussion of Jeavons and *Limits to Growth* in Paehlke, *Environmentalism*.

16. This is not to say that *Diet for a Small Planet* is a world that should provoke fear or even concern, though obviously overfishing and forest depletion rates are alarming.

17. See e.g. P. Ekins (ed.), *The Living Economy: A New Economics in the Making* (London: Routledge, 1986); D. Pearce, *Economic Values and the Natural World* (London: Earthscan, 1993); as well as the journal *Ecological Economics*.

18. Milbrath, L. W. (1984), *Environmentalists: Vanguard for a New Society*, Albany: State University of New York Press.

19. Gurr, 'On the Political Consequences of Scarcity', 58.

20. R. Kazis and R. L. Grossman, *Fear at Work* (New York: Pilgrim Press, 1982).

21. Several relevant studies are cited in F. H. Buttel, C. C. Geisler and I. W. Wiswall (eds), *Labor and the Environment* (Westport, Conn.: Greenwood Press, 1984); see, in particular, their annotations 016, 017, 040, 050, 064, 105, and 159.

22. Regarding recycling and refillable containers and employment, see W. U. Chandler, *Materials Recycling: The Virtue of Necessity* (Washington, DC: Worldwatch Institute, 1984); C. M. Gudger and J. C. Bailes, *The Economic Impact of Oregon's Bottle Bill* (Corvallis: Oregon State University Press, 1974). Regarding energy conservation and employment, see e.g. sources annotated in Buttel, Geisler, and Wiswall (eds), *Labor and the Environment*.

23. B. Hannon and F. Puleo, *Transferring from Urban Cars to Buses: The Energy and Employment Impacts* (Urbana: University of Illinois, Center for Advanced Computation, 1974).

24. See e.g. R. D. Bullard, *Dumpling in Dixie: Race, Class, and Environmental Quality* (Boulder, Colo.: Westview Press, 1991); C. Lee, *Toxic Waste and Race in the United States* (New York: United Church of Christ Commission

for Racial Justice, 1987); L. Blumberg and R. Gottlieb, 'The New Environmentalists: Saying No to Mass Burn', *Environmental Action*, 20 (January/February 1989), 28–30.

25. See R. D. Bullard, *Unequal Protection: Environmental Justice and Communities of Color* (San Francisco: Sierra Club Books, 1994).

26. Ophuls, *Ecology and the Politics of Scarcity*, 145.

27. Heilbroner, *An Inquiry into the Human Prospect*, 161.

28. World Commission on Environment and Development, *Our Common Future* (New York: Oxford University Press, 1987).

29. See K. Boulding, 'The Encounters of the Coming Spaceship Earth', in H. E. Daly (ed.), *Economics, Ecology, Ethics* (San Francisco: W. H. Freeman, 1980), 253–63.

30. World Commission, *Our Common Future*, 6–7. See also International Union for Conservation of Nature and Natural Resources (IUCN), *World Conservation Strategy* (Gland, Switzerland: IUCN, 1980); Independent Commission on Disarmament and Security Issues (Olaf Palme, Chairman),

Common Security A Blueprint for Survival (New York: Simon & Schuster, 1982); W. Brandt, *World Armament and World Hunger* (London: Victor Gollancz, 1986).

31. World Commission, *Our Common Future*, 290.

32. A. B. Lovins and L. Hunter Lovins, *Energy/War: Breaking the Nuclear Link* (New York: Harper & Row, 1980), 153.

33. J. Passmore, *Man's Responsibility for Nature* (London: Duckworth, 1974), 183.

34. For a broad consideration of environmentalism and administration, including the issue of openness, see R. Paehlke and D. Torgerson (eds), *Managing Leviathan: Environmental Politics and the Administrative State* (Peterborough, Ontario: Broadview Press, (1990).

35. See e.g. G. McConnell, 'The Conservation Movement—Past and Present', *Western Political Quarterly*, 7 (1954), 470–1.

36. The broad issue of participation and the right to know is discussed in S. G. Hadden, *A Citizen's Right to Know: Risk Communication and Public Policy* (Boulder, Colo.: Westview Press, 1989).

12   The German Greens: Preparing for Another New Beginning?

Helmut Wiesenthal

I. Introduction

The German Greens are an exception. Not because their career as a political party began relatively early and thus secured attention for ecological issues in the political system of their country as early as the first half of the 1980s but because they have become, much more than any other green party in Western Europe, the object, indeed the victim, of a myth. Although the well-intentioned myths about Germany's Greens have fostered a positive view of the chances of Green parties in other countries, they nevertheless hinder understanding of the convoluted and irritating course of development followed by the party 'Die Grünen'. Unless one knows the background to the Greens' emergence, and the problems associated with their organisation, their assimilation of experience, and their elaboration of strategy, one cannot understand why, in the process of German unification, the Greens ended up on the periphery of political events, and even lost their seats in the Bundestag.

One of the chief myths is the notion that the foundation and early electoral successes of the German Greens were due to a particularly strong ecological/pacifist mood in West German society. 'Ecological issues' have indeed become a 'standard topic' in the media and amongst a large number of younger people, but this is not sufficient to account for the existence of the 'Greens'. Unconditional pacifism and the tendency to engage in an ecological critique of civilisation are features confined to a tiny segment of the population, and to only a minority of green voters. Combative commitment to the environment was, in any case, not a German speciality. The anti-nuclear and environmental movement in 1970s France was markedly stronger, but it was only about ten years later that a viable green party came into being there. Again, the West German subcultural milieu never attained the creativity and radiating power of the new age 'consciousness revolution' which began on the west coast of the United States in the 1960s and left its mark all over the world, even in places where green parties have remained unheard of to this day.

Also mythical is the belief that the German Greens are the successful creation of charismatic personalities such as Petra Kelly or Rudolf Bahro. However important the role of such personalities was in bringing together groups and individuals during 1979 and 1980, the fate of the Greens took shape largely uninfluenced by the wishes and actions of their prominent founders.[1] Another myth, finally, is the notion that the activities and conflicts of the Greens were always, and primarily, concerned with the issue of ecology, with ecological values and the critique of industrialism. There is a very important difference here between the picture which the media painted of the Greens (and which for many years determined public perception of them) and the issues on which they actually concentrated as they formulated their objectives and conducted their disputes. Thus, until very recently, the Greens were accused of being a single-issue party, although from the very beginning they had concerned themselves with the full range of global and social themes, as well as pursuing the ambitious programme of a movement of democratic and moral renewal.

The real Greens, both members and party officials, experienced a different reality—a deep gulf between favourable opportunities for effective social action on the one hand, and immense internal party difficulties on the other. Many an internal conflict gave rise to hostilities that were more intense than any dispute with other parties. If, despite this, one can currently observe a positive trend in the development of the Greens, this is due primarily to the commitment and sacrifice of countless local activists, who refused to trust in any favourable-looking trend, and who, despite the factional disputes going on in all the different bodies, sought repeatedly to give public proof of the Greens' political potential.

This chapter attempts to plot an interpretive framework within which questions about organisational development and organisational structure may be answered. What were the institutional conditions under which the unique phenomenon of 'greenness' emerged (section II)? What marks have the Greens left on society (section III)? What is the explanation for their dual ideological identity (section IV), and for the ambivalent results of the grass-roots experiment (section V)? And finally, where do the Greens stand today, twelve years or so after their foundation and in an unexpectedly united Germany (section VI)? The chapter closes with an analytical summary of the problems which any party of reform now faces in shaping itself (section VII).

II. Attractions and Handicaps: The Opportunity Structure

Comparative political science views the emergence of the new social movements and green parties in Western Europe as part of a profound change in the social structures of industrial society. From this standpoint, the environmental movements and parties appear as new forms of participation by new social categories, in particular the new middle classes.[2] Unfortunately, however, this characterisation can only capture the common aspects of a phenomenon which presents itself in nationally and culturally highly varied permutations. Since the phenomenon does not exist anywhere in a 'generalised' or 'average' form, it becomes interesting, and comprehensible, only through its peculiarities. Thus it should come as no surprise that the emergence, development, and prospects of the German Greens have all been influenced to a great degree by the peculiar historical and cultural features of the Federal Republic.

Naturally, the influence exerted on the Greens by historical/cultural factors can be seen clearly only when one looks back over a sizeable stretch of development. As far as the shaping of political image is concerned, this influence has manifested itself in a decidedly 'left–green' bias, with strong traits of a 'generation-based party'. For one thing, the party has maintained an outlook on society and political conflict that was prevalent amongst substantial sections of its membership at the time of its foundation. In addition, the generations associated with the party's foundation, these are primarily contingents with birth-years falling between 1945 and 1965, form a dispro-portionate percentage of the membership in relation to the population as a whole. In somewhat overstated terms, one can say that the Greens still 'think' like their founders, and, since their way of thinking is shared less and less by younger generations, they are also 'ageing' with their founders.

In order to understand the political and cultural image of the Greens, one has to recall some of the peculiar features of German post-war history. West Germany, here for once regarded not as a symbol of the economic miracle, but as a political/cultural syndrome, was obliged to 'rein-vent' the Germans' collective view of themselves, their social and political values, following the downfall of the Hitler regime. As is well known, early post-war policy (i.e. the governments of Chancellor Adenauer) discharged this task through unconditional political and economic attachment to the West, and through two equally resolute 'separations'. One was the dissociation from National Socialism, and the other was the strict rejection of all things 'communist' or 'socialist'. These latter were equated with Stalinist domination and repression.[3]

Both the climate of opinion, characterised as it was by repression and taboo, and the political leanings of the Christian Democrat governments prevented the demarcation from National Socialism and from the crimes of the Hitler regime from being carried out as honestly and consistently as was the rejection of everything that could be associated, however remotely, with any manifestation of 'Soviet domination'. Thus it was that until well into the 1960s, official policy displayed an obsessive McCarthy-like anti-communism, whereas the National Socialist past was treated as a taboo subject (i.e. was suppressed from public discussion). It is one of the paradoxes of post-war Germany that in 1956 the Communist Party (KPD) was outlawed, whilst associations of former SS and SA members were tolerated, and met with considerable success in their socio-political demands. Later on, the infamous Berufsverbot or professional ban was intro-duced for use against any members of the German Communist Party (DKP), labelled 'extremists', who wanted to work as teachers, railway workers, postmen, or civil/public servants. During this same time, former Nazi judges were still at work, and concentration-camp superintendents who were being sought for murder and torture could expect their crimes eventually to come under the statute of limitations (until its application to Nazi murder was abolished in 1979).

Post-war Germany was characterised not so much by social divisions as by moral/cultural and political 'cleavages'. In comparison with the majority, probably 90 per cent—of consumer-minded, security-oriented, and politically abstinent citizens, there was only a small minority of left-wing, left-liberal souls. They had an eye for the past and a critical attitude to cultural devel-opments, though they were no more interested in institutional politics than were the majority. It was only in the years around '1968' (now the symbol of democratic awakening) and as a 'joint product' of internal political democratisation and the external relaxation of relations with the East, and also as a belated effect of the student movement[4] that the present liberal, pluralist society of the Federal Republic, with its capacity for self-critical analysis, emerged. Only a generation after '1945', in the 1970s and 1980s, did knowledge of the National Socialist past combine with moral horror at the fact that this past had been possible and was irreparable.

Only once did that Old German authoritarian state, with its unashamed propensity for stirring nationalist emotion, for snooping into people's political convictions, and for conducting witch-hunts against intellectuals, seem to resurrect itself. This was in 1977, a year of 'extreme events' in politics, the high point of a wave of left-wing terrorist actions[5] and the last surge of the mass movement against the construction of nuclear power stations. A number of large-scale demonstrations were literally fought down by police using quasimilitary means. If '1968' had been the symbol of a phase of liberalisation overloaded with utopian revolutionary ideas, '1977' became the negative symbol of a 'German autumn' which not only provoked justified worries in civil society about politically motivated terror, but also served as a reminder of the dangers that emanate from a ruling elite that is unnerved but, equally, has great power of interpretation and repression.

When, after 1977, following the blossoming of the 'citizens' initiative' movement, 'green' electoral associations began to be formed at local and state level, the protagonists of these groups regarded themselves as being motivated not only by ecological considerations of the natural 'limits to growth', by the fear of a 'silent spring' (Rachel Carson), and by the risks of nuclear energy, but also by their desire for a genuinely democratic kind of politics, open to participation and moral scrutiny. However, the greater willingness to take part in collective action which manifested itself in the extensive participation in civil action groups and mass demonstrations was not transmitted to the political parties. Whereas the social democrats had still managed, at the end of the 1960s, to recruit young people as members and supporters with their watchword of 'daring more democracy', the Greens developed, from 1979, from a very small base of members who were ready to undertake organising activities. These were representatives of the first 'green' lists, individual pioneers of the ecological critique of civilisation, disillusioned social democrats, and, last but not least, the remains of the groups and small-scale parties left over from the student movement, some of undogmatic 'socialist' bent, others of decidedly 'Marxist–Leninist' outlook.

With this mixture of policy-related motives for participation and 'anti-capitalist' standpoints (as is well known, the student movement was accompanied not only by the expansion of the education system, but also by the return, with considerable impact, of Marxist and 'critical' theories to the universities), the Greens became the first party to succeed in defining itself discursively and independently[6] in terms of a quest for social reform, of criticism of the repression of National Socialism, and of an anti-institutional understanding of politics and democracy. In so doing, they filled a gap in supply of a kind that was unknown in the political systems of other Western European states, namely the specific German lack of a socialist opposition, resulting from the division of the country, the Cold War, and the semi-official anti-communism. They found themselves pushed into this role, and were simultaneously the subject and object of an unexpected 'push effect': as interlocutors and representatives of social minorities,[7] as systematic advocates of the effective enforcement of equal rights for women, as champions of egalitarian principles and morally sound decisions.[8] It goes without saying that this brought pitfalls as well as opportunities. 'Structural' overstrain of the Greens was to some extent pre-programmed. The more pleasant consequences of the task of multiple representation will be discussed in the next section.

The fact that the Greens did not collapse under this strain but managed rather to establish themselves within the network of political actors in the Federal Republic might be described as an effect of various institutional 'pull-factors'. Thanks to comparative political research, these factors are well known, and mention of four special features of the Federal German political system will therefore suffice to give a rough picture of what, for many sceptical observers, was an unexpected chance of institutionalisation for the Greens.

(1) The first, and probably most important, condition of success is satisfied by German electoral law, under which all parties at the various levels of representation obtain parliamentary seats in proportion to the votes cast. Whether a member of Parliament has stood for election in a constituency and and won that constituency, or whether she owes her mandate (parliamentary seat) solely to her place on her party's list of candidates (the so-called *Landesliste*) is of no significance once the election is over. This means that even parties with only small reserves of voters have some chance of success, and the securing of absolute majorities by a single party are the exception rather than the rule in the multi-party system that results from these arrangements. Thus the various Parliaments are, in principle, open to any interest that shows itself capable of organisation and is able to win at least 5 per cent of the votes (this is the so-called *Sperrklausel* or 'barring clause'). In addition, because in certain circumstances majorities come about only when coalitions are formed between a number of parties, the 'small parties' also come in for consideration as potential participants in government.

(2) The '5 per cent clause' performs the function of preventing a fragmentation of the party system. It is supposed to ensure continuity and predictability. Not every viewpoint, not every minority interest is to be able to send its own representative (or handful of representatives) to Parliament. As far as the creation of the Greens is concerned (who incidentally support the abolition of the *Sperrklausel*), this rule was a strong incentive, perhaps the decisive incentive, to construct the party as an alliance of at least four variously oriented forces. In addition to green, the 'spectrum of green colour-theory' contains a hefty dash of 'red' (in the form of Marxist, Leninist, Maoist, Trotskyist, anarchist, and Spontaneist groups), as well as the somewhat weaker streak of 'lilac' of the feminist movement.[9] At any rate, had it not been for the institutional pressure to put aside the many differences that existed, the Greens would not have emerged in 1980, and not in this form. Neither could any single current have asserted itself alone.

(3) The party system in the Federal Republic owes its stability not only to the 'constitutional patriotism' (Jürgen Habermas) of its citizens, but also to systematic precautions taken by the political parties, who were keen to safeguard themselves against unwelcome competition.[10] The CDU/CSU and SPD, operating as 'catch-all parties', came to an agreement very early on with the much smaller, and therefore organisationally very weak Liberals (FDP) to 'unshackle' themselves from the fluctuating commitment of their members in regard to participation and financial support. They created a legally based system of party finance, the stoutest pillar of which is the so-

called *Wahlkampfkostenerstattung*, or refund of electoral campaign costs. According to this, all parties taking part in state or federal parliamentary election campaigns and receiving at least 0.5 per cent of the vote are awarded a certain sum of money for every vote,[11] although on the one hand this arrangement makes the older parties markedly less dependent on voluntary commitment, and thus less dependent on the political will of their members. It also constitutes a kind of spur to innovation, operating to the benefit of small-scale parties which cannot themselves finance repeated candidacies. Because, in accordance with democratic principles, the system of subsidy to parties begins to operate a long way below the 5 per cent hurdle, parties with shares of the vote between 1 and 5 per cent receive a reliable aid to organisation. This explains why twenty to thirty other parties, besides the four parties in the Bundestag, regularly woo the voters. And it also explains how an initially small party like the Greens, despite many handicaps and the absence of any donations by financially strong members (let alone industry), managed to build up a network of party offices and an electoral campaign organisation.

(4) Finally, the federative structure of the German political system provides comparatively favourable opportunities for new parties to develop. It is relatively easy to acquire initial experience and a public profile through participation in local elections (for seats in the city council) or in elections for the State Parliament. The State Parliaments and governments may be subject to federal decisions in many important areas, but because of their responsibility for education, for the promotion of the economy, for developmental and structural planning, and for monitoring local-authority operations, they offer many opportunities for 'new' political approaches to make their mark. Less striking are the effects of the principle of democratic proportional representation which is part of German federalism. According to this, representatives of all the parties present in Parliament are, in time, sent to take part in consultative and supervisory organs of the most varied kinds. In addition, members of Parliament receive invitations to discussions and educational events, by no means uninfluential, at academic institutions associated with the Church, the trade unions, or the universities. Thanks to the many opportunities for participation, even small parties can benefit from the multiplicatory effect of media coverage.

Summarising the combined effect of these four elements of relative openness in the political system, one can say that the 'political opportunity structure' is definitely favourable as far as a green party is concerned. As regards the chances of success for social movements, the responsiveness of established politics may appear slight, as Herbert Kitschelt[12] observes, but for newly arrived political actors the institutional obstacles are perfectly capable of being overcome. Indeed, as long as it is possible to mobilise increased potential support and secure re-election, self-assertion within the political system brings a series of 'feelings of achievement'. The new actor receives incentives to view his survival as an endorsement of his political programme and of his interpretation of reality, even though they contradict those of the other parties. In the case of the Greens, this meant not only that they were subject to the temptation to satisfy society's 'demand' for a resolutely left-wing party, but also that they found themselves being 'rewarded' with institutional recompenses and increasing opportunities for influence, the more they played this role. In addition to the various advantages flowing from a gradual adaptation to the set forms and routines of the political system (on this, see the detailed analysis by Claus Offe[13], there were also premiums for non-adaptation and for the demonstrative pursuit of 'otherness'.

III. The Greens as a Stimulus to Social Learning Processes

Society and politics in the 1980s were characterised not only by the revival of conservative and liberal forces but also by the rise of the Greens. In 1983 they succeeded in getting into the Bundestag and won seats in nine out of eleven regional parliaments.[14] Here and in countless municipal and district councils the agenda and style of political debates was transformed under the influence of the Greens. It sometimes seemed as if the journalists in the press and in broadcasting, and even individual civil servants in the various administrations, had just been waiting for the change initiated by the Greens. They seized on quite a few 'green' themes, provided the Greens with useful background information, and thus secured greater public attention for the Greens. The Greens did not function only as vehicles for environmental interests and the concerns of disadvantaged groups but also as monitors of the conduct of governments, mayors, and administrations. With great persistence they set about uncovering corruption, tacit partnerships between politicians and business, and instances where competencies had been exceeded. The influence of the Greens is thus scarcely measurable in terms of votes. Their very presence, their politics, and even their internal disputes have left unmistakable marks. Four points illustrate this.

(1) The general acceptance and 'normalisation' of the environmental issue, including the related problems of the link between the industrialised and developing countries, of agricultural policy, of energy policy, etc., are not, of course, due solely to the Greens. Nevertheless, their effect as a catalyst and reinforcer of this set of issues was and is enormous. By transporting the doubts, critical viewpoints, and anxieties of the social movements into the political system and securing a hearing for 'counter-experts', they ensured greater variety in the relevant information and arguments. Thus, although the nuclear industry's abandonment of three large-scale projects[15] during the second half of the 1980s is not attributable directly to the activity of the Greens, the fact that politicians regarded the continuation of these projects as too costly is due chiefly to the changes which the Greens brought about in the criteria for determining political legitimacy and economic reasonableness. A similarly unchartable strand of influence reaches into the environmental ministries at state and federal level. Because the SPD was forced, under competitive pressure from the Greens, to develop a comprehensive environmental programme, the ruling CDU/CSU also found itself unable to carry on with its purely symbolic policy. Measured against the situation in the 1970s, or the environmental policies of other countries, the 'material' effects brought about by the Greens appear considerable. Measured against the much more rapid growth in the problems themselves and in the need for action, they continue to be inadequate. Even in Germany, ecological factors are far from being regarded as the self-evident premisses for decisions relating to economic innovation and investment. Thus, although German environmental policy has attained a quite high level (as far as the strictness of standards for emission and licensing procedures are concerned), the majority of the population quite rightly

considers that environmental problems are the most urgent and least satisfactorily handled political issues.

(2) Somewhat less striking but no less important is the political 'change of style' fostered (again, not caused solely) by the Greens. Initially, the Greens had a tendency to champion their ideas of egalitarian political participation, of openness and transparency in the political debate, and of unmediated self-expression by concerned interests in a way that was not only provocative but also dogmatic and formalistic. Nevertheless, positive effects of this confrontation are visible in many areas of politics, and even within rival parties. Naturally, the established parties at first tried to deflect the barrage of 'radical' arguments against economic growth, against militarily based concepts of security, and against the multiplicity of social inequalities, and to classify green reasoning as naïve, one-sided, and failing to take consequences into account. They did not, however, succeed for very long with this approach. Whether because of the dialectic of communicative understanding or because of the career opportunities which up and coming 'non-green' politicians saw in a 'serious' approach to green issues. The forms as well as the themes of 'green' politics, and indeed something of the radical impetus of the early Greens, became part of political culture. At the same time, toleration of unusual or differing views has also increased in civilian society. A positive view of pluralism established itself, in which even the representatives of the 'fundamentalist' position enjoyed respect and achieved a certain prominence in the media. Mention should also be made of the successes brought about by the green-inspired 'feminisation' of politics, initially confined to the symbolic but now a yardstick for women's demands and women's presence in all political bodies (women are often more strongly represented than men in the official bodies of the Greens). The Greens' intensive experiments with 'grass-roots' forms of operation had a similar effect. It seems as if the predictability of the lower levels has gradually diminished in other parties as well, as if those at the top of the organisation can no longer rely so easily on the 'obedience' of their members, or ensure discipline simply via the allocation of official positions and career opportunities.

(3) One of the surprising, and perhaps paradoxical, effects brought about by the Greens is the reinforcement of left–right polarisation in inter-party rivalry. This has several causes. One is related to the 'political ecology' developed by the Greens. The ecological approach would be doomed to failure if there were not simultaneous and equally serious attempts to champion the material needs of the poorest members of society. An environmental policy that relied solely on change in individual behaviour appeared ineffective, whereas comprehensive intervention by the State in the economic process seemed indispensable. Given that environmental interventions are necessarily mainly restrictive in character, it was calculated that there would have to be trade-offs in terms of income and employment. The Greens therefore attached great importance to social guarantees for workers. They pledged to offset the material burdens occasioned by environmental policy.

In order to fulfil this promise, the Greens had to enter into competition with social democracy in the field of social policy, thus contributing further to the new left–right polarisation. Following its fall from government in 1982, the SPD was in the process of trying, by means of comprehensive employment and social programmes, to suppress recollection of the fact that it was not a conservative but a social democratic government—that of Helmut Schmidt—which had initiated the roll-back in social policy. Because the SPD was afraid it would lose voters to the Greens, it declared itself to be the only socially responsible party and castigated its new rival, the Greens, for focusing exclusively on the environment and for not paying any attention to the unemployed or to workers affected by crisis. The unjust accusation of hostility to the workers greatly affected the Greens, who saw themselves as both critical of capitalism and socially oriented. They responded with even more voluminous programmes of social action, which, like those of the Social Democrats, adhered to Keynesian logic. Because both business and a majority of the electorate were against the idea of higher taxes and higher public borrowing, the Greens soon fell into the same attractiveness and credibility trap as the SPD. An intense competition for precedence in determining opinion within the left-wing spectrum of voters widened the gulf with the government and hindered the updating of both the SPD's and the Greens' programmes.[16]

Finally, the internal competition between Green 'pragmatists' and the ethically motivated 'fundamentalists', may be seen as a fourth causative factor in the increased polarisation. The latter group, who lost their dominant position in the formation of the Greens' political goals and objectives only in 1989, did not just reject any form of continuous political co-operation between Greens and Social Democrats but attempted to depict the SPD as a party of 'right-wing' bent, which now differed only in minor traits from the ruling conservatives. Under fundamentalist dominance, the Greens narrowed down the ecological dispute to class conflict and assumed the role of 'linesman' in the party system. They disallowed any other lines of conflict, besides the crude left–right dimension, along which political alliances, particularly with the Social Democrats, might have been concluded.

(4) The most significant success produced by this competition between Greens and Social Democrats is undoubtedly the transformation in programme and 'style' undergone by the SPD. The one-time bastion of 'socio-technocratic' state-interventionism, as represented by ex-Chancellor Helmut Schmidt and the former Defence Minister Hans Apel, is scarcely recognisable any longer. As well as 'green' terminology, the SPD adopted various items from the Greens' programme of action in the areas of energy and environmental policy, global economic policy and policy on development, and even peace and (military) security policy. This was both the result of an unconscious 'learning response' to changes in the SPD's constituency, and the intentional effect of a competitive strategy initiated by Oskar Lafontaine. Lafontaine, who, with his unorthodox political proposals and enthusiasm for controversy, has contributed greatly to the revival of German politics (yet was defeated in the 1990 federal elections by Kohl, the 'chancellor of unity'), had from the outset regarded the Greens as a force to be reckoned with, and had overstrained them with his strategy of tactical embrace. Those sections of the SPD which drew their inspiration from Lafontaine (notably in the states of Saarland, Berlin, Schleswig-Holstein, Niedersachsen, Hessen, and Rheinland-Pfalz) adapted a part of the green range of ideas and surprised the Greens, whenever the electoral results seemed to permit this, by putting forward proposals for the formation of joint administrations. By so doing, they stoked up the internal dispute between the co-operation-minded Realos and the identity-obsessed Fundis, each of whom occupied diametrically opposed positions on the question of a 'red–green' coalition.

Whatever the result of the conflict, it redounded to the advantage of the SPD. If the fundamentalists won the day, this seemed to prove to the voters that the Greens were politically incapable, and the SPD could then regularly reap a substantial percentage of the 'green' vote for itself at the next election. If, on the other hand, the pragmatists amongst the Greens got their way, the SPD gained a coalition partner with which it shared a greater area of agreement than with the Free Democrats (FDP). It then had a good chance, working on the basis of joint successes, of building up a new, 'ecological' image, which would improve its prospects with younger voters. One problematic consequence of this double game, however, is that the SPD is transforming itself rather too quickly into a 'post-modern' party, i.e. the rate at which it is modernising its image is greater than that of the (post-) modernisation of attitudes amongst its constituency. In the working-class milieu, which is traditionally union-oriented and of industrial–conservative bent, 'Auntie SPD's' new style is frowned upon. One section of the constituency is migrating to the conservatives. The poor figure cut by the SPD in the five 'new' federal states is a sign of this dilemma. The modern SPD, which was sceptical in regard to German unity, which would like to see a change in the Federal Republic's 'tried and tested' constitution, and which for the most part condemned the Gulf War and regards the delegation of German soldiers to take part in UN operations as a prelude to the remilitarisation of German politics. This party is regarded by many classical SPD voters as a populist version of the Greens. The competition from the Greens, the 'Lafontaine' strategy of adopting green issues, and a number of very successful red–green coalitions in various states have helped the SPD achieve a new and, in the long term, promising image.[17] That what is involved here is not mere superficial retouching of the party image but irreversible changes is demonstrated by the fate of the right-wing Social Democrats. They have lost some of the key positions of influence in the parliamentary party, the national executive, and the cabinets of the state governments.

IV. The Greens' Dual Identity

A brief glance has already been cast, in the second point of the last section, at the history of the Greens' internal conflict. Because the background to this conflict, and the forms it has taken, are one of the most misunderstood aspects of the Greens, it deserves somewhat closer inspection. For this, we may turn to social-scientific analyses which deal with the Greens' fundamental conflict not (or not only) from the point of view of committed green activists,[18] but (also) from that of a critical observer concerned to understand the phenomenon. This is the approach that characterises the empirical studies conducted by Herbert Kitschelt[19] and Joachim Raschke[20] from which at least the first two of the following three points derive.

In contrast to what uncritical admirers of the Greens (e.g. Fritjof Capra and Charlene Spretnak)[21] suggest, there is almost no proof of the development of a common basic stance or central idea amongst the German Greens. This thesis naturally does not dispute the existence of diverse proposals for a unified green philosophy; it simply records the differences, indeed the rivalry, between these. The great susceptibility of the Greens to ideological conflict is to be explained by the peculiar nature of issues in the 'new politics'.[22] There is no central 'cleavage' along the lines of the 'labour versus capital' split. Instead there is a multiplicity of conflictual aspects touching on almost all social spheres, from production, through upbringing and education, state and law, science and technology, to patterns of consumption and individual lifestyles. Dichotomies between 'true and false', 'good and evil', 'us and them', are of little use. What is required is well-considered decisions that take account of reciprocal relations and learning-processes.[23] The unclear and fluctuating conflictual structure manifests itself in problems of orientation; after all, a party can secure its existence only if it can rely on the stable involvement of its members, and those members, in their turn, are most easily recruited where there are a number of fundamental shared convictions. Given that the Greens' orientation problem springs from a 'simultaneous radicalisation of problems and deradicalisation of the means available for solving these',[24] radicalisation of thought and desire is one way of still being able to stabilise group-identity and involvement.

This is one reason, probably the main reason, why catastrophic scenarios, apocalytpic forecasts, and an impassioned critique of civilisation and capitalism were such marked features of the 'philosophy' of the early Greens. Radicalness in diagnoses and therapies promised to offset the lack of a fully-developed theory, a lack of which those concerned had been painfully aware of since the crisis of Marxism. Also, reference to a radicalised concept of politics provided a means of containing the difficulties occasioned by the model of identity prevalent in the new social movements. That model is subjective, particularist, and marked by a strong preference for autonomy which runs counter to the requirements of any kind of formal organisation. There was another reason why ecological fundamentalism became the most influential current of opinion during the Greens' initial phase. The income from official party funding did not suffice to establish local party-offices with paid officials in every locality. Quite apart from the fact that paying party workers an appropriate wage would have violated grass-roots principles, it was vital to recruit committed members for voluntary, unpaid work. As Herbert Kitschelt[25] shows, only those members who derived some 'private benefit', the corroboration of their own philosophical standpoint by others, or involvement in important organisational decisions, would undertake poorly paid, or even unpaid, work for the party.[26]

Of course, the fundamentalists did not have a monopoly on the organisation. They had to share power with adherents of a basically moderate view of politics, who, because they had participated in the foundation of the party and because conditions of entry to the party were 'lax', could not be refused membership. However, because the fundamentalists were the ones who continually devoted themselves to the development of the organisation and, until very recently, held the majority in party congresses, they had a monopoly on the intellectual interpretation of the party's image. It was thanks to this monopoly that there occurred what for outsiders was an astonishing reversion to the traditions of the early workers' movement, to its rhetoric and its schemes of institutional reform (expropriation and socialisation of the means of production, establishment of a system of councils in addition to Parliament, integration and equalisation of systems of social security). At the same time, issues concerning the organisational 'form' of politics were declared to be key political issues, on the one hand via the establishment and impassioned defence of grass-roots principles (the problems associated with this will be discussed in the next section), and on the other hand by a fetishisation of the role of the parliamentary opposition. True to the principle that political practice consists primarily in the manifestation of identities and intentions, Parliament was to be used only as a 'stage', not as a means of participating in the elaboration of political decisions, let alone the formation of governmental coalitions.

Strictly speaking, the ideological predominance of fundamentalism was broken not so much by 'better' arguments from the pragmatists, but by side-effects of the growth in the green constituency. Lobbysism and parliamentarism contributed greatly to the change in image and in the processes whereby demands and objectives were formulated. I shall deal first with the function of green 'lobbyists', who come in two versions. The first are advocates of the kinds of specific collective interests which figure in the list of issues of 'new politics', for example, representatives of citizens' initiatives, of environmental or conservation groups, of women's refuges. The second group consists of lobbyists who represent not only collective interests but also legitimate individual interests, namely those involved in self-managed businesses or projects (production companies, bookshops, alternative newspapers, cultural centres, music and theatre groups). The 'lobby faction' regularly succeeded in persuading the fundamentalists to support particularised, more realistic and more short-term political objectives. In return, they gave their backing to the fundamentalists when it was a question of occupying positions of influence or of defending 'radical' formulas of identity against the pragmatists' practical view of politics.

However, because the 'lobbyists' now and again, e.g. before important election dates, allied themselves with the 'pragmatists', they were able to hold fundamentalism in check and to stop the pragmatists leaving the Greens. Although the champions of ecological and social special interests began by being scarcely less radical than the convinced fundamentalists, as they experienced the (individual and collective) benefits of parliamentarism, their view of politics came closer to that of the pragmatists. As experts or 'specialist politicians', they enjoyed a certain amount of attention in the media and were respected even by officials of other parties. A fact which had a beneficial effect on the interests which they represented. It gradually became obvious how much social influence the Greens were throwing away when they did not, like the other parties, steer their followers towards vacant posts in civil and public service (e.g. as mayors, public administrators, judges, or school heads). As the political weight of the 'lobby politicians' in the Greens increased, so too did their dissatisfaction with the fundamentalists' anachronistic approach to conflict, which threatened to squander the hard-won influence that had been gained within the political system. It was only in 1988 that they determined to organise a third green current, under the name 'Aufbruch' or 'New Beginning'.[27]

Given the triply fragmented way in which the Greens' experience was shaped, it is no surprise that their image continues to be a disunited one. The tendency to identify adversaries solely as a means of reinforcing the party's own identity, and to evoke an inexorable apocalypse has, it is true, been curbed. Nevertheless the makeshift solution of borrowing various elements from the labour movement (expropriation, council systems) is still current practice. The 'anti-capitalist' impetus is also kept alive through ideological 'rivalry' with certain sections of the unions and of social democracy which see themselves as (eco)socialist. For a long time, this meant that radical but politically ineffective criticism was regarded as an alternative to practicable environmental intervention (e.g. in the spheres of energy, waste, and transport policy).

The internal party scepticism in regard to a policy of reform that is necessarily incrementalist but is rejected by the other parties as 'going too far' has now given way to a positive attitude. The Greens too have learned to appreciate the 'effects' of their parliamentarians and ministers. However, the competition to appear as 'left wing' as possible, from which even the pragmatists could not escape, has prevented the elaboration of all those proposals which aim at a loosening of society's dependence on economic development and thus damage the vested interests of workers as well.[28] Again, the idea that at the end of the twentieth century capitalism should more appositely be thought of as a kind of drug-dependency of the whole of society, and no longer as a kind of fist-fight involving only capital and labour, was one that did not occur to the majority of Green politicians.

V. Organisational Democracy as a Test of Self

As is well known, the Greens' approach to politics has a formal as well as a material (or policy-oriented) side. There has been an attempt, through the choice of organisational structures and procedural rules, to take account of the fact that attitudes and preferences do not simply flow into the party from outside but are also shaped by the party itself, indeed are in some cases self-generated. What the party wants and how it acts is dependent to an important degree on how it is organised. In order to guarantee the effective operation of members' interests, which in bureaucratic organisations and hierarchical decision-making structures are often at a disadvantage, the Greens expressly pledged themselves to the principles of 'grass-roots democracy'. These principles are familiar from the anarchist and syndicalist traditions of the labour movement. The Greens established the principle of the rotation of official posts, which allows for short periods of office (from one to two years)[29] and excludes re-election of office-holders. They prohibited the simultaneous holding of a number of offices, particularly the combination of a party office and a parliamentary mandate (the 'incompatibility rule'). They experimented with the imperative mandate, which binds delegates to the resolutions of the body that has delegated them. And they tried (prompted also by a lack of money) to fulfil most organisational tasks using voluntary, honorary, and unpaid workers rather than a paid staff.[30] Not much importance was attached to the decisions of executive committees and elected functionaries. What was expected of the latter was not so much political initiative and organisational capacity but a readiness to ensure that the resolutions taken by members' and delegates' conferences were put into practice.

The effects of green grass-roots democracy were, to put it cautiously, highly ambivalent. Above all, one has to distinguish between the effects which it had outside the Greens and those which it had inside, for the Greens themselves. The 'external' effects of the green experiment in democracy can be adjudged to have been unreservedly positive, and may be said to continue to be felt to this day. The fact that organisations could not only function but also be politically effective without permanent functionaries, provided members occupied a 'strong' position and there was a high degree of transparency in all (formal) procedures, came as a positive surprise. There was a 'radiating power', which affected many other organisations (e.g. tenants' and consumers' associations), setting them under pressure to democratise. One has to bear this in mind when one assesses the internal effects, which appear much less favourable.

Grass-roots principles are typically justified with arguments such as those developed by the party sociologist Robert Michels[31] in explaining the emergence of an 'iron law of oligarchy'. Division of labour, power hierarchies, and expert knowledge alienate elected leaders from their constituency, so that the latter's will is either ignored or, indeed, changed into its opposite. It was principally the fundamentalists amongst the Greens who wished to preclude this kind of scenario of detachment, in which those who represent members' interests are wont to change into charismatic leaders who end up managing to impose their own personal will on the membership. In fact, however, the situation of the Greens, as Herbert Kitschelt's precise analysis shows,[32] cannot be likened to the relationship between members and leaders in the Social Democratic Party of the Kaiserreich. Members of the Green Party have access to sufficient information and resources to be able to ensure that their interests are enforced. The party does not have an organisational monopoly, with no alternative available. Its members are not prevented by any subjective or institutional factors from themselves seeking higher-ranking offices within it. Quite the contrary, provided they act jointly and not purely individually, members who are at all informed or articulate have a relatively good chance of helping to determine the course of the party by means of 'voice' and (the threat of) 'exit'.

The problems posed by the relationship between members and party are quite different ones in the case of the Greens. Because the overwhelming majority of the members come from the new middle classes, the Greens are presented with some very varied subjective motives for participation. The members do have some normative attitudes in common, but their commitment is based not on any binding ethic but on a desire for self-fulfilment and on high expectations as to the direct benefit of political action. The preconditions for stable group-solidarity are thus scarcely satisfied. If party life makes great demands on members (e.g. by having meetings dominated by ideological controversies and an excess of formal issues), the commitment of the 'average' member quickly dissipates. This discontinuous pattern of participation, punctuated by 'shifting involvements,[33] became a typical feature of the Greens. Problems developed which were not healed but aggravated by grass-roots principles.

The formal application of the principle of rotation, of the incompatibility rule, and of various other forms of 'grass-roots monitoring' of elected party representatives produced the same sort of tendencies to alienation and detachment as are claimed for a rigid ruling hierarchy. Instead of a lively organisational democracy, what often developed was a 'culture of distrust'.[34] The most serious effects were those brought about by rotation and the incompatibility rule. They prevented the accumulation of experience and the building-up of stable informational and communication links with other actors inside and outside the party. The tight chronological and functional restriction on the mandates ran counter to the interdependent nature of the problems with which green politics is concerned. Because party functionaries and members of Parliament were not allowed to stand for office again, they lost an important incentive to communicate with the grass roots, they 'became detached' and concerned themselves only with that which they personally considered to be important. Accountability and willingness to assume responsibility dwindled. Because there was a strict ban on plurality even of party offices (e.g. a member of the regional executive committee could not also be treasurer of the local party organisation), an important channel of communication between the different levels of the organisation was lost.

Two fatal consequences in particular are to be regretted. In the first place, a disproportion developed between the large number of posts that had to be filled and the meagre stock of members that were sufficiently qualified and motivated to fill them. As a result, individuals had to be called on who appeared unsuitable. The only rudiments of competition to be observed, if there was any competition at all, emerged when candidates had to be selected for parliamentary seats. In the second place, the party soon became fragmented into a multiplicity of different spheres of action, in which actors operated in parallel or against each other, instead of co-operating. At local, state, and federal levels the bodies in which posts had to be filled included not only executive committees and delegates' conferences, but also supervisory forums (finance and steering committees) and twenty to thirty specialist working-parties. Because delegates and grass-roots representatives are only willing to commit themselves on a discontinuous basis, the various conferences have a greatly fluctuating make-up, with a high proportion of first-timers and last-timers. In 1990, the executive committee chairperson Ruth Hammerbacher complained in her farewell speech that the basic principle which the Greens had established, namely the 'principle of division' rather than that of meaningful connection, was a false one, indeed that they had made the 'lopping-off of connections into a systematic practice'.[35] She identified a structure of 'fragmented, compartmentalised "stratarchies"'.

Grass-roots democracy became an arena chiefly for two groups of actors. On the one hand, there were those who regarded the formal principles of grass-roots democracy as having great value in themselves, these were the (mainly younger) fundamentalists. Their concern to pledge the party to strict definitions of identity coincided with the opportunities made available to them for gaining self-knowledge and self-fulfilment in public roles and in exciting party conferences. On the other hand, informal networks began to form within the different wings, the members of which prepared the formal decisions through covert arrangements and took it in turns to occupy the most influential posts. The latter happened in full accord with the rotation principle, since this only prohibited standing again for the last-held post, but not for a different one. These two groups determined the shape of the party's work in many areas, and they furnish most of the delegates who are present on a continuous basis. A certain mismatch already exists between the motives for participation in a strongly reform minded party and the complexity of the problems and tasks which are to be considered. Also the difficulties associated with the design of the organisation are multiplied if the party is seen as a means of attaining direct satisfaction of 'aesthetic organisational' interests, in addition to comprehensive social reforms. The directness and ease of evaluation of organisation-related objectives gives such objectives almost automatic precedence over the complex, long-term social goals. Bureaucratic rule is not the only regime able to pervert the claim to a viable and worthwhile society. Grass-roots democracy can also do this.

If the well-considered balancing of different democratic principles (such as representation, participation, pluralism, and accountability) is abandoned in favour of one single principle, this may satisfy participatory desires but it also frustrates participatory motives. The motives of those who wish to participate not so much for reasons of self-fulfilment but more in the interests of long-term collective goals remain unrealised. The predominance of the one democratic principle destroys the others' chances of being realised. When one looks at the situation from this point of view, the fundamental problem of the Greens become clear. 'They are unable to combine legitimacy and efficiency.'[36] What they regard as legitimate, namely laxer rules of membership and a high degree of fluctuation, institutionalised distrust and intense self-reflection is inefficient as far as intervention in society is concerned. The things that would be efficient, the fostering of creativity, the ability to communicate and co-operate, the delegation of responsibility for a fixed term, the acknowledgement and corroboration of successful work, are considered illegitimate. When the Greens failed to secure entry into the first all-German Parliament in December 1990, they were not just paying the penalty with the voters for having shown themselves indecisive and petty-minded *vis-à-vis* the historic opportunity offered by unification. Their predicament was also a consequence of their irritating 'performance', a result of the distrust fomented by Greens against other Greens.

VI. Where do the Greens Stand Today?

The failure in the federal elections of 1990 profoundly shocked the Greens. All wings of the party, apart from the fundamentalist 'radical ecologists' around Jutta Ditfurth, reacted with impassioned self-criticism. In spring 1991 the organisation's constitution was reformed by a national delegates' conference. Compulsory rotation was abolished, the incompatibility rule was toned down,[37] conditions of pay for executive committee members were changed, a procedure for postal ballots was introduced, and the filling of posts on the national steering committee was assigned to the regional executives. These organisational modifications are being applied to a party which, under the pressure of considerable changes in its milieu, is beginning to project a different ideological image.[38] These changes are: (1) The erosion of green fundamentalism; (2) The consequences of the break-up of the GDR.

THE EROSION OF GREEN FUNDAMENTALISM

Fundamentalism started to lose support when the option of red–green coalitions began to appear a viable one in more and more states. This in its turn was due more to the growing dissatisfaction of the voters with conservative–liberal coalitions than to any attractive proposals of reform put forward by the SPD and Greens. A certain weariness with the same old fundamentalist plea for a critical attitude to the system and for abstinence from politics, a fall in the number of votes won in the fundamentalist strongholds, and the seemingly attractive opportunitites offered by participation in government meant that even in erstwhile 'radical' regional executive committees majorities emerged in favour of political co-operation and policies of reform.

The readiness of the West Berlin Greens (AL) to form a municipal administration with the SPD in 1989 gave the impression of a real breakthrough to a productive conception of politics.[39] It was the second instance of a red–green administration, the first being the red–green coalition in Hessen, renewed in 1990. The pattern was followed shortly afterwards by the Greens in Niedersachsen. The traditional alliance between fundamentalists and 'left-wingers' in the regional executives of Nordrhein-Westfalen, Schleswig-Holstein and Hamburg began to collapse. As late as 1990, the 'eco-socialists' around Rainer Trampert and Thomas Ebermann left the Greens; in spring 1991 the 'radical ecologists' around Jutta Ditfurth announced their departure.[40] The rump consisted of moderate 'left-wingers', now transformed into critics of the fundamentalism which they had previously supported. There is now a ubiquitous willingness amongst them to team up with the pragmatists, their erstwhile pet enemies, a factor which strengthens the party's capacity for integration and action in most states. Since spring 1991, the national executive committee itself has been made up of a majority of pragmatic 'left-wingers', and these are striving to establish a relationship of co-operation with prominent pragmatists of ministerial status (in particular Joschka Fischer, the Green Environment Minister in Hessen).

Any appraisal of this change of image will necessarily register a 'narrowing-down' of the spectrum of green positions. On the one hand, the Greens have seen the departure not only of the spokespersons of fundamentalism but also of prominent pragmatists (such as Thea Bock and Otto Schily, who are now SPD MPs in the Bundestag). On the other hand, the internal conclusion of peace between pragmatists and left-wingers has meant that the middle-of-the-road current operating under the label 'New Beginning' now feels itself pushed to the periphery. Since it began in 1988, the 'New Beginning' itself has changed character. Originally intended as a melting-pot for specialised (lobby) interests and as a mediator between the mutually hostile Realo and Fundi camps, it is now the sole group in which any reflection occurs about the central ideas and fundamental issues relating to the green concept of politics, an activity that occurs in opposition both to the simplistic left–right thinking of the 'left-wingers' and to the pragmatism of the Real-politiker.

THE COLLAPSE OF THE GDR

The collapse of the socialist states of Eastern Europe, the flow of refugees from the GDR, the end of the SED regime, and, finally, the unification of the two German states constituted another shock for which the Greens were unprepared. Their political activity was geared to overcoming confrontation between the blocs and achieving equality of rights and understanding between them. It did not aim for the 'triumph of the West'. They had always advocated acceptance of the dual statehood of Germany and the extension of co-operative relations between the GDR and FRG. The Greens were far from being supporters of state socialism, and, through their long years of support for civil rights activists in the USSR, Czechoslovakia, Poland, and the GDR, they had helped reinforce the movement for democracy. At the same time, however, they appreciated real socialism as a counterweight to the power pretensions of the Western alliance and also as a symbol of the 'counter-system'. There was always the idea that at least the experiences that had been gathered under socialism could be used as material for a fundamental restructuring of capitalism. Even Gorbachev's 'Perestroika' evoked ambivalent feelings, because it was unclear whether its aim was to improve or to abolish Soviet communism. The actual end of the socialist system initially left the Greens utterly speechless.[41]

Understandably, the West German Greens felt affinities primarily with the left-wing and ecological sections of the civil rights movements in the GDR. They supported both their attempts to organise themselves as well as the goal of converting the GDR into what would be a second democratic but the first 'social-ecological' (because non-capitalist) German state. The explosive growth in the East German population's desire for arrangements to be made as quickly as possible for them to live in the same state and enjoy the same living-conditions as the West Germans astonished the whole left-wing movement in West Germany, including the Social Democrats. East German civil rights movements, East and West German Greens, and the majority of Social Democrats opposed the course to unification which the government and Chancellor Helmut Kohl succeeded in pushing through in the face of the erstwhile allies and, in particular, the USSR. However, the standpoint of the German left, which was somewhat romantic and sidestepped the real needs, was not well received by the voters in West or East Germany. Because the East German Greens and social movements also gave in to the temptation to indulge in profuse self-reflection, they have as yet been unable to solve the problem of their fragmentation into a handful of parallel, small-scale organisations. They managed to overthrow a state, but their influence on the subsequent process of unification and on current developments in the new Germany has been minimal. There is, quite rightly, talk of the decline of the West German left.[42] Even if one adds the votes of the post-communist PDS to the votes of the SPD, Greens, and citizens' movements, the 'strength' of the left at the national level now amounts to only 41 per cent of total votes. The German parties of the left are currently stuck in the minority ghetto.

This means that there is for the present no prospect of the Greens and Social Democrats ousting the Kohl Government and bringing a 'social and ecological turnaround' to the Federal Republic. The 'narrowing' of the Green spectrum, the loss of seats in the Bundestag[43] and a jading of the willingness to enter into grand debates about future schemes make the Greens currently appear weaker than they really are. All observers do believe however, that the Greens will 'survive', even if they do not reappear that quickly in the seat of government. The voters have long since come to regard them as an indispensable part of local and regional politics. At the level of the national party, where the great issues of world-view and strategy were debated, the Greens have caused as much disappointment as they have attracted attention. All in all, therefore, their absence from national politics need not be adjudged negative. One feature that is problematic, however, is the lack of incentives in the present situation for overcoming weakness of ideas and for developing an autonomous left–ecological strategy of reform, independent of the distributive interests of the Social Democrats and trade unions. Confining oneself to ecological reforms which at best impinge only on the purses of big earners no longer seems appropriate, given the state of the problem and the wealth of Western industrial societies. However, any other, more thoroughgoing reforms presuppose a transformation of priorities and institutions, and these, in their turn, can be brought about only by well-founded arguments, attractive partial goals, and judicious strategies based on a well-developed awareness of one's opponents. Only in the wake of institutional change can desires for more thoroughgoing changes develop. The first phase of this endogenous moulding of political preferences was inaugurated by the Greens during the 1980s. Will they also be able to give the signal for a second new beginning?

VII. Two analytical conclusions

The green experiment contains a wealth of valuable experience. This seems as yet scarcely to have been tapped, let alone put to use by the Green party in shaping itself. Instead of providing a summary, I should like to close this chapter by outlining two perspectives on key problems of the Greens. These relate to the particular problems associated with rational operation in ambient conditions which, from the one perspective may be viewed as systemic links, i.e. a web of non-linear causalities, and from the other as an interdependence between strategic actors.

(1) The prolific attempts of the social movements (and the early Greens) to awaken a sense of 'involvement' amongst people and to move them to take part in collective protest actions or to become members of the party through exaggerated diagnoses of problems, catastrophic scenarios, and a radicalised conception of the enemy, were by no means unsuccessful. Fundamentalist arguments appear neither illogical nor ineffective. Yet they have no effect on the causal structure of the problems which are the object of their disapproval. There is no channel of influence leading from intensely felt involvement and moral rigorism to causal therapies in the form of institutional changes aimed at bringing about certain effects. Every material or institutional change (of laws, of the premises on which legal decisions are based, or of collective interpretations of how things hang together) seems to be indebted to at least one additional factor, namely knowledge of the existence of alternatives that can be implemented with a reasonable amount of effort. Moral reasoning may strive to raise the threshold of reasonableness, but success is dependent on realisable alternatives. Alternatives that are inadequate or lacking in credibility do not appear to be increased in value by being linked to an appeal for greater individual sacrifice. The fact that the moral fundamentalism of radical ecology, or of 'deep ecology', is geared to the generation only of the need for action but not of alternatives for action, is what makes it politically weak. Viewed thus, fundamentalism is parasitic, because it remains dependent on the readiness of those with 'other' motives to engage in pragmatic action.

What we have here is probably a problem located in the overlap between individual psychology and cognitive science, one that we regularly observe when emotional affectedness *vis-à-vis* 'global' problems is accompanied by a resolute rejection of the decision-making calculus relating to 'local' political alternatives. Even where this state of affairs is occasionally acknowledged by the relevant actors to be a problem, the latter see this not as a compelling reason to analyse their situation as regards social (or political) action but rather as an invitation to expound their emotions. One explanation for this is that the emotional actor has an intense need to indulge in cognitive simplification and therefore comes to the conclusion that problems regarded as 'big' can only be tackled with 'big' solutions. However, since 'big' solutions themselves again present one with 'big' problems, the emotional actor becomes the victim of circular thinking. Matching up 'big' problems with what are the only available solutions, namely 'little' ones, is, in contrast, a task that requires not emotionality, but a readiness to tolerate ambiguity. Given the inherent uncertainty, the notion of a chain of 'small' steps precludes any allusion to success. Only such a notion can open one's eyes to the conditions that permit a type of action that is geared to effect and is, to this extent, causally adequate.

The inability to tolerate ambiguities that are real and rooted in the operational context has considerably hindered the Greens in their attempt to develop their potential for influencing society. This was demonstrated in the quasi-confessional formulas used to comment on peace policy (e.g. 'Out of NATO!'), on women's policy (which was always modelled on the lifestyle of the 'most radical' feminists of the day), on German unity (which was declared to be the resurrection of the German Reich), or on the Gulf War (which was regarded as an example of the material colonialism of the West, not as a response to the Iraqi occupation and not as having anything to do with Israel's interest in survival). Abstracting equally well-founded interests, which clearly appear to bear some relation to the one interest that is championed, may relieve one of the effort of having to weigh up all the factors and to present a discriminating case, but it leads to an arbitrary simplification of the true complexity of the world. This in its turn brings about a reduction in potential support, because it expressly excludes—or indeed declares as enemies—those who hold a more differentiated view of the world yet agree on many concrete proposals for action.[44] It is a well-attested sociological finding that voluntary organisations are wont to ensure their cohesiveness by means of emotionally satisfying collective interpretations which regularly prove to be insufficiently complex and of little instructive value when it comes to selecting strategies of action. Sociologists can be content with the elucidatory value of this finding, but actors who wish to influence society in a purposeful and responsible manner face a hard task. They must be constantly guarding against the temptations and consequences of simplification.

(2) A look back at the 'fundamentalist' phase of green politics seems to prove the case for developing an awareness of ambiguity, for a 'culture of the scale-pan', and for tolerance of multiple rationalities. Indeed, for some time now a number of Greens of academic bent, most of whom consider themselves as belonging to the 'New Beginning' group or to the smaller, pragmatist section, have been expressing great disquiet at the Greens' crudely simplified perspective on problems, and at their rigid 'zero-sum game' understanding of political conflicts. These critics of ecological and political fundamentalism (with whom the author sympathises) cannot acquiesce in a situation where political strategy, whose targets are complex systemic reciprocal relations (e.g. between science, the economy, and culture), is still based on patterns of thought deriving from Newtonian mechanics (i.e. notions of linear causality), on a mechanistic model of social interaction, and an antagonistic conception of conflict. They point to findings in system-theory and evolutionary theory[45] and draw attention to the 'social construction of reality' through interpretive action that has no firm anchor in absolute truths or exogenous preferences.

Resisting the temptation of biologistic 'naturalism', which seeks to explain politics and society on the pattern of non-cognitive organic processes,[46] these critics, aware of the complexity of reality, tend to call for attention to be focused on the procedures and rules of 'sensible' politics. This deferment of issues follows on from a fruitful renaissance of 'institutional' approaches in political theory,[47] and shifts attention towards issues raised in present-day theory of democracy and towards the debate about the preconditions for the development of 'civil society'. Its significance for political actors lies in the way in which procedural norms influence the quality of the outcomes of political decision-making. It is obvious that a more complex knowledge of context and a higher level of reflection within politics would also make possible 'more' consideration of consequences, as well as more accurate strategies. The only 'residual' problem would appear to be the emotional and expressive needs of the members of the organisation, which up to now have been satisfied by crudely simplified world-views and 'gratificatory' organisational routines (e.g. party conferences). These, it is suggested, would have to be 'diverted' into a new democratic organisational culture, such as would appear to be achievable by replacing 'in person' democracy with plebiscitary procedures for participation (e.g. postal ballots).

However attractive such ideas may appear at first glance, they do not offer a way out of the dilemma faced by a party of reform in resolving the issues of participation and the determination of objectives. It only seems as if the substantial fundamentalism that is based on the need to express identity could profitably be exchanged for a procedural fundamentalism which attempts to follow the ethics of communicative understanding as formulated by Jürgen Habermas.[48] A party of reform that wishes to act as the agent of new issues and as the promoter of comprehensive democratisation cannot confine itself to reflexive decision-making and ethical deliberations. Even to win support for such an approach it would need to take strategic decisions in which the strategic options and probable moves of other actors were taken into account.

On the realistic assumption that actors have non-identical preferences and do not share the same world-view (this is not to say which of them must be regarded as 'right' and which 'wrong'), politics will always be a game of strategy, in which 'true' intentions should not be laid bare without consideration of the consequences. In other words, duplicating social complexity in the discourses of the collective actor threatens to make that actor incapable of joining in the strategic game with other actors. The successes, and they are urgently needed, of ecological and social politics will be successes brought about by judicious politics, or they will not be brought about at all. Green politics cannot afford to confine itself to the joys of communicative aesthetics. When some part of the basis of life disappears every day, when lives begin and end without hope, before a single trace of happiness has been experienced, ecological politics cannot display the kind of patience suited to a philosophy seminar. Equally, it must not become addicted to the pleasures of emotion.

The correct response to emotional reductionism is therefore not to be found solely in an increased awareness of complexity and in ethical reflection. It can only come as a result of weighing up defensible against indefensible simplifications, co-operative against antagonistic urges, mobilising against paralysing 'truths', in other words, weighing up 'good' against 'bad' politics. Because the name of that response is 'politics', it has no transcendental premisses. It need wait on nothing and no one.

Notes

1. Although Petra Kelly was one of the three chairpersons of the Greens from 1980 to 1982, and was a member of the Bundestag from 1983 to 1990, she took no part in the impassioned factional disputes and debates about strategy which took place in this period. The few (oral) comments which she did make on the development of the organisation had little influence. The same is true of her suggestion—which aroused a lot of interest

outside the Greens—that the Greens should be thought of as an 'anti-party party', the object of which was by no means simply to 'freshen up' the other parties by introducing Green ideas to them (Kelly 1983: 21).

In contrast, Rudolf Bahro, who was a member of the national executive committee from 1982 to 1984, strove to give the Greens the image of a radical force that was critical of civilisation and which, although it determined the topics of public debate, resisted the temptation to participate in political decision-making and the exercise of power. Bahro left the party in 1985, following the party conference's rejection of his proposal of an unconditional ban on animal experiments. In his most recent published work, where he advocates a spiritualistic avant-garde concept of the radical reform of civilisation, the Greens figure merely as 'factotums' of the industrial system (cf. Bahro 1987).

2. On this, see Müller-Rommel and Pridham 1989; Dalton and Kuechler 1990; and Kitschelt 1989.

3. This was comprehensible both to the extent that the assessments of the situation which prevailed at the time—and which were reinforced by the Cold War—saw grave threats emanating from the Soviet sphere of power (one should not forget the Korean War and the blockade of Berlin), and to the extent that the Iron Curtain put up by the hostile power-blocs ran right through the middle of Germany until autumn 1989. Both post-war German states—the FRG and GDR—regarded themselves (though not always explicitly) as 'front-line' states, in the strict sense of the term.

4. The first two factors cited are directly attributable to the participation of the Social Democrats in government, whereas the third factor, namely the student movement, was expressly targeted against the limits to development and notions of order implied in the social democratic model of society.

5. The president of the German employers' federation, Hans-Martin Schleyer, was kidnapped and murdered by terrorist commandos of the Red Army Faction (RAF).

The passengers travelling in an aircraft hijacked by RAF supporters and made to fly to Mogadishu were freed by force. Immediately after this, three prominent members of the RAF (Baader, Ensslin, and Raspe) died in mysterious circumstances in prison in Stuttgart-Stammheim. These events, and the circumstances surrounding the death of the prisoners, came to be regarded by a small circle of young militant *Autonomer* (non-conformists) as mystical high-points in the struggle against 'the State'. The German Left, on the other hand, saw them as marking the end of the romantic notion of revolution.

6. i.e. not like the still-marginal DKP, which was duty-bound to criticise German capitalism and the national–socialist past on account of its 'unswerving loyalty' to the USSR.

7. In line with their inclusive concept of representation, the Greens give particular support to the rights of children, young people, and the elderly. Their commitment, as expressed in parliamentary initiatives (parliamentary questions, draft legislation), has been concerned with the social situation of the jobless, of recipients of welfare, of migrant workers, of asylum-seekers, of refugees, and of ethnic and sexual minorities. For example, the Green parliamentary group in the Bundestag took up the case of the Roma and Sinti peoples, who are still being refused compensation for the injustice perpetrated against them by the Nazis in the concentration camps.

8. One of the earliest appraisals of their work in the Bundestag bears the title *Ankläger im Hohen Haus* ('pointing the finger in the house') (Cornelsen 1986).

9. Raschke 1991.

10. And were successful in doing this until the appearance of the Greens. Hence the various extreme right-wing and crypto-Fascist parties have not yet succeeded in getting elected to the Bundestag. All they have managed to do is get elected—temporarily—to one or two regional Parliaments. The pro-Soviet left (DKP) has also until recently been present in only a very small number of local councils (and will have to quit these positions, now

that its followers have been surprised by the collapse of real socialism).

11. Parties currently pay themselves DM3.50 per vote. This so-called 'refund of electoral costs' makes up more than half of the total income of all parties.
12. Kitschelt 1989.
13. Offe 1990.
14. The Greens are not represented in the Parliaments of either Saarland or Schleswig-Holstein. These two cases display interesting parallels. Before the election, the fundamentalist-dominated regional executives rejected the offer of co-operation put to them (for thoroughly tactical reasons) by the SPD. The regional SPD groups, led by younger 'carriers of hope' (as Oskar Lafontaine called Björn Engholm), won absolute majorities. As far as the state Parliaments elected in October 1990 in what was formerly the GDR are concerned, the Greens are represented by their own members of Parliament in Sachsen, Sachsen-Anhalt, and Thüringen. In the state of Brandenburg, where no alliance was formed between the Greens and the democratic citizens' movements, only the latter are represented in the Parliament. In Mecklenburg-Vorpommern both the Greens and the citizens movements, having fought the election separately, failed to clear the 5 per cent hurdle.
15. These were the fast-breeder reactor in Kalkar, the high-temperature reactor in Hamm, and the reprocessing plant in Wackersdorff.
16. Cf. the excellent account of the decline of the party-political left in Germany recently produced by Padgett and Patterson 1991.
17. This development has also been reflected in political science, where the concept of 'catch-all' parties that has prevailed up to now has been revised: *Volksparteien* now no longer appear as slothful and hostile to innovation but as compelled, at the risk of going under, to show sensitivity to changes in society (cf. Czada and Lehmbruch 1990; Wolinetz 1991). They only survive if they react flexibly to social change and ensure that new social interests are carried over into the political system.

18. The reader will have noted that the author is inclined to see himself as belonging to the group of the committed activists, although he likes to adopt the position of a neutral and detached observer—ultimately returning to the battlefield with the insights and arguments he has gained. The observations that follow do not claim anything more than this kind of 'tactical' objectivity.
19. Kitschelt 1989.
20. Raschke 1991.
21. Capra and Spretnak 1984.
22. Hildebrandt and Dalton 1978.
23. It is no coincidence that normative theories of ecological politics readily borrow from concepts relating to biological systems, and argue the case for 'interwoven thinking'. Cf. Hinchman and Hinchman 1989.
24. Raschke 1991.
25. Kitschelt 1989.
26. 'For ideologues, party organization is a laboratory to explore new forms of social solidarity and decision-making. Because the gratifications derived from organizational experiments are immediate and the collective benefits or comprehensive social change are more likely to be realized only in the distant future, ideologues may be more concerned with the party's appropriate organization than with its long-term program' (Kitschelt 1989: 50).
27. The most prominent politician associated with the 'New Beginning' is the former member of the Bundestag and chairperson of the parliamentary party Antje Vollmer.
28. Thus almost all attempts to develop an independent Green labour and social policy—e.g. the elaboration of a scheme of guaranteed basic income—have failed. The adoption of current union demands in relation to wages and working-time, on the other hand, have met with approval.
29. The members of the first federal parliamentary party had to give up their seats after two years and were replaced by the so-called 'follow-on brigade'.
30. It is sometimes said that the Greens were to have reached their decisions according to the consensus principle, i.e. they would seek to secure the agreement of all those involved. But

this is not the case. Even in the highest bodies such as the national executive committee, majority decision-making was the rule from the outset.

31. Michels 1962.
32. Kitschelt 1989: 72.
33. Hirschman 1982.
34. Kitschelt 1989: 72.
35. Ibid. 72.
36. Raschke 1991: 10.
37. However, members of the Bundestag may still not stand for a seat on the national executive committee, and vice versa.
38. However, developments have given the lie to those optimistic observers who, like Elim Papadakis (1988: 433–54), believed that the Greens had managed to develop 'a reflexive and analytical approach both to issues of organization and political ideology', and thus to spare themselves the choice between radicalism and reformism. In contradiction to what Papadakis thought, what one observes instead is that Green radicalism did allow itself to be tamed by means of various self-restricting arrangements that were capable of commanding consensus, but only after it had caused considerable losses in terms of power of attraction and effectiveness.
39. The alliance was badly prepared in terms of its political programme, and it lasted only a short time. It was terminated by the SPD on tactical grounds, a few weeks before new elections were held in autumn 1990.
40. A number of prominent adherents of 'eco-socialism' (like Jürgen Reents and Michael Stamm) acted as electoral advisers or press spokespersons for the PDS, the party which succeeded the official East German SED and currently has seventeen members in the Bundestag. The radical ecologists, for their part, are seeking to establish an organisation engaged chiefly in extra-parliamentary work.
41. Speechlessness seems to have become the hallmark of green politics in relation to the fundamental upheavals in Europe. Neither the complex processes of transformation in the new Eastern European democracies, nor the nationality disputes that are erupting at every turn, nor even the bloody civil war between Serbs and Croats had elicited a single clear comment from the diligent Euro-Greens in Brussels and Strasburg before summer 1992.
42. Padgett and Patterson 1991.
43. There are nine individuals from the East German Greens and citizens' movements sitting as MPs in the Bundestag, but because of their origins, the emphases of their individual interests, and the looseness of their links with the Green Party, they are not perceived as representing the West German Greens.
44. In the examples cited above, a number of people felt offended: (a) those who thought Germany had a useful role to play in the transformation of NATO; (b) those who thought women's choice of lifestyle should be left to women themselves to decide; (c) those who recognised in the desire for a united Germany the needs of people who felt frustrated and had suffered years of disadvantage; and (d) those who realised that Iraqi-cum-German poison-gas represented a real threat to the Israeli population.
45. e.g. on multiple causality, autopoietic self-referential processes, paradoxal emergence phenomena, perverse effects of purposive action, and evolutionary selection mechanisms.
46. Hinchman and Hinchman 1989.
47. March and Olsen 1989.
48. Dryzek 1990: 195–210.

References

Bahro, Rudolf (1987), *Logik der Rettung* (Stuttgart: Thienemanns Verlag).

Capra, Fritjof, and Spretnak, Charlene (1984), *Green Politics: The Global Promise* (London: Hutchinson).

Cornelsen, Dirk (1986), *Ankläger im Hohen Haus: Die Grünen im Bundestag* (Essen: Klartext Verlag).

Czada, Roland, and Lehmbruch, Gerhard (1990), 'Parteienwettbewerb, Sozialstaatspostulat und gesellschaftlicher Wertewandel', in Udo Bermbach et al. (eds), *Spaltungen der Gesellschaft und die Zukunft des Sozialstaats* (Opladen: Leske & Budrich), 55–84.

Dalton, Russell J., and Kuechler, Manfred (1990) (eds), *Challenging the Political Order: New Social and Political Movements in Western Democracies* (Cambridge: Polity Press).

Dryzek, John S. (1990), 'Green Reason: Communicative Ethics for the Biosphere', *Environmental Ethics*, 12: 195–210.

Hildebrandt, Kai, and Dalton, Russell (1978), 'The New Politics: Political Change or Sunshine Politics?', in Max Kaase (ed.), *Election and Parties* (London and Beverly Hills: Sage).

Hinchman, Lewis P., and Hinchman, Sandra K. (1989), ' "Deep Ecology" and the Revival of Natural Right', *Western Political Quarterly*, 42: 201–28.

Hirschman, Albert O. (1982), *Shifting Involvements: Private Interest and Public Action* (Princeton: Princeton University Press).

Kelly, Petra K. (1983), *Um Hoffnung Kämpfen* (Bornheim-Merten: Lamuv Verlag).

Kirchheimer, Otto (1966), 'The Transformation of West European Party Systems', in Joseph LaPalombara and Myron Weiner (eds), *Political Parties and Political Development* (Princeton: Princeton University Press), 177–200.

Kitschelt, Herbert P. (1986), 'Political Opportunity Structures and Political Protest: Anti-Nuclear Movements in Four Democracies', *British Journal of Political Science*, 16: 57–85.

—— (1989), *The Logics of Party Formation: Ecological Politics in Belgium and West Germany* (Ithaca and London: Cornell University Press).

March, James G., and Olsen, Johan P. (1989), *Rediscovering Institutions: The Organizational Basis of Politics* (New York: Free Press).

Michels, Robert (1962), *Political Parties: A Sociological Study of the Oligarchical Tendencies of Modern Democracy* (1911) (London: Collier-Macmillan).

Müller-Rommel, Ferdinand, and Pridham, Geoffrey (1989) (eds), *Small Parties in Western Europe: Comparative and National Perspectives* (London and Beverly Hills: Sage).

Offe, Claus (1990), 'Reflections on the Institutional Self-Transformation of Movement Politics: A Tentative Stage Model', in Russell J. Dalton and Manfred Kuechler (eds), *Challenging the Political Order: New Social and Political Movements in Western Democracies* (Cambridge: Polity Press), 233–50.

Padgett, Stephen, and Patterson, William (1991), 'The Rise and Fall of the West German Left', *New Left Review*, 186 (Mar./Apr.): 46–77.

Papadakis, Elim (1988), 'Social Movements, Self-Limiting Radicalism and the Green Party in West Germany', *Sociology*, 22: 433–54.

Raschke, Joachim (1991), *Krise der Grünen: Bilanz und Neubeginn* (Marburg: Schüren).

Wolinetz, Steven B. (1991), 'Party System Change: The Catch-all Thesis Revisited', *West European Politics*, 14: 113–28.

13 The American Political Economy II: The Non-Politics of Laissez Faire

William P. Ophuls with A. Stephen Boyan, Jr.

The invisible hand is no longer to be relied on for social decisions; we shall be obliged to make explicit political choices in order to meet the challenges of ecological scarcity. This is an embarrassing conclusion, for we Americans have never had a genuine politics—that is, something apart from economics that gives direction to our community life. Instead, American politics has been but a reflection of its laissez-faire economic system.

The Political Functions of Economic Growth

From our earliest colonial beginnings, rising expectations have been a fundamental part of the American credo, each generation expecting to become richer than the previous one. Thanks to this expectation of growth, the class conflict and social discontent typical of early nineteenth-century Europe were all but absent in America; politics was accordingly undemanding, pragmatic, and laissez-faire. Thus, said Alexis de Tocqueville in his classic study of American civilization *Democracy in America*, we were indeed a "happy republic."

Growth is still central to American politics. In fact, it matters more than ever, for the older social restraints (the Protestant ethic, deference, isolation) have all been swept away. Growth is the secular religion of American society, providing a social goal, a basis for political solidarity, and a source of individual motivation. The pursuit of happiness has come to be defined almost exclusively in material terms, and the entire society—individuals, enterprises, the government itself—has an enormous vested interest in the continuation of growth.

The Economic Basis of Pragmatic Politics

Growth continues to be essential to the characteristic pragmatic, laissez-faire style of American politics, which has always revolved around the question of fair access to the opportunity to get on financially. Indeed, American political history is but the record of a more or less amicable squabble over the division of the spoils of a growing economy. Even social problems have been handled by substituting economic growth for political principle, transforming non-economic issues into ones that could be solved by economic bargaining. For example, when labor pressed its class demands, the response was to legitimize its status as a bargaining unit in the division of the spoils. Once labor had to be bargained with in good businesslike fashion, compromise, in terms of wages and other costable benefits, became possible. In return for labor's abandonment of uncompromising demands for socialism, others at the economic trough "squeezed over" enough for labor to get its share. Similarly, new political demands by immigrants, farmers, and so on were bought off by the opportunity to share in the fruits of economic growth. The only conflict that we failed to solve in this manner was slavery and its aftermath, and it is typical that once the legitimacy of black demands was recognized in the 1960s, the reflex response was to promote economic opportunity via job training, education, "black capitalism," and fair hiring practices—that is, the wherewithal to share the affluence of the envied whites. If blacks prosper economically, says our intuitive understanding of politics, racial problems will vanish.

As a political mode, economic reductionism has many virtues. Above all, it is a superb means of channeling and controlling social conflict. Economic bargaining is a matter of a little more or a little less. Nobody loses on issues of principle, and even failure to get what you want today is tolerable, for the bargaining session is continuous, and the outcome of the next round may be more favorable. Besides, everybody's share is growing, so that even an unfair share is a more-than-acceptable bird in the hand. Most people understand that in a growth economy, individuals or groups have more to gain from increases in the size of the enterprise as a whole than from any feasible change in distribution. Furthermore, people have gotten what was of primary interest to them—access to income and wealth—and with their chief aim satisfied, they were able to repress desires for community, social respect, political power, and other values that are not so easily divisible as money.

This characteristic style of conflict resolution presupposes agreement on the primacy of economics and a general willingness to be pragmatic and to accept the bargaining approach to political and social as well as economic issues. Unfortunately, the arrival of ecological scarcity places issues on the political agenda that are not easily compromisable or commensurable, least of all in terms of money. Trade-offs are possible, of course, but environmental imperatives are basically matters of principle that cannot be bargained away in an economic fashion. Environmental management is therefore a role for which our political institutions are miscast, because it involves deciding issues of principle in favor of one side or another rather than merely allocating shares in the spoils. Worse, a cessation or even a slowing of growth will bring opposing interests into increasingly stark conflict. Economic growth has made it possible to satisfy the demands of new claimants to the spoils without taking anything away from others. Without significant growth, however, we are left with a zero-sum game, in which there will be winners and losers instead of big winners and little winners. Especially in recent years, growth has become an all-purpose "political solvent" (Bell 1974: 43), satisfying rapidly rising expectations while allowing very large expenditures for social welfare and defense. Without the political solvent of growth to provide quasi-automatic solutions to many of our domestic social problems, our political institutions will be called on to make hard choices about how best to use relatively scarce resources to meet a plethora of demands. More important, long-suppressed social issues can now be expected to surface—especially the issue of equality.

Ecological Scarcity versus Economic Justice

To state the problem succinctly, growth and economic opportunity have been substitutes for equality of income and wealth. We have justified large differences in income and wealth on the grounds that they promote growth and that all members of society would receive future advantage from current inequality as the benefits of development "trickled down" to the poor. (On a more personal level, economic growth also ratifies the ethics of individual self-seeking: You can get on without concern for the fate of others, for they are presumably getting on too, even if not so well as you.) But if growth in production is no longer of overriding importance, the rationale for differential rewards gets thinner, and with a cessation of growth it virtually disappears. In general, anything that diminishes growth and opportunity abridges the customary substitutes for equality. Because people's demands for economic betterment are not likely to disappear, once the pie stops growing fast enough to accommodate their needs, they will begin making demands for redistribution.

Even more serious than the frustration of rising expectations is the prospect of actual deprivation as substantial numbers of people get worse off in terms of real income as a result of scarcity-induced inflation and the internalization of environmental costs. Indeed, the eventual consequence of ecological scarcity is a lower standard of living, as we currently define it, for almost all members of society. One does not need a gloomy view of human nature to realize that this will create enormous political and social tension. It is, in fact, the classic prescription for revolution. At the very least, we can expect that our politics will come to be dominated by resentment and envy—or "emulation," to use the old word—just as it has many times in the past in democratic polities.

To make the revolutionary potential of the politics of emulation more concrete, let us imagine that the current trend toward making automobile ownership and operation more expensive continues to the point where the car becomes once again a luxury item, available only to "the carriage trade." How will the average person, once an economic aristocrat with his or her own private carriage but now demoted to a scooter or a bicycle, react to this deprivation, especially in view of the fact that the remaining aristocrats will presumably continue to enjoy their private carriages?

Of course, such an extreme situation is probably a long way off (although many would be priced out of the market today if all the social costs attributable to the automobile were internalized). Yet it is toward such a situation that the rising costs due to ecological scarcity are pushing us. Already, in striking contrast to the not-too-distant past, the price of a detached house in the most populous areas of the country is more than the average family can afford to pay. Also, as the cost of food and other basic necessities continues to increase, less disposable income will be left for the purchase of automobiles and other highly desired goods. In sum, deprivation is inevitable, even in the short term.

This point has not been lost on advocates for the disadvantaged, who have already protested vehemently against the regressive impact of even modest increases in the cost of energy (through increased gasoline taxes, for example) and goods.[1] More generally, they fear that lessened growth will tend to restrict social mobility and freeze the status quo, or even turn the clock back in some areas, such as minority rights.

The political stage is set, therefore, for a showdown between the claims of ecological scarcity on the one hand and socioeconomic justice on the other. If the impact of scarcity is distributed in a laissez-faire fashion, the result will be to intensify existing inequalities. Large-scale redistribution, however, is almost totally foreign to our political machinery, which was designed for a growth economy and which has used economic surplus as the coin of social and political payoff. Thus the political measures necessary to redistributing income and wealth such that scarce commodities are to a large degree equally shared will require much greater social cooperation and solidarity than the system has exhibited in the past.

They will also require greater social control. Under conditions of scarcity, there is a trade-off between freedom and equality, with perfect equality necessitating almost total social control (as was attempted in Maoist China). However, even partial redistribution will involve wholesale government intervention in the economy and major transfers of property rights, as well as other infringements of liberty in general, that will be resisted bitterly by important and powerful interests.

Thus either horn of the dilemma—laissez faire or redistribution—would toss us into serious difficulties that would strain our meager political and moral resources to or beyond capacity. American society is founded on competition rather than cooperation, and scarcity is likely to aggravate rather than ameliorate the competitive struggle to gain economic benefits for oneself or one's group. Similarly, our political ethic is based on a just division of the spoils, defined almost purely in terms of fair access to the increments of growth; once the spoils of abundance are gone, little is left to promote social cooperation and sharing. As Adam Smith pointed out, the "progressive state" is "cheerful" and "hearty"; by contrast, the stationary state is "hard," the declining state "miserable" (Smith 1776: 81). How well will a set of political institutions completely predicated on abundance and molded by over 200 years of continuous growth cope with the "hardness" of ecological scarcity?

The Non-Politics of Due Process

This dilemma is only a specific instance of a more general problem. In many areas, the American government will be obliged to have genuine policies—that is, specific measures or programs designed to further some particular conception of the public interest. This will require radical changes, because in our laissez-faire political system, ends are subordinated to political means. In other words, we practice "process" politics as opposed to "systems" politics (Schick 1971). As the name implies, process politics emphasizes the adequacy and fairness of the rules governing the process of politics. If the process is fair, then, as in a trial conducted according to due process, the outcome is assumed to be just—or at least the best that the system can achieve. By contrast, systems politics is concerned primarily with desired outcomes; means are subordinated to predetermined ends.

The process model has many virtues. Keeping the question of ends out of politics greatly diminishes the intensity of social conflict. People debate the fairness of the rules, a matter about which they find it relatively easy to agree, and they do not confront each other with value demands, which may not be susceptible to compromise. However, by some standards, the process model hardly deserves the name of politics, for it evades the whole issue of the common interest simply by declaring that the "will of all" and the "general will" are identical. The common interest is thus, by definition, whatever the political system's invisible hand cranks out, for good or ill.

Of course, we have found that pure laissez-faire politics, like pure laissez-faire economics, produces outcomes that we find intolerable, but our instinct has always been to curb the social costs of laissez faire by reforms designed to preserve its basic features: We check practices that prevent the efficient or fair operation of the market rather than converting to a planned economy; we promote equal opportunity rather than redistributing wealth or income. Planning with certain ends in mind does take place in such a political system. Each separate atom or molecule in the body politic (individuals, corporations, government agencies, advisory commissions, and supreme courts) plans in order to maximize its own ends, and the invisible hand produces the aggregated result of action on these private plans. But the central government does not plan in any systematic way, even though its ad hoc actions—VA and FHA home loans, tax breaks for homeowners, and the like—do in a sense constitute a "plan" for certain outcomes—in this case, suburban sprawl.

In reality, "the American political system" is almost a misnomer. What we really have is congeries of unintegrated and competitive subsystems pursuing conflicting ends—a non-system. And our overall policy of accepting the outcome of due process means that in most particulars we have non-policies. Now, however, just as in economics, the externalities produced by this laissez-faire system of non-politics have become unacceptable. Coping with the consequences of ecological scarcity will require explicit, outcome-oriented political decisions taken in the name of some conception of an ecological, if not a political and social, common interest. What likelihood is there of this happening?

Who Dominates the Political Marketplace?

Critics of the American political system almost never question the necessity (or superiority) of process politics. If bad outcomes are generated, it must be because powerful interests dominate the political marketplace and prevent the will of the majority from being fully and fairly translated into outcomes. There has been, say the critics, a wholesale expropriation of the public domain by private interests (Lowi 1969; McConnell 1966). Nevertheless, although much of this criticism is incontrovertible, the general preferences of the American people are in fact quite well reflected in political output. People want jobs, economic opportunities, and a growing economy. Indeed, to the extent that the system has had a guiding policy goal at all, it has been precisely to satisfy the rising expectations of its citizens. Even if special interests have benefited disproportionately from the measures taken to promote this end, most of the benefit has been transmitted to the vast majority of the population. The problem, then, is not that our political institutions are unresponsive to our wills but that what we desire generates the tragedy of the commons.

Naturally, to the extent that our government is largely a brokerage house for special interests, the situation is much worse, because such interests have an even bigger stake in continued economic growth. But within a process system of politics, government decisions that consistently favor producer over consumer interests are all but inevitable, for the political marketplace is subject to the public-goods problem. For example, those who have a direct and substantial financial interest in legislation and regulation are strongly motivated to organize, lobby, make campaign contributions, advertise, litigate, and so forth in pursuit of their interests. By comparison, the great mass of the people, who will be indirectly affected and whose personal stake in the outcome is likely to be negligible, have very little incentive to organize in defense of their interests. After all, the "right" decision may be worth $10 million to General Motors but will cost each individual only a few pennies. Thus those who try to stand up to special interests on environmental issues find themselves up against superior political resources all across the board.

The gross political inequality of profit and nonprofit interests is epitomized by the favorable tax treatment accorded the former. By law, tax-deductible donations cannot be used for lobbying or other attempts to influence legislation (for example, by advertising). Thus the nonprofit organizations that depend very heavily on donations are severely handicapped; if they lobby, they undercut their financial support. Businesses, by contrast, can deduct any money spent for the same purpose from their taxable income and pass on the remaining expense in the form of higher prices. The public, both as consumers and as taxpayers, therefore subsidizes one side in environmental disputes. Moreover, the law is self-protecting, for public-interest groups cannot even lobby to have it changed without losing their tax-exempt status.

Thus the outcome of the process of American politics faithfully reflects the will of the people and their desire for economic growth. However, just as in the economic marketplace, the public suffers from certain negative externalities as a result of the inordinate political power of producer interests; political power tends to be used to ratify and reinforce, rather than countermand, the decisions of the economic market. In sum, the American political system has all the drawbacks of laissez faire, wherein individual decisions add up to an ecologically destructive macro-decision, as well as a structural bias in favor of producers that tends to make this macro-decision even more destructive of the commons than it would otherwise be.

The Ecological Vices of Muddling Through

The logic of the commons is enshrined in a system of process politics obedient to the demands of both consumer and producer for economic growth. The ecological vices of this system are further intensified by the decision-making style characteristic of all our institutions—disjointed incrementalism or, to use the more honest and descriptive colloquial term, "muddling through."

Incremental decision making largely ignores long-term goals; it focuses on the problem immediately at hand and tries to find the solution that is most congruent with the status quo. It is thus characterized by comparison and evaluation of marginal changes (increments) in current policies, not radical departures from them; by consideration of only a restricted number of policy alternatives (and of only a few of the important consequences for any given alternative);

by the adjustment of ends to means and to what is "feasible" and "realistic"; by serial or piece-meal treatment of problems; and by a remedial orientation in which policies are designed to cure obvious immediate ills rather than to bring about some desired future state. Moreover, analysis of policy alternatives is not disinterested, for it is carried out largely by partisan actors who are trying to improve their bargaining position with other partisan actors.

Muddling through is therefore a highly economic style of decision making that is well adapted to a pragmatic, laissez-faire system of politics. Moreover, it has considerable virtues. Like the market itself, disjointed incrementalism promotes short-term stability by minimizing serious conflict over ultimate ends, by giving everybody something of what they want, and by bringing bargained compromises among political actors, satisfying their needs reasonably well at mini-mal intellectual and financial cost. At the same time, it promotes the consensus and legitimacy needed to support public policy. It is also basically democratic; like the economic market, it reflects the preferences of those who participate in the political market (assuming that all legiti-mate interests can participate equally, which is not always the case). Disjointed incrementalism is also conservative in a good sense: It does not slight traditional values, it encourages apprecia-tion of the costs of change, and it prevents overly hasty action on complex issues. It may also avoid serious or irreversible mistakes, for an incremental measure that turns out to be mistaken can usually be corrected before major harm has been done. Under ideal circumstances, dis-jointed incrementalism therefore produces a succession of policy measures that take the system step by step toward the policy outcome that best reflects the interests of the participants in the political market.

Unfortunately, muddling through has some equally large vices. For example, it does not guar-antee that all relevant values will be taken into account, and it is likely to overlook excellent poli-cies not suggested by past experience. In addition, disjointed incrementalism is not well adapted to handling profound value conflicts, revolutions, crises, grand opportunities, and the like—in other words, any situation in which simple continuation of past policies is not an appropriate response. Most important, because decisions are made on the basis of immediate self-interest, muddling through is almost guaranteed to produce policies that will generate the tragedy of the commons. It is perfectly possible to come up with a series of decisions that all seem eminently reasonable on the basis of short-term calculation of costs and benefits and that satisfy current preferences but that yield unsatisfactory results in the long run, especially because the future is likely to be discounted in the calculation of costs and benefits. In fact, that is just how we have gotten ourselves into an ecological predicament. Thus the short-term adjustment and stability achieved by muddling through is likely to be achieved at the expense of long-term stability and welfare.

A perfect illustration of the potential dangers of muddling through is our approach to global warming. As a result of millions of separate decisions made by industry and individuals, 6 billion tons of carbon dioxide are emitted into the atmosphere each year, and emissions are increasing by 3% annually. Yet no real congressional debate has occurred on whether to control these private decisions in order to reduce carbon emissions. Even worse, the executive branch blithely ignores the problem and advocates a more aggressive pursuit of the traditional energy and growth policies that have brought about the rise in carbon dioxide emissions. As a result, we go on unwittingly pursuing business as usual, making short-term calculations of costs and benefits, and bring upon ourselves the greenhouse effect almost by default.

Indeed, in its purest form, muddling through *is* policy making by default instead of by conscious choice—simply an administrative device for aggregating individual preferences into a "will of all" that may bear almost no resemblance to the "general will." Unfortunately, the contrasting synoptic, or outcome-oriented, style of decision making cannot be fully achieved in the real world because of limits to our intellectual capacities (even with computers), lack of information (plus the cost of remedying it), uncertainty about our values and conflicts between them, and time constraints, as well as many lesser factors. Moreover, in its pure form, synoptic decision making could lead to irreversible and disastrous blunders, obliviousness to people's values, and the destruction of political consensus. Thus some measure of muddling through is a simple administrative necessity in any political system.

However, we Americans have taken muddling through, along with laissez faire and other prominent features of our political system, to an extreme. We have made compromise and short-term adjustment into ends instead of means, have failed to give even cursory consideration to the future consequences of present acts, and have neglected even to try to relate current policy choices to some kind of long-term goal. Worse, we have taken the radical position that there can be no common interest beyond what muddling through produces. In brief, we have elevated what is an undeniable administrative necessity into a philosophy of government, becoming in the process an "adhocracy" virtually oblivious to the implications of our governmental acts and politically adrift in the dangerous waters of ecological scarcity.

Disjointed incrementalism, then, provides an almost sufficient explanation of how we have proceeded step by step into the midst of ecological crisis and of why we are not meeting its challenges at present. As a normative philosophy of government, it is a program for ecological catastrophe; as an entrenched reality with which the environmental reformer must cope, it is a cause for deep pessimism. At the very least, the level or quality of muddling through must be greatly upgraded, so that ecology and the future are given due weight in policy making. But goal-oriented muddling through comes close to being a contradiction in terms (especially within a basically democratic system). Moreover, incrementalism is adapted to status-quo, consensus politics, not to situations in which policy outcomes are of critical importance or in which the paradigm of politics itself may be undergoing radical change (Dror 1968: especially pp. 300–4; Lindblom 1965; Schick 1971: especially p. 158). Thus steering a middle course will be difficult at best, and it may not be possible at all during the transition to a steady-state society.

Policy Overload, Fragmentation, and Other Administrative Problems

Disjointed incrementalism is not the only built-in impediment to an effective response to ecological scarcity. In the first place, the growing scale, complexity, and interdependence of society make the decision-making environment increasingly problematic, for the greater the number of decisions (and, above all, the greater the degree of risk they entailed), the greater the social effort necessary to make them. Given the size and complexity of the task of environmental management alone, especially with the declining margin for ecological or technological error, there would be a danger of administrative overload. But the crisis of ecological scarcity is only one crisis among many—part of a crisis of crises that will afflict decision makers in the decades ahead (Platt 1969). An allied crisis of priorities also impends, as burgeoning demands for environmental cleanup, more and better social services, and so on compete for the tiny portion of government resources remaining after the "fixed" demands of defense, agricultural supports, and other budgetary sacred cows are satisfied, so that decision makers will simply lack sufficient funds to act effectively across the board. (In the United States, this has been true throughout the 1980s and early 1990s.) In addition, there may be critical shortfalls in labor power, especially technical and scientific labor power. In short, the problems are growing faster than the wherewithal to handle them, and political and administrative overload is therefore a potentially serious problem for the future, if not right now.

A second serious problem is fragmented and dispersed administrative responsibility. The agency in charge of decisions on air pollution, for example, usually has no control over land-use policy, freeway building, waste disposal, mass transit, and agriculture! Also, some elements of policy are handled at the federal level, whereas others belong to the state and local governments; the boundaries of local governments, especially, have no relationship to ecological realities. As a result, it frequently happens that one agency or unit of government works at cross-purposes with another, or even with itself, as in the old Atomic Energy Commission, which was charged with both nuclear development and radiation safety.[2] Furthermore, each agency has been created to perform a highly specialized function for a particular constituency, which leads to a single-mindedness or tunnel vision that deliberately ignores the common interest. In brief, we have as many different policies as we have bureaus and it is difficult to get them to pull together.

A third major defect of our policy-making machinery is that decisions inevitably lag behind events—usually far behind. In part, the problem is that the decision makers' information and knowledge are deficient and out of date. Owing to the complexity and scope of the problems of environmental management, these deficiencies are either impossible to remedy or too costly. Thus, even if they are inclined to be forward-looking, decision makers are virtually obliged to muddle through critical problems with stopgap measures that provoke disruptive side effects. Much the larger part of the time-lag problem, however, is that the procedural checks and balances built into our basically adversary system of policy making can subject controversial decisions to lengthy delays. For example, Congress in 1977 amended the Clean Air Act to protect visibility in large national parks and wilderness areas; it took until 1990, however, for the EPA to issue draft regulations to implement the law. Thereafter, before the EPA issued its final regulations, the White House weakened them, sacrificing two-thirds of the visibility reductions that the EPA had proposed (Rauber 1991: 28). The matter may still end up in court. By presidential decree, the White House Office of Management and Budget subjects all EPA regulations to cost-benefit analysis. But the 1977 law requires power plants to install "the best available retrofit technology" to eliminate the air pollution impairing visibility in the parks. Opponents argue that insofar as cost-benefit analysis causes regulations to be issued that do not require the use of the best available technology, the use of such analysis is illegal. They also argue a proper cost-benefit analysis, in any event, supports the original EPA draft regulations—that OMB simply manipulated the data to weaken them. This example suggests that the best we can expect in most cases is long wars of legal attrition against environmental despoilers. However, the adversary legal system is already having difficulty coping with environmental issues,[3] and there is some risk that environmental policy making may simply bog down in a morass of hearings, suits, counter-suits, and appeals, as government agencies, business interests, and environmentalist groups use all the procedural devices available to harass each other. And even if total stalemate is avoided, there are bound to be significant delays—an ominous prospect now that an anticipatory response to problems has become essential for their solution.

Additional hindrances to effective environmental decision making abound. The narrowly rationalistic norms and *modus operandi* of bureaucracies, for example, are at odds with the eco-logical holism needed for the task of environmental management. History also shows that regu-latory agencies tend to be captured by the interests they are supposed to be regulating, so that they rapidly turn into guardians of special interest instead of public interest. In addition, the institutions charged with environmental management are frequently so beholden to their own institutional vested interests or so dominated by sheer inertia that they actively resist change, employing secrecy, special legal advantages available to government agencies, and other devices to squelch the efforts of critics and would-be reformers (for example, Lewis 1972). In recent years, environmental decision making has been hindered by nonstatutory mechanisms established in the White House. The President's Council on Competitiveness, for example, is a non-statutory body that, after closed meetings with industry, has repeatedly forced the Environmental Protection Agency to rewrite regulations to make them hospitable to industry interests. As of this writing, the Council has successfully forced the EPA to gut four major pro-visions—some say the "pillars"—of the 1990 Clean Air Act (Weisskopf 1991: A1).[4] These dif-ficulties suggest that the problem is not simply to overcome inertia and vested interest but rather to arrest the institutional momentum in favor of growth created by two centuries of pro-development laws, policies, and practices. This will require across-the-board institutional reform, not merely new policies.

In sum, administrative overload, fragmented and dispersed authority, protracted delays in making and enforcing social decisions, and the institutional legacy of the era of growth and exploitation are likely to obstruct timely and effective environmental policy making.

How Well Are We Doing?

None of the tendencies and trends we have just considered inspires much optimism that our political institutions at any level are adequate to the challenges of dealing with ecological scarcity. Although the final verdict is not yet in, this conclusion is certainly reinforced by the quality of their performance so far.

Energy policy is a good illustration. Despite a consensus that a coherent national energy policy is absolutely essential to avoid economic and social turmoil, a menacing international trade deficit, and even the compromise of its political independence, the United States has no genuine policy, much less a coherent one. Instead, the past decade has seen almost continual dithering and muddle and devotion to business as usual. In 1989 President Bush called for a long-term comprehensive policy, but what he proposed in 1991 was a mere grab-bag of favored projects of the oil, coal, gas, and nuclear power industries. Among these was more off-shore oil drilling, drilling in environmentally pristine areas, and the doubling of nuclear power capacity by 2030. The President proposed few conservation measures, only a minuscule increase in research on renewable energy, and support only for selected alternative fuels (ethanol and methanol but not for hydrogen, fuel cells, or electric vehicles). He proposed nothing to combat greenhouse gas emissions, except as an incidental consequence of his support for nuclear power.

When the Reagan administration made similar proposals during its years in office, it and Congress fought each other to a stalemate on energy conservation, environmental protection, and the relative support for renewable energy and fuels versus the support for fossil fuel and nuclear energy development. For example, a majority in Congress has thus far rejected oil drilling in the Arctic and other wilderness areas; instead it favors raising automobile fuel-efficiency standards to 40 miles per gallon by 2001, which would save 5 to 10 times the oil expected to be produced by oil drilling in the Arctic. But the Congressional majority is not veto-proof and the result is a stalemate. Continued stalemate, regrettably, sets the stage for an eventual general collapse of our energy economy because of either rising costs of petroleum or intolerable levels of pollution.

Similarly, our political institutions have so far conspicuously failed to meet the challenge represented by the automobile. The decline in air quality was sufficiently alarming to cause Congress to pass the Clean Air Act in 1970. For all its faults, this was a landmark piece of environmental legislation, and acting under the law's authority, government agencies forced emission control on a reluctant automobile industry. However, Detroit several times succeeded in winning delayed compliance. Moreover, the air-quality standards mandated by Congress in the 1970 Clean Air Act simply could not be achieved through technology alone. Yet when the Environmental Protection Agency tried to impose on key municipalities pollution-control plans that would have penalized or restricted car use (through gas rationing and parking surcharges, for instance), the resulting political ruckus soon forced the EPA into retreat, and all pretense of meeting the original standards was abandoned. At the same time, Congress tried to control emissions through Corporate Fuel Economy Standards (CAFE). A 1975 law required manufacturers to raise the average efficiency of the cars they sold to 27.5 miles per gallon by 1985. Again, the executive branch granted the automobile industry many delays in complying with the law, and by 1990, efficiency standards had reached only 26.5 miles per gallon (which meant that the hoped-for reduction in pollution was nullified by a doubling, since the law was passed, of the number of vehicle miles driven). The 1990 Clean Air Act does tighten emission standards further and hopes to achieve its objectives via technological changes such as the use of reformulated gasoline in the nine most polluted metropolitan regions by 1995. But although the 1990 law will help, cleaning up the air and reducing greenhouse gas emissions cannot be achieved by more stringent emissions standards alone, because improvements in clean-air technology are more than eaten up by growth in the automobile fleet and increases in vehicle miles driven. In short, Americans must simply drive much less than they do now (with much more efficient vehicles) and use mass transit much more. Unfortunately, having allowed the automobile so completely to dominate our lives that to restrict its use would produce instant economic and social crisis, we are repeatedly reduced to the desperate hope that some kind of technological fix will turn up in time to prevent natural feedback mechanisms—extreme price rises, national bankruptcy, intolerable levels of air pollution—from taking matters out of our hands.

Thus in these and other critical areas we are failing to meet the challenges. Everybody wants clean air and water, but nobody wants to pay the price. Nor do we wish to give up the appurtenances of a high-energy style of life or to accept the major restructuring of the economy and society that would be needed to reduce greenhouse-gas emissions significantly. Even modest invasion of sacrosanct private property rights—for example, in the form of vitally needed land-use law—has also proved to be well beyond our current political capacity. In fact, since the beginning of the 1980s there has been considerable backlash and backsliding on environmental issues, leading to relaxed standards and blatant denial of problems. In short, although there has been genuine progress since environmental issues first became a matter for political concern, our political institutions have so far largely avoided the tasks of environmental management and have for the most part done too little too late in those efforts they have undertaken.

As we have seen, the basic institutional structure and *modus operandi* of the American political system are primarily responsible for this. Nevertheless, the lack of courage and vision displayed by the current set of political actors should not escape notice. Neither Congress nor the executive branch has provided real leadership or faced up to crucial issues. To the extent that they have acted, as in the area of pollution control, they have acted faintheartedly or, what is almost worse, expediently rather than effectively. Say what one will about the institutional impediments and the difficulty of the problems, it is hard to conclude that our political leaders are doing the job they were elected to do. But of course, the inability or reluctance of our political officials to act simply reflects the desires of the majority of the American people, who have so far evinced only modest willingness to make minor sacrifices (for example, to support and engage in recycling) for the sake of environmental goals, but no willingness to accept fundamental changes in their way of life (for example, to restrict development to areas where public transit is available, or to support and use public transit and drive less). Our public officials can hardly be expected to commit political suicide by forcing unpopular environmental measures on us. Until the will of the people ordains otherwise or fundamental changes are quite literally forced on us, the best we can expect is piecemeal, patchwork, ineffective reform that lags ever farther behind onrushing events.

The Necessity for Paradigm Change

Our political institutions, predicated almost totally on growth and abundance, appear to be no match for the mounting challenges of ecological scarcity. This is a shocking conclusion about a political system that was once regarded, even by many foreigners, as marvelously progressive. For all its faults, the virtues of the American political system are undeniable: It worked well for nearly two hundred years, and it was eminently just and humane by any reasonable historical standard. Unfortunately, the problems of scarcity that confront the system today are problems that *it was never designed to handle.* Many of its past virtues are therefore irrelevant; what we must now address are its equally undeniable failings in the face of ecological scarcity.

Efforts to patch up the current paradigm of politics with new modes of decision making and planning—or even with new policies—will not succeed. These can only delay, and perhaps intensify, the ultimate breakdown. Only a new politics based on a set of values that are morally and practically appropriate to an age of scarcity will do. To achieve this new politics will require a revolution even more fundamental than that which created our nation in the first place, for the characteristic features of American civilization, not merely the nature of the regime, must be transformed. A great question stands before the American polity: Will we make the effort to translate our ideals of equality and freedom into forms appropriate to the new age of scarcity, or will we not even try, continuing prodigally to sow as long as we can and leaving the future to reap the consequences? Only time will tell whether the return of scarcity must inevitably presage retrogression to the classical scenario of inequality, oppression, and conflict, but one way or another, we Americans are about to find out what kind of people we really are.

Notes

1. For every $1.00 increase in the price of oil, about 78,000 jobs are lost in the United States. Yet if the gasoline tax were adjusted to pay the cost of all public subsidies to the automobile, Americans would have to pay $4.50 per gallon of gas (Schaeffer 1990: 15).
2. The Nuclear Regulatory Commission, whose mission is protection of the public from nuclear and radiation hazards, in practice also promotes nuclear energy. It has become, as do most government agencies, the captive of the industry it is charged to regulate.
3. Increased volume is only part of the problem. The traditional legal machinery for redressing civil wrongs, designed for two-party litigation, is having trouble with standing to sue and other issues that crop up in the typical environmental suit, where society as a whole is one of the parties. Also, technology creates new situations faster than the courts can work out precedents, and much of the scientific evidence used in environmental litigation is of a probabilistic and statistical nature that ill accords with the standards of proof traditionally demanded by courts.
4. Industry and administration lobbyists had tried to persuade Congress to adopt their substitutes for all four provisions when the legislation was being considered, but Congress had refused to adopt them. Environmentalists may thus be in a strong position to challenge these regulations as illegal, but even if they prevail, implementation of the law's requirements will be substantially delayed.

References

Abelson, Philip H. (1972a), "Environmental Quality," *Science*, 177: 655.

——(1972b), "Federal Statistics," *Science*, 175: 1315.

Bachrach, Peter (1967), *The Theory of Democratic Elitism: A Critique* (Boston: Little, Brown).

Bell, Daniel (1974), "The Public Household—On 'Fiscal Sociology' and the Liberal Society," *Public Interest*, 37: 29–68.

Brown, Harrison, Bonner, James, and Weir, John (1963), *The Next Hundred Years* (New York: Viking), esp. chaps. 14–17, which discuss manpower.

Bruce-Briggs, B. (1974), "Against the Neo-Malthusians," *Commentary*, July: 25–9.

Burch, William R., Jr. (1971), *Daydreams and Nightmares: A Sociological Essay on the American Environment* (New York: Harper and Row).

Caldwell, Lynton K. (1971), *Environment: A*

Challenge to Modem Society (Garden City, NY: Doubleday).

—— and Siddiqi, Toufiq A. (1974), *Environmental Policy, Law and Administration: A Guide to Advanced Study* (Bloomington: University of Indiana School of Public and Envrionmental Affairs).

Carpenter, Richard A. (1972), "National Goals and Environmental Laws," *Technology Review*, 74 (3): 58–63.

Carter, Luther J. (1973a), "Environment: A Lesson for the People of Plenty," *Science*, 182: 1323–24.

—— (1973b), "Environmental Law (I): Maturing Field for Lawyers and Scientists," *Science*, 179: 1205–09.

—— (1973c), "Environmental Law (II): A strategic Weapon Against Degradation?," *Science*, 179: 1310–12, 1350.

—— (1973d), "Pesticides: Environmentalists Seek New Victory in a Frustrating War," *Science*, 181: 143–5.

—— (1974a), "Cancer and the Environment (I): A Creaky System Grinds On," *Science*, 186: 239–42.

—— (1974b), "Con Edison: Endless Storm King Dispute Adds to Its Troubles," *Science*, 194: 1353–58.

—— (1974c), "The Energy Bureaucracy: The Pieces Fall into Place," *Science*, 185: 44–5.

—— (1974d), "Energy: Cannibalism in the Bureaucracy," *Science*, 186: 511.

—— (1974e), "Pollution and Public Health: Taconite Case Poses Major Test," *Science*, 186: 31–6.

—— (1975a), "The Environment: A 'Mature' Cause in Need of a Lift," *Science*, 187: 45–8.

—— (1975b), *The Florida Experience: Land and Water Policy in a Growth State* (Baltimore: Johns Hopkins).

Cohn, Victor (1975), "The Washington Energy Show," *Technology Review*, 77 (3): 8, 68.

Conservation Foundation (1972), "Wanted: A Coordinated, Coherent National Energy Policy Geared to the Public Interest," *CF Letter*, No. 6–72.

Cooley, Richard A., and Wandesforde-Smith, Geoffrey (eds), *Congress and the Environment* (Seattle: Washington).

Crossland, Janice (1974), "Cars, Fuel, and Pollution," *Environment*, 16 (2): 15–27.

Dahl, Robert A. (1970), *After the Revolution?:*

Authority in a Good Society (New Haven: Yale).

Davies, Barbara S., and Davies, Clarence J., III (1975), *The Politics of Pollution*, 2nd edn. (New York: Pegasus).

Davis, David H. (1974), *Energy Politics* (New York: St Martin's).

Dexter, Lewis A. (1969), *The Sociology and Politics of Congress* (Chicago: Rand McNally).

Downs, Anthony (1972), "Up and Down with Ecology—The 'Issue-Attention Cycle,'" *Public Interest*, 28: 38–50.

Dror, Yehezkel (1968), *Public Policymaking Reexamined* (San Francisco: Chandler).

Edelman, Murray (1964), *The Symbolic Uses of Politics* (Urbana: Illinois).

Forrester, Jay W. (1971), *World Dynamics* (Cambridge: Wright–Allen), esp. chaps. 1 and 7 for a radical critique of nonsystematic, incremental decision making.

Forsythe, Dall W. (1974), "An Energy-Scarce Society: The Politics and Possibilities," *Working Papers for a New Society*, 2 (1): 3–12, an excellent short analysis.

Gillette, Robert (1973a), "Energy: The Muddle at the Top," *Science*, 182: 1319–21.

—— (1973b), "Western Coal: Does the Debate Follow Irreversible Commitment?," *Science*, 182: 456–8.

—— (1975), "In Energy Impasse, Conservation Keeps Popping Up," *Science*, 187: 42–5.

Goldstein, Paul, and Ford, Robert (1973), "On the Control of Air Quality: Why the Laws Don't Work," *Bulletin of the Atomic Scientists*, 29 (6): 31–4.

Green, Charles S., III (1973), "Politics, Equality and the End of Progress," *Alternatives*, 2 (2): 4–9.

Haefele, Edwin T. (1974), *Representative Government and Environmental Management* (Baltimore: Johns Hopkins).

Hartz, Louis (1955), *The Liberal Tradition in America: An Interpretation of American Political Thought Since the Revolution* (New York: Harcourt, Brace).

Henning, Daniel H. (1974), *Environmental Policy and Administration* (New York: American Elsevier).

Hirschman, Albert O. (1970), *Exit, Voice and Loyalty* (Cambridge: Harvard), esp. chap. 8 on frontier-style decision making and problem avoidance.

Horowitz, Irving L. (1972), "The Environmental Cleavage: Social Ecology versus Political Economy," *Scoial Theory and Practice*, 2 (1): 125–34.

Jacobsen, Sally (1974), "Anti-Pollution Backlash in Illinois: Can a Tough Protection Program Survive?" *Bulletin of the Atomic Scientists*, 30 (1): 39–44.

Jones, Charles O. (1975), *Clean Air: The Policies and Polities of Pollution Control* (University of Pittsburgh Press).

Kohlmeier, Louis M., Jr. (1969), *The Regulators: Watchdog Agencies and the Public Interest* (New York: Harper and Row).

Kraft, Michael (1972), "Congressional Attitudes Toward the Environment," *Alternatives*, 1 (4): 27–37, congressional avoidance of the environmental issue.

—— (1974), "Ecological Politics and American Government: A Review Essay," in Nagel (1974), 139–59, the best critical review of the political science literature in the light of environmental problems.

Lecht, L. A. (1966), *Goals, Priorities and Dollars* (New York: Free Press).

—— (1969), *Manpower Needs for National Goals in the 1970's* (New York: Praeger).

Lewis, Richard (1972), *The Nuclear Power Rebellion* (New York: Viking).

Lindblom, Charles E. (1965), *The Intelligence of Democracy: Decisionmaking Through Mutual Adjustment* (New York: Free Press).

—— (1969), "The Science of 'Muddling Through,'" *Public Administration Review*, 19 (2): 79–88.

Little, Charles E. (1973), "The Environment of the Poor: Who Gives a Damn?," *Conservation Foundation Letter*, July.

Loveridge, Ronald O. (1971), "Political Science and Air Pollution: A Review and Assessment of the Literature," in Paul B. Downing (ed.), *Air Pollution and the Social Sciences* (New York: Praeger), 45–85, why we are not coping with the problem.

—— (1972), "The Environment: New Priorities and Old Politics," in Harlan Hahn (ed.), *People and Politics in Urban Society* (Los Angeles: Sage), 499–529.

Lowi, Theodore (1969), *The End of Liberalism: Ideology, Policy, and the Crisis of Public Authority* (New York: Norton).

McConnell, Grant (1966), *Private Power and American Democracy* (New York: Knopf).

McLane, James (1974), "Energy Goals and Institutional Reform," *The Futurist*, 8: 239–42.

Michael, Donald N. (1968), *The Unprepared Society: Planning for a Precarious Future* (New York: Harper and Row).

Miller, John C. (1957), *Origins of the American Revolution* (Stanford, Calif.: Stanford University Press).

Moorman, James W. (1974), "Bureaucracy v. The Law," *Sierra Club Bulletin*, 59 (9): 7–10, how agencies evade or flout their legal responsibilities.

Murphy, Earl F. (1967), *Governing Nature* (Chicago: Quadrangle).

Nagel, Stuart S. (1974) (ed.), *Environmental Politics* (New York: Praeger).

Nelkin, Dorothy (1974), "The Role of Experts in a Nuclear Siting Controversy," *Bulletin of the Atomic Scientists*, 30 (9): 29–36.

Neubaus, Richard (1971), *In Defense of People* (New York: Macmillan).

de Nevers, Noel (1973), "Enforcing the Clean Air Act of 1970," *Scientific American*, 228 (6): 14–21.

Odell, Rice (1975a), "Automobiles Keep Posing New Dilemmas," *Conservation Foundation Letter*, March.

—— (1975b), "Should Americans Be Pried Out of Their Cars?," *Conservation Foundation Letter*, April.

Pirages, Dennis C., and Paul, R. Ehrlich (1974), *Ark II: Social Response to Environmental Imperatives* (New York: W. H. Freeman and Co.).

Platt, John (1969), "What We Must Do," *Science*, 166: 1115–21.

Potter, David M. (1954), *People of Plenty: Economic Abundance and the American Character* (Chicago: University of Chicago).

Quarles, John (1974), "Fighting the Corporate Lobby," *Environmental Action*, 7 December: 3–6, how the political and other resources of corporations overwhelm the environmental regulators.

Quigg, Philip W. (1974), "Energy Shortage Spurs Expansion of Nuclear Fission," *World*

Environment Newsletter in SIR World, 29 June: 21–2.

Rauber, Paul (1991), "O Say, Can You See," *Sierra*, July/August: 24–9.

Roos, Leslie L., Jr. (1971) (ed.), *The Politics of Ecosuicide* (New York: Holt, Rinehart and Winston).

Rose, David J. (1974), "Energy Policy in the U.S.," *Scientific American*, 230 (1): 20–9.

Rosenbaum, Walter A. (1973), *The Politics of Environmental Concern* (New York: Praeger).

Ross, Charles R. (1970), "The Federal Government as an Inadvertent Advocate of Environmental Degradation," in Harold W. Helfiich, Jr. (ed.), *The Environmental Crists* (New Haven: Yale), 171–87.

Ross, Douglas, and Wolman, Harold (1971), "Congress and Pollution—The Gentleman's Agreement," in Warren A. Johnson and John Hardesty (eds), *Economic Growth vs. the Environment* (Belmont, Calif.: Wadsworth), 134–44.

Schaeffer, Robert (1990), "Car Sick," *Greenpeace*, May/June: 13–17.

Schick, Allen (1971), "Systems Politics and Systems Budgeting," in Roos (1971), 135–58.

Shapley, Deborah (1973), "Auto Pollution: Research Group Charged with Conflict of Interest," *Science*, 181: 732–5.

Shubik, Martin (1967), "Information, Rationality, and Free Choice in a Future Democratic Society," *Daedalus*, 96: 771–8.

Sills, David L. (1975), "The Environmental Movement and Its Critics," *Human Ecology*, 3: 1–41.

Smith, Adam (1776), *An Inquiry into the Nature and Causes of the Wealth of Nations*, ed. Edwin Cannan (New York: Modern Library, 1937).

Smith, James N. (1974) (ed.), *Environmental Quality and Social Justice* (Washington, DC: Conservation Foundation).

Sprout, Harold, and Sprout, Margaret (1971), *Ecology and Politics in America: Some Issues and Alternatives* (New York: General Learning Press).

——(1972), "National Priorities: Demands, Resources, Dilemmas," *World Politics*, 24: 293–317.

Weisskopf, Michael (1991), "Rule-Making Process Could Soften Clean Air Act," *Washington Post*, 21 September, A1.

White, Lawrence J. (1973), "The Auto Pollution Muddle," *Public Interest*, 32: 97–112.

Wolff, Robert Paul (1968), *The Poverty of Liberalism* (Boston: Beacon).

PART THREE

ENVIRONMENT AND ECONOMICS

Environmental values and economic values have long been treated as pointing in opposite directions. Survivalists have always claimed that economic values must yield to ecological ones; reformists have implicitly assumed that the best we could hope for is some reasonable compromise between the two opposites. In Part Three we introduce literatures that point to the essential compatibility of environment and economics. Section V focuses on the possibility of putting economic instruments (especially quasi-market schemes) to the service of environmental values. Sections VI and VII deal with arguments that economic growth and environmental conservation can proceed hand-in-hand, provided that intelligent political action can redirect the structure and development of global and national political-economic systems.

Section V: Market Liberalism

While environmental policy in practice has generally featured some combination of administrative and liberal democratic procedures, environmental policy in theory has seen a great deal more of market liberalism. Market liberals believe that the key to effective resolution of environmental problems is the intelligent deployment of markets and quasi-markets. They have nothing but scorn for the kind of professional resource management advocated by administrative rationalists, and believe that liberal democratic politics is little more than licence for special interests to poke their snouts into the public trough.

Hard-line market liberals believe that all environmental problems have a common origin: the failure to specify appropriate private property rights. If it is a truism that people tend to take care of their private property much more carefully than they care for what they hold in common with others, why not, then, convert the environment into private property too? Market liberals have devoted a great deal of effort to exploring how property rights might be established in land, fisheries, air, and water. Once established, such rights can be exchanged in the market, available to the highest bidder and so to the most socially and economically beneficial use. The classic statement of this hard-line position appears in our selection from Terry Anderson and Donald Leal. William Mitchell and Randy Simmons provide some specific examples of just how far this position can be extended.

Not all proponents of market and quasi-market schemes share this hard-line position. As Robert Goodin notes, such schemes are also attractive to a broad spectrum of environmentalists. The difference here is that these environmentalists want to keep the schemes under tight governmental control. So rather than simply turning everything into private property, quasi-market schemes would involve (say) managed markets in pollution rights, with government free to increase or decrease the number of rights available for auction. Other proposals involve the use of 'green taxes' which provide an incentive to polluters to cut back on their emissions or other environmentally-damaging activities. One of the best-known such proposals is a carbon tax levied on fossil fuels in order to reduce emissions of greenhouse gases. Such managed markets are scorned by Mitchell and Simmons, but in general they find broad support. Given this support, it is perhaps surprising that they do not appear more frequently in the real world. Market liberal schemes of all sorts are attacked by Goodin, who likens the selling of rights to pollute to the selling of indulgences to sinners by the medieval Catholic Church.

Further Reading

Anderson and Leal's *Free Market Environmentalism* (1991) remains the best comprehensive statement of hard-line market liberalism. This position is also developed in Roger E. Meiners and Bruce Yandle (eds), *Taking the Environment Seriously* (1993). Herman E. Daly shows why environmentalists might reject this hard-line position while still making use of market-type policies in 'Free

Market Environmentalism: Turning a Good Servant into a Bad Master', *Critical Review*, 6 (1992), 171–83. A comprehensive regime of green taxes is advocated in a British context in David Pearce, Anil Markandya, and Edward R. Barbier, *Blueprint for a Green Economy* (1989). A critical account of economists and their schemes, which helps to explain why many environmentalists are uneasy with them, is developed by Steven Kelman in *What Price Incentives? Economists and the Environment* (1981). Mark Sagoff's *The Economy of the Earth* (1988) is a sustained attack on environmental and natural resource economists. Elinor Ostrom in *Governing the Commons* (1990) shows that dividing the commons into chunks of private property is not the only way to solve the tragedy of the commons. Perspective on the varieties of market liberalism and their critics is provided in Robyn Eckersley (ed.), *Markets, the State and the Environment: Towards Integration* (1995).

14 Visions of the Environment and Rethinking the Way We Think

Terry L. Anderson and Donald T. Leal

I. Visions of the Environment

Many people see free markets and the environment as incompatible; for them, the very notion of free market environmentalism is an oxymoron. Even many "free marketeers" find themselves on opposite sides of the fence when it comes to governmental regulation of the environment. Some will hold fast to the conviction that markets work best to allocate most of the goods and services we enjoy, but they will also argue that the environment is different and is too precious to be allocated on the basis of profits.

The view that markets and the environment do not mix is buttressed by the perception that resource exploitation and environmental degradation are inextricably linked to economic growth. This view, which first emerged with industrialization, builds on fears that we are running out of resources because economic growth based on materialistic values is tempting us to squander our natural endowment. During the Industrial Revolution in England, the Reverend Thomas Malthus articulated this view by hypothesizing that exponential population growth would eventually result in famine and pestilence; productivity simply would not be able to keep up with population. The human propensity to reproduce, according to Malthus, would eventually surpass our ability to feed ourselves.

Modern-day Malthusians have given such dire predictions an aura of credibility by using complex computer models to predict precisely when Malthusian calamities will occur. In early 1974, a group of scientists from the Massachusetts Institute of Technology predicted:

If the present growth trends in world population, industrialization, pollution, food production, and resource depletion continue unchanged, the limits to growth on this planet will be reached sometime within the next one hundred years. The most probable result will be a rather sudden and uncontrollable decline in both population and industrial capacity.[1]

In a graph generated by its computer model, the scientific team showed that the "uncontrollable decline" would begin shortly after the turn of the century—in 2005, to be exact—with a precipitous decline in industrial output, food supplies, and population.[2]

The Global 2000 Report commissioned by President Jimmy Carter arrived at similar conclusions in its prediction of what the state of the world's population and natural resources would be at the turn of the next century. "If present trends continue," the report claimed, "the world in 2000 will be more crowded, more polluted, less stable ecologically, and more vulnerable to disruption than the world we live in now. Serious stresses involving population, resources, and environment are clearly visible ahead." In every resource category, Global 2000 predicted overuse and declines in quantity and quality.

But there is no indication that these predictions will come to pass, and many of them have already been proven wrong.[3] The problem rests in the acceptance of Malthus's initial premise that demands on resources will be exponential while the supply is finite. All of these forecasts fail to take account of the ability of humans to react to problems of scarcity by reducing consumption, finding substitutes, and improving productivity. As economist Julian Simon observed, the "ultimate resource" is the human mind, which has allowed us to avoid Malthusian cycles.[4]

Neo-Malthusians might agree with Simon about the value of the human mind, but they generally see political controls of resource use as the only way to implement this human ingenuity. If markets that promote resource consumption are the cause of the problem, then government must be the solution. When nineteenth-century timber harvests denuded portions of the upper Midwest, there was a call to nationalize the forests to ensure against predicted timber famines. Although there has been no timber famine and private forests continue to be more productive than public forests, the political response has endured. From land to water to air, governmental control—which means political control—is seen as a necessary check on the environmental ravages of free markets.

Here we will challenge this common perception and offer an alternative way of thinking about environmental issues, markets, and political choice. This way of thinking does not always provide solutions; instead, it concentrates on how alternative processes link information about the environment with individual incentives to interact with it. Here, the environment and the market are inextricably connected in a positive rather than a negative way.

At the heart of free market environmentalism is a system of well-specified property rights to natural resources. Whether these rights are held by individuals, corporations, non-profit environmental groups, or communal groups, a discipline is imposed on resource users because the wealth of the owner of the property right is at stake if bad decisions are made. Of course, the further a decision maker is removed from this discipline—as he is when there is political control—the less likely it is that good resource stewardship will result. Moreover, if well-specified property rights are transferable, owners must not only consider their own values, they must also consider what others are willing to pay.

The Nature Conservancy's private land management program offers an excellent example of how free market environmentalism works.[5] When the Conservancy obtains title to a parcel of land, the group's wealth, defined in terms of preserving habitat for a rare or endangered species, depends on good stewardship. When The Wisconsin Nature Conservancy was given title to forty acres of beachfront property on St. Croix, Virgin Islands, some may have thought that the group would protect that pristine beach at all costs. But the Conservancy traded the property (with covenants) for a larger parcel of rocky hillside in northern Wisconsin. The trade allowed the Conservancy to protect an entire watershed containing many endangered plant species. To be sure, trade-offs were made, but through the exchange of well-defined and enforced property rights—that is, markets—The Nature Conservancy's wealth in the form of environmental amenities was enhanced.

Free market environmentalism emphasizes an important role for government in the enforcement of property rights. With clearly specified titles—obtained from land recording systems, strict liability rules, and adjudication of disputed property rights in courts—market processes can encourage good resource stewardship. It is when rights are unclear and not well enforced that over-exploitation occurs.

This way of thinking will be alien to some and acceptable to others largely because of the different "visions" each person brings to the issue. In *A Conflict of Visions* Thomas Sowell described a vision as

what we sense or feel *before* we have constructed any systematic reasoning that could be called a theory, much less deduced any specific consequences as hypotheses to be tested against evidence. . . . Visions are the foundations on which theories are built.[6]

The theory of free market environmentalism is founded on certain visions regarding human nature, knowledge, and processes. A consideration of these visions helps explain why some people accept this way of thinking as the only alternative to bureaucratic control and why others reject it as a contradiction in terms.

Human nature. Free market environmentalism views man as self-interested. This self-interest may be enlightened to the extent that people are capable of setting aside their own well-being for close relatives and friends or that they may be conditioned by moral principles. But beyond this, good intentions will not suffice to produce good results. Developing an environmental ethic may be desirable, but it is unlikely to change basic human nature. Instead of intentions, good resource stewardship depends on how well social institutions harness self-interest through individual incentives.

Knowledge. In addition to incentives, good resource stewardship depends on the information available to self-interested individuals. Free market environmentalism views this information or knowledge as diffuse rather than concentrated. Because ecosystems depend on the interaction of many different natural forces, they cannot be "managed" from afar. The information necessary for good management varies significantly from time to time and from place to place, and resource management requires knowledge that can only be obtained "on the ground." Therefore, knowledge cannot be gathered into a single mind or group of minds that can then capably manage all of society's natural resources.

The difference between perceptions of knowledge under centralized, political resource management and free market environmentalism centers on the distribution of knowledge among individuals. In visions of centralized, political control, the distribution has a low mean with a high variance. That is, the common man is not perceived as knowing much about the environment, and what he does know (including knowledge of his own values) is incorrect; the high variance means that experts can manage for the good of the masses. Free market environmentalism sees a much smaller knowledge gap between the experts and the average individual. In this view, individual property owners, who are in a position and have an incentive to obtain time- and place-specific information about their resource endowments, are better suited than centralized bureaucracies to manage resources.

Processes or solutions. These visions of human nature and knowledge combine to make free market environmentalism a study of process rather than a prescription for solutions. If man can rise above self-interest and if knowledge can be concentrated, then the possibility for solutions through political control is more likely. But if there are self-interested individuals with diffuse knowledge, then processes must generate a multitude of solutions conditioned by the checks and balances implicit in the process. By linking wealth to good stewardship through private ownership, the market process generates many individual experiments; and those that are successful will be copied. The question is not whether the right solution has been achieved but whether the relevant trade-offs are being considered in the process.

These three elements of free market environmentalism also characterize the interaction of organisms in ecosystems. Since Charles Darwin's revolutionary study of evolution, most scientific approaches have implicitly assumed that self-interest dominates behavior for higher as well as lower forms of life. Individual members of a species may act in "altruistic" ways and may cooperate with other species, but species survival depends on adjustments to changing parameters in ways that enhance the probability of survival. To assume that man is not self-interested or that he can rise above self-interest because he is part of a political process requires heroic assumptions about homo sapiens vis-à-vis other species.

Ecology also emphasizes the importance of time- and place-specific information in nature. Because the parameters to which species respond vary considerably within ecosystems, each member of a species must respond to time- and place-specific characteristics with the knowledge that each possesses. These parameters can vary widely, so it is imperative for survival that responses utilize the diffuse knowledge. Of course, the higher the level of communication among members of a species, the easier it is to accumulate and concentrate time- and place-specific knowledge. Again, however, it requires a giant leap of faith to assume that man's ability to accumulate and assimilate knowledge is so refined that he can centrally manage the economy or the environment for himself and for all other species. Recent evidence from Eastern Europe underscores the environmental problems that can arise with centralized management.

Ecology is also the study of processes and interaction among species; it is not a scientific prescription for solutions to environmental changes. Like free market environmentalism, ecology focuses on the information and incentives that reach the members of a species. When a niche in an ecosystem is left open, a species can "profit" from filling that niche and other species can benefit as well. If an elk herd grows, there is additional food for bears and wolves and the number of predators will expand as they take advantage of this "profit" opportunity. Individual elk will suffer at the expense of predators, but elk numbers will be controlled. In the process, plant species will survive and other vertebrates will retain their place in the ecosystem. No central planner knows the best solution for filling niches; it is the individualistic process that rewards the efficient use of time- and place-specific information.

Comparing free market environmentalism with ecosystems serves to emphasize how market processes can be compatible with good resource stewardship and environmental quality. As survival rewards species that successfully fill a niche, increased wealth rewards owners who efficiently manage their resources. Profits link self-interest with good resource management by attracting entrepreneurs to open niches. If bad decisions are being made, then a niche will be open. Whether an entrepreneur sees the opportunity and acts on it will depend on his ability to assess time- and place-specific information and act on his assessment. As with an ecosystem, however, the diffuse nature of this information makes it impossible for a central planner to determine which niches are open and how they should be filled. If the link between self-interest and good resource stewardship is broken because good stewards cannot reap the benefits, do not bear the costs of their decisions, or receive distorted information through political intervention, then the efficacy of free market environmentalism will be impaired in the same way that the efficacy of an ecosystem would be impaired by centralized planning.

Visions of what makes good environmental policy are not easily changed; if they are to change, it will be because we recognize that our visions are not consistent with reality. We must ask ourselves whether well-intentioned individuals armed with sufficient information dominate the political decisions that affect natural resources and the environment. Environmentalist Randal O'Toole answered this question in the context of the US Forest Service:

While the environmental movement has changed more than the Forest Service, I would modestly guess that I have changed more than most environmental leaders. . . . In 1980, I blamed all the deficiencies in the markets on greed and big business and thought that government should correct these deficiencies with new laws, regulatory agencies, rational planning, and trade and production restrictions. When that didn't work, I continued to blame the failure on greed and big business.

About 1980, someone suggested to me that maybe government didn't solve environmental or other social problems any better than markets. That idea seemed absurd. After all, this is a democracy, a government of the people, and what the people want they should be able to get. Any suggestion that government doesn't work was incomprehensible.

But then I was immersed in the planning processes of one government agency for ten years (sort of like taking a Berlitz course in bureau-speaking). I learned that the decisions made by government officials often ignored the economic and other analyses done by planners. So much for rational planning. Their decisions also often went counter to important laws and regulations. So much for a democratic government.

Yet I came to realize that the decisions were all predictable, based mainly on their effects on forest budgets. . . .

I gradually developed a new view of the world that recognized the flaws of government as well as the flaws in markets. Reforms should solve problems by creating a system of checks and balances on both processes. . . . The key is to give decision makers the incentives to manage resources properly.[7]

We seek to provide a "Berlitz course in free market environmentalism." We challenge entrenched visions. The development of free market environmentalism has progressed from an examination of the relatively easy problems of land and energy development to the tougher problems of water quality and quantity. The evolution of land and water rights on America's frontier illustrates how the creation of property rights responds to scarcity. Massive reservations of land as public domain halted this privatization movement and often subsidized environmental destruction. There is good evidence that political land management has ignored important recreational and amenity values and that there is a potential for providing them through markets in ways that promote harmony between development and ecology. Free market environmentalism has caught on in the area of water policy, and it holds the promise of a more efficient and environmentally acceptable allocation of that scarce resource. If land use constitutes an "easy" problem for free market environmentalism, pollution problems challenge the paradigm. But there is a clear advantage to using the paradigm of free market environmentalism to examine air pollution problems ranging from acid rain to global warming.

By confronting our entrenched visions, we can move beyond the status quo of political control of the environment and unleash environmental entrepreneurs on the tougher problems we face. The popularity of Earth Day 1990 illustrated the heightened environmental consciousness of people around the world. Most of the proposed solutions to perceived environmental problems, however, call for centralized approaches that are not consistent with the science of ecology. Moreover, these solutions pit winners against losers in a zero-sum game that tears at the social fabric. Free market environmentalism depends on a voluntary exchange of property rights between consenting owners and promotes cooperation and compromise. In short, it offers an alternative that channels the heightened environmental consciousness into win-win solutions that can sustain economic growth, enhance environmental quality, and promote harmony.

II. Rethinking the Way We Think

Most natural resource and environmental policy has been premised on the assumption that markets are responsible for resource misallocation and environmental degradation and that centralized, political processes can correct these problems. In general, the failure of markets is attributed to private decision makers who do not take into account all costs and benefits, to the unequal availability of information to all buyers and sellers, or to monopolies distorting prices and outputs.[8] In essence, market failure is blamed on the lack of information, inappropriate incentives, or both. To counter market failures, centralized planning is seen as a way of aggregating information about social costs and social benefits in order to maximize the value of natural resources. Decisions based on this aggregated information are to be made by disinterested resource managers whose goal is to maximize social welfare.

Economic analysis in general and natural resource economics in particular have approached resource policy as if there is a "socially efficient" allocation of resources that will be reached when scientific managers understand the relevant trade-offs and act to achieve the efficient solution. For example, forest resources are supposed to be managed to achieve the "greatest good for the greatest number" through "multiple use management" undertaken by an "elite corps of professionals." When problems with management are recognized, they are attributed to "bad people in government" and the solution is to replace them with better trained, better financed managers.

But there is a more realistic way of thinking about natural resource and environmental policy. This alternative recognizes and emphasizes the costs of coordinating human actions. There is no assumption that costs of engaging in a transaction are zero or that there is perfect competition. To the contrary, understanding alternative policies requires that we specify coordination costs and discover why and where competitive forces may not be working.[9]

This analytical framework applies equally to markets and politics. If all people lived alone on remote islands, there would be no costs of coordination; but in a complex society where people gain from trade, interacting individuals must measure and monitor the actions of one another. In the marketplace, consumers must signal to suppliers what quantity and quality of products they demand at what prices; suppliers must determine which products to produce and which input combinations to use. Both demanders and suppliers must monitor one another to ensure that products are delivered and paid for. To the extent that actions can be effectively measured and monitored, demanders and suppliers will internalize costs and benefits, profits will be made, and efficient resource allocation will be a by-product.

Similarly, citizens who demand goods and services from government must monitor the politicians and bureaucrats who supply them. Like a consumer displeased with food purchased from the supermarket, a citizen who is unhappy with the actions of his political representative has experienced the cost of measuring and monitoring supplier performance. Outcomes do not always reflect citizens' desires; the political process may supply too many of goods like nuclear arms or too little of goods like quality education. As with market analysis, policy analysis must focus on how well the political process internalizes costs and benefits to citizens and their political agents so that resources will not be squandered.

In rethinking natural resource and environmental policy, two facts must be recognized. First, *incentives matter to all human behavior*. No matter how well intended professional resources managers are, incentives affect their behavior. Like it or not, individuals will undertake more of an activity if the costs of that activity are reduced; this holds as much for bureaucrats as it does for profit-maximizing owners of firms. Everyone accepts that managers in the private sector would dump production wastes into a nearby stream if they did not have to pay for the cost of their action. Too often, however, we fail to recognize the same elements at work in the political arena. If a politician is not personally accountable for allowing oil development on federal lands or for permitting an agency to dump hazardous wastes into the environment, then we can expect too much development or too much dumping. Moreover, when the beneficiaries of these policies do not have to pay the full cost, they will demand more of each from political representatives.

Second, *information costs are positive in both the private and political sectors*. In a world of scarcity, both private and political resource managers must obtain information about the relative values of alternative uses. When one resource use rivals another, trade-offs must be made. Resource managers can only make these trade-offs based on the information coming to them or on their own values. If they believe lumber is more valuable than wildlife habitat, trees will be cut. Timber managers may know how fast trees grow under certain conditions, but they cannot know what the value of the growth is without incurring some cost in obtaining that information. The lumber market provides information on timber value as a commodity, but information about the value of wildlife habitat and environmental amenities is more costly because those markets are less developed. Private timber managers for International Paper, for example, are being forced to consider wildlife habitat in their timber production decisions because prices tell them that consumers are willing to pay increasingly more for hunting, camping, and recreation. Political managers who "give away" recreational services from political lands lack this price information and have less incentive to react to changing values.

When incentives matter and information is costly, resource management is complicated so that it is not sufficient to rely on good intentions. Even if the superintendent of national parks believes that grizzly bear habitat is more valuable than more campsites, his good intentions will not necessarily yield more grizzly bear habitat. In a political setting where camping interests have more influence over a bureaucrat's budget, his peace and quiet, or his future promotion, intentions will have to override incentives if grizzly bear habitat is to prevail. But if a private resource owner believes that grizzly bear habitat is more valuable and can capitalize on that value, then politics will not matter. Moreover, if those who demand grizzly habitat are willing to pay more than those who demand campsites, then incentives and information reinforce one another. Management simply cannot be adequately analyzed without careful attention to the information and incentives that actors face under alternative institutional arrangements.

SCIENTIFIC MANAGEMENT OR ECONOMICS WITHOUT PRICES

For years economists have tried to use computer modeling techniques to simulate the market allocation of natural resources. The US Forest Service, for example, developed FORPLAN, a forest simulation model, to specify the necessary conditions for efficient national forest use. The rationale of such models is simply that if the additional or marginal value of one resource use is greater than another, then allocation will be improved if the resource is reallocated from the latter to the former. This form of analysis teaches us that there are many margins for adjustment and that few decisions have all-or-nothing consequences. When water is allocated for fish or irrigation, trade-offs must be made; it is not an either or decision. Put simply, neither demand nor supply is unresponsive to price changes. If prices rise, then demanders will make marginal adjustments by shifting consumption to the nearest substitutes; suppliers will adjust by substituting among resources and technologies.

The logic of this analysis combined with models and computers that can simulate resource use can lure policy analysts into believing that the maximization of resource value is a simple matter. Unfortunately, in this case logic and simplicity are not good guides because they mask the information costs and incentives. Consider the case of multiple use management of the national forests, where the scientific manager is supposed to trade off timber production, wildlife habitat, aesthetic values, water quality, recreation, and other uses to maximize the value of the forest. Because the managers are not supposed to be motivated by profit or self-interest, it is assumed that they will impartially apply economic theory and quantitative methods to accomplish efficient resource allocation. The scientific manager, armed with the economic concepts of marginal analysis, is supposed to be "always analytical. . . . Always, the economist's reasoning, his analytical framework . . . , and his conclusions are exposed forthrightly to the examination and criticism of others. In these ways, *scientific objectivity* is actively sought."[10]

To apply marginal analysis to multiple use, decision makers must attach values to the relevant margins. Scientific management assumes that these values are known and, therefore, that there is an efficient solution. The decision maker must only acquire the "correct" information about resource values in alternative uses and reallocate those resources until marginal equalities hold. Management is simply the process of finding the socially optimal allocation. Thomas Sowell has captured the traditional resource economics perspective on information:

Given that explicitly articulated knowledge is special and concentrated . . . the best conduct of social activities depends upon the special knowledge of the few being used to guide the actions of the many. . . . Along with this has often gone a vision of intellectuals as disinterested advisors. . . . [11]

If knowledge of values that must be traded off against one another were "special and concentrated," then scientific management might be possible. But as F. A. Hayek has pointed out,

the economic problem of society is . . . not merely a problem of how to allocate "given resources"—if "given" is taken to mean given to a single mind which deliberately solves the problem set by these "data." It is rather a problem of how to secure the best use of resources known to any of the members of society, for ends whose relative importance only these individuals know. Or, to put it briefly, it is a problem of utilization of knowledge not given to anyone in its totality.[12]

The very information and knowledge necessary for trade-offs made using scientific management are subjective and are only revealed through human action.

As analytical tools, economic models focus on the importance of marginal adjustments, but they cannot instruct managers in which trade-offs to make or which values to place on a resource. In the absence of subjective individual evaluations, the marginal solutions derived by sophisticated efficiency maximization models are unachievable ideals. Unfortunately, these models have been used as guides to tell resource managers how to achieve efficient allocation; in fact, they can only provide a way of thinking about trade-offs. Managers argue that these models have added sophistication and authority to political management efforts, allowing shadow prices (that is, prices that are not real but images of what would exist if there was a market) to be derived and used in lieu of actual market processes. The Forest Service and the Bureau of Land Management, enamored with these models, assume that with sufficient data and large enough computers it is possible to produce wise and efficient management plans. Forest economist Richard Behan stated that the planning acts that guide the Forest Service mandate "with the force of law that forest plans can be rational, comprehensive, and essentially perfect."[13] But no matter how rational or comprehensive they may be, models built on marginal analysis will always be constrained by information requirements.

The market process generates information on the subjective values that humans place on alternative resource use as individuals engage in voluntary trades. The decentralized decisions made in markets are crucial, because "practically every individual has some advantage over all others in that he possesses unique information of which beneficial use might be made, but of which use can be made only if the decisions depending on it are left to him or are made with his active cooperation." Once we understand that most knowledge is fragmented and dispersed, then "systemic coordination among the many supersedes the special wisdom of the few." Traditional economic analysis has failed to recognize this fundamental point. The information necessary for "efficient" resource allocation depends on the knowledge of the special circumstance of time and place.[14]

The idea of scientific management has also misguided public policy because it ignores the incentives of decision makers in the political sector. The economic analysis of markets focuses on incentives in the form of prices that determine the benefits and costs that decision makers face. Market failure is said to result when any benefits are not captured or costs are not borne by decision makers. The existence of these externalities or third-party effects means that either too little of a good is produced in the case of uncaptured benefits or too much in the case of unborne costs. A system of private water allocation, for example, may not provide a sufficient supply of instream flows for wildlife habitat and environmental quality because owners of water cannot easily charge recreationalists and environmentalists who benefit from free-flowing water. And too much pollution exists because firms do not have to pay the full cost of waste disposal, so they "overuse" the air or water as a garbage dump. Such under- or over-production is often taken as a sufficient condition for taking political control of resource allocation.

There is, however, an asymmetry in the analysis of market and political processes because of a failure to recognize that the *political sector operates by externalizing costs*. Consider the reasoning that political agents apply to scientific management. When land is diverted from timber production to wilderness, there is an opportunity cost associated with the reallocation. Private landowners interested in maximizing the value of the resource must take this cost into account in the "price" of wilderness. The bureaucratic manager or politician who does not own the land, however, does not face all the opportunity costs of his decisions. He will take the values forgone into account only if the political process makes him do so. If we assume that the political process worked perfectly (which is the equivalent of *assuming* that markets work perfectly), then the countervailing powers of the opposing sides would internalize the benefits and costs for the decision maker.

But there is little reason to believe that the political process works perfectly or even tolerably well. Because politicians and bureaucrats are rewarded for responding to political pressure groups, there is no guarantee that the values of unorganized interests will be taken into account *even if* they constitute a majority of the population. For example, most Americans will pay marginally higher prices for petroleum products if oil production is not allowed in the Arctic National Wildlife Refuge. Because this cost to each individual is low and the costs of information and action are high relative to the benefits, each person will remain rationally ignorant; that is, he will not become informed on the issue. But organized groups that favor preserving wildlife habitat in the pristine tundra can gain by stopping drilling in the refuge. To the extent that those who benefit from wildlife preservation do not have to pay the opportunity costs of forgone energy production, they will demand "too much" wildlife habitat. In the absence of a perfect political process, we must depend on good intentions to overpower the special interest incentives built into the imperfect system. This takes a giant leap of faith.

Traditional thinking about natural resource and environmental policy ignores the most basic economic tenet: *incentives matter*. Markets with positive costs of eliminating third-party effects have been compared with a political process where those costs are ignored or assumed to be zero. Consider the approach taken in a leading natural resource economics textbook:

> . . . "the government" is a separate agent acting in the social interest when activity by individuals fails to bring about the social optimum. . . . we discuss some limits of this approach, but it permits us to abstract from the details of the political process.[15]

When we abstract from the details of the political process, we ignore incentives inherent in that process. Daniel Bromley claimed that government agencies are

> politically responsible to the citizenry through the system of . . . elections and ministerial direction. However imperfect this may work, the *presumption* must be that the wishes of the full citizenry are more properly catered to than would be the case if all environmental protection were left to the ability to pay by a few members of society given to philanthropy.[16]

But why must we "presume" that the "wishes of the full citizenry are more properly catered to"? And what does "full citizenry" mean? Is there unanimous consent? Does a majority constitute the "full citizenry" when voting turnout is traditionally low? Bromley also charged that "claims for volitional exchange are supported by appeal to a body of economic theory that is not made explicit," but there is little made explicit when we "abstract from the details of the political process" by presuming "that the wishes of the full citizenry are more properly catered to" in the political process.[17]

Because traditional thinking about resource and environmental policy pays little attention to the institutions that structure and provide information and incentives in the political sector, practitioners often seem surprised and puzzled that efficiency implications from their models are ignored in the policy arena. In the private sector, efficiency matters because it influences profits; in the political sector, prices and incentives are often very different. Political resource managers make trade-offs in terms of political currencies measured in terms of special interest support; at best, this unit of account provides imprecise measures of the subjective values of citizens.

The incentive structure in the political sector is complicated because the bottom line depends on the electoral process where votes matter, not efficiency. Because voters are rationally ignorant, because benefits can be concentrated and costs diffused, and because individual voters seldom (and probably never) influence the outcome of elections, there is little reason to expect that elections will link political decisions to efficiency in the same way that private ownership does in the market process.[18]

Under private ownership, profits and losses are the measure of how well decision makers are managing. Even where shareholders in a large company have little effect on actual decisions, they can observe stock prices and annual reports as a measure of management's performance. In other words, private ownership gives owners both the information and the incentive to measure performance. In the political sector, however, both information and incentives are lacking. Annual budget figures offer information about overall expenditures and outlays, but it is not clear who is responsible and whether larger budgets are good or bad. Even when responsibility can be determined, there is no easy way for a citizen to "buy and sell shares" in the government. Therefore, citizens remain rationally ignorant about most aspects of political resource allocation and rationally informed about issues that directly affect them. The rewards for political resource managers depend not on maximizing net resource values but on providing politically active constituents with what they want with little regard for cost. Although it may not be possible to state precisely what is maximized by politicians and bureaucrats, it is clear that efficiency is not the main goal. If political resource managers were to follow the tenets of traditional natural resource economics, it would have to be because there were honest, sincere people (professional managers) pursuing the public interest.

Anthony Fisher has provided perhaps the best summary of the problem:

We have already abandoned the assumption of a complete set of competitive markets. . . . But if we now similarly abandon the notion of a perfect planner, it is not clear, in my judgment, that the government will do any better. Apart from the question of the planner's motivation to behave in the way assumed in our models, to allocate resources efficiently, there is the question of his ability to do so.[19]

Without information and incentives, scientific management becomes economics without prices.

GETTING THE INCENTIVES RIGHT

The constraint on the gains from trade in market processes is that each party to a transaction must measure and monitor the activities of the other. If individuals were self-sufficient, these costs disappear, but they would also forgo the gains from specialization and trade. Hence, the problem we all face is to trade off the gains from specialization against the costs of measuring and monitoring the performance of those with whom we interact.

This framework is useful for examining relationships in the political sector where citizens "hire" politicians or bureaucrats to produce certain goods and services. At a minimum, this relationship grants to the government a monopoly on the use of coercion, which enables it to enforce voluntary contracts between individuals. In addition, citizens may assign to the state the role of producing goods for which coercion is necessary because the costs of measuring and monitoring voluntary transactions are prohibitive. For example, if the costs of excluding fishermen from a free-flowing stream are high, then there will be little incentive for the private sector to provide this amenity; market failure is said to result in the underproduction of these "public goods." By using the coercive power of government to charge all citizens (or at least all fishermen), this problem can be overcome. Unfortunately, this solution raises another problem: How can the citizens be certain that the state is producing the desired bundle of public goods? Indeed, the fundamental dilemma of political economy is: Once the state has the coercive power to do what voluntary (market) action cannot do, how can that power be constrained from being usurped by special interests?

At least two variables are important in determining the resolution of this dilemma. First, the complexity of the good in question will have a direct bearing on the ability of a consumer or citizen to measure the performance of suppliers. If lands managed by the political sector produce timber, measuring the board feet of production may be simple; but if those same lands are for "multiple use," then it is much more costly to determine how closely actual results approximate the results desired. Goods such as environmental quality, risk management, soil conservation, national heritage, and wilderness values are all costly to measure.

The second determinant will be the costs of monitoring political agents who provide public goods, and these costs will be directly related to the proximity, both in time and space, of the agent to the citizen. Monitoring the behavior of a local zoning board is less costly than monitoring the behavior of the director of the National Park Service. Furthermore, before we had telephones and computers, monitoring agent behavior was more costly because of the time required for communication. A free press and free access to governmental information reduced these costs. At the same time however, the multitude of decisions made at various levels of government and the large number of constituents represented by each political agent raised the cost of monitoring.

Because the same kinds of costs exist with market transactions, we must complete the analysis by comparing the measurement and monitoring costs of the political sector with those of the private sector. For all market transactions, both buyers and sellers must incur measurement and monitoring costs. The buyer must consider a product's value in quantity and quality terms and weigh that value against alternative goods. The seller must monitor production and discover mechanisms for making sure buyers cannot enjoy the benefits of the good without paying. For example, a hunter purchasing hunting rights must consider the value of the hunting experience relative to other opportunities. The seller must determine whether it is worth enhancing hunting opportunities and whether nonpaying hunters can avoid paying the fee (that is, trespassing) while still reaping the benefits. If the costs for either buyer or seller are sufficiently high, the potential net gains from trade will be reduced and trades may not take place.

There are three important characteristics of private sector transactions, however, that tend to mitigate these costs. First, measurement costs are greatly reduced in market transactions by prices. Prices convey valuable, condensed information that allows consumers to compare and aggregate inputs and outputs. In the absence of price information that transforms subjective values into an objective measure, comparing values of alternative resource uses is difficult. Because many governmental goods and services are not priced, transaction costs are higher in the political sector.

Prices also allow a measure of efficiency through profits and losses. If a shareholder wants to know how well the management of his firm is performing, he can at least consult the profit-and-loss statement. This is not a perfect measure of performance, but continual losses suggest that actual results differ from those that are desired. This can tell the shareholder that he should consider alternative managers who can produce the product at a lower cost or he should reconsider the market for the product. Compared to the political sector where the output of government is not priced and where agency performance is not measured by the bottom line, profits and losses in the private sector provide concise information with which owners can measure the performance of their agents.

Second, the political and private sectors differ in the degree to which measurement and monitoring costs are borne by those who demand the goods. In the political process, voters ultimately decide who the suppliers will be. In order to make good decisions, voters must gather information about alternative candidates or referenda issues and vote on the basis of that information. If an individual invests a great deal of effort into becoming informed and votes on what is best for society, he does a service for his fellow citizens. If the voter is not well informed and votes for things that will harm the society, then this cost is spread among all voters. In other words, well-informed voters produce a classic public good, and, as with any public good, we can expect voters to under-invest in becoming informed, thus remaining "rationally ignorant." In contrast, consumers in the private sector bear the costs of being informed, but they also reap the benefits of good choices and bear the costs of bad ones. When a landowner hires a forest manager, he will seek information on the manager's ability and he will monitor his performance. If the landowner assumes none of the costs and gets a bad manager, then the owner will bear the costs directly; if he pays the costs and management quality is improved, then the benefits are internalized to the landowner in the form of higher profits. It is the clear assignment of these profits and losses that distinguishes the private from the political sector.

Third, private sector relationships differ from those in the political sector in terms of the cost of choosing alternative suppliers. In the political sector, if a citizen does not believe he is getting from government the goods and services he desires, then he can attempt to sway a majority of the voters and elect new suppliers or he can physically move from one location to another. In either case, the costs of changing suppliers is much higher than in the private sector, where there is greater competition among potential agents. For example, if a local supermarket does not sell what a customer desires, then he has many alternative producers from whom to choose. Even in the more complex case of corporate managers, a stockholder can easily change agents by selling shares in one company and purchasing shares in another. In short, because changing suppliers in the private sector does not require agreement from a majority of the other consumers, change is less costly. This condition imposes a strong competitive discipline. In general, information through prices, internalization of costs and benefits from monitoring by individuals, and agent discipline imposed by competition reduce measurement and monitoring costs.

Where market transactions fail to occur for natural resources and environmental amenities, it is usually because the costs of measuring and monitoring resource use are high. For example, suppose a landowner is deciding whether to forgo one type of production to enhance an aesthetic quality. If the aesthetic quality is a beautiful flower garden, a high fence may be sufficient to exclude free riders and capture the full benefits from the product. If the trade-off is between cutting trees and preserving a beautiful mountainside, however, excluding casual sightseers may be far too costly.

The key, therefore, to effective markets in general and free market environmentalism in particular is the establishment of well-specified and transferable property rights. When a conservation group purchases a conservation easement on a parcel of land, the exchange requires that property rights be well defined, enforced, and transferable. The physical attributes of the resources must be specified in a clear and concise manner; they must be measurable. For example, the rectangular survey system allows us to define ownership rights over land and clarifies disputes over ownership. The system may also help us define ownership to the airspace over land, but more questions arise here because of the fluidity of air and the infinite vertical third dimension above the ground. If property rights to resources cannot be defined, then they obviously cannot be exchanged for other property rights.

Property rights also must be defendable. A rectangular survey may define surface rights to land, but conflicts are inevitable if there is no way to defend the boundaries and prevent other incompatible uses. Barbed wire provided an inexpensive way to defend property rights on the western frontier; locks and chains do the same for parked bicycles. But enforcing one's rights to peace and quiet by "fencing out" sound waves may be much more difficult, as will keeping other people's hazardous wastes out of a groundwater supply. Whenever the use of property cannot be monitored or enforced, conflicts are inevitable and trades are impossible.

Finally, property rights must be transferable. In contrast to the costs of measuring and monitoring resource uses, which are mainly determined by the physical nature of the property and technology, the ability to exchange is determined largely by the legal environment. Although well-defined and enforced rights allow the owner to enjoy the benefits of using his property, legal restrictions on the sale of that property preclude the potential for gains from trade. Suppose that a group of fishermen values water for fish habitat more highly than farmers value the same water for irrigation. If the fishermen are prohibited from renting or purchasing the water from the farmers, then gains from trade will not be realized and potential wealth will not be created. Moreover, the farmer will have less incentive to leave the water in the stream.

In sum, free market environmentalism presupposes well-specified rights to take actions with respect to specific resources. If those rights cannot be measured, monitored, and marketed, then there is little possibility for exchange. Garbage disposal through the air, for example, is more of a problem than solid waste disposal in the ground because property rights to the Earth's surface are better defined than property rights to the atmosphere. Private ownership of land works quite well for producing timber, but measuring, monitoring, and marketing the land for endangered species habitat requires entrepreneurial imagination.

Imagination is crucial to free market environmentalism, because it is in the areas where property rights are evolving that resource allocation problems occur. Where environmental entrepreneurs can devise ways of marketing environmental values, market incentives can have dramatic results. It is important to recognize that any case of external benefits or costs provides fertile ground for an entrepreneur who can define and enforce property rights. A stream owner who can devise ways of charging fishermen can internalize the benefits and costs and gain an incentive to maintain or improve the quality of his resource. The subdivider who puts covenants on deeds that preserve open space, improve views, and generally harmonize development with the environment establishes property rights to these values and captures the value in higher asset prices.

The property rights approach to natural resources recognizes that property rights evolve depending on the benefits and costs associated with defining and enforcing rights. This calculus will depend on such variables as the expected value of the resource in question, the technology for measuring and monitoring property rights, and the legal and moral rules that condition the behavior of the interacting parties. At any given time, property rights will reflect the perceived benefits and costs of definition and enforcement. To observe actions that are not accounted for in market transactions—that is, for which property rights have not been specified—and call them externalities or market failure ignores the evolutionary nature of property rights.[20] As the perceived costs and benefits of defining and enforcing property rights change, property rights will evolve.

This does not mean that there is no role for government in the definition and enforcement process or that property rights will always take all costs and benefits into account. The costs of establishing property rights are positive and *potentially* can be reduced through governmental institutions, such as courts. Furthermore, because transaction costs are positive, contracts that take costs into account will not always be forthcoming. In the case of water pollution from sources that cannot be identified (with current technology) at low costs, for example, the definition and enforcement of property rights governing water use may be impossible. And excluding non-payers from enjoying a scenic view may be costly enough that a market cannot evolve under current technologies and institutions. In these cases, there is a utilitarian argument for considering government intervention. But there is still no guarantee that the results from political allocation will work very well. If markets produce "too little" clean water because dischargers do not have to pay for its use, then political solutions are equally likely to produce "too much" clean water because those who enjoy the benefits do not pay the cost.

CONCLUSION

Traditional economic analysis stresses the potential for market failure in the natural resource and environmental arena on the grounds that externalities are pervasive. Free market environmentalism explicitly recognizes that this problem arises because it is costly to define and enforce rights in both the private and political sectors. In fact, the symmetry of the externality argument requires that specific attention be paid to politics as the art of diffusing costs and concentrating benefits. Assuming that externality problems in the environment can be solved by turning to the political sector ignores the likelihood that government will externalize costs. Just as pollution externalities can generate too much dirty air, political externalities can generate too much water storage, clear-cutting, wilderness, or water quality.

Free market environmentalism emphasizes the importance of market processes in determining optimal amounts of resource use. Only when rights are well-defined, enforced, and transferable will self-interested individuals confront the trade-offs inherent in a world of scarcity. As entrepreneurs move to fill profit niches, prices will reflect the values we place on resources and the environment. Mistakes will be made, but in the process a niche will be opened and profit opportunities will attract resource managers with a better idea. Remember that even externalities offer profit niches to the environmental entrepreneur who can define and enforce property rights to the unowned resource and charge the free-riding user. In cases where definition and enforcement costs are insurmountable, political solutions may be called for. Unfortunately, however, those kinds of solutions often become entrenched and stand in the way of innovative market processes that promote fiscal responsibility, efficient resource use, and individual freedom.

Notes

1. Donnella H. Meadows, Dennis L. Meadows, Jorgen Randers, William W. Behrens III, *The Limits to Growth: A Report for the Club of Rome's Project on the Predicament of Mankind* (New York: A Potomac Associates Book, New American Library, 1974), pp. ix–x.

2. For a discussion of additional apocalyptic predictions, see Edith Efron, *The Apocalyptics* (New York: Simon and Schuster, 1984), chap. 1.

3. *Global 2000 Report to the President* (Washington, DC: Government Printing Office, 1980), 1. For a critique of the *Global 2000* findings and for data refuting the predictions, see Julian Simon and Herman Kahn, *The Resourceful Earth: A Response to Global 2000* (Oxford: Basil Blackwell, 1984).

4. Julian Simon, *The Ultimate Resource* (Princeton: Princeton University Press, 1981).

5. The Nature Conservancy controls thousands of acres of private land that fit the free-market environmentalism model. But the Conservancy also turns many of its lands over to public agencies, thereby perpetuating political control of resources.

6. Thomas Sowell, *A Conflict of Visions* (New York: William Morrow and Company, 1987), 14.

7. Randal O'Toole, "Learning the Lessons of the 1980s," *Forest Watch*, 10 (January–February 1990), 6.

8. For a summary of the standard criticisms of natural resource markets, see Charles Howe, *Natural Resource Economics* (New York: John Wiley and Sons, 1979), 103.

9. This framework for thinking about the environment has been called the New Resource Economics and was first formally discussed in Terry L. Anderson, "New Resource Economics: Old Ideas and New Applications," *American Journal of Agricultural Economics*, 64 (December 1982), 928–34.

10. Alan Randall, *Resource Economics* (Columbus, Oh.: Grid Publishing Company, 1981), 36.

11. Sowell, *Conflict of Visions*, 46.

12. F. A. Hayek, "The Use of Knowledge in Society," *American Economic Review*, 35 (September 1945), 519–20.

13. Richard W. Behan, "RPA/NFMA—Time to Punt," *Journal of Forestry*, 79 (1981), 802.

14. Hayek, "Use of Knowledge," 80; Sowell, *Conflict of Visions*, 48.

15. John M. Hartwick and Nancy D. Olewiler, *The Economics of Natural Resource Use* (New York: Harper and Row, 1986), 18.

16. Daniel W. Bromley, *Property Rights and the Environment: Natural Resource Policy in Transition* (Wellington, New Zealand: Ministry for the Environment, 1987), 55.

17. Ibid. 54.

18. For a more detailed discussion, see James Gwartney and Richard Stroup, *Economics: Private and Public Choice*, 4th edn. (New York: Harcourt Brace & Jovanovich, 1987), 687–99.

19. Anthony C. Fisher, *Resource and Environmental Economics* (Cambridge: Cambridge University Press, 1981), 54.

20. See Terry L. Anderson and P. J. Hill, "The Evolution of Property Rights: A Study of the American West," *Journal of Law and Economics*, 12 (October 1975), 163–79.

15 Political Pursuit of Private Gain: Environmental Goods

William C. Mitchell and Randy T. Simmons

If the volume of legislation and political rhetoric is a good indicator, we might dub the 1980s the Environmental Decade. Never before were so much attention and so many resources devoted to "saving" the environment, reducing pollution, preserving wildlife, creating more environmental amenities, keeping fit, vacationing in the wilderness, and purchasing fashionable hiking shoes, backpacks, bicycles, and ski equipment. Morally enraged attacks on industrial polluters and obscene profiteers were and remain fashionable in dinner-table conversations. Humans, we are told, do not live on bread alone; poetry, the mind, and environmental amenities must also be cultivated in civilized societies. In short, what economists label as externalities, social costs, or neighborhood effects have become a staple of daily conversation as well as of modern textbooks.

This new-found concern over the amenities of life is made possible, paradoxically, because of the tremendous economic growth engendered by capitalism. As material goods have become more plentiful, their marginal value has, as the law says, diminished; at the same time, the "quality-of-life" attributes have increased in value, posing further allocative choices. The problem becomes one of determining that combination of material and quality-of-life goods we wish to consume. For example, poor people place higher values on scarce material things, whereas those who take high incomes for granted seek the less available, more costly amenities. But any sacrifices from preserving environmental amenities are expected to be shared by all.

Public opinion polls do show continuing support from all income classes for the government to "do something" about environmental degradation and to protect environmental amenities. But the methods government officials have chosen and continue to choose are often failures. Some policies create the illusion of creating improvement while actually making things worse. Others succeed at protecting or improving environmental amenities but at costs that are greater than the value of the amenities.

A Primer

Ever since Paul Samuelson first wrote about public goods in the 1950s, political scientists and policy analysts have asserted that voluntary collective action in large groups and markets will fail to produce the socially optimal level of those private goods having external costs or benefits in production and/or consumption. The market overproduces a good when external costs exist because not all costs are incurred by the producers and consumers of the good. In effect, consumers of the good are subsidized by the damaged third parties. Conversely, the market underproduces a good whenever external benefits exist because all benefits are not captured by market demand for the product. In competitive markets, especially those consisting of large numbers of people, there will be little or no incentive for individuals to voluntarily do anything about negative externalities; everyone is induced to become a free rider. On the basis of this argument, the standard approach has been to apply extensive and forceful governmental action to remedy the situation.

This discussion will gain in precision if we consider an elementary graph that will enable us to pinpoint the nature of the problem and locate possible solutions. Consider Figure 15.1. Let the line ABC represent the marginal spillover costs of an industry and the line DBE_m the marginal costs of abatement by the industry. In an uncontrolled market the industry will emit a total of $0E_m$ units of pollution even though the socially optimal level is $0E_s$ where the two sets of marginal costs are equal.

The standard approach suggests two responses. The first, preferred by most environmental groups and politicians, is to mandate $0E_s$. This approach, known as "command and control," is characteristic of most of the environmental legislation enacted during the past two decades. The second response is to tax the industry by the amount of $0T$ or BE_s. A tax will encourage the industrialists to produce the correct combination of products and pollution. Each firm will reduce its level of pollution until the marginal cost of abatement equals the tax rate. Any further reduction of pollution would be more costly than paying the tax, so $0E_s$ is the optimal level.

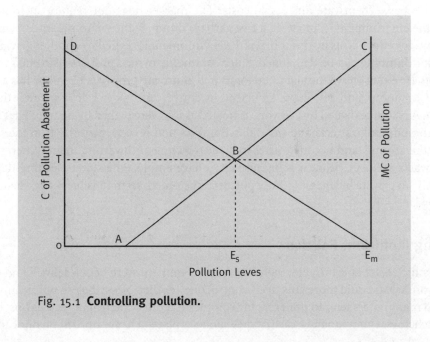

Fig. 15.1 **Controlling pollution.**

Presumably, the marginal cost of abatement will be equalized for all firms minimizing the costs of pollution control.

Economists tend to favor the taxing scheme because enforcement costs are lower and innovation encouraged. But taxing an undesirable or even "immoral" activity is seen by many environmental activists as a social statement of indifference to environmentally destructive behavior. Taxing an activity fails to stigmatize it the way prohibiting or controlling it would, at least in the minds of the environmental elite. Both schemes are bound to be highly inefficient. Choosing taxes or command-and-control policies is dictated in the first place by an incorrect diagnosis of the sources or causes of externalities and second by political considerations honored by politicians and bureaucrats.

Faith in government's ability to raise social welfare through cost-benefit analysis and adopting command-and-control or tax policies is unwarranted. It is unwarranted because environmental problems must be understood more as failures by government to specify property rights than as offshoots of private profit-seeking. Most politicians and many welfare economists do not agree with this argument, however, and instead view private property and profits as the culprits and imply that if government restricted or controlled them, society and the environment would be better off.

We emphasize the elementary but crucial fact that externalities, both good and bad, are *unintended* consequences of *useful*, purposive actions. Polluters do not go into business in order to pollute; they go into business to make money by satisfying consumer demands. Private firms as well as individual citizens take account of their own direct business costs in making decisions; they do not often take account of social effects. As a consequence, the prices attached to products reflect only the former and not the latter costs. That is what economists mean when they write of divergences between private and social costs. The market does not require such accounting because the environment is, in effect, a free garbage dump. If the environment is owned by no one, it pays to reduce costs by dumping; if the environment is owned by another private person, charges for dumping can be demanded. Since commonly owned property is owned by no one, the results are clear—it will not be cared for as well as private property. Everyone has a powerful incentive to dump and few have sufficient incentives and power to prevent others from dumping. A resource owned by everyone is treated as if it were owned by no one. That is why we notice litter on public streets and sidewalks. Smokers find it convenient to drop their cigarette butts on the ground, and no one wishes to incur the costs of thwarting them. Wherever streets and sidewalks are kept clean, it is because cities have employed a street-cleaning department and/or rely on private businesses whose potential customers seem to value ready, clean access to their shops.

Choosing Inefficient Policies

Efficiency dictates that if property rights to the environment were better defined and enforced, private transactors could more effectively control one another. Nevertheless, politicians, bureaucrats, and many voters tend to prefer highly complex but often inefficient regulations, taxes, and subsidy schemes. Unfortunately, each of these policies places a heavy burden on our capacities to gather and process information and multiplies the administrative costs of supervising polluters. At the same time, command-and-control or taxation solutions ignore the incentives and capacities of private parties to bargain with one another.

Politicians may prefer direct controls because controls enhance their own power and because many voters mistakenly believe that regulation through law is the simplest and most effective way to discourage antisocial behavior. Since politicians must honor electoral myths, passing a law seems to demonstrate their deep concern and forcefulness in attacking outstanding problems.

Whenever large numbers of people are involved in polluting, politicians are notably reluctant to enact tough antipollution legislation. The Oregon state legislature, for example, summoned up a great deal of courage and imagination in devising statutes to limit the number two polluter in Oregon, the wood-burning stove. The law permits people to use existing inefficient stoves and does not mandate costly improvements for them; however, manufacturers of new wood-burning stoves will be required to meet the higher standards beginning several years in the future. Needless to say, most homeowners will not voluntarily pay for more expensive but less polluting stoves. Old stoves will, accordingly, command a higher price in the second-hand market and pollution will not be reduced for a decade or more. Now politicians claim to have "done something," yet the net costs imposed on present voters are minimal.

Likewise, politicians are reluctant to make drivers the culprits in auto pollution and traffic accidents. Industry serves as a convenient scapegoat. And many politicians of the highest rank blame drug abuse not on users but on suppliers, foreign producers, and disreputable local pushers.

Bureaucrats, too, prefer environmental controls over market solutions; controls provide them with something useful to do and give them a ready claim to larger budgets to meet further unmet social needs. When they institute controls, they may be seen as dedicated servants of the public, hard-working officials protecting the environment; that they restrict the choices and behavior of others is of lesser concern. And, although their activities may be costly in the long run and, worse, ineffectual, few people notice the long run. Since higher costs of abatement appear to fall on the wealthy, corporate "malefactors" rather than the small taxpayer and consumer, politicians and bureaucrats gain support among voters.

In addition to the political attractiveness of illusory control policies, conventional approaches ignore the technical problem of identifying the optimal level of pollution. Without this information, it is impossible to calculate what amount of tax or level of control will best succeed in bringing social costs and benefits into line. Moral suasion on the part of government presents even more problems, for it calls for nothing less than an ethical revolution. Besides being impractical, such a government policy is devoid of a mechanism to achieve the optimal level of pollution. Still, governments resort to moral suasion where enforcement is impossible (littering) or where immediate action is required in brief emergencies (temperature inversions in Los Angeles). Outright bans may be more reliable than moral suasion so long as they are limited in scope. But outright bans cannot work if the ban affects nearly everyone, as is the case with pollution from internal combustion engines. In any event, such prohibitions are unlikely to achieve the optimal amount of the externality—unless, of course, the optimum is zero pollution. In general, risk-averse governments have chosen the ban when the cost of discovering the optimum level was in itself prohibitive and they had to choose an arbitrary level between zero and unchecked, highly dangerous pollution.

Setting standards seems to be the most popular environmental policy, at least in the United States. Whether the standards pertain to resource inputs, emissions, or ambient standards, all have a serious drawback; they are likely to be extremely costly and, for the most part, unnecessarily so. Since it is inordinately difficult for governments to catch, prosecute, and convict violators, administrative costs are high. And compliance costs are also apt to be high because standards must be tailored to the special circumstances of each polluter. Governments faced with this administrative nightmare therefore enact uniform standards but enforce them selectively.

Governments may also use a variety of subsidy instruments, including income-tax credits, accelerated depreciation privileges, low-interest loans, and exemptions from various taxes to purchasers of pollution-abatement equipment. These are only partial bribes and are therefore highly ineffective in encouraging installation of the equipment. A substantial private sacrifice on the part of the polluters is still required. Such programs also introduce a powerful bias toward the use of control equipment that may not be the least costly.

The Clean Air Act of 1970 and its 1977 amendments provide a useful guide to the politics of environmental protection. Prior to 1970, coal-fired generating plants produced about one-half of all electric power generated in the United States and, according to Environmental Protection Agency estimates, produced 65 percent of the sulfur oxides emitted. Sulfur oxides (sulfur dioxide—SO_2—in particular) are the pollutants believed to be the major cause of acid rain, so reducing their production was a major goal of the clean air legislation. In fact, the Act required that SO_2 emissions be reduced to no more than 1.2 pounds of SO_2 per million BTU of energy produced.

What the Act did not specify until the 1977 amendments was how the reductions were to be attained. Utility companies could install flue gas de-sulfurization mechanisms (scrubbers) in their smokestacks, wash crushed coal to remove most of the sulfur-bearing particles (coal washing), or burn coal with a lower sulfur content. The least effective and most costly of the alternatives was scrubbing, and the least costly was burning low-sulfur coal.

But burning low-sulfur coal presented a political problem because most of the nation's low-sulfur coal is located in the mountain states. The East and Midwest have mostly high-sulfur coal. If utilities shifted to low-sulfur, western coal in order to meet the clean air standards, jobs would be lost in the eastern coalfields where the United Mine Workers Union's membership is concentrated. Thus, the Clean Air Act amendments of 1977 became a legislative battle over regional protectionism.

Environmental groups joined the battle on the side of eastern "dirty coal" interests. The National Clean Air Coalition, the Environmental Policy Center, the Sierra Club, and the Natural Resources Defense Council supported a mandate for scrubbing *regardless of the coal's sulfur content*. Some environmentalists apparently favored forced scrubbing as a means of reducing the amount of strip mining in the West. Another rationale was the belief that scrubbing might reduce emissions below the 1.2-pound target.

Like the Oregon legislation that applied only to new wood-burning stoves, forced scrubbing, mandated by the 1977 amendments, only applied to new plants; existing plants were allowed to continue to emit four or five pounds of SO_2 per MBTU. Since adding scrubbers increases the cost of a new power plant by about 15 percent, old plants were being kept in production far longer than they would have been otherwise. And this "old plant effect" outweighs the extra benefits for air quality of forcing all new plants to scrub.

As modified by the 1977 amendments, the Clean Air Act is a model of political symbolism. Environmental groups won new standards; politicians, notably Senator Howard Metzenbaum of Ohio, appeared to protect the environment; and the United Mine Workers in the eastern coalfields reduced the competition for their jobs. But the air is not cleaner. As Bruce A. Ackerman and William T. Hassler maintained in their book *Clean Coal/Dirty Air* (1981):

As far as the West is concerned, scrubbing is an exceedingly expensive way of achieving minor reductions in sulfates; in the East, scrubbing is not only far more expensive, but may be positively counterproductive. Even on optimistic assumptions, forcing new plants to scrub will lengthen the life of dirty plants and may generate increases in emissions of sulfur oxides in the industrial Midwest for the next twenty years. And once a realistic view of enforcement is taken, forced scrubbing may make the sulfate problem worse, not better, for even larger portions of the nation's vulnerable northeastern quadrant. (pp. 77–8)

The cost of such symbolism is not trivial. Paul Portney (1990*b*) of Resources for the Future, a Washington, DC, think tank, estimates that by the year 2000 utility companies will have spent anywhere from $400,000 to $800,000 annually for each job saved in the eastern coalfields. Portney's estimate was generated by comparing the cost of scrubbing with the cost of coal washing and burning low-sulfur coal. Portney points out that the miners could be bought out at their present salaries for less than one-tenth of the cost of the regulation. Instead, the East gets dirtier air and consumers of electricity produced in the Midwest get to pay for dirty air and political symbolism through their utility bills.

These effects of the Clean Air Act have not changed the tactics of the Washington, DC, environmental community. In fact, the effects appear to have encouraged more of the same behavior. When one of us (Simmons) asked the lead person on acid rain at the Natural Resources Defense Council (NRDC) whether NRDC would promote a form of legislation more satisfactory than the 1977 amendments in its efforts to have acid rain controlled, she snapped, "You must have been reading Ackerman's book. It's easy for him to accuse us from the comfort of New Haven but he was not here needing to get legislation passed!" Apparently passing legislation was more important than the legislation's effects, at least to her. During the Reagan administration, several bills seeking to mandate reduced emissions circulated in Congress. They typically proposed installing more and better scrubbers on new and existing plants. In one version sponsored by Representatives Jerry Sikorski and Henry Waxman (HR3400, 98th Congress), 90 percent of the cost would come from a tax on all consumers of electricity regardless of whether the source of their electricity was coal, nuclear, solar, or hydro plants. The bill's sponsors argued that "a nationwide fee system is necessary . . . to lessen utility rate increases and avoid economic disruption or increased unemployment." The provisions of this bill would increase the cost of forced scrubbing another $70,000 annually per job saved.

The 101st Congress amended the Clean Air Act and, although there are some important improvements, in most instances the new amendments make the same mistakes as the 1977 amendments. Portney's (1990b) analysis is as instructive as his previous analysis. He estimates the annual cost of compliance by the year 2005 at between $29 billion and $36 billion, with annual benefits ranging from $6 billion to $25 billion. He estimates the most likely value of the benefits to be about $14 billion, which is in line with other studies. Thus, costs exceed benefits by almost two to one. Nevertheless, President Bush trumpeted this legislation as landmark environmental legislation.

Pollution by Government Agencies

Pollution is produced by government agencies as well as the private sector. A somewhat straight-forward example illustrates governmental externalities and the applicability of economic reasoning to public bureaucracies. The agency is the US Army Corps of Engineers and the activity is the pollution of Lake Michigan. Chicago is linked to the Mississippi waterway system and Lake Michigan by a series of ship and barge canals. These canals also transport sewage away from Lake Michigan. The Corps has been assigned the task of maintaining the canals, including dredging the garbage that accumulates in them. Because the Corps is required to operate within a fixed budget, economies were practised. Among them was the practice of dumping the dredgings in Lake Michigan. The Corps did this for a simple reason: The cost of such dumping was much lower than any other means of disposal. And, since the Corps was obligated to keep the canals clean but not Lake Michigan, the response was rational. By our analysis, the Corps of Engineers had a kind of "property right" in the canals but not in the lake. A clean lake could not, under the legal arrangements, be an objective. At the same time, no single citizen or organization had any incentive to protect the lake: Why should they bear all the costs and share the benefits with everyone?

One finds the same sort of behavior among other agencies. Similar behavior is documented, for instance, in several recent studies by authors who have impeccable credentials—not the least of which is their dedication to the environment. Marc Reisner, in *Cadillac Desert* (1986), writes in a most compelling and moving way about the public mismanagement of water supplies in the far western states. Reisner's analysis of the roles of the Bureau of Reclamation and the Army Corps of Engineers in the Iron Triangle, while depressing, is familiar indeed. Their sponsorship of dams and other water-control projects displays the usual hocus-pocus of saving the world, concealing enormous costs, including externalities, and exaggerating the benefits for all. In the San Joaquin Valley in California, for example, the bureau charges the typical farmer less than $20 per acre-foot for Central Valley Project water that farmers value at about $50 per acre-foot. The cost to the taxpayers for just the irrigation portions of the Central Valley Project range from $300 to $500 per acre-foot. Such subsidies made those who owned the farmland at the time the project was built very wealthy at taxpayers' expense. A severe depletion of natural water resources has been one consequence; another is the accumulation of salts in the soil, which has killed farmland, created further drainage crises, and poisoned wildlife.

The environmental costs of government actions so eloquently documented by Reisner and others have been somewhat more dispassionately analyzed by economists making more rigorous cost-benefit studies of all sorts of public projects. Among others, University of Wisconsin economist Robert Haveman (1965) has shown that no matter what cost-benefit procedures are employed, most of the 147 water resource projects authorized by Congress during the post-World War II period (1946–1962) were highly inefficient and egregiously inequitable in the distribution of costs and benefits. And even though the Bureau of Reclamation recently announced that it has completed its prime mission since 1902—building dams to make western US deserts bloom—the costs to society of the bureau's continuing to supply water at subsidized prices will exceed the benefits.

Water policy is one area where substantial progress is being made to use property rights to manage a resource. As it has become abundantly clear that eastern members of Congress are unwilling to support more, massive water subsidies for the West, those wanting more water have turned to markets. The Western Governors' Association, for example, has called for an increase in water marketing—allowing water to be bought and sold. Although firm, private-property rights have not been established for water from federal projects, experimentation is under way. The Imperial Water District in California, for example, is attempting to contract with the Municipal Water District to have Municipal pay the costs of lining Imperial's canals in exchange for 100,000 acre-feet of water annually. The water traded is part of what is currently lost to seepage from the unlined canals and is more than Imperial would have gotten if the bureau, or anyone else, had built a new dam.

Water marketing could really begin to allocate and conserve water currently supplied in federal projects if current water allocations were converted into property rights and issued to existing irrigators. Currently, water allocations not used are taken away from the irrigator so he or she has little incentive to conserve or to seek out those who place a higher value on an alternative use of the water. Allowing farmers to sell water at a profit, by contrast, would enforce conservation because it would prevent farmers from wasting water; instead they could sell it and increase their personal income. Municipalities, instream recreational users, other farmers, and transport users could all buy water for their purposes.

Trading Dirty Air: Markets for Optimal Pollution

In 1960, an English economist at the University of Chicago published one of the most remarkable papers in the history of economic theory—a paper entitled simply "The Problem of Social Cost." In this paper, Ronald Coase shattered previous analyses and offered an entirely new way of approaching social costs and the policies needed to deal with them. The idea, once understood, is fairly simple. Coase claimed that externalities are not caused by markets. Instead, they are caused by a failure to specify property rights so that markets can internalize all costs and benefits. Once such rights are well-defined, if not fully defined, the allocation of scarce resources is accomplished efficiently. As Coase said, the only time externalities can result in market failure, if property rights exist, is when exchange costs are high.

What happens in most pollution situations is this: The polluter emits costly emissions into space occupied by others who have no control over the polluter. Since the persons damaged by the pollution do not "own" the airspace or waterways adjacent to their surface property, they cannot legally claim damages. If they could assert legal ownership to that space, they could either sue for damages or demand a price from the polluter in a regular market transaction. From an efficiency perspective, it makes no difference who is the initial owner of the rights so long as transactions are permitted. If the polluter is assigned the property rights, the pollutee must pay the polluter not to pollute; if the pollutee is given the rights, the polluter must pay to pollute. Fully informed utility maximizers will then arrange a mutually beneficial exchange and arrive at the "correct" amounts of pollution and production. Establishing property rights causes costs and benefits to be internalized and thereby aids in the calculation of efficient courses of action.

Some city governments are creating pollution rights to the airspace above their cities. These rights are also transferable, an important ingredient for their success. In addition to specifying property rights, the government also specifies the maximum amount of emissions that may be generated by polluters. Once these pollution rights are decided, businesses have a powerful market incentive to reduce their own emissions because they can then sell their excess rights to others. A company that closes a plant, reduces operations, or installs more efficient antipollution devices receives emissions credits that may be purchased by new or old firms. The idea is to permit industry to negotiate the prices and details of the tradeoffs as long as the overall level of air pollution in the shed is not increased. When the City of Portland, Oregon, adopted such a policy, businesses quickly learned how to operate in the new market. As might be expected, some individuals soon became brokers in pollution rights. Thus, the traditional function of the middleman has been extended in a most novel way. Companies that propose to build new plants and add to pollution may be established; other concerns are encouraged to reduce their emissions, and everyone is made better off, except perhaps the bureaucrats who might have regulated the matter.

An imaginative restaurateur in Portland, Oregon, who had probably never heard of Coase, applied the theory, in part, to the running of his establishment by offering his patrons a 5 percent discount for not smoking. One of the authors can testify from personal experience that the policy is working well. The owner claims that his business has improved since he adopted the practice: He makes better profits and reduces pollution, and his customers enjoy better dining.

The 1990 Clean Air Act included some innovations along these lines. It allowed polluters to meet SO_2 emissions standards any way they liked, including buying "excess" emissions reductions from other sources able to cut back more than the amount required by the legislation. In this new pollution market, the EPA grants pollution credits to the nation's 101 dirtiest power plants—credits that total just 30 to 50 percent of the sulfur dioxide they now emit. The credits can be swapped or sold. The EPA has chosen the Chicago Board of Trade to run treasury-style auctions in credits that are in addition to those granted the utilities. The auction will be held each March and is open to anyone, including speculators who want to buy pollution credits as investments or environmentalists who want to retire the credits. Portney (1990a) estimates that this approach will save $2 billion to $3 billion annually compared to the amount spent under the 1977 Clean Air Act amendments.

The State of Wisconsin, the City of New York, and Japan have all enacted legislation that enables ownership and transference of airspace rights, and Japan also enacted a sunshine law that guarantees rights to scarce sunshine. New York City's Museum of Modern Art recently helped finance an expansion plan by selling its air rights for $17 million to a developer who will construct a forty-four-story apartment tower above the museum. Again, everyone is made better off—the museum, art patrons, tenants, the developer, and investors in the apartment building. And, lest we forget, the coffers of New York City will gain millions in property taxes.

Market Limitations

Although markets can address water, sunshine, air, and pollution problems, we cannot simply assume that all is well. The Coase theorem has abstract problems that are not easily shed and even if they were the theorem would still face considerable political problems of implementation. At the abstract level, critics have pointed to some highly restrictive conditions, including the fact that transaction and administrative costs must be on the low side. Others have argued that the assignment of the initial rights has profound wealth effects and that everyone will therefore want the original title. The original allocation is also critical because in general the amount that someone will pay to acquire something (say, pollution rights) is often less than the amount we demand to give it up. Who can demand compensation is exceedingly important.

A crucial issue for pollution control is determining the total amount of pollution permitted within the bubble. The decision may and should be influenced by scientific considerations but should not be dominated by such considerations. In democratic processes, citizens are being asked to collectively determine the absolute pollution level. Arriving at a common decision will not be easy, nor is the outcome likely to be optimal. And there have been bitter political battles over attempts to change the levels. These battles, in many instances, spilled over into the rules governing the airshed until the regulations made it nearly impossible for the pollution market to function. Given these public choice problems, we still do not know how effective pollution markets will be.

Even with these difficulties, when compared to the alternatives of taxation, subsidies, and regulation, markets for pollution have much to commend them. One problem with taxation is the obvious one—who will become the tax setters and how will the many tax rates be set? Any such system is bound to become immensely complex and will be subject, of course, to political battles at every session of the legislature or city council. Although a tax system may be efficient in theory, its implementation presents a hornet's nest of logistical problems. Another problem with the tax scheme is its failure to encourage the kind of entrepreneurship and creativity stimulated by property rights.

But the worst consequence of political controls is that they do not get at the heart of the pollution problem; they deal with symptoms. We have argued that the basic problem is that our system incompletely assigns property rights. Markets for pollution provide a way of requiring polluters to pay the costs they impose on others. And by polluters, we mean the ultimate consumers of goods that give rise to pollution. The prices they pay must include the social costs not now taken into account in price setting. Markets for pollution accomplish that end with a minimum of red tape, coercion, and monetary outlays.

Other Environmental Markets

Water markets and markets for pollution are two of the more dramatic applications of property-rights and market principles; there are many others, some of which also test the credulity of conventional thinkers. One example is that proposed by John Baden and Tom Blood (1984) in which they extend these ideas to the preservation and propagation of wild animals. They note that US landowners often support game and other wildlife without compensation and at considerable personal cost. They suggest that such helpful ranchers be rewarded for increasing their conservation practices. This could be done by permitting them to act as wildlife entrepreneurs able to recoup their costs of production by selling their products. Hunting fees should be charged hunters, as is done with conventional private goods. Ranchers and other landowners providing wildlife habitat might be granted tax credits, just as are owners of historical buildings who maintain and refurbish them. "Fee hunting" is being more widely practised in the United States, especially as the hunting quality on public lands diminishes. But landowners cannot yet sell the animals, although they can sell the right to pursue them, since the animals are owned by the state. Thus, state agencies set bag limits and establish seasons.

Markets for wildlife are widely employed in other nations, including seemingly "socialist" Britain, where private clubs hold fishing rights to certain streams and rivers. The owners of these valuable resources maintain them in far better condition than is usually the case for commonly held properties. Much of Africa's wildlife is threatened with extinction; the wildlife on private game ranches and in a few national parks, however, is the exception. Even Zimbabwe's Marxist regime actively promotes private game ranching as a means of preserving wildlife and bringing in desired foreign currency. In one variation of game ranching, the government granted peasants property rights to wildlife, including elephants, on the communal lands so that they would have incentives to protect "their" animals. Zimbabwe's elephant herds are increasing at a rate in excess of 5 percent per year, whereas Kenya's herds (which are owned only by the government) have become so depleted that they will, in all likelihood, be gone in ten years (Simmons and Kreuter 1989). Zimbabwe and other southern African countries opposed the international ivory trade ban instituted in 1989 because they claimed their programs for moving wildlife into markets was far more effective than programs to remove them from markets.

A powerful example of property rights in action in the United States occurred on the 200,000-acre Deseret Ranch in Utah. The ranch manages cows, sheep, deer, elk, and bison for a profit. Because the ranchers can control the habitat itself and access by hunters, they are able to manage the elk and deer much as they manage the cows, sheep, and bison and charge significant fees for hunting. Although the ranch contains just 0.6 of 1 percent of the elk habitat in the state, it produces 15 percent of Utah's elk. The elk and deer herds have better age-class stratification than those on public lands. The average mule deer buck on the ranch, for example, is a four-point (western count) with a 22-inch spread. On the public lands, by contrast, the average is a two-point with a 12-inch spread.

Baden and Blood note that at present cows are "hardier" than elk; the reason is simple—private-property arrangements. Elk, whales, buffalo, snail darters, and birds will all increase in proportion to the property rights held in them by profit-oriented entrepreneurs. Need we beat the point into the ground by observing that there is no shortage of dogs, cats, horses, sheep, cows, chickens, and pigs?

It has also been proposed, notably by Milton Friedman (1962), that public parks be sold to private investors. Richard Stroup (1990) went one step further and suggested that the national parks be given to "park endowment boards" managed by the leadership of such environmental organizations as the Sierra Club and the Audubon Society. These boards would treat the lands as privately held property. Stroup contends that the parks would be better managed under this arrangement, not because the board's members would care more for the natural resources than the National Park Service does, but because the board would soon adopt such efficient practices as increasing the park fees. Fees would reduce the damages of overuse by the price mechanism, not by fiat. Furthermore, the boards would also begin to "exploit" other currently unused resources found within the parks, including oil and coal deposits, timber, and so on. Revenues from these sales would doubtless be used to maintain and improve the recreational resources and services of the parks as well as to acquire new properties. As the preference of US citizens move away from plastic goods to natural amenities, Stroup believes, the market for park and environmental services will become a growth industry. One need only note that private entrepreneurs are already in the recreational business: ski lodges, motels, hotels, private lodges, golf and tennis clubs, RV parks, and the like are but a few of the facilities everyone takes for granted.

Why, then, must parks be in the public domain? And why are so many public parks in disrepair, dangerous, and accorded low status? Perhaps property rights have been misplaced. The Nature Conservancy has for more than three decades purchased and protected ecologically valuable properties for preservation and public use. One of the authors has hiked the lovely trails of a Conservancy property located along the Oregon coast not far from Salishan Lodge, one of the top five lodges in the nation and itself a sensitive owner and manager of beautiful forests and ocean beaches, not to speak of restaurants, tennis courts, a golf course, hiking trails, and art galleries. The Nature Conservancy, Salishan Lodge, Deseret Ranch, and Zimbabwe's elephants are just a few examples suggesting that private-property holders can be at least as dedicated as public agencies in protecting the environment and usually can do so more efficiently.

Conclusions

Current environmental policies are based on antipathy for business, support for increasing government intervention and regulation, and a belief that the ecology and economy are conflicting systems. We have suggested just the opposite, that environmental protection would be best achieved by enabling entrepreneurs to hold property rights to environmental resources and relying on market forces. Economy and ecology harmonize when property rights are clear.

It should be clear why we believe that only a private, decentralized system can enlist the dispersed knowledge necessary for wise resource management and why we have concluded that a property-rights system is the best way to create the incentives for people to act on that information. The information and incentive problems so easily handled by markets are at the heart of government mismanagement.

Obviously, there are many difficulties with extending markets and property rights that are now controlled politically, but those difficulties are not unique to the environmental arena. And the creative student might attempt to apply lessons from successful privatization programs worldwide to extending property-rights principles to the environment.

References

Ackerman, Bruce A., and Hassler, William T. (1981), *Clean Coal/Dirty Air* (New Haven: Yale University Press).

Baden, John, and Blood, Tom (1984), "Wildlife Habitat and Economic Institutions: Feast or Famine for Hunters and Game," *Western Wildlands*, 10 (Spring): 8–13.

Coase, Ronald H. (1960), "The Problem of Social Cost," *Journal of Law and Economics*, 3 (October): 1–44.

Friedman, Milton (1962), *Capitalism and Freedom* (Chicago: University of Chicago Press).

Haveman, Robert H. (1965), *Water Resource Investment and the Public Interest* (Nashville: Vanderbilt University Press).

Portney, Paul R. (1990a) "Air Pollution Policy," in Paul R. Portney (ed.), *Public Policies for*

Environmental Protection (Washington, DC: Resources for the Future), 27–96.

—— (1990b), "Policy Watch: Economics and the Clean Air Act," *Journal of Economic Perspectives*, 4 (Fall): 173–81.

Reisner, Marc (1986), *Cadillac Desert* (New York: Viking Press).

Simmons, Randy T., and Kreuter, Urs (1989), "Save an Elephant—Buy Ivory," *Washington Post*, 1 October; D3.

Stroup, Richard L. (1990), "Rescuing Yellowstone from Politics: Expanding Parks While Reducing Conflict," in John A. Baden and Donald Leal (eds), *The Yellowstone Primer: Land and Resource Management in the Greater Yellowstone Ecosystem* (San Francisco: Pacific Research Institute for Public Policy), 169–84.

16   Selling Environmental Indulgences

Robert E. Goodin

According to a common and currently influential diagnosis, the environmental crisis has essentially economic roots. The problem is not just that there are too many people, or even that they are on average enjoying too high a standard of living. All that is true, too, of course. More fundamentally, however, problems of environmental despoliation are said to derive from skewed incentives facing agents as they pursue their various goals.

For some things, people must pay full price. For others, they pay only partially or indirectly or belatedly. To an economist, it goes without saying that the lower the costs the more people will consume of any particular commodity. Where some of the costs of their activities will be borne by others, agents looking only to their own balance sheets will over-engage in those activities. Because some of the costs are 'external' (which is to say, are borne by others, rather than themselves) agents will undertake more of those activities than they would have done, had they been forced to pay their full costs. They will do more of them than is socially optimal, taking due account of costs and benefits to everyone concerned (Pigou 1932).

Environmental despoliation poses problems of economic externalities of just that sort. Environmental inputs are typically 'common property resources'. Clean air and water, fisheries, the ozone layer, the climate are everyone's business—and no one's. No one 'owns' those things. There is no one with standing to sue you if you take them without paying; nor is there anyone you could pay for permission to impinge on them, even if you wanted to do so. That fact inevitably gives rise to a divergence between the full social costs created by your actions and the portion of those costs sheeted back to you as private costs, to be entered on your own ledger. It is, of course, only the latter sorts of costs to which economically rational agents can be expected to respond (Freeman et al. 1973; Fisher 1981; Pearce et al. 1989: see esp. p. 5).

Either of two prescriptions might follow from that economistic diagnosis of the environmental problem. Both would put government in control of—cast it in the role of 'owner' of—common property resources. Both vest in government the power to authorise the use of environmental resources, and to punish people for using them without authorisation. The two prescriptions differ, principally, over the form that those authorisations and punishments would take.

The standard 'legalistic' approach operates by manipulating rights and duties. It is essentially a command-and-control strategy, specifying what people may or must or must not do and attaching penalties to violation of those commands. The newer 'economistic' approach works by

From *Kyklos*, 47 (1994), 573–96. Reprinted with permission.

manipulating incentives. In the limiting case, nothing is required or prohibited: everything just has a higher or lower price; and so long as you are willing to pay that price, you are perfectly welcome to do just as you please. Any actual control system may well combine both modes, of course, but for analytic purposes it pays to treat them separately.

The most dramatic form of the economistic strategy is to sell transferable permits to pollute, which permit-holders can then resell to others in turn.[1] Imposing 'green taxes', conceived essentially as charges for using the environment in certain ways, constitutes a less dramatic and politically more acceptable form of the same basic strategy. In that form, economistic logic attracts the endorsement of a surprisingly wide range of political players: from, on the one side, the OECD (1975; Opschoor and Vos 1988), national Treasuries and their advisers (Pearce et al. 1989: chap. 7) and economic think tanks (Epstein and Gupta 1990; Weimer 1990); to, on the other side, various Green Parties across Europe (Die Grünen 1983: sec. iv.1; European Greens 1989: sec. 1; Spretnak and Capra 1986). The 'carbon tax' in particular is now the instrument of choice among the widest possible range of policymakers for controlling emissions of greenhouse gases.[2]

In all variations on that economistic strategy, the highest aspiration is to set the price of licenses/permits/fees/taxes at a rate that would force polluters to internalise, in their own cost calculations, the full measure of environmental damage that they do. Of course, calculating that price will never be easy; many of the complaints with these economistic strategies will amount to little more than the (often, perfectly proper) complaint that the price has been set too low (Pearce et al. 1989: chaps. 3, 4, and 7). But once we have calculated total social costs correctly, and once we have forced the creators of those costs to internalise them fully, then objections to environmental despoliation should (on the economistic diagnosis of the problem) cease. Once despoilers have been made to repay fully the environmental costs of their activities, there would be no further reason to stop them from proceeding with those activities.

From an economic point of view, that case for 'green taxes' seems well nigh indisputable.[3] Environmental economists are therefore frankly dumbfounded when such 'unassailable' proposals nonetheless come under attack from fellow environmentalists. The latter, in turn, have proven particularly inept at articulating exactly what they see wrong with green taxes, though. The exchange amounts to a veritable dialogue of the deaf (Kelman 1981, 1983; Frey 1986).

This article is thus devoted essentially to bridging a gap within environmentalist discourse. Whilst fully acknowledging all the advantages that environmental economists see in green taxes, I hope to explain in terms congenial to them what other environmentalists have against them. The running analogy which will figure centrally in my discussion is that between green taxes and medieval indulgences. The former amount, in effect, to 'selling rights to destroy nature'; the latter amount, in effect, to 'selling God's grace'.

This analogy, like all analogies, is far from perfect in various respects. Perhaps the most obvious and important point of disanalogy is just this. There is a general ban on sin: a sin is always wrong. Environmental emissions, in contrast, are not always necessarily thought to be wrong. There is, or it is generally thought there should be, no general ban on them. (On the contrary, green taxes and such like are offered as *alternatives* to bans.) Religious indulgences are set against the background assumption of a prohibition on sin, the function of indulgences there being to forgive sinners their lapses. Environmental indulgences seem to be set against the background assumption that some pollution will be permitted, the function of environmental indulgences being to allocate those permissions to particular people.

Equating environmental pollution with sin seems to suggest that zero emissions should be our ideal goal. To most practical people, that seems plainly crazy—just the sort of thing that gives philosophy in general a bad name. But it pays to pause to reflect exactly why we think that a zero emission standard is so plainly crazy. In part, that is merely because a zero emission standard seems unrealistic (so, too, are the Ten Commandments, but they are nonetheless attractive as ideal standards for that). In part, it is because some emissions—ones in certain circumstances, or below certain levels—actually do no harm. The implication there is merely that it is environmental despoliation (an outcome) rather than environmental emissions (an act) that should be counted as the sin. Finally, even some genuinely despoiling emissions seem misdescribed as sins because, though harmful, they cause harm unavoidably and in the service of some greater good. The implication of there, however, is not that certain genuinely despoiling emissions are perfectly all right. The implication is, instead, that we are there operating in the realm of 'tragedy': even if we have done 'the right thing on balance', we will nonetheless have committed a wrong.[4]

These are only preliminary remarks, designed not so much to motivate the analogy as to defuse any strong initial sense of disanalogy, between religious indulgences and environmental ones. Arguments of a more positive sort for treating (certain sorts of) environmental despoliation as akin to a sin will be offered in Section II below.[5] There it will be shown that, while less than perfect, the analogy is closer that one might initially suppose. Despite the various points of (often important) disanalogy, it nonetheless remains a telling way into this troubled debate.

The upshot of those arguments is to dash the highest hopes of economistic advocates of green taxes. As I hope will be clear from those discussions, we may not legitimately use green taxes and cognate economistic mechanisms as optimising devices in directly guiding 'policy choice'. Such techniques may nonetheless retain a secondary use as tools of 'policy enforcement'. There, they would be serving merely to provide incentives and disincentives for people to achieve certain 'target' levels of maximum permissible environmental damage—levels that have been set elsewhere, by other means, in the political system.[6] That fallback position has much to be said for it. But as shown in Section III, that more modest case for green taxes must be sharply distinguished from the other, for it amounts to falling back a very long way indeed from those bolder claims often made on behalf of green taxes.

I. Religious Indulgences: A Potted History

The function of indulgences, in Catholic theology, is to remit time to be served by a sinner in purgatory. Indulgences were granted *by* church officials (originally popes, latterly bishops). They were granted *to* those who have sinned (by definition the only ones in need of them).

The practice of *granting* such indulgences goes back to the early history of the Church. The practice of *selling* them can be traced, fairly precisely, to the need of popes to provide incentives for Crusades—in the first instance for people to participate in them, in the second instance for people to pay for them (Purcell 1975). From the eve of the Third Crusade in 1187 to the Council of Trent which finally abolished the practice in 1563, selling indulgences became an increasingly common phenomenon. Indulgences were increasingly awarded in exchange for assistance, of an increasingly crassly material sort, rendered to the church and, increasingly, its temporal allies (Boudinhon 1940).

Increasingly, in turn, the practice became the subject of controversy among theologians of all stripes. Notable critics included Jan Hus, who in 1412 crossed the King Wenceslas on the matter (Boudinhon 1940). Most famous of all was Martin Luther (1517), whose 'Ninety-five Theses' nailed to the door of the Wittenberg Cathedral were largely devoted to an attack on the practice.

This is no place for a detailed examination of either the history or the theology of the matter, though. (On that, see Eliade (1987).) Present purposes will be better served by a more stylised account of generic sorts of possible objections to the sale of indulgences. As is only to be expected, these generic styles of objections track actual Church history only very imperfectly. But this being an exercise in moral philosophy rather than in theology, still less in Church history, that is just as it should be.

II. Grounds for Objecting to the Sale of Indulgences

Surveying the many possible grounds for objecting to the sale of indulgences for sin in religious affairs, surprisingly many of them might apply, *mutatis mutandis*, to the sale of indulgences (in the form of 'green taxes' or 'pollution permits') for activities degrading the natural environment.

Many environmentalists, of course, would take a vaguely spiritual attitude toward nature (Spretnak 1986). For them, the analogy between the sacrilege of selling nature's benefice and that of selling God's grace might be felt particularly powerfully. It would be wrong, however, to think that this analogy literally works only by implicitly or explicitly giving environmental values a spiritual twist.

1. SELLING WHAT IS NOT YOURS TO SELL

One of the recurring themes in opposition to the selling of religious indulgences, even by popes, was that they were selling what was not truly theirs to sell. The item on auction was God's grace: His forgiveness. When it comes to grace and forgiveness, what is at issue is not God's commandments (which popes are indeed empowered to interpret) but rather the exercise of His discretionary powers. Those are for Him alone to exercise. It is simply presumptuous—preempting prerogatives properly reserved to Him—for others, however high their Churchly station, to act on His behalf.[7]

There are important elements of this sort of logic at work within objections to selling environmental indulgences. Those elements figure particularly importantly in the objections of those who take a vaguely mystical view of nature, of course. It is not our place to grant (much less to sell) indulgences for violations of what, on this view, would be regarded as almost literally Mother Nature's physical integrity. It would be simply presumptuous of any human agents to grant indulgences on behalf of Mother Nature. Forgiveness is the prerogative of the party who has been wronged.

There is no need to give environmental ethics a spiritual twist to find an echo of this objection to the selling of indulgences, however. Many, for example, suppose merely that we have 'steward-ship' responsibilities—either toward nature, or perhaps just toward future generations and their interests in the natural environment (Passmore 1980: chaps. 4 and 5; Goodin 1985: 169–86; Barry 1989: chaps. 17–19; Sax 1970). It would be objectionable for such stewards to sell environmental indulgences in much the same way, and for much the same reason. They, too, would be selling something that is not theirs to sell. Stewards would then be permitting people to destroy irrevo-cably that which those stewards are duty-bound to preserve, either for its own sake or for the sake of future generations.

2. SELLING THAT WHICH CANNOT BE SOLD

The objection just canvassed deals in terms of a breach of stewardship responsibilities per se. As such, it applies with equal force whatever the reasons for allowing those responsibilities to be breached or whatever form the breach takes. Stewards are bound to protect that which indulgers would allow to be destroyed. Hence granting indulgences, for whatever reason, would seem equally illegitimate.

There is, however, a variation on that objection which applies with peculiar force to the *sale* of indulgences—to the indulging of wrongful behaviour for reason of money. The objection there is not (or not just) that the impermissible is permitted. It is instead that the impermissible is per-mitted for a peculiarly sordid (pecuniary) motive. The objection is to the sale of the unsaleable, more than (and, indeed, often instead of) to the permitting of the impermissible.

The spiritual analogy is again illuminating here. It is not unreasonable to suppose, someone like Luther might say, that God forgives people their sins. It is not even unreasonable for those versed in God's words and His ways to second-guess (in a way that is of course utterly non-binding on Him) the circumstances in which he might do so. What *is* unreasonable, however, is to suppose that God's grace can be bought. What counts with Him is the purity of the heart, not the size of the purse (Luther 1517: prop. 27).

By the same token in the environmental case, it might be thought that there are indeed cir-cumstances in which it is perfectly proper for the environment to be despoiled. Suppose that were the only way of securing a decent life (or, indeed, life at all) for a great many people who would otherwise lead miserable lives or face even more miserable deaths. Then chopping down large portions of the Amazonian rain forest might well be forgivable, if nonetheless unfortunate. But what makes it forgivable has nothing to do with (or, as in the case here sketched, may even be negatively related to) the size of the purse of those chopping down the forests. Certainly permis-sion to chop down the forests should not be publicly auctioned to the highest bidder, any more than should remission of time in purgatory for sins committed.

A religious indulgence is granted upon condition of the indulged feeling true contrition for their sins. The environmental indulgence may be granted, by the same token, upon condition of the indulged showing that they have no other choice and that they have made good-faith (albeit unsuccessful) efforts to avoid damage to the environment.[8] The objection here in view is not to conditionality as such, but rather to making the granting of the indulgence conditional upon payment of hard, cold cash. God may grant His favours freely and simply; but God cannot be bought. By the same token, we might forgive people who despoil the environment for certain sorts of reasons—but the pursuit of pure profit (as represented in 'willingness to pay' green taxes) is not one of them.

Why that should be so is an open question that admits of various different styles of answer. One might have to do with distributive justice. We might suppose that the present distribution of cash holdings is without justification or that it is positively unjustified. For that reason, we might be reluctant to let one person's environmental quality be determined, in part, by another's unwarranted riches.

Alternatively, the argument might work in terms of 'blocked exchanges'. We may think that, even if the distribution of cash is morally unexceptionable, there are nonetheless certain things that money ought not be able to buy. Why the category should exist at all is, perhaps, philosophically mysterious; what falls into it certainly is sociologically variable (Simmel 1907/1978; Tobin 1970; Douglas and Isherwood 1979; Walzer 1983). Still, that the category exists seems both sociologically undeniable and ethically (not just ethnographically) interesting.

One way of justifying the category—and of rationalising much of its sociological content—is this. It is a clear affront to practical reason to engage in an exchange that secures you cash only at the cost of depriving you of the material and nonmaterial prerequisites for making use of that cash. So selling yourself into slavery is wrong (irrational) because once a slave you will no longer have the legal capacity to dispose of the money thereby acquired. By the same token, trading all your foodstuffs for money is self-defeating insofar as without sustenance you will not survive to spend the money.

Perhaps the objection to trading environmental quality for money derives from a similar thought. If you trade away (all) the environmental prerequisites for human existence, then the money acquired in exchange for that will do you no good; the trade makes no sense, at least in that limiting case. Perhaps, by extension, it makes little sense in many other much less extreme cases for something of the same sorts of reasons. Private affluence, of certain sorts anyway, may simply be pragmatically impossible to enjoy, under circumstances of sufficiently severe public squalor (Barry 1989: chap. 20).

Another way of justifying a category of things which ought not be bought and sold is in terms of the corruption of public morals. There is a well-known tendency, firmly established in the literature of empirical social psychology, for extrinsic rewards to drive out otherwise strong intrinsic motivations to perform the same actions. The precise psychological mechanisms at work are many and varied, and the precise nature of the interactions among them is none too clear. What is nonetheless clear is that there are many worthy actions that people would originally have done 'for their own sake', but which they will no longer do simply for their own sake once extrinsic material (especially monetary) rewards are also offered for doing them. Putting certain sorts of good deeds on the auction block, so to speak, demeans them and diminishes their intrinsic value in the eyes of those initially most sensitive to such intrinsic moral values (Goodin 1981, 1982: chap. 6; Lane 1991: chaps. 19–21; Frey 1986: 552–6, 1992, 1993).

What people value in that very special way is, as I have said, sociologically variable. Still, insofar as any appreciable part of the population does regard the value of the environment in that special way—and there seem to be reasons to think both that they should and that they do (Sagoff 1988)—then there is likely to be an efficiency cost that will potentially offset any efficiency gain in offering material incentives for environmental protection. Just as in Titmuss's (1971) famous case of blood donation, so too with the 'free' supply of voluntary environmental protection: it is likely to dry up the more we pay people (those same people, or others) for undertaking the same or similar actions.

3. RENDERING WRONGS RIGHT

Environmentalists sometimes say that they have no objection to *fining* despoilers of the environment: their objection is merely to charging, licensing, or taxing them. Economists scratch their heads at that. In terms of corporate balance sheets, there is no important difference between fines, charges, and taxes. In strictly economic terms, exactly the same disincentive is provided by a $100,000 fine as a $100,000 charge as a $100,000 tax on any given activity. To careful watchers of the profit-and-loss statements, it is a distinction without a difference.

To others, however, the difference is very real. With a fine, the wrongness remains even after the payment of a fine. It is wrong to have done what you have been fined for doing; you may have 'paid your debt to society' and be a member in good standing once again after having done so; but what you did nonetheless remains wrong. Not so with a mere license fee or charge. If you buy a pollution permit, then you are permitted to do what you have paid for permission to do: there is nothing wrong with it. The same is true of a 'charge'. There is nothing wrong with people dumping wastes in a sanitary landfill, once they have paid the charge for doing so. Similarly, with a 'tax', there is nothing wrong with doing most of the things for which we are ordinarily taxed. Quite the contrary, the ordinary activities giving rise to tax liability—like turning a profit or earning a wage—are very much socially approved.[9]

The problem with green taxes or pollution charges or permits, on this model, is that they seem to say, 'It is okay to pollute, provided you pay', when the proper message is instead, 'It is wrong to pollute, even if you can afford to pay'. (The reasons that is the right message are elaborated in Section 11.6 below.) On the religious analogy, this comes through very strongly. There, an indulgence is forgiveness of sins. The sins clearly remain wrong things to have done. It is the punishment that is being remitted, not the wrongness of the action that is being cancelled, by the indulgence.[10]

The bottom line, here, is that putting indulgences up for sale makes them too easy to come by. In the religious case, remission for sin is granted too easily, and consequently sins are taken insufficiently seriously (Luther 1517: prop. 40). Much the same objection applies there as in the case of selling environmental indulgences (Frey 1992: 170–2; see similarly McCarthy 1990). In both cases, the problem with being able to buy your way out of the consequences of a nefarious activity is that anyone with sufficient ready cash is consequently led to take the nefariousness of the activity insufficiently seriously.

4. MAKING WRONGS ALL RIGHT

Maybe the point of buying an indulgence is not to make a wrong right, but merely to make it all right. Advocates of environmental charges emphasise that we license and tax all sorts of things we vaguely disapprove of, including gambling, smoking, drinking. What payment of the requisite price has done is not to make wrongs right but, rather, to make them 'all right'—permissible, if still undesirable in some ideal world.[11]

Classic religious indulgences did something less than that, though. Religious indulgences granted forgiveness for sins past, on condition of penance and a genuine intention not to do it again. Indulgences once granted made it all right to *have* sinned, but that indulgence stopped well short of making it all right to *sin*. The religious formula offered a mechanism for forgiving past wrongs without encouraging future ones. Through religious indulgences, past wrongs were rendered all right but present or future ones were not.

The whole point (in religious, if not necessarily pragmatic terms) of buying a religious indulgence was backward-looking, to wipe one's slate clean of past sins. The whole point of buying an environmental indulgence is forward-looking, to secure permission to despoil the environment now and in the future. Whereas the religiously indulged are seeking merely forgiveness for things past, the environmentally indulged seek permission for future actions. If buying an environmental indulgence is tantamount to buying a permission to commit a wrong, it is continuing permission (conditional on continuing payment) to commit continuing wrongs.

The reason the wrong remains wrong, even after payment, is simply that the wrong done to the environment and to people using it is not an economic wrong. It is not as if it (or we) are 'poorer' for those acts, at least not in any way that can be made good by any transfer of financial resources. Yet while the wrong remains, even after payment of taxes, that wrong is nonetheless permitted on a continuing basis, on continuing payment of the taxes. I return to these themes in Section 11.6 below.

5. INDULGING SOME BUT NOT ALL

In granting indulgences there is a further problem of fairness to confront. Crudely put, it might be thought unfair, somehow, to indulge some but not all sinners. If not all can be (or, anyway, not all will be) indulged, then perhaps it is wrong—unfair—to indulge any at all. And that unfairness might be felt to be especially strong when indulgences are being sold in situations in which some but not all are willing or able to pay the asking price. Less crudely put, it might be thought a matter of elementary fairness that if any sinners are to be indulged, then all with relevantly similar characteristics should be. Of course not all sinners should be indulged: some are unreconstructed reprobates who really ought be punished. But all who are in the same boat ought, in fairness, be treated similarly.[12]

In the religious case, the issue of fairness arguably does not arise. There, indulgences merely reflect God's grace, understood as His purely discretionary whimsy. He can choose to indulge whomsoever He pleases, without a thought for constraints of consistency (although few would be attracted to a vision of so purely capricious a God, perhaps). Insofar as we are making a *social* practice of granting indulgences (environmental or otherwise), however, the practice surely ought be grounded in principles that are more regular and publicly defensible than that.

The particular problem of fairness arises, in the environmental case, from the fact that we can often afford a few—but only a few—environmental renegades (Kennan 1970). A few countries can continue to hunt whales, for example, without causing the extinction of any species, just so long as not all do. A few countries can continue generating greenhouse gases or emitting CFCs without altering the climate or destroying the ozone layer, just so long as most countries do not. In short, nature can tolerate some but not all misbehaving (Goodin 1995: chap. 18).

In such cases, the question immediately becomes how to choose who gets to play this role of environmental renegade. Advocates of green taxes suggest that these slots should be sold to the highest bidder: others suggest other ways in which this determination might be made (Taylor and Ward 1982). Behind all such schemes, however, is an unspoken assumption that we ought make sure that all those slots are taken—that we ought allow just as many renegades as nature itself will tolerate.

Critiques couched in terms of fairness query precisely that proposition. The root idea there is that if we cannot allow everyone to do something, then we ought not allow anyone to do it. That may not appeal much as a general principle: it seems perfectly reasonable that I should be able to allow some people to share my house without allowing everyone to do so. But that principle seems considerably more apt when it comes to the exploitation of genuinely collective goods: it seems far less reasonable to allow some co-owners of a common property resource to use it in certain ways, without allowing all co-owners to use it similarly.

The impetus to economic efficiency leads us to regard such opportunities to exploit common property resources (by some but not all) as things to be allocated—somehow, to someone. The impetus to fairness leads us to regard such opportunities as things to be eschewed, rather than being allocated at all. Granting environmental indulgences, upon payment of a suitable price, is essentially an allocation device. On the fairness critique, it allocates what ought not be allocated at all. Those are efficiency gains that, in all fairness, we ought not pursue.

That rejoinder is not always compelling. Efficiency ought not always be eschewed in the interests of fairness. The fact that we do not have food enough to feed everyone does not mean that we should let such food as we do have go to waste, with the consequence that everyone starves. Rather, we ought ration scarce necessities in such a way that they do as much good as possible.

Still, in circumstances of rationing, we are characteristically highly sensitive to the precise mechanisms employed for allocating rights to use hyper-scarce, necessary resources. We generally want to ensure that the distribution of those rationed commodities is more equal than the distribution of cash holdings or of other commodities in general. That is reflected in the fact that the buying and selling of ration coupons is almost invariably prohibited: and necessarily so, if the ration coupons are to serve their social function as an independent 'second' currency, distinct from and restraining on the operation of ordinary economic forces (Tobin 1952, 1970; Neary 1987; Hirshleifer 1987: esp. chap. 1).

6. GROUNDS FOR INDULGENCE

Many of those objections ultimately turn on questions of appropriate (relevant) criteria for granting indulgences. In the religious case, and on one telling of the environmentalist case, it is an inerasable wrong that is being indulged. In the economistic telling of the environmentalist tale, it is merely a previously uncompensated external cost that is being indulged, upon condition of payment of some sum adequate to compensate those who would otherwise have to bear that cost.

In the case of religious indulgences, what is wrong with their being bought and sold is that money payments are the wrong basis for granting them. It is not how much people pay, but rather their regret for what they have done, that is there relevant. Not every penitent can afford to pay, nor are all those who can afford to pay truly penitent. Granting indulgences only to those who pay (or even to all those who pay) would result in a maldistribution of indulgences, by the only standard that is really relevant there.

What ought be the relevant standards for granting indulgences depends upon the nature of the wrong being indulged, though. The salient feature of sin, in this regard, is that it can never be undone. It is a blot that can never be erased or wiped clean. So the most we can be looking for, in deciding whether to indulge any particular sinner, is a genuinely penitent attitude: sincere regret, and a deep commitment not to sin again.

On one account, the wrong done in despoiling the environment is just like that: a presumptuous intrusion into, and destruction of, the creation of another's hand. On that view, it would be wrong for the same reasons to grant environmental indulgences to all, or to any, who were prepared to pay for them. There, as in the religious case, what we should be looking for in granting indulgences is genuine remorse and a firm commitment not to harm nature again. There, as in the religious case, granting indulgences in return for monetary payment would be to grant them for wrong (anyway, irrelevant) reasons. Worse, it would encourage the continued wronging of nature, since knowing you can always buy your way out of trouble tempts you to do it again.

Others, environmental economists conspicuously among them, take a different view of the nature of the wrong done by despoiling the environment. They would say that the wrong is an economic wrong. The wrong is the destruction, or diminution, of a collective good. It is a cost that one person's activities impose upon everyone sharing in those collective goods. Furthermore, environmental economists tend to conceive of that harm as a cost or 'welfare loss' which can in principle be recompensed.

That conjunction of attitudes carries important implications for one's view of the power of environmental indulgences to rectify wrongs. If environmental despoilers can and do fully compensate others for the harm that they have done them, then that on this view wipes the slate clean. On that view of the sort of wrong done by environmental despoilers, ability/willingness to pay for indulgences would indeed be a relevant criteria for allocating indulgences. By paying the price, despoilers would—quite literally—have undone the wrong.

Clearly, there are some deep issues at stake in deciding between these interpretations of the wrongs done by environmental despoilers. For those who view the wrong as being done to nature, righting the wrong requires recompensing nature, somehow; and if it is naturalness that is of value, most obvious forms of recompense are not viable—or anyway are not as valuable— options (Goodin 1992: 26–41). Only those who are prepared to view the wrong as one done to other people might conceivably regard paying them a suitable price in exchange for an indulgence as suitable recompense.

It is important to note, however, that not everyone who views the wrong as one done to other people would necessarily regard paying the right price as suitable recompense. That is to say, this difference of opinion does not map easily onto the difference—easily relegated to the 'too hard' basket—between deep and shallow ecologists (Devall and Sessions 1985; Sylvan 1985). Even anthropocentric analysts might regard cash transfers, of the sort entailed in buying indulgences through payment of green taxes and such like, as inadequate recompense for environmental harms. Anthropocentric analysts might, for example, have a more nuanced notion of human interests, such that people cannot be compensated for losses in one category (e.g. environmental quality) by gains in another (e.g. money, or even any of the things that money can buy) (Goodin 1989, 1995: chap. 11).

My own view of the value of nature is very much like that. The value of natural processes is to provide a context, outside of ourselves (individually, or even collectively), in which to set our lives (see similarly Hill 1983). What is wrong with environmental despoliation is that it deprives us of that context; it makes the external world more and more one of our own (perverse) creation. That is ultimately a wrong to humans, rather than to nature as such, to be sure. It is, nonetheless, a wrong that cannot be recompensed by cash payments. The humans wronged by such practices might be made better off in some sense or another by such payments. But they will be better off, if at all, in dimensions altogether different from those in which their losses have been sustained. The cash offered in payment for environmental indulgences—through green taxes and such like—cannot possibly recompense them for the loss of that context that provided meaning, of a sort, to their lives (Goodin 1992: 41–54).

III. Economistic Backtracking

From an economist's point of view, making environmental despoilers pay for indulgences might serve two quite distinct functions. The first and more modest function is one of 'policy enforcement'. The idea here is to use green taxes simply to provide a disincentive for despoiling. The higher the charges are, for whatever reason, the greater the disincentive effect: that is the end of the story (Baumol and Oates 1971). How much despoliation we want to tolerate, and how much we want to deter, is a matter for determination by other non-economistic means (by politicians, theologians, or moralists).

I shall return to that more modest version of the tale shortly. First, however, let us consider the more ambitious function that might be served by selling environmental indulgences—one of actual 'policy choice'. The aim here would be to use green taxes and associated economistic techniques to determine 'optimal' levels of despoliation. This second argument subsumes the first; the whole idea is to provide an incentive for (certain) would-be despoilers to desist. But this second argument transcends the first, in acknowledging that certain despoilers ought be allowed to persist and in providing some mechanism for determining who they should be and how much they should be allowed to despoil.

For purposes of this more ambitious argument, we are required to make the following assumptions:

(1) the price of indulgences fully reflect social costs of the activity;
(2) the activity occurs only upon payment of that price; and
(3) that payment is actually used to compensate or correct for the harm done.

Under those assumptions, environmental despoliation would be a socially optimal activity which actually ought be engaged in by anyone who can afford to pay for the indulgence out of the proceeds of that despoliation. The sense in which it would be optimal is the weak and unexceptionable Paretian sense of no one being worse off (thanks to the compensation in clause 3 above) and at least one person being better off (that is, despoilers who want to persist even after having had to pay the price of the indulgence).[13]

It is of course the latter, more ambitious defence of the sale of environmental indulgences that is the more attractive to defenders of the economistic faith. It is the selfsame defence that is the greater anathema to their detractors. What is problematic, in particular, is the presumption that money payments can ever correct or compensate for environmental despoliation.

For those who attach great importance to environmental integrity, 'correcting' environmental despoliation is simply not a feasible option. No doubt, even for them, restoration and reclamation might be preferable to letting a despoiled bit of nature remain utterly despoiled. But for those who attach great importance to authenticity, the process by which a bit of nature came to be as it is matters greatly; and restored or reclaimed bits of nature, however effective the restoration or reclamation, will necessarily be of less value than they would have been had they never been despoiled in the first place. The reason, quite simply, is that they will have come to be as they are in part through artificial human interventions rather than through more purely natural processes.[14]

Neither, many would say, can cash transfers of the sort received in payment for environmental indulgences compensate for the harms involved in environmental despoliation. If, as just argued, they cannot be used to correct the damage, they could 'compensate' if at all only by making people better off in some other respect altogether. Their environment might be worse, but their wine cellar better; and, on balance, they think themselves better off in consequence. Surely it is true that overall well-being is a composite of roughly that sort; and surely some of its components are tradeable, at the margins, for one another in just that way. The question is whether environmental quality is of that character. On at least some of the arguments canvassed above, it is not: it is more fundamental; it is a precondition for valuing, rather than merely a source of values which can be set alongside and traded against other values. If so, neither money nor anything that money can buy can compensate for its loss.[15]

Of course, there are also a great many practical difficulties in calculating (or, rather, in defending any particular calculation of) the cash value of environmental quality. More in deference to those practicalities than in deference to any matters of high principle, environmental economists are sometimes prepared (and governments are often keen) to fall back onto the first 'policy-enforcement' defence of green taxes alone.[16]

This fallback position amounts to using a 'market-based incentive system to meet preordained environmental quality standards' (Pearce et al. 1989: 165, after Baumol and Oates 1971). The basic idea goes something like this. Let there be some independent social determination of the environmental standards that we want to attain. Let those be given by the political process, rather than by any economistic calculation of 'social cost' or 'optimal' despoliation. Let us merely use the price system to enforce that standard, floating the price up or down until the desired level of environmental quality has been achieved.

There is, on this model, no independent justification of the particular price charged. It is all just a matter of what it takes to get people to cut back on their activities sufficiently to achieve our environmental targets.[17] While there is nothing special about the particular price being charged, however, there is nonetheless a good economistic reason to use price mechanisms to enforce those standards. The rationale is just that, insofar as the standards can be attained in ways that admit of partial noncompliance, pricing mechanisms evoke compliance from those whom economists would regard as the 'right' people—those who gain relatively less from environmental despoliation or whom it costs relatively less to desist from it.

This fallback position effectively insulates economists against the criticism that, in selling environmental indulgences, they are auctioning off nature's bounty too cheaply. If too much environmental despoliation is occurring, they would say, then that can only be for either of two reasons: either the price has been set too low to achieve the desired standard (and advocates of green taxes and such like would be the first to agree that it should be raised as high as necessary to achieve that goal); or else the standard has been set too low (which is the fault of politicians, and ought not be taken as criticism of the price mechanism as a way of securing compliance with the standard). Either way, the complaint seems not to touch the practice of selling environmental indulgences, as such.

Of course, efficiency gains from using the pricing mechanism even in this minimal way arise only in very particular circumstances. They presuppose that we can afford to tolerate some people, but not all people, acting as environmental despoilers. Sometimes, though, the situation is such that we cannot—or cannot be sufficiently confident that we can—afford any slackers at all. (Whaling negotiations are often like that: we do not know just how close we are to the limits of a successful breeding population, and given the real risks of destroying the whole species we do not want to take any chances.) Other times, considerations of fairness of the sort discussed in Section 11.5 above would lead us to say that, purely as a matter of principle, we should not tolerate any slackers even if practicalities would allow. For reasons either of practicality or principle, we might thus set the desired standard at zero despoliation. And if that is the goal, there is no advantage to pursuing it through the price mechanism.

The more fundamental point to be made here, though, is that in retreating to this fallback position environmental economists really have given away their strongest claims on behalf of green taxes. Their proudest boast was that the buying of an environmental indulgence made despoliation not merely all right but actually right—socially optimal. But that boast was predicated on the assumption that the price was right, that it was a true reflection of the full social costs of environmental despoliation. If there is no social-cost based rationale for the particular price being set for environmental indulgences, then their sale cannot perform that role of serving as a solvent turning wrongs into rights.[18]

IV. Conclusions

How attractive we find green taxes and the 'polluter pays' principle more generally depends, in large part, upon what we see as their alternative. If, realistically, the alternative is polluters not paying, then the 'polluter pays' principle looks to be the relatively more restrictive option. Most of us would probably prefer a regime in which polluters at least be made to pay something—however inadequate that sum (or any sum) might be—if the alternative realistically in view were that otherwise they be allowed to continue polluting with gay abandon.

Suppose, however, the alternative in view were instead that polluters desist from polluting altogether. Then a rule that the 'polluter pays' looks to be the relatively more permissive option. If absent the option to pay the alternative is that people not pollute, then giving them permission to pollute upon payment is actually a mechanism for allowing more pollution than would otherwise occur. Seen in that light, many of us may well hesitate to endorse the 'polluter pays' principle that, in that other light, looked relatively attractive.

Which is the correct comparison—which, realistically, is the alternative to polluters paying (their not paying, or their not polluting)—is essentially a political question. As such, it varies according to time and place, policy arena and issue area. That in itself is an important lesson. Perhaps it is right that environmentalists should endorse green taxes, in circumstances where stronger prohibitions are not yet in sight. But they ought not turn that into blanket endorsement or an unalterable policy commitment, debarring them from the pursuit of stronger measures should they ever come politically into view.

Therein lies, perhaps, a larger lesson for green politics. True, perhaps environmentalists ought be realists. They ought not go tilting at windmills; they ought not let the best be the enemy of the good; they ought get what they can, here and now, rather than holding out in all-or-nothing fashion when doing so only guarantees that nothing will be achieved. Be all that as it may, it is nonetheless equally true that environmentalists ought not be so sensitive to current political realities as to render them insensitive to shifting political realities. Shifting alliances and provisional policy commitments—as to green taxes—ought be very much part of the environmentalist's political repertoire.[19]

Notes

1. For discussions of such proposals, see Dales (1968: 93–7); Hahn (1982); Hahn and Hester (1987, 1989); Ackerman and Stewart (1988); and Pearce et al. (1989: 165–6). Note that, by setting upper limits on the amount of allowable pollution, these permits are more limiting than charges or taxes, which in principle dictate no such upper limit on the amount of allowable pollution (although in practice, of course, they price it out at some point).

2. Elaborating such proposals, see Epstein and Gupta (1990); Weimer (1990); and Pearce et al. (1989: 165–6). On the political uptake, see Palmer (1992) and Taylor (1992).

3. This is the cumulative conclusion of, e.g., Dales (1968: chap. 6); Kneese and Schultze (1975); Schultze (1977); Schelling (1983); Rhoads (1985: 40–56); Pearce et al. (1989: chap. 7).

4. Poisoning one person so that thousands may lives is, by most standards, the obviously right thing to do in the desperately unfortunate circumstances. But there is something obviously wrong with someone who is not even vaguely apologetic to the bereaved family for the sad necessity of that sacrifice (Nussbaum 1984).

5. See in particular Section 11.2 and 6 below. Another tack, unexplored here, is Hill's (1983) observation that certain sorts of character traits hang together, so the environmentally insensitive are likely also to be morally insensitive in ways classically linked to sin.

6. That is precisely the use made of permits under the most familiar instantiation of these techniques, in the US Emissions Trading Program and the Clean Air Act and Amendments of 1990 (US EPA 1986; US Congress 1990). See Hahn and Hester (1989) for discussion of those policies and Ackerman and Steward (1988) for elaboration of the 'democratic' roots underlying their rationale.

7. In the Eastern and the older Western Church, 'the priest invoked divine forgiveness but could not himself declare the sinner to be absolved'; it was only 'after the Papal Revolution' in the eleventh century that 'a new formula was introduced in the West: *Ego te absolvo* ('I absolve you'). This was at first interpreted as the priest's certification of God's action . . . In the twelfth century, however, it was interpreted as having a performative, that is, a sacramental as well as a declarative, effect' (Berman 1983: 173). Luther's (1517) fifth and sixth propositions especially hark back to this older understanding.

8. Some such 'good-faith' condition is built into the US offset policy: emissions permits can be sold only by those who have controlled their own emissions more than they are legally required to do; and potential buyers must as a precondition of purchase demonstrate that they have already installed the best available control technology, and they must buy 20 percent more permits than they will actually use (US EPA 1986; Hahn and Hester 1989).

9. Not always: see Section 11.4 below.

10. Even God might not be able to make wrongs right or bads good. On the so-called 'Euthyphro argument', His will does not make things good; rather, He wills what He does because it is good independently of His will. In Socrates' formulation, 'Is what is holy holy because the gods approve it, or do they approve it because it is holy?' (Plato nd/1961: sec. 10a/p. 178).

11. This may have to do with limits of criminal sanction. Much that we regard as morally wrong remains legally permissible, because it would be wrong (inappropriate, given the limits of the criminal sanction) literally to outlaw it—so we merely tax it instead.

12. What counts as 'the same boat' comes down to a matter of what are the characteristics that would make them 'relevantly similar'. The question of fairness, posed that way, quickly transforms itself into one of appropriate (relevant) criteria for granting indulgences. That issue is taken up in Section 11.6 below.

13. The more standard welfare-economic phrasing of that point would substitute hypothetical compensation for actual in clause 3 above: the test, there, is whether gainers *could* compensate losers (Kaldor 1939; Hicks 1939). Nothing is lost rephrasing the arguments of this article in those terms. Nor is anything gained by advocates of optimal despoilation, for the whole point of those opposing such optimization is that certain forms of damage could not even in principle be corrected or compensated by cash payments of any sort.

14. Elliot (1982). Humanity is part of nature, too, of course: but surely we ought not infer from that that any human intervention, however destructive of the rest of creation, is acceptable because it is just part of a natural process. Those intuitions seem firm and clear. How to justify them—and with them, any sharp distinction between human and non-human parts of nature—is less straightforward, perhaps. One way is to say that the value that humans derive from being able to set their lives in some context outside of themselves, either individually or collectively; and for this purpose, it is precisely the non-human part of nature that is crucial (Goodin 1992: chap. 2).

15. Even the OECD (1975: 28), acknowledges that 'direct controls' of a more legalistic, command-and-control sort are preferable to incentives of a 'green tax' sort as a 'means of preventing *irreversible effects* or *unacceptable pollution* (mercury, cadmium, etc.)'.

16. Even the OECD's (1975) *Polluter Pays Principle* proceeds in this way. Its 'Guiding Principles' state that 'the polluter should bear the expenses of carrying out . . . measures decided by public authorities to ensure that

the environment is in an *acceptable* state' (pp. 12–13, emphasis added). A rather confused 'Note' glossing those guidelines elaborates, 'The notion of an "acceptable state" decided by public authorities.' The 'collective choice' of what is an 'acceptable' should be made with due regard to comparative social costs of the pollution and of its abatement, but those determinations are to be made politically rather than literally economically; it therefore follows that 'the Polluter-Pays Principle is no more than an efficiency principle for allocating costs and does not (necessarily) involve bringing pollution down to an optimum level of any type' (p. 15). See further Pearce et al. (1989: 157–8; cf. chap. 3).

17. In similar vein, the US Comptroller General (1979) reported to Congress that the then-existing limits on fines that the Nuclear Regulatory Commission could impose on operators of nuclear power plants for safety violations were inadequate deterrents: allowing a maximum penalty of $5,000 for each violation up to a maximum of $25,000 for all violations over a period of 30 consecutive days is a derisory deterrent, when it would cost the operators of the power plant something on the order of $300,000 to purchase power from the grid every day it is shut down to make repairs.

18. Environmental economists, of course, see themselves retreating to this fallback position purely for reasons of pragmatism—purely because of practical difficulties in calculating costs. The imposition of 'standards' which the price mechanism is then used to enforce is nonetheless justified, at root, in terms of social costs, even if they cannot be calculated precisely. Even on this minimal understanding of why the retreat was necessary, however, paying the price still cannot right wrongs. As those environmental economists themselves would be the first to concede (indeed, insist, as a criticism of standard-setting ungrounded in hard economic calculations more generally), standards will only accidentally if at all correspond to what is socially optimal, defined as the level of environmental despoilation that would follow from a proper calculation of social costs. (See Pearce et al. 1989: chap. 7.) Hence paying a price set merely to achieve those standards will only accidentally if at all provide recompense for the damage done. The price is essentially arbitrary, even from the environmental economist's point of view; and paying an *arbitrarily* high price cannot, even from their point of view, serve to right any wrongs.

19. Earlier versions were read at the Universities of Queensland and Melbourne and at various venues around the Australian National University. I am particularly grateful for valuable comments, then and later, from John Dryzek, Patrick Dunleavy, Bruno S. Frey, René L. Frey, Daniel Hausman, Max Neutze, Alan Ryan, Rob Sparrow, and Cass Sunstein.

References

Ackerman, Bruce A., and Stewart, Richard B. (1988), 'Reforming Environmental Law: The Democratic Case for Market Incentives', *Columbia Journal of Environmental Law*, 13: 171–99.

Barry, Brian (1989), *Democracy, Power and Justice* (Oxford: Clarendon Press).

Baumol, William J., and Oates, Wallace E. (1971), 'The Use of Standards and Prices for Protection of the Environment', *Swedish Journal of Economics*, 73: 42–54.

Berman, Harold J. (1983), *Law and Revolution: The Formation of the Western Legal Tradition* (Cambridge, Mass.: Harvard University Press).

Boudinhon, A. (1940), 'Indulgences', in James Hastings (ed.), *Encyclopedia of Religion and Ethics* (Edinburgh: T. & T. Clark), vii. 252–5.

Dales, J. H. (1968), *Pollution, Property & Prices* (Toronto: University of Toronto Press).

Devall, Bill, and Sessions, George (1985), *Deep Ecology* (Salt Lake City: Peregrine Smith Books).

Die Grünen (1983), *Programme of the German Green Party*, trans. Hans Fernbach (London: Heretic Books).

Douglas, Mary, and Isherwood, Brian (1979), *The World of Goods* (London: Allen Lane).

Eliade, Mircea (1987) (ed.), *The Encyclopedia of Religion* (New York: MacMillan).

Elliot, Robert (1982), 'Faking Nature', *Inquiry*, 25: 81–94.

Epstein, Joshua M., and Gupta, Raj (1990), *Controlling the Greenhouse Effect: Five Global Regimes Compared* (Washington, DC: Brookings Institution).

European Greens (1989), *Common Statement of the European Greens for the 1989 Elections to the European Parliament* (Brussels: European Greens).

Fisher, Anthony C. (1981), *Resource and Environmental Economics* (Cambridge: Cambridge University Press).

Freeman, A. Myrick, III, Haveman, Robert H., and Kneese, Allen V. (1973), *The Economics of Environmental Policy* (New York: Wiley).

Frey, Bruno S. (1986), 'Economists Favour the Price System—Who Else Does?', *Kyklos*, 39: 537–633.

—— (1992), 'Tertium Datur: Pricing, Regulating and Intrinsic Motivation', *Kyklos*, 45: 161–84.

—— (1993), 'Motivation as a Limit to Pricing', *Journal of Economic Psychology*, 14: 635–64.

Goodin, Robert E. (1981), 'Making Moral Incentives Pay', *Policy Sciences*, 12: 131–45.

—— (1982), *Political Theory and Public Policy* (Chicago: University of Chicago Press).

—— (1985), *Protecting the Vulnerable* (Chicago: University of Chicago Press).

—— (1989), 'Theories of Compensation', *Oxford Journal of Legal Studies*, 9: 56–75.

—— (1992), *Green Political Theory* (Oxford: Polity Press).

—— (1995), *Utilitarianism as a Public Philosophy* (Cambridge: Cambridge University Press).

Hahn, Robert W. (1982), 'Marketable Permits: What's all the Fuss About?', *Journal of Public Policy*, 2: 395–412.

—— and Hester, Gordon L. (1987), 'The Market for Bads: EPA's Experience with Emissions Trading', *Regulation*, 3/4: 48–53.

—— —— (1989), 'Marketable Permits: Lessons for Theory & Practice', *Ecology Law Quarterly*, 16: 361–406.

Hicks, John R. (1939), 'The Foundations of Welfare Economics', *Economic Journal*, 49: 696–712.

Hill, Thomas E., Jr. (1983), 'Ideals of Human Excellence and Preserving Natural Environments', *Environmental Ethics*, 5: 211–24.

Hirshleifer, Jack (1987), *Economic Behaviour in Adversity* (Brighton: Harvester-Wheatsheaf).

Kaldor, Nicholas (1939), 'Welfare Propositions of Economics and Interpersonal Comparisons of Utility', *Economic Journal*, 49: 549–52.

Kelman, Steven (1981), *What Price Incentives? Economists and the Environment* (Boston: Auburn House).

—— (1983), 'Economic Incentives and Environmental Policy: Politics, Ideology and Philosophy', in Thomas C. Schelling (ed.), *Incentives for Environmental Protection* (Cambridge, Mass.: MIT Press), 291–332.

Kennan, George F. (1970), 'To Prevent a World Wasteland', *Foreign Affairs*, 48: 401–13.

Kneese, Allen V., and Schultze, Charles L. (1975), *Pollution, Prices and Public Policy* (Washington, DC: Brookings Institution).

Lane, Robert E. (1991), *The Market Experience* (Cambridge: Cambridge University Press).

Luther, Martin (1963), 'Ninety-five Theses' (1517), in Carl S. Meyer (trans.), *Luther's and Zwingli's Propositions for Debate* (Leiden: E. J. Brill), 3–21.

McCarthy, Eugene J. (1990), 'Pollution Absolution', *New Republic*, 3: 9.

Neary, J. Peter (1987), 'Rationing', in *The New Palgrave: A Dictionary of Economics* (London: MacMillan), iv. 92–6.

Nussbaum, Martha C. (1984), *The Fragility of Goodness* (Cambridge: Cambridge University Press).

Opschoor, J. B., and Vos, H. (1988), *The Application of Economic Instruments for Environmental Protection in OECD Member Countries* (Paris: OECD).

Organisation for Economic Co-operation and Development (1975), *The Polluter Pays Principle* (Paris: OECD).

Palmer, John (1992), 'Community Plans Carbon Fuel Tax', *Guardian Weekly*, 146(21): 11.

Passmore, John (1980), *Man's Responsibility for Nature*, 2nd edn. (London: Duckworth).

Pearce, David, Markandya, Anil, and Barbier, Edward B. (1989), *A Blueprint for a Green Economy: A Report to the UK Department of the Environment* (London: Earthscan).

Pigou, A. C. (1932), *The Economics of Welfare*, 4th edn. (London: MacMillan).

Plato, *Euthyphro*. Reprinted in E. Hamilton and H. Cairns (eds), *The Collected Dialogues of Plato* (Princeton, NJ: Princeton University Press, 1961).

Purcell, Maureen (1975), *Papal Crusading Policy, 1244–1291* (Leiden: E. J. Brill).

Rhoads, Steven E. (1985), *The Economists's View of the World* (Cambridge: Cambridge University Press).

Sagoff, Mark (1988), *The Economy of the Earth* (Cambridge: Cambridge University Press).

Sax, Joseph L. (1970), 'The Public Trust Doctrine in Natural Resource Law', *Michigan Law Review*, 68: 471–566.

Schelling, Thomas C. (1983) (ed.), *Incentives for Environmental Protection* (Cambridge, Mass.: MIT Press).

Schultze, Charles (1977), *The Public Use of Private Interest* (Washington, DC: Brookings Institution).

Simmel, Georg (1978), *The Philosophy of Money*, trans. T. B. Bottomore and D. Frisby (London: Routledge & Kegan Paul) (originally published 1907).

Spretnak, Charlene (1986), *The Spritual Dimension of Green Politics* (Santa Fe, N. Mex.: Bear & Co).

——and Capra, Fritjof (1986), *Green Politics: The Global Promise* (Santa Fe, N. Mex.: Bear & Co).

Sylvan, Richard (1985), 'A Critique of Deep Ecology', *Radical Philosophy*, 40: 2–12 and 41: 10–22.

Taylor, Jeffrey (1992), 'Global Market in Pollution Rights Proposed by U.N.', *New York Times*, 31 January: C1 and C12.

Taylor, Michael, and Ward, Hugh (1982), 'Chickens, Whales and Lumpy Public Goods: Alternative Models of Public-Goods Provision', *Political Studies*, 30: 350–70.

Titmuss, R. M. (1971), *The Gift Relationship* (London: Allen and Unwin).

Tobin, James (1952), 'A Survey of the Theory of Rationing,' *Econometrica*, 20: 521–53.

——(1970), 'On Limiting the Domain of Inequality', *Journal of Law and Economics*, 13: 363–78.

United States, Comptroller General (1979), *Higher Penalities Could Deter Violations of Nuclear Regulations*, Report to the Congress number EMD-79-9 (Washington, DC: General Accounting Office).

United States, Congress (1990), Clean Air Act, Amendments, Public Law 101–549 (S. 1630), 15 November 1990, *Statutes*, 104: 2399–2712.

United States, Environmental Protection Agency (1986), Emissions Trading Policy Statement, *Federal Register*, 51: 43–814.

Walzer, Michael (1983), *Spheres of Justice* (Oxford: Martin Robertson).

Weimer, David L. (1990), 'An Earmarked Fossil Fuels Tax to Save the Rain Forests', *Journal of Policy Analysis and Management*, 9: 254–9.

Section VI: Sustainable Development

As we saw in Section V, market liberals believe that economic mechanisms can serve environmental values, provided only that the appropriate set of private property rights is in place. Sustainable development too is a doctrine that believes in the integration of economic and environmental values, but in a somewhat different dimension. The era of sustainable development began in earnest on the global stage in the 1980s, when it largely displaced the more established discourse of limits and survivalism. The ecological limits stressed by the latter were in no sense disproved by sustainable development; rather, these limits were assumed away. Sustainable development begins from the contention that economic growth and environmental protection can be brought into productive harmony on a global scale, though only by concerted collective action (of the sort that horrifies market liberals). A commitment to redistribution from rich to poor now and in the future is thrown in for good measure, though this redistribution should not prove especially painful for the rich.

While sustainable development is nowhere an accomplished fact, as a concept and a framework it informs the efforts of international organizations, environmental groups, and governments, especially in international environmental affairs. Its hold on the global environmental imagination was confirmed in 1987 with the publication of *Our Common Future*, the report of the World Commission on Environment and Development chaired by Norwegian Prime Minister Gro Harlem Brundtland, whose basic statement we reprint here. Since then it has gone from strength to strength. Perhaps its finest hour was the 1992 Earth Summit in Rio de Janeiro, where heads of state from all over the world gathered to endorse a broad global strategy for sustainable development. While that agenda has flagged and occasionally languished in its implementation, it still has no real competitor in international environmental politics.

Sceptics charge that the popularity of sustainable development stems only from the fact that it can mean all things to all people. To the World Business Council on Sustainable Development it means mainly continued economic growth. To the international environmental groups that endorse the concept it means deeper commitment to ecological values in redesigning the world's political economy. To the sceptics William Lafferty replies that for environmentalists there is simply no other game worth playing. If we want to advance environmental values, we had better use this best available vehicle. Lafferty believes that sustainable development is about all that stands in the way of market liberalism wreaking environmental havoc.

Herman Daly strikes a note of dissent. He criticizes the popular equation of sustainable development with sustainable growth; the latter, he avers, is impossible in our very finite world. At some point we still have to come to terms with the kinds of ecological limits that energize survivalists. Vandana Shiva for her part is critical of the whole idea of development as an attempt to impose alien Western imperatives on the Third World and advocates a more indigenous notion of sustainability.

Further Reading

Aside from the Brundtland report, key documents advancing the cause of sustainable development published by international organizations include the lengthy *Agenda 21* coming out of the 1992 Earth Summit, and *Caring for the Earth: A Strategy for Sustainable Living*, produced jointly in 1991 by the International Union of the Conservation of Nature, United Nations Environment Program, and World Wildlife Fund. Michael Jacobs in *The Green Economy: Environment, Sustainable Development and the Future* (1991) gives an environmentalist's account of how economics might be re-oriented in the interests of sustainable development. Frank Fischer and Michael Black (eds), *Greening Environmental Policy: The Politics of a Sustainable Future* (1995) is a good collection oriented to environmental policy and politics. Stephan Schmidheiny in *Changing Course: A Global Business Perspective on Development and the Environment* (1992) shows how sustainable development can be accommodated to the interests of large corporations. Michael Redclift's *Sustainable Development: Exploring the Contradictions* (1987) demonstrates the variety of uses to which the concept can be put. Tim Luke's 'Sustainable Development as a Power Knowledge System: The Problem of Governmentality', in Fischer and Black (1995) is an uncompromising critique of the concept.

17 From One Earth to One World

An Overview by the World Commission on Environment and Development

In the middle of the twentieth century, we saw our planet from space for the first time. Historians may eventually find that this vision had a greater impact on thought than did the Copernican revolution of the sixteenth century, which upset the human self-image by revealing that the Earth is not the centre of the universe. From space, we see a small and fragile ball dominated not by human activity and edifice but by a pattern of clouds, oceans, greenery, and soils. Humanity's inability to fit its doings into that pattern is changing planetary systems, fundamentally. Many such changes are accompanied by life-threatening hazards. This new reality, from which there is no escape, must be recognized—and managed.

Fortunately, this new reality coincides with more positive developments new to this century. We can move information and goods faster around the globe than ever before; we can produce more food and more goods with less investment of resources; our technology and science gives us at least the potential to look deeper into and better understand natural systems. From space, we can see and study the Earth as an organism whose health depends on the health of all its parts. We have the power to reconcile human affairs with natural laws and to thrive in the process. In this our cultural and spiritual heritages can reinforce our economic interests and survival imperatives.

This Commission believes that people can build a future that is more prosperous, more just, and more secure. Our report, *Our Common Future*, is not a prediction of ever-increasing environmental decay, poverty, and hardship in an ever more polluted world among ever-decreasing resources. We see instead the possibility for a new era of economic growth, one that must be based on policies that sustain and expand the environmental resource base. And we believe such growth to be absolutely essential to relieve the great poverty that is deepening in much of the developing world.

But the Commission's hope for the future is conditional on decisive political action now to begin managing environmental resources to ensure both sustainable human progress and human survival. We are not forecasting a future; we are serving a notice—an urgent notice based on the latest and best scientific evidence—that the time has come to take the decisions needed to secure the resources to sustain this and coming generations. We do not offer a detailed blueprint for action, but instead a pathway by which the peoples of the world may enlarge their spheres of co-operation.

I. The Global Challenge

SUCCESSES AND FAILURES

Those looking for success and signs of hope can find many: Infant mortality is falling; human life expectancy is increasing; the proportion of the world's adults who can read and write is climbing; the proportion of children starting school is rising; and global food production increases faster than the population grows.

But the same processes that have produced these gains have given rise to trends that the planet and its people cannot long bear. These have traditionally been divided into failures of 'development' and failures in the management of our human environment. On the development side, in terms of absolute numbers there are more hungry people in the world than ever before, and their numbers are increasing. So are the numbers who cannot read or write, the numbers without safe water or safe and sound homes, and the numbers short of woodfuel with which to cook and warm themselves. The gap between rich and poor nations is widening—not shrinking—and there is little prospect, given present trends and institutional arrangements, that this process will be reversed.

There are also environmental trends that threaten to radically alter the planet, that threaten the lives of many species upon it, including the human species. Each year another 6 million hectares of productive dryland turns into worthless desert. Over three decades, this would amount to an area roughly as large as Saudi Arabia. More than 11 million hectares of forests are destroyed yearly, and this, over three decades, would equal an area about the size of India. Much of this forest is converted to low-grade farmland unable to support the farmers who settle it. In Europe, acid precipitation kills forests and lakes and damages the artistic and architectural heritage of nations; it may have acidified vast tracts of soil beyond reasonable hope of repair. The burning of fossil fuels puts into the atmosphere carbon dioxide, which is causing gradual global warming. This 'greenhouse effect' may by early next century have increased average global temperatures enough to shift agricultural production areas, raise sea levels to flood coastal cities, and disrupt national economies. Other industrial gases threaten to deplete the planet's protective ozone shield to such an extent that the number of human and animal cancers would rise sharply and the oceans' food chain would be disrupted. Industry and agriculture put toxic substances into the human food chain and into underground water tables beyond reach of cleansing.

There has been a growing realization in national governments and multilateral institutions that it is impossible to separate economic development issues from environment issues; many forms of development erode the environmental resource upon which they must be based, and environmental degradation can undermine economic development. Poverty is a major cause and effect of global environmental problems. It is therefore futile to attempt to deal with environmental problems without a broader perspective that encompasses the factors underlying world poverty and international inequality.

These concerns were behind the establishment in 1983 of the World Commission on Environment and Development by the UN General Assembly. The Commission is an independent body,

The World Commission on Environment and Development first met in October 1984, and published its report 900 days later, in April 1987. Over those few days:

- The drought-triggered, environment-development crisis in Africa peaked, putting 35 million people at risk, killing perhaps a million.
- A leak from a pesticides factory in Bhopal, India, killed more than 2,000 people and blinded and injured over 200,000 more.
- Liquid gas tanks exploded in Mexico City, killing 1,000 and leaving thousands more homeless.
- The Chernobyl nuclear reactor explosion sent nuclear fallout across Europe, increasing the risks of future human cancers.
- Agricultural chemicals, solvents, and mercury flowed into the Rhine River during a warehouse fire in Switzerland, killing millions of fish and threatening drinking water in the Federal Republic of Germany and the Netherlands.
- An estimated 60 million people died of diarrhoeal diseases related to unsafe drinking water and malnutrition; most of the victims were children.

linked to but outside the control of governments and the UN system. The Commission's mandate gave it three objectives: to re-examine the critical environment and development issues and to formulate realistic proposals for dealing with them; to propose new forms of international cooperation on these issues that will influence policies and events in the direction of needed changes; and to raise the levels of understanding and commitment to action of individuals, voluntary organizations, businesses, institutes, and governments.

Through our deliberations and the testimony of people at the pubic hearings we held on five continents, all the commissioners came to focus on one central theme: many present development trends leave increasing numbers of people poor and vulnerable, while at the same time degrading the environment. How can such development serve next century's world of twice as many people relying on the same environment? This realization broadened our view of development. We came to see it not in its restricted context of economic growth in developing countries. We came to see that a new development path was required, one that sustained human progress not just in a few places for a few years, but for the entire planet into the distant future. Thus 'sustainable development' becomes a goal not just for the 'developing' nations, but for industrial ones as well.

THE INTERLOCKING CRISES

Until recently, the planet was a large world in which human activities and their effects were neatly compartmentalized within nations, within sectors (energy, agriculture, trade), and within broad areas of concern (environmental, economic, social). These compartments have begun to dissolve. This applies in particular to the various global 'crises' that have seized public concern, particularly over the past decade. These are not separate crises: an environmental crisis, a development crisis, an energy crisis. They are all one.

The planet is passing through a period of dramatic growth and fundamental change. Our human world of 5 billion must make room in a finite environment for another human world. The population could stabilize at between 8 billion and 14 billion sometime next century, according to UN projections. More than 90 per cent of the increase will occur in the poorest countries, and 90 per cent of that growth in already bursting cities.

Economic activity has multiplied to create a $13 trillion world economy, and this could grow five- or tenfold in the coming half-century. Industrial production has grown more than fiftyfold over the past century, four-fifths of this growth since 1950. Such figures reflect and presage profound impacts upon the biosphere, as the world invests in houses, transport, farms, and industries. Much of the economic growth pulls raw material from forests, soils, seas, and waterways.

A mainspring of economic growth is new techology, and while this technology offers the potential for slowing the dangerously rapid consumption of finite resources, it also entails high risks, including new forms of pollution and the introduction to the planet of new variations of life forms that could change evolutionary pathways. Meanwhile, the industries most heavily reliant on environmental resources and most heavily polluting are growing most rapidly in the developing world, where there is both more urgency for growth and less capacity to minimize damaging side effects.

These related changes have locked the global economy and global ecology together in new ways. We have in the past been concerned about the impacts of economic growth upon the environment. We are now forced to concern ourselves with the impacts of ecological stress—degradation of soils, water regimes, atmosphere, and forests—upon our economic prospects. We have in the more recent past been forced to face up to a sharp increase in economic interdependence among nations. We are now forced to accustom ourselves to an accelerating ecological interdependence among nations. Ecology and economy are becoming ever more interwoven—locally, regionally, nationally, and globally—into a seamless net of causes and effects.

Impoverishing the local resource base can impoverish wider areas: Deforestation by highland farmers causes flooding on lowland farms; factory pollution robs local fishermen of their catch. Such grim local cycles now operate nationally and regionally. Dryland degradation sends environmental refugees in their millions across national borders. Deforestation in Latin America and Asia is causing more floods, and more destructive floods, in downhill, downstream nations. Acid precipitation and nuclear fallout have spread across the borders of Europe. Similar phenomena are emerging on a global scale, such as global warming and loss of ozone. Internationally traded hazardous chemicals entering foods are themselves internationally traded. In the next century, the environmental pressure causing population movements may increase sharply, while barriers to that movement may be even firmer than they are now.

Over the past few decades, life-threatening environmental concerns have surfaced in the developing world. Countrysides are coming under pressure from increasing numbers of farmers and the landless. Cities are filling with people, cars, and factories. Yet at the same time these developing countries must operate in a world in which the resources gap between most developing and industrial nations is widening, in which the industrial world dominates in the rule-making of some key international bodies, and in which the industrial world has already used much of the planet's ecological capital. This inequality is the planet's main 'environmental' problem; it is also its main 'development' problem.

International economic relationships pose a particular problem for environmental management in many developing countries. Agriculture, forestry, energy production, and mining generate at least half the gross national product of many developing countries and account for even larger shares of livelihoods and employment. Exports of natural resources remain a large factor in their economies, especially for the least developed. Most of these countries face enormous economic pressures, both international and domestic, to overexploit their environmental resource base.

The recent crisis in Africa best and most tragically illustrates the ways in which economics and ecology can interact destructively and trip into disaster. Triggered by drought, its real causes lie deeper. They are to be found in part in national policies that gave too little attention, too late, to the needs of smallholder agriculture and to the threats posed by rapidly rising populations. Their roots extend also to a global economic system that takes more out of a poor continent than it puts in. Debts that they cannot pay force African nations relying on commodity sales to overuse their fragile soils, thus turning good land to desert. Trade barriers in the wealthy nations—and in many developing ones—make it hard for Africans to sell their goods for reasonable returns, putting yet more pressure on ecological systems. Aid from donor nations has not only been inadequate in scale, but too often has reflected the priorities of the nations giving the aid, rather than the needs of the recipients. The production base of other developing world areas suffers similarly both from local failures and from the workings of international economic systems. As a consequence of the 'debt crisis' of Latin America, that region's natural resources are now being used not for development but to meet financial obligations to creditors abroad. This approach to the debt problem is short-sighted from several standpoints: economic, political, and environmental. It requires relatively poor countries simultaneously to accept growing poverty while exporting growing amounts of scarce resources.

A majority of developing countries now have lower per capita incomes than when the decade began. Rising poverty and unemployment have increased pressure on environmental resources as more people have been forced to rely more directly upon them. Many governments have cut back efforts to protect the environment and to bring ecological considerations into development planning.

The deepening and widening environmental crisis presents a threat to national security—and even survival—that may be greater than well-armed, ill-disposed neighbours and unfriendly alliances. Already in parts of Latin America, Asia, the Middle East, and Africa, environmental decline is becoming a source of political unrest and international tension. The recent destruction of much of Africa's dryland agricultural production was more severe than if an invading army had pursued a scorched-earth policy. Yet most of the affected governments still spend far more to protect their people from invading armies than from the invading desert.

Globally, military expenditures total about $1 trillion a year and continue to grow. In many countries, military spending consumes such a high proportion of gross national product that it itself does great damage to these societies' development efforts. Governments tend to base their approaches to 'security' on traditional definitions. This is most obvious in the attempts to achieve security through the development of potentially planet-destroying nuclear weapons systems. Studies suggest that the cold and dark nuclear winter following even a limited nuclear war could destroy plant and animal ecosystems and leave any human survivors occupying a devastated planet very different from the one they inherited.

The arms race—in all parts of the world—pre-empts resources that might be used more productively to diminish the security threats created by environmental conflict and the resentments that are fuelled by widespread poverty.

Many present efforts to guard and maintain human progress, to meet human needs, and to realize human ambitions are simply unsustainable—in both the rich and poor nations. They draw too heavily, too quickly, on already overdrawn environmental resource accounts to be affordable far into the future without bankrupting those accounts. They may show profits on the balance sheets of our generation, but our children will inherit the losses. We borrow environmental capital from future generations with no intention or prospect of repaying. They may damn us for our spendthrift ways, but they can never collect on our debt to them. We act as we do because we can get away with it: future generations do not vote; they have no political or financial power; they cannot challenge our decisions.

But the results of the present profligacy are rapidly closing the options for future generations. Most of today's decision makers will be dead before the planet feels the heavier effects of acid precipitation, global warming, ozone depletion, or widespread desertification and species loss. Most of the young voters of today will still be alive. In the Commission's hearings it was the

The Commission has sought ways in which global development can be put on a sustainable path into the twenty-first century. Some 5,000 days will elapse between the publication of our report and the first day of the twenty-first century. What environmental crises lie in store over those 5,000 days?

During the 1970s, twice as many people suffered each year from 'natural' disasters as during the 1960s. The disasters most directly associated with environment/development mismanagement—droughts and floods—affected the most people and increased most sharply in terms of numbers affected. Some 18.5 million people were affected by drought annually in the 1960s, 24.4 million in the 1970s. There were 5.2 million flood victims yearly in the 1960s, 15.4 million in the 1970s. Numbers of victims of cyclones and earthquakes also shot up as growing numbers of poor people built unsafe houses on dangerous ground.

The results are not in for the 1980s. But we have seen 35 million afflicted by drought in Africa alone and tens of millions affected by the better managed and thus less-publicized Indian drought. Floods have poured off the deforested Andes and Himalayas with increasing force. The 1980s seem destined to sweep this dire trend on into a crisis-filled 1990s.

young, those who have the most to lose, who were the harshest critics of the planet's present management.

SUSTAINABLE DEVELOPMENT

Humanity has the ability to make development sustainable—to ensure that it meets the needs of the present without compromising the ability of future generations to meet their own needs. The concept of sustainable development does imply limits—not absolute limits but limitations imposed by the present state of technology and social organization on environmental resources and by the ability of the biosphere to absorb the effects of human activities. But technology and social organization can be both managed and improved to make way for a new era of economic growth. The Commission believes that widespread poverty is no longer inevitable. Poverty is not only an evil in itself, but sustainable development requires meeting the basic needs of all and extending to all the opportunity to fulfil their aspirations for a better life. A world in which poverty is endemic will always be prone to ecological and other catastrophes.

Meeting essential needs requires not only a new era of economic growth for nations in which the majority are poor, but an assurance that those poor get their fair share of the resources required to sustain that growth. Such equity would be aided by political systems that secure effective citizen participation in decision making and by greater democracy in international decision making.

Sustainable global development requires that those who are more affluent adopt life-styles within the planet's ecological means—in their use of energy, for example. Further, rapidly growing populations can increase the pressure on resources and slow any rise in living standards; thus sustainable development can only be pursued if population size and growth are in harmony with the changing productive potential of the ecosystem.

Yet in the end, sustainable development is not a fixed state of harmony, but rather a process of change in which the exploitation of resources, the direction of investments, the orientation of technological development, and institutional change are made consistent with future as well as present needs. We do not pretend that the process is easy or straightforward. Painful choices have to be made. Thus, in the final analysis, sustainable development must rest on political will.

THE INSTITUTIONAL GAPS

The objective of sustainable development and the integrated nature of the global environment/development challenges pose problems for institutions, national and international, that were established on the basis of narrow preoccupations and compartmentalized concerns. Governments' general response to the speed and scale of global changes has been a reluctance to recognize sufficiently the need to change themselves. The challenges are both interdependent and integrated, requiring comprehensive approaches and popular participation.

Yet most of the institutions facing those challenges tend to be independent, fragmented, working to relatively narrow mandates with closed decision processes. Those responsible for managing natural resources and protecting the environment are institutionally separated from those responsible for managing the economy. The real world of interlocked economic and ecological systems will not change; the policies and institutions concerned must.

There is a growing need for effective international co-operation to manage ecological and economic interdependence. Yet at the same time, confidence in international organizations is diminishing and support for them dwindling.

The other great institutional flaw in coping with environment/development challenges is governments' failure to make the bodies whose policy actions degrade the environment responsible for ensuring that their policies prevent that degradation. Environmental concern arose from damage caused by the rapid economic growth following the Second World War. Governments, pressured by their citizens, saw a need to clean up the mess, and they established environmental ministries and agencies to do this. Many had great success—within the limits of their mandates—in improving air and water quality and enhancing other resources. But much of their work has of necessity been after-the-fact repair of damage: *re*forestation, *re*claiming desert lands, *re*building urban environments, *re*storing natural habitats, and *re*habilitating wild lands.

The existence of such agencies gave many governments and their citizens the false impression that these bodies were by themselves able to protect and enhance the environmental resource base. Yet many industrialized and most developing countries carry huge economic burdens from inherited problems such as air and water pollution, depletion of ground-water, and the proliferation of toxic chemicals and hazardous wastes. These have been joined by more recent problems—erosion, desertification, acidification, new chemicals, and new forms of waste—that are directly related to agricultural, industrial, energy, forestry, and transportation policies and practices.

The mandates of the central economic and sectoral ministries are also often too narrow, too concerned with quantities of production or growth. The mandates of ministries of industry include production targets, while the accompanying pollution is left to ministries of environment. Electricity boards produce power, while the acid pollution they also produce is left to other bodies to clean up. The present challenge is to give the central economic and sectoral ministries the responsibility for the quality of those parts of the human environment affected by their decisions, and to give the environmental agencies more power to cope with the effects of unsustainable development.

The same need for change holds for international agencies concerned with development lending, trade regulation, agricultural development, and so on. These have been slow to take the environmental effects of their work into account, although some are trying to do so.

The ability to anticipate and prevent environmental damage requires that the ecological dimensions of policy be considered at the same time as the economic, trade, energy, agricultural, and other dimensions. They should be considered on the same agendas and in the same national and international institutions.

This reorientation is one of the chief institutional challenges of the 1990s and beyond. Meeting it will require major institutional development and reform. Many countries that are too poor or small or that have limited managerial capacity will find it difficult to do this unaided. They will need financial and technical assistance and training. But the changes required involve all countries, large and small, rich and poor.

18 The Politics of Sustainable Development: Global Norms for National Implementation

William M. Lafferty

The notion of 'sustainable development' has in recent years achieved a popularity approaching that of 'democracy'. Just as every country and ideology after the Second World War wished to profile itself as 'democratic', we find the same trend today with respect to 'sustainable development'. The underlying idea of sustainability is, of course, much older than the 1987 report from the Brundtland Commission. It is, however, only since the publication of *Our Common Future* (OCF 1987) that sustainability, coupled to the notion of 'development', has become a rhetorical talisman for our common present. Pity the politician, the party programme, the long-term plan, or the international agreement that does *not* pay respect to the idea. The prospect of a non-sustainable society is on a par with that of a non-democratic society. It is simply not on.

Yet there is a tremendous diversity of definitions and interpretations.[1] Competing understandings of 'sustainable development' are surely as numerous as competing understandings of 'democracy'.[2] The idea has evolved into an 'essentially contested concept' (Gallie 1962; Connolly 1983), an idea characterised by different types of 'vagueness' (Kaplan 1964) over which we pursue endless semantic debates.[3] For many, this points towards a relatively simple solution: avoidance. Unclear concepts lead to unclear communication, and unclear communication is the source of both nonsense and trouble. Any idea that attempts to attach relatively simple normative connotations to the complex notion of 'development' as applied to widely diverse global settings and populations, deserves to be scrapped.

There is, of course, much to be said for this position, particularly from a scientific and analytic point of view. The matter can, however, be viewed in another light. As conceived here, the most significant potential of the concept lies in neither science nor academic analysis but in politics. The promulgation of the idea by politicians and bureaucrats is in inverse proportion to its rejection by critical social scientists. The more the politicians use it—the less the intellectuals like it. There is surely an interesting problematic here for political psychologists, but this is less important in the present context than the problem of implementation. Denying the usefulness of 'sustainable development' as an analytic concept, or the attractiveness of it as a normative concept, does nothing to affect either its popularity or import as a political concept.

The world has use for political scientists only insofar as political scientists can help us to make a better world. If a concept such as sustainable development is being used to manipulate political values and emotions, then we must be prepared to demonstrate this in a systematic and effective way. But we must also allow for the very real possibility that the term *can* be used in good faith, and that some of us, at any rate, have a responsibility to assist in the conversion of values and goals into specific results which conform with the normative aspirations.

This is a very different—more constructive and pragmatic—approach from that usually taken to the concept by academics. There can be little doubt that the majority of books and articles on sustainable development run from the sceptical to the outright critical.[4] By way of illustration, let me cite a very recent critique, one of particular interest in that it specifically attempts to link the concept to politics. In a recent paper Dick Richardson offers the following assessment:

So what, then, is the future of sustainable development? The concept as defined by Brundtland is not only a political fudge, it is a sham. It attempts to theoretically obscure the basic contradiction between the finiteness of the Earth, with natural self-regulating systems operating with limits, and the expansionary nature of industrial society. . . . The divide between the anthropocentric and biocentric approaches is unbridgeable, and the attempt by Brundtland to obfuscate the incongruity by promoting a new terminology was foredoomed to failure.[5]

Richardson's views are representative of those who feel that the concept of sustainable development (SD) is both garbled and deceptive. Such views are usually anchored in some form of 'deeper' environmental understanding (biocentrism, deep ecology, eco-socialism, eco-feminism, and so on) where there is a conviction as to the real essence of the environment-and-development (E&D) problem, and where it is felt that the official lip-service to sustainable development merely detracts from a more correct understanding.

There are, of course, other lines of criticism—lines which focus more on the operationalisation and practicality of the concept without getting into the issue of correctness—but they are less relevant for the political context chosen here. My interest is to focus on the idea's normative-political implications rather than its potential usage for generating descriptive indicators. As I see it, there are a number of very good reasons for taking the politics of sustainable development seriously, regardless of how individual politicians and bureaucrats may use or abuse the idea. The structure of the argument is as follows:

(1) the concept of sustainable development, as originally expressed in *Our Common Future*, is both more coherent and potentially more radical than both its political adherents and critics seem to be aware of;

(2) the concept can be viewed as expressing essential normative standards for a global ethics of environment-and-development. As such, it fulfils two important criteria for ethical legitimacy—consensualism and realism;

(3) the more general normative standards of the concept have been translated into relatively specific and wide-ranging operational goals;

(4) there exist political fora, institutions and procedures for realising these goals;

(5) these political mechanisms are imperfect and incremental, but there is, at present, no more effective way to seek progress with respect to global environment-development problems.

Sustainable Development: The Concept

Though the idea of 'sustainability' has relatively deep historical roots (O'Riordan 1993), its meaning in an environment-and-development context, seems to derive from German forestry (Stenseth 1991). A sustainable harvest of trees is one that reasonably covers current needs while preserving the integrity and productivity of a forest for many generations to come. The concept gained popularity among environmentalists in the 1960s and 1970s, and gradually became part of the more 'official' E&D programme with its adoption by the Brundtland Commission in 1987. Dixon and Fallon (1989) capture the development of the concept by identifying three different connotations: first, sustainability as a purely physical concept with respect to a single national resource (e.g. forestry); secondly, sustainability as a broader physical-biological concept with respect to the regenerative capacity of resource-systems or whole ecosystems (e.g. a harvest with respect to the impact on biodiversity); and thirdly, sustainability as a physical-biological-social concept, where the notion of ongoing 'maintainability' attaches to the relationship between nature, human welfare, and society.

The Brundtland report can be seen as the first internationally sanctioned document that attempts to elaborate on the third connotation, its goal being to establish sustainable development as a central normative concept for both assessing and changing global relationships. The report states forthrightly that: 'The issues we have raised . . . are inevitably of far-reaching importance to the quality of life on earth—indeed, to life itself. We have tried to show how human survival and well-being could depend on success in elevating sustainable development to a global ethic' (OCF: 308). The Brundtland Commission defines the idea as follows:

Sustainable development is development that meets the needs of the present without compromising the ability of future generations to meet their own needs. It contains within it two key concepts: the concept of 'needs', in particular the essential needs of the world's poor, to which overriding priority should be given; and the idea of limitations imposed by the state of technology and social organisation on the environment's ability to meet present and future needs. (OCF 1987: 43)

There are two characteristics of the Brundtland definition that distinguish it from other concepts that build on the notion of 'sustainability'. First, the Brundtland approach places human beings and human welfare above concepts of environmental or ecological sustainability; and, second, it introduces an aspect of social equity directly into the connotation. We thus find three basic elements in the Commission's usage. First, there is an element of so-called 'physical sustainability', whereby human development must be assessed with respect to the limits of nature and overall global ecological balance. There is, secondly, an element of 'global equity', whereby the extractive and distributional aspects of environment-and-development should be equitably divided among living generations, both locally and globally, and thirdly, there is an element of 'generational equity', whereby the environment-and-development relationship must be assessed with respect to the needs of future generations.

In addition to these three elements, the report also raises the issue of knowledge and risk with respect to environmental interventions. Later formulated as the 'precautionary principle', this element basically stipulates that a lack of adequate knowledge as to potential environmental effects shall not be used to hinder policies and actions designed to prevent environmental degradation. The benefit of scientific doubt must, in other words, always be applied to the advantage of environmental protection.

Combining these four elements, we can define sustainable development (as a relevant political concept) as follows:

> Sustainable development is a normative concept used to prescribe and evaluate changes in living conditions. Such changes are to be guided by four principles:
> (1) They aim to satisfy basic human needs and reasonable standards of welfare for all living beings (Development I);
> (2) They aim to achieve more equitable standards of living both within and among global populations (Development II);
> (3) They should be pursued with great caution as to their actual or potential disruption of biodiversity and the regenerative capacity of nature, both locally and globally (Sustainability I);
> (4) They should be achieved without undermining the possibility for future generations to attain similar standards of living and similar or improved standards of equity (Sustainability II).[6]

The inclusion of both physical and social aspects of sustainability in the Brundtland approach has led to numerous critiques and debates as to whether there is, or should be, a certain priority among the different elements. Should sustainability in relation to nature be given priority over global and/or generational equity, or should the orders be reversed? The report itself seems to stipulate physical sustainability as a minimalist standard, but it also states explicitly that 'even the narrow notion of physical sustainability implies a concern for social equity between generations, a concern that must logically be extended to equity within each generation' (OCF 1987: 43).

For present purposes (to establish a meaningful discourse on the politics of sustainable development), these issues are less important than the fact that the Brundtland report establishes standards for environment-and-development which aim to integrate and bring to bear all four elements simultaneously, and that the same standards have also been given more specific expression in numerous treaties, documents, declarations, and plans of action. This is the basis for viewing sustainable development as a new standard for political action and change. The idea provides a core set of values, norms, and goals which has the potential of engaging and mobilising citizens, at the same time that there are specific programmes for integrated action at the local, national, and global levels. Though there may be clear differences in opinion as to the internal ordering of the normative elements of the Brundtland concept, the importance of the work lies in its attempt to differentiate *its* notion of development from alternative notions that do not integrate the four basic elements.

In this light, the idea and its documentation can be said to have the potential of fulfilling an ideological and mobilising function. There is a theoretical foundation describing the relationship between man and nature; there are a limited number of integrated guiding principles; there is a clear identification of problems to be solved and the actors who must take responsibility for solving them; and there is a multifaceted and relatively specific agenda for change.[7]

None of this is meant to imply that the idea of sustainable development is intuitively simple, logically coherent, and normatively straightforward. The critique of the concept has clearly not been groundless. But there has been, I believe, a general lack of willingness, particularly on the part of environmental activists and their academic supporters, to give the concept its due in an ideological and ethical context. Perhaps this has to do with the fact that the idea was launched at a time when environmental concern was peaking in the West, and there was a feeling that the gradualist, managerial approach was inadequate. Or maybe it has to do with the fact that the idea emerged from an official United Nations commission, and commissions are hardly popular sources for ideology. Whatever the reason, the idea has clearly not been adopted as a focal symbol for political mobilisation and change. Its potential remains largely within the realm of rhetoric, and the follow-up from the Earth Summit is both less focused and less impressive than anticipated in Rio. Much of this comes. I believe, from a lack of analytic attention to the concept's ethical and political possibilities.

Sustainable Development as a Global Ethic

Given the prospect that the above definition expresses a reasonable summary of what *Our Common Future* intended, why and how can we understand the position as a global ethic? What force does it have as moral prescription, and why should we endorse it as a potentially effective norm-set for positive environment-and-development change?

There are, of course, numerous views as to the nature of ethics. Moral statements aim to convince us of good and bad behaviour, but they do so in different ways, with different arguments as to the legitimacy of their claims. For present purposes, we can be extremely simplistic by identifying two major modes for achieving ethical legitimacy and compliance: 'realism' and 'consensualism'.[8] The choice of these two orientations is conditioned by two vital premises as to how change should be accomplished. The first is that compliance should be achieved through rational argument directly related to the problematic, and the second is that any sanctions involved must derive from reasonable democratic procedures.

The realist mode argues for compliance on the basis of presumed ontological truth. What is right or wrong is derivable from a correct understanding of the phenomena relevant to the problematic. The oldest and most resilient form of this mode of ethics is the morality of natural law. Once we have understood the innate workings of the real world (as discoverable by science), we will then know how to act with respect to that world. Goodness attaches to the natural, badness to the unnatural. Both positivist and phenomenological approaches to the real world support ethics in this mode.

The consensual mode seeks moral validity through collective agreement. Theories of the real world are too indecisive and contingent to provide adequate ethical foundations. The debate as to correct epistemology leads to the deconstruction of scientific method as a decisive criterion for truth. Morality as a guide for action can only be secured through critical dialogue and consensual acknowledgment. The greater the degree of consensus as to right or wrong, the greater the force of moral prescription, and the greater the chances of moral compliance.

As outlined above, the concept of sustainable development can be shown to derive force from both of these modes of ethical legitimacy. With respect to the aspect of 'physical sustainability', the norm-set is validated by the enormous weight of scientific evidence and argument as to the degenerative effects on the environment from human intervention. It is clearly no accident that several of the more decisive texts and many of the most prominent activists of the early environmental movement came from the natural sciences. Natural science arguments, supported by natural-science data, have been at the core of demands for global environmental change from the start. They have provided these demands with a legitimacy and force that modern humanism lacked in its attempt to reverse the negative effects of industrialism. It is an interesting commentary on the foibles of ideological development and change, that modern environmentalism should anchor its moral appeal in positivist science at a point in history when the critical-scientific basis of Marxism was being definitively undermined. Where indeed would the argument for environmentalism-as-progress be if it were not for the natural scientists—a point which the Brundtland report makes explicit in its admonition for more direct links between the scientific community and NGOs (OCF 1987: 326–9).

In addition to its realist appeal, however, the demand for sustainable development, in both its physical and equity aspects, derives clear moral support from its widespread endorsement as a consensual norm. Regardless of which school of ethics one adheres to, there can be no doubt that if the goal is mobilisation for change within the realm of democratic procedures and institutions, the stronger the potential for consensus the better. And whereas philosophers of consensual ethics promote the correctness of their position in terms of abstract consensus, the concept of sustainable development has been the subject of very real and widespread agreement. We need only mention the Rio Declaration, *Agenda 21*, the Maastricht Treaty, and the numerous other conventions and action programmes within both the United Nations and the European Union, to illustrate the point. When, previously, has such a clearly prescriptive idea received such diverse and comprehensive voluntary support? Regardless of differences of interpretation, and making no presumptions as to sincerity of commitment, the worldwide acknowledgment of the principle of sustainable development gives credence to the claim of a global ethic. A foundation has been laid which ideological purists may reject, and cynical politicians exploit, but which normative pragmatists can and should work with.

Admittedly, the entire complex of values, declarations, conventions, and institutions may reflect no more than rhetorical inflation and political expediency. The 'consensus', it could be argued, is a consensus in word only. The understandings of the more than 170 governments assembled in Rio as to what sustainable development *actually* implies vary so much as to belie the image of a coordinated commitment. A political compromise does not constitute either a common goal or a consensual plan of action.

No one would want to deny the potential validity of such a perspective. Yet the import of the critique is neither new nor decisive. Democratic majorities are always subject to interpretation and second-guessing. In the present case, however, we are not dealing with a simple majority, but with global unanimity. Furthermore, we are not dealing with highly vague, rambling and usually neglected party-political platforms, but with specific documents which, in most cases, have been meticulously negotiated over many years. If we are to admit the open nature of the Rio documents because they reflect political compromise, we must also admit the relatively high degree of specificity and commitment which results from the long and intense preparatory process leading up to Rio.

Negotiations among the fundamental global interests represented in Rio led not only to problems of interpretation and the assessment of potential change, but to a broad scope of principles and action directives which *only* such a process of negotiation could produce. In contrast to the partisan bodies which normally author political platforms, the body that first composed and then signed off on the Rio Declaration, *Agenda 21* and two binding conventions (on climate change and biodiversity), constituted an Assembly of the Whole. In this fact alone lies a unique consensual mandate: unique in its breadth of representation; unique in its adherence to the principle of sustainable development; unique in the specificity of both its prescriptions and admonitions for change; and unique in the scope and purpose of its newly established mechanisms for implementation.

None of this is to say, of course, that the goal of sustainable development is unanimously understood, or that the changes advocated at Rio are sufficient to halt and reverse global environment-and-development degradation. What it does say is that the UNCED process has established new standards for global politics in this area, and that it has also put into place a network of fora and arenas for pursuing these standards within specific action frameworks. The process in no way guarantees progress toward a global sustainable society. But the prospect of resolving the trade-off between global ecological balance and global welfare equity in a relatively peaceful and democratic fashion under any *other* normative regime, is surely less likely.

From Ethics to Implementation

What is contended, therefore, is that the politics of sustainable development are at once more normatively constrained and more instrumentally specific than any form of global politics thus far developed. Furthermore, it is maintained that there are clear possibilities of exploiting the normative position to exert political pressure on domestic regimes. Governmental leaders become bound up, and to a certain degree carried away by the momentum of international and regional environment-and-development processes. They either compete in capturing, or belatedly give their active support to, the moral cutting edge of the persuasion. The role of environmental journalists and NGOs has been crucial in forcing this development, but the functional need for creating 'new politics' at home has also been a factor.

What is important however, is that when the leaders return home they leave behind a wealth of publicly recorded statements, documents, accords, procedures, and institutions—records which clearly can be used to press for domestic political compliance. The politics of sustainable development are not only the politics of UNCED, UNEP, UNDP, CSD, and the EU. They are also the *potential* politics of national and local change under the onus of supranational commitments. Gro Harlem Brundtland may, as a national politician and Prime Minister of Norway, regret her reference to the results of Rio as 'promises made by world leaders' (COCF 1993). But her observation in the same context that the promises in question 'can only be fulfilled in time to secure our future if governments are inspired and pressured by their citizens' stands as a rallying cry for political mobilisation and change.

It thus becomes increasingly important to objectify, analyse, and make better known the parameters for sustainable-development politics. The emerging global game is of great significance in its own right, but there are also important implications for regional, national, and local development. The slogan 'Think globally, act locally' can only be given more widespread and concrete meaning if voters become better schooled in the intricacies of the environment-and-development relationship, and more aware of the moral and practical potential for local-global linkages.

During the past twenty years or so, the global arena for environment-and-development politics has emerged as a clearly identifiable political system. There are actors, roles, routines, settings, and an increasingly distinct political culture. Each major political milestone, from the Stockholm Conference in 1972 to the Rio Summit in 1992, has established new precedents for how future events and procedures should be structured. A pattern of relationships between governments, international administrative organisations, business groups, voluntary organisations, and the media has emerged within a common historical framework.

Of special interest for the politics of implementation at present, is the latest addition to the environment-and-development arena, the United Nations Commission on Sustainable Development (CSD). Established by the General Assembly in December of 1992 under the umbrella of the UN Economic and Social Council (ECOSOC), CSD has a small secretariat and an assembly of representatives from 53 governments. Its specific mandate is to follow up and implement the massive *Agenda 21*. More than any other document, *Agenda 21* is the successor to *Our Common Future*. Its categories are, to a large degree, those established by the Brundtland Commission. The document addresses (in 470 pages and 40 chapters) topics varying from radioactive waste and toxic chemicals to 'Children and Youth in Sustainable Development'. It was endorsed by virtually all national delegations to Rio as a 'global partnership for sustainable development', with the signatories committing their respective governments to the development and implementation of national 'plans of action'. It is this process that CSD is designed to monitor and promote.

There are already numerous versions of the Agenda available (original, short, annotated, critical), and it has quickly superseded *Our Common Future* as the most quoted, misrepresented, widely discussed, and little-read document of the UNCED process. Without going into detail, I would like to stress one feature of the document which is, I believe, underplayed— namely, that the prescriptions and coverage of the Agenda are as much devoted to the political, economic, and financial aspects of sustainable development as they are to environmental degradation and conservation. This differentiation is clearly visible in the structure and content of the report itself, with 25 of the 40 chapters devoted to issues *other than* biogeospheric degradation. But it emerges even more clearly in the operative standards and procedures adopted by the CSD at its initial session in New York in May of 1993.

Figure 18.1 lists the 13 general guidelines which the Commission has laid down for the secretariat's analytic reports and recommendations for national implementation. A quick run-down of the list shows that it is more concerned with issues of political and economic relevance than with issues related to the natural environment. Part of this has to do with the fact that CSD has limited resources and cannot be expected to monitor environmental phenomena which are already under observance by other international bodies. More specifically, however, the profile is attributable to what can be referred to as CSD's 'compensatory role' *vis à vis* Rio. It was widely acknowledged in the aftermath of the Rio conference that two issues of key concern for Southern countries were not adequately covered by the concluding documents: the financing of sustainable development in the South, and the transfer of technologies necessary for more sustainable economic production. CSD was implicitly given responsibility for these tasks, and proceeded forthwith to establish high-profile 'work-groups' on both issues.

Fig. 18.1 UN Commission for Sustainable Development: General guidelines for monitoring implementation of Agenda 21.

1. Policies and measures at national level to meet *Agenda 21* objectives, including national sustainable-development strategies and major activities and projects undertaken;
2. Institutional mechanisms to address sustainable-development issues, including the participation of NGOs and major groups in these mechanisms;
3. Assessments of progress achieved to date, with statistical sheets and tables;
4. Measures taken and progress achieved to reach sustainable production and consumption patterns and life-styles, to combat poverty, and limit demographic impact on the planet's life-supporting capacity;
5. The impact of the environmental measures undertaken on the national economy, including the social impact of such measures;
6. Experiences gained, for example, descriptions of successful policies and projects that can serve as models, and particularly strategies that improve both social conditions and environmental sustainability;
7 Specific problems and constraints encountered, including those related to finance and technology and to the adverse impact of economic and trade policies and measures, particularly on developing countries;
8. The adverse impact on sustainable development of trade-restrictive and distortive policies and measures, and progress in making trade and environment policies, mutually supportive in favour of sustainable-development;
9. Assessments of capacity, or the availability of domestic human, technological, and financial resources;
10. Assessments of needs and priorities for external assistance in finance, technology transfer, co-operation, and capacity building, and human-resources development;
11. Implementation of *Agenda 21* commitments related to finance (including the 0.7 per cent of GNP aid target) and to technology transfer, co-operations, and capacity building;
12. Assessments of the effectiveness of activities and projects of international organisations, including international financial institutions and funding mechanisms;
13. Other environment-and-development issues, including those affecting youth, women, and other major groups.

Source: Martin Khor 1994: 106–7.

These developments mean that CSD has been placed in the front line of sustainable-development implementation. Not only is the Commission to monitor and highlight national efforts with regard to the overall goals of *Agenda 21*, it must also bear the responsibility of carrying forward the crucial North–South issues of financial aid and the transfer of technology. The CSD must, in other words, keep UNCED 'honest' with respect to both its public and hidden agendas. From the point of view of political analysis, it is not too strong a proposition, I believe, to maintain that the long-term implications of UNCED now rest with the CSD. The new body has been entrusted with a heavy responsibility for securing progress on the key issues of Rio. If it fails (and a discontinuation has already been aired in open session), the future of both *Agenda 21* and the Rio Declaration will be dim indeed.[9]

'Sustainable Production and Consumption': A Test Case for the UNCED Process

Of the numerous issues covered by 'sustainable development', one of the far most crucial is the nature and level of consumption in the overdeveloped North. UNDP (United Nations Development Programme) has estimated that the Northern 20 per cent of the world's population accounts for more than 80 per cent of consumed natural resources. While the wealthy of the North prefer to focus on population growth in the South as a major cause of environmental degradation, the poor of the South point out that each American birth represents a level of consumption that is hundreds of times that of each birth in Nepal, Vietnam, or Madagascar. The sustainability of Northern consumption patterns has long been on the lips of representatives of Southern NGOs, but has only very recently been moved to a more action-oriented place on the agenda. The political 'processing' of the issue since 1987 provides important insights into the politics of sustainable development.

Though the level and type of consumption in wealthy Northern countries is implicitly problematised in the Brundtland report, there is very little mention of the problem itself. I have, in fact, found only two direct references to the issue. The second of the two references provides, however, a number of the core aspects of the perspective:

Sustainable global development requires that those who are more affluent adopt life-styles within the planet's ecological means in their use of energy, for example. (OCF 1987: 9) . . . Living standards that go beyond the basic minimum are sustainable only if consumption standards everywhere have regard for long-term sustainability. Yet many of us live beyond the world's ecological means, for instance in our patterns of energy use. Perceived needs are socially and culturally determined, and sustainable development requires the promotion of values that encourage consumption standards that are within the bounds of the ecological *possible* (my emphasis) and to which all can reasonably aspire.

Meeting essential needs depends in part on achieving full growth potential, and sustainable development clearly requires economic growth in places where such needs are not being met. Elsewhere, it can be consistent with economic growth, *provided the content of growth reflects the broad principles of sustainability and non-exploitation of others*. But growth by itself is not enough. High levels of productive activity and widespread poverty can coexist, and can endanger the environment. *Hence sustainable development requires that societies meet human needs both by increasing productive potential and by ensuring equitable opportunities for all.* (OCF 1987: 44, my emphasis)

We see here a direct problematisation of life-styles in the North; a clear differentiation as to the nature and justifiability of growth in poor and rich countries; and a general reminder that sustainability also implies social justice.

The signals on consumption in the Brundtland report were picked up during the initial follow-up process, and were given more specific treatment in the regional conferences which were held in 1990. These conferences were designed to move beyond the generalities of *Our Common Future* toward more specific proposals which would then be adopted at Rio. Given the context of the paper, I will concentrate only on the conference held for the Economic Commission for Europe region.[10] This was held in Bergen, Norway in May 1990 under the title 'Action for a Common Future'. Given the ECE auspices, the conference focused on four main themes: (1) consciousness-raising and public participation, (2) sustainable industrial activity, (3) sustainable energy use, and (4) the economics of sustainability.

The two principal documents from the conference were the 'Bergen Ministerial Declaration on Sustainable Development in the ECE Region' and the NGO-inspired 'Joint Agenda for Action'. The issue of sustainable consumption is given specific treatment in both documents.

The *Ministerial Declaration*, for example, stated that: 'Unsustainable patterns of production and consumption, particularly in industrialised countries, are at the root of numerous environmental problems, notably foreclosing options for future generations by depletion of the resource base' (ACF 1990: 15) and: 'We believe that the attainment of sustainable development on the national, regional and global levels requires fundamental changes in human values towards the environment and in patterns of behaviour and consumption as well as the establishment of necessary democratic institutions and processes' (ACF 1990: 16) whilst the *Joint Agenda for Action* demanded that: 'Future economic development should not be based on increases in consumption of energy and raw materials, but instead must stress greater efficiency and reduced inputs. ECE governments should give high priority to reducing excess consumption and waste in their own societies in order to achieve sustainable development' (ACF 1990: 24).

Beyond these statements and admonitions, there are, of course, numerous other passages which encourage more environmentally friendly behaviour, but these expressions are in general terms and do not focus on the differences between the rich and poor countries. In this respect, it is interesting to note that the NGOs did not succeed in Bergen in getting a stronger and more specific statement into the Joint-Agenda document. The preliminary version prepared by the NGOs at their preparatory conference ('Bridging the Gap', *The Danube*, 29–31 March 1990) contains a separate section on North–South relations. Here it is stated that:

It is ecologically impossible for 75 per cent of the world's population living in the South to achieve the same level of consumption of fossil fuels, raw materials and agricultural resources as that of the North. In order to eliminate the economic discrimination against the South, Northern countries must give high priority to changing lifestyles in their own societies in order to become real models for sustainable development. (ACF 1990: 47)

What they did not achieve in Bergen in 1990, however, they managed to achieve to a much greater degree in Rio in 1992. Though the issue is given little direct attention in the very terse Rio Declaration (United Nations 1993), the formulations are expressed as relatively clear-cut 'principles':

Principle 7: . . . The developed countries acknowledge the responsibility that they bear in the international pursuit of sustainable development in view of the pressures their societies place on the global environment and of the technologies and financial resources they command.

Principle 8: To achieve sustainable development and a high quality of life for all people, states should reduce and eliminate unsustainable patterns of production and consumption and promote appropriate demographic policies.

These principles place a clear burden on Northern countries to examine their production and consumption patterns with respect to standards of sustainable development.[11] The burden is then spelled out more specifically in chapter 4 of *Agenda 21*, 'Changing Consumption Patterns'. It is here pointed out that the issue is also addressed in other parts of the Agenda dealing with energy, transportation, waste, and the transfer of technology. But it is clear that the framers of the document also wanted to give the topic particular attention in its own moral context. We thus read that:

Poverty and environmental degradation are closely interrelated. While poverty results in certain kinds of environmental stress, *the major cause of the continued deterioration of the global environment is the unsustainable pattern of consumption and production, particularly in industrialised countries*, which is a matter of grave concern, aggravating poverty and imbalances. (United Nations 1993: 34, my emphasis)

The chapter goes on to spell out objectives and activities related to the problem, placing, for example, emphasis on the promotion of 'patterns of consumption and production that reduce environmental stress and will meet the basic needs of humanity', and advocating 'domestic policy framework(s) that will encourage a shift to more sustainable patterns of production and consumption'. The chapter also calls for greater scientific analysis of the implications of consumption patterns for sustainable development, and recommends that the achievement of sustainable consumption be given 'high priority'.

It was in response to these requests that the Norwegian Minister of the Environment, Thorbjørn Berntsen, took an initiative at the first session of the CSD to facilitate further development on sustainable production and consumption within the Working Group on Financial Resources. Without mincing words, Berntsen addressed the session as follows:

Our consumption patterns, and our efforts to multiply them world-wide, will undermine the environmental resource base even if we were to introduce the best available technology world-wide. I am convinced that without real change in our consumption patterns we will not be able to reach the goals in the climate and biodiversity conventions, nor will we effectively fight poverty. (as quoted in Khor 1994: 110)

The Norwegian minister also used the occasion to announce a working conference of experts on the topic, to be held in Oslo in February 1994. The 'Oslo Symposium on Sustainable Consumption' attracted considerable media attention in Norway, revealing in the process clear differences of opinion between Berntsen on the one hand and his own Prime Minister, government, and labour movement on the other.[12] Berntsen's pronouncements to the media at the opening of the conference must clearly stand as the most critical indictment of Northern consumption patterns that a Northern (or at least Western) minister has ever expressed.[13]

The Oslo Symposium marked a clear turning point in the politics of sustainable development. The crucial importance of Northern life-styles and patterns of consumption for sustainable development was clearly established. The simplistic emphasis on population growth as the major threat to global ecological balance was undermined. The message was that it is the current patterns and levels of production and consumption *by Northern populations* that is more threatening than the relatively meagre consumption levels of the numerically superior South.

The papers presented to the Symposium, as well as the summary of the proceedings, raised issues which had been previously voiced only by the most critical of NGOs.[14] Of particular significance was the way in which the conference lived up to the aspirations of *Agenda 21* by introducing new analytic and scientific perspectives which provided a much more solid basis for further negotiations and action frameworks. Of particular importance in this regard was the introduction into the political debate of two key concepts: *environmental space* and *the ecological footprint*.

The former was presented by the head of Friends of the Earth, Netherlands, Max van Brakel (in tandem with the Dutch Minister of the Environment). Environmental space is the core idea of the project 'Sustainable Netherlands', an ambitious attempt to calculate equitable national per-capita shares of vital natural resources (Milieudefensie 1993). The idea was so successfully promoted in Oslo that there was immediately established a project for 'Sustainable Europe' with the goal of preparing national reports on the 'environmental space' of other European countries. The project has received funding from the European Commission and is being coordinated by the Wüppertal Institute in Germany.[15]

The second concept aired at the Symposium was that of 'the ecological footprint'. As outlined in a paper by Nick Robbins (1994) (which builds on the work of William E. Rees (1992, 1994), the 'footprint' concept adds the notion of trying to trace the consequences of consumption patterns in the North through to ecological impact on the South. If successfully developed empirically, the 'ecological footprint' could provide a useful tool for operationalising North–South interdependencies.

The work done in Oslo led to the tabling of a draft document on sustainable production and consumption at the second 'normal' session of the CSD in New York in May 1994. The document proved to be more controversial than expected, with a major part of the opposition coming from Southern representatives. Interestingly enough, the major thrust of their negativism was related to the prospect of *limiting growth in the North*. Far from echoing Thorbjørn Berntsen's call for a ceiling on welfare and further growth in the most wealthy countries, the representatives from the more economically expansive Southern states were concerned that any slow-down in Northern development would affect their chances for continued growth at home. The conflict threatened, at one point, to torpedo the entire effort on the theme, and—according to Berntsen's own account in the Oslo newspapers—was only resolved by a resolute intervention from the representative from the European Union.

The issue was, however, resolved, and the CSD gave its assent to continue with the work on an action plan for sustainable production and consumption. The next stage in the process was the 'Oslo Ministerial Roundtable'. Following up on the symposium, the Oslo Roundtable was designed to be both more pragmatic and more political. With governmental representatives from 26 countries and the European Union (including 14 Ministers/Commissioners of Environment), the conference aimed 'to prepare elements for an international work programme on sustainable production and consumption'. The tone for the meeting was once again set by the Norwegian Minister who welcomed the delegates to the meeting with a quote from Mahatma Gandhi: 'The Earth has enough for everyone's need, but not for everyone's greed.'

The Roundtable was conducted under what has now become a relatively standard procedure for the politics of sustainable development. The accredited places around the table were allocated to 50 invited representatives from: national governments and their bureaucracies; the United Nations and European Commission; other international organisations; business and labour organisations; environment-and-development NGOs; and selected academics. In addition, there was an equal number of 'observers', many of whom had participated in a preliminary session on the draft document prior to the ministerial meeting. The draft document itself was a result of the continuous consultations since the initial session of the CSD in 1993. It consisted of two sets of texts, one devoted to the specifics of the work programme itself, and one devoted to parallel commentaries and perspectives ('windows') from different organisations and official bodies.

The final document from the Oslo Roundtable was submitted to the third session of the CSD in April 1995, where it received general support as a basis for further specification and implementation. In addition to outlining several of the basic conceptual issues involved, the Oslo document identifies 'a menu of possible actions' for the 'key actors' involved. These are generally focused around three types of activity: first, improving understanding and analysis; secondly, applying tools for modifying behaviour; and thirdly, monitoring, evaluating and reviewing performance. The structure of the document is relatively specific as to both goals and initiatives for each of the topics.[16]

In his address to the Oslo Roundtable, the Chairman of the CSD, Klaus Töpfer, added further specifics to what he saw as the future development of the programme: first, a systematic analysis of individual country experiences—with five to ten countries reviewed each year—in the design and implementation of policy measures intended to make an impact in the short- and medium-term on their most pressing problems requiring changes in consumption and production patterns; secondly, systematic analysis of the impact on developing countries of changes in consumption and production patterns anticipated in the developed countries; thirdly, reviews (every three to five years) of the results of quantitative analysis, including the use of global models for long-term projections linking resource use to economic activity in order to assess their policy implications at the national and international levels; and fourthly, the further development and compilation of indicators of sustainable development (MoE 1995: 43).

As with all international agreements and projects, the fate of the joint CSD efforts in this area will depend on the follow-up activities of the individual member states. What the activities and results thus far indicate, however, is that this particular area of *Agenda 21* is being pursued with a vigour and directness which few would have anticipated in the immediate post-Rio period. The CSD process on sustainable production and consumption has focused the burden of environment-and-development responsibility on the Northern countries in a dramatic way, at the same time that it has revealed a much more complex picture with respect to differing interests in the South. In both tone and content, the two Oslo conferences with their resulting documents mark a turning point in coming to grips with the unsustainable production and consumption patterns of the North.

Conclusion

The purpose of the present article has been, first, to suggest a more constructive and pro-active approach to the notion of sustainable development; secondly, to outline the general parameters of the international political arena for sustainable-development politics; and thirdly, to illustrate the workings of the arena with reference to a single institution (the UN Commission on Sustainable Development) and a single issue (sustainable production and consumption). The major argument of the paper is that the politics of sustainable development provide a new and potentially effective way to pursue global environment-and-development change. Given the normative strength of the sustainable-development position, with ethical legitimacy deriving from both 'realist' and 'consensualist' meta-theories, there is a definite potential for concerted action along two dimensions.

Representatives for NGOs and concerned scientists can, in the first instance, exert direct influence on the formulation of sustainable-development goals and action plans. The political culture that has arisen in and through the UNCED process involves a strengthened role for civil society. At a time when market liberalism continues to undermine the role of interest groups in national governance, the politics of UNCED point in an opposite direction. Representatives for business, labour and environmental organisations are not only welcomed to UNCED's 'lobbies', they are increasingly drawn directly into the halls of deliberation.

This marks an interesting anomaly in the notion of 'political development'. In the 1960s, at a time when international politics was generally perceived as an exclusive realm for diplomats and power brokers, 'corporate pluralism' was being promoted as an important adjunct to national democratic governance (Rokkan 1966; Heisler 1974). Today the emphases are reversed. The ideological dominance of market liberalism has weakened the participatory role of interest groups at the national level, while the politics of environment-and-development have created new models and opportunities for an emerging global civil society.

Equally important, however, is the fact that the politics of sustainable development can also be seen as the politics of post-industrial morality. The new global arena is not only open to input from concerned scientific experts and environmental activists, it also sets new standards for domestic politics. Though the language and results of UNCED are necessarily imbued with rhetoric, it is a rhetoric which offers promise of more substantial gains at home. Though many would claim that there are no limits to political dissembling, and that politicians thrive on moralist posturing, it is the argument of the present paper that the public record on sustainable-development goals is a useful tool for promoting change. Ministers and prime ministers who seek the moral high-ground as a vantage point for the pursuit of global political recognition, can be pressured to make good on their promises before their own constituencies.

Environmental concern among democratic publics may have declined in recent years, but the levels are still considerable (Dunlap 1994) and constitute a strong potential for implementation politics. The goals and prescriptions that have emerged from the UNCED process are in many respects insufficient to the problems they address. But the process itself has imbued the 'new agenda' with a moral urgency and an ethical legitimacy which concentrated effort and political mobilisation should be able to exploit. The development of the political agenda after Rio with respect to sustainable production and consumption is but one area where the new mode of normative politics has made an impact (at least in Scandinavia). Having taken the commitments of their governments in Rio seriously, all three Scandinavian Ministers of Environment were instrumental in pushing for positive follow-up action to *Agenda 21*. The efforts of the Norwegian minister were clearly above and beyond what his own Cabinet was prepared for, but by constantly referring to the commitments from Rio, and with strong backing from the media and environmental organisations, he was able to push the issue to the forefront of Norwegian politics. Two outcomes which were strongly affected by these efforts, were the appointment of an independent 'Green Tax Commission' to look at the structure of environmental fees and tax incentives, and the initiation of a relatively large new research programme on 'sustainable production and consumption' within the Research Council of Norway.

In sum, the concept of sustainable development has survived both its worst rhetoricians and best critics. It has proved itself to be neither panacea nor fiasco, and it is beginning a serious move from ideal to reality. Whereas the ideological discourse of the 1980s was largely an exercise in negativist futures—post-industrial, post-capitalist, post-liberal, post-welfare-state—the discourse of the 1990s has gradually focused on the more positive notion of a sustainable global society. The momentum of UNCED has developed side by side with the momentum of neo-market liberalism. Though the latter frequently tries to borrow the phraseology and moral urgency of the former, it has been argued here that such a transaction is both logically and ethically unsound.

Notes

1. See e.g. Brown et al. (1988); Dixon and Fallon (1989); Mähler (1990). Moxnes (1989); Pearce et al. (1990); Pezzey (1992); Redclift (1987, 1993); Soussan (1992); and Stokke (1990). The usage in the present paper is derived from Lafferty and Langhelle (1995).

2. It could easily be argued that we now need an effort for the conceptual clarification of 'sustainable development' which corresponds with the UNESCO project on 'democracy' from the 1950s. See e.g. Næss et al. (1956); Christophersen (1966); and McKeon (1955).

3. Connolly's summary perspective on the original idea of Gallie (1962) is formulated as follows: 'When the concept involved is *appraisive* in that the state of affairs it describes is a valued achievement, when the practice described is *internally complex* in that its characterisation involves reference to several dimensions, and when the agreed and contested rules of application are relatively *open*, enabling parties to interpret even those shared rules differently as new and unforseen situations arise, then the concept in question

is an "essentially contested concept". Such concepts (quoting Gallie) "essentially involve endless disputes about their proper uses on the part of their users" ' (Connolly 1983: 10).

4. A representative selection is available in Sachs (1993), and an excellent bibliography in Pezzey (1992).

5. Richardson mentions the possibility that we may, in the future, view Brundtland 'in a better light', that is by 'considering the concept of sustainable development not as an end in itself but as a tentative first step which took politicians along the road from anthropocentricity to biocentricity' (1994: 12). But should such an unlikely development take place, he feels that we would nonetheless have to replace the concept with terminology more compatible with the biocentric approach. It is, in other words, the biocentric approach that is correct, and the concept of sustainable development is viewed as irreconcilable with this approach.

6. It will be noticed that the definition offered here incorporates 'reasonable standards of welfare for all living beings'. Such a formulation expands the connotation of SD to include the 'interests' and 'needs' of non-human beings. Though the Brundtland report is generally portrayed as having an anthropocentric bias, there are at least some passages which open for a more biocentric ethic. The report points out, for example, that there are 'moral, ethical, cultural, aesthetic, and purely scientific reasons for conserving wild beings' (p. 13), and, more pointedly, that '. . . the case for the conservation of nature should not rest only with development goals. It is part of our moral obligation to other living beings and future generations' (p. 57). For a more thorough assessment of the report with respect to biocentric norms, see Wetlesen (1995). As used here, sustainable development prescribes a pragmatic concern for non-human species with respect to the preservation of biodiversity, without further stipulation as to intra-species rights and/or duties.

7. These aspects correspond roughly with the categories developed by Michael Mann (1974) in his analysis of Western working-class consciousness.

8. The argument in this section builds on the work of Jon Wetlesen (1995).

9. For profiles on the CSD, see Khor (1994) and Roddick (1994). Users of Internet can monitor the developments of the CSD by accessing proceedings and documents through any one of a number of WWW sites (for example, ProSus in Europe: http://www.prosus.nfr.no/; or the International Institute for Sustainable Development in Canada: http://iisd1.iisd.ca/).

10. The ECE is the United Nations Economic Commission for Europe. In 1990, there were 34 member states, including the then Soviet Union, the United States, and representation from the European Community. The report from the conference is entitled *Action for a Common Future: Conference Report* (here referred to as ACF). Regional conferences were also held in Africa, Asia, and Latin America.

11. It is an important feature of the pro-active potential inherent in the politics of sustainable development that the goals are defined in relation to standards which are presumed to be empirically operational. If existing conditions do not measure up to normative standards, they should be altered. Herein lies the potential for combining the 'realist' and 'consensual' ethical foundations of the concept.

12. It should be pointed out that Thorbjørn Berntsen is a highly atypical minister of environment. Having begun his career as a shipyard labourer, he gradually moved up through the labour-union apparatus, became an active and unconventional member of parliament, and ultimately developed a solid hands-on knowledge of environmental questions. He has a tendency to do things 'his way', which is sometimes successful, always colourful.

13. Some examples: To the magazine 'Occupation' (*Yrke*, No. 2: 1993): 'Any discussion of the quality of life and alternative values must address the question of what kind of growth we really want and which goals growth should serve. Most Norwegians today have more than

enough, and much of it is just garbage. It provides growth in the GNP, but that's not the kind of growth we want!' To the newspaper *Aftenposten* (19 January 1994): 'The type of growth we are trying to achieve in Norway today implies increased need and poverty for many areas in the rest of the world. This in turn means further environmental degradation, the opposite of sustainable development . . . At least one thing is certain: Goals which aim towards a doubling of Norwegian consumption by the year 2030 [that is, the goals put forth in the "Long-Term Plan" of Berntsen's own government] are completely crazy. If India tries to keep up with us, the world will collapse. We Norwegians have to acknowledge that there is no room for further increases in welfare'.

14. The papers presented to the Symposium, along with other documentation, are available in English from the Norwegian Ministry of Environment. PO Box 8013 Dep, 0030 Oslo, Norway. Title: *Symposium—Sustainable Consumption: 19–20 January 1994, Oslo, Norway*, 180 pages.

15. Norway was the second country to complete an overview of 'environmental space'. The report (prepared by John Hille for The Project for an Alternative Future (PAF) and the Norwegian Forum for Development and Environment) is available from the successor project to PAF—ProSus, Sognsveien 700855 Oslo. The report is also available at the ProSus 'home page' on the World Wide Web: http://www.prosus.nfr.no/. The larger project, 'Sustainable Europe', disseminates information through Friends of the Earth, Netherlands, E-mail: susteur@foenl.antenna.nl.

16. The recommended 'tools for modifying behaviour' for national governments, for example, are divided into three separate categories: 'regulatory measures' (e.g. 'comprehensive product policies, including the broadening of producer responsibility targets for re-use, recycling, durability and resource efficiency'); 'economic incentives' (e.g. 'the reform of fiscal and pricing policies to internalise environmental costs so that effective incentives are given for sustainable consumption and production, while introducing effective mitigating measures to protect poorer sections of society'); and 'social instruments'(e.g. 'the development of a code of conduct to control the use of environmental claims in advertising').

References

ACF (1990), *Action for a Common Future: Conference Report*, Regional Conference on the follow-up to the Brundtland Report in the ECE Region, Bergen, Norway, 8–16 May 1990 (Oslo: Ministry of Environment).

Brown, B. J., et al. (1988), 'Global Sustainability: Toward Definition', *Environmental Management*, 11 (6): 713–19.

Christophersen, Jens A. (1966), *The Meaning of Democracy as Used in European Ideologies* (Oslo: University Press).

COCF (Centre for Our Own Common Future) (1993), *Agenda for Change: A Plain Language Version of Agenda 21 and the Other Rio Agreements*, written by Michael Keating (Geneva).

Connolly, W. E. (1983), *The Terms of Political Discourse* (Princeton: Princeton University Press).

Dixon, J. A., and Fallon, L. A. (1989), *The Concept of Sustainability: Origins, Extensions and Usefulness for Policy* (Division Working Paper, No. 1; Washington, DC: World Bank, Environment Department).

Dunlap, Riley (1994), 'International Attitudes towards Environment and Development', in *Green Globe Yearbook 1994* (Oslo and Oxford: Scandinavian University Press and Oxford University Press), 115–26.

Gallie, W. B. (1962), 'Essentially Contested Concepts', in Max Black (ed.), *The Importance of Language* (Englewood Cliffs, NJ: Prentice Hall).

Heisler, Martin O. (1974) (ed.), *Politics in Europe: Structures and Processes in Some Post-Industrial Democracies* (New York: David McKay).

Hille, John (1995), *Sustainable Norway: Exploring the Scope and Equity of Environmental Space* (Oslo: Project for an Alternative Future (now ProSus) and ForUM).

Kaplan, Abraham (1964), *The Conduct of Inquiry* (San Francisco: Chandler Publishing Co.).

Khor, Martin (1994), 'The Commission on Sustainable Development: Paper Tiger or Agency to Save the Earth?', in *Green Globe Yearbook 1994* (Oslo and Oxford: Scandinavian University Press and Oxford University Press), 103–13.

Lafferty, William M., and Langhelle, Oluf (1995) (eds.), *Bærekraftig Utvikling: Om Utviklingens Mål og Bærekraftens Betingelser* ('Sustainable Development: On the Goals of Development and Conditions of Sustainability') (Oslo: Ad Notam/Gyldendal).

McKeon, R. P. (1955) (ed.), *Democracy in a World of Tensions* (New York: UNESCO).

Mähler, K. G. (1990), 'Sustainable Development', in *Sustainable Development, Science and Policy*, The Conference Report, Bergen, 8–12 May 1990 (Oslo: Norwegian Research Council for Science and the Humanities (NAVF)), 239–48.

Mann, Michael (1974), *Consciousness and Action among the Western Working Class* (London: Macmillan).

Milieudefensie (1993), *Action Plan Sustainable Netherlands* (Amsterdam: Milieudefensie).

MoE (Ministry of Environment, Norway) (1995), 'Oslo Ministerial Roundtable: Conference on Sustainable Production and Consumption', Report (Oslo).

Moxnes, E. (1989), *Sustainable Development*, Report No. 30701-1 (Bergen: Christian Michelsen Institute).

Næss, Arne, et al. (1956), *Democracy, Ideology and Objectivity* (Oslo: Oslo University Press).

OCF (1987), *Our Common Future: World Commission on Environment and Development* (Oxford: Oxford University Press).

O'Riordan, Timothy (1993), 'The Politics of Sustainability', in R. Kerry Turner (ed.), *Sustainable Environmental Economics and Management: Principles and Practice* (London: Belhaven Press).

Pearce, D., et al. (1990), *Sustainable Development: Economics and Environment in the Third World* (London: Earthscan Publications).

Pezzey, J. (1992), 'Sustainability', *Environmental Values*, 1 (4): 321–62.

Redclift, M. (1987), *Sustainable Development: Exploring the Contradictions* (London: Routledge).

—— (1993), 'Sustainable Development: Needs, Values, Rights', *Environmental Values*, 2 (1): 3–20.

Rees, William E. (1992), 'Ecological Footprints and Appropriated Carrying Capacity: What Urban Economics Leaves Out', *Environment and Urbanization*, 4 (2): 121–30.

—— (1994), 'Ecological Footprints and Appropriated Carrying Capacity: Measuring the Natural Capital Requirements of the Human Economy', in A. -M. Jannson, M. Hammer, C. Folke, R. Costanza (eds), *Investing in Natural Capital: The Ecological Economics Approach to Sustainability* (Washington, DC: Island Press).

Richardson, Dick (1994), 'The Politics of Sustainable Development', paper presented to the International Conference on The Politics of Sustainable Development within the European Union, University of Crete, 21–23 Oct. 1994.

Robbins, Nick (1994), 'Tracking the Ecological Footprint: A Discussion Paper and Research Agenda' (London: International Institute for Environment and Development).

Roddick, J. (1994), 'Second Session of the Commission on Sustainable Development', *Environmental Politics*, 3 (3): 503–12.

Rokkan, Stein (1966), 'Norway: Numerical Democracy and Corporate Pluralism', in Robert A. Dahl (ed.), *Political Oppositions in Western Democracies* (New Haven and London: Yale University Press), 70–115.

Sachs, Wolfgang (1993) (ed.), *Global Ecology: A New Arena of Political Conflict* (London: Zed Books).

Soussan J. G. (1992), 'Sustainable Development', in S. R. Bowlby and A. M. Mannion (eds), *Environment Issues in the 1990s* (London: John Wiley & Sons), 21–36.

Stenseth, Nils Christian (1991), 'Bærekraftig utvikling: Bak flosklene' ('Sustainable Development: Getting Behind the Jargon'), in Nils Chr. Stenseth and Karine Hertzberg (eds), *Ikke Bare Si Det, Men Gjøre Det!* ('Don't Just Say It—Do It!') (Oslo: Oslo University Press), 19–36.

Stokke, O. (1990) (ed.), *Sustainable Development* (London: Frank Cass).

United Nations (1993), *Report of the United Nations Conference on Environment and Development, Rio de Janeiro 3–14 June 1992*, i. *Resolutions Adopted by the Conference* (New York).

Wetlesen, Jon (1995), 'A Global Ethics of Sustainability', in William M. Lafferty and Oluf Langhelle (eds), *Bærekraftig Utvikling: Om Utviklingens Mål og Bærekraftens Betingelser* ('Sustainable Development: On the Goals of Development and Conditions of Sustainability') (Oslo: Ad Notam/Gyldendal), 41–58.

19 Sustainable Growth: An Impossibility Theorem

Herman E. Daly

Impossibility statements are the very foundation of science. It is impossible to: travel faster than the speed of light; create or destroy matter-energy; build a perpetual motion machine, etc. By respecting impossibility theorems we avoid wasting resources on projects that are bound to fail. Therefore economists should be very interested in impossibility theorems, especially the one to be demonstrated here, namely that it is impossible for the world economy to grow its way out of poverty and environmental degradation. In other words, sustainable growth is impossible.

In its physical dimensions the economy is an open subsystem of the earth ecosystem, which is finite, nongrowing, and materially closed. As the economic subsystem grows it incorporates an ever greater proportion of the total ecosystem into itself and must reach a limit at 100 percent, if not before. Therefore its growth is not sustainable. The term "sustainable growth" when applied to the economy is a bad oxymoron—self-contradictory as prose, and unevocative as poetry.

Challenging the Economic Oxymoron

Economists will complain that growth in GNP in a mixture of quantitative and qualitative increase and therefore not strictly subject to physical laws. They have a point. Precisely because quantitative and qualitative change are very different it is best to keep them separate and call them by the different names already provided in the dictionary. *To grow* means "to increase naturally in size by the addition of material through assimilation or accretion." *To develop* means "to expand or realize the potentialities of; to bring gradually to a fuller, greater, or better state." When something grows it gets bigger. When something develops it gets different. The earth ecosystem develops (evolves), but does not grow. Its subsystem, the economy, must eventually stop growing, but can continue to develop. The term "sustainable development" therefore makes sense for the economy, but only if it is understood as "development without growth"—i.e. qualitative improvement of a physical economic base that is maintained in a steady state by a throughput of matter-energy that is within the regenerative and assimilative capacities of the ecosystem. Currently the term "sustainable development" is used as a synonym for the oxymoronic "sustainable growth." It must be saved from this perdition.

From *Development*, nos. 3/4 (1990), 45–7. Reprinted with permission.

Politically it is very difficult to admit that growth, with its almost religious connotations of ultimate goodness, must be limited. But it is precisely the nonsustainability of growth that gives urgency to the concept of sustainable development. The earth will not tolerate the doubling of even one grain of wheat 64 times, yet in the past two centuries we have developed a culture dependent on exponential growth for its economic stability (Hubbert 1976). Sustainable development is a cultural adaptation made by society as it becomes aware of the emerging necessity of nongrowth. Even "green growth" is not sustainable. There is a limit to the population of trees the earth can support, just as there is a limit to the populations of humans and of automobiles. To delude ourselves into believing that growth is still possible and desirable if only we label it "sustainable" or color it "green" will just delay the inevitable transition and make it more painful.

Limits to Growth?

If the economy cannot grow forever then by how much can it grow? Can it grow by enough to give everyone in the world today a standard of per capita resource use equal to that of the average American? That would turn out to be a factor of seven,[1] a figure that is neatly bracketed by the Brundtland Commission's call (Brundtland et al. 1987) for the expansion of the world economy by a factor of five to ten. The problem is that even expansion by a factor of four is impossible if Vitousek et al. (1986: 368–73) are correct in their calculation that the human economy currently preempts one-fourth of the global net primary product of photosynthesis (NPP). We cannot go beyond 100 percent, and it is unlikely that we will increase NPP since the historical tendency up to now is for economic growth to reduce global photosynthesis. Since land-based ecosystems are the more relevant, and we preempt 40 percent of land-based NPP, even the factor of four is an overestimate. Also, reaching 100 percent is unrealistic since we are incapable of bringing under direct human management all the species that make up the ecosystems upon which we depend. Furthermore it is ridiculous to urge the preservation of biodiversity without being willing to halt the economic growth that requires human takeover of places in the sun occupied by other species.

If growth up to the factor of five to ten recommended by the Brundtland Commission is impossible, then what about just sustaining the present scale—i.e. zero net growth? Every day we read about stress-induced feedbacks from the ecosystem to the economy, such as greenhouse buildup, ozone layer depletion, acid rain, etc., which constitute evidence that even the present scale is unsustainable. How then can people keep on talking about "sustainable growth" when: (a) the present scale of the economy shows clear signs of unsustainability, (b) multiplying that scale by a factor of five to ten as recommended by the Brundtland Commission would move us from unsustainability to imminent collapse, and (c) the concept itself is logically self-contradictory in a finite, nongrowing ecosystem? Yet sustainable growth is the buzz word of our time. Occasionally it becomes truly ludicrous, as when writers gravely speak of "sustainable growth in the rate of increase of economic activity." Not only must we grow forever, we must accelerate forever! This is hollow political verbiage, totally disconnected from logical and physical first principles.

Alleviating Poverty, Not Angelizing GNP

The important question is the one that the Brundtland Commission leads up to, but does not really face: How far can we alleviate poverty by development without growth? I suspect that the answer will be a significant amount, but less than half. One reason for this belief is that if the five- to tenfold expansion is really going to be for the sake of the poor, then it will have to consist of things needed by the poor—food, clothing, shelter—not information services. Basic goods have an irreducible physical dimension and their expansion will require growth rather than development, although development via improved efficiency will help. In other words, the reduction in resource content per dollar of GNP observed in some rich countries in recent years cannot be heralded as severing the link between economic expansion and the environment, as some have claimed. Angelized GNP will not feed the poor. Sustainable development must be development without growth—but with population control and wealth redistribution—if it is to be a serious attack on poverty.

In the minds of many people, growth has become synonymous with increase in wealth. They say that we must have growth to be rich enough to afford the cost of cleaning up and curing poverty. That all problems are easier to solve if we are richer is not in dispute. What is at issue is whether growth at the present margin really makes us richer. There is evidence that in the US it now makes us poorer by increasing costs faster than it increases benefits (Daly and Cobb 1989: appendix). In other words we appear to have grown beyond the optimal scale.

Defining the Optimal Scale

The concept of an optimal scale of the aggregate economy relative to the ecosystem is totally absent from current macroeconomic theory. The aggregate economy is assumed to grow forever. Microeconomics, which is almost entirely devoted to establishing the optimal scale of each microlevel activity by equating costs and benefits at the margin, has neglected to inquire if there is not also an optimal scale for the aggregate of all micro activities. A given scale (the product of population times per capita resource use) constitutes a given throughput of resources and thus a given load on the environment, and can consist of many people each consuming little, or fewer people each consuming correspondingly more.

An economy in sustainable development adapts and improves in knowledge, organization, technical efficiency, and wisdom; and it does this without assimilating or accreting, beyond some point, an ever greater percentage of the matter-energy of the ecosystem into itself, but rather stops at a scale at which the remaining ecosystem (the environment) can continue to function and renew itself year after year. The nongrowing economy is not static—it is being continually maintained and renewed as a steady-state subsystem of the environment.

What policies are implied by the goal of sustainable development, as here defined? Both optimists and pessimists should be able to agree on the following policy for the US (sustainable development should begin with the industrialized countries). Strive to hold throughput constant at present levels (or reduced truly sustainable levels) by taxing resource extraction, especially energy, very heavily. Seek to raise most public revenue from such resource severance taxes, and compensate (achieve revenue neutrality) by reducing the income tax, especially on the lower end of the income distribution, perhaps even financing a negative income tax at the very low end. Optimists who believe that resource efficiency can increase by a factor of ten should welcome this policy, which raises resource prices considerably and would give powerful incentive to just those technological advances in which they have so much faith. Pessimists who lack that technological faith will nevertheless be happy to see restrictions placed on the size of the already unsustainable throughput. The pessimists are protected against their worst fears; the optimists are encouraged to pursue their fondest dreams. If the pessimists are proven wrong and the enormous increase in efficiency actually happens, then they cannot complain. They got what they most wanted, plus an unexpected bonus. The optimists, for their part, can hardly object to a policy that not only allows but gives a strong incentive to the very technical progress on which their optimism is based. If they are proved wrong at least they should be glad that the throughput-induced rate of environmental destruction has been slowed. Also severance taxes are harder to avoid than income taxes and do not reduce incentives to work.

At the project level there are some additional policy guidelines for sustainable development. Renewable resources should be exploited in a manner such that:

(1) harvesting rates do not exceed regeneration rates; and
(2) waste emissions do not exceed the renewable assimilative capacity of the local environment.

Balancing Nonrenewable and Renewable Resources

Nonrenewable resources should be depleted at a rate equal to the rate of creation of renewable substitutes. Projects based on exploitation of nonrenewable resources should be paired with projects that develop renewable substitutes. The net rents from the nonrenewable extraction should be separated into an income component and a capital liquidation component. The capital component would be invested each year in building up a renewable substitute. The separation is made such that by the time the nonrenewable is exhausted, the substitute renewable asset will have been built up by investment and natural growth to the point where its sustainable yield is equal to the income component. The income component will have thereby become perpetual, thus justifying the name "income," which is by definition the maximum available for consumption while maintaining capital intact. It has been shown (El Serafy 1989: 10–18) how this division of rents into capital and income depends upon: (1) the discount rate (rate of growth of the renewable substitute); and (2) the life expectancy of the nonrenewable resource (reserves divided by annual depletion). The faster the biological growth of the renewable substitute and the longer the life expectancy of the nonrenewable, the greater will be the income component and the less the capital set-aside. "Substitute" here should be interpreted broadly to include any systemic adaptation that allows the economy to adjust the depletion of the nonrenewable resource in a way the maintains future income at a given level (e.g. recycling in the case of minerals). Rates of return for the paired projects should be calculated on the basis of their income component only.

However, before these operational steps toward sustainable development can get a fair hearing, we must first take the conceptual and political step of abandoning the thought-stopping slogan of "sustainable growth."

Note

1. Consider the following back-of-the-envelope calculation, based on the crude estimate that the US currently uses 1/3 of annual world resource flows (derived from National Commission on Materials Policy 1973). Let R be current world resource consumption. Then $R/3$ is current US resource consumption, and $R/3$ divided by 250 million is present per capita US resource consumption. Current world per capita resource consumption would be R divided by 5.3 billion. For future world per capita resource consumption to equal present US per capita consumption, assuming constant population, R must increase by some multiple, call it M. Then M times R divided by 5.3 billion must equal $R/3$ divided by 250 million. Solving for M gives 7. World resource flows must increase sevenfold if all people are to consume resources at the present US average.

But even the sevenfold increase is a gross underestimate of the increase in environmental impact, for two reasons. First, because the calculation is in terms of current flows only with no allowance for the increase in accumulated stocks of capital goods necessary to process and transform the greater flow of resources into final products. Some notion of the magnitude of the extra stocks needed comes from Harrison Brown's estimate that the "standing crop" of industrial metals already embodied in the existing stock of artifacts in the ten richest nations would require more than 60 years' production of these metals at 1970 rates. Second, because the sevenfold increase of net, usable minerals and energy will require a much greater increase in gross resource flows, we must mine ever less accessible deposits and lower grade ores. It is the gross flow that provokes environmental impact.

References

Brundtland, G. H., et al. (1987), *Our Common Future: Report of the World Commission on Environment and Development* (Oxford: Oxford University Press).

Daly, H. E., and Cobb, Jr., J. B. (1989), *For the Common Good: Redirecting the Economy toward Community, the Environment and a Sustainable Future* (Boston: Beacon Press).

El Serafy, S, (1989), "The Proper Calculation of Income from Depletable Natural Resources," in Y. J. Ahmad, S. El Serafy, and E. Lutz (eds), *Environmental Accounting for Sustainable Development*, a UNEP–World Bank Symposium (Washington, DC: World Bank).

Hubbert, M. King (1976), "Exponential Growth as a Transient Phenomenon in Human History," in Margaret A. Storm (ed.), *Societal Issues: Scientific Viewpoints* (New York: American Institute of Physics).

National Commission on Materials Policy (1973), *Material Needs and the Environment Today and Tomorrow* (Washington, DC: US Government Printing Office).

Vitousek, Peter M., Ehrlich, Paul R., Ehrlich, Anne H., and Matson, Pamela A. (1986), "Human Appropriation of the Products of Photosynthesis," *BioScience*, 34 (6 May).

20 Development, Ecology, and Women

Vandana Shiva

Development as a New Project of Western Patriarchy

'Development' was to have been a post-colonial project, a choice for accepting a model of progress in which the entire world remade itself on the model of the colonising modern West, without having to undergo the subjugation and exploitation that colonialism entailed. The assumption was that Western-style progress was possible for all. Development, as the improved well-being of all, was thus equated with the Westernisation of economic categories—of needs, of productivity, of growth. Concepts and categories about economic development and natural resource utilisation that had emerged in the specific context of industrialisation and capitalist growth in a centre of colonial power, were raised to the level of universal assumptions and applicability in the entirely different context of basic needs satisfaction for the people of the newly independent Third World countries. Yet, as Rosa Luxemberg has pointed out, early industrial development in Western Europe necessitated the permanent occupation of the colonies by the colonial powers and the destruction of the local 'natural economy'.[1] According to her, colonialism is a constant necessary condition for capitalist growth: without colonies, capital accumulation would grind to a halt. 'Development' as capital accumulation and the commercialisation of the economy for the generation of 'surplus' and profits thus involved the reproduction not merely of a particular form of creation of wealth, but also of the associated creation of povety and dispossession. A replication of economic development based on commercialisation of resource use for commodity production in the newly independent countries created the internal colonies.[2] Development was thus reduced to a continuation of the process of colonisation; it became an extension of the project of wealth creation in modern Western patriarchy's economic vision, which was based on the exploitation or exclusion of women (of the West and non-West), on the exploitation and degradation of nature, and on the exploitation and erosion of other cultures. 'Development' could not but entail destruction for women, nature, and subjugated cultures, which is why, throughout the Third World, women, peasants, and tribals are struggling for liberation from 'development' just as they earlier struggled for liberation from colonialism.

The UN Decade for Women was based on the assumption that the improvement of women's economic position would automatically flow from an expansion and diffusion of the development process. Yet, by the end of the Decade, it was becoming clear that development itself was the problem. Insufficient and inadequate 'participation' in 'development' was not the cause for

From Vandana Shiva, *Staying Alive: Women, Ecology and Development* (London: Zed Books, 1988), 1–13. Reprinted with permission of Zed Books Ltd.

women's increasing under-development; it was rather, their enforced but asymmetric participation in it, by which they bore the costs but were excluded from the benefits, that was responsible. Development exclusivity and dispossession aggravated and deepened the colonial processes of ecological degradation and the loss of political control over nature's sustenance base. Economic growth was a new colonialism, draining resources away from those who needed them most. The discontinuity lay in the fact that it was now new national elites, not colonial powers, that masterminded the exploitation on grounds of 'national interest' and growing GNPs, and it was accomplished with more powerful technologies of appropriation and destruction.

Ester Boserup[3] has documented how women's impoverishment increased during colonial rule; those rulers who had spent a few centuries in subjugating and crippling their own women into de-skilled, de-intellectualised appendages, disfavoured the women of the colonies on matters of access to land, technology, and employment. The economic and political processes of colonial under-development bore the clear mark of modern Western patriarchy, and while large numbers of women and men were impoverished by these processes, women tended to lose more. The privatisation of land for revenue generation displaced women more critically, eroding their traditional land-use rights. The expansion of cash crops undermined food production, and women were often left with meagre resources to feed and care for children, the aged, and the infirm, when men migrated or were conscripted into forced labour by the colonisers. As a collective document by women activists, organisers, and researchers stated at the end of the UN Decade for Women, 'The almost uniform conclusion of the Decade's research is that with a few exceptions, women's relative access to economic resources, incomes and employment has worsened, their burden of work has increased, and their relative and even absolute health, nutritional and educational status has declined.'[4]

The displacement of women from productive activity by the expansion of development was rooted largely in the manner in which development projects appropriated or destroyed the natural resource base for the production of sustenance and survival. It destroyed women's productivity both by removing land, water, and forests from their management and control, as well as through the ecological destruction of soil, water, and vegetation systems so that nature's productivity and renewability were impaired. While gender subordination and patriarchy are the oldest of oppressions, they have taken on new and more violent forms through the project of development. Patriarchal categories which understand destruction as 'production' and regeneration of life as 'passivity' have generated a crisis of survival. Passivity, as an assumed category of the 'nature' of nature and of women, denies the activity of nature and life. Fragmentation and uniformity as assumed categories of progress and development destroy the living forces which arise from relationships within the 'web of life' and the diversity in the elements and patterns of these relationships.

The economic biases and values against nature, women and indigenous peoples are captured in this typical analysis of the 'unproductiveness' of traditional natural societies:

Production is achieved through human and animal, rather than mechanical, power. Most agriculture is unproductive; human or animal manure may be used but chemical fertilisers and pesticides are unknown. . . . For the masses, these conditions mean poverty.[5]

The assumptions are evident: nature is unproductive; organic agriculture based on nature's cycles of renewability spells poverty; women and tribal and peasant societies embedded in nature are similarly unproductive, not because it has been demonstrated that in cooperation they produce *less* goods and services for needs, but because it is assumed that 'production' takes place only when mediated by technologies for commodity production, even when such technologies destroy life. A stable and clean river is not a productive resource in this view: it needs to be 'developed' with dams in order to become so. Women, sharing the river as a commons to satisfy the water needs of their families and society are not involved in productive labour: when substituted by the engineering man, water management and water use become productive activities. Natural forests remain unproductive till they are developed into monoculture plantations of commercial species. Development thus, is equivalent to maldevelopment, a development bereft of the feminine, the conservation, the ecological principle. The neglect of nature's work in renewing herself, and women's work in producing sustenance in the form of basic, vital needs is an essential part of the paradigm of maldevelopment, which sees all work that does not produce profits and capital as non or unproductive work. As Maria Mies[6] has pointed out, this concept of surplus has a patriarchal bias because, from the point of view of nature and women, it is not based on material surplus produced *over and above* the requirements of the community: it is stolen and appropriated through violent modes from nature (who needs a share of her produce to reproduce herself) and from women (who need a share of nature's produce to produce sustenance and ensure survival).

From the perspective of Third World women, productivity is a measure of producing life and sustenance; that this kind of productivity has been rendered invisible does not reduce its centrality to survival—it merely reflects the domination of modern patriarchal economic categories which see only profits, not life.

Maldevelopment as the Death of the Feminine Principle

In this analysis, maldevelopment becomes a new source of male–female inequality. 'Modernisation' has been associated with the introduction of new forms of dominance. Alice Schlegel[7] has shown that under conditions of subsistence, the interdependence and complementarity of the separate male and female domains of work is the characteristic mode, based on diversity, not inequality. Maldevelopment militates against this equality in diversity, and superimposes the ideologically constructed category of Western technological man as a uniform measure of the worth of classes, cultures, and genders. Dominant modes of perception based on reductionism, duality, and linearity are unable to cope with equality in diversity, with forms and activities that are significant and valid, even though different. The reductionist mind superimposes the roles and forms of power of Western male-oriented concepts on women, all non-Western peoples, and even on nature, rendering all three 'deficient', and in need of 'development'. Diversity, and unity and harmony in diversity, become epistemologically unattainable in the context of maldevelopment, which then becomes synonymous with women's underdevelopment (increasing sexist domination), and nature's depletion (deepening ecological crises). Commodities have grown, but nature has shrunk. The poverty crisis of the South arises from the growing scarcity of water, food, fodder and fuel, associated with increasing maldevelopment and ecological destruction. This poverty crisis touches women most severely, first because they are the poorest among the poor, and then because, with nature, they are the primary sustainers of society.

Maldevelopment is the violation of the integrity of organic, interconnected, and interdependent systems, that sets in motion a process of exploitation, inequality, injustice, and violence. It is blind to the fact that a recognition of nature's harmony and action to maintain it are preconditions for distributive justice. This is why Mahatma Gandhi said, 'There is enough in the world for everyone's need, but not for some people's greed.'

Maldevelopment is maldevelopment in thought and action. In practice, this fragmented, reductionist, dualist perspective violates the integrity and harmony of man in nature, and the harmony between men and women. It ruptures the co-operative unity of masculine and feminine, and places man, shorn of the feminine principle, above nature and women, and separated from both. The violence to nature as symptomatised by the ecological crisis, and the violence to women, as symptomatised by their subjugation and exploitation arise from this subjugation of the feminine principle. I want to argue that what is currently called development is essentially maldevelopment, based on the introduction or accentuation of the domination of man over nature and women. In it, both are viewed as the 'other', the passive non-self. Activity, productivity, creativity which were associated with the feminine principle are expropriated as qualities of nature and women, and transformed into the exclusive qualities of man. Nature and women are turned into passive objects, to be used and exploited for the uncontrolled and uncontrollable desires of alienated man. From being the creators and sustainers of life, nature and women are reduced to being 'resources' in the fragmented, anti-life model of maldevelopment.

Two Kinds of Growth, Two Kinds of Productivity

Maldevelopment is usually called 'economic growth', measured by the Gross National Product. Porritt, a leading ecologist has this to say of GNP:

Gross National Product—for once a word is being used correctly. Even conventional economists admit that the hey-day of GNP is over, for the simple reason that as a measure of progress, it's more or less useless. GNP measures the lot, all the goods and services produced in the money economy. Many of these goods and services are not beneficial to people, but rather a measure of just how much is going wrong; increased spending on crime, on pollution, on the many human casualties of our society, increased spending because of waste or planned obsolescence, increased spending because of growing bureaucracies: it's all counted.[8]

The problem with GNP is that it measures some costs as benefits (e.g. pollution control) and fails to measure other costs completely. Among these hidden costs are the new burdens created by ecological devastation, costs that are invariably heavier for women, both in the North and South. It is hardly surprising, therefore, that as GNP rises, it does not necessarily mean that either wealth or welfare increase proportionately. I would argue that GNP is becoming, increasingly, a measure of how real wealth—the wealth of nature and that produced by women for sustaining life—is rapidly decreasing. When commodity production as the prime economic activity is introduced as development, it destroys the potential of nature and women to produce life and goods and services for basic needs. More commodities and more cash mean less life—in nature (through ecological destruction) and in society (through denial of basic needs). Women are devalued first, because their work cooperates with nature's processes, and second, because work which satisfies needs and ensures sustenance is devalued in general. Precisely because more growth in maldevelopment has meant less sustenance of life and life-support systems, it is now imperative to recover the feminine principle as the basis for development which conserves and is ecological. Feminism as ecology, and ecology as the revival of Prakriti, the source of all life, become the decentred powers of political and economic transformation and restructuring.

This involves, first, a recognition that categories of 'productivity' and growth which have been taken to be positive, progressive, and universal are, in reality, restricted patriarchal categories. When viewed from the point of view of nature's productivity and growth, and women's production of sustenance, they are found to be ecologically destructive and a source of gender inequality. It is no accident that the modern, efficient, and productive technologies created within the context of growth in market economic terms are associated with heavy ecological costs, borne largely by women. The resource and energy-intensive production processes they give rise to demand ever-increasing resource withdrawals from the ecosystem. These withdrawals disrupt essential ecological processes and convert renewable resources into non-renewable ones. A forest, for example, provides inexhaustible supplies of diverse biomass over time if its capital stock is maintained and it is harvested on a sustained yield basis. The heavy and uncontrolled demand for industrial and commercial wood, however, requires the continuous overfelling of trees which exceeds the regenerative capacity of the forest ecosystem, and eventually converts the forests into non-renewable resources. Women's work in the collection of water, fodder, and fuel is thus rendered more energy and time-consuming. (In Garhwal, for example, I have seen women who originally collected fodder and fuel in a few hours, now travelling long distances by truck to collect grass and leaves in a task that might take up to two days.) Sometimes the damage to nature's intrinsic regenerative capacity is impaired not by over-exploitation of a particular resource but, indirectly, by damage caused to other related natural resources through ecological processes. Thus the excessive overfelling of trees in the catchment areas of streams and rivers destroys not only forest resources, but also renewable supplies of water, through hydrological destabilisation. Resource-intensive industries disrupt essential ecological processes not only by their excessive demands for raw material, but by their pollution of air and water and soil. Often such destruction is caused by the resource demands of non-vital industrial products. In spite of severe ecological crises, this paradigm continues to operate because for the North and for the elites of the South, resources continue to be available, even now. The lack of recognition of nature's processes for survival *as factors in the process of economic development* shrouds the political issues arising from resource transfer and resource destruction, and creates an ideological weapon for increased control over natural resources in the conventionally employed notion of productivity. All other costs of the economic process consequently become invisible. The forces which contribute to the increased 'productivity' of a modern farmer or factory worker for instance, come from the increased use of natural resources. Lovins has described this as the amount of 'slave' labour presently at work in the world.[9] According to him, each person on earth, on an average, possesses the equivalent of about 50 slaves, each working a 40-hour week. Man's global energy conversion from all sources (wood, fossil fuel, hydroelectric power, nuclear) is currently approximately 8×10^{12} watts. This is more than 20 times the energy content of the food necessary to feed the present world population at the FAO standard diet of 3,600 cal/day. The 'productivity' of the Western male compared to women or Third World peasants is not intrinsically superior; it is based on inequalities in the distribution of this 'slave' labour. The average inhabitant of the USA, for example, has 250 times more 'slaves' than the average Nigerian. If Americans were short of 249 of those 250 'slaves', one wonders how efficient they would prove themselves to be?

It is these resource and energy-intensive processes of production which divert resources away from survival, and hence from women. What patriarchy sees as productive work, is, in ecological terms highly destructive production. The second law of thermodynamics predicts that resource-intensive and resource-wasteful economic development must become a threat to the survival of the human species in the long run. Political struggles based on ecology in industrially advanced countries are rooted in this conflict between *long-term survival options* and *short-term over-production and over-consumption*. Political struggles of women, peasants, and tribals based on ecology in countries like India are far more acute and urgent, since they are rooted in the *immediate threat to the options for survival* for the vast majority of the people, *posed by resource-intensive and resource-wasteful economic growth* for the benefit of a minority.

In the market economy, the organising principle for natural resource use is the maximisation of profits and capital accumulation. Nature and human needs are managed through market mechanisms. Demands for natural resources are restricted to those demands registering on the market; the ideology of development is in large part based on a vision of bringing all natural resources into the market economy for commodity production. When these resources are already being used by nature to maintain her production of renewable resources and by women for sustenance and livelihood, their diversion to the market economy generates a scarcity condition for ecological stability and creates new forms of poverty for women.

Two Kinds of Poverty

In a book entitled *Poverty: the Wealth of the People*,[10] an African writer draws a distinction between poverty as subsistence, and misery as deprivation. It is useful to separate a cultural conception of subsistence living as poverty from the material experience of poverty that is a result of dispossession and deprivation. Culturally perceived poverty need not be real material poverty: subsistence economies which satisfy basic needs through self-provisioning are not poor in the sense of being deprived. Yet the ideology of development declares them so because they do not participate overwhelmingly in the market economy, and do not consume commodities produced for and distributed through the market *even though they might be satisfying those needs through self-provisioning mechanisms*. People are perceived as poor if they eat millets (grown by women) rather than commercially produced and distributed processed foods sold by global agri-business. They are seen as poor if they live in self-built housing made from natural material like bamboo and mud rather than in cement houses. They are seen as poor if they wear hand-made garments of natural fibre rather than synthetics. Subsistence, as culturally perceived poverty, does not necessarily imply a low physical quality of life. On the contrary, millets are nutritionally far superior to processed foods, houses built with local materials are far superior, being better adapted to the local climate and ecology, natural fibres are preferable to man-made fibres in most cases, and certainly more affordable. This cultural perception of prudent subsistence living as poverty has provided the legitimisation for the development process as a poverty removal project. As a culturally biased project it destroys wholesome and sustainable lifestyles and creates real material poverty, or misery, by the denial of survival needs themselves, through the diversion of resources to resource-intensive commodity production. Cash crop production and food processing take land and water resources away from sustenance needs, and exclude increasingly large numbers of people from their entitlements to food.

The inexorable processes of agriculture-industrialisation and internationalisation are probably responsible for more hungry people than either cruel or unusual whims of nature. There are several reasons why the high-technology-export-crop model increases hunger. Scarce land, credit, water and technology are pre-empted for the export market. Most hungry people are not affected by the market at all. . . . The profits flow to corporations that have no interest in feeding hungry people without money.[11]

The Ethiopian famine is in part an example of the creation of real poverty by development aimed at removing culturally perceived poverty. The displacement of nomadic Afars from their traditional pastureland in Awash Valley by commercial agriculture (financed by foreign companies) led to their struggle for survival in the fragile uplands which degraded the ecosystem and led to the starvation of cattle and the nomads.[12] The market economy conflicted with the survival economy in the Valley, thus creating a conflict between the survival economy and nature's economy in the uplands. At no point has the global marketing of agricultural commodities been assessed against the background of the new conditions of scarcity and poverty that it has induced. This new poverty moreover, is no longer cultural and relative: it is absolute, threatening the very survival of millions on this planet.

The economic system based on the patriarchal concept of productivity was created for the very specific historical and political phenomenon of colonialism. In it, the input for which efficiency of use had to be maximised in the production centres of Europe, was industrial labour. For colonial interest therefore, it was rational to improve the labour resource *even at the cost of wasteful use of nature's wealth*. This rationalisation has, however, been illegitimately universalised to all contexts and interest groups and, on the plea of increasing productivity, labour-reducing technologies have been introduced in situations where labour is abundant and cheap, and resource-demanding technologies have been introduced where resources are scarce and already fully utilised for the production of sustenance. Traditional economies with a stable ecology have shared with industrially advanced affluent economies the ability to use natural resources to satisfy basic vital needs. The former differ from the latter in two essential ways: first, the same needs are satisfied in industrial societies through longer technological chains requiring higher energy and resource inputs and excluding large numbers without purchasing power; and second, affluence generates new and artificial needs requiring the increased production of industrial goods and services. Traditional economies are not advanced in the matter of non-vital needs satisfaction, but as far as the satisfaction of basic and vital needs is concerned, they are often what Marshall Sahlins has called 'the original affluent society'. The needs of the Amazonian tribes are more than satisfied by the rich rainforest; their poverty begins with its destruction. The story is the same for the Gonds of Bastar in India or the Penans of Sarawak in Malaysia.

Thus are economies based on indigenous technologies viewed as 'backward' and 'unproductive'. Poverty, as the denial of basic needs, is not necessarily associated with the existence of traditional technologies, and its removal is not necessarily an outcome of the growth of modern ones. On the contrary, the destruction of ecologically sound traditional technologies, often created and used by women, along with the destruction of their material base is generally believed to be responsible for the 'feminisation' of poverty in societies which have had to bear the costs of resource destruction.

The contemporary poverty of the Afar nomad is not rooted in the inadequacies of traditional nomadic life, but in the *diversion of the productive pastureland of the Awash Valley*. The erosion of the resource base for survival is increasingly being caused by the demand for resources by the market economy, dominated by global forces. The creation of inequality through economic activity which is ecologically disruptive arises in two ways: first, inequalities in the distribution of privileges make for unequal access to natural resources—these include privileges of both a political and economic nature. Second, resource-intensive production processes have access to subsidised raw material on which a substantial number of people, especially from the less privileged economic groups, depend for their survival. The consumption of such industrial raw material is determined purely by market forces, and not by considerations of the social or ecological requirements placed on them. The costs of resource destruction are externalised and unequally divided among various economic groups in society, but are borne largely by women and those who satisfy their basic material needs directly from nature, simply because they have no purchasing power to register their demands on the goods and services provided by the modern production system. Gustavo Esteva has called development a permanent war waged by its promoters and suffered by its victims.[13]

The paradox and crisis of development arises from the mistaken identification of culturally perceived poverty with real material poverty, and the mistaken identification of the growth of commodity production as better satisfaction of basic needs. In actual fact, there is less water, less fertile soil, less genetic wealth as a result of the development process. Since these natural resources are the basis of nature's economy and women's survival economy, their scarcity is impoverishing women and marginalised peoples in an unprecedented manner. Their new impoverishment lies in the fact that resources which supported their survival were absorbed into the market economy while they themselves were excluded and displaced by it.

The old assumption that with the development process the availability of goods and services will automatically be increased and poverty will be removed, is now under serious challenge from women's ecology movements in the Third World, even while it continues to guide development thinking in centres of patriarchal power. Survival is based on the assumption of the sanctity of life; maldevelopment is based on the assumption of the sacredness of 'development'. Gustavo Esteva asserts that the sacredness of development has to be refuted because it threatens survival itself. 'My people are tired of development', he says, 'they just want to live.'[14]

The recovery of the feminine principle allows a transcendance and transformation of these patriarchal foundations of maldevelopment. It allows a redefinition of growth and productivity as categories linked to the production, not the destruction, of life. It is thus simultaneously an ecological and a feminist political project which legitimises the way of knowing and being that create wealth by enhancing life and diversity, and which delegitimises the knowledge and practise of a culture of death as the basis for capital accumulation.

Notes

1. Rosa Luxemberg, *The Accumulation of Capital* (London: Routledge and Kegan Paul, 1951).
2. An elaboration of how 'development' transfers resources from the poor to the well-endowed is contained in J. Bandyopadhyay and V. Shiva, 'Political Economy of Technological Polarisations', in *Economic and Political Weekly*, 18 (1982), 1827–32; and J. Bandyopadhyay and V. Shiva, 'Political Economy of Ecology Movements', in *Economic and Political Weekly*.
3. Ester Boserup, *Women's Role in Economic Development* (London: Allen and Unwin, 1970).
4. DAWN, *Development Crisis and Alternative Visions: Third World Women's Perspectives* (Bergen: Christian Michelsen Institute, 1985), 21.
5. M. George Foster, *Traditional Societies and Technological Change* (Delhi: Allied Publishers, 1973).
6. Maria Mies, *Patriarchy and Accumulation on a World Scale* (London: Zed Books, 1986).
7. Alice Schlegel (ed.), *Sexual Stratification: A Cross-Cultural Study* (New York: Columbia University Press, 1977).
8. Jonathan Porritt, *Seeing Green* (Oxford: Blackwell, 1984).
9. A. Lovins, cited in S. R. Eyre, *The Real Wealth of Nations* (London: Edward Arnold, 1978).
10. R. Bahro, *From Red to Green* (London: Verso, 1984), 211.
11. R. J. Barnet, *The Lean Years* (London: Abacus, 1981), 171.
12. U. P. Koehn, 'African Approaches to Environmental Stress: A Focus on Ethiopia and Nigeria', in R. N. Barrett (ed.), *International Dimensions of the Environmental Crisis* (Boulder, Colo.: Westview, 1982), 253–89.
13. Gustavo Esteva, 'Regenerating People's Space', in S. N. Mendlowitz and R. B. J. Walker, *Towards a Just World Peace: Perspectives from Social Movements* (London: Butterworths and Committee for a Just World Peace, 1987).
14. G. Esteva, Remarks made at a Conference of the Society for International Development, Rome, 1985.

Section VII: Ecological Modernization

Ecological modernization shares sustainable development's interest in reconciling economic growth and environmental protection, but is much more explicit on how this might be done—at least in highly developed countries. The concept first saw the light of day in Germany in the early 1980s, and has since spread to several other European countries, which have now displaced the English-speaking countries as the leaders in environmental conservation. The essential idea is that a clean environment is actually good for business, for it connotes happy and healthy workers, profits for companies developing conservation technologies or selling green products, high-quality material inputs into production (e.g. clean air and water), and efficiency in materials usage. Pollution, on the other hands, indicates wasteful use of materials. In addition, it is cheaper to tackle environmental problems before they get out of hand and require expensive remedial action. The extent to which such a reorientation of the economy will require a helping hand from government remains an open question.

The selection from Albert Weale describes the rise of ecological modernization in Europe, with a focus on Germany. Weale contrasts German progress with British resistance and stagnation, as Britain established a reputation as Western Europe's dirtiest country. The ecological modernization concept is not yet used outside Europe. However, the kind of green capitalism advocated by US Vice-President Al Gore is entirely consistent with the concept, and we present here a selection from his book in which he advocates a global programme along these lines, more ambitious than any current efforts confined within countries such as Germany and the Netherlands. Gore's programme has not been adopted in the United States, least of all by the administration in which he serves. A cleaner and greener capitalism is emerging in Japan, though again without explicit appeal to the European concept of ecological modernization.

Gore does not believe that much in the way of political and economic restructuring is necessary. Our selection from Ulrich Beck, in contrast, believes that radical restructuring is absolutely necessary. Beck agrees with the ecological modernizers that we are entering a new phase of modernization, which he calls a reflexive modernity, as we move beyond semi-modern industrial society. The essence of this new phase is that questions about the basic trajectory of the economy and technology, long treated as off-limits to democratic control, are being called into question because people are increasingly sensitive to the environmental risks being generated. To Beck, politics is increasingly centred around these issues of risk, and existing institutions are called into question because of their complicity in the production of risks. Beck looks forward to a future in which risks, economy, science, and technology are brought under participatory democratic control, though he is a little vague as to what these new institutions might actually look like. Such a future would be consistent with a radicalized version of ecological modernization, something much more than the re-tooling of industry along environmentally sensitive lines.

Further Reading

Maarten Hajer in *The Politics of Environmental Discourse: Ecological Modernization and the Policy Process* (1995) provides a comprehensive analysis of the rise of ecological modernization in the Netherlands, and resistance to it in the United Kingdom. Peter Christoff in 'Ecological Modernisation, Ecological Modernities', *Environmental Politics*, 5 (1996) nicely contrasts 'weak' and 'strong' versions of ecological modernization. Christoff's strong version is consistent with Ulrich Beck's ideas about reflexive modernization, which are developed at length in Becks's *Risk Society* (1992). Arthur P. J. Mol in 'Ecological Modernisation and Institutional Reflexivity: Environmental Reform in the Late Modern Age', *Environmental Politics*, 5 (1996), 302–23 believes that ecological modernization, whatever its virtues, is not going to lead in this Becksian direction.

21 The Politics of Ecological Modernization

Albert Weale

The new politics of pollution have not developed at the same pace everywhere. Some countries have been able to adapt their systems of pollution control and environmental policy more rapidly than others. In all countries some aspects of pollution control have been adapted more extensively than others, and in no country is the transformation anywhere near complete. Yet, we can learn much by comparing systems that have responded differently to the new environmental challenges. In this chapter we shall compare the experience of Britain and Germany in the 1980s.[1] The reason for taking this pair is, in the words of Sonja Boehmer-Christiansen and Jim Skea, 'the widely divergent policy stances which were taken by the two countries on the acid rain issue'.[2]

Acid rain became an important issue of international and comparative policy in the 1980s. 'The term "acid rain" refers to the dilute sulphuric and nitric acids which, many believe, are created when fossil fuels are burned in power stations, smelters, and motor vehicles, and which fall over long distances downwind of possible sources of the pollutants.'[3] Its basic ingredients are sulphur dioxide, nitrogen oxides, and ozone, which can be deposited in dry form, and in a wet form in solution with rain or snow or by suspension in fog.[4]

Policy towards acid rain is a good test of the differences in policy development for a number of reasons. Unlike air pollution by particulates, its effects were often widespread and remote. Moreover, although the phenomenon of acid rain has long been identified as a problem of transboundary air pollution, there are considerable scientific controversies about its effects alone or in combination with other pollutants. As we shall see, the widely divergent stances on the issue of acid rain in Britain and Germany involved and reflected a whole series of other institutional and ideological differences, and the difference in policy position over acid rain was replicated across a wide variety of issues. As case studies in contrasting policy approaches to environmental policy, therefore, Britain and Germany provide excellent examples.

Yet the contrast is in many ways a surprising one. At the time of the second oil price explosion in 1979, an observer of comparative environmental policy would have been most likely to conclude that Britain and Germany had a roughly similar position on environmental policy questions. Both countries were more preoccupied with the problems of maintaining economic growth than they were with the protection of the environment, so that the upsurge in environ-

From Albert Weale, *The New Politics of Pollution* (Manchester: Manchester University Press, 1992), 66–92. Reprinted with permission.

mental interest that had characterised the late 1960s and early 1970s appeared to have receded. Although both countries had legislation and administration in place for controlling pollution, the systems were patchy and prone to failures of implementation. In Britain significant portions of the 1974 Control of Pollution Act had not been put into effect, including those dealing with public access to registers of emission levels, and there was a continuing uncertainty about the future administrative arrangements for pollution control.[5] In Germany the principal legislation for air pollution control at national level, the 1974 Federal Immission Control Act was in place, but regulators were finding it difficult to advance more stringent emission standards under the legislation, and there were many other aspects of pollution that were weakly or inadequately regulated.[6] In both countries the day to day work of enforcing pollution control regulation was prone to bargaining and negotiation over the setting of standards and the timetable for their application. In Germany this phenomenon became identified by the term 'implementation deficit'.[7] At the international level it was a similar story. There was little use of the European Community (EC) as an instrument for internationalising environmental regulation and the governments of both countries were sceptical of the need for further reductions in sulphur-dioxide emissions under international agreements and protocols, for example the 1979 Convention on Long-Range Transboundary Air Pollution of the UN's Economic Commission for Europe. In short, Britain and Germany together presented the spectacle of two, medium-sized and industrialised countries that had put in place the legislation and policy instruments to cope with the most obvious and visible problems of environmental degradation, but who were unwilling to become pace-setters in a comparative context.

Slowly building up from 1979, however, German environmental policy entered what Edda Müller has termed its 'recovery phase' and revived its 'offensive' potential, and German policy positions on a whole range of environmental questions have come to diverge considerably from those in the UK.[8] The most important and most vivid symbol of this divergence was the adoption in 1983 by the German government of the Large Combustion Plant Ordinance in the wake of the public concern over forest die-back (*Waldsterben*).[9] The 1983 Ordinance, implemented under the Federal Immission Control Act, imposed stringent limits on emissions of sulphur dioxide on large furnaces, affecting most significantly those plants generating electricity from the burning of coal. The Ordinance required that existing plants meet the new standards within five years, so that expensive flue-gas desulphurisation equipment had to be retrofitted. By contrast, the British government's decision to retrofit flue-gas desulphurisation equipment to a small number of power stations run by the Central Electricity Generating Board in September 1986 was tardy, and taken after much domestic and international campaigning. The lack of public commitment to the programme was shown when it was revealed in the aftermath of electricity privatisation that the government would allow the newly privatised electricity generators to meet emission targets by burning low sulphur coal rather by the installation of flue-gas desulphurisation equipment.

Although the most dramatic symbol of change in policy stance, the legislation on air pollution was not the only example of Germany's move to a more stringent pollution control policy. Restrictions on vehicle emissions, including lead, have been pursued, and Germany favoured the development of an EC directive requiring the fitting of catalytic converters on cars. Waste recycling programmes have been implemented at local level, and in 1991 an Ordinance on packaging was introduced making producers and retailers responsible for the disposal of their packaging waste. There have been point source reductions in water pollution by the application of more stringent standards, and water quality maps show signs of improvement. In 1986 a new federal ministry of the environment was created and, although it took some months to establish its style and political resource base, it became a powerful force for environmental improvement by the late 1980s.[10] In international negotiations, Germany became anxious to use existing institutional regimes, like that of the European Community, to advance the international regulation of pollution, and it took the initiative in convening the first International Conference on the Protection of the North Sea in Bremen in 1984, thereby inaugurating a new regime of international environmental protection. In regard to problems of global climate change and the control of greenhouse gases, Germany had by the beginning of the 1990s committed itself to the ambitious target of a unilateral reduction in carbon-dioxide emissions of between 25 and 30 per cent by the year 2005.

This is not to say that German environmental policy is solving the substantial problems of environmental protection that still exist. Whereas total sulphur-oxide emissions fell by some 46 per cent between 1985 and the late 1980s, total nitrogen-oxide emissions were more or less stable over the same period.[11] This discrepancy is consistent with a continuing decline in German forest health and reflects the growth of private vehicle use in the period. In the agricultural sector there is a neglect of non-point sources of pollution. The problem of hazardous waste has often been solved by the simple expedient of exporting it to countries with less stringent environmental regulation. Despite these weaknesses, it remains true to say that within Europe Germany has earned for itself the title of an environmental leader during the 1980s. In many ways the unification of Germany in 1990 consolidated the impetus towards stringent environmental standards. The discovery of the magnitude of the clean-up costs resulting from the environmental neglect of the former East German regime was shocking in itself and galvanised action, resulting in the federal government allocating DM800 million over two years for pollution control measures related primarily to drinking water and waste.

Britain's reputation as an environmental policy laggard or 'dirty man of Europe' has been won through a dogged determination not to take action in fields with international repercussions, most notably action to reduce emissions of sulphur dioxide. Although the UK's total emissions of sulphur dioxide fell by some 23 per cent in the first half of the 1980s,[12] the principal explanation for this was the downturn in the economy following Sir Geoffrey Howe's deflationary budget of 1981. By the late 1980s, rapid rates of economic growth led to speculation that official sulphur-dioxide projections were too optimistic and would be exceeded. During the 1980s the UK government put up fierce resistance to the adoption of an EC large combustion plant directive that had been originally modelled on the German Large Combustion Plant Ordinance of 1983. The UK's resistance was prolonged over five years, and the issue was only resolved in 1988 after much manipulation of timetables and reduction targets by those responsible for drafting the directive.[13] Since the UK was given a relatively generous target figure because of the comparatively high costs it faced in installing flue-gas desulphurisation equipment, any attempt to meet the target by alternative measures like the burning of low sulphur coal will increase scepticism in Europe about the UK's environmental commitment.

In other areas of EC and international policy, the UK has also been a laggard. The UK has been an unwilling participant in the EC's efforts to clean up Europe's rivers and coastal waters, for example by initially identifying only twenty-seven beaches under the Bathing Waters Directive, fewer than land-locked Luxembourg.[14] For some time the British government held up the process that eventually led to the Montreal Protocol, to the Vienna Convention and an international agreement to phase out the use of chlorofluorocarbons.[15] The British government has also been reluctant to commit itself to the reduction of carbon-dioxide emissions unilaterally, tying its willingness to take action to simultaneous action by others. It is true that, at the International Conference on the Protection of the North Sea in The Hague in 1990, Britain did accept the case for ending the dumping of sewage sludge in the North Sea, but this was a relatively late change of heart, and it can be interpreted less as a sign of long-term commitment and more as a desire to avoid politically embarrassing public exposure.

These international dimensions of the UK's policy record have been mirrored in domestic aspects of its pollution control policy. Administrative arrangements have been reformed in ad hoc and incremental ways, following on the privatisation of the water supply companies and the creation of Her Majesty's Inspectorate of Pollution in 1987. The latter never settled into its stride, and there have been continuing difficulties in its relationship with the National Rivers Authority which acquired the responsibility for water pollution control with the breakup of the former Regional Water Authorities as a result of privatisation. The new water companies were allowed to breach water pollution standards to sustain their profitability. Continuing doubts have been raised about the management of hazardous waste. And the much vaunted White Paper on the environment, published in September 1990, was generally regarded as a damp squib.[16]

Since 1980, therefore, Britain and Germany's environmental policies have followed divergent paths of development. Germany has moved from a position of reluctant environmentalism to one in which it is now legislating some of the most stringent pollution control standards in Europe and pressing internationally for more vigorous action on a wide range of issues. The UK, by contrast, has been laggardly in its adoption of environmental measures, and has acquired the reputation in international negotiations of resisting the development of more forceful pollution control.

It is useful at this point to consider the underlying political structure of those groups that have traditionally dominated air pollution control policy, and here a comparison with the USA is useful. In the case of US air pollution policy, Sabatier has shown that there were two competing interests over clean air policy.[17] On the one hand there was the 'clean air coalition', which was dominated by environmental and public health groups, their allies in Congress, a few labour unions, many state and local pollution control officials (especially those in large cities with serious problems), and some researchers. This clean air coalition was united around a set of propositions concerning the role of industry and the state in respect of environmental protection. These propositions included a belief about the inability of markets to deal with pollution externalities and an assumption that the serious health problems created by these externalities would be ignored by state and local governments in their attempts to attract and retain industry.

Against this clean air coalition was an 'economic feasibility' coalition that was dominated by industrial emissions sources, energy companies, their allies in Congress, several labour unions, some state and local pollution control officials, and a few economists. This coalition was united around a belief system that gave high place to the role of markets in promoting economic welfare in general and also involved a mistrust of federal government involvement in regulation and an insistence that the benefits of human health gains be traded-off against the costs of making the necessary capital and technical investments. This pattern of coalitions around the elements of those competing belief systems could be replicated in the clean air case for both Britain and Germany in the 1970s. For example, during the 1970s and 1980s in the UK, the clean air coalition comprised a wide range of environmental and public health groups, some elements of the Labour Party, and some members of the policy elite including influential members of the scientific advisory system. On the other side was a coalition of groups who stressed the uncertainties attached to the benefits supposedly flowing from costly investments in acid rain abatement policies, including the Central Electricity Generating Board, the industrial emitters, the Confederation of British Industry, most of the Conservative Party, and some members of the policy advisory elite.[18] The debate between these two coalitions was essentially framed in terms of costs and benefits, with much attention being paid to the question of how far the putative benefits had to be discounted in light of the scientific uncertainties that attached to them. A similar constellation of interests formed around competing belief systems in the Federal Republic of Germany. In the clean air coalition could be found the environmental movement, pollution control officials, some parts of the Social Democrats, and members of the policy elite. In the economic feasibility coalition could be found the power-generating companies, the industrial emitters, the Christian Democrats, some Social Democrats particularly from North Rhine-Westphalia, the German Industrial Federation (BDI), and some members of the policy elite.[19] But in Germany, unlike Britain, the balance of advantage shifted to the clean air coalition.

It is no doubt possible to give an account of these contrasting developments in the idioms of rational choice theory and institutional analysis. Within these idioms, the most obvious factor to point to as explaining these divergent policy developments is the difference in the party systems between the two countries and the effects of Germany's system of proportional representation upon the incentives facing office-seeking politicians by comparison with the UK's system of simple plurality voting. A system of proportional representation like that used in Germany will typically deprive any one political party of a majority in the legislature, and indeed in the 1987 elections German voters showed great sophistication in casting their second list votes in such a way as to deprive the CDU/CSU of an overall majority. The UK's system of simple plurality has the opposite effect, magnifying an electoral plurality into a legislative majority. Thus, throughout the 1980s Germany was governed by parties in coalition, and for a large part of the decade the Greens were a potential threat to the Christian-Liberal coalition at federal level and pivotal in the formation of a number of governments at *Land* level. For rational choice analysts it is a well-known result within the theory of political coalitions that small, pivotal groups can extract large concessions from potential coalition partners, and from this perspective it is not surprising that environmental issues become prominent on the political agenda.[20] Britain's electoral system, by contrast, allowed a political party with little more than 40 per cent of the vote to remain in office throughout the 1980s, free to pursue its overriding ideological objective of seeking to transform the ailing state of the British economy by reducing the scope of public intervention in its management. From this viewpoint the divergent policy developments corresponded to quite distinct political incentives and institutional constraints.

Notice, incidentally, that in such an account we do not need to posit any underlying difference of political culture or citizen preference about environmental policy in order to account for differences in policy trends, but we merely need to locate rational action within distinct institutional settings. To be sure, Germany has consistently scored a higher level of post-materialism than Britain among members of its population since the phenomenon was first identified in the mid-1970s, and some observers have pointed to potentially more deep-seated cultural differences between the two societies.[21] But against this must be set other evidence, most notably the share of the vote received by the British Green Party in the European Parliament elections of 1989, which at 15 per cent was the largest in any country. Moreover, a committed wielder of Occam's razor would not need to invoke these factors within the rational choice idiom. From the basis of social choice theory it is clear that identical preference profiles will yield quite distinct collective choices, provided only that the processes for amalgamating popular preferences vary sufficiently.[22] The institutional differences of electoral and party systems, by themselves, would be quite capable of explaining the divergence of public policies, without resorting to hypothetical conjectures about underlying cultural differences, or observed differences in the prevalence of post-materialist values.

Although the simplest model of office-seeking politicians within different institutional contexts goes some way to explaining divergent policy developments between Britain and Germany, it may be said to miss an important dimension of the story, namely how German policy initiatives were legitimised and justified within the relevant policy communities and in society at large. For a complex variety of historical reasons there are elaborate mechanisms of political accountability built into the German system of government. The influential ideological traditions associated with the idea of the *Rechtsstaat*, by which public action should take place through lawful procedures and with explicit justification in terms of principles, form one element of this historical complex. Another is formed by reaction to the totalitarian excesses of the Third Reich, leading post-war constitution builders to design a system in which public accountability for public action was high. As a result of these historical pressures there is in Germany a striking (to the outsider at least) amount of institutional attention devoted to the detailing and elaboration of policy principles and programmes, and there are firm institutional safeguards to ensure that administrative and political action is underpinned by an account of its rationale. Together with the frequently observed juridification of politics in Germany, by which for example the courts play a significant part in reviewing and defining the permissible scope of administrative measures, there are powerful processes of policy legitimisation built into the German policy system. These discursive features of policy development are ignored within the conventional idiom of rational choice analysis.

In their famous opening to *The German Ideology* Marx and Engels describe how, according to German ideologists, Germany underwent an unparalleled intellectual revolution within a short period 'principles ousted one another, intellectual heroes overthrew each other with unheard-of rapidity and in a three year period more was cleared away in Germany than at any other time in three centuries'.[23] Yet the problem with the German ideology, according to Marx and Engels, was that all this was supposed to have taken place in the realm of pure thought, and it did not occur to any of the philosophers to enquire into the connection of the new critical ideology with the philosophers' material surroundings.

In seeking to understand the divergent policy developments of Britain and Germany, we need to understand how a transformation took place in the legitimating discourse of German environmental policy but not British environmental policy if we are to capture the processes of policy justification and rationalisation in the German case. Unlike the German ideological revolution that Marx and Engels described, the contemporary revolution in intellectual orientation is still incomplete and it has been taking place more slowly. It is also unlike the earlier revolution in one respect: it can only be understood once we place it in the context of its material surroundings, for it is by reference to the interaction of ideas and institutional context that we can best appreciate how and in what ways this ideology has developed. Along with other commentators I shall refer to this ideology as one of 'ecological modernisation'. In the next section I turn to the principal features of this body of ideas.

Ecological Modernisation as an Ideology

There is no one canonical statement of the ideology of ecological modernisation as *The General Theory* is a source for Keynesianism. It is a view about the relationships between the environment, the economy, society, and public policy that has to be pieced together from various sources. One way to understand it is by way of reflection upon and reaction to the assumptions underlying the policy strategies of the 1970s. Previously, I argued that there were a number of assumptions presupposed in the pollution control strategies of the 1970s: that environmental problems could be dealt with adequately by a specialist branch of the machinery of government; that the character of environmental problems was well understood; that environmental problems could be handled discretely; that end-of-pipe technologies were typically adequate; and that in the setting of pollution control standards a balance had to be struck between environmental protection and economic growth and development.

The structure of ecological modernisation as an ideology is given by the denial of the general validity of these assumptions. According to the proponent of ecological modernisation, serious environmental problems are frequently not obvious and the link from cause to effect is often long and indirect. Fundamental problems of environmental protection cannot be dealt with by end-of-pipe technologies, but need to be tackled at source. One reason for this is that from the perspective of the mass balance approach to pollution the solution of one disposal problem will merely displace the problem into another medium. Indeed, if anything forms the leitmotif of the modernist's critique of 1970s environmental policy it is that the policy strategies adopted characteristically resulted in problem displacement, across time and place, rather than problem solution.

However, it is in reconceptualising the relationship between economy and environment that the ideology of ecological modernisation probably marks the most decisive break with the assumptions that informed the first wave of environmental policy. There are a number of themes that are pursued in the reconceptualisation. One of these takes the form of a simple critique. If the 'costs' of environmental protection are avoided the effect is frequently to save money for present generations at the price of an increased burden for future generations. In other words, the costs do not disappear, they are merely pushed forward and possibly magnified in the process. Thus, a failure to regulate industrial waste disposal or agricultural pesticide use in one generation will simply have the effect of creating soil clean-up costs for future generations.

The claims of ecological modernisation go deeper than this, however. Instead of seeing environmental protection as a burden upon the economy the ecological modernist sees it as a potential source for future growth. Since environmental amenity is a superior good, the demand for pollution control is likely to increase and there is therefore a considerable advantage to an economy to have the technical and production capacity to produce low polluting goods or pollution control technology. For example, the EC's *Fourth Environmental Action Programme* makes the point that its proposals:

are rooted in the generally acknowledged fact that, as a key factor in economic decision-making, environmental protection policy and strict environmental protection standards are no longer an optional extra but a *sine qua non* for the quality of life which the Community's citizens expect.[24]

The point is sometimes linked to the fact that skilled workers in new technology industries (electronics, biotechnology, software, and so on) have shown a tendency to wish to live in attractive and pleasant surroundings that do not display the environmental degradation of traditional industrial areas. Thus, Baden-Württemberg and Bavaria have seen a growth of the new middle classes precisely because of their environmental appeal.

Moreover, with the advent of global markets, the standards of product acceptability will be determined by the country with the most stringent pollution control standards. Hence the future development of a post-industrial economy will depend upon its ability to produce high-value, high-quality products with stringent environmental standards enforced. This aspect of the ideology of ecological modernisation was well brought out by Mr Laurens Brinkhorst, the Director-General of the environment directorate of the European Commission, speaking before a House of Lords select committee about the draft *Fourth Environmental Action Programme*:

Secondly—and here it is the old Japan hand who is speaking—I have become very much concerned—and I think this is a view largely shared by other departments—that environment and technology, environment and competition, have become brothers and sisters. It is not because of the low prices of Japanese products that the Japanese are making inroads in all kinds of areas (whether we speak about cars or computers), but it is largely because of the quality of their products and in the field of cars, for instance, the very high emissions standards.[25]

The same point is made in the *Fourth Environmental Action Programme* itself:

The Commission is convinced that hte (*sic*) future competitiveness of Community industry on world markets will depend heavily upon its ability to offer goods and services causing no pollution and achieving standards at least as high as its competitors. Small firms in particular can play their part. Technological innovation allied with a commitment to high supply standards can open up new opportunities, by developing new markets and putting to work the technologies of the future.[26]

Both of these passages are explicit in linking the prospects for future economic development in an era of global markets with higher standards of pollution control and environmentally safe products and processes.

This account of the relationship between economic competitiveness and environmental regulation is also linked to a view about the proper role of the public authorities in ensuring the condition for economic development. Public intervention, along with other decision processes, is an essential part of ensuring a progressive relationship between industry and the environment. Mr Brinkhorst put it as follows to the House of Lords Select Committee:

proper care and environmental standards actually make our society more competitive . . . Europe as a technological power is falling behind because we do not put enough pressure from the government and industry, together with the consumer, in seeing that an effective environmental policy is a necessity for our industrial survival in many areas.[27]

Implicit in this account is a positive role for public authority in raising the standards of environmental regulation, as a means of providing a spur to industrial innovation.

In stating the ideology of ecological modernisation I do not want to present it as a coherent, well-formulated doctrine on which there is substantial agreement by many of those active in environmental politics. Each of the central propositions is capable of great elaboration and illustration, and the relative stress and importance given to each one of them will yield different styles of critique with quite distinct policy implications. For example, if more stress is laid upon the need to move from effects to causes then a radical version of policy is likely to emerge, whereas if the stress is the potential growth stimulated by an environmentally sound economy, then a more pro-industry version of policy is likely. However, despite the undoubted differences of emphasis that these distinct propositions will receive, ecological modernisation forms a category of discourse that is a flexible and powerful instrument for criticising the assumptions built into the first wave of environmental protection.

This body of ideas became appealing to many members of the policy elite in European countries and international organisation during the 1980s. Not only the EC, but also the World Commission on Environment and Development and the OECD took up the themes. Part of its appeal, I conjecture, is that it has the potential to break the political stalemate between the clean air advocacy and economic feasibility advocacy coalitions. Once it is recognised that pollution control can itself be a source of economic growth, both in terms of a rising demand for clean products and in terms of an emerging high-tech pollution control industry, then the balance of argument in terms of economic feasibility is tipped towards clean air rather than away from it. In particular, it weakens the economic feasibility arguments against anticipatory environmental policy, since it will highlight the costs of failing to act as much as the costs of acting. This does not imply that all actors in the policy system will recognise the case for improved pollution control. On the contrary, those who incur the costs of stringent pollution control will have an incentive to argue against its introduction if they cannot capture the economic benefits, and undoubtedly the operators of many coal-fired power stations fall into this category. All they see are economic benefits to pollution control companies or nuclear power operators arising from higher prices for coal-fired electricity generation. Nevertheless, it becomes more difficult to argue the economic feasibility case when there are economic, as well as political, arguments in favour of clean air.

My main thesis can now be stated. It is that there were elements in the ideological and institutional traditions of German public policy that made certain elements of ecological modernisation both a legitimising device of public policy developments and a potential source of policy principles. In making this claim I am not saying that the ideology of ecological modernisation was absorbed wholesale by German policy elites in the 1980s. Indeed it will be part of my purpose to claim that the ideological and institutional features of German public policy that found ecological modernisation congenial also predisposed the discourse towards certain specific elements of the new programme. Nevertheless, by comparison with the equivalent ideological and institutional traditions in the UK, ecological modernisation had a much better opportunity in Germany.

Ecological Modernisation in Britain and Germany

The basic principle in terms of which German policy developments were justified in the 1980s was the *Vorsorgeprinzip*, or principle of precaution. There is no simple or single meaning to be given to the principle of precaution. Indeed one analyst has distinguished no less than eleven different meanings assigned to the principle of precaution within German policy discourse.[28] However, the typical context within which the principle of precaution is used in which policy-makers are forced to go 'beyond science' in the sense of being required to make decisions where the consequences of alternative policy options are not determinable within a reasonable margin of error and where potentially high costs are involved in taking action. The installation of flue-gas desulphurisation equipment conforms to this pattern. At the time at which the decision on the Large Combustion Plant Ordinance was taken, there was considerable scientific controversy over the extent to which sulphur deposition was the cause of forest die-back, so that it was unclear how much environmental benefit would be derived from the implementation of a costly measure. Another example, where similar levels of uncertainty pertains, is the dumping of wastes in the seas, in connection with which the German Council of Experts on Environmental Questions argued for a principle of precaution in relation to the North Sea, even though the complexity of the natural system was such that it would be difficult to bring the costs of measures into any clear relationship with putative benefits. A final example is provided by the uncertainties surrounding global climate change, where the costs and benefits of either action or inaction are difficult to conceptualise, let alone quantify. In all these cases, proponents of the principle of precaution would argue that precaution would indicate possibly costly measures to prevent the possibility of serious environmental degradation.

During the 1980s in Germany the principle of precaution became a widely used justificatory principle among members of the environmental policy community, but the idea was also taken up by other policy elites in Europe, including those who drafted the EC's *Fourth Environmental Action Programme*, who sought to develop an approach to environmental policy that was preventive rather than reactive. Commenting upon a draft of this programme Mr William Walde-grave, as Minister of State at the UK's Department of Environment, said:

I have been struck by how often we appear to be dealing with subjects not really on the basis of an objective assessment of environmental priorities but as a result of the changing fashions in pressures from outside. It is necessary in an area which should be science-based to put up pretty formidable hurdles and tests of a scientific nature if we are to make rational priorities . . .[29]

In stating this view, Mr Waldegrave was only expressing an established feature of the British approach to environmental policy, namely that scientific understanding of cause-and-effect relationships in natural systems is a necessary condition for adequate and rational policy-making. This emphasis was restated in the British government's 1990 White Paper on the environment, where it was asserted that precipitate action on the basis of inadequate evidence is the wrong response.[30]

There are here, therefore, two competing principles of action: the principle of precaution and the principle of the scientific burden of proof. It is clear that these principles will pull in opposite directions over issues like acid rain or the protection of the seas. Why do we find that one principle is favoured in one country and a contrary principle in another?

The beginnings of an answer to this question can be found by contrasting German and British policy styles.[31] By tradition British policy making is conducted in a mode appropriate to a 'flexible' rather than a 'rigid' constitution (to use Bryce's vocabulary[32]). Policy is conceived as a series of problems, constituting cases that have to be judged on their merits. General norms are to be avoided if the decision can be left to the exercise of continuous administrative discretion. There is a desire to avoid programmatic statements or expositions of general principles governing particular areas of policy. The preference is for the particular over the general, the concrete over the abstract and the commonsensical over the principled. These features of policy-making lead to the absence of principled policy choice in many sectors of policy, including economic and health policy as well as environmental policy. Thus Hayward has characterised the British style in terms of an absence of explicit and medium- or long-term objectives on the one hand and unplanned, and incremental decision-making in which policies are arrived at by a continuous process of mutual adjustment between a plurality of actors on the other.[33] As Richardson and Watts point out, the specialised knowledge co-opted via the advisory group system is an essential element in this plurality of actors.[34]

The German policy style, by contrast, is consistent with the operation of a rigid constitution. A programmatic statement of general principles is seen as an essential prologue to legislation and policy development, a tendency that is probably reinforced by the practice of coalition government in which political parties of different ideological persuasions have to come to some agreement on the running of government. Moreover, the emphasis upon constitutionalism in the conduct of government also has the effect of making the policy process more formal. Thus, as part of the process involved in securing constitutional changes enabling it to legislate on air pollution, the federal German government set out the principled basis of its programme in a general statement in 1971.[35] The programme established the principles of the polluter pays, the common burden principle in cases where it would not be possible to identify the polluting source, the principle of social co-operation in environmental policy and the principle of international co-operation. Within the logic of German policy discourse, particular policy measures are seen as the 'concretisation' of general principles, by contrast with the logic of British policy discourse in which principles are seen as a generalisation of particular policies.

However, it may be argued that these differences of policy style show that issues of policy principle will be handled by different methods and under different assumptions within the two systems, but they do not explain why particular principles, like the principle of precaution, could play a creative role in German policy developments but not in British ones. After all, the principle of precaution addresses an aspect of many contemporary pollution problems where the science is generally only poorly understood. Since this is an intrinsic feature of problems, how was the British government able to side-step the challenges that it produces?

One answer here is to look at the composition and background of typical members of the policy communities that gather around pollution control. The high esteem accorded to respecting the finding of science in the British system in part reflects a procedural reality. Given the non-technical background of virtually all civil servants involved in environmental policy-making, many elements of choices are simply remitted to expert advisory committees or the office of the chief scientist in the department. The intellectual disposition of those with such a background is to look for evidence to confirm a hypothesis, and if no evidence is to hand to suspend judgement until it can be accumulated. By contrast the system of uniform emissions set according to the principle of *Stand der Technik*, as it operates in Germany, relies heavily upon the expertise of lawyers and engineers, reinforced by the role that the Federation of German Engineers has traditionally played in the setting of pollution control standards. From these backgrounds the intellectual predisposition is not to ask for confirmation of an hypothesis, but to ask whether there is an enforceable technical proposal for dealing with a pollution problem and then ask whether policy can be built around that solution.

In one important respect, however, the policy community for pollution control is usually wider in Germany than the UK. The constitutional formalism of German policy-making means that the courts play an important role in the setting of standards, since proposed regulations or decisions may be referred to the courts by interested parties under procedures for judicial review of constitutional or administrative issues. Two important court decisions affected the interpretation of the precautionary principle.[36] In its decision on the licensing of the nuclear reactor at Whyl, the Federal Administrative Court refused to accept a distinction between the principle of precaution on the one hand and the generally accepted principle of protection from hazards on the other. The logic of the court's judgement was to argue that potential risks and known hazards are on a continuum, and that both protection from hazards and the principle of precaution required an approach in which the dangers and risks associated with nuclear power should be reduced as far as possible taking into account the state of science and technology. The logic of this position is to refuse to draw a sharp distinction between dangers that have been demonstrated and risks that are suggested but about which there is little current evidence. In the Federal Administrative Court's *Voerde* judgement, where the court held that a district heating scheme should be subject to more stringent air pollution controls, it was held that stringent controls were justified because the costs of pollution abatement had to be considered from the point of view of the economy as a whole, and air quality standards had to be taken into account beyond the immediate vicinity of the plant. In this latter judgement, in particular, there is therefore an acknowledgement of one of the key propositions within the ideology of ecological modernisation, namely that a failure to address a pollution problem does not save costs but merely displaces them elsewhere around the economy, for example in the form of forest damage or damage to buildings.

The net effect of the development of the principle of precaution was the tightening of emission standards within the framework of traditional legal regulations. The stress upon anticipation essentially entailed a movement away from a narrow cost-benefit calculation when considering the implementation of stricter standards and a willingness to see costs as part of a wider process of improving the social environment.

In addition to the development of these specific regulatory policies, another traditional instrument of German public policy has been used to promote environmental protection, namely public investment and subsidy. For example, between 1979 and 1985 the German government subsidy for environmental research and development rose from the equivalent of $144.3 m to $236.4 m, or from 2.1 per cent of R and D expenditures to 3.1 per cent. (The equivalent figures for Britain were $51.6 m, that is 0.8 per cent of R and D, to $76.4 m, or 1.1 per cent of R and D.) By 1985 German public subsidy had in fact taken over from the US as being the largest absolute level of expenditure.[37] German public investment has also been used to provide financial support in the field of energy conservation, including investment help for firms installing energy-saving devices.[38] The use of public investment subsidies and tax concessions is a familiar element of German public policy. As Andrew Shonfield pointed out in his discussion of the phenomenon in *Modern Capitalism*, such a use of public funds derives from two sources: an ideological tradition of national economics, in which the aim of public policy is seen as that of building up the basic capacity of the national economy; and close organisational and institutional links between government and peak associations in which bargains can be struck about the terms of subsidies and performance targets.[39]

Looked at from this viewpoint, we would expect that certain elements only within the ideology of ecological modernisation were to be taken up and used in the course of policy arguments, and that other elements would be discarded or ignored. For example, the stress upon setting emissions standards implies a focus on effects, rather than causes, and hence a focus upon end-of-pipe solutions. We should not expect a great emphasis, then, in policy discourse on the need for structural changes in production and consumption to reduce pollution. It is striking in this context how much emphasis has been placed in German policy strategies on the installation of pollution control technologies, and how little on behavioural change, for example the imposition of strict speed limits on *Autobahnen*. By contrast we might expect a more positive responsiveness to the theme that there was a potential complementarity between economic growth and environmental protection, and hence a willingness to see the pollution control industry as a part of the expanding sector of the economy. The rise in expenditure on environmental research and development is consistent with this approach.

Of course this does not mean that arguments about the costs of environmental protection are redundant. Even if there is a net gain to the economy from investment in environmental protection, we should still expect some sectors to lose, especially if they are required to under-take new investment to upgrade existing plant. But the existence of costs, and hence of political arguments about costs, is consistent with a positive internalisation of environmental responsi-bility by leading economic actors, and one symptom has been the willingness of German firms to undertake environmental protection. The conception of the state playing a developmental role has, thus, provided an ideological framework within which elements of ecological moderni-sation could be incorporated into the thinking of policy elites.

When we turn to the contrasting case of Britain, there are a a number of reasons why there was a lack of policy momentum. Scientific scepticism about the effectiveness of measures like flue-gas desulphurisation rested on the claim that the proposed reduction in sulphur dioxide and nitrogen oxides would not yield significant benefits to forest health, and this in turn rested on the claim that the observed damage to forests could not be clearly related to sulphur deposi-tion. It is tempting to take this as a bad faith argument on the part of the CEGB, but there are grounds for doubting this interpretation. One reason for doubt is that the scientific scepticism was not confined to CEGB scientists. Scientists at the Forestry Commission, whose institutional affiliation ought perhaps to sensitise them to forest health, were equally sceptical of the sulphur-dioxide hypothesis.[40] Moreover, when CEGB-funded research revealed that continual sulphur deposition was contributing to the build-up of sulphur banks with potentially long-term conse-quences, this finding proved to be a turning point in CEGB policy.[41]

Even without the scientific scepticism, however, there were other trends at work that made it difficult to develop vigorous environmental policy. One was a preoccupation with machinery of government questions among policy elites. As part of the creation of the Health and Safety Exec-utive, the Industrial Air Pollution Inspectorate, that is the old Alkali Inspectorate, was integrated with the inspectorates that had been responsible for occupational health and safety. The Royal Commission inveighed against this decision in its 1976 report on air pollution, but it took eleven years for the decision to be reversed and a new location to be found for the air inspectorate along with other inspectorates in Her Majesty's Inspectorate of Pollution.[42] This preoccupation with machinery of government issue was not confined to this one case. A continuation of the theme can be seen in the 1990 strategic White Paper, *This Common Inheritance*, the bulk of whose posi-tive proposals were procedural rather than substantive, and directed to improving the co-ordination of policy within government. Current Labour Party thinking duplicates the preoccupation.

This was reinforced by the Royal Commission's pursuit of one of its principal themes during this period, namely its concern with the cross-media effects of pollution control. The development of this theme by the Royal Commission is of interest, since it clearly has a strong relationship to one of the central themes of ecological modernisation that stresses the intercon-nectedness of natural systems. In its 1976 report on *Air Pollution* the Royal Commission high-lighted the problem of cross-media transfers by pointing out that the solution to an air pollution problem can sometimes involve a technology that worsens pollution in some other medium.[43] Its solution to this problem was to create a unified pollution inspectorate which would operate under the principle of best practicable environmental option. In effect they Royal Commission was recommending an incremental adaptation to the traditional British approach to pollution control, by which an inspectorate in central government could use its wide discretion and powers of negotiation to secure optimal reductions of pollution from operators of scheduled works at low cost. No doubt had the recommendations of the Royal Commission been accepted shortly after they were made, Britain would have entered the 1980s with a more efficient and effective system of environmental administration than it did, although it is questionable whether with the widespread attachment to the old informal procedures it still would have been adequate to meet the environmental challenges that the international context was beginning to impose.

One way of highlighting this point is to note how wide in formal, legal terms was the discretion of the air pollution inspectorate to regulate in matters of atmospheric emissions. Under the legislation operators of licensed premises, known as 'scheduled works', were required to use the 'best practical means' to reduce their pollution within specified limits. The head of the air pollution inspectorate, the chief inspector, had the discretion to say what constituted 'best practicable means' for any given type of process. Formally, therefore, the chief inspector could simply have decided that flue-gas desulphurisation was the best practicable means for reducing sulphur-dioxide emissions from large combustion plants. The absence of action at this level reflects the constraints of governing party preference under which all civil servants work.

There were, in addition, two features of the Thatcher Government programme that were always going to make to vigorous development of pollution control unlikely. The first was its desire to maintain strict controls on public expenditure. The second was its adherence to neo-liberal, laissez-faire economics. The control of public expenditure was relevant because the electricity-generating industry was in public ownership throughout most of the 1980s, and technically any investment undertaken by a nationalised industry adds to the level of public expenditure. Similar considerations applied to water pollution control, which was the responsibility of the Regional Water Authorities. In order to meet improved environmental standards for either water or air, new investment would have been needed, and the public expenditure implications of this encountered resistance from the Thatcher Government's desire tightly to constrain public spending.

But the policy of the Thatcher Government was informed not simply by a desire to balance expenditure against income but also by a vision of the role of the state in relation to the economy and civil society. According to this conception the role of the state is to provide the framework within which economic agents can pursue their own goals; it is not to impose some collective view about where and how economic development is to take place. According to the most sophisticated account of the theory behind this view, in the work of Hayek, public officials are simply unable to know enough about the detailed workings of the economy to substitute their view of what will be profitable to pursue for the view of private entrepreneurs. It follows from this assumption that it ought not to be the role of the state to plan for the future or to promote new technologies. In so doing, it would merely be trying to second guess the outcomes of future market transactions, and this it will inevitably do badly. In this respect the libertarian conservatism of the Thatcher administration was unable to grasp one of the central elements of the ideology of ecological modernisation, namely that the public authorities needed to promote high environmental quality standards, in order to accomplish the goal of promoting greater global competitiveness. In this respect too, ecological modernisation is mercantilism with a green twist; libertarian conservatism is its antithesis.

For a variety of ideological and institutional reasons, therefore, the German policy process provided a more hospitable environment for the ideas of ecological modernisation than did the British policy process. British debates never escaped the belief that there was an inevitable tension between environmental protection and economic development. German debates did, but they selected those elements of the ideology of ecological modernisation they found most congenial. We have in these contrasting examples, then, identified some of the main sources of policy development and sought to understand the political dynamics of the Anglo-German comparison. What does the case study say about more general analytic issues?

Implications for Analysis

I have argued in this chapter that the widely divergent stances of the British and German governments cannot be understood solely in the idiom of rational choice politics, even when that idiom is supplemented by an emphasis upon institutional variations that would make it rational for politicians and policy-makers to develop policies in one way in one country and in a contrary way in another country. Such an approach threatens to obscure the discursive and justificatory aspects of policy development, and therefore threatens to understate how changing ideological perceptions can tilt the balance of argument in favour of one advocacy coalition rather than another. This is not to say that changes at the level of ideology provide the sole basis for understanding policy developments. Rational choice analysis may provide key actors within the policy system with the incentive to take up some arguments rather than others, and institutional contexts may provide circumstances within which some arguments carry greater weight than others. Indeed, it will be true that the possibility of mounting some arguments, for example those connected with constitutional principles, are only possible given a certain institutional context, because their use depends upon an ability of the courts to intervene in the processes of environmental standard-setting. Policy argument does not take place in an 'ideal speech situation', but in the rough and tumble of political competition and in the historically determined circumstances of those institutions given and transmitted from the past. Nevertheless, although the self-interested motivations of key policy actors and the institutional realities of bureaucratic politics may limit the rationality of policy discourse they do not entirely supplant it, and ideas and principles may play an independent role in the determination of policy outputs.

Such a conclusion also has implications for the idiom of systems analysis. There is no doubt that the functions of legitimating state action and securing mass loyalty do have to be discharged by the political-administrative subsystem, and it may be that these functions are in tension with the imperative of capital accumulation. But the emergence of the ideology of ecological modernisation may show that this conflict is not as fundamental as may be thought. In societies in which one of the central legitimating devices rests upon the ability to deliver to populations increasing standards of living, the capacity to redefine the terms under which that will be accomplished is a potentially important political weapon. The challenge of environmental protection suggests that how the function of legitimation is carried out is as important as whether it is carried out. Moreover, it may be significant that the home of the theory of the legitimation crisis has been Germany, a society in which a high emphasis has traditionally been placed both on capital accumulation and on the processes of public accountability through the principles of the *Rechtsstaat*. Hence, the specification of system functions may well itself depend upon an intellectual understanding of political cultures that are themselves affected by the dominant ideologies within any particular political system.

The contrast between Britain and Germany suggests therefore that our idioms of analysis may need to be combined in complex ways when we examine the effects of new conceptions of pollution control policy. But, as critics of the strategy of the 1970s will point out, there are other dimensions to the critique of pollution control policy apart from technology enhancement and economic competitiveness.

Notes

1. Since unification in 1990, the nomenclature for the Federal Republic has become confused and tortuous. To avoid having always to refer to the 'former Federal Republic' or 'the former West Germany', I shall most often simply speak of 'Germany' meaning the Federal Republic established in 1949 and contained in the same boundaries until 1990.

2. S. Boehmer-Christiansen and J. Skea, *Acid Politics* (London and New York: Belhaven Press, 1991), 4.

3. C. C. Park, *Acid Rain* (London and New York: Routledge, 1987), 1–2.

4. Strictly the term to describe the phenomenon should be 'acid deposition', since this covers the variety of pathways that acidification takes. However, the term 'acid rain' is so widely used that it is rather pedantic to stick to the strictly scientific designation.

5. R. Levitt, *Implementing Public Policy* (London: Croom Helm, 1980) and A. Weale, T. O'Riordan, and L. Kramme, *Controlling Pollution in the Round* (London: Anglo-German Foundation, 1991), chap. 5. See also A. Blowers, 'Transition or Transformation? Environmental Policy under Thatcher', *Public Administration*, 65: 3 (1987), 277–94; H. Weidner, *Clean Air Policy in Great Britain: Problem-Shifting as Best Practicable Means* (Berlin: Edition Sigma, 1987).

6. For a good discussion reflecting the experience of the late 1970s as well as the 1980s in Germany, see H. Weidner, *Air Pollution Control Strategies and Policies in the Federal Republic of Germany* (Berlin: Edition Sigma, 1986).

7. R. Mayntz u.a., *Vollzugsprobleme der Umweltpolitik* (Wiesbaden: Rat Van Sachverständigen Umweltfragen, 1978).

8. E. Müller, *Innenwelt der Unweltpolitik* (Opladen: Westdeutscher Verlag, 1986), esp. 114–43.

9. Boehmer-Christiansen and Skea, *Acid Politics*, chap. 10.

10. Weale, O'Riordan, and Kramme, *Controlling Pollution in the Round*, chap. 4.

11. OECD, *Environmental Indicators: A Preliminary Set* (Paris: OECD, 1991), 21–3.

12. Ibid. 21.

13. Boehmer-Christiansen and Skea, *Acid Politics*, chap. 12.

14. N. Haigh, *EEC Environmental Policy and Britain* (London: Longman, 1987 edition, revised 1989), 61–9.

15. G. Lean, 'The Role of the Media', in L. Roberts and A. Weale (eds.), *Innovation and Environmental Risk* (London and New York: Belhaven Press, 1991), 23.

16. Compare Albert Weale, *The New Politics of Pollution* (Manchester: Manchester University Press, 1992), chap. 5.

17. P. A. Sabatier, 'Knowledge, Policy-Oriented Learning and Policy Change', *Knowledge: Creation, Diffusion, Utilization*, 8: 4 (1987), 661–2.

18. Compare Park, *Acid Rain*, chap. 10.

19. Boehmer-Christiansen and Skea, *Acid Politics*, chap. 10.

20. W. H. Riker, *The Theory of Political Coalitions* (New Haven and London: Yale University Press, 1962).

21. R. Inglehart, *The Silent Revolution* (Princeton: Princeton University Press, 1977) and 'Value Change in Industrial Societies', *American Political Science Review*, 81: 4 (1987), 1289–1303; for the alleged cultural difference between Britain and Germany, see Boehmer-Christiansen and Skea, *Acid Politics*, 58–63.

22. W. H. Riker, *Liberalism versus Populism* (San Francisco: W. H. Freeman and Co., 1982).

23. K. Marx and F. Engels, *The German Ideology*, in K. Marx and F. Engels, *Collected Works*, v (London: Lawrence and Wishart, 1976), 27–8. Marx and Engels note in this passage that '. . . when the German market was glutted . . . the business was spoiled in the usual German manner by cheap and spurious production, deterioration in quality, adulteration of the raw materials, falsification of labels, fictitious purchases, bill-jobbing and a credit system devoid of any real basis.' It will be no part of my argument to uphold this as an accurate account of the contemporary German economy, whatever may have been true in the 1840s.

24. Commission of the European Communities, *Fourth Environmental Action Programme*, 1987–92, COM (86) 485 final (Luxembourg: Office for Official Publications of the European Communities, 1986), 3.

25. House of Lords, Select Committee on the European Communities, *Fourth Environmental Action Programme* (London: HMSO, 1987), 1986–7 Sessions, HL 135, 53–4.

26. Commission of the European Communities, *Fourth Environmental Action Programme*, 1987–92, COM (86) 485 final.

27. House of Lords Select Committee on the European Communities, *Fourth Environmental Action Programme*, 54.

28. E. Rehbinder, 'Vorsorgeprinzip in Umweltrecht und präventive Umweltpolitik', in U. E. Simonis (Hg.), *Präventive Umweltpolitik* (Frankfurt: Campus Verlag, 1988).

29. House of Lords Select Committee on the European Communities, *Fourth Environmental Action Programme*, 85.

30. Her Majesty's Government, *This Common Inheritance* (London: HMSO, 1990), Cm. 1200, 11.

31. For the discussion on policy styles, see also J. J. Richardson (ed.), *Policy Styles in Western Europe* (London: George Allen and Unwin, 1982).

32. J. Bryce, *Studies in History and Jurisprudence* (New York: Oxford University Press, 1991), chap. 3.

33. J. E. S. Hayward, 'National Aptitudes for Planning in Britain, France and Italy', *Government and Opposition*, 9: 4 (1974), 398, quoted in J. J. Richardson and N. S. J. Watts, 'National Policy Styles and the Environment', International Institute for Environment and Society, Wissenschaftszentrum Berlin, Discussion Paper 85–16.

34. Ibid. 12.

35. *Umweltprogramm der Bundesregierung*, BT-Druck 6/2710, reprinted as *Umweltschtuz* (Stuttgart: Kohlhammer, 1972).

36. See, in particular, the *Voerde* judgement, B VerG, Urt. v. 17.2.1984–7C 8/82, Mannheim, esp. 373–4.

37. A. J. Heidenheimer et al., *Comparative Public Policy*, 3rd edn. (London and Basingstoke: Macmillan, 1990), 343.

38. S. Boehmer-Christiansen, *Forests versus Fossil Fuels?* (Brighton: Science Policy Research Unit, University of Sussex, 1989), 71.

39. A. Shonfield, *Modern Capitalism* (London: Oxford University Press, 1969).

40. Interview evidence by author from member of Forestry Commission.

41. Weale, O'Riordan, and Kramme, *Controlling Pollution in the Round*, 181.

42. Ibid., chap. 5.

43. Royal Commission on Environmental Pollution, *Air Pollution Control: An Integrated Approach*, Fifth Report (London: HMSO, 1976), Cmnd. 6371.

22   A Global Marshall Plan

Al Gore

Human civilization is now so complex and diverse, so sprawling and massive, that it is difficult to see how we can respond in a coordinated, collective way to the global environmental crisis. But circumstances are forcing just such a response; if we cannot embrace the preservation of the earth as our new organizing principle, the very survival of our civilization will be in doubt.

That much is clear. But how should we proceed? How can we create practical working relationships that bring together people who live in dramatically different circumstances? How can we focus the energies of a disparate group of nations into a sustained effort, lasting many years, that will translate the organizing principle into concrete changes—changes that will affect almost every aspect of our lives together on this planet?

We find it difficult to imagine a realistic basis for hope that the environment can be saved, not only because we still lack widespread agreement on the need for this task, but also because we have never worked together globally on any problem even approaching this one in degree of difficulty. Even so, we must find a way to join this common cause, because the crisis we face is, in the final analysis, a global problem and can only be solved on a global basis. Merely addressing one dimension or another or trying to implement solutions in only one region of the world or another will, in the end, guarantee frustration, failure, and a weakening of the resolve needed to address the whole of the problem.

While it is true that there are no real precedents for the kind of global response now required, history does provide us with at least one powerful model of cooperative effort: the Marshall Plan. In a brilliant collaboration that was itself unprecedented, several relatively wealthy nations and several relatively poor nations—empowered by a common purpose—joined to reorganize an entire region of the world and change its way of life. The Marshall Plan shows how a large vision can be translated into effective action, and it is worth recalling why the plan was so successful.

Immediately after World War II, Europe was so completely devastated that the resumption of normal economic activity was inconceivable. Then, in the early spring of 1947, the Soviet Union rejected US proposals for aiding the recovery of German industry, convincing General George Marshall and President Harry Truman, among others, that the Soviets hoped to capitalize on the prevailing economic distress—not only in Germany but also in the rest of Europe. After much discussion and study, the United States launched the basis for the Marshall Plan, technically known as the European Recovery Program (ERP).

The commonly held view of the Marshall Plan is that it was a bold strategy for helping the nations of Western Europe rebuild and grow strong enough to fend off the spread of communism. That popular view is correct—as far as it goes. But the historians Charles Maier and Stanley Hoffman, both professors at Harvard, emphasize the strategic nature of the plan, with its emphasis on the structural causes of Europe's inability to lift itself out of its economic, political, and social distress. The plan concentrated on fixing the bottlenecks—such as the damaged infrastructure, flooded coal mines, and senseless trade barriers—that were impeding the potential for growth in each nation's economy. ERP was sufficiently long-term that it could serve as an overall effort to produce fundamental structural reorientation, not just offer more emergency relief or another "development" program. It was consciously designed to change the dynamic of the systems to which it extended aid, thus facilitating the emergence of a healthy economic pattern. And it was brilliantly administered by Averell Harriman.

Historians also note the Marshall Plan's regional focus and its incentives to promote European integration and joint action. Indeed, from the very beginning the plan tried to facilitate the emergence of a larger political framework—unified Europe; to that end, it insisted that every action be coordinated with all the countries in the region. The recent creation of a unified European Parliament and the dramatic steps toward a European political community to accompany the European Economic Community (EEC) have all come about in large part because of the groundwork of the Marshall Plan.

But when it was put in place, the idea of a unified Europe seemed even less likely than the collapse of the Berlin Wall did only a few years ago—and every bit as improbable as a unified global response to the environmental crisis seems today. Improbable or not, something like the Marshall Plan—a Global Marshall Plan, if you will—is now urgently needed. The scope and complexity of this plan will far exceed those of the original; what's required now is a plan that combines large-scale, long-term, carefully targeted financial aid to developing nations, massive efforts to design and then transfer to poor nations the new technologies needed for sustained economic progress, a worldwide program to stabilize world population, and binding commitments by the industrial nations to accelerate their own transition to an environmentally responsible pattern of life.

But despite the fundamental differences between the late 1940s and today, the model of the Marshall Plan can be of great help as we begin to grapple with the enormous challenge we now face. For example, a Global Marshall Plan must, like the original, focus on strategic goals and emphasize actions and programs that are likely to remove the bottlenecks presently inhibiting the healthy functioning of the global economy. The new global economy must be an inclusive system that does not leave entire regions behind—as our present system leaves out most of Africa and much of Latin America. In an inclusive economy, for instance, wealthy nations can no longer insist that Third World countries pay huge sums of interest on old debts even when the sacrifices necessary to pay them increase the pressure on their suffering populations so much that revolutionary tensions build uncontrollably. The Marshall Plan took the broadest possible view of Europe's problems and developed strategies to serve human needs and promote sustained economic progress; we must now do the same on a global scale.

But strategic thinking is useless without consensus, and here again the Marshall Plan is instructive. Historians remind us that it would have failed if the countries receiving assistance had not shared a common ideological outlook, or at least a common leaning toward a set of similar ideas and values. Postwar Europe's strong preference for democracy and capitalism made the regional integration of economies possible; likewise, the entire world is far closer to a consensus on basic political and economic principles than it was even a few short years ago, and as the philosophical victory of Western principles becomes increasingly apparent, a Global Marshall Plan will be increasingly feasible.

It is fair to say that in recent years most of the world has made three important choices: first, that democracy will be the preferred form of political organization on this planet; second, that modified free markets will be the preferred form of economic organization; and, third, that most individuals now feel themselves to be part of a truly global civilization—prematurely heralded many times in this century but now finally palpable in the minds and hearts of human beings throughout the earth. Even those nations that still officially oppose democracy and capitalism—such as China—seem to be slowly headed in our philosophical direction, at least in the thinking of younger generations not yet in power.

Another motivation for the Marshall Plan was a keen awareness of the dangerous vacuum created by the end of the Axis nations' totalitarian order and the potential for chaos in the absence of any positive momentum toward democracy and capitalism. Similarly, the resounding philosophical defeat of communism (in which the Marshall Plan itself played a significant role) has left an ideological vacuum that invites either a bold and visionary strategy to facilitate the emergence of democratic government and modified free markets throughout the world—in a truly global system—or growing chaos of the kind that is already all too common from Cambodia to Colombia, Liberia to Lebanon, and Zaire to Azerbaijan.

The Marshall Plan, however, depended in part for its success on some special circumstances that prevailed in postwar Europe yet do not prevail in various parts of the world today. For example, the nations of Europe had developed advanced economies before World War II, and they retained a large number of skilled workers, raw materials, and the shared experience of modernity. They also shared a clear potential for regional cooperation—although it may be clearer in retrospect that it was at the time, when the prospect of warm relations between, say, Germany and England seemed remote.

In contrast, the diversity among nations involved in a Global Marshall Plan is simply fantastic, with all kinds of political entities representing radically different stages of economic and political development—and with the emergence of "post-national" entities, such as Kurdistan, the Balkans, Eritrea, and Kashmir. In fact, some people now define themselves in terms of an ecological criterion rather than a political subdivision. For example, "the Aral Sea region" defines people in parts of several Soviet republics who all suffer the regional ecological catastrophe of the Aral Sea. "Amazonia" is used by peoples of several nationalities in the world's largest rain forest, where national boundaries are often invisible and irrelevant.

The diversity of the world's nations and peoples vastly complicates the model used so success-fully in Europe. Even so, another of the Marshall Plan's lessons can still be applied: within this diversity, the plans for catalyzing a transition to a sustainable society should be made with regional groupings in mind and with distinctive strategies for each region. Eastern Europe, for example, has a set of regional characteristics very different from those of the Sahel in sub-Saharan Africa, just as Central America faces challenges very different from those facing, say, the Southeast Asian archipelago.

Many of the impediments to progress lie in the industrial world. Indeed, one of the biggest obstacles to a Global Marshall Plan is the requirement that the advanced economies must undergo a profound transformation themselves. The Marshall Plan placed the burden of change and transition only on the recipient nations. The financing was borne entirely by the United States, which, to be sure, underwent a great deal of change during those same years, but not at the behest of a foreign power and not to discharge any sense of obligation imposed by an inter-national agreement.

The new plan will require the wealthy nations to allocate money for transferring environmen-tally helpful technologies to the Third World and to help impoverished nations achieve a stable population and a new pattern of sustainable economic progress. To work, however, any such effort will also require wealthy nations to make a transition themselves that will be in some ways more wrenching than that of the Third World, simply because powerful established patterns will be disrupted. Opposition to change is therefore strong, but this transition can and must occur—both in the developed and developing world. And when it does, it will likely be within a frame-work of global agreements that obligate all nations to act in concert. To succeed, these agreements must be part of an overall design focused on devising a healthier and more balanced pattern in world civilization that integrates the Third World into the global economy. Just as important, the developed nations must be willing to lead by example; otherwise, the Third World is not likely to consider making the required changes—even in return for substantial assistance. Finally, just as the Marshall Plan scrupulously respected the sovereignty of each nation while requiring all of them to work together, this new plan must emphasize coopera-tion—in the different regions of the world and globally—while carefully respecting the integrity of individual nation-states.

This point is worth special emphasis. The mere mention of any plan that contemplates worldwide cooperation creates instant concern on the part of many—especially conservatives—who have long equated such language with the advocacy of some supranational authority, like a world government. Indeed, some who favor a common global effort tend to assume that a supra-national authority of some sort is inevitable. But this notion is both politically impossible and practically unworkable. The political problem is obvious: the idea arouses so much opposition that further debate on the underlying goals comes to a halt—especially in the United States, where we are fiercely protective of our individual freedoms. The fear that our rights might be jeopardized by the delegation of even partial sovereignty to some global authority ensures that it's simply not going to happen. The practical problem can be illustrated with a question: What conceivable system of world governance would be able to compel individual nations to adopt environmentally sound policies? The administrative problems would be gargantuan, not least because the inefficiency of governance often seems to increase geometrically with the distance between the seat of power and the individuals affected by it; and given the chaotic state of some of the governments that would be subject to that global entity, any such institution would most likely have unintended side effects and complications that would interfere with the underlying goal. As Dorothy Parker once said about a book she didn't like, the idea of a world government "should not be tossed aside lightly; it should be thrown with great force."

But if world government is neither feasible nor desirable, how then can we establish a successful cooperative global effort to save the environment? There is only one answer: we must negotiate international agreements that establish global constraints on acceptable behavior but that are entered into voluntarily—albeit with the understanding that they will contain both incentives and legally valid penalties for noncompliance.

The world's most important supranational organization—the United Nations—does have a role to play, though I am skeptical about its ability to do very much. Specifically, to help monitor the evolution of a global agreement, the United Nations might consider the idea of establishing a Stewardship Council to deal with matters relating to the global environment—just as the Security Council now deals with matters of war and peace. Such a forum could be increasingly useful and even necessary as the full extent of the environmental crisis unfolds.

Similarly, it would be wise to establish a tradition of annual environmental summit meetings, similar to the annual economic summits of today, which only rarely find time to consider the environment. The preliminary discussions of a Global Marshall Plan would, in any event, have to take place at the highest level. And, unlike the economic summits, these discussions must involve heads of state from both the developed and developing world.

In any global agreement of the kind I am proposing, the single most difficult relationship is the one between wealthy and poor nations; there must be a careful balance between the burdens and obligations imposed on both groups of nations. If, for example, any single agreement has a greater impact on the poor nations, it may have to be balanced with a simultaneous agreement that has a greater impact on the wealthy nations. This approach is already developing naturally in some of the early discussions of global environmental problems. One instance is the implicit linkage between the negotiations to save the rain forests—which are found mostly in poor countries—and the negotiations to reduce greenhouse gas emissions—which is especially difficult for wealthy nations. If these negotiations are successful, the resulting agreements will become trade-offs for each other.

The design of a Global Marshall Plan must also recognize that many countries are in different stages of development, and each new agreement has to be sensitive to the gulf between the countries involved, not only in terms of their relative affluence but also their various stages of political, cultural, and economic development. This diversity is important both among those nations that would be on the receiving end of a global plan and among those expected to be on the giving end. Coordination and agreement among the donor countries might, for example, turn out to be the most difficult challenge. The two donor participants in the Marshall Plan, the United States and Great Britain, had established a remarkably close working relationship during the war, which was then used as a model for their postwar collaboration. Today, of course, the United States cannot conceivably be the principal financier for a global recovery program and cannot make the key decisions alone or with only one close ally. The financial resources must now come from Japan and Europe and from wealthy, oil-producing states.

The Western alliance has frequently been unwieldy and unproductive when large sums of money are at stake. Nevertheless, it has compiled an impressive record of military, economic, and political cooperation in the long struggle against communism, and the world may be able to draw upon that model just as the United States and Great Britain built upon their wartime cooperation in implementing the Marshall Plan. Ironically, the collapse of communism has deprived the alliance of its common enemy, but the potential freeing up of resources may create the ideal opportunity to choose a new grand purpose for working together.

Still, a number of serious obstacles face cooperation among even the great powers—the United States, Japan, and Europe—before a Global Marshall Plan could be considered. Japan, in spite of its enormous economic strength, has been reluctant to share the responsibility for world political leadership and thus far seems blind to the need for it to play such a role. And Europe will be absorbed for many years in the intricacies of becoming a unified entity—a challenge further complicated by the entreaties of the suddenly free nations in Eastern Europe that now want to join the EEC.

As a result, the responsibility for taking the initiative, for innovating, catalyzing, and leading such an effort, falls disproportionately on the United States. Yet in the early 1990s our instinct for world leadership often seems not nearly so bold as it was in the late 1940s. The bitter experience of the Vietnam War is partly responsible, and the sheer weariness of carrying the burden of world leadership has taken a toll. Furthermore, we are not nearly as dominant in the world economy as we were then, and that necessarily has implications for our willingness to shoulder large burdens. And our budget deficits are now so large as to stifle our willingness to consider even the most urgent of tasks. Charles Maier points out that the annual US expenditures for the Marshall Plan between 1948 and 1951 were close to 2 percent of our GNP. A similar percentage today would be almost $100 billion a year (compared to our total nonmilitary foreign aid budget of about $15 billion a year).

Yet the Marshall Plan enjoyed strong bipartisan support in Congress. There was little doubt then that government intervention, far from harming the free enterprise system in Europe, was the most effective way to foster its healthy operation. But our present leaders seem to fear almost any form of intervention. Indeed, the deepest source of their reluctance to provide leadership in creating an effective environmental strategy seems to be their fear that if we do step forward, we will inevitably be forced to lead by example and actively pursue changes that might interfere with their preferred brand of laissez-faire, nonassertive economic policy.

Nor do our leaders seem willing to look as far into the future as did Truman and Marshall. In that heady postwar period, one of Marshall's former colleagues, General Omar Bradley, said, "It is time we steered by the stars, not by the lights of each passing ship." This certainly seems to be another time when that kind of navigation is needed, yet too many of those who are responsible for our future appear to be distracted by such "lights of passing ships" as overnight public opinion polls.

In any effort to conceive of a plan to heal the global environment, the essence of realism is recognizing that public attitudes are still changing—and that proposals which are today considered too bold to be politically feasible will soon be derided as woefully inadequate to the task at hand. Yet while public acceptance of the magnitude of the threat is indeed curving upward—and will eventually rise almost vertically as awareness of the awful truth suddenly makes the search for remedies an all-consuming passion—it is just as important to recognize that at the present time, we are still in a period when the curve is just starting to bend. Ironically, at this stage, the maximum that is politically feasible still falls short of the minimum that is truly effective. And to make matters worse, the curve of political feasibility in advanced countries may well look quite different than it does in developing countries, where the immediate threats to well-being and survival often make saving the environment seem to be an unaffordable luxury.

It seems to make sense, therefore, to put in place a policy framework that will be ready to accommodate the worldwide demands for action when the magnitude of the threat becomes clear. And it is also essential to offer strong measures that are politically feasible now—even before the expected large shift in public opinion about the global environment—and that can be quickly scaled up as awareness of the crisis grows and even stronger action becomes possible.

With the original Marshall Plan serving as both a model and an inspiration, we can now begin to chart a course of action. The world's effort to save the environment must be organized around strategic goals that simultaneously represent the most important changes and allow us to recognize, measure, and assess our progress toward making those changes. Each goal must be supported by a set of policies that will enable world civilization to reach it as quickly, efficiently, and justly as possible.

In my view, five strategic goals must direct and inform our efforts to save the global environment. Let me outline each of them briefly before considering each in depth.

The first strategic goal should be **the stabilizing of world population**, with policies designed to create in every nation of the world the conditions necessary for the so-called demographic transition—the historic and well-documented change from a dynamic equilibrium of high birth rates and death rates to a stable equilibrium of low birth rates and death rates. This change has taken place in most of the industrial nations (which have low rates of infant mortality and high rates of literacy and education) and in virtually none of the developing nations (where the reverse is true).

The second strategic goal should be **the rapid creation and development of environmentally appropriate technologies**—especially in the fields of energy, transportation, agriculture, building construction, and manufacturing—capable of accommodating sustainable economic progress without the concurrent degradation of the environment. These new technologies must then be quickly transferred to all nations—especially those in the Third World, which should be allowed to pay for them by discharging the various obligations they incur as participants in the Global Marshall Plan.

The third strategic goal should be **a comprehensive and ubiquitous change in the economic "rules of the road" by which we measure the impact of our decisions on the environment.** We must establish—by global agreement—a system of economic accounting that assigns appropriate values to the ecological consequences of both routine choices in the marketplace by individuals and companies and larger, macroeconomic choices by nations.

The fourth strategic goal should be **the negotiation and approval of a new generation of international agreements** that will embody the regulatory frameworks, specific prohibitions, enforcement mechanisms, cooperative planning, sharing arrangements, incentives, penalties, and mutual obligations necessary to make the overall plan a success. These agreements must be especially sensitive to the vast differences of capability and need between developed and undeveloped nations.

The fifth strategic goal should be **the establishment of a cooperative plan for educating the world's citizens about our global environment**—first by the establishment of a comprehensive program for researching and monitoring the changes now under way in the environment in a manner that involves the people of all nations, especially students; and, second, through a massive effort to disseminate information about local, regional, and strategic threats to the environment. The ultimate goal of this effort would be to foster new patterns of thinking about the relationship of civilization to the global environment.

Each of these goals is closely related to all of the others, and all should be pursued simultaneously within the larger framework of the Global Marshall Plan. Finally, the plan should have as its more general, integrating goal **the establishment, especially in the developing world—of the social and political conditions most conducive to the emergence of sustainable societies**—such as social justice (including equitable patterns of land ownership); a commitment to human rights; adequate nutrition, health care, and shelter; high literacy rates; and greater political freedom, participation, and accountability. Of course, all specific policies should be chosen as part of serving the central organizing principle of saving the global environment.

23 From Industrial Society to the Risk Society: Questions of Survival, Social Structure, and Ecological Enlightenment

Ulrich Beck

Are Risks Timeless?

Aren't risks at least as old as industrial society, possibly even as old as the human race itself? Isn't all life subject to the risk of death? Aren't and weren't all societies in all epochs 'risk societies'?

One the contrary, should we not (or must we not) be discussing the fact that since the beginning of industrialization, threats—famines, epidemics, or natural catastrophes—have been continually reduced? To list only a few key words: the reduction of infant mortality, the 'bonus years' (Imhof), the achievements of the welfare state, the enormous progress in technological perfection over the past hundred years. Isn't the Federal Republic of Germany, in particular, an Eldorado of bureaucratically organized care and caution?

Certainly there are 'new risks', such as nuclear power, chemical and biotechnical production, and the like. But, considered mathematically or physically, are these not dangers of great scope, but also of exceedingly small, actually negligible probability? Looking at them coolly and rationally, does that not imply that they should be given a lesser status than long accepted risks, such as the incredible carnage on the highways or the risks to smokers?

Certainly, ultimate security is denied to us human beings. But is it not also true that the unavoidable 'residual risks' are the downside of the opportunities—for prosperity, relatively high social security, and general comfort—that developed industrial society offers to the majority of its members in a historically unparalleled manner? Is the dramatization of such risks not in the end a typical media spectacle, ignoring established expert opinion, a 'new German anxiety', as untenable and just as short-lived as the debacle regarding the 'railroad sickness' from the end of the preceding century?

And finally, aren't risks a central concern of the engineering and physical sciences? What business has the sociologist here? Isn't that once again typical?

From *Theory, Culture, and Society*, 9: 1 (1992), 97–123. Reprinted with permission of Sage Publications Ltd.

The Calculus of Risk: Predictable Security in the Face of an Open Future

Human dramas—plagues, famines, and natural disasters, the looming power of gods and demons—may or may not quantifiably equal the destructive potential of modern mega-technologies in hazardousness. They differ essentially from 'risks' in my sense, since they are not based on decisions, or more specifically, decisions that focus on techno-economic advantages and opportunities and accept hazards as simply the dark side of progress. This is my first point: risks presume industrial, that is, techno-economic decisions and considerations of utility. They differ from 'war damage' by their 'normal birth', or more precisely, their 'peaceful origin' in the centres of rationality and prosperity with the blessings of the guarantors of law and order. They differ from pre-industrial natural disasters by their origin in decision-making, which is of course never conducted by individuals but by entire organizations and political groups.[1]

The consequence is fundamental: pre-industrial hazards, no matter how large and devastating, were 'strokes of fate' raining down on mankind from 'outside' and attributable to an 'other'—gods, demons, or Nature. Here too there were countless accusations, but they were directed against the gods or God, 'religiously motivated', to put it simply, and not—like industrial risks—politically charged. For with the origin of industrial risks in decision-making the problem of social accountability and responsibility irrevocably arises, even in those areas where the prevailing rules of science and law permit accountability only in exceptional cases. People, firms, state agencies, and politicians are responsible for industrial risks. As we sociologists say, the social roots of risks block the 'externalizability' of the problem of accountability.[2]

Therefore, it is not the number of dead and wounded, but rather a social feature, their industrial self-generation, which makes the hazards of mega-technology a political issue. The question remains however: must one not view and assess the past 200 years as a period of continual growth in calculability and precautions in dealing with industrially produced insecurities and destruction? In fact, a very promising approach, and one barely explored to date, is to trace the (political) institutional history of evolving industrial society as the conflict-laden emergence of a system of rules for dealing with industrially produced risks and insecurities (see Ewald 1986; Evers and Nowotny 1987; Böhret 1987; Lau 1988).

The idea of reacting to the uncertainties that lie in opening and conquering new markets or in developing and implementing new technologies with collective agreements—insurance contracts for instance, which burden the individual with general fees just as much as they relieve him from dramatic damage cases—is hardly a new social invention. Its origins go back to the beginnings of intercontinental navigation, but with the growth of industrial capitalism, insurance was continually perfected and expanded into nearly all problem areas of social action. Consequences that at first affect only the individual become 'risks', systematically caused, statistically describable and in that sense 'predictable' types of events, which can therefore also be subjected to supra-individual and political rules of recognition, compensation, and avoidance.

The calculus of risks connects the physical, the engineering, and the social sciences. It can be applied to completely disparate phenomena not only in health management—from the risks of smoking to those of nuclear power—but also to economic risks, risks of old age, of unemployment, of traffic accidents, of certain phases of life, and so forth. In addition, it permits a type of 'technological moralization' which no longer need employ moral and ethical imperatives directly. To give an example, the place of the 'categorical imperative' is taken by the mortality rates under certain conditions of air pollution. In this sense, one could say that the calculus of risk exemplifies a type of ethics without morality, the mathematical ethics of the technological age. The triumph of the calculus of risks would probably not have been possible if fundamental advantages were not tied to it.

The first of these lies in the fact that risks open the opportunity to document statistically consequences that were at first always personalized and shifted onto individuals. In this way they are revealed as systematic events, which are accordingly in need of a general political regulation. Through the statistical description of risks (say in the form of accident probabilities) the blinkers of individualization drop off—and this is not yet sufficiently the case with environmental diseases such as pseudo-croup, asthma, or even cancer. A field for corresponding political action is opened up: accidents on the job, for instance, are not blamed on those whose health they have already ruined anyway, but are stripped of their individual origin and related instead to the plant organization, the lack of precautions and so on.

A second advantage is closely connected to the first: insurance payments are agreed on and guaranteed on a no-fault basis (setting aside the extreme cases of gross negligence or intentional damage). In that way, legal battles over causation become unnecessary and moral outrage is moderated. Instead, an incentive for prevention is created for businesses, in proportion to the magnitude of the insurance costs—or perhaps not.

The decisive thing, however, is ultimately that in this manner the industrial system is made capable of dealing with its own unforeseeable future. The calculus of risks, protection by insurance liability laws and the like promise the impossible: events that have not yet occurred become the object of current action—prevention, compensation or precautionary after-care. As the French sociologist François Ewald (1986) shows in detailed studies, the 'invention' of the calculus of risks lies in making the incalculable calculable, with the help of accident statistics, through generalizable settlement formulae as well as through the generalized exchange principle of 'money for damages'. In this way, a norm system of rules for social accountability, compensation, and precautions, always very controversial in its details, creates present security in the face of an open uncertain future. Modernity, which brings uncertainty to every niche of existence, finds its counter-principle in a *social compact against industrially produced hazards and damages*, stitched together out of public and private insurance agreements.

Politically and programmatically, this pact for the containment and 'just' distribution of the consequences of the standard industrial revolution is situated somewhere between socialism and liberalism, because it is based on the systematic creation of consequences and hazards, but at the same time involves individuals in preventing and compensating for them. The consensus that can be achieved with it always remains unstable, conflict-laden and in need of revision. For that very reason, however, it represents the core, the inner 'social logic' of the consensus on progress, which—in principle—legitimated techno-economic development in the first phase of industrialism. Where this 'security pact' is violated wholesale, flagrantly and systematically, the consensus on progress itself is consequently at stake.

Risk and Threat: On the Overlapping of Normal and Exceptional Conditions

My decisive idea, and the one that leads us further, is that this is precisely what has happened in a series of technological challenges with which we are concerned today—nuclear power, many types of chemical and bio-technological production as well as the continuing and threatening ecological destruction. The foundations of the established risk logic are being subverted or suspended.[3]

Put another way, since the middle of this century the social institutions of industrial society have been confronted with the historically unprecedented possibility of the destruction through decision-making of all life on this planet. This distinguishes our epoch not only from the early phase of the industrial revolution, but also from all other cultures and social forms, no matter how diverse and contradictory these may have been in detail. If a fire breaks out, the fire brigade comes; if a traffic accident occurs, the insurance pays. This interplay between beforehand and afterwards, between the future and security in the here and now, because precautions have been taken even for the worst imaginable case, has been revoked in the age of nuclear, chemical, and genetic technology. In all the brilliance of their perfection, nuclear power plants have suspended the principle of insurance not only in the economic, but also in the medical, psychological, cultural, and religious sense. *The residual risk society has become an uninsured society*, with protection paradoxically diminishing as the danger grows.

There is no institution, neither concrete nor probably even conceivable, that would be prepared for the 'WIA', the 'worst imaginable accident', and there is no social order that could guarantee its social and political constitution in this worst possible case.[4] There are many, however, which are specialized in the only remaining possibility: denying the dangers. For after-care, which guarantees security even against hazards, is replaced by the dogma of technological infallibility, which will be refuted by the next accident. The queen of error, science, becomes the guardian of this taboo. Only 'communist' reactors, but not those in West Germany, are empirical creations of the human hand which can toss all their theories onto the scrap-heap. Even the simple question 'What if it does happen after all?' ends up in the void of unpreparedness for after-care. Correspondingly, political stability in risk societies is the stability of not thinking about things.

Put more precisely, nuclear, chemical, genetic, and ecological mega-hazards abolish the four pillars of the calculus of risks. First, one is concerned here with global, often irreparable damage that can no longer be limited; the concept of monetary compensation therefore fails. Second, precautionary after-care is excluded for the worst imaginable accident in the case of fatal hazards; the security concept of anticipatory monitoring of results fails. Third, the 'accident' loses its delimitations in time and space, and therefore its meaning. It becomes an event with a beginning and no end; an 'open-ended festival' of creeping, galloping, and overlapping waves of destruction. But that implies: standards of normality, measuring procedures and therefore the basis for calculating the hazards are abolished; incomparable entities are compared and calculation turns into obfuscation.

The problem of the incalculability of consequences and damage becomes clear with particular vividness in the lack of accountability for them. The scientific and legal recognition and attribution of hazards takes place in our society according to the principle of causality, the polluter-pays principle. But what strikes engineers and lawyers as self-evident, even virtually demanded by ethics, has extremely dubious, paradoxical consequences in the realm of mega-hazards. One example: the legal proceedings against the lead crystal factory in the community of Altenstadt in the Upper Palatinate (reported in *Der Spiegel*, 46 (1986): 32 ff.).

Flecks of lead and arsenic the size of a penny had fallen on the town, and fluoride vapours had turned leaves brown, etched windows and caused bricks to crumble away. Residents were suffering from skin rashes, nausea, and headaches. There was no question where all of that originated. The white dust was pouring visibly from the smokestacks of the factory. A clear case. A clear case? On the tenth day of the trial the presiding judge offered to drop charges in return for a fine of DM 10,000, a result which is typical of environmental crimes in the Federal Republic (1985: 13,000 investigations, twenty-seven convictions with prison terms, twenty-four of those suspended, the rest dropped).

How is that possible? It is not only the lack of laws and not merely the legendary shortcomings in applying them which protect the criminals. The reasons lie deeper and cannot be eliminated by the staunch appeals to the police and the law-makers that issue ever more loudly from the ranks of the environmentalists. A conviction is blocked by the very thing that was supposed to achieve it: the strict application of the (individually interpreted) polluter-pays principle.

In the case of the lead crystal factory, the commission of the crime could not be and was not denied by anyone. A mitigating factor came into play for the culprits: there were three other glass factories in the vicinity which emitted the same pollutants. Notice: the more pollution is committed, the less is committed.

More precisely: the more liberally the acceptable levels are set, the greater the number of smokestacks and discharge pipes through which pollutants and toxins are emitted, the lower the 'residual probability' that a culprit can be made responsible for the general sniffling and coughing, that is to say, the less pollution is produced. Whereas at the same time—one does not exclude the other—the general level of contamination and pollution is increasing. Welcome to the real-life travesty of the hazard technocracy![5]

This organized irresponsibility is based fundamentally on a confusion of centuries. The hazards to which we are exposed date from a different century than the promises of security which attempt to subdue them. Herein lies the foundation for both phenomena: the periodic outbreak of the contradictions of highly organized security bureaucracies and the possibility of normalizing these 'hazard shocks' over and over again. At the threshold of the twenty-first century, the challenges of the age of atomic, genetic, and chemical technology are being handled with concepts and recipes that are derived from early industrial society of the nineteenth and the early twentieth centuries.[6]

Is there an operational criterion for distinguishing between risks and threats? The economy itself reveals the boundary line of what is tolerable with economic precision, through the refusal of private insurance. Where the logic of private insurance disengages, where the economic risks of insurance appear too large or too unpredictable to insurance concerns, the boundary that separates 'predictable' risks from uncontrollable threats has obviously been breached again and again in large and small ways.

Two types of consequences are connected in principle to this overstepping of the bounds. First, the *social* pillars of the calculus of risks fail; security degenerates into mere technical safety. The secret of the calculus of risks, however, is that technical *and* social components work together: limitation, accountability, compensation, precautionary after-care. These are now running in neutral, and social and political security can be created solely by means of a contradictory maximizing of technical superlatives.

Second, a central part of this political dynamic is the social contradiction between highly developed safety bureaucracies on the one hand, and the open legalization of previously unseen, gigantic threats on the other, without any possibility of after-care. A society which is oriented from top to toe toward security and health is confronted with the shock of their diametrical opposites, destruction and threats which scorn any precautions against them.

Two contrary lines of historical development are converging in late twentieth-century Europe: a level of security founded on the perfection of techno-bureaucratic norms and controls, and the spread and challenge of historically new hazards which slip through all the meshes of law, technology, and politics. This contradiction, which is not of a technical, but a social and political character, remains hidden in the 'confusion of centuries' (Günther Anders). And this will continue so long as the old industrial patterns of rationality and control last. It will break up to the extent that improbable events become probable. 'Normal catastrophes' is the name Charles Perrow (1988) gives in his book to this predictability with which what was considered impossible occurs—and the more emphatically it is denied, the sooner, more destructively and shockingly it occurs. In the chain of publicly revealed catastrophes, near-catastrophes, whitewashed security faults, and scandals the technically centred claim to the control of governmental and industrial authority shatters—quite independently of the established measure of hazards: the number of dead, the danger of the contaminations, and so on.

The central social-historical and political potential of ecological, nuclear, chemical, and genetic hazards lies in the collapse of administration, in the collapse of techno-scientific and legal rationality and of institutional political security guarantees which those hazards conjure up for everyone. That potential lies in the unmasking of the concretely existing anarchy which has grown out of the denial of the social production and administration of mega-hazards.[7]

Hazards of the nuclear and chemical age, therefore, have a social as well as a physical explosiveness. As the hazards appear, the institutions which are responsible for them, and then again not responsible, are pressed into competition with the security claims they are compelled to issue, a competition from which they can only emerge as losers. On the one hand, they come under permanent pressure to make even the safest things safer; on the other hand, this overtaxes expectations and sharpens attention, so that in the end not only accidents, but even the suspicion of them, can cause the façades of security claims to collapse. The other side of the recognition of hazards is the failure of the institutions that derive their justification from the non-existence of hazard. That is why the 'social birth' of a hazard is an event which is equally improbable and dramatic, traumatic and unsettling to the entire society.

Precisely because of their explosiveness in the social and political space, hazards remain distorted objects, ambiguous, interpretable, resembling modern mythological creatures, which now appear to be an earthworm, now again a dragon, depending on perspective and the state of interests. The ambiguity of risks also has its basis in the revolutions which their official unambiguity had to provoke. The institutions of developed industrial society—politics, law, engineering sciences, industrial concerns—accordingly command a broad arsenal for 'normalizing' non-calculable hazards. They can be under-estimated, compared out of existence or made anonymous causally and legally. These instruments of a symbolic politics of detoxification enjoy correspondingly great significance and popularity (this is shown by Fischer 1989).

Ministers of the Environment, no matter what their party affiliation, are not to be envied. Hampered by the scope of their ministry and its financial endowment, they must keep the causes largely constant and counter the cycle of destruction in a primarily symbolic fashion. A 'good' minister of the environment ultimately is the one who stages activities in a publicity-grabbing way, piling up laws, creating bureaucratic jurisdications, centralizing information. He may even dive into the Rhine with a daredevil smile or try a spoonful of contaminated whey powder, provided the media eyes of a frightened public are trained upon him. Dogged adherence to a line must be sold with the same TV smile and 'good arguments' as a 180-degree shift in direction. First the nuclear reprocessing plant at Wackersdorf is flogged through with police power, only to have to shout 'April Fools!' after others who obviously know more about it have turned it down.

But gradually, one accident at a time, the logic of the institutionalized non-management of problems can turn into its opposite: what does probability-based safety—and thus the entire scientific diagnosis—mean for the evaluation of the worst imaginable accident, whose occurrence would leave the experts' theories intact but destroy their lives?

Sooner or later the question will arise as to the value of a legal system that regulates and pursues every detail of the technically manageable minor risks, but legalizes the mega-hazards by virtue of its authority, to the extent they cannot be minimized technically, and burdens everyone with them, including those who resist?

How can a democratic political authority be maintained which must counter the escalating consciousness of hazards with energetic safety claims, but in that very process puts itself constantly on the defensive and risks its entire credibility with every accident or sign of an accident?

The Role of Technology and the Natural Sciences in the Risk Society

There is a public dispute over a new ethics of research in order to avoid incalculable and inhuman results. To limit oneself to that debate is to misunderstand the degree and type of involvement of the engineering sciences in the production of hazards. An ethical renewal of the sciences, even if it were not to become entangled in the thicket of ethical viewpoints, would be like a bicycle brake on an intercontinental jet, considering the autonomization of technological development and its interconnections with economic interests. Moreover, we are not concerned merely with the ethics of research, but also with its logic and with the unity of culprits and judges (experts) of the engineering sciences in the technocracy of hazards.

An initial insight is central: in matters of hazards, no one is an expert—particularly not the experts. Predictions of risk contain a double fuzziness. First, they presume cultural acceptance and cannot produce it. There is no scientific bridge between destruction and protest or between destruction and acceptance. Acceptable risks are ultimately accepted risks. Second, new knowledge can turn normality into hazards overnight. Nuclear energy and the hole in the ozone layer are prominent examples. Therefore: the advancement of science refutes its original claims of safety. *It is the successes of science which sow the doubts as to its risk predictions.*

But conversely, it is also true that acute danger passes the monopoly of interpretation to those who caused it, of all people. In the shock of the catastrophe, people speak of rem, Becquerels or ethylene glycol as if they know what such words mean and they must do so in order to find their way in the most everyday matters. This contradiction must be exposed: on the one hand the engineering sciences involuntarily enact their own self-refutation in their contradictory risk diagnoses. On the other, they continue to administer the privilege handed down to them from the Kaiser's days, the right to determine according to their own internal standards the global social question of the most intensely political nature: how safe is safe enough?

The power of the hard sciences here rests on a simple social construct. They are granted the binding authority—binding for law and politics—to decide on the basis of their own standards what the 'state of technology' demands. But since this general clause is the legal standard for safety, private organizations and committees (for instance, the Society of German Engineers, the Institute for Standards) decide in Germany the amount of hazards to which everyone can be subjected (see Wolf 1987).

If one asks, for instance, what level of exposure to artificially produced radioactivity must be tolerated by the populace, that is, where the threshold of tolerance separating normality from hazardousness is situated, then the Atomic Energy Act gives the general answer that the necessary precautions are to correspond to 'the state of technology' (Sec. 7 II No. 3). This phrase is fleshed out in the 'Guidelines' of the Reactor Safety Commission—an 'advisory council' of the Ministry of the Environment in which representatives of engineering societies hold sway.

In air pollution policy, noise protection, and water policy one always finds the same pattern: laws prescribe the general programme. But anyone who wishes to know how large a continuing ration of standardized pollution citizens are expected to tolerate needs to consult the 'Ordinance on Large Combustion Facilities' or the 'Technical Instructions: Air Quality' and similar works for the (literally) 'irritating' details.

Even the classical instruments of political direction—statutes and administrative regulations—are empty in their central statements. They juggle with the 'state of technology', thus undercutting their own competence, and in its place they elevate 'scientific and technical expertise' to the throne of the civilization of threat.

This *monopoly of scientists and engineers in the diagnosis of hazards*, however, is simultaneously being called into question by the 'reality crisis' of the natural and engineering sciences in their dealings with the hazards they produce. It has not been true only since Chernobyl, but there it first became palpable to a broad public: safety and probable safety, seemingly so close, are worlds apart. The engineering sciences always have only probable safety at their command. Thus, even if two or three nuclear reactors blow up tomorrow, their statements remain true.

Wolf Häfele, the dean of the German reactor industry, wrote in 1974:

It is precisely the interplay between theory and experiment or trial and error which is no longer possible for reactor technology . . . Reactor engineers take account of this dilemma by dividing the problem of technical safety into sub-problems. But even the splitting of the problem can only serve to approximate ultimate safety . . . The remaining 'residual risk' opens the door to the realm of the 'hypothetical' . . . The interchange between theory and experiment, which leads to truth in the traditional sense, is no longer possible . . . I believe it is this ultimate indecisiveness hidden in our plans which explains the particular sensitivities of public debates on the safety of nuclear reactors. (Häfele 1974)

What one hears here is nothing less than the contradiction between experimental logic and atomic peril. Just as sociologists cannot force society into a test tube, engineers cannot let people's reactors blow up all around them in order to test their safety, unless they turn the world into a laboratory. Theories of nuclear reactor safety are testable only after they are built, not beforehand. The expedient of testing partial systems amplifies the contingencies of their interaction, and thus contains sources of error which cannot themselves be controlled experimentally.

If one compares this with the logic of research that was originally agreed upon, this amounts to its sheer reversal. We no longer find the progression, first laboratory then application. Instead, testing comes after application and production precedes research. The dilemma into which the mega-hazards have plunged scientific logic applies across the board; that is, for nuclear, chemical, and genetic experiments *science hovers blindly above the boundary of threats*. Test-tube babies must first be produced, genetically engineered artificial creatures released and reactors built, in order that their properties and safety can be studied. The question of safety, then, must be answered affirmatively before it can even be raised. The authority of the engineers is undermined by this 'safety circle'.

Through the anticipation of application before it has been fully explored, science has itself abolished the boundary between laboratory and society (Beck 1988: chap. 5; Kohn and Weyer 1989). Along with that, the conditions of freedom of research have shifted. Freedom of research implies freedom of application. Today, anyone who demands or grants only freedom of research abolishes research. The power of technology is based in its command of practice. Engineers can directly apply things, where politics must first advise, convince, vote, and then push them through against resistance. This makes technology capable of conducting a policy of the *fait accompli*, which not only puts all the others under constant pressure to react, but also puts them at the mercy of the engineers' judgment for assessment and avoidance of disaster. This power grows with the velocity of the innovations, the lack of clarity regarding their consequences and hazards, and it grows even though the credibility of technological promises of safety is thereby undermined.

Where the monopoly of technology becomes a monopoly on concealed social change, it must be called into question and cancelled by the principle of division of powers—like the earlier 'legal transcendence of the sovereign'. Internally, this implies a redistribution of the burdens of proof and, externally, the liberation of doubt (see Beck 1988: chap. 8, 1990). In all central social issues and committees relative to technological development, systematic alternatives, dissenting voices, dissenting experts, and an interdisciplinary diversity would have to be combined. The exposure of scientific uncertainty is the liberation of politics, law, and the public sphere from their patronization by technocracy.

The Ecological Conflict in Society

If the risk society does not mean only a technical challenge, then the question arises: what political dynamics, what social structure, what conflict scenarios arise from the legalization and normalization of global and uncontrollable systematic threats? To reduce things to an admittedly crude formula: hunger is hierarchical. Even following the Second World War, not everyone went hungry. Nuclear contamination, however, is egalitarian and in that sense 'democratic'. Nitrates in the ground water do not stop at the general director's water tap (see Beck 1986: 48 ff.).[8]

All suffering, all misery, all violence inflicted by people on other people to this point recognized the category of the Other—workers, Jews, blacks, asylum seekers, dissidents, and so forth—and those apparently unaffected could retreat behind this category. *The 'end of the Other', the end of all our carefully cultivated opportunities for distancing ourselves, is what we have become able to experience with the advent of nuclear and chemical contamination.* Misery can be marginalized, but that is no longer true of hazards in the age of nuclear, chemical, and genetic technology. It is there that the peculiar and novel political force of those threats lies. Their power is the power of threat, which eliminates all the protective zones and social differentiations within and between nation states.

It may be true that in the storm tide of threat 'we're all in the same boat', as the cliché goes. But, as is so often the case, here too there are captains, passengers, helmsmen, engineers, and men and women overboard. In other words, there are countries, sectors, and enterprises which *profit* from the production of risk, and others which find their economic existence threatened together with their physical well-being. If, for instance, the Adriatic or the North Sea dies or they are perceived socially as 'hazardous to health'—this difference is cancelled with respect to economic effects— then it is not just the North Sea or the Adriatic which die, along with the life those seas contain and make possible. The economic life in all the towns, sectors, and coastal countries that live directly or indirectly from the commercialization of the sea is also extinguished. At the apex of the future, which reaches into the horizon of the present day, industrial civilization is transformed into a kind of 'world cup' of the global risk society. Destruction of nature and destruction of markets coincide here. It is not what one has or is able to do that determines one's social position and future, but rather where and from what one lives and to what extent others are permitted in a prearranged unaccountability to pollute one's possessions and abilities in the guise of 'environment'.

Even passionate denial, which can certainly count on full official support, has its limits. The revenge of the abstract expert dispute on hazards is its geographic concretion. One can dispute everything, operating the official whitewashing machinery in high gear. That does not prevent, but only accelerates the destruction. In this way, 'toxin-absorbing regions' come into being, crossing national boundaries and old institutional lines of conflict, creating geographical positions whose 'fate' coincides with the industrial destruction of nature (see Beck 1988: 247 ff.).

The greenhouse effect, for example, will raise temperatures and sea levels around the world through the melting of the polar icecaps. The period of warming will submerge entire coastal regions, turn farmland into desert, shift climatic zones in unpredictable ways and dramatically accelerate the extinction of species. *The poorest in the world will be hit the hardest.* They will be least able to adapt themselves to the changes in the environment. Those who find themselves deprived of the basis of their economic existence will flee the zone of misery. A veritable Exodus of eco-refugees and climatic asylum-seekers will flood across the wealthy North; crises in the Third and Fourth Worlds could escalate into wars. Even the climate of world politics will change at a faster pace than is imaginable today. So far, all these are just projections, but we must take them seriously. When they have become reality, it will already be too late to take action.

Many things would be easier here if those countries on the way to industrialization could be spared the mistakes of the highly industrialized countries. But the unchecked expansion of the industrial society is still considered the *via regia* that promises the mastery of many problems— not only those of poverty—so that the prevailing misery often displaces the abstract issues of environmental destruction.

'Threats to nature' are not only that; pointing them out also threatens property, capital, jobs, trade union power, the economic foundation of whole sectors and regions, and the structure of nation states and global markets. Put another way: there is a major distinction between the conflict field of wealth production, from which the nineteenth century derived the experience and premises of industrial and class society, and the conflict field of hazard production in the developed nuclear and chemical age, to which we are only just beginning to become sensitive in sociology. It probably lies in the fact that wealth production produced the antagonisms between capital and labour, while the systematic chemical, nuclear, and genetic threats bring about polarizations between capital and capital—and thus also between labour and labour—cutting across the social order. If the social welfare state had to be forced through against the concerted resistance of the private investors, who were called on to pay in the form of wage and fringe-benefit costs, then *ecological threats split the business camp*. At first glance, it is impossible to discern where and how the boundary runs; or more accurately, who receives the power, and from where, to cause the boundary to run in what way.

While it may still be possible to speak of the 'environment' on the level of an individual operation, this talk becomes simply fictitious on the level of the overall economy, because there a type of 'Russian roulette' is being played behind the increasingly thin walls of the 'environment'. If it is suddenly revealed and publicized in the mass media that certain products contain certain 'toxins' (information policy is receiving a key importance considering the fact that hazards are generally imperceptible in everyday life), then entire markets may collapse and invested capital and effort are instantly devalued.

No matter how abstract the threats may be, their concretizations are ultimately just as irreversible and regionally identifiable. What is denied collects itself into geographical positions, into 'loser regions' which have to pay the tab for the damage and its 'unaccountability' with their economic existence. In this 'ecological expropriation', we are facing the historical novelty of a devaluation of capital and achievement, while relationships of ownership and sometimes even the characteristics of the goods remain constant. Sectors that had nothing or very little causally to do with the production of the threat—agriculture, the food industry, tourism, fisheries, but also retail trade and parts of the service industry—are also among those most affected.

Where the (world) economy splits into risk winners and risk losers—in a manner difficult to define—this polarization will also make its mark upon the structure of employment. First, new types of antagonisms that are specific to countries, sectors, and enterprises arise between groups of employees and correspondingly within and between trade union interest organizations. Second, these are, so to speak, third-hand antagonisms, derived from those between factions of capital, which turn the 'fate of workers' into 'fate' in a further and fundamental dimension. Third, with the intensified consciousness of the corresponding lines of conflict, a sector-specific alliance of the old 'class opponents', labour and capital, may arise. The consequence may be a confrontation between this union–management bloc and other mixed factions over and above the divisions of class differences which have been narrowed under the pressure of 'ecological politicization'.[9]

One has to wonder what an ecological labour movement would really mean. The production and definition of hazards aims largely at the level of products, which escapes almost completely from the influence of the works councils and workers' groups and falls completely under the jurisdiction of management. And this is still at the intra-organizational level. Hazards are produced by business operations, to be sure, but they are defined and evaluated socially—in the mass media, in the experts' debate, in the jungle of interpretations and jurisdications, in courts or with strategic-intellectual dodges, in a milieu and in contexts, that is to say, to which the majority of workers are totally alien. We are dealing with 'scientific battles' waged over the heads of the workers, and fought out instead by intellectual strategies in intellectual milieux. The definition of hazards eludes the grasp of workers and even, as things stand, the approach of trade unions for the most part. Workers and unions are not even those primarily affected; that group consists of the enterprises and management. But as secondary targets they must count on losing their jobs if worst comes to worst.

Even a latent risk definition hits them in the centre of their pride in achievement, their promise of a usable commodity. Labour and labour power can no longer conceive of themselves only as the source of wealth, but must also be perceived socially as the motive force for threat and destruction. The labour society is not only running out of labour, the only thing which gives meaning and solidity to life, as Hannah Arendt puts it ironically, it is also losing even this residual meaning.

Somewhat crudely, one can say in conclusion: what is 'environment' for the polluting industry, is the basis of economic existence for the affected loser regions and loser sectors. The consequence is: political systems in their architecture as nation states on the one hand, and large-scale ecological conflict positions on the other, become mutually autonomous and create 'geopolitical' shifts which place the domestic and international structure of economic and military blocs under completely new stresses, but also offer new opportunities. *The phase of risk society politics which is beginning to make itself heard today in the arena of disarmament and detente in the East–West relationship can no longer be understood nationally, but only internationally, because the social mechanics of risk situations disregards the nation state and its alliance systems.* In the sense, apparently iron-clad political, military, and economic constellations are becoming mobile, and this forces or, better, permits, a new 'European global domestic policy' (Genscher).

Political Reflexivity: The Counterforce of Threat and the Opportunities for Influence by Social Movements

Where progress and fate appear interwoven, the goals of social development are spelled antithetically from the highest to the lowest floor. This is certainly not the first conflict which modern societies have had to master, but it is one of the most fundamental. Class conflicts or revolutions change power relations and exchange elites, but they hold fast to the goals of techno-economic progress and clash over mutually recognized civil rights. The double face of 'self-annihilating progress', however, produces conflicts that cast doubt on the social basis of rationality—science, law, democracy. In that way, society is placed under permanent pressure to negotiate foundations without a foundation. It experiences an institutional destabilization, in which all decisions—from local government policy on speed limits and 'parking lots' to the manufacturing details of industrial goods to the fundamental issues of energy supply, law and technological development—can suddenly be sucked into fundamental political conflicts.

While the façades remain intact, quasi-governmental power positions arise in the research laboratories, nuclear power plants, chemical factories, editorial offices, courts, and so on, in the milieu of hazards dependent on definitions and publicity. Put another way: as the contradictions of the security state are stirred up, systems come to require action and become subject-dependent. The courageous Davids of this world get their chance. The colossal interdependence of threat definitions—the collapse of markets, property rights, trade union power, and political responsibility—brings about key positions and media of 'risk-definition' which cross the social and professional hierarchy.

On the one hand, one can use all one's powers of conviction to pile up arguments for the institutional non-existence of suicidal threats, one need not deny one iota of hope to the institutional hegemony, one can even draw on the distraction of the social movements and the limitations of their political effectiveness, and one must still recognize with equal realism: all this is countered by the opposing power of threat. It is constant and permanent, not tied to interpretations denying it, and even present in places demonstrators have long since abandoned. The probability of improbable accidents grows with time and the number of implemented megatechnologies. Every 'event' arouses memories of all the other ones, not only in Germany, but all over the world.

Different types of revolutions have been contrasted: coups d'état, the class struggle, civilian resistance, and so on. They all have in common the empowering and disempowering of social subjects. Revolution as an autonomized process, as a hidden, latent, permanent condition, in which conditions are involved against their own interests, while political structures or property and power relations remain unchanged—this is a possibility which so far, to my knowledge, has neither been taken into consideration nor thought through. But it is precisely this conceptual scheme into which the *social power of threat* fits. It is the product of the deed, requiring no political authorization and no authentication. Once in existence, awareness of it endangers all institutions—from business to science, from law to politics—which have produced and legitimated it.

Everyone asks: from where will the opposing forces come? It is probably not very promising to place large or small ads for the missing 'revolutionary subject' in hip papers of the subculture. It feels good, of course, to appeal to reason with all the strictness at one's command, and it can do no harm, for the very reason that a realistic view of experience has shown that it leaves few traces behind. One could also found another circle for the solution of global problems. Certainly, it is to be hoped that political parties will catch on.

If all this does not suffice to stimulate alternative political action however, then there remains the knowledge of the activatable political reflexivity of the hazard potential.[10] Three Mile Island, Chernobyl, Hanau, Biblis, Wackersdorf, and so forth: the global experiment of nuclear energy (toxic chemistry) has by now taken over the roles of its own critics, perhaps even more convincingly and effectively than the political counter-movements could ever have managed on their own. This becomes clear not only in the worldwide, unpaid negative advertising at peak news times and on the front pages of papers, but also in the fact that everyone between the Alpine chalets and the North Sea mud flats now understands and speaks the language of the nuclear critics. Under the dictates of necessity, people have passed a kind of crash course in the contradictions of hazard administration in the risk society: on the arbitrariness of acceptable levels and calculation procedures or the unimaginability of the long-term consequences and the possibilities of making them anonymous through statistics. They have learned more information, more vividly, and more clearly than even the most critical critique could have ever taught them or demanded of them.

The most enduring, convincing, and effective critics of nuclear energy (or the chemical industry and so forth) are not the demonstrators outside the fences or the critical public (no matter how important and indispensable they may be). The most influential opponent of the threat industry is the threat industry itself.

To put it differently, the power of the new social movements is not based only on themselves, but also on the quality and scope of the contradictions in which the hazard producing and administering industries are involved in the risk society. Those contradictions become public and scandalous through the needling activities of the social movements. Thus, there is not only an autonomous process of the suppression of dangers, but also opposite tendencies to uncover this suppression, even though they are much less marked and always dependent on the civil courage of individuals and the vigilance of social movements. Catastrophes that touch the vital nerves of society in a context of highly developed bureaucratic safety and welfare arouse the sensationalist greed of the mass media, threaten markets, make sales prospects unpredictable, devalue capital and set streams of voters in motion. Thus the evening news ultimately exceeds even the fantasies of countercultural dissent; daily newspaper reading becomes an exercise in technology critique.

This oppositional power of the unintended revelation of hazards depends of course on overall social conditions, which have so far been fulfilled in only a few countries: parliamentary democracy, (relative) independence of the press, and advanced production of wealth in which the invisible threat of cancer is not overridden for the majority of the populace by acute under-nourishment and famine.

In the co-operation from within and without over and above the boundary lines of the subsystems there are in this sense also symptoms of a strength, which have so far remained almost unnoticed. The socially most astonishing, most surprising and perhaps least understood phenomenon of the 1980s in West Germany is the unexpected renaissance of an 'enormous subjectivity'—inside and outside the institutions (see Beck 1986: chaps. 2 and 4; Beck and Beck-Gernsheim 1990). In this sense it is not an exaggeration to say that *citizens' groups have taken the initiative thematically in this society*. It was they who put the themes of an endangered world on the social agenda, against the resistance of the established parties. Nowhere does this become so clear as in the spectre of the 'new unity' which is haunting Europe. The compulsion to perform ecological lip-service is universal. It unites the Christian Social Union with the Communists, and the chemical industry with its Green critics. All products, absolutely all products, are 'safe for the environment' to say the least. There are rumours that the chemical concerns plan to take out full-page ads announcing themselves as a registered conservation association.

Admittedly this is all just packaging, programmatic opportunism, and perhaps really intentional rethinking now and then. The actions and the points of origin of the facts are largely untouched by it. Yet it remains true: the themes of the future, which are now on everyone's lips, have not originated from the farsightedness of the rulers or from the struggle in Parliament—and certainly not from the cathedrals of power in business, science, and the state. They have been put on the social agenda against the concentrated resistance of this institutionalized ignorance by the entangled, moralizing groups and splinter groups fighting each other over the proper way, split and plagued by doubts. *Democratic subversion has won a quite improbable thematic victory*. And this in Germany, rupturing with an authoritarian everyday culture which, historically, has enabled all official nonsense and insanity with its anticipatory obedience.

Even the surprising aspect of the events in Eastern Europe is after all the rebellion of the really existing individuals against a 'system' that had allegedly dominated them into the very capillaries of daily life. The tiny groups of avowed civil libertarians swell into popular movements that redraw the plans of the civic structure. It is not only the planned economy which is bankrupt. Systems theory, which conceives of society independent of subjects, has also been thoroughly refuted. In a society devoid of consent, revealed as virtually legitimatory, even a gust of wind that brings on the call for freedom can topple the powerful like a house of cards. The soft—orientations, hopes, ideas, people's interests—triumphs over the hard—the organizations, the established, the powerful, and the armed. Eastern Europe is one big citizens' group exulting in a success that is overrunning it.

The differences between protesting citizens in the East and the West are evident and have often been mentioned, but this is less true of the considerable common ground they share. Both are oriented to the grassroots, non-parliamentary, not tied to any particular class or party, and programmatically diffuse or even fragmented. Their Horatio Alger careers in both places are also similar: criminalized, fought, patronized but in the end part of party programmes and inaugural speeches. This has happened with environmental issues, women's issues, and the peace movement, now outstripped by the galloping democratization in Eastern Europe. The 'democracy issue' has reawakened—in the struggles over there for the most basic human rights, here for the enforcement of rights that were only granted partially even in our countries (Rödel et al. 1989). The question, however, of how the universal challenge of an industrial system producing wealth *and* destruction is to be solved democratically remains completely open, both theoretically and practically.

The Utopia of Ecological Democracy

Europe is called to a new social project and has already set off on it. The East–West antagonism as an ideological fortress mentality is breaking up on both sides. The international themes of the risk civilization could move into the resulting vacuum. One sign of this is the pressure for global arrangements which technology, science, and business produce. Another is the dawning of the large and small, the creeping and the galloping suicidal hazards everywhere in the world, and a final sign comes from the elevated standards of promised safety and rationality in developed welfare state capitalism.

These are the horrendous opportunities that offer themselves to a European global domestic policy, not only in the foundation and building of the 'European house', but also by the highly industrialized countries assuming a large portion of the costs for the necessary corrective measures. In the place where the dynamic of industrial development had its origin, in Europe, enlightenment on and against industrial society could also begin. This project of an ecological enlightenment would have to be designed and fought for both on the macro and micro levels. Even in everyday life, because the threats overturn well-worn routine everywhere and represent a spectacular challenge for civil courage—at jobs in industry, in the practices of doctors where people come with their fears and questions, in research which can block off or reveal, in the courts, in the monitoring of the administration and, not least, in the editorial offices of the mass media, where the invisible can be made culturally discernible. There are many concrete concerns in the relationship of the 'European house' to its neighbours on this planet. Among them is the impossibility of appearing any longer with the self-confidence of the donating wealthy, but rather admitting our destructive industrial role and correcting it in thought and action.

The technological project, the technological dogmatism of industrialism must not simply be extended to the ecological crisis, lest an ever more perfect technocracy result from the public dramatization of the dangers. *Industrial society has produced a 'truncated democracy', in which questions of the technological change of society remain beyond the reach of political-parliamentary decision-making.* As things stand, one can say 'no' to techno-economic progress, but that will not change its course in any way. It is a blank check to be honoured—beyond agreement or refusal. That is a manufactured 'natural force' in civilization, an 'industrial middle ages', that must be overcome by more democracy—the production of accountability, redistribution of the burdens of proof, division of powers between the producers and the evaluators of hazards, public disputes on technological alternatives (see Beck 1988: chap. 7).[11] This in turn requires different organizational forms for science and business, science and the public sphere, science and politics, technology and law, and so forth.

The ecological extension of democracy then means: playing off the concert of voices and powers, the development of the independence of politics, law, the public sphere, and daily life against the dangerous and false security of a 'society from the drawing board'.

My suggestion contains two interlocking principles: first, carrying out a division of powers and second, the creation of a public sphere. Only a strong, competent public debate, 'armed' with scientific arguments is capable of separating the scientific wheat from the chaff and allowing the institutions for directing technology—politics and law—to reconquer the power of their own judgement.

The means: with regard to all issues that are central to society dissenting voices, alternative experts, an interdisciplinary variety and, not least, alternatives to be developed systematically must always be combined. The public sphere in co-operation with a kind of 'public science' would be charged as a second centre of the 'discursive checking' of scientific laboratory results in the crossfire of opinions. Their particular responsibility would comprise all issues that concern the broad outlines and dangers of scientific civilization and are chronically excluded in standard science. The public would have the role of an 'open upper chamber'. It would be charged to apply the standard, 'How do we wish to live?' to scientific plans, results, and hazards.

That presupposes that research will fundamentally take account of the public's questions and be addressed to them and not just multiply our common problems in an economic short circuit with industry. Perhaps it would be possible that through these two steps—an opening of science from within and the filtering out of its limitations in a public test of its practice—that politics and science could successively hone their direction-finding and self-monitoring instruments—instruments that are now largely inactive.

The cultural blindness of daily life in the civilization of threat can ultimately not be removed; but culture 'sees' in symbols. The images in the news of skeletal trees or of dying seals have opened people's eyes. Making the threats publicly visible and arousing attention in detail, in one's own living space—these are cultural eyes through which the 'blind *citoyens*' can perhaps win back the autonomy of their own judgement.

To conclude with a question: what would happen if radioactivity itched? Realists, also called cynics, will answer: people would invent something, perhaps a salve, to 'turn off' the itching. A good business then. Certainly, explanations would soon arise and would enjoy great public effect: they would claim that the itching had no meaning, that it might be correlated to other factors besides radioactivity, and that it was harmless in any case, unpleasant but provably harmless. If everyone ran around scratching themselves and with rashes on their skin, and if photo sessions with fashion models as well as management meetings of the united denial institutes took place with all participants scratching themselves, it would have to be assumed that such explanations would have little chance of surviving. In that case, nuclear policy as well as dealings with modern mega-hazards in general, would confront a completely changed situation: the object being disputed and negotiated would be culturally perceptible.[12]

That is precisely where the future of democracy is being decided: are we dependent in all the details of life and death issues on the judgement of experts, even dissenting experts, or will we win back the competence to make our own judgement through a culturally created perceptibility of the hazards? Is the only alternative still an authoritarian technocracy or a critical one? Or is there a way to counter the incapacitation and expropriation of daily life in the civilization of threat?

Translated by Mark Ritter

Notes

This essay is a revised and expanded version of a text entitled 'Risk Society: Questions of Survival, Social Structure and Ecological Enlightenment' ('Risikogesellschaft. Überlebensfragen, Sozialstruktur und ökologische Aufklärung') which appeared in *Aus Politik und Zeitgeschicte*, B (36/1989): 3–13.

1. Niklas Luhmann (1990) has pointed out this difference between pre-industrial hazards, which are not controllable, but also not caused by decisions, and industrial risks, which come from decisions and considerations of utility. Here Luhmann, the systems theorist, ascribes the decisions exclusively to individuals, who otherwise are never presented as within organizations and bureaucracies in his theory.

2. This occurs in a historical amalgam of nature and society, where even natural catastrophes such as floods, landslides, and so on, which are apparently externally caused, appear to be caused by human beings (see Beck 1988: chap. 2).

3. This idea was first worked out in case studies of major accidents by Lagadec (1987), deepened by Ewald (1986) and Perrow (1988); the argument was also developed in the German linguistic area by Evers and Nowotny (1987). For details, see Beck (1988) and Lau (1988).

4. In this respect the disputes over so-called 'catastrophic medicine' have an exemplary character.

5. The debate over the duties and function of law in risk societies has increased accordingly in recent years. See Wolf (1987 and 1988); Meyer-Abich and Schefold (1986); Ritter (1987); Blanke (1986); Heinz and Meinberg (1988); Calliess (1981); Bruggemeier (1988).

6. Later on we will not be concerned only, nor primarily, with issues of a new ethics of civilizational action, but with the fact that the established categories and criteria for institutional action stem from a different world.

7. Until Chernobyl, protection against catastrophes, for example, was planned only within a radius of 29 km around a power plant; foreign accidents were officially excluded (cf. Czada and Drexler 1988; Gottweis 1988).

8. The conflicts and crises of classical industrial society have not ended after all, so that realistically, overlaps will occur between the social structure and conflict dynamics of industrial and risk society. These are excluded here.

9. 'That there are symptoms of such a bloc-formation is seen in the West German nuclear industry following Chernobyl: works councils and employers' representatives jointly defended prevailing West German energy policy against any change of course' (Schumann 1987). Contrary to the prevailing assumptions, Heine and Mautz (1989) in a corresponding study on 'industrial workers contra environmentalism', reach the conclusion: 'With the trend to professionalization of production work in the chemical industry, chemical workers could in future constitute a growing potential of ecologically vigilant production workers, who are capable of reflecting critically upon the ecological conditions and consequences of their own labour, and represent a supporting force for ecologically motivated political interventions' (1989: 187).

10. This view is based generally on the theoretical distinction between simple and reflexive modernization, which has not yet been adequately worked out. To put it crudely, simple modernization runs within the framework of categories and principles of industrial society. In the second case, however, we are concerned with a phase of social transformation in which, by dint of its own dynamics, modernization changes its shape within industrial society. Class, stratum, occupation, sex roles, businesses, sectoral structure, and in general the presuppositions and the course of 'natural' techno-economic progress are all affected. The world of classical industrial society is becoming just as much a tradition to be run over and demystified as, in the nineteenth century, industrial

modernization ran over and demystified status-based feudal society. Unconsciously, acting against its own plan, modernization is undercutting modernization. In that way however, restratifications in social structures arise, along with power shifts, new lines of conflict, possibilities and constraints for coalitions. Social movements, the public sphere, ethics, the civil courage of individuals and the networks of differential politics get their chances to exert historical influence (cf. Beck 1986: 176 ff.; chaps. 7, 8).

11. The arguments developed in Beck (1988) are often misunderstood as suggested political solutions, whereas they actually aim to stimulate institutional re-learning by political means.

12. In figurative terms: making radioactivity itch is a central task of political education in the risk society (cf. Claussen 1989; Ackermann et al. 1988).

References

Ackermann, H., et al. (1988) (eds), *Technikentwicklung und politische Bildung* (Opladen: Westdeutscher Verlag).

Beck, U. (1986), *Risikogesellschaft: Auf dem Weg in eine andere Moderne* (Frankfurt/Main; English translation published by Sage Publications 1992).

——(1988), *Gegengifte: Die organisierte Unverantwortlichkeit* (Frankfurt/Main: Suhrkamp; English translation published by Polity 1992).

——(1990), 'Praxis als Forschung', *Forschungsjournal Neue Soziale Bewegungen*, 3 (1).

——and Beck-Gernsheim, E. (1990), *Das ganz normale Chaos der Liebe* (Frankfurt: Suhrkamp).

Blanke, T. (1986), 'Autonomie und Demokratie', *Kritische Justiz*, 4: 406–22.

Böhret, C. (1987) (ed.), *Herausforderungen an die Innovationskraft der Verwaltung* (Opladen: Leske & Budrich).

Bruggemeier, G. (1988), 'Umwelthaftsrecht: Ein Beitrag zum Recht in der "Risikogesellschaft"', *Kritische Justiz*, 2: 209–30.

Calliess, R.-P. (1981), 'Strafzweck und Strafrecht: 40 Jahre Grundgesetz—Entwicklungstendenzen vom freiheitlichen zum sozial-autoritären Rechtsstaat?', *Neue Juristische Wochenschrift*, 21: 1338–43.

Claussen, B. (1989), 'Politische Bildung in der Risikogesellschaft', *Aus Politik und Zeitgeschichte*, B 36.

Czada, R., and Drexler, A. (1988), 'Konturen einer politischen Risikoverwaltung', *Österreichische Zeitschrift für Politikwissenschaft*, 1: 52 ff.

Evers, A., and Nowotny, H. (1987), *Über den Umgang mit Unsicherheit* (Frankfurt: Suhrkamp).

Ewald, F. (1986), *L'Etat Providence* (Paris).

Fischer, J. (1989), *Der Umbau der Industriegesellschaft* (Berlin).

Gottweis, H. (1988), 'Politik in der Risikogesellschaft', *Österreichische Zeitschrift für Politikwissenschaft*, 1: 3 ff.

Häfele, W. (1974), 'Hypotheticality and the New Challenges: The Pathfinder Role of Nuclear Energy', *Minerva*, 12 (1): 313 ff.

Heine, H., and Mautz, R. (1989), *Industriearbeiter contra Umweltschutz* (Frankfurt: Campus).

Heinz, G., and Meinberg, U. (1988), 'Empfehlen sich Änderungen im strafrechtlichen Umweltschutz, insbes. in Verbindung mit dem Verwaltungstrecht. Gutachten D für den 57. Dt. Juristentag', in Staendige Deputation des Dt. Juristentages (ed.), *Verhandlungen des 57. Dt. Juristentages in Mainz*, vol. I. Part D.

Kohn, W., and Weyer, J. (1989), 'Gesellschaft als Labor', *Soziale Welt*, 3: 349–73.

Lagadec, P. (1987), *Das grosse Risiko* (Nördlingen: Greno; French original 1982).

Lau, C. H. (1988), 'Risikodiskurse', *Soziale Welt*, 3: 418–36.

Luhmann, Niklas (1990), 'Die Moral des Risikos und das Risiko der Moral', in G. Bechmann (ed.), *Risiko und Gesellschaft*.

Meyer-Abich, K. M. (1989), 'Von der Wohlstands- zur Risikogesellschaft', *Aus Politik und Zeitgeschichte*, B 36: 3 ff.

—— and Schefold, B. (1986), *Die Grenzen der Atomwirtschaft* (Munich).

Perrow, C. (1988), *Normale Katastrophen* (Frankfurt: Campus).

Ritter, E. H. (1987), 'Umweltpolitik und Rechtsentwicklung', *Neue Zeitschrift für Verwaltungsrecht*, 11: 929–38.

Rödel, U., Frankenberg, G., and Dubiel, H. (1989), *Die demokratische Frage* (Frankfurt/Main: Suhrkamp).

Schumann, M. (1987), 'Industrielle Produzenten in der ökologischen Herausforderung', Research proposal, Göttingen.

Wolf, R. (1987), 'Die Antiquiertheit des Rechts in der Risikogesellschaft', *Leviathan*, 15: 357–91.

—— (1988), ' "Herrschaft kraft Wissen" in der Risikogesellschaft', *Soziale Welt*, 2: 164–87.

PART FOUR

GREEN SOCIAL CRITIQUES

We turn now to a number of radical ecologies, their analyses of the sources of and solutions to ecological problems, and their accounts of the relationship between social practices and ecological problems. These critiques consider the way we think about nature, and the institutionalization of that thought in social and economic practices. Such practices turn out to dominate not only nature, but also the poor and working classes, women, and people of colour. For these schools of ecological thought, neither piecemeal reform nor economic tinkering is enough to deal with the dire problems we face. The ecological crisis is related to a number of other social problems, and it will take both radical rethinking and radical restructuring of political procedures and institutions to address our current predicament. The schools of thought represented in the following sections, however, are divided on the extent to which we should emphasize political structure rather than social consciousness.

Section VIII: Deep Ecology and Bioregionalism

Of the eco-philosophies that inform the more radical part of the spectrum of ecological politics, the most popular, or at least well-known, is Deep Ecology. The Norwegian philosopher Arne Naess founded this school of ecological thought in 1973, with the publication of his classic differentiation between mainstream environmentalism—shallow ecology—and his ideal of deeper, more long-range notion of ecology. For deep ecology, the environmental crisis is, at its centre, a crisis of consciousness. The way we *think* about nature and our relations with it is, pure and simple, wrong. A change in the way we understand and relate to nature is the top priority for addressing the environmental crisis. Deep ecologists seek a major reduction in human arrogance when it comes to dealing with the natural world.

Some deep ecologists focus on two "ultimate norms" articulated by Naess, two key ways to think more deeply about nature. The first is a recognition of the necessity of the self-realization of one's potential—for both humans and the rest of the natural world. Everyone and everything, in this view, should develop and live without interference, as all life has a value and a potential in and for itself, and not just for others. Secondly, deep ecology calls for 'biocentric equality', or what others have called variously 'biocentrism' or 'ecocentrism'. This notion elevates the self-realization to a *right*, such that all creatures, and the earth itself, have a right to be and to develop to their full potential. Does this mean that humans are *equal* to worms? For deep ecologists, this may not necessarily be the case *legally*, but we should be considered equal in the sense that we are both members of a larger biotic community.

Naess's founding essay is essentially a list of seven normative tenets of deep ecology—what he calls a 'value priority system' that has been 'inspired' by knowledge of ecological systems. While the focus is on values, Naess does attempt to explore what a deep ecological *politics* would look like, with a cursory mention of class egalitarianism, local autonomy, and decentralization. The selection by Robyn Eckersley, written nearly two decades after Naess's, demonstrates the evolution and diversity of ecocentric thought. Her discussion differentiates and defines three key varieties of ecocentrism, and addresses the relationship between ecocentric and ecofeminist thought. If ecofeminism is based on an assertion about the similarities between the domination of nature and the domination of women, then ecofeminists have something to gain from theories of ecocentrism, and vice versa. Eckersley adds to the discussion of deep ecology a more thorough defence of *social* justice and *human* emancipation, in addition to a change in the way of thinking about the natural world.

Both Naess and Eckersley are theorists, but a number of environmental activists have used notions of deep ecology to define and defend radical political action in defence of nature. To follow up on this more political theme, we have included two essays which translate the philosophy of deep ecology into political action and relations. The selection by Dave Foreman, one of the founders of the radical environmental group Earth First!, articulates the type of politics he believes deep ecology requires. Foreman argues that a biocentric worldview necessitates putting the Earth and its wildlands before human welfare in any political decision making, emphasizes a change in personal lifestyles, and defends the sabotage of projects which threaten the wild. Jim Dodge offers a less flashy, but just as radical, implementation of the ideals of radical ecology in his discussion of the theory and practice of bioregionalism. Bioregionalism is the philosophy and practice of living in place. Dodge distills bioregional practice down into two key elements: resistance and renewal. Resistance is to any practice that continues the destruction of natural systems; renewal is achieved through political participation at the local level.

Finally, we offer a critical selection by Martin Lewis, in which he chides the 'green delusions' of all forms of radical ecology. Lewis is an environmental moderate—and self-professed Promethean—who marries Julian Simon's faith in technology with Dave Foreman's passion to save wilderness. In the selection here, Lewis argues that the thought and actions of radical ecologists threaten the necessary, though incremental, environmental reforms that need public support. As his argument cuts a broad path across radical ecology generally, it should be kept in mind as a counter to Section IX as well as this one.

Further Reading

Deep Ecology and Bioregionalism have many definers and defenders. The canon of deep ecology includes Bill Devall and George Sessions *Deep Ecology: Living as if Nature Mattered* (1985), Naess's own *Ecology, Community, and Lifestyle* (1989), and Warwick Fox's *Toward a Transpersonal Ecology* (1990). Some of the links and contrasts between deep ecology and ecofeminism are explored in various essays in Irene Diamond and Gloria Orenstein (eds), *Reweaving the World: The Emergence of Ecofeminism* (1990). Three classics of bioregionalism are Kirkpatrick Sale's *Dwellers in the Land: The Bioregional Vision* (1985), and the edited volumes *Thinking Like a Mountain: Toward a Council of All Beings* (1988), and *Home! Reinhabiting North America: A Bioregional Reader* (1992). A more recent collection, *Bioregionalism* (1998), edited by Michael McGinnis, brings together bioregional theory and practice in one volume.

Deep ecology in practice, embodied in Earth First! and other groups, is explored in *The Earth First Reader: Ten Years of Radical Environmentalism* (1991), edited by Dave Foreman and John Davis; and Rik Scarce, *Eco-Warriors: Understanding the Radical Environmental Movement* (1990). Both deep ecological action and bioregional understanding have been defined and inspired by literary works. See, for example, Ed Abbey's classic *The Monkey Wrench Gang* (1976), and Gary Snyder's *Turtle Island* (1974).

Deep ecology, however, has its share of critics from *within* radical ecology. Murray Bookchin and James O'Connor, both included in the following section on Social and Socialist Ecology, have argued the limitations of a political philosophy based on bio- or ecocentrism. Bookchin has been the most vocal critic, though his concerns are mostly with the anti-left and misanthropic writings of Earth First!ers like Dave Foreman and Christopher Manes. See his essay 'Social Ecology Versus Deep Ecology', in *Socialist Review*, 18: 3 (1988), 9–29. Bookchin and Foreman did 'make-up' after this heated conflict; their illuminating debate is in Bookchin and Foreman, *Defending the Earth* (1991).

24 The Shallow and the Deep, Long-Range Ecology Movement: A Summary

Arne Naess

Ecologically responsible policies are concerned only in part with pollution and resource depletion. There are deeper concerns which touch upon principles of diversity, complexity, autonomy, decentralization, symbiosis, egalitarianism, and classlessness.

The emergence of ecologists from their former relative obscurity marks a turning-point in our scientific communities. But their message is twisted and misused. A shallow, but presently rather powerful movement, and a deep, but less influential movement, compete for our attention. I shall make an effort to characterize the two.

1. The Shallow Ecology Movement

Fight against pollution and resource depletion. Central objective: the health and affluence of people in the developed countries.

2. The Deep Ecology Movement

(1) Rejection of the man-in-environment image in favour of the relational, total-field image. Organisms as knots in the biospherical net or field of intrinsic relations. An intrinsic relation between two things *A* and *B* is such that the relation belongs to the definitions or basic constitutions of *A* and *B*, so that without the relation, *A* and *B* are no longer the same things. The total-field model dissolves not only the man-in-environment concept, but every compact thing-in-milieu concept—except when talking at a superficial or preliminary level of communication.

(2) Biospherical egalitarianism—in principle. The 'in principle' clause is inserted because any realistic praxis necessitates some killing, exploitation, and suppression. The ecological field-worker acquires a deep-seated respect, or even veneration, for ways and forms of life. He reaches an understanding from within, a kind of understanding that others reserve for fellow men and for a narrow section of ways and forms of life. To the ecological field-worker, *the equal right to*

Reprinted from Arne Naess, 'The Shallow and the Deep, Long-Range Ecology Movement: A Summary', *Inquiry* 16 (1983), 95–100, by permission of Scandinavian Univerrsity Press, Oslo, Norway.

live and blossom is an intuitively clear and obvious value axiom. Its restriction to humans is an anthropocentrism with detrimental effects upon the life quality of humans themselves. This quality depends in part upon the deep pleasure and satisfaction we receive from close partnership with other forms of life. The attempt to ignore our dependence and to establish a master–slave role has contributed to the alienation of man from himself.

Ecological egalitarianism implies the reinterpretation of the future-research variable, 'level of crowding', so that *general* mammalian crowding and loss of life-equality is taken seriously, not only human crowding. (Research on the high requirements of free space of certain mammals has, incidentally, suggested that theorists of human urbanism have largely underestimated human life-space requirements. Behavioural crowding symptoms (neuroses, aggressiveness, loss of traditions . . .) are largely the same among mammals.)

(3) Principles of diversity and of symbiosis. Diversity enhances the potentialities of survival, the chances of new modes of life, the richness of forms. And the so-called struggle of life, and survival of the fittest, should be interpreted in the sense of ability to coexist and cooperate in complex relationships, rather than ability to kill, exploit, and suppress. 'Live and let live' is a more powerful ecological principle than 'Either you or me'.

The latter tends to reduce the multiplicity of kinds of forms of life, and also to create destruction within the communities of the same species. Ecologically inspired attitudes therefore favour diversity of human ways of life, of cultures, of occupations, of economies. They support the fight against economic and cultural, as much as military, invasion, and domination, and they are opposed to the annihilation of seals and whales as much as to that of human tribes or cultures.

(4) Anti-class posture. Diversity of human ways of life is in part due to (intended or unintended) exploitation and suppression on the part of certain groups. The exploiter lives differently from the exploited, but both are adversely affected in their potentialities of self-realization. The principle of diversity does not cover differences due merely to certain attitudes or behaviours forcibly blocked or restrained. The principles of ecological egalitarianism and of symbiosis support the same anti-class posture. The ecological attitude favours the extension of all three principles to any group conflicts, including those of today between developing and developed nations. The three principles also favour extreme caution towards any overall plans for the future, except those consistent with wide and widening classless diversity.

(5) Fight against pollution and resource depletion. In this fight ecologists have found powerful supporters, but sometimes to the detriment of their total stand. This happens when attention is focused on pollution and resource depletion rather than on the other points, or when projects are implemented which reduce pollution but increase evils of the other kinds. Thus, if prices of life necessities increase because of the installation of anti-pollution devices, class differences increase too. An ethics of responsibility implies that ecologists do not serve the shallow, but the deep ecological movement. That is, not only point (5), but all seven points must be considered together.

Ecologists are irreplaceable informants in any society, whatever their political colour. If well organized, they have the power to reject jobs in which they submit themselves to institutions or to planners with limited ecological perspectives. As it is now, ecologists sometimes serve masters who deliberately ignore the wider perspectives.

(6) Complexity, not complication. The theory of ecosystems contains an important distinction between what is complicated without any Gestalt or unifying principles—we may think of finding our way through a chaotic city—and what is complex. A multiplicity of more or less lawful, interacting factors may operate together to form a unity, a system. We make a shoe or use a map or integrate a variety of activities into a workaday pattern. Organisms, ways of life, and interactions in the biosphere in general, exhibit complexity of such an astoundingly high level as to colour the general outlook of ecologists. Such complexity makes thinking in terms of vast systems inevitable. It also makes for a keen, steady perception of the profound *human ignorance* of biospherical relationships and therefore of the effect of disturbances.

Applied to humans, the complexity-not-complication principle favours division of labour, *not fragmentation of labour*. It favours integrated actions in which the whole person is active, not mere reactions. It favours complex economies, an integrated variety of means of living. (Combinations of industrial and agricultural activity, of intellectual and manual work, of specialized and non-specialized occupations, of urban and non-urban activity, of work in city and recreation in nature with recreation in city and work in nature . . .)

It favours soft technique and 'soft future-research', less prognosis, more clarification of possibilities. More sensitivity towards continuity and live traditions, and—most importantly—towards our state of ignorance.

The implementation of ecologically responsible policies requires in this century an exponential growth of technical skill and invention—but in new directions, directions which today are not consistently and liberally supported by the research policy organs of our nation-states.

(7) Local autonomy and decentralization. The vulnerability of a form of life is roughly proportional to the weight of influences from afar, from outside the local region in which that form has obtained an ecological equilibrium. This lends support to our efforts to strengthen local self-government and material and mental self-sufficiency. But these efforts presuppose an impetus towards decentralization. Pollution problems, including those of thermal pollution and recirculation of materials, also lead us in this direction, because increased local autonomy, if we are able to keep other factors constant, reduces energy consumption. (Compare an approximately self-sufficient locality with one requiring the importation of foodstuff, materials for house construction, fuel, and skilled labour from other continents. The former may use only 5 per cent of the energy used by the latter.) Local autonomy is strengthened by a reduction in the number of links in the hierarchical chains of decision (For example a chain consisting of local board, municipal council, highest sub-national decision-maker, a state-wide institution in a state federation, a federal national government institution, a coalition of nations, and of institutions, e.g. EEC top levels, and a global institution, can be reduced to one made up of local board, nation-wide institution, and global institution.) Even if a decision follows majority rules at each step, many local interests may be dropped along the line, if it is too long.

Summing up, then, it should, first of all, be borne in mind that the norms and tendencies of the Deep Ecology movement are not derived from ecology by logic or induction. Ecological knowledge and the lifestyle of the ecological field-worker have *suggested, inspired, and fortified* the perspectives of the Deep Ecology movement. Many of the formulations in the above seven-point survey are rather vague generalizations, only tenable if made more precise in certain directions. But all over the world the inspiration from ecology has shown remarkable convergencies. The survey does not pretend to be more than one of the possible condensed codifications of these convergencies.

Secondly, it should be fully appreciated that the significant tenets of the Deep Ecology movement are clearly and forcefully *normative*. They express a value priority system only in part based on results (or lack of results, cf. point (6)) of scientific research. Today, ecologists try to influence policy-making bodies largely through threats, through predictions concerning pollutants and resource depletion, knowing that policy-makers accept at least certain minimum *norms* concerning health and just distribution. But it is clear that there is a vast number of people in all countries, and even a considerable number of people in power, who accept as valid the wider norms and values characteristic of the Deep Ecology movement. There are political potentials in this movement which should not be overlooked and which have little to do with pollution and resource depletion. In plotting possible futures, the norms should be freely used and elaborated.

Thirdly, insofar as ecology movements deserve our attention, they are *ecophilosophical* rather then ecological. Ecology is a *limited* science which makes *use* of scientific methods. Philosophy is the most general forum of debate on fundamentals, descriptive as well as prescriptive, and political philosophy is one of its subsections. By an *ecosophy* I mean a philosophy of ecological harmony or equilibrium. A philosophy as a kind of *sofia* wisdom, is openly normative, it contains *both* norms, rules, postulates, value priority announcements, *and* hypotheses concerning the state of affairs in our universe. Wisdom is policy wisdom, prescription, not only scientific description and prediction.

The details of an ecosophy will show many variations due to significant differences concerning not only 'facts' of pollution, resources, population, etc., but also value priorities. Today, however, the seven points listed provide one unified framework for ecosophical systems.

In general system theory, systems are mostly conceived in terms of causally or functionally interacting or interrelated items. An ecosophy, however, is more like a system of the kind constructed by Aristotle or Spinoza. It is expressed verbally as a set of sentences with a variety of functions, descriptive and prescriptive. The basic relation is that between subsets of premises and subsets of conclusions, that is, the relation of derivability. The relevant notions of derivability may be classed according to rigour, with logical and mathematical deductions topping the list, but also according to how much is implicitly taken for granted. An exposition of an ecosophy must necessarily be only moderately precise considering the vast scope of relevant ecological and normative (social, political, ethical) material. At the moment, ecosophy might profitably use models of systems, rough approximations of global systematizations. It is the global character, not preciseness in detail, which distinguishes an ecosophy. It articulates and integrates the efforts of an ideal ecological team, a team comprising not only scientists from an extreme variety of disciplines, but also students of politics and active policy-makers.

Under the name of *ecologism*, various deviations from the deep movement have been championed—primarily with a one-sided stress on pollution and resource depletion, but also with a neglect of the great differences between under- and over-developed countries in favour of a vague global approach. The global approach is essential, but regional differences must largely determine policies in the coming years.

Selected Literature

Commoner, B., *The Closing Circle: Nature, Man, and Technology* (New York: Alfred A. Knopf, 1971).

Ehrlich, P. R., and Ehrlich, A. H., *Population, Resources, Environment: Issues in Human Ecology*, 2nd edn. (San Francisco: W. H. Freeman & Co., 1972).

Ellul, J., *The Technological Society*, English edn. (New York: Alfred A. Knopf, 1964).

Glacken, C. J., *Traces on the Rhodian Shore: Nature and Culture in Western Thought* (Berkeley: University of California Press, 1967).

Kato, H., 'The Effects of Crowding', Quality of Life Conference, Oberhausen, April 1972.

McHarg, Ian L., *Design with Nature* (New York: Doubleday & Co., 1969; paperback 1971).

Meynaud, J., *Technocracy*, English edn. (Chicago: Free Press of Glencoe, 1969).

Mishan, E. J., *Technology and Growth: The Price We Pay* (New York: Frederick A. Praeger, 1970).

Odum, E. P., *Fundamentals of Ecology*, 3rd edn. (Philadelphia: W. E. Saunders Co., 1971).

Shepard, Paul, *Man in the Landscape* (New York: A. A. Knopf).

25 Putting the Earth First

Dave Foreman

These are the times that try men's souls; the summer soldier and the sunshine patriot will, in this crisis, shrink from the service of his country, but he that stands it now, deserves the love and thanks of man and woman.

(Thomas Paine)

In July 1987, seven years after the campfire gathering that spawned Earth First!, I rose among the Ponderosa Pines and scattered shafts of sunlight on the North Rim of the Grand Canyon and mounted a stage festooned with Earth First! banners and American flags. Before me sat several hundred people: hippies in tie-dyed shirts and Birkenstocks, rednecks for wilderness in cowboy boots and hats, middle-class hikers in waffle stompers, graybeards, and children. The diversity was impressive. The energy was overpowering. Never in my wildest dreams had I imagined the Earth First! movement would attract so many. Never had I hoped that we would have begun to pack such a punch. We were attracting national attention; we were changing the parameters of the debate about ecological issues; we had become a legend in conservation lore.

Yet, after seven years, I was concerned we were losing some of our clarity of purpose, and blurring our focus. In launching Earth First!, I had said, "Let our actions set the finer points of our philosophy." But now I was concerned that the *what* of our actions might be overwhelming the *why*. For some of those newly attracted to Earth First!, action seemed to be its own justification. I felt a need to return to wilderness fundamentalism, to articulate what I thought were the principles that defined the Earth First! movement, that gave it a specific identity. The response to the principles I offered that day was so overwhelmingly positive that I elaborated on them in the *Earth First! Journal* later that fall. Here they are.

A placing of Earth first in all decisions, even ahead of human welfare if necessary. Our movement is called "Earth First!" not "People First!" Sometimes what appears to be in the short-term interest of human beings as a whole, a select group of human beings, or individual human beings is detrimental to the short-term or long-term health of the biosphere (and to the actual long-term welfare of human beings). Earth First! does not argue that native diversity should be preserved if it can be done without negatively impacting the material "standard of living" of a group of human beings. We simply state that native diversity should be preserved, that natural diversity building for three and a half billion years should be left unfettered. Human beings must adjust to the planet; it is supreme arrogance to expect the planet and all it contains to adjust to the demands of humans. In everything human society does, the primary consideration should be for the long-term health and biological diversity of Earth. After that, we can consider the welfare of humans. We should be kind, compassionate, and caring with other people, but Earth comes first.

A refusal to use human beings as the measure by which to value others. An individual human life has no more intrinsic value than does an individual Grizzly Bear life. Human suffering resulting from drought and famine in Ethiopia is tragic, yes, but the destruction there of other creatures and habitat is even more tragic. This leads quickly into the next point:

An enthusiastic embracing of the philosophy of Deep Ecology or biocentrism. This philosophy states simply and essentially that all living creatures and communities possess intrinsic value, inherent worth. Natural things live for their own sake, which is another way of saying they have value. Other beings (both animal and plant) and even so-called "inanimate" objects such as rivers and mountains are not placed here for the convenience of human beings. Our biocentric worldview denies the modern concept of "resources." The dominant philosophy of our time (which contains Judeo-Christianity, Islam, capitalism, Marxism, scientism, and secular humanism) is anthropocentrism. It places human beings at the center of the universe, separates them from nature, and endows them with unique value. EF!ers are in direct opposition to that philosophy. Ours is an ecological perspective that views Earth as a community and recognizes such apparent enemies as "disease" (e.g. malaria) and "pests" (e.g. mosquitoes) not as manifestations of evil to be overcome but rather as vital and necessary components of a complex and vibrant biosphere.

A realization that wilderness is the real world. The preservation of wilderness is the fundamental issue. Wilderness does not merely mean backpacking parks or scenery. It is the natural world, the arena for evolution, the caldron from which humans emerged, the home of the others with whom we share this planet. Wilderness is the real world; our cities, our computers, our airplanes, our global business civilization all are but artificial and transient phenomena. It is important to remember that only a tiny portion of the history of the human species has occurred outside of wilderness. The preservation of wildness and native diversity is *the* most important issue. Issues directly affecting only humans pale in comparison. Of course, ecology teaches us that all things are connected, and in this regard all other matters become subsets of wilderness preservation—the prevention of nuclear war, for example—but the most important campaigns being waged today are those directly on behalf of wilderness.

A recognition that there are far too many human beings on Earth. There are too many of us everywhere—in the United States, in Nigeria; in cities, in rural areas; with digging hoes, with tractors. Although there is obviously an unconscionable maldistribution of wealth and the basic necessities of life among humans, this fact should not be used—as some leftists are wont to do— to argue that overpopulation is not the problem. It *is* a large part of the problem; there are far too many of us *already*—and our numbers continue to grow astronomically. Even if inequitable distribution could be solved, six billion human beings converting the natural world to material goods and human food would devastate natural diversity.

This basic recognition of the overpopulation problem does not mean that we should ignore the economic and social causes of overpopulation, and shouldn't criticize the accumulation of

wealth in fewer and fewer hands, the maldistribution of "resources," and the venality of multinational corporations and Third World juntas alike, but simply that we must understand that
Great Blue Whales, Jaguars, Black Rhinoceroses, and rain forests are not compatible with an
exploding human population.[1]

A deep questioning of, and even an antipathy to, "progress" and "technology." In looking at
human history, we can see that we have lost more in our "rise" to civilization than we have
gained. We can see that life in a hunter-gatherer society was on the whole healthier, happier, and
more secure than our lives today as peasants, industrial workers, or business executives. For
every material "achievement" of progress, there are a dozen losses of things of profound and
ineffable value. We can accept the pejoratives of "Luddite" and "Neanderthal" with pride. (This
does not mean that we must immediately eschew all the facets of technological civilization. We
are *of* it, and use it; this does not mean that we can't critique it.)

A refusal to accept rationality as the only way of thinking. There is room for great diversity
within Earth First! on matters spiritual, and nowhere is tolerance for diversity more necessary.
But we can all recognize that linear, rational, logical left brain thinking represents only part of
our brain and consciousness. Rationality is a fine and useful tool, but it is just that—a tool, one
way of analyzing matters. Equally valid, perhaps more so, is intuitive, instinctive awareness. We
can become more cognizant of ultimate truths by sitting quietly in the wild than by studying in
a library. Reading books, engaging in logical discourse, and compiling facts and figures are necessary in the modern context, but they are not the only ways to comprehend the world and our
lives. Often our gut instincts enable us to act more effectively in a crisis than does careful rational
analysis. An example would be a patient bleeding to death in a hospital emergency room—you
can't wait for all the tests to be completed. Your gut says, "Act!" So it is with Earth First!'s actions
in Earth's current emergency.

**A lack of desire to gain credibility or "legitimacy" with the gang of thugs running human
civilization.** It is basic human nature to want to be accepted by the social milieu in which you
find yourself. It hurts to be dismissed by the arbiters of opinion as "nuts," "terrorists," "wackos,"
or "extremists." But we are not crazy; we happen to be sane humans in an insane human society
in a sane natural world. We do not have "credibility" with Senator Mark Hatfield or with
Maxxam chairman Charles Hurwitz—but they do not have credibility with us! (We do have
their attention, however.) They are madmen destroying the pure and beautiful. Why should we
"reason" with them? We do not share the same worldview or values. There is, however, a dangerous pitfall here that some alternative groups fall into. That is that we gain little by being consciously offensive, by trying to alienate others. We can be strong and unyielding without being
obnoxious.

The American system is very effective at co-opting and moderating dissidents by giving them
attention and then encouraging them to be "reasonable" so their ideas will be taken seriously.
Putting a critic on the evening news, on the front page of the newspaper, in a national magazine—all of these are methods the establishment uses to entice one to share their worldview and
to enter the negotiating room to compromise. The actions of Earth First!—both the bold and
the comic—have gained attention. If they are to have results, we must resist the siren's offer of
credibility, legitimacy, and a share in the decision-making. We are thwarting the system, not

reforming it. While we are therefore not concerned with political credibility, it must be remembered that the arguments and actions of Earth First! are based on the understandings of ecology. It is vitally important that we have biological credibility.

An effort to go beyond the tired, worn-out dogmas of left, right, and middle-of-the-road. These doctrines, whether blaming capitalism, communism, or the devil for all the problems in the world, merely represent internecine squabbles between different factions of humanism. Yes, multinational corporations commit great evil (the Soviet Union is essentially a state-run multinational corporation); there is a great injustice in the world; the rich are getting richer and the poor poorer—but all problems cannot be simplistically laid at the feet of evil capitalists in the United States, Europe, and Japan. Earth First! is not left or right; we are not even in front. Earth First! should not be in the political struggle between humanist sects at all. We're in a wholly different game.

An unwillingness to set any ethnic, class, or political group of humans on a pedestal and make them immune from questioning. It's easy, of course, to recognize that white males from North America and Europe (as well as Japanese males) hold a disproportionate share of responsibility for the mess we're in; that upper- and middle-class consumers from the First World take an excessive portion of the world's "resources" and therefore cause greater per capita destruction than do other peoples. But it does not follow that everyone else is blameless.

The Earth First! movement has great affinity with aboriginal groups throughout the world. They are clearly in the most direct and respectful relationship with the natural world. Earth First! should back such tribes in the common struggle whenever possible without compromising our ideals. For example, we are supportive of the Dine (Navajo) of Big Mountain against relocation, but this does not mean we overlook the severe overgrazing by domestic sheep on the Navajo Reservation. We may be supportive of subsistence life-styles by natives in Alaska, but we should not be silent about clearcutting old-growth forest in southeast Alaska by native corporations, or about the Eskimo Doyon Corporation's push for oil exploration and development in the Arctic National Wildlife Refuge. It is racist either to condemn or to pardon someone based on their ethnic background.

Similarly, we are inconsistent when we castigate Charles Hurwitz for destroying the last wilderness redwood forest, yet feel sympathy for the loggers working for him. Industrial workers, by and large, share the blame for the destruction of the natural world. They may be yoked by the big-money boys, but they are generally willing servants who share the worldview of their bosses that Earth is a smorgasbord of resources for the taking. Sometimes, in fact, it is the sturdy yeoman from the bumpkin proletariat who holds the most violent and destructive attitudes toward the natural world (and toward those who would defend it).[2] Workers are victims of an unjust economic system, but that does not absolve them of what they do. This is not to deny that some woods workers oppose the destruction of ancient forests, that some may even be Earth First!ers, but merely that it is inappropriate to overlook abuse of the natural world simply because of the rung the perpetrators occupy on the economic ladder.

Some argue that workers are merely struggling to feed their families and are not delighting in destroying the natural world. They say that unless you deal with the needs of loggers to make a living, you can't save the forest. They also claim that loggers are manipulated by their bosses to express anti-wilderness viewpoints. I find this argument to be patronizing to loggers and other workers. When I read comments from timber fellers expressing hatred toward pristine forests and toward conservationists, it is obvious that they willingly buy into the worldview of the lumber barons. San Francisco's *Image Magazine* reports on a letter to the editor written by one logger: "Working people trying to feed their families have little time to be out in the woods acting like children and making things hard for other working people. . . . Anyone out there have a recipe for spotted owl? Food stamps won't go far, I'm afraid. And since they're always being shoved down my throat, I thought I'd like mine fried."[3] Bumper stickers proclaiming "Kill an owl. Save a logger." are rife in the Northwest. I at least respect the logger who glories in felling a giant tree and who hunts Spotted Owls enough to grant him the mental ability to have his own opinions instead of pretending he is a stupid oaf, manipulated by his bosses and unable to think for himself.

Of course the big timber companies do manipulate their workers with scare tactics about mill closings and wilderness lockups, but many loggers (or cat-skinners, oilfield workers, miners, and the like) simply hate the wild and delight in "civilizing" it. Even educating workers about ecological principles will not necessarily change the attitudes of many; there are basic differences of opinion and values. Conservationists should try to find common ground with loggers and other workers whenever possible, but the sooner we get rid of Marxist views about the noble proletariat, the better.

A willingness to let our actions set the finer point of our philosophy and a recognition that we must act. It is possible to debate endlessly the finer points of dogma, to feel that every nuance of something must be explored before one can act. Too often, political movements become mere debating societies where the participants engage in philosophical masturbation and never get down to the vital business at hand. Others argue that you have no right to argue for environmental preservation until you are living a pure, non-impacting life-style. We will never figure it all out, we will never be able to plan any campaign in complete detail, none of us will ever entirely transcend a polluting life-style—but we can act. We can act with courage, with determination, with love for things wild and free. We can't be perfect, but we can *act*. We are warriors. Earth First! is a warrior society. We have a job to do.

An acknowledgment that we must change our personal life-styles to make them more harmonious with natural diversity. We must eschew surplusage. Although to varying degrees we are all captives of our economic system and cannot break entirely free, we must practice what we preach to the best of our ability. Arne Naess, the Norwegian philosopher and originator of the term "Deep Ecology," points out that we are not able to achieve a true "Deep Ecology" life-style, but it is the responsibility of each of us to move in that direction. Most of us still need to make a living that involves some level of participation in " the system." Even for activists, there are trade-offs—flying in a jetliner to help hang a banner on the World Bank in Washington, DC, in order to bring international attention to the plight of tropical rain forests; using a computer to write a book printed on tree pulp that will catalyze people to take action; driving a pickup truck down a forest road to gain access to a proposed timber sale for preventive maintenance. We need to be aware of these trade-offs, and to do our utmost to limit our impact.

A commitment to maintaining a sense of humor, and a joy in living. Most radicals are a dour, holier-than-thou, humorless lot. Earth First!ers strive to be different. We aren't rebelling against the system because we're losing in it. We're fighting for beauty, for life, for joy. We kick up our heels in delight in the wilderness, we smile at a flower and a hummingbird. We laugh. We laugh at our opponents—and, more important, we laugh at ourselves.

An awareness that we are animals. Human beings are primates, mammals, vertebrates. EF!ers recognize their animalness; we reject the New Age eco-la-la that says we must transcend our base animal nature and take charge of our evolution in order to become higher, moral beings. We believe we must return to being animal, to glorying in our sweat, hormones, tears, and blood. We struggle against the modern compulsion to become dull, passionless androids. We do not live sanitary, logical lives; we smell, taste, see, hear, and feel Earth; we live with gusto. We *are* Animal.

An acceptance of monkeywrenching as a legitimate tool for the preservation of natural diversity. Not all Earth First!ers monkeywrench, perhaps not even the majority, but we generally accept the idea and practice of monkeywrenching. Look at an EF! T-shirt. The monkeywrench on it is a symbol of resistance, an heir of the *sabot*—the wooden shoe dropped in the gears to stop the machine, from whence comes the word *sabotage*. The mystique and lore of "night work" pervades our tribe, and with it a general acceptance that strategic monkeywrenching is a legitimate tool for defense of the wild.

And finally: Earth First! is a warrior society. In addition to our absolute commitment to and love for this living planet, we are characterized by our willingness to defend Earth's abundance and diversity of life, even if that defense requires sacrifices of comfort, freedom, safety, or, ultimately, our lives. A warrior recognizes that her life is not the most important thing in her life. A warrior recognizes that there is a greater reality outside her life that must be defended. For us in Earth First!, that reality is Earth, the evolutionary process, the millions of other species with which we share this bright sphere in the void of space.

Not everyone can afford to make the commitment of being a warrior. There are many other roles that can—and must—be played in defense of Earth. One may not constantly be able to carry the burden of being a warrior; it may be only a brief period in one's life. There are risks and pitfalls in being a warrior. There may not be applause, there may not be honors and awards from human society. But there is no finer applause for the warrior of the Earth than the call of the loon at dusk or the sigh of wind in the pines.

Later that evening as I looked out over the darkening Grand Canyon, I knew that whatever hardships the future might bring, there was nothing better and more important for me to do than to take an intransigent stand in defense of life, to not compromise, to continue to be a warrior for the Earth. To be a warrior for the Earth regardless of the consequences.

Notes

1. Two excellent books on the population issue that are also sensitive to social and economic issues are William R. Catton, Jr.'s *Overshoot: The Ecological Basis of Revolutionary Change* (Urbana, Ill. and Chicago: University of Illinois Press, 1982), and *The Population Explosion*, by Paul and Anne Ehrlich (New York: Simon and Schuster, 1990). No one concerned with the preservation of biological diversity should be without these.

2. A case in point involves the Spotted Owl, a threatened species dependent on ancient forests. These little owls are easily attracted by playing tapes of their call. Loggers in the Northwest are going into old-growth forests with tape recorders and shotguns to exterminate Spotted Owls. They feel that if they do so, they will eliminate a major reason to stop the logging of these pristine forests.

3. Jane Kay, "Tree Wars," *San Francisco Examiner Image Magazine* (17 December 1989).

26 Living By Life: Some Bioregional Theory and Practice

Jim Dodge

I want to make it clear from the outset that I'm not all that sure what bioregionalism is. To my understanding, bioregionalism is an idea still in loose and amorphous formulation, and presently is more hopeful declaration than actual practice. In fact, "idea" may be too generous: bioregionalism is more properly a notion, which is variously defined as a general idea, a belief, an opinion, an intuition, an inclination, an urge. Furthermore, as I think will prove apparent, bioregionalism is hardly a new notion; it has been the animating cultural principle through 99 percent of human history, and is at least as old as consciousness. Thus, no doubt, the urge.

My purpose here is not really to define bioregionalism—that will take care of itself in the course of things—but to mention some of the elements that I see composing the notion, and some possibilities for practice. I speak with no special privilege on the matter other than my longstanding and fairly studious regard for the subject, a regard enriched by my teachers and numerous bioregional friends. My only true qualification is that I'm fool enough to try.

"Bioregionalism" is from the Greek *bios* (life) and the French *region* (region), itself from the Latin *regia* (territory), and earlier, *regere* (to rule or govern). Etymologically, then, bioregionalism means life territory, place of life, or perhaps by reckless extension, government by life. If you can't imagine that government by life would be at least 40 billion times better than government by the Reagan administration, or Mobil Oil, or any other distant powerful monolith, then your heart is probably no bigger than a prune pit and you won't have much sympathy for what follows.

A central element of bioregionalism—and one that distinguishes it from similar politics of place—is the importance given to natural systems, both as the source of physical nutrition and as the body of metaphors from which our spirits draw sustenance. A natural system is a community of interdependent life, a mutual biological integration on the order of an ecosystem, for example. What constitutes this community is uncertain beyond the obvious—that it includes all interacting life forms, from the tiniest fleck of algae to human beings, as well as their biological processes. To this bare minimum, already impenetrably complex, bioregionalism adds the influences of cultural behavior, such as subsistence techniques and ceremonies. Many people further insist—sensibly, I think—that this community/ecosystem must also include the planetary processes and the larger figures of regulation: solar income, magnetism, gravity, and so forth. Bioregionalism is simply biological realism; in natural systems we find the physical truth of our

From *CoEvolution Quarterly*, 32 (1981), 6–12. Reprinted with permission.

being, the real obvious stuff like the need for oxygen as well as the more subtle need for moon-light, and perhaps other truths beyond those. Not surprisingly, then, bioregionalism holds that the health of natural systems is directly connected to our own physical/psychic health as individuals and as a species, and for that reason natural systems and their informing integrations deserve, if not utter veneration, at least our clearest attention and deepest respect. No matter how great our laws, technologies, or armies, we can't make the sun rise every morning nor the rain dance on the goldenback ferns.

To understand natural systems is to begin an understanding of the self, its common and particular essences—literal self-interest in its barest terms. "As above, so below," according to the old-tradition alchemists; natural systems as models of consciousness. When we destroy a river, we increase our thirst, ruin the beauty of free-flowing water, forsake the meat and spirit of the salmon, and lose a little bit of our souls.

Unfortunately, human society has also developed technologies that make it possible to lose big chunks all at once. If we make just one serious mistake with nuclear energy, for instance, our grandchildren may be born with bones like overcooked spaghetti, or torn apart by mutant rats. Global nuclear war is suicide: the "losers" die instantly; the "winners" inherit slow radiation death and twisted chromosomes. By any sensible measure of self-interest, by any regard for life, nuclear war is abhorrent, unthinkable, and loathsomely stupid, and yet the United States and other nations spend billions to provide that possibility. It is the same mentality that pooh-poohs the growing concentration of poisons in the biosphere. It's like the farmer who was showing off his prize mule to a stranger one day when the mule suddenly fell over sideways and died. The farmer looked at the body in bewildered disbelief: "Damn," he said, "I've had this mule for 27 years and it's the first time he's ever done this." To which the stranger, being a biological realist, undoubtedly replied, "No shit."

While I find an amazing depth of agreement among bioregionalists on what constitutes *bios*, and on what general responsibilities attend our place in the skein of things, there is some disagreement—friendly but passionate—on what actually constitutes a distinct biological region (as opposed to arbitrary entities, like states and counties, where boundaries are established without the dimmest ecological perception, and therefore make for cultural incoherence and piecemeal environmental management). Since the very gut of bioregional thought is the integrity of natural systems and culture, with the function of culture being the mediation of the self and the ecosystem, one might think "bioregion" would be fairly tightly defined. But I think it must be kept in mind that, to paraphrase Poe and Jack Spicer, we're dealing with the grand concord of what does not stoop to definition. There are, however, a number of ideas floating around regarding the biological criteria for a region. I'll mention some of them below, limiting the example to Northern California.

One criterion for determining a biological region is biotic shift, a percentage change in plant/animal species composition from one place to another—that is, if 15 to 25 percent of the species where I live are different from those where you live, we occupy different biological regions. We probably also experience different climates and walk on different soils, since those differences are reflected in species composition. Nearly everyone I've talked with agrees that biotic shift is a fairly slick and accurate way to make bioregional distinctions; the argument is over the percentage, which invariably seems arbitrary. Since the change in biotic composition is usually gradual, the biotic shift criterion permits vague and permeable boundaries between regions, which I personally favor. The idea, after all, is not to replace one set of lines with another, but simply to recognize inherent biological integrities for the purpose of sensible planning and management.

Another way to biologically consider regions is by watershed. This method is generally straightforward, since drainages are clearly apparent on topographical maps. Watershed is usually taken to mean river drainage, so if you live on Cottonwood Creek you are part of the Sacramento River drainage. The problem with watersheds as bioregional criteria is that if you live in San Francisco you are also part of the Sacramento (and San Joaquin) River drainage, and that's a long way from Cottonwood Creek. Since any long drainage presents similar problems, most people who advance the watershed criterion make intradrainage distinctions (in the case of the Sacramento: headwaters, Central Valley, west slope Sierra, east slope Coast Range, and delta/bay). The west slope of the Coast Range, with its short-running rivers and strong Pacific influence, is often considered as a whole biological area, at least from the Gualala River to the Mattole River or, depending on who you're talking to, from the Russian River to the Eel River, though they aren't strictly west slope Coast Range rivers. The Klamath, Smith, and Trinity drainages are often considered a single drainage system, with the arguable inclusion of the Chetco and the Rogue.

A similar method of bioregional distinction is based upon land form. Roughly, Northern California breaks down into the Sierra, the Coast Range, the Central Valley, the Klamath Range, the southern part of the Cascade Range, and the Modoc Plateau. Considering the relationship between topography and water, it is not surprising that land form distinctions closely follow watersheds.

A different criterion for making bioregional distinctions is, awkwardly put, cultural/phenomenological: you are where you perceive you are; your turf is what you think it is, individually and collectively. Although the human sense of territory is deeply evolved and cultural/perceptual behavior certainly influences the sense of place, this view seems to me a bit anthropocentric. And though it is difficult *not* to view things in terms of human experience and values, it does seem wise to remember that human perception is notoriously prey to distortion and the strange delights of perversity. Our species hasn't done too well lately working essentially from this view; because we're ecological dominants doesn't necessarily mean we're ecological determinants. (In fairness, I should note that many friends think I'm unduly cranky on this subject.)

One of the more provocative ideas to delineate bioregions is in terms of "spirit places" or psyche-tuning power-presences, such as Mount Shasta and the Pacific Ocean. By this criterion, a bioregion is defined by the predominate physical influence where you live. You have to live in its presence long enough to truly feel its force within you and that it's not mere descriptive geography.

Also provocative is the notion that bioregion is a vertical phenomenon having more to do with elevation than horizontal deployment—thus a distinction between hill people and flatlanders, which in Northern California also tends to mean country and city. A person living at 2,000 feet in the Coast Range would have more in cultural common with a Sierra dweller at a similar altitude than with someone at sea level 20 miles away.

To briefly recapitulate, the criteria most often advanced for making bioregional distinctions are biotic shift, watershed, land form, cultural/phenomenological, spirit presences, and elevation. Taken together, as I think they should be, they give us a strong sense of where we're at and the life that enmeshes our own. Nobody I know is pushing for a quick definition anyway. Bioregionalism, whatever it is, occupies that point in development (more properly, renewal) where definition is unnecessary and perhaps dangerous. Better now to let definitions emerge from practice than impose them dogmatically from the git-go.

A second element of bioregionalism is anarchy. I hesitate using that fine word because it's been so distorted by reactionary shitheads to scare people that its connotative associations have become bloody chaos and fiends amok, rather than political decentralization, self-determination, and a commitment to social equity. Anarchy doesn't mean out of control; it means out of *their* control. Anarchy is based upon a sense of interdependent self-reliance, the conviction that we as a community, or a tight, small-scale federation of communities, can mind our own business, and can make decisions regarding our individual and communal lives and gladly accept the responsibilities and consequences of those decisions. Further, by consolidating decision-making at a local, face-to-face level without having to constantly push information through insane bureaucratic hierarchies, we can act more quickly in relation to natural systems and, since we live there, hopefully with more knowledge and care.

The United States is simply too large and complex to be responsibly governed by a decision-making body of perhaps 1,000 people representing 220,000,000 Americans and a large chunk of the biosphere, especially when those 1,000 decision makers can only survive by compromise and generally are forced to front for heavy economic interests (media campaigns for national office are expensive). A government where one person represents the interests of 220,000 others is absurd, considering that not all the people voted for the winning representative (or even voted) and especially considering that most of those 220,000 people are capable of representing themselves. I think people do much better, express their deeper qualities, when their actions matter. Obviously one way to make government more meaningful and responsible is to involve people directly day by day, in the processes of decision, which only seems possible if we reduce the scale of government. A bioregion seems about the right size: say close to a small state, or along the lines of the Swiss canton system or American Indian tribes.

If nothing else, bioregional government—which theoretically would express the biological and cultural realities of people-in-place—would promote the diversity of biosocial experimentation; and in diversity is stability. The present system of national government seems about to collapse on the weight of its own emptiness. Our economy is dissolving like wet sugar. Violence is epidemic. The quality of our workmanship—always the hallmark of a proud people—has deteriorated so badly that we're ashamed to classify our products as durable goods. Our minds have been homogenized by television, which keeps our egos in perpetual infancy while substituting them for a sense of the self. Our information comes from progressively fewer sources, none of them notably reliable. We spend more time posturing than we do getting it on. In short,

American culture has become increasingly gutless and barren in our lifetimes, and the political system little more than a cover for an economics that ravages the planet and its people for the financial gain of very few. It seems almost a social obligation to explore alternatives. Our much-heralded standard of living hasn't done much for the quality of our daily lives; the glut of commodities, endlessly hurled at us out of the vast commodity spectacle, is just more shit on the windshield.

I don't want to imply that bioregionalism is the latest sectarian addition to the American Left, which historically has been more concerned with doctrinal purity and shafting each other than with effective practice. It's not a question of working within the system or outside the system, but simply of working, *somewhere*, to pull if off. And as I mentioned at the beginning, I'm not so sure bioregionalism even has a doctrine to be pure about—it's more a sense of direction (uphill, it seems) than the usual leftist highway to Utopia . . . or Ecotopia for that matter.

Just for the record, and to give some credence to the diversity of thought informing bioregionalism, I want to note some of the spirits I see at work in the early formulation of the notion: pantheists, Wobs, Reformed Marxists (that is, those who see the sun as the means of production), Diggers, liberterreans, Kropotkinites (mutual aid and coevolution), animists, alchemists (especially the old school), lefty Buddhists, Situationists (consummate analysts of the commodity spectacle), syndicalists, Provos, born-again Taoists, general outlaws, and others drawn to the decentralist banner by raw empathy.

A third element composing the bioregional notion is spirit. Since I can't claim any spiritual wisdom, and must admit to being virtually ignorant on the subject, I'm reluctant to offer more than the most tentative perceptions. What I think most bioregionalists hold in spiritual common is a profound regard for life—all life, not just white Americans, or humankind entire, but frogs, roses, mayflies, coyotes, lichens: all of it: the gopher snake and the gopher. For instance, we don't want to save the whales for the sweetsie-poo, lily-romantic reasons attributed to us by those who profit from their slaughter; we don't want them saved merely because they are magnificent creatures, so awesome that when you see one close from an open boat your heart roars; we want to save them for the most selfish of reasons; without them we are diminished.

In the bioregional spirit view we're all one creation, and it may seem almost simple-minded to add that there is a connection—even a necessary unity—between the natural world and the human mind (which may be just a fancy way of saying there is a connection between life and existence). Different people and groups have their own paths and practices and may describe this connection differently—profound, amusing, ineluctable, mysterious—but they all acknowledge the importance of the connection. The connection is archaic, primitive, and so obvious that it hasn't received much attention since the rise of Christian dominion and fossil-fuel industrialism. If it is a quality of archaic thought to dispute the culturally enforced dichotomy between the spiritual and the practical, I decidedly prefer the archaic view. What could possibly be of more *practical* concern than our spiritual well-being as individuals, as a species, and as members of a larger community of life? The Moral Majority certainly isn't going to take us in that direction; they're interested in business as usual, as their golden boy, James Watt, has demonstrated. We need fewer sermons and more prayers.

This sense of bioregional spirit isn't fixed to a single religious form or practice. Generally it isn't Christian-based or noticeably monotheistic, though such views aren't excluded. I think the main influences are the primitive animist/Great Spirit tradition, various Eastern and esoteric religious practices, and plain ol' paying attention. I may be stretching the accord, but I also see a shared awareness that the map is not the journey, and for that reason it is best to be alert and to respond to the opportunities presented rather than waste away wishing life would offer some worthy spiritual challenge (which it does, constantly, anyway). Call it whatever seems appropriate—enlightenment, fulfillment, spiritual maturity, happiness, self-realization—it has to be earned, and to be earned it has to be lived, and that means bringing it into our daily lives and working on it. Instant gratifications are not the deepest gratifications, I suspect, though Lord knows they certainly have their charms. The emphasis is definitely on the practice, not the doctrine, and especially on practicing what you preach; there is a general recognition that there are many paths, and that they are a further manifestation of crucial natural diversity. I might also note for serious backsliders that the play is as serious as the work, and there is a great willingness to celebrate; nobody is interested in a spirit whose holiness is constantly announced with sour piety and narrow self-righteousness.

Combining the three elements gives a loose idea of what I take to be bioregionalism: a decentralized, self-determined mode of social organization; a culture predictated upon biological integrities and acting in respectful accord; and a society which honors and abets the spiritual development of its members. Or so the theory goes. However, it's not mere theory, for there have been many cultures founded essentially upon those principles; for example, it has been the dominant cultural mode of inhabitation on this continent. The point is not to go back, but to take the best forward. Renewal, not some misty retreat into what was.

Theories, ideas, notions—they have their generative and reclamative values, and certainly a loveliness, but without the palpable intelligence of practice they remain hovering in the nether regions of nifty entertainments or degrade into more flamboyant fads and diversions like literary movements and hula-hoops. Practice is what puts the heart to work. If theory establishes the game, practice is the gamble, and the first rule of all gambling games has it like this: you can play bad and win; you can play good and lose; but if you play good over the long haul you're gonna come out alright.

Bioregional practice (or applied strategy) can take as many forms as the imagination and nerves, but for purpose of example I've hacked it into two broad categories; resistance and renewal. Resistance involves a struggle between the bioregional forces (who represent intelligence, excellence, and care) and the forces of heartlessness (who represent a greed so lifeless and forsaken it can't even pass as ignorance). In a way, I think it really is that simple, that there is, always, a choice about how we will live our lives, that there is a state of constant opportunity for both spiritual succor and carnal delight, and that the way we choose to live is the deepest expression of who we truly are. If we consistently choose against the richest possibilities of life, against kindness, against beauty, against love and sweet regard, then we aren't much. Our only claim to dignity is trying our best to do what we think is right, to put some heart in it, some soul, flower and root. We're going to fall on our asses a lot, founder on our pettiness and covetousness and sloth, but at least there is the effort, and that's surely better than being just another quivering piece of the national cultural jello. Or so it seems to me.

However, the primary focus of resistance is not the homogeneous American supraculture—that can be resisted for the most part simply by refusing to participate while at the same time trying to live our lives the way we think we should (knowing we'll get no encouragement whatsoever from the colonial overstructure). Rather, the focus of resistance is against the continuing destruction of natural systems. We can survive the ruthless homogeneity of national culture because there are many holes we can slip through, but we cannot survive if the natural systems that sustain us are destroyed. That has to be stopped if we want to continue living on this planet. That's not "environmentalism"; it's ecology with a vengeance. Personally, I think we should develop a Sophoclean appreciation for the laws of nature, and submit. Only within the fractional time frame of fossil-fuel industrialization have we begun to seriously insult the environment and impudently violate the conditions of life. We've done a great deal of damage in a very short time, and only because of the amazing flexibility of natural systems have we gotten away with it so far. But I don't think we'll destroy the planet; she will destroy us first, which is perhaps only to say we'll destroy ourselves. The most crucial point of resistance is choosing not to.

And then we must try to prevent others from doing it for us all, since by allowing monopoly-capital centralized government (which, like monotheism, is not so much putting all your eggs in one basket as dropping your one egg in a blender), we have given them the power to make such remote-control decisions. The way to prevent it is five-fold: by being a model for an alternative; by knowing more than they do; by being politically astute; by protecting what we value; and by any means necessary. (I think it's important to note that there is nearly complete agreement that nonviolence is the best means available, and that the use of violence is always a sad admission of desperation. Besides, they have all the money, guns, and lawyers. People advocating violent means are probably not very interested in living much longer.)

I think political smarts are best applied in the local community and county. Most crucial land use decisions, for instance, are made at the county level by boards of supervisors. The representative-to-constituent ratio is obviously much better in a county than in a country, and therefore informed and spirited constituents have a far greater influence on decisions and policies. Work to elect sympathetic representatives. Put some money where your heart is. Go to your share of the generally boring meetings and hearings. Challenge faulty information (thus the importance of knowing more than they do). Create alternatives. Stand your ground.

Buying land is also a strong political move; "ownership" is the best protection against gross environmental abuse, just as living on the land is the best defence against mass-media gelatin culture, assuming the quality of information influences the quality of thought. Owning land also affords increased political leverage within the present system. Besides, bioregionalism without a tangible land base would be like love without sex; the circuits of association wouldn't be complete. (Of course, it isn't necessary to own land to either appreciate it or resist its destruction, and I hope nobody infers that bioregionalism is for land aristocracy.)

The growth and strength of the "environmental movement" in the past decade has encouraged awareness about the destruction of natural systems and the consequences of such callous disregard. This is all to the good, and we should continue to stay in their faces on critical issues. But it's going to be continual crisis ecology unless we come up with a persuasive economic alternative; otherwise, most people will go on choosing progress over maturity, for progress is deeply equated with payroll, and money, to most people, means life. It's that cold. It's also basically true, and many friends share my chagrin that it took us so long to grasp that truism. It now seems painfully obvious that the economic system must be transformed if we hope to protect natural systems from destruction in the name of Mammon. Economics seems to baffle everyone, especially me. I have no prescriptions to offer, except to note that it doesn't have to be one economic system, and that any economics should include a fair measure of value. What's needed is an economy that takes into true account the cost of biospheric destruction and at the same time feeds the family. People must be convinced that it's in their best economic interest to maintain healthy biological systems. The best place to meet this challenge is where you live—that is, personally and within the community.

It's probably also fairly plain that changing the economic system will involve changing our conception of what constitutes a fulfilled life and cracking the cultural mania for mindless consumption and its attendant waste. To realize what is alive within us, the who of who we are, we have to know what we truly need, and what is enough. As Marshall Sahlins has pointed out, affluence can be attained either through increasing production or reducing needs. Since increased production usually means ravaged natural systems, the best strategy seems the reduction of needs, and hopefully the consequent recognition that enough is plenty. A truly affluent society is one of material sufficiency and spiritual riches.

While we're keeping up this resistance in our daily lives—and I think it is in the quality of daily life rather than momentary thrills that the heart is proven—we can begin repairing the natural systems that have been damaged. Logged and mined watersheds need to be repaired. Streams have to be cleared. Trees planted. Checkdams built to stop gully erosion. Long-term management strategies developed. Tough campaigns waged to secure funding for the work. There's a strong effort in this direction happening in Northern California now, much of it through worker co-ops and citizens' groups, with increasingly cooperative help from local and state agencies. This work has really just begun, and the field is wide open. So far it seems to satisfy the two feelings that prompted it: the sense that we have a responsibility to renew what we've wasted and the need to practice "right livelihood," or work that provides a living while promoting the spirit.

Natural system renewal (or rehabilitation, or enhancement, or whatever other names it goes by) could well be our first environmental art. It requires a thorough knowledge of how natural systems work, delicate perceptions of specific sites, the development of appropriate techniques, and hard physical work of the kind that puts you to bed after dinner. What finer work than healing the Earth, where the rewards are both in the doing and the results? It deserves our participation and support. For the irrefutable fact of the matter is that if we want to explore the bioregional possibility, we've got to work, got to get dirty—either by sitting on our asses at environmental hearings or by busting them planting trees in the rain. Sniveling don't make it.

The chances of bioregionalism succeeding, like the chances of survival itself, are beside the point. If one person, or a few, or a community of people, live more fulfilling lives from bioregional practice, then it's successful. This country has a twisted idea of success: it is almost always a quantitative judgment—salary, wins, the number of rooms in the house, the amount of people you command. Since bioregionalism by temperament is qualitative, the basis of judgment should be shifted accordingly. What they call a subculture, we call friends.

Most of the people I talk with feel we have a fighting chance to stop environmental destruction within 50 years and to turn the culture around within 800 to 1,000 years. "Fighting chance" translates as long odds but good company, and bioregionalism is obviously directed at people whose hearts put a little gamble in their blood. Since we won't live to see the results of this hoped-for transformation, we might as well live to start it right, with the finest expressions of spirit and style we can muster, keeping in mind that there's only a functional difference between the flower and the root, that essentially they are part of the same abiding faith.

The Sun still rises every morning. Dig in.

27   Ecocentrism Explained and Defended

Robyn Eckersley

....

Introduction

So far, I have been concerned to distinguish a general ecocentric approach from the other major streams of modern environmentalism, namely, resource conservation, human welfare ecology, preservationism, and animal liberation. It still remains to explore the theoretical framework of ecocentrism in a little more detail and address some of the common criticisms and misunderstandings that are often levelled against, or associated with, a general ecocentric perspective. I will also use this opportunity to compare and discuss three distinctive types of ecocentrism within the Western tradition: autopoietic intrinsic value theory, transpersonal ecology, and ecofeminism.

Ecocentrism Explained

Ecocentrism is based on an ecologically informed philosophy of *internal relatedness*, according to which all organisms are not simply interrelated with their environment but also *constituted* by those very environmental interrelationships.[1] According to Birch and Cobb, it is more accurate to think of the world in terms of "events" or "societies of events" rather than "substances":

Events are primary, and substantial objects are to be viewed as enduring patterns among changing events. . . . The ecological model is a model of internal relations. No event first occurs and then relates to its world. The event is a synthesis of relations to other events.[2]

According to this picture of reality, the world is an intrinsically dynamic, interconnected web of relations in which there are no absolutely discrete entities and no absolute dividing lines between the living and the nonliving, the animate and the inanimate, or the human and the nonhuman. This model of reality undermines anthropocentrism insofar as whatever faculty we choose to underscore our own uniqueness or specialness as the basis of our moral superiority (e.g. rationality, language, or our tool-making capability), we will invariably find either that there are some humans who do *not* possess such a faculty or that there are some nonhumans who *do*.[3] Nonanthropocentric ethical theorists have used this absence of any rigid, absolute dividing line between humans and nonhumans to point out the logical inconsistency of conventional anthropocentric ethical and political theory that purports to justify the exclusive moral

From Robyn Eckersley, *Environmentalism and Political Theory: Toward an Ecocentric Approach* (Albany, NY: SUNY, 1992), 49–71. Reprinted with permission.

considerability of humans on the basis of our separateness from, say, the rest of the animal world. Indeed, we saw in the previous chapter how Singer used this kind of argument to criticize human-centered ethical theory and defend animal liberation. While there are undoubtedly many important differences in *degree* (as distinct from kind) between all or some humans and nonhumans, as Fox points out, this cuts both ways; for example, there are countless things that other animals do better than us.[4] (And there are also innumerable differences in capacities that separate nonhuman life-forms from each other.) From an ecocentric perspective, to single out only *our* special attributes as the basis of our exclusive moral considerability is simply human chauvinism that conveniently fails to recognize the special attributes of other life-forms: it assumes that what is distinctive about humans is *more worthy* than, rather than simply *different* from, the distinctive features of other life-forms.[5] John Rodman has called this the "differential imperative," that is, the selection of what humans do best (as compared to other species) as the measure of human virtue and superiority over other species. Rodman traces this idea in Western thought as far back as Socrates, who saw the most virtuous human as "the one who most fully transcends their animal and vegetative nature."[6] The upshot, of course, is that one becomes a better human if one reinforces the differential imperative by maximizing one's "species-specific differentia." (Moreover, as Benton points out, the putative human/animal opposition may sometimes be seen as serving "as a convenient symbolic device whereby we have attributed to animals the dispositions we have not been able to contemplate in ourselves."[7])

Ecocentric theorists have also pointed out how new scientific discoveries have served to challenge long-standing anthropocentric prejudices. As the Copernican and Darwinian revolutions have shown, scientific discoveries can have a dramatic impact on popular conceptions of, and orientations toward, nature. This is not to argue that science can or ought to determine ethics or politics but merely to acknowledge that in modern times the credibility of any Western philosophical worldview is seriously compromised if it is not at least cognizant of, and broadly consistent with, current scientific knowledge. It is indeed ironic that while an ecocentric orientation is often wrongly criticized for resting on an "anti-science," mystical idealization of nature, many proponents of ecocentrism are quick to point out that the philosophical premises of ecocentrism (i.e. the model of internal relations) are actually *more* consistent with modern science than the premises of anthropocentrism, which posit humans as either separate from and above the rest of nature (or if not separate from the rest of nature then nonetheless the acme of evolution). In this respect, ecocentric theorists, far from being anti-science, often *enlist* science to help undermine deeply ingrained anthropocentric assumptions that have found their way into many branches of the social sciences and humanities, including modern political theory. As George Sessions has argued, modern science has "been the single most decisive non-anthropocentric intellectual force in the Western world."[8] Indeed, it has been the mechanistic, materialistic worldview of the Enlightenment (which has shaped so much modern political theory) that has most come under challenge by these new scientific discoveries. Just as the Copernican and Darwinian revolutions helped to undermine the Judeo-Christian, medieval worldview of the "great chain of being" (according to which all life-forms were fixed in a static hierarchy with humans standing above the beasts and below the angels), the picture of ecological and subatomic reality that has emerged from new discoveries in biology and physics has now made inroads into many of the assumptions of the Newtonian worldview.[9] The most pervasive of these are *technological optimism*—the confident belief that with further scientific research we can rationally manage (i.e. predict, manipulate, and control) all the negative unintended consequences of large-scale human interventions in nature; *atomism*—the idea that nature is made up of discrete building blocks and that the observer is therefore completely separate from the observed; and *anthropocentrism*—the belief that there is a clear and morally relevant dividing line between humankind and the rest of nature, that humankind is the only or principal source of value and meaning in the world, and that nonhuman nature is there for no other purpose but to serve humankind.[10]

Clearly, ecocentric theorists are not against science or technolgy per se; rather they are against scientism (i.e. the conviction that empiric-analytic science is the only valid way of knowing) and technocentrism (i.e. anthropocentric technological optimism). The distinction is crucial. Indeed, many ecocentric theorists are keenly interested in the history and philosophy of science and are fond of pointing out the reciprocal interplay between dominant images of nature (whether derived from science, philosophy, or religion) and dominant images of society.[11] This mutual reinforcement is reflected in the resonance between medieval Christian cosmology and the medieval political order (both of which emphasized a hierarchy of being) and between the Newtonian worldview and the rise of modern liberal democracy (both of which emphasized atomism). Ecocentric theorists are now drawing attention to what Fox has referred to as the "structural similarity" between the ecological model of internal relatedness and the picture of reality that has emerged in modern biology and physics, although it is too early to say what the societal implications of these developments might be.[12] Unlike Capra, I see nothing *inevitable* about the possibility of a new, ecologically informed cultural transformation, although there are certainly many exciting possibilities "in the wind."[13]

The structural similarity between the ecological model of internal relatedness that informs ecocentrism and the picture of reality delivered to us by certain branches of modern science is, of course, no substitute for an ethical and political justification of an ecocentric perspective (although it does serve to undermine the opposing perspective of anthropocentrism). As I noted earlier, in modern times general consistency with science is merely a necessary—as distinct from a sufficient—condition for the acceptance of an alternative philosophical worldview in the West. In this respect, I agree with Michael Zimmerman's observations concerning the relevance of science to environmental ethics and politics: that it may help to inspire and prepare the ground for a new orientation toward nature and "give humanity prudential reasons for treating the biosphere with more care" but that "a change in scientific understanding alone cannot produce the needed change of consciousness."[14] It is no argument, then, simply to appeal to the authority of nature as a justification for a particular political worldview. It is, on the other hand, perfectly reasonable to question an opposing worldview on the ground that the assumptions on which it is based have been shown by science to be erroneous.

The ecocentric recognition of the interrelatedness of all phenomena together with its prima facie orientation of inclusiveness of all beings means that it is far more protective of the Earth's life-support system than an anthropocentric perspective. As Michael Zimmerman has argued in addressing the practical consequences of an anthropocentric perspective:

If humankind is understood as the goal of history, the source of all value, the pinnacle of evolution, and so forth, then it is not difficult for humans to justify the plundering of the natural world, which is not human and therefore "valueless."[15]

When anthropocentric assumptions of this kind are combined with a powerful technology, the capacity for environmental destruction increases dramatically.

Anthropocentrism of this extreme kind may be seen as a kind of ecological myopia or unenlightened self-interest that is blind to the ecological circularities between the self and the external world, with the result that it leads to the perpetuation of unintended and unforeseen ecological damage. An ecocentric perspective, in contrast, recognizes that nature is not only more complex than we presently know but also quite possibly more complex, in principle, than we *can* know—an insight that has been borne out in the rapidly expanding field of chaos theory.[16]

Although the anthropocentric resource conservation and human welfare ecology streams of environmentalism adopt a general ethic of prudence and caution based on an ecologically enlightened self-interest, they differ from an ecocentric perspective in that they see the ecological tragedy as essentially a *human* one. Those belonging to the ecocentric stream, on the other hand, see the tragedy as *both* human and nonhuman. This is because a thoroughgoing ecocentric perspective is one that, "within obvious kinds of practical limits, allows all entities (including humans) *the freedom to unfold in their own way unhindered by the various forms of human domination*."[17] Such a general perspective may be seen as seeking "emancipation writ large." In according ontological primacy to the internal relatedness of all phenomena, an ecocentric perspective adopts an "existential attitude of mutuality" in recognition of the fact that one's personal fulfilment is inextricably tied up with that of others.[18] This is not seen as a resignation or self-sacrifice but rather as a *positive affirmation* of the fact of our embeddedness in ecological relationships.

The ecological model of internal relatedness upon which ecocentrism rests applies not only in respect of human-nonhuman relations but also in respect of relations among humans: in a biological, psychological, and social sense we are all constituted by our interrelationships between other humans, and our political, economic, and cultural institutions. As Birch and Cobb emphasize, we do not exist as separate entities and *then* enter into these relations. From the moment we are born, we are constituted by, and coevolve within the context of, such relations.[19] According to this model, we are neither completely passive and determined beings (as crude behaviorists would have it) nor completely autonomous and self-determining beings (as some existentialists would have it). Rather, we are *relatively* autonomous beings who, by our purposive thought and action, help to constitute the very relations that determine who we are.[20] Of course, this kind of social interactionist model is hardly new to the social sciences. For example, in social psychology it is found in the theories of symbolic interactionism and phenomenology. In political philosophy a similar social model is implicit in the many communitarian and socialist political philosophies that seek the mutual self-realization of all in preference to the individual self-realization of some. This helps to explain why there is a much greater elective affinity—and hence a much greater potential for theoretical synthesis—between ecocentrism and communitarian and socialist political philosophies than there is between ecocentrism and individualistic political philosophies such as liberalism. Ecocentric political theorists have generally discarded what Callicott has aptly described as "the threadbare metaphysical cloth from which classical utilitarianism [and, I would add, Lockean liberalism] is cut." This is because, as Callicott puts it,

Utilitarianism [indeed liberalism in general] assumes a radical individualism or rank social atomism completely at odds with the relational sense of self that is consistent with a more fully informed evolutionary and ecological understanding of terrestrial and human nature.[21]

It should be clear, however, that ecocentric theorists are not seeking to discard the central value of autonomy in Western political thought and replace it with something completely new. Rather, ecocentric theorists are merely concerned to revise the notion of autonomy and incorporate it into a broader, ecological framework.

The word autonomy is derived from the Greek *autos* (self) and *nomos* (law) and means, literally, to live by one's own laws. This is similar to Immanuel Kant's influential formulation according to which an autonomous person is someone who acts from self-imposed principle (as distinct from personal whim or externally imposed commands). Ecocentric theorists have carried forward this basic notion of autonomy as self-determination. However, they have extended the interpretation and application of the notion by radically revising the notion of "self." After all, if we take autonomy to mean self-determination, this still begs the question as to what kind of "self" we are addressing. In lieu of the atomistic and individualistic self of liberalism or the more social self of socialism, ecocentric theorists have introduced a broader, ecological notion of self that incorporates these individual and social aspects in a more encompassing framework. From the perspective of the ecological model of internal relations, the liberal idea of autonomy as independence from (or "freedom from") others is seen as philosophically misguided. (To the extent that interconnectedness with others is acknowledged under this particular liberal interpretation, it is likely to be experienced as threatening, as causing a loss of self.) While socialists tend to adopt a more relational model of self (which sometimes encompasses our relations with the nonhuman world), this still remains embedded in an anthropocentric framework.

Of course, the ecocentric reformulation of autonomy does not mean that the boundary between one's individual self and others completely falls away. Rather, the reformulation merely seeks to emphasize the flexible or soft nature of the boundaries between self and other (which is why ecocentric theorists often refer to the individual self as forming part of a "larger self"). Evelyn Fox Keller encapsulates the permeable nature of the boundaries between self and other in her concept of "dynamic autonomy." As Keller explains, this dynamic concept of autonomy "is a product at least as much of relatedness as it is of delineation; neither is prior."[22] From an ecocentric perspective, the exercise of dynamic autonomy requires psychological maturity and involves a sensitive mediation between one's individual self and the larger whole. This does not mean having control over others but rather means having *a sense of competent agency in the world* in the context of an experience of continuity with others. In contrast, the quest for radical independence from others, or power over others, leads to an objectification of others, and a denial of their own modes of relative autonomy or subjectivity.

What is new about an ecocentric perspective (and Keller shares this perspective) is that it extends the notion of autonomy (and the interactionist model of internal relations on which it is based) to a broader and more encompassing pattern of layered interrelationships that extend beyond personal and societal relations to include relations with the rest of the biotic community. This means that the nonhuman world is no longer posited simply as the background or means to the self-determination of individuals or political communities, as is the case in most modern political theorizing. Rather, the different members of the nonhuman community are also appreciated as important in their own terms, as having their own (varying degrees of) relative autonomy and their own modes of being. The implications of applying this expanded model of internal relations to social and political thought are far-reaching. As Zimmerman has put it, "the paradigm of internal relations lets us view ourselves as manifestations of a complex universe; we are not apart but are moments in the openended, novelty-producing process of cosmic evolution."[23]

Some Common Criticisms and Misunderstandings

Ecocentrism's challenge to cultural and political orthodoxy has been widely resisted and misunderstood by critics for a variety of reasons: that it is impossible, misanthropic (or at least insulting to some humans, notably the oppressed), impractical, and/or based on an all too convenient idealization of nature. Some resistance is, of course, to be expected of a perspective that, as George Sessions has put it, is mounting a philosophical challenge to "the pervasive metaphysical and ethical anthropocentrism that has dominated Western culture with classical Greek humanism and the Judeo-Christian tradition since its inception."[24] But is such resistance warranted? In the remainder of this section I address five common objections that have contributed to this resistance to ecocentrism.

One common criticism is that it is impossible to perceive the world *other* than from an anthropocentric perspective, since we are, after all, *human* subjects. This criticism, however, entirely misses the point of the critique of anthropocentrism by conflating the identity of the perceiving subject with the content of what is perceived and valued, a conflation that Fox has called the "anthropocentric fallacy."[25] In particular, this kind of understanding conflates the trivial and tautological sense of the term anthropocentrism (i.e. that we can only ever perceive the world as human subjects—who can argue against this?) and the substantive and informative sense of the term (the unwarranted, differential treatment of other beings on the basis that they do not belong to our *own* species).[26] Ecocentric theorists are not claiming that we must, or indeed can, know *exactly* what it is like to be, say, a kangaroo (although there are meditation traditions and forms of shamanic journeying that enable humans to experience the world as other beings).[27] As Barbara Noske explains, "there is a sense in which we cannot know the Other (whether it be other species, other cultures, the other sex or even each other) [however] we must remind ourselves that other meanings exist, even if we may be severely limited in our understanding of them."[28] As Fox points out, to say that humans cannot be nonanthropocentric is like saying that a male cannot be nonsexist or that a white person cannot be nonracist because they can only perceive the world as male or white subjects.[29] This understanding ignores the fact that males and whites are quite capable of cultivating a nonsexist or nonracist consciousness or, in this case, that humans are quite capable of cultivating a nonanthropocentric consciousness.

A second misconception of ecocentrism is to interpret its sustained critique of anthropocentrism as anti-human and/or as displaying an insensitivity to the needs of the poor and the oppressed by collectively blaming the human species as a whole for the ecological crisis (rather than singling out specific nations, groups, or classes). However, this criticism fails to appreciate the clear distinction between a *non*anthropocentric and a *mis*anthropic perspective.[30] Ecocentrism is not against humans per se or the celebration of humanity's special forms of excellence; rather, it is against the ideology of human chauvinism. Ecocentric theorists see each human individual and each human culture as just as entitled to live and blossom as any other species, *provided* they do so in a way that is sensitive to the needs of other human individuals, communities, and cultures, and other life-forms generally. Moreover, many critics of ecocentrism fail to realize that a perspective that seeks emancipation writ large is one that *necessarily* supports social justice in the human community. Given that it is patently the case that not all humans are implicated in ecological destruction to the same degree, then it follows that ecocentric theorists would not expect the costs of environmental reform to be borne equally by all classes and nations, regardless of relative wealth or privilege. That many ecocentric theorists have given special theoretical attention to human–nonhuman relations arises from the fact that these relations are so often neglected by theorists in the humanities and social sciences. It does not arise from any lack of concern or lack of theoretical inclusiveness with regard to human emancipatory struggles.

Before leaving this point, it should be noted that some ecophilosophically minded writers (e.g. David Ehrenfeld in *The Arrogance of Humanism*) have been critical of humanism in general, rather than just anthropocentrism. This can be misleading, however, since humanism does not represent one single idea, such as human self-importance or the celebration of humanity as the sole and sufficient source of value and inspiration in the world, although these have been central ideas in humanism and are the main bone of contention of nonanthropocentric ecophilosophers.[31] Rather, humanism is a complex tapestry of ideas, many strands of which are anthropocentric, yet some strands of which remain worthwhile and consistent with an ecocentric perspective. As Blackham explains, "the 'open mind,' the 'open society,' and the sciences and 'humanities' are the glory of humanism and at the same time a widely shared inheritance."[32] In view of this, it is more to the point simply to criticize the many anthropocentric assumptions embedded in our humanist heritage rather than to equate anthropocentrism with humanism and thereby condemn humanism in its entirety.

A third criticism is that ecocentrism is a passive and quietistic perspective that regards humans as no more valuable than, say, ants or the AIDS virus. However, ecocentrism merely seeks to cultivate a prima facie orientation of nonfavoritism; it does not mean that humans cannot eat or act to defend themselves or others (including other threatened species) from danger or life-threatening diseases.[33] In this respect, the degree of sentience of an organism and its degree of self-consciousness and capacity for richness of experience are relevant factors (as distinct from exclusive criteria) in any ethical choice situation alongside other factors, such as whether a particular species is endangered or whether a particular population is crucial to the maintenance of a particular ecosystem.[34] A nonanthropocentric perspective is one that ensures that the interests of nonhuman species and ecological communities (of varying levels of aggregation) are not ignored in human decision making *simply* because they are not human or because they are not of instrumental value to humans. It does not follow from this prima facie orientation of nonfavoritism, however, that the actual outcome of human decision making must necessarily favor noninterference with other life-forms. Humans are just as entitled to live and blossom as any other species, and this inevitably necessitates some killing of, suffering by, and interference with, the lives and habitats of other species.[35] When faced with a choice, however, those who adopt an ecocentric perspective will seek to choose the course that will minimize such harm and maximize the opportunity of the widest range of organisms and communities—*including ourselves*—to flourish in their/our own way. This is encapsulated in the popular slogan "live simply so that others [both human and nonhuman] may simply live."[36]

A fourth criticism against ecocentrism is that it is difficult to translate into social, political, and legal practice. How, many sceptics ask, can we ascribe rights to nonhumans when they cannot reciprocate? My primary answer to this kind of criticism is that it is neither necessary nor ultimately desirable that we ascribe legal rights to nonhuman entities to ensure their protection. However, it also needs to be pointed out that there is no a priori reason why legal rights cannot be ascribed to nonhuman entities. As Christopher Stone has argued, the idea of conferring legal rights on nonhumans is not "unthinkable" when it is remembered that legal rights are conferred on "nonspeaking" persons such as infants and fetuses, on legal fictions such as corporations, municipalities and trusts, and on entities such as churches and nation states.[37] Given that there is no common thread or principle running through this anomalous class of right holders, Stone argues that there is no good reason *against* extending legal rights to natural entities. Stone proposes that the rights of nonhuman entities (or, in his language, "natural objects") be defended in the same way as "human vegetables" that is, by the appointment of a Guardian or Friend who would ensure that the natural entity's interests were protected (e.g. by administering a trust fund and instigating legal actions on its behalf in order to make good any injury inflicted on it). Stone's proposal may be seen as an even more daring adventure in liberalism than animal liberation insofar as it seeks to provide the means of legally protecting the special interests of nonhuman and nonsentient entities such as forests, rivers, and oceans.

While Stone's proposals may serve an important educative and protective purpose in respect of nonhuman interests, there is nonetheless an element of absurdity in the notion of extending rights to nonhumans on the basis of a *contractarian* notion of rights, whereby a right must be accompanied by a correlative duty. Stone appears to lean toward such a view in his suggestion that the trust funds established for the benefit of a natural entity might also be used to satisfy judgments *against* that entity (e.g. a river might be liable for the damage inflicted by its flooding and destroying crops!) although he admits that such an idea would prove to be troublesome. As Stone asks: "When the Nile overflows, is it the 'responsibility' of the river? the mountains? the snow? the hydrological cycle?"[8] Stone also canvasses the possibility of "an electoral apportionment that made some systematic effort to allow for the representative 'rights' of nonhuman life."[39] Of course, the first kind of scenario could be avoided by employing a noncontractarian theory of rights (i.e. as not necessarily entailing reciprocal duties), yet there is still something strained and ungainly in the attempt to extend to the nonhuman world political concepts that have been especially tailored over many centuries to protect *human* interests. This highlights the need to search for simpler and more elegant ways of enabling the flourishing of a rich and diverse nonhuman world without resorting to the extension to the nonhuman realm of peculiarly *human* political and legal models such as justice, equality, and rights.[40] As John Livingston points out, extending liberal egalitarian ideals in this way "anthropomorphizes the nonhuman world in order to include it in a human ethical code."[41] Similarly, John Rodman has suggested that the "liberation of nature" requires not the extension of human-like rights to nonhumans but the liberation of the nonhuman world from "the status of human resource, human product, human caricature."[42] It is indeed noteworthy that one of the doyens of modern liberal theory— John Rawls—in discussing the limits of his liberal theory of justice, has stated in passing that

it does not seem possible to extend the contract doctrine so as to include them [i.e. creatures lacking a capacity for a sense of justice] in a natural way. A correct conception of our relations to animals and to nature would seem to depend [instead] upon a theory of the natural order and our place in it.[43]

The above reservations concerning the appropriateness of extending legal rights to nonhumans are hardly fatal to ecocentrism; nor do they provide any argument for resorting to anthropocentrism through want of appropriate legal mechanisms. Rather, they emphasize the importance of a general change in consciousness and suggest that a gradual cultural, educational, and social revolution involving a reorientation of our sense of place in the evolutionary drama is likely to provide a better long-term protection of the interests of the nonhuman world than a more limited legal revolution of the kind envisaged by Stone. In the short term, the above reservations concerning the applicability of liberal categories to the nonuman world highlight the needs for us to rethink the ways in which we might legally protect the interests of the nonhuman world. Indeed, there are already existing alternative legislative precedents that avoid the language of rights but nonetheless ensure that government departments and courts consider both human *and* nonhuman interests when administering environmental legislation or adjudicating land-use conflicts.[44]

Finally, some critics are cynical of ecocentrism because they consider that it interprets nature selectively as something that is essentially harmonious, kindly, and benign (ignoring suffering, unpredictability, and change), thus providing an all too convenient model for human relations. Alternatively, critics have argued that the popular ecological views of some Green thinkers lean toward an idealization of nature or employ outmoded ecological notions (such as the "balance of nature") that have little to do with the way nature in fact operates.[45] My response to these criticisms is that ecocentric theorists simply do not need to depict nature as having a kindly human face or to show that nature is essentially benevolent or benign in order that humans respect it and regard it as worthy. If we try to judge the nonhuman world by human standards as to what is "kindly," we will invariably find it wanting.[46] Nonhuman nature knows no human ethics, it simply *is*.

In any event, appealing to the authority of nature (as known by ecology) is no substitute for ethical argument.[47] Ecological science cannot perform the task of normative justification in respect of an ecocentric political theory because it does not tell us why we *ought* to orient ourselves toward the world in a particular way. It can inform, inspire, and redirect our ethical and political theorizing, but it cannot justify it. *That* is the task of ethical and political theory. However, a general familiarity with new developments in science is important to an ecocentric perspective (the employment of outmoded concepts of nature *does* serve to detract from the force and credibility of ecopolitical argument). As we have already seen, a general familiarity with new developments in science by social and political theorists can enhance our understanding of the world around us, improve the general grounding and credibility of a political theory, and provide the basis for challenging opposing worldviews on the grounds that the assumptions on which they are based have been shown to be erroneous.

Three Varieties of Ecocentrism

Having explained and defended a general ecocentric perspective, it now remains to explore some particular theoretical and cultural expressions of ecocentrism. Indeed, there is a wide range of different approaches that are consistent with a general ecocentric perspective. Examples include axiological (i.e. value theory) approaches that argue for the intrinsic value of all living entities *as well* as such "systemic" entities as populations, species, ecosystems, and the ecosphere; the psychological-cosmological approach that is being developed under the name of "deep ecology" or, more recently, "transpersonal ecology"; the antihierarchical and personal ethic of care and reciprocity defended by ecofeminism; certain Eastern philosophies such as Taoism and Buddhism that emphasize the interconnectedness of all phenomena and the importance of humility and compassion; and the animistic cosmologies of many indigenous peoples who see and respect the nonhuman world as alive and enspirited.

I will explore three complementary expressions of ecocentrism within the Western tradition: autopoietic intrinsic value theory (which I see as an improvement on the popular, ecosystem-based "land ethic" of Aldo Leopold), transpersonal ecology, and ecofeminism.[48] In view of the increasing influence and popularity of both deep/transpersonal ecology and ecofeminism within Green circles, particular attention will be given to clarifying the areas of overlap and difference between these two distinctive ecocentric approaches.

AUTOPOIETIC INTRINSIC VALUE THEORY

Autopoietic intrinsic value theory—outlined by Fox under the name of "autopoietic ethics"—represents one kind of intrinsic value theory approach that is capable of providing a sound theoretical basis for ecocentrism. An autopoietic approach attributes intrinsic value to all entities that display the property of *autopoiesis*, which means "self-production" or "self-renewal" (from the Greek *autos*, "self," and *poiein*, "to produce").[49] Autopoietic entities are entities that are "primarily and continuously concerned with the regeneration of their own organizational activity and structure."[50] It is precisely this characteristic of self-production or self-renewal (as distinct from merely self-organization) that distinguishes living entities from self-correcting machines that appear to operate in a purposive manner (such as guided missiles). In other words, the primary product of the operations of living systems, as distinct from mechanical systems, is themselves, not some goal or task external to themselves.[51] Autopoietic entities are therefore *ends in themselves*, which as Fox points out, "amounts to the classical formulation of intrinsic value."[52] This means that autopoietic entities (e.g. populations, gene pools, ecosystems, and individual living organisms) are deserving of moral consideration in their own right.

An autopoietic approach provides a sounder theoretical basis for ecocentrism than the ethical holism of Aldo Leopold's famous land ethic, which declares that "A thing is right when it tends to preserve the integrity, stability and beauty of the biotic community. It is wrong when it does otherwise."[53] The problem with this ethic, as animal liberation proponents point out, is that it is vulnerable to the charge of "environmental fascism" in that is provides no recognition of the value of *individual* organisms. This is because, considered on its own, it can be interpreted as suggesting that individuals are dispensible—indeed, might need to be sacrificed for the good of the whole.[54]

An autopoietic approach to intrinsic value is not vulnerable to the objections that are associated with either extreme atomism or extreme holism. Whereas atomistic approaches attribute intrinsic value only to individual organisms, and whereas an unqualified holistic approach attributes intrinsic value only to whole ecosystems (or perhaps only the biosphere or ecosphere itself), an autopoietic approach recognizes the value of *all* process-structures that "continuously strive to produce and sustain their own organizational activity and structure."[55] That is, an autopoietic approach recognizes the value not only of individual organisms but also of species, ecosystems, and the ecosphere ("Gaia").

TRANSPERSONAL ECOLOGY

In contrast to the autopoietic approach, which proceeds via an axiological (i.e. value theory) route, transpersonal ecology proceeds by way of a cosmological and psychological route and is concerned to address the way in which we understand and experience the world.[56] The primary concern of transpersonal ecology is the cultivation of a wider sense of self through the common or everyday psychological process of *identification* with others. This should not be understood simply as a reformulation of the Kantian Categorical Imperative (i.e. dutiful altruism) or the Golden Rule (i.e. do unto others as you would have others do unto you) since these remain axiological approaches that are concerned with moral *obligations* that may or may not correspond with one's personal (or "heartfelt") inclinations.[57] (In any event, it should be noted here that Kant regarded *only* humans as ends in themselves.[58]) In contrast to axiological approaches, which issue in moral injunctions or a code of conduct (i.e. "you *ought* to respect other beings, regardless of how you might personally experience them"), transpersonal ecology is concerned to find ways in which we may experience a *lived sense* of identification with other beings. Indeed, as Fox points out, transpersonal ecology explicitly rejects approaches that issue in moral injunctions and advances instead an approach that seeks "to *invite* and *inspire* others to realize, in a this-worldly sense, as expansive a sense of self as possible."[59] As Arne Naess explains, if your sense of self embraces other beings, then "you need no moral exhortation to show care" toward those beings.[60] The cultivation of this kind of expansive sense of self means that compassion and empathy naturally flow as part of an individual's way of being in the world rather than as a duty or obligation that must be performed regardless of one's personal inclination.[61]

The transpersonal ecology approach is described as both cosmological *and* psychological because it proceeds from a particular picture of the world or cosmos—that we are, in effect, all "leaves" on an unfolding "tree of life"—to a psychological identification with all phenomena (i.e. with all leaves on the tree). Fox refers to this approach as *transpersonal* ecology because it is concerned to cultivate a sense or experience of self that extends *beyond* one's egoistic, biographical, or personal sense of self to include all beings.[62] This should not be confused with a generalized form of narcissism as this simply involves the projection of one's ego into a larger sphere (i.e. the self that is revered is still confined to the narrow, egoistic, particle-like sense of self). In contrast, transpersonal ecology (which draws on insights from, among other sources, transpersonal psychology and the teachings of Mahatma Gandhi) is addressing a much broader, transpersonal (i.e. transegoistic) sense of "ecological self" that embraces other beings (human and nonhuman) and ecological processes. The movement from an atomistic, *ego*centric sense of self toward an expansive, *eco*centric or transpersonal sense of self is seen as representing a process of psychological maturing.[63] In other words, transpersonal ecology is concerned to expand the circle of human compassion and respect for others beyond one's particular family and friends and beyond the human community to include the entire ecological community. The realization of this expansive, ecocentric sense of self is brought about by the process of identification with other beings (i.e. the cultivation of an empathic orientation toward the world) in recognition of the fact that one's own individual or personal fate is intimately bound up with the fate of others. It is noteworthy that deep/transpersonal ecology theorists provide a sophisticated theoretical articulation of the experience of many environmental activists as revealed in empirical research. As Lester Milbrath found in his sociological survey, "environmentalists, much more than non-environmentalists, have a generalized sense of compassion that extends to other species, to people in remote communities and countries, and to future generations."[64]

Some critics might object that this kind of approach attempts to derive an "ought" from an "is," in that it proceeds from the fact of our interconnectedness with the world to a particular kind of normative orientation toward the world. However, transpersonal ecologists do not seek to argue that the fact of our interconnectedness *logically* implies a caring orientation toward the world (indeed, this fact does not *logically* imply *any* kind of normative orientation). Rather, transpersonal ecologists are offering an "experiential invitation" rather than issuing a moral injunction. As Fox explains:

For transpersonal ecologists, given a deep enough understanding of the way things are, the response of being inclined to care for the unfolding of the world in all its aspects follows "naturally"—not as a *logical* consequence but as a *psychological* consequence; as an expression of the spontaneous unfolding (development, maturing) of the self.[65]

The autopoietic intrinsic value theory approach and the transpersonal ecology approach each have different advantages and are appropriate in different contexts. For example, the autopoietic approach is more suitable to translation into legal and political practice than the transpersonal ecology approach. After all, it makes sense to enact legislation that demands the recognition of certain intrinsic values, whereas it makes no sense to enact legislation that demands that people identify more widely with the world around them.[66] Indeed, there are already existing legislative precedents that are consistent with an autopoietic intrinsic value theory approach rather than an atomistic intrinsic value approach in that they value for their own sake both individual living organisms as well as entities such as ecosystems.[67]

The transpersonal ecology approach, in contrast, is more appropriately pursued in the community through educational and cultural activities (although these activities can, of course, be encouraged and financially supported by the state). Transpersonal ecology, in other words, lends itself far more to a "bottom-up" rather than a "top-down" approach to social change. Transpersonal ecology may thus be seen as forming part of the vanguard of the cultivation of a new worldview, a new culture and character, and new political horizons that are appropriate to our times. This emphasis on cultural renewal and reenvisioning our place in nature forms an essential component of ecocentric emancipatory thought. In this respect, transpersonal ecology may be seen as being more expressive of the cultural aspirations of ecocentric emancipatory thought than an autopoietic intrinsic value theory approach, although the latter is an essential complement. That is, cultural renewal and legislative reform must go hand in hand.

ECOFEMINISM

Like transpersonal ecology, ecofeminism is concerned with our sense of self and the way in which we experience the world rather than with formal value theory. Like transpersonal ecology, ecofeminism also proceeds from a process oriented, relational image of nature and seeks mutualistic social and ecological relationships based on a recognition of the interconnectedness, interdependence, and diversity of all phenomena.[68]

However, unlike transpersonal ecology, ecofeminism has taken the historical/symbolic association of women with nature as demonstrating a special convergence of interests between feminism and ecology. The convergence is seen to arise, in part, from the fact that patriarchal culture has located women somewhere between men and the rest of nature on a conceptual hierarchy of being (i.e. God, Man, Woman, Nature). This has enabled ecofeminists to identify what they see as a similar logic of domination between the destruction of nonhuman nature and the oppression of women. Indeed, it is a central claim of many ecofeminists (writing mostly, but not exclusively, from a radical feminist perspective) that "the larger culture's devaluation of natural processes was a product of masculine consciousness."[69] As Simone de Beauvoir observed in her wide-ranging exploration of the "second sex," women—like nonhuman animals—have usually been more preoccupied with the regeneration and repetition of life, whereas men have usually been free to seek ways of transcending life by remodelling, reshaping, and recreating the future through technology and symbols. Whereas women's activity has usually been perishable, involving "lower level" transformations of nature, men's activity has usually beem more lasting, involving major transformations of nature and culture.[70]

Although many feminists have rejected the association of women and nature as burdensome, ecofeminists, while recognizing that the association has been used to oppress women in the past, have nonetheless embraced it as a source of empowerment for women and the basis of a critique of the male domination of women *and* nonhuman nature. This is an explicitly ecofeminist project because it exposes and celebrates what has traditionally been regarded as Other—both woman *and* nonhuman nature—in the context of a far-reaching critique of hierarchical dualism and "masculine" culture. Ecofeminists seek to subvert the dominant valuation of what human characteristics and activities are most valuable. This project entails a rejection of many of the "advances" of patriarchal culture and a celebration of the previously undervalued nurturing characteristics of women.

In contrast to the more secular leanings of socialist and liberal feminists, many ecofeminists are vitally interested in cultivating an ecofeminist spirituality, whether it be through retrieving the insights of nonhierarchical pre-Christian cultures or reviving other Earth-based traditional practices (e.g. celebrating the Goddess-oriented culture of Old Europe, pagan rituals, Gaia, the body, natural cycles, and the experience of connectedness and embodiment in general).[71] In this respect, most ecofeminists would have much sympathy with Gary Snyder's sentiment that "our troubles began with the invention of male deities located off the planet."[72] Indeed, both ecofeminist and deep/transpersonal ecology theorists have been particularly critical of the Judeo-Christian heritage. As the ecofeminist theologian Elizabeth Dodson Gray explains, we need to move toward an "embodied ecospirituality" and re-myth Genesis in a way that honors diversity by moving our culture "to *a creation-based valuing of all parts of nature.*"[73]

There is a great deal in common between the particular ecological sensibility or sense of self defended by ecofeminists and deep/transpersonal ecologists. Indeed, many ecofeminist insights are indistinguishable from the "wider indentification" approach of transpersonal ecology. For example, Elizabeth Dodson Gray has suggested that the root of the modern ecological crisis is that "*we do not understand who we are*"; when we realize that we are intimately connected with the larger whole then "what hurts any part of my larger system will hurt me."[74]

Notwithstanding these important commonalities, ecofeminism tends to diverge from transpersonal ecology in two significant ways (although these tendencies are far from uniform among different ecofeminist writers). The first relates to the *kinds of identification* that are emphasized and the *kinds of self* that identify; the second relates to the kinds of theoretical explanation offered to account for the environmental crisis.

Most ecofeminists emphasize a form of identification with the world that is gender specific and based on, or at least begins with, personal contact and familiarity. Indeed, some ecofeminists have criticized the kind of identification defended by transpersonal ecologists for being abstract, impersonal, and preoccupied with the whole at the expense of the parts.[75] However, these criticisms overlook the fact that the transpersonal ecology approach to identification encompasses the personal by including both the whole *and* the parts in what Fox describes as an "outside-in" rather than "inside-out" approach. (Indeed, many ecofeminists arrive at a similar position to transpersonal ecology, albeit from an "inside-out" rather than "outside-in" route.) As Fox explains, it is an approach that "proceeds from a sense of the cosmos (such as that provided by the image of the tree of life) and works inward to each particular individual's sense of commonality with other entities."[76] Fox argues that cosmologically based identification represents a more impartial, inclusive, and, hence, more egalitarian approach to identification than does a *purely* personally based approach, in that it leads one to identify with all of the human and nonhuman world irrespective of one's personal involvement. Moreover, Fox argues that purely personally based forms of identification can lead to excessive partiality, attachment, possessiveness, and parochialism.[77] This does not mean, however, that transpersonal ecologists wish to deny the significance of personally based identification—indeed, Fox acknowledges that this kind of identification is the easiest and most immediate experience of identification available to humans. Rather, transpersonal ecologists simply seek to locate personally based identification in a wider social and ecological context. Moreover, this kind of identification does not seek to draw specific gender boundaries; rather it addresses a kind of identification that is available to both women and men.[78]

Nonetheless, some ecofeminists have argued that there is something special about women's experience that make women better placed than men to identify with nonhuman beings, ecological processes, and the larger whole. This argument takes two forms (although these are not always clearly differentiated). On the one hand, it is often claimed, or more usually implied, that this ease of identification with the rest of nature arises by virtue of what is unique about women's bodies (e.g. ovulation, menstruation, pregnancy, childbirth, and suckling the young). Here, the special connection between women and nature is usually presented as something that is grounded in women's reproductive and associated nurturing capabilities. On the other hand, it is often claimed that this readiness to identify with the rest of nature arises by virtue of women's oppression. That is, the separate social reality of women that has resulted from the division of labor in patriarchal societies (i.e. between the spheres of reproduction (women) and production (men)) is heralded as the basis of an alternative, nurturing, and more caring morality.[79] I will refer to these two arguments as the "body-based argument" and the "oppression argument" respectively. In both cases, the closer connection between woman and nature (whether biologically based or culturally assigned) is embraced as a source of special insight and empowerment for women.

Depending on how they are formulated, these two arguments carry significant insights that can assist in the task of ecological and social reconstruction. However, these arguments also raise a number of problems if pressed too far. While it cannot be denied that male and female bodily experiences do differ in a number of important respects, it is problematic to suggest that the particular bodily experiences that are unique to women confer on women a *superior* (as distinct from merely special) insight into our relatedness with life.[80] Such an argument effectively introduces a new hierarchical dualism that subtly condemns men to an inferior status (of Otherness) on the ground that men's bodily differences render them incapable of participating in the particular kind of body-based consciousness that is believed to confer on women a keener psychological awareness of ecological connectedness. Yet, as transpersonal ecologists and some ecofeminists show, there is no a priori reason why men *and* women cannot both participate in body-based forms of identification (whether personal *or* cosmological).[81] To the extent that bodily experiences may differ between men and women, there is no reason why either should be *socially* elevated as superior to the other. Moreover, the nurturing qualities usually associated with women can for the most part be attributed to the social division of labor and therefore can be made more culturally diffuse through shared parenting (the latter reform is, of course, strongly supported by feminists and ecofeminists). Finally, as Joan Griscom observes,

simply because women are *able* to bear children does not mean that doing so is *essential* to our nature. Contraception clarifies this distinction: the ability to give birth can now be suppressed, and there are powerful ecological pressures in favor of this. In this context, it is important that biology *not* be our destiny.[82]

The oppression argument—that women are in a better position to critically evaluate ecological practices and envision an alternative society by virtue of their *oppression* rather than their biology per se—provides a more defensible reason for paying special attention to the experiences of women. That women have been less implicated than men in major activities and centers of ecological destruction (e.g. the military, the boardroom, science, and bureaucracy) is itself an excellent reason to hear what women have to say on the subject of ecological reconstruction. Most women do occupy a vantage point of "critical otherness" from which they can offer a different way of looking at the problems of both patriarchy *and* ecological destruction. Of course, the same can be said for many other minority groups and classes such as indigenous tribespeople, ethnic minorities, and other oppressed groups—a point that is of crucial importance if we are to develop a *general* ecocentric emancipatory theory. Here, ecofeminist theorists need to be wary of the problem of over-identifying with, and hence accepting uncritically, the perspective of women. Such an over-identification can sometimes *inhibit* the general emancipatory process by offering an analysis that can (i) deny the extent to which many women may be complicit in the domination of nature; (ii) overlook the various ways in which men have been oppressed by limiting "masculine stereotypes"; and (iii) be blind to other social dynamics, institutions, and prejudices that do not bear on the question of gender. Moreover, privileging—rather than simply rendering visible and *critically* incorporating—the special insights of women can sometimes lead to a lopsided and reductionist analysis of social and ecological problems.

For example, an uncritical identification with the female stereotype can sometimes lead to a simple reversal of the human characteristics that are considered to be valuable, that is, a replacement of the hyperrational, impersonal, and abstract "male" standard of human excellence with an excessively particular, personal, and emotional "female" standard. Indeed, many ecofeminists, drawing on theories of gender and self-development (such as object relations theory), have argued that the "feminine" sense of self is preferable to the "masculine" sense of self on the ground that it gives rise to a personal, reciprocal, emotional, and contextualized "caring ethic" as opposed to an abstract, rights-based ideal of justice.[83] While we certainly need to discredit the masculine stereotype we also need to be wary of certain aspects of the feminine stereotype. Indeed, if the speculative theory of object relations tells us anything, it is that the prevailing stereotypical male and female senses of self are both deficient—that the former is excessively delineated whereas the latter is *not delineated enough*.[84] This would seem to undermine the claim that a new environmental ethic ought to speak in the "different voice" of women (to adopt Carol Gilligan's phrase, although this is not her claim), suggesting instead that both the masculine and feminine stereotypes need to be transcended (at least in part and not necessarily to the same degree), not only by shared parenting but also by other kinds of social and cultural change.[85]

A further tendency toward reductionism is illustrated by the argument maintained, or implied, by some ecofeminists that it is patriarchy that lies at the root of the domination of women *and* nature. This argument suggests that the principal focus of an emancipatory *ecological* praxis must be patriarchy rather than anthropocentrism (indeed, this charge has been levelled against deep ecology).[86] However, it is one thing to note parallels in the logic or symbolic structure of different kinds of domination (surely this is enough to explain the strong resonance in the egalitarian orientations of the radical feminist and ecology movements) and another thing to argue that the kinds of domination that radical feminists and radical ecologists are addressing stem from the *one* source. To maintain this causal explanation, it must be shown that patriarchy not only *predated* but also gave rise to anthropocentrism—in other words, that there is a necessary connection between the two phenomena. How, then, do we explain the existence of patriarchy in traditional societies that have lived in harmony with the natural world?[87] How do we explain Engels' vision of "scientific socialism," according to which the possibility of egalitarian social/sexual relations is premised on the instrumental manipulation and domination of the nonhuman world?[88] Clearly, patriarchy and the domination of nonhuman nature can each be the product of quite different conceptual and historical developments. It follows that the emancipation of women need not necessarily lead to the emancipation of the nonhuman world and vice versa.

The above criticisms are not intended to deny that patriarchy and anthropocentrism can be mutually reinforcing when they do occur together. In this respect, both women and the nonhuman world can indeed be seen to have a mutual "interest" in emancipation from the status of Otherness. Moreover, at the symbolic and conceptual levels, both women and nonhuman nature have been associated and downgraded in the God-Man-Woman-Nature hierarchy of being—a conceptual schema that has served to *legitimize* the greater social status and power held by men vis-à-vis women and nonhuman nature. However, as Fox has argued, a variety of human/nonhuman distinctions have served as the fundamental legitimating ideology not only for patriarchy but also for other kinds of human oppression. For example, the fundamental legitimating ideology of racism and imperialism has been that whites and Westerners are seen to possess—or possess to a greater extent than their counterparts (i.e. blacks or non-Westerners)—certain qualities that are deemed to be of the essence of humanness (e.g. rationality, civilization, or being more favored by God). In other words, not only men but also whites and Westerners (both men and women) have sought to legitimate their superior social position by claiming that they are somehow "more fully human" than, and hence morally superior to, women, blacks, and non-Westerners.[89] Of course, as Val Plumwood has pointed out, the success of this kind of legitimation in relation to patriarchy depends on a general acceptance of a concept of the human that is set apart from the rest of the animal world on a hierarchy of being.[90] Replacing such a hierarchical mode of perceiving the world with an ecological sense of self that affirms others (both humans and nonhumans) in a state of reciprocal interdependence serves to undermine the conceptual apparatus that has legitimated not only patriarchy and other forms of human oppression but also anthropocentrism. In other words, patriarchy may be seen as not the root of the ecological crisis but rather a subset of a more general problem of philosophical dualism that has pervaded Western thought (e.g. mind/body, reason/emotion, human/nonhuman) from the time of the classical Greek philosophers.[91]

Such a recognition has led many ecocentric theorists (including transpersonal ecologists and many ecofeminists) to argue that we need to transcend masculine and feminine stereotypes and cultivate a new kind of *person* that possesses "the *human* characteristics of gentleness and caring" (my emphasis).[92] This does not mean that the new ecological person must be thoroughly androgynous or gender neutral (there is no reason why the differences between men and women should not be celebrated), *only that a person's sex is not considered to have an important bearing on the human qualities that are needed to heal the rift between humans and the rest of nature.* As Don E. Marietta has put it, "We are talking about people who cultivate the best qualities of human beings, regardless of the traditional assignment of those to one sex. These qualities of character and behaviour indicate, I believe, the values supported by feminism."[93] Similarly, Val Plumwood has argued that what we now need is "an account of the human ideal for both sexes, which accepts the undesirability of the domination of nature associated with masculinity."[94] Such an ideal must flow from a critique of *both* masculinity and femininity and be linked to a "systematic transcendence of the wider set of dualisms" (e.g. mind/body, reason/emotion, public/private).[95]

To recapitulate, then, ecofeminists have drawn attention to the conceptual parallels, symbolic resonances, and areas of practical overlap in both the critical and constructive tasks of the radical wings of the ecology movement and the women's movement. However, in those areas where ecofeminism diverges from a deep/transpersonal ecology perspective (i.e. in emphasizing purely personally based forms of identification; in sometimes *uncritically* privileging the experience of women; and in sometimes overstating the links between patriarchy and the domination of nature) it is vulnerable to criticism. Of course, not all ecofeminists make these claims and, of those who have, not all have pursued them in the same way or to the same end. Indeed, given that there are many different kinds of feminism (e.g. liberal, Marxist, socialist, radical, existentialist, psychoanalytical, and postmodern), it is hardly surprising to find that there is more than one kind of ecofeminism.

However, when we turn to those particular expressions of ecofeminism that are *not* vulnerable to the above criticisms, we find an ecophilosophical orientation that is almost indistinguishable from that of transpersonal ecology. That is, we find a similar ecophilosophical orientation of inclusiveness, albeit from an "inside-out" rather than an "outside-in" route. The qualification "almost" remains important, however, when it comes to deciding on an ecophilosophical framework and label for a *general* emancipatory theory. Such a framework must be able to critically incorporate the special experiences and perspectives of all oppressed social groups, not just women. Now an ecofeminist perspective is quite capable of doing this—indeed, Karen Warren has defended an inclusive and pluralistic version of ecofeminism that is concerned to end *all* forms of oppression (and which provides a general ecocentric emancipatory theory).[96] Yet some ecofeminists might want to argue that ecofeminism *should* remain a specifically feminist project in the sense of providing a special voice to women in view of the pervasiveness of patriarchal culture and its links with the domination of nature. (In any event, this is what is suggested by the label "eco*feminist*.") This is, I believe, a valid case, although it would mean that ecofeminism would then become a major and essential tributary of a general ecocentric emancipatory framework rather than serve as *the* general emancipatory framework. Moreover, a case might be made that a general ecocentric emancipatory theory must be one that in both purpose *and* name does not privilege the concerns of any particular human emancipatory movement.

Whatever label is ultimately adopted, however, a general ecocentric emancipatory theory must accommodate all human emancipatory struggles within a broader, ecological framework. That is, it must be able to provide the context for establishing the outer ecological limits within which the different needs of human emancipatory movements can be addressed and harmonized in order to ensure that the interests of the nonhuman world are not continually sacrificed in the name of human emancipation. The emancipatory concerns of new social movements—including the women's movement—may thus be seen *as nesting within* such an ecocentric framework. Transpersonal ecology provides one such general theoretical articulation of ecocentrism. As we have seen, autopoietic intrinsic value theory provides a complementary general theory of ecocentrism. Ecofeminism can provide, at a minimum, an essential component of a general ecocentric theory by pointing to the links between the domination of women and the domination of nature, or, alternatively, it can be formulated in such a way as to provide a general theory of ecocentrism. However, all of these approaches provide only the *ecophilosophical* underpinnings of ecocentrism. It remains to explore how this inclusive ecophilosophical framework might be fleshed out in a political and economic direction.

Notes

1. For a clear exposition of this model, see Charles Birch and John B. Cobb, Jr., *The Liberation of Life: From the Cell to the Community* (Cambridge: Cambridge University Press, 1981). See also J. Baird Callicott, "The Metaphysical Implications of Ecology," *Environmental Ethics*, 8 (1986), 301–16 and Andrew McLaughlin, "Images and Ethics of Nature," *Environmental Ethics*, 7 (1985), 293–19.

2. Birch and Cobb, *Liberation of Life*, 95.

3. See Richard Routley and Val Routley, "Human Chauvinsim and Environmental Ethics" in Don Mannison, Michael McRobbie, and Richard Routley (eds), *Environmental Philosophy*, (Monograph Series, No. 2; Department of Philosophy, Research School of the Social Sciences, Australian National University, Canberra, Australia), 96–189. See also Warwick Fox, *Toward a Transpersonal Ecology: Developing New Foundations for Environmentalism* (Boston: Shambhala, 1990), 15–17.

4. Fox, *Transpersonal Ecology*, 15.

5. R. Routley and V. Routley, "Against the Inevitability of Human Chauvinism," in K. E. Goodpaster and K. M. Sayre (eds), *Ethics and Problems of the 21st Century* (Notre Dame, Ind.: University of Notre Dame Press, 1979), 36–59. For an excellent discussion of supposed human–animal discontinuities, see Barbara Noske, *Humans and Other Animals* (London: Pluto, 1989), chap. 6.

6. John Rodman, "Paradigm Change in Political Science," *American Behavioral Scientist*, 24 (1980), 54.

7. Ted Benton, "Humanism = Speciesism: Marx on Humans and Animals," *Radical Philosophy*, Autumn 1988, 11. Benton is summarizing here an argument of Mary Midgley's from *Animals and Why They Matter* (Harmondsworth: Penguin, 1983), chap. 2.

8. George Sessions, "Anthropocentrism and the Environmental Crisis," *Humboldt Journal of Social Relations*, 2 (1974), 73.

9. See Fritjof Capra, *The Turning Point: Science, Society, and the Rising Culture* (London: Fontana, 1983; reprint edn., 1985) and Rupert Sheldrake, *The Rebirth of Nature: The Greening of Science and God* (London: Century, 1990). As George Sessions has pointed out ("Ecocentrism and the Greens: Deep Ecology and the Environmental Task," *The Trumpeter*, 5 (1988), 67), the idea of a hierarchical chain of being can be traced back to Aristotle, who "rejected the Presocratic ideas of an infinite universe, cosmological and biological evolution, and heliocentrism, and proposed instead an Earth-centered, finite universe, wherein humans were differentiated from, and seen as superior to, the rest of the animals by virtue of their rationality. Also found in Aristotle is the hierarchical concept of the 'great chain of being' which holds that Nature made plants for the use of animals, and animals were made for the sake of

humans (*Politics I*, 88)." Sessions notes that the Presocratics, on the other hand, had been much more interested in cosmological inquiry and nature in general.

10. For three sustained critiques of anthropocentrism, see Routley and Routley, "Against the Inevitability of Human Chauvinism"; David Ehrenfeld, *The Arrogance of Humanism* (New York: Oxford University Press, 1981); and Fox, *Transpersonal Ecology*, 13–22. Fox concludes that anthropocentrism is not only self-serving but also "empirically bankrupt and theoretically disastrous, practically disastrous, logically inconsistent, morally objectionable, and incongruent with a genuinely open approach to experience" (18–19).

11. Rodman, "Paradigm Change in Political Science," 67; Capra, *Turning Point*; Sessions, "Anthropocentrism and the Environmental Crisis"; and Sessions, "Ecocentrism and the Greens."

12. Warwick Fox, "Deep Ecology: A New Philosophy of Our Time?", *The Ecologist*, 14 (1984): 194–200. See also J. Baird Callicott, "Intrinsic Value, Quantum Theory, and Environmental Ethics," *Environmental Ethics*, 7 (1985), 257–75 and Capra, *Turning Point*.

13. For Capra's somewhat deterministic conclusions, see *Turning Point*, 464–6.

14. Michael Zimmerman, "Quantum Theory, Intrinsic Value, and Panentheism," *Environmental Ethics*, 10 (1988), 5.

15. Michael Zimmerman, "Marx and Heidegger on the Technological Domination of Nature," *Philosophy Today*, 23 (1979), 103.

16. The complexity and unpredictability of many physical and social phenomena are underscored by the new body of scientific inquiry known as chaos theory, which shows that dynamic biological and social systems that behave deterministically (i.e. according to laws that can be described mathematically) are nonetheless inherently unpredictable beyond a certain point. This is due to the fact that these systems exhibit nonlinear dynamical properties (which means that they are extraordinarily sensitive to initial conditions) together with the fact that it is impossible in principle to specify the initial conditions of any system precisely. That is, some degree of approximation is always involved. For a general introduction, see James Gleick, *Chaos: Making a New Science* (New York: Viking, 1987).

17. Warwick Fox, "The Deep Ecology–Ecofeminism Debate and its Parallels," *Environmental Ethics*, 11 (1989), 6. The term *unfold* is used here and throughout this inquiry to mean "develop" or "grow" and is not intended imply any predestination.

18. Trevor Blake, "Ecological Contradiction: The Grounding of Political Ecology," *Ecopolitics II Proceedings* (Hobart: Centre for Environmental Studies, University of Tasmania, 1987), 79.

19. Birch and Cobb, *Liberation of Life*, 95.

20. For more on the concept of relative autonomy, see Warwick Fox, *Approaching Deep Ecology: A Response to Richard Sylvan's Critique of Deep Ecology* (Environmental Studies Occasional Paper, No. 20; Hobart: Centre for Environmental Studies, University of Tasmania, 1986), Section 3.

21. J. Baird Callicott, "What's Wrong with the Case for Moral Pluralism," paper presented to the Pacific Division Meeting of the American Philosophy Association, Berkeley, 23 March 1989, 32–3.

22. Evelyn Fox Keller, *Reflections on Gender and Science* (New Haven: Yale University Press, 1985), 99.

23. Zimmerman, "Quantum Theory, Intrinsic Value, and Panentheism," 17.

24. George Sessions, "The Deep Ecology Movement: A Review," *Environmental Review*, 11 (1987), 105.

25. Fox, *Transpersonal Ecology*, 21.

26. Routley and Routley, "Against the Inevitability of Human Chauvinism," 36 and Fox, *Transpersonal Ecology*, 21.

27. I am grateful to Alan Drengson for drawing my attention to these practices.

28. Noske, *Humans and Other Animals*, 160.

29. Fox, *Transpersonal Ecology*, 21.

30. Fox calls this misinterpretation "the fallacy of misplaced misanthropy" (*Transpersonal Ecology*, 19).

31. See e.g. Sessions, "Anthropocentrism and the Environmental Crisis."

32. H. J. Blackham, *Humanism* (New York: International Publishing Service, 1976), 102.

33. For a discussion of how respect for humans' rights can nest within an ecocentric framework, see Peter S. Wenz, *Environmental Justice* (Albany: State University of New York Press, 1988).

34. For an example of a nonanthropocentric intrinsic value approach that seeks to maximize richness of experience while taking into account populations and ecosystems, see Birch and Cobb, *Liberation of Life*, esp. 173–4.

35. See Naess, "The Shallow and the Deep, Long-Range Ecology Movement: A Summary," *Inquiry*, 16 (1973), 95.

36. See Bill Devall, *Simple in Means, Rich in Ends: Practicing Deep Ecology* (Layton, Utah: Gibbs M. Smith, 1988).

37. Christopher Stone, *Should Trees Have Standing?: Toward Legal Rights for Natural Objects* (Los Altos, Calif.: Kaufmann, 1974).

38. Ibid. 34.

39. Ibid. 40.

40. Paul Shepard, "Animal Rights and Human Rites," *North American Review*, Winter 1974, 35.

41. John Livingston, *The Fallacy of Wildlife Conservation* (Toronto: McClelland and Stewart, 1981), 62–3.

42. Rodman, "The Liberation of Nature?", *Inquiry*, 20 (1970), 101.

43. John Rawls, *A Theory of Justice* (London: Oxford University Press, 1976), 512.

44. New Zealand is in the forefront of comprehensive environmental legislation of this kind. For example, the preamble to the New Zealand Environment Act 1986 states that the purpose of the Act is, *inter alia*, to "ensure that, in the management of natural and physical resources, full and balanced account is taken of (i) the intrinsic value of ecosystems; and (ii) all values which are placed by individuals and groups on the quality of the environment; and (iii) the principles of the Treaty of Waitangi (i.e. an agreement between White settlers and Maories); and (iv) the sustainability of natural and physical resources; and (v) the needs of future generations." A further example is the New Zealand Conservation Act 1987, which defines conservation to mean "the preservation and protection of natural and historic resources *for the purpose of maintaining their intrinsic values*, providing for their appreciation and recreational enjoyment by the public, and safeguarding the options of future generations" (Section 2(1)—my emphasis). "Natural resources" are defined in the Act to include not only plants and animals, but landscapes and landforms, geological features and "systems of interacting living organisms, and their environment."

45. Charles Elton, the founder of modern animal ecology, has bluntly stated that "the balance of nature does not exist and perhaps never has existed" (Charles Elton, *Animal Ecology and Evolution* (Oxford: Oxford University Press, 1930), 17, quoted in Birch and Cobb, *Liberation of Life*, 36–7). Birch and Cobb suggest that it is more precise to speak of certain kinds of activity as being "unsustainable" rather than as upsetting the "balance of nature," since the latter suggests that nature is static, that is, that the distribution and abundance of plants and animals in a community does not change. See also Frank N. Egerton, "Changing Concepts of the Balance of Nature," *Quarterly Review of Biology*, 48 (1978), 322–50.

46. Livingston, *Fallacy of Wildlife Conservation*, 75.

47. Elsewhere I have been critical of this tendency in the work of Murray Bookchin (see Robyn Eckersley, "Divining Evolution: The Ecological Ethics of Murray Bookchin," *Environmental Ethics*, 11 (1989), 107). Indeed, ecoanarchism in general is prone to this kind of reasoning.

48. Although I do not discuss Taoism, Buddhism, and animistic cosmologies, it should be pointed out that autopoietic intrinsic value theory, transpersonal ecology, and ecofeminism are obviously broadly sympathetic with these non-Western approaches. On Taoist and Buddhist approaches, see Ip Po-Keung, "Taoism and the Foundations of Environmental Ethics," *Environmental Ethics*, 5 (1983), 335–43, and McLaughlin, "Images and Ethics of Nature," 293–319; and on animistic cosmologies, see J.

Donald Hughes, *American Indian Ecology* (El Paso, Tex.: Texas Western Press, 1983) and J. Baird Callicott, "Traditional American Indian and Western European Attitudes Toward Nature: An Overview," *Environmental Ethics*, 4 (1982), 293–318.

49. The concept of "autopoiesis" derives from the biological work of Francisco Varela, Humberto Maturana, and Ricardo Uribe. See Francisco J. Varela, Humberto R. Maturana, and Ricardo Uribe, "Autopoiesis: The Organization of Living Systems, Its Characterization and a Model," *Biosystems*, 5 (1974), 187–96, and Humberto R. Maturana and Francisco J. Varela, *The Tree of Knowledge: The Biological Roots of Human Understanding* (Boston: Shambhala, 1988). Fox is responsible for introducing this idea to the environmental philosophy literature (see *Transpersonal Ecology*, 165–76).

50. Fox, *Transpersonal Ecology*, 171.

51. Ibid. 171–2.

52. Ibid. 172. On the meaning of intrinsic value, see also William Godfrey-Smith, "The Value of Wilderness," *Environmental Ethics*, 1 (1979), 309.

53. Aldo Leopold, *A Sand County Almanac* (Oxford: Oxford University Press, 1949), 224–5. See also J. Baird Callicott, "The Conceptual Foundations of the Land Ethic," in J. Baird Callicott (ed.), *Companion to A Sand County Almanac* (Madison: University of Wisconsin Press, 1987), 186–217 and James D. Heffernan, "The Land Ethic: A Critical Appraisal," *Environmental Ethics*, 4 (1982), 235–47.

54. Defenders of Leopold's land ethic have sought to get around this problem by presenting the ethic as a much-needed *addition*, rather than alternative, to atomistic approaches to intrinsic value theory such as animal liberation or life-based ethics. See e.g. Callicott, "Conceptual Foundations of the Land Ethic," 207.

55. Fox, *Transpersonal Ecology*, 169.

56. Bill Devall and George Sessions, *Deep Ecology: Living as if Nature Mattered* (Layton, Utah: Gibbs M. Smith, 1985) and Fox, *Transpersonal Ecology*, esp. chaps. 7 and 8. In the following discussion I draw on many of the categories and arguments presented by Fox in *Transpersonal Ecology* on the differences between intrinsic value theory approaches and psychological-cosmological approaches (these approaches are explained in the text).

57. For a helpful discussion on the distinction between acting according to moral principle and acting "according to the heart," see Alan R. Drengson, "Compassion and Transcendence of Duty and Inclination," *Philosophy Today*, Spring (1981), 34–45.

58. See Elizabeth M. Pybus and Alexander Broadie, "Kant and the Maltreatment of Animals," *Philosophy*, 53 (1978), 560–1.

59. Warwick Fox, "The Meanings of 'Deep Ecology,'" *Island Magazine*, Autumn 1989, 34 (this article has also appeared in *The Trumpeter*, 7 (1990), 48–50).

60. Arne Naess, "Self-Realization: An Ecological Approach to Being in the World," *The Trumpeter*, 4 (1987), 39.

61. Fox, *Transpersonal Ecology*, chap. 7.

62. Transpersonal ecology should *not* be confused with a "New Age" perspective. Indeed, deep/transpersonal ecologists have been quite critical of New Age ideas, particularly those of the Christian theologian Pierre Teilhard de Chardin. See George Sessions, review of *The Soul of the World: An Account of the Inwardness of Things*, by Conrad Bonifazi, *Environmental Ethics*, 3 (1981), 275–81; Sessions, review of *Eco-Philosophy: Designing New Tactics for Living*, by Henryk Skolimowski, *Environmental Ethics*, 6 (1984), 167–74; and Devall and Sessions, *Deep Ecology*, 5–6 and 138–44. For the historical roots of the transpersonal ecology approach one needs to look in the direction of people as diverse (in some senses) as Spinoza and Gandhi (see Fox, *Transpersonal Ecology*, chap 4).

63. Alan R. Drengson, "Developing Concepts of Environmental Relationships," *Philosophical Inquiry*, 8 (1986), 50–65.

64. Lester Milbrath, *Environmentalists: Vanguard for a New Society* (Albany: State University of New York Press, 1984), 28.

65. Fox, *Transpersonal Ecology*, 247.

66. See Warwick Fox, "New Philosophical

Directions in Environmental Decision-Making," in P. R. Hay, R. Eckersley, and G. Holloway (eds), *Theoretical Issues in Environmentalism: Essays from Australia* (Hobart: University of Tasmania, 1991).

67. See e.g. the New Zealand Environment Act 1986 and Conservation Act 1987, discussed above.

68. For general introductions to ecofeminism, see Rosemary Radford Ruether, *New Woman New Earth: Sexist Ideologies and Human Liberation* (New York: Seabury, 1975); Susan Griffin, *Woman and Nature: The Roaring Inside Her* (New York: Harper and Row, 1978); Elizabeth Dodson Gray, *Green Paradise Lost* (Wellesley, Mass.: Roundtable, 1981); Brian Easlea, *Science and Sexual Oppression: Patriarchy's Confrontation with Woman and Nature* (London: Weidenfeld and Nicolson, 1981); Carolyn Merchant, *The Death of Nature: Women, Ecology and the Scientific Revolution* (London: Wildwood House, 1982); Isaac D. Balbus, *Marxism and Domination: A Neo-Hegelian, Feminist, Psychoanalytical Theory of Sexual, Political and Technological Liberation* (Princeton: Princeton University Press, 1982); Leonie Caldecott and Stephanie Leland (eds), *Reclaim the Earth: Women Speak Out for Life on Earth* (London: Women's Press, 1983); Joan Rothschild (ed.), *Machina Ex Dea: Feminist Perspectives on Technology* (New York: Pergamon, 1983); Val Plumwood, "Ecofeminism: An Overview and Discussion of Positions and Arguments," *Australasian Journal of Philosophy*, 64 (1986), 120–38; Patsy Hallen, "Making Peace with Nature: Why Ecology Needs Feminism," *The Trumpeter*, 4 (1987), 3–14; Val Plumwood, "Women, Humanity and Nature," *Radical Philosophy*, Spring 1988, 16–24; Judith Plant (ed.), *Healing the Wounds: The Promise of Ecofeminism* (Philadelphia: New Society Publishers, 1989); Irene Diamond and Gloria Feman Orenstein (eds), *Reweaving the World: The Emergence of Ecofeminism* (San Francisco: Sierra Club Books, 1990); Karen J. Warren, "Feminism and Ecology: Making Connections," *Environmental Ethics*, 9 (1987), 3–20; and also by Warren, "The Power and the Promise of Ecological Feminism," *Environmental Ethics*, 12 (1990), 125–46.

69. Irene Diamond and Gloria Feman Orenstein, "Introduction," *Reweaving the World*, p. ix. Similarly, Ynestra King has argued that the domination of women is "the prototype of other forms of domination" of which the domination of nature is but one example. Ynestra King, "Toward an Ecological Feminism and a Feminist Ecology," in Rothschild (ed.), *Machina Ex Dea*, 119.

70. Simone de Beauvoir, *The Second Sex*, trans. and ed. H. M. Parshley (New York: Knopf, 1978; reprint edn., Harmondsworth: Penguin, 1982). Although de Beauvoir was a feminist existentialist and not an *eco*feminist (indeed, she rejected the association of women with nature on the grounds that it inhibited women's own process of becoming free, independent existents), her observations on the relationship between woman, man, and nature in *The Second Sex* have been widely drawn upon by contemporary ecofeminist theorists.

71. See e.g. Charlene Spretnak, *The Spiritual Dimension of Green Politics* (Santa Fe, N. Mex.: Bear and Company, n.d.); reprinted as Appendix C in Charlene Spretnak and Fritjof Capra, *Green Politics: The Global Promise* (London: Paladin, 1986), 230–58; Starhawk, *Dreaming the Dark: Magic, Sex, and Politics* (Boston: Beacon, 1982); and Judith Plant (ed.), *Healing the Wounds*, Part 3 ("She is Alive in You: Ecofeminist Spirituality"), 115–88.

72. Gary Snyder, "Anarchism, Buddhism, and Political Economy," lecture delivered at the Fort Mason Center, San Francisco, 27 February 1984 (quoted by Charlene Spretnak, *The Spiritual Dimensions of Green Politics*, in Spretnak and Capra, *Green Politics*, 238).

73. Dodson Gray, *Green Paradise Lost*, 148.

74. Ibid. 84 and 85.

75. Ariel Kay Salleh, "Deeper than Deep Ecology: The Ecofeminist Connection," *Environmental Ethics*, 6 (1984): 339–45; Jim Cheney, "Eco-Feminism and Deep Ecology," *Environmental Ethics*, 9 (1987), 115–45; and Marti Kheel, "Ecofeminism and Deep Ecology: Reflections

on Identity and Difference," in Irene Diamond and Gloria Feman Orenstein (eds), *Reweaving the World*, 128–37.

76. Fox, *Transpersonal Ecology*, 258.

77. Ibid. 262–3. See also Fox, "The Deep Ecology-Ecofeminism Debate," 11–12.

78. See Fox, "The Deep Ecology-Ecofeminism Debate," 12–13. See also Dolores LaChapelle, *Sacred Land, Sacred Sex: Rapture of the Deep* (Silverton, Colo.: Finn Hill Arts, 1988),

79. Salleh, "Deeper than Deep Ecology," 342–3; King, "Toward an Ecological Feminism," 123; and Cheney, "Eco-feminism and Deep Ecology."

80. Elizabeth Dodson Gray has gone so far as to claim "that there is a definite limit to the perception of men. It is a limit imposed upon their consciousness by the lack of certain bodily experiences which are present in the life of woman. . . . the male's is simply a much diminished experience of body, of natural processes, and of future generations" (Gray, *Green Paradise Lost*, 113–14). See also Salleh, "Deeper than Deep Ecology," 340.

81. See e.g. Spretnak, "The Spiritual Dimension of Green Politics"; LaChapelle, *Earth Wisdom* (Los Angeles: Guild of Tutors Press, 1978); LaChapelle, *Sacred Land, Sacred Sex*; and John Seed, Joanna Macy, Pat Fleming, and Arne Naess, *Thinking like a Mountain: Towards a Council of All Beings* (Santa Cruz, Calif.: New Society Publishers, 1988) .

82. Joan L. Griscom, "On Healing the Nature/History Split in Feminist Thought," *Heresies*, 13 (1981), 8.

83. Object relations theory is a branch of psychoanalytic theory concerned with the development of the self in relation to others. For two feminist approaches, see Dorothy Dinnerstein, *The Mermaid and the Minotaur: Sexual Arrangements and Human Malaise* (New York: Harper and Row, 1977) and Nancy Chodorow, *The Reproduction of Mothering* (Berkeley and Los Angeles: University of California Press, 1978). Ecofeminists who draw on object relations theory to defend a "feminine sense of self" include Isaac D. Balbus, "A Neo-Hegelian, Feminist, Psychoanalytic Perspective on Ecology," *Telos*,

52 (1982), 140–55; Balbus, *Marxism and Domination*; and Marti Kheel, "Ecofeminism and Deep Ecology," 130–1.

84. See e.g. Keller, *Reflections on Gender and Science*, 89.

85. Carol Gilligan, *In a Different Voice* (Cambridge: Harvard University Press, 1982.)

86. See e.g. Ariel Salleh, "Deeper than Deep Ecology." For replies to this charge, see Michael E. Zimmerman, "Feminism, Deep Ecology, and Environmental Ethics," *Environmental Ethics*, 9 (1987), 21–44; Warwick Fox, "Deep Ecology–Ecofeminism Debate"; and Alan E. Wittbecker, "Deep Anthropology: Ecology and Human Order," *Environmental Ethics*, 8 (1986), 261–70.

87. See Joan Babberger, "The Myth of Matriarchy: Why Men Rule in Primitive Societies," in Michelle Zimbalist Rosaldo and Louise Lamphere (eds), *Woman, Culture, and Society* (Stanford, Calif.: Stanford University Press, 1974), 263–80 and Marilyn French, *Beyond Power: Women, Men and Morality* (London: Abacus, 1986), 96–100.

88. See Friedrich Engels, *The Origin of the Family, Private Property and the State*, trans. Alick West and Dona Torr (London: Lawrence and Wishart, 1940; reprint edn., 1946).

89. Fox, "Deep Ecology–Ecofeminism Debate," 21–5.

90. Plumwood, "Women, Humanity and Nature," 18.

91. See e.g. Sessions, "Anthropocentrism and the Environmental Crisis."

92. Judith Plant, "Introduction," *Healing the Wounds*, 3.

93. Don E. Marietta, "Environmentalism, Feminism, and the Future of American Society," *The Humanist*, 44 (1984), 18. Other theorists sympathetic with this kind of approach include Warwick Fox, Joan Griscom, Patsy Hallen, Evelyn Fox Keller, Val Plumwood, Karen Warren, Alan Wittbecker, and Michael Zimmerman.

94. Plumwood, "Women, Humanity and Nature," 22.

95. Ibid. 23.

96. Warren, "The Power and the Promise of Ecological Feminism."

28 Introduction to *Green Delusions*

Martin W. Lewis

The global environment currently faces two profound ideological threats. The first, and most serious, stems from the work of anti-environmentalists who would have us believe that the ecological crisis is a mirage. Such modern-day Pollyannas as Ben Wattenberg (1987), Dixy Lee Ray (1990), and Julian Simon and Herman Kahn (1984) present a comforting vision to those who shudder at the thought of the sacrifices that will be necessary to ensure the ecological health of the planet. But as their writings reveal, this cadre evidently considers human beings the only organisms worthy of consideration. To anyone who deems the survival of other species important, such "optimism" offers cold comfort indeed.

Despite ritual protestations to the contrary, these attacks on ecological concern are blatant enough to receive fierce opposition from all environmental quarters. But there is a much less visible ideological threat at work as well, one that masquerades under the mantle of environmentalism itself. In my view, many of the most committed and strident "greens" unwittingly espouse an ill-conceived doctrine that has devastating implications for the global ecosystem: so-called radical environmentalism. It is the purpose of this book to distinguish the five main variants of eco-extremism currently being forwarded, to expose the fallacies upon which such views ultimately flounder, and to demonstrate that the policies advocated by their proponents would, if enacted, result in unequivocal ecological catastrophe.

I would emphasize at the onset that in attacking eco-radicalism I seek not to assail but rather to defend the broad-based environmental movement. The great majority of environmental organizations shun extremism, remaining committed to reforming our economy and society through dogged work within normal political and legal channels. Such groups deserve, and require, widespread public praise and support. But eco-extremism, based on a doctrine of radical ecological salvation, has been gaining strength rapidly over the past several years. In fact, the environmental mainstream is itself now under assault from the eco-radicals, as extremists denounce such steadfast organizations as the Sierra Club or the Audubon Society for having "sold out to the despoilers." It is precisely to defend environmentalism—a term that many radicals tellingly disdain as reeking of accommodation—that I have chosen to speak out against environmental extremism. The latter must be countered, for in seeking to dismantle modern civilization it has the potential to destroy the very foundations on which a new and ecologically sane economic order must be built.

Throughout this work I will argue vigorously, at times fiercely, against the many doctrines of green radicalism. I do this because I am convinced that such ideas are beginning to lead the environmental movement toward self-defeating political strategies, preventing society from making the reforms it so desperately needs. This does not by any means entail denouncing all of the committed activists holding eco-radical views. To the contrary, many of them deserve praise for their genuine concern and for the personal sacrifices they are making on behalf of the earth. It is rather their ill-conceived *ideas* with which I am concerned. If at times my aspersions are caustic, it is because I have had to battle against these seductive ideas myself. Until a few years ago, I too endorsed all of the main platforms of the radical greens.

■ Environmentalism: Radical and Mainstream Positions

Radical environmentalism is a multistranded philosophy. But beneath their many differences, eco-radicals concur in one central proposition: that human society, as it is now constituted, is utterly unsustainable and must be reconstructed according to an entirely different socio-economic logic. The dominant school of radical green thought argues specifically that a sustainable society must be small in scale and modest in technology. Eco-radicals, therefore denounce anyone seeking merely to reform, and thus perpetuate, a society that they regard as intrinsically destructive if not actually evil.

THE POSTULATES OF ECO-RADICALISM

Radicalism, as the term is employed here, is the notion that society must be attacked "at the root" and reinvented whether through revolution, enlightenment (the massive ideological conversion of the populace), or the rebuilding that would follow upon an ecological holocaust. Most radical greens, to their credit, forswear revolution and hope to avoid Armageddon. But the movement as a whole consistently questions and often disparages the struggle for environmental reform within the framework of liberal democracy (Manes 1990: 19; Pell 1990). Such reform, extremists argue, would only allow a terminally sick society to persist in its fundamentally destructive habits, forestalling the drastic rebuilding necessary for long-term survival.

The dominant version of radical environmentalism rests on four essential postulates: that "primal" (or "primitive") peoples exemplify how we can live in harmony with nature (and with each other); that thoroughgoing decentralization, leading to local autarky, is necessary for ecological and social health; that technological advance, if not scientific progress itself, is inherently harmful and dehumanizing; and that the capitalist market system is inescapably destructive and wasteful. These views, in turn, derive support from an underlying belief that economic growth is by definition unsustainable, based on a denial of the resource limitations of a finite globe.

In accordance with these tenets, radical environmentalists would have us abandon urban, industrial, capitalist civilization and return to the earth. Here our modern social maladies will be healed as we find true harmony between land and life. The call is for a simpler existence and a more direct relationship between humanity and nature, one in which natural landscapes are transformed by human agency as little as possible. People must never be so arrogant as to "manage" nature; rather, nature should always be allowed to exemplify its own essential harmonies.

Within the human community, according to this doctrine, economic relationships likewise should be unmediated. Radical green thinkers usually consider trade to be alien and finance positively wicked. Third World countries are urged not only to shun industrialization but also to isolate themselves from the intrinsically exploitative global economic system. According to one prominent theory, only village-based, low-tech, agrarian development strategies will allow poor societies to fulfill basic human needs.

Most importantly, eco-radicals inform us that economic growth must simply come to an end. The larger the human economy becomes, the more nature suffers. Whereas moderate environmentalists see some benefits to economic growth (a more prosperous society being able to afford more environmental protection), green stalwarts consider this proposition self-canceling "We do not cure treatment-induced diseases by increasing the treatment dosage," writes Herman Daly (1977: 101). Or, as Arne Naess (1989: 211), the founder of the "deep ecology" movement, frames it: "One per cent increase in Gross National Product today inflicts far greater destruction of nature than one per cent 10 or 20 years ago because it is one per cent of a far larger product. And the old rough equivalency of GNP with 'Gross National Pollution' still holds. And the efforts to increase GNP create more formidable pressure against ecological policies every year." Fortunately, we need not fear that the end of economic growth will diminish human well-being—quite the contrary, for our obsession with economic growth, and more generally, the possession of material goods, has only hidden from our view an underlying spiritual impoverishment (Daly 1977: 44). By relinquishing our mad drive for progress we may at last begin to build a truly humane and genuinely prosperous community.

CONTEMPORARY ENVIRONMENTALISM: MODERATE AND RADICAL

While these radical notions seem to be beginning to dominate the environmental discourse, they by no means monopolize it. In fact, a pragmatic philosophy continues to inform most of the movement's large organizations. In *An Environmental Agenda for the Future*, for example, leaders of the country's ten most influential conservation groups explicitly accept capitalism and expressly endorse economic growth (Cahn 1985). Robert Repetto and others at the World Resources Institute argue powerfully that environmental health depends on sustainable development—on ecologically sound economic programs that aim to increase human "wealth and well-being" (Repetto 1986: 10). Other advocates of sustainable development, such as R. Kerry Turner, stress "the need to view environmental protection and continued economic growth . . . as mutually compatible and not necessarily conflicting objectives" (Turner 1988: 5). Piasecki and Asmus (1990) similarly propose a moderate course in seeking "environmental excellence," while Henning and Mangun (1989: 203) claim that the presumed conflict between economic growth and environmental salvation rests on a false dichotomy. Still other theorists might be described as "techno-environmentalist." Oppenheimer and Boyle (1990), for example, propose that technical advances in power generation and in transportation systems offer the best hope for protecting the atmosphere.

But, as Peter Borrelli (1988: 19) shows, the larger environmental community increasingly suspects that the mainstream organizations have compromised too much, falling into the trap of "creeping conservatism." The moderate stance of the established lobbying organizations seems far too weak to those who are most distraught over the planet's failing health. Seeking to avoid this pit, the most vociferous of the mainstream groups, Greenpeace, has recently called for a grassroots revolution against pragmatism and compromise (*Greenpeace*, July–August 1990). Many radical greens have even begun to view institutional conservation groups as enemies, or at best as allies of convenience only. As one noted radical put it, "The worldview of the executive director of the Sierra Club is closer to that of James Watt or Ronald Reagan [than it is to our own]" (quoted in Manes 1990: 225). Such views appear to have seized the movement's heart already, and they may soon be poised to grasp its political initiative as well.

RADICALISM'S FILLIP: THE ENVIRONMENTAL CRISIS

The attractions of a radical perspective are very real. As signs of impending disaster mount, it is not at all surprising that concerned individuals should seek forceful action—and the strident philosophies that would justify it. Those who espouse radical notions, though gravely mistaken in the solutions they propose, are not wrong about the magnitude of the problem.

The signals of impending disaster are many. Global warming and especially the depletion of stratospheric ozone are extraordinary threats to life on earth. The need to graduate from fossil fuels and move into a solar age is paramount, as is the necessity to recycle, rather than discard, our material artifacts. Equally worrisome are contemporary agricultural practices. The bombarding of croplands with life-destroying chemicals is unconscionable and, in the long run, economically self-defeating as well.

Perhaps most appalling is the mass extermination of plant and animal species presently occurring in many reaches of the world. Environmental extremists do clearly occupy the moral high ground here in arguing that life should be protected for its own sake, rather than merely for the benefits that it might someday proffer to humanity. Furthermore, it is not just extinction per se that should concern us; as Soulé (1980) has shown, the reduction of the numbers and the geographical ranges of large mammals has effectively ended their ongoing evolution. Wildlife must be not merely saved but restored—a monumental task, to say the least.

Environmental radicals also have a compelling point when they argue that the earth's human population is already too large. While the Malthusian vision of humanity soon exceeding global carrying capacity is probably fantasy, the simple fact that some 30 percent of the planet's primary production is now devoted to sustaining our species (Ehrlich 1988: 23) is reprehensible. I too believe that we have a moral obligation to share this world with its other inhabitants, which the very weight of our own numbers is making increasingly difficult.

And finally, all environmentalists should applaud certain nonviolent acts of civil disobedience undertaken by eco-extremists. Whether they are harassing Icelandic whaling vessels or chaining themselves to ancient trees in the Pacific Northwest, green radicals show great courage in trying to stop needless destruction. But in lauding these actions one is by no means obligated to endorse the beliefs that presently lie behind them. In fact, as I will argue, only by renouncing those beliefs can we begin to create a truly effective environmental movement.

■ The Fatal Flaws of Eco-Radicalism

Those who condemn radical environmentalism usually do so on the grounds that it represents a massive threat to human society, to civilization, and material progress as we have come to know them. This is hardly surprising, since many eco-radicals proudly claim this to be their intent. But the core argument of this work is that green extremism should be more deeply challenged as a threat to nature itself. Because this thesis is seemingly paradoxical, it is necessary to outline in unambiguous terms how nature's most fervent champions could also unwittingly be among its most dangerous foes.

A GREEN THREAT TO NATURE

The most direct way in which eco-extremists threaten the environment is simply by fueling the anti-environmental countermovement. When green radicals like Christopher Manes (1990) call for the total destruction of civilization, many begin to listen to the voices of reaction. Indeed, the mere linking of environmental initiatives to radical groups such as Earth First! often severely dampens what would otherwise be widespread public support (see Gabriel 1990: 64).

As radicalism deepens within the environmental movement, the oppositional anti-ecological forces accordingly gain strength. The Center for the Defense of Free Enterprise, a think tank for the so-called wise use movement, has, for example, recently published a manifesto calling for such outrages as the opening of all national parks to mineral production, the logging of all old-growth forests, and the gutting of the Endangered Species Act. This group's ideologues contend that certain environmental philosophies represent nothing less than mental illnesses, a theory anonymously propounded in the "intellectual ammunition department" of their *Wise Use Memo* (Center for the Defense of Free Enterprise 1990: 2). Even more worrisome is the fact that a former high-ranking CIA agent is now spreading rumors that environmental scientists are presently attempting to concoct a virus that could destroy humankind (See "Tale of a Plot to Rid Earth of Humankind," *San Francisco Examiner*, 14 April 1991, A-2). My fear is that if green extremism captures the environmental movement's upper hand, the public would be much less likely to recognize such a claim as paranoid fantasy; while a handful of eco-radicals would be happy to destroy humanity, such individuals also reject science and thus would never be able to act on such convictions.

More frightening, and more immediate, is the specter of a few radicals actually opposing necessary environmental reforms. Such individuals conclude that "reform environmentalism" is "worse than useless because by correcting short-term symptoms it postpone[s] the necessary reconstruction of the entire human relationship with the natural world" (Nash 1989: 150). From here it is a short step to argue that reform would only forestall an ecological apocalypse—which some evidently believe is a necessary precondition for the construction of an environmentally benign social order. The insanity of pushing the planet even closer to destruction in order to save it in the future should be readily apparent.

While such are the fantasies only of the most moonstruck extremists, even moderate radicals (if one may be permitted the oxymoron) espouse an ideology that would preclude the development of an ecologically sustainable economy. Most environmentalists, for instance, aver that a sustainable economy must be based on solar power. Yet the radicals' agenda, calling for total decentralization, deurbanization, economic autarky, a ban on most forms of high technology, and the complete dismantling of capitalism, would not only prevent future improvements in solar power but would actually destroy the gains that have already been made. While most radical greens embrace "appropriate technologies" (just as anti-environmentalists denounce "pollution"), their program would, if enacted, undercut the foundations of all technological research and development. Appropriate technology, in fact, often turns out to mean little more than well-engineered medieval apparatuses: we may expect crude mechanical power from the wind, but certainly not electricity from the sun. Equally important, the systematic dismantling of large economic organizations in favor of small ones would likely result in a substantial increase in pollution, since few small-scale firms are able to devise, or afford, adequate pollution abatement equipment.

Radical environmentalism is similarly culpable on the issue of demography. While adherents argue powerfully that the reduction of human numbers is necessary for ecological health, all indications are that their envisaged social program would only lead to further growth. Reverting to small, self-sustaining rural communities would only recreate the conditions that have historically led, in most cases, to steady population gains. Precluding industrialization in the Third World is also likely to ensure that high fertility rates remain the global norm.

Radical environmentalism presents yet another threat to the earth in its unyielding opposition to the human management of nature. The notion that "nature knows best" is meaningless in a world already remade to anthropogenic contours. Pristine nature is nonexistent—and has been, except perhaps in a few remote islands, for thousands of years (Goudie 1981; Simmons 1989). Only thoroughgoing human intervention can preserve remaining biological diversity until the time comes when a more advanced human society can begin to let nature reclaim more of the earth (see e.g. Janzen 1988). In particular, while some eco-radicals evidently believe that "liberating zoos" will help "save the earth" (G. Smith 1990), responsible environmentalists fully realize that such actions would, at present, only ensure the extinction of numerous endangered animal species currently being bred in zoological gardens (Conway 1988).

Finally, the radical green movement threatens nature by advocating a return to the land, seeking to immerse the human community even more fully within the intricate webs of the natural world. Given the present human population, this is hardly possible, and even if it were to occur it would result only in accelerated destruction. Ecological philosophers may argue that we could follow the paths of the primal peoples who live in intrinsic harmony with nature, but they are mistaken. Tribal groups usually do live lightly on the earth, but often only because their population densities are low. To return to preindustrial "harmony" would necessarily entail much more than merely decimating the human population.

Yet unless our numbers could be reduced to a small fraction of present levels, any return to nature would be an environmental catastrophe. The more the human presence is placed directly on the land and the more immediately it is provisioned from nature, the fewer resources will be available for nonhuman species. If all Americans were to flee from metropolitan areas, rural populations would soar and wildlife habitat would necessarily diminish.

An instructive example of the deadly implications of returning to nature may be found when one considers the issue of fuel. Although more common in the 1970s than the 1990s, "split wood not atoms" is still one of the green radicals' favored credos. To hold such a view one must remain oblivious to the clearly devastating consequences of wood burning, including suffocating winter air pollution in the enclosed basins of the American West, widespread indoor carbon monoxide poisoning, and the ongoing destruction of the oak woodlands and savannahs of California. If we were all to split wood, the United States would be a deforested, soot-choked wasteland within a few decades. To be sure, the pollution threat of wood stoves can be mitigated by the use of catalytic converters, but note that these are technologically sophisticated devices developed by capitalist firms.

If the most extreme version of the radical green agenda were to be fully enacted without a truly *massive* human die-off first, forests would be stripped clean of wood and all large animals would be hunted to extinction by hordes of neo-primitives desperate for food and warmth. If, on the other hand, eco-extremists were to succeed only in paralyzing the economy's capacity for further research, development, and expansion, our future could turn out to be reminiscent of the environmental nightmare of Poland in the 1980s, with a stagnant economy continuing to rely on outmoded, pollution-belching industries. A throttled steady-state economy would simply lack the resources necessary to create an environmentally benign technological base for a populace that shows every sign of continuing to demand electricity, hot water, and other conveniences. Eastern Europe shows well the environmental devastation that occurs when economic growth stalls out in an already industrialized society.

THE SHAKY FOUNDATIONS OF RADICAL ENVIRONMENTALISM

In the pages that follow I will argue that each of the four essential postulates of radical environmentalism outlined above is directly contradicted by the empirical record. "Primal" economies have rarely been as harmonized with nature as they are depicted; many have actually been highly destructive. Similarly, decentralized, small-scale political structures can be just as violent and ecologically wasteful as large-scale, centralized ones. Small is sometimes ugly, and big is occasionally beautiful. Technological advance, for its part, is clearly necessary if we are to develop less harmful ways of life and if we are to progress as a human community. And finally, capitalism, despite its social flaws, presents the only economic system resilient and efficient enough to see the development of a more benign human presence on the earth.

But a critique of these notions, however sound, misses the fundamental point. Ultimately, green extremism is rooted in a single, powerful conviction: that continued economic growth is absolutely impossible, given the limits of a finite planet. Only if this notion is discredited can the edifice of eco-radical philosophy be shaken.

It can logically be shown that the supposed necessity of devising a steady-state economy is severely misconstrued. Economic growth, strictly speaking, is defined as an increase in the *value* of goods *and* services produced. Yet as noted almost twenty years ago by Mancur Olson (1973: 4), radical greens have a significantly different conception, one that largely ignores services and that substitutes mass for value. To read some of their tracts, one could only conclude that economic growth requires producing ever larger quantities of steel, wheat, and similar material goods (e.g. Ornstein and Ehrlich 1989: 227).

The more sophisticated advocates of a steady-state economy do, however, take care to distinguish between qualitative economic growth (which they sometimes support) and quantitative economic growth (which they denounce), holding ultimately that only human bodies and material artifacts must be held at a constant level (Daly 1977). But in the end, the bias against even nonconsumptive forms of economic growth remains. The provision of services must stabilize, warns Daly (1977: 17–18), because services too require physical maintenance, while Kassiola (1990: 121) cautions that services are further suspect because they are "part of the materialist value structure of industrialism." Porritt (1985: 37, 183) even worries about the economic expansion entailed by the growth of the pollution abatement and recycling industries.

Services do indeed require maintenance. Yet it appears that as services become more sophisticated, they often require less physical support rather than more. More importantly, recent economic progress has come to demand a certain dematerialization of value, based on miniaturization and the development of lightweight, energy efficient, composite materials. Growth has also been repeatedly stimulated as relatively abundant resources are substituted for rare ones, the replacement of copper wire by fiber optic (glass) cables being a prime example. While the global economy certainly cannot grow indefinitely in *volume* by pouring out an ever mounting cavalcade of consumer disposables, in *can* continue to expand in *value* by producing better goods and services ever more efficiently.

As I shall argue repeatedly throughout this work, economic growth of this type is absolutely essential. Only a strongly expanding economic base can generate the capital necessary to retool our economy into one that does not consume the earth in feeding itself. Ecological sanity will be expensive, and if we cannot pay the price we may well perish. This proposition is even more vital in regard to the Third World; only steady economic expansion can break the linkages so often found in poor nations between rural desperation and land degradation. Genuine development, in turn, requires both certain forms of industrialization as well as participation in the global economy.

The major portion of this work is devoted to examining and criticizing the key postulates of radical environmentalism. To put it bluntly, I will argue that the foundations of green extremism are constructed upon erroneous ideas fabricated from questionable scholarship. Radical environmentalism's ecology is outdated and distorted, its anthropology stems from naive enthusiasms of the late 1960s and early 1970s, and its geography reflects ideas that were discredited sixty years ago. Moreover, most eco-radicals show an unfortunate ignorance of history and a willful dismissal of economics.

THE STRATEGIC BLUNDERING OF ECO-RADICALISM

Such are the bases of the ideological critique. At the same time, it is essential to examine the realm of radical environmental action. Here I will argue that eco-radical political strategy, if one may call it that, is consummately self-defeating. The theoretical and empirical rejection of green radicalism is thus bolstered by a series of purely pragmatic objections.

Many eco-radicals hope that a massive ideological campaign can transform popular perceptions, leading both to a fundamental change in lifestyles and to large-scale social reconstruction. Such a view is highly credulous. The notion that continued intellectual hectoring will eventually result in a mass conversion to environmental monasticism (Roszak 1979: 289)—marked by vows of poverty and nonprocreation—is difficult to accept. While radical views have come to dominate many environmental circles, their effect on the populace at large has been minimal. Despite the greening of European politics that recently gave stalwarts considerable hope, the more recent green plunge suggests that even the European electorate lacks commitment to environmental radicalism. In the United States several decades of preaching the same eco-radical gospel have had little appreciable effect; the public remains, as before, wedded to consumer culture and creature comforts.

The stubborn hope that nonetheless continues to inform green extremism stems from a pervasive philosophical error in radical environmentalism. As David Pepper (1989) shows, most eco-radical thought is mired in idealism: in this case the belief that the roots of the ecological crisis lie ultimately in *ideas* about nature and humanity. As Dobson (1990: 37) puts it: "Central to the theoretical canon of Green politics is the belief that our social, political, and economic problems are substantially caused by our intellectual relationship with the world" (see also Milbrath 1989: 338). If only such ideas would change, many aver, all would be well. Such a belief has inspired the writing of eloquent jeremiads; it is less conducive to designing concrete strategies for effective social and economic change.

It is certainly not my belief that ideas are insignificant or that attempting to change others' opinions is a futile endeavor. If that were true I would hardly feel compelled to write a polemic work of this kind. But I am also convinced that changing ideas alone is insufficient. Widespread ideological conversion, even if it were to occur, would hardly be adequate for genuine social transformation. Specific policies must still be formulated, and specific political plans must be devised if those policies are ever to be realized.

Many of the more sophisticated eco-radicals would agree with this notion. But even the political moves advocated by the more savvy among them remain committed to a radicalism that the great majority of the American public finds unpalatable. Radical green strategists may call for alliances with new social movements or with radical political parties, but even a concerted coalition of the disaffected would be unable to approach the critical mass needed to gain effective power. And several radical thinkers have proposed that much narrower constituencies form potentially eco-revolutionary groups that might lead society as a whole to its necessary transformation. According to one theory, only the unemployed can seek real change, rather than just a redistribution of spoils, because only they do not participate in the wicked system (Dobson 1990: 163). Although this represents a fringe view, the general process of seeking ever more radical foundations for social reinvention leads eco-extremists to reduce their own potential bases for political power to ever more minuscule, and powerless, groups. At the same time, most green extremists overtly denounce more moderate environmentalists who are willing to seek compromises with individuals or groups of opposing political philosophies. Since compromise, in one form or another, is necessary for any kind of effective political action, the quest for purity will in the end only undercut the prospects for change.

Even moderate environmentalists often adopt an unnecessarily exclusive political strategy. Robert Paehlke, whose *Environmentalism and the Future of Progressive Politics* stands as a monument to reason within the field, insists on attaching the movement firmly to the traditional left, urging environmentalists to appeal primarily to "industrial workers, public servants, and those employed in health, education, and the arts" (1989: 276, 263). Since in the United States this traditional liberal constituency by itself has no immediate chance of gaining national power, such a tactic would again only diminish the prospects for much needed reform. At the same time, the pernicious fear of compromise seriously diminishes the possibility of creating a broader coalition for environmental action. Barry Commoner, for example, warns environmentalists that if they compromise with corporations they may become "hostages" and eventually even assume "the ideology of [their] captors" (1990: 177). The end result of this kind of thinking—to which we are painfully close in the United States—is an ideological stalemate in which opposed camps are increasingly unable even to communicate. In such a political environment, the creation of an ecologically sustainable society becomes little more than an impossible dream.

AGAINST NAIVE GLOBALISM

Finally, while radical environmentalists are right to argue that the most pressing ecological problems are global in scale, the need for international cooperation does not mean that one can ignore the existing geopolitical framework of competing sovereign states. Leading countries—those boasting economic and technological prowess—will unavoidably play key roles in determining whether an ecologically sustainable socioeconomic order is ever to be created. By merely condemning rather than coming to terms with international competition, radical greens again undermine the prospects for creating a sustainable global economy.

While the United States has for some time been the world's predominant economic power, the 1980s saw that dominance severely challenged, especially by Japan. In attempting to discern the possible future economic-environmental directions to be taken by global society, it is therefore necessary to examine the relative positions and current trajectories of both countries.

The United States is currently hesitating on the threshold of a high-tech future. Its economy is in perilous straits, a vocal minority of its population wishes to dismantle the engines of technological growth, and its financial structures remain deeply biased against long-range planning and growth. Japan, on the other hand, is rushing headlong, yet with some foresight, into an ever more mechanized and synthesized future. The question is no longer whether America can remain the world's foremost economic power, but rather whether it can hope to be Japan's equal. Japan, with half our population, now invests more money annually in its basic industrial infrastructure than does the United States, and America's premier research laboratories are beginning to do as much work for Japanese as for US firms. Political developments within this country may well turn out to be irrelevant to the global economic system. As Paul Krugman (1990: 41) bitterly writes, "The vision of the United States as a giant Argentina may be unlikely, but no one should dismiss it out of hand."

By attacking the foundations of scientific research and technical development, radical environmentalism would hasten the decline of the United States relative to Japan. In so doing, I believe it would threaten the ecological future of the planet. Rough parity between the United States and Japan is highly desirable, in part because the two countries' environmental strengths and weaknesses are mirror images of each other. While Japan is far ahead in basic energy and resource efficiency, Americans as a whole are more concerned about the preservation of nature—for nature's sake—than are the Japanese. Japanese protests over such outrages as the mass slaughtering of dolphins are the merest of whispers. In a world economy dominated by Japan, energy and resource conservation would likely be high priorities, but not the preservation of biological diversity.

The best hope, economically as well as environmentally, lies in increasing cooperation between the United States and Japan as equals (see Rosecrance 1990). But unless the American economy is restructured to enhance long-range investments—and unless the American public unreservedly embraces continuing advances in technology—the best position we will be able to maintain will be that of a resource-rich but technologically dependent junior partner. Even if eco-extremists were to gain power in the United States, under such circumstances their ability to influence the evolutionary path of global society would be nil.

ENVIRONMENTALISM'S CURRENT CHALLENGE

At present, radical environmentalism is a marginal movement that presents little threat to the status quo. Although the radicalized intellectuals of the Vietnam generation have been almost universally converted to one or another variety of eco-extremism, their influence over the electorate at large remains minimal.

One hears repeated laments that the generation coming of age now is more concerned with high wages and career security than with social change. Yet it is precisely to this cynical generation that an effective environmental philosophy must appeal. To galvanize a young electorate whose primary political act to date has been to throw in its lot with capitalism, environmentalism must reconstitute itself with an entirely new philosophical foundation.

References

Borrelli, Peter (1988) (ed.), *Crossroads: Environmental Priorities for the Future* (Covelo, Calif.: Island).

Cahn, Robert (1985) (ed.), *An Environmental Agenda for the Future* (Covelo, Calif.: Island).

Center for the Defense of Free Enterprise (1990), *The Wise Use Memo* (Bellevue, Wash.).

Commoner, Barry (1990), *Making Peace with the Planet* (New York: Pantheon).

Conway, William (1988), "Can Technology Aid Species Preservation?," in E. O. Wilson and F. Peter (eds), *Biodiversity* (Washington, DC: National Academy), 263–8.

Daly, Herman (1977), *Steady-State Economics: The Economics of Biophysical Equilibrium* (San Francisco: W. H. Freeman).

Dobson, Andrew (1990), *Green Political Thought* (London: Unwin Hyman).

Ehrlich, Paul (1988), "The Loss of Diversity: Causes and Consequences," in E. O. Wilson and F. Peter (eds), *Biodiversity* (Washington, DC: National Academy), 21–7.

Gabriel, Trip (1990), "If a Tree Falls in the Forest, They Hear It," *New York Times Magazine*, 4 November, 34 ff.

Goudie, Andrew (1981), *The Human Impact: Man's Role in Environmental Change* (Cambridge, Mass.: MIT Press).

Henning, Daniel, and Mangun, William (1989), *Managing the Environmental Crisis: Incorporating Competing Values in Natural Resource Administration* (Durham, NC: Duke University Press).

Janzen, Daniel (1988), "Tropical Dry Forests: The Most Endangered Major Tropical Ecosystem," in E. O. Wilson and F. Peter (eds), *Biodiversity* (Washington, DC: National Academy), 130–7.

Kassiola, Joel Jay (1990), *The Death of Industrial Civilization: The Limits of Economic Growth and the Repoliticization of Advanced Industrial*

Society (Albany: State University of New York Press).

Krugman, Paul (1990), *The Age of Diminished Expeciations: U.S. Economic Policy in the 1990s* (Cambridge, Mass.: MIT Press).

Manes, Christopher (1990), *Green Rage: Radical Environmentalism and the Unmaking of Civilization* (Boston: Little, Brown).

Milbrath, Lester (1989), *Envisioning a Sustainable Society: Learning Our Way Out* (Albany: State University of New York Press).

Naess, Arne (1989), *Ecology, Community and Lifestyle: Outline of an Ecosophy*, translated and edited by David Rothenberg (Cambridge: Cambridge University Press).

Nash, Roderick (1989), *The Rights of Nature: A History of Environmental Ethics* (Madison: University of Wisconsin Press).

Olson, Mancur, and Landsberg, Hans (1973) (eds), *The No Growth Society* (New York: W. W. Norton).

Oppenheimer, Michael, and Boyle, Robert (1990), *Dead Heat: The Race against the Greenhouse Effect* (New York: Basic Books).

Ornstein, Robert, and Ehrlich, Paul (1989), *New World, New Mind: Moving toward Conscious Evolution* (New York: Simon and Schuster).

Paehlke, Robert (1989), *Environmentalism and the Future of Progressive Politics* (New Haven, Conn.: Yale University Press).

Pell, Eve (1990), "Buying In: How Corporations Keep an Eye on Environmental Groups that Oppose Them–By Giving Them Money," *Mother Jones*, April–May 1990: 23–7.

Pepper, David (1989), *The Roots of Modern Environmentalism* (London: Routledge).

Piasecki, Bruce, and Asmus, Peter (1990), *In Search of Environmental Excellence: Moving Beyond Blame* (New York: Simon & Schuster).

Porritt, Jonathon (1985), *Seeing Green: The Politics of Ecology Explained* (Oxford: Basil Blackwell).

Ray, Dixy Lee (1990), *Trashing the Planet: How Science Can Help Us Deal with Acid Rain, Depletion of Ozone, and Nuclear Waste (among Other Things)* (Washington, DC: Regenery Gateway).

Repetto, Robert (1986), *World Enough and Time: Successful Strategies for Resource Management* (New Haven, Conn.: Yale University Press).

Rosecrance, Richard (1990), *America's Economic Resurgence: A Bold New Strategy* (New York: Harper and Row).

Roszak, Theodore (1979), *Person/Planet: The Creative Disintegration of Industrial Society* (Garden City, NY: Anchor).

Simmons, I. G. (1989), *Changing the Face of the Earth: Culture, Environment, History* (Oxford: Basil Blackwell).

Simon, Julian, and Kahn, Herman (1984) (eds), *The Resourceful Earth: A Response to Global 2000* (New York: Basil Blackwell).

Smith, Gar (1990) (compiler), "50 Difficult Things You Can Do to Save the Earth," *Utne Reader*, July–August: 56.

Soulé, Michael (1980), "Conservation Biology: Its Scope and Challenge," in M. Soulé and B. Wilcox (eds), *Conservation Biology: An Evolutionary-Ecological Perspective*. (Sunderland, Mass.: Sinauer).

Turner, R. Kerry (1988), "Sustainability, Resource Conservation and Pollution Control: An Overview," in R. K. Turner (ed.), *Sustainable Environmental Management: Principles and Practice* (London: Bellhaven), 1–28.

Wattenberg, Ben (1984), *The Good News Is the Bad News Is Wrong* (New York: Simon and Schuster).

Section IX: Social and Socialist Ecology

As demonstrated by the readings in the previous section, deep ecology and bioregionalism focus on forging a new relationship between humans and their environment, and denounce human arrogance towards nature. Social and socialist ecologists agree with the need to radicalize ecology and our understanding of nature. However, their central concern is with the social, cultural, and economic sources of ecological problems. It is not enough to deal with our understanding of, and feelings about, the natural world; we must analyse what it is in contemporary capitalist and industrial societies that has brought environmental crisis. Only with a thorough social and economic critique can we really understand *why* we abuse nature in the way that we do, and, so, develop ways of relating to nature—and each other—in less dominating and destructive ways.

Murray Bookchin is the intellectual founder of social ecology. His writings about human society's effects on the natural world span three and a half decades, beginning with *Our Synthetic Environment* in 1962. For Bookchin, the central ecological problem is not our lack of reverence or respect for nature. Rather, it is that we justify as 'natural' the whole range of social and economic inequalities, hierarchies, and dominating relationships which damage human societies as well as ecological ones. Bookchin argues that if you understand nature as a nasty, brutish, and competitive world, then the only possible structure of human society is one that attempts to dominate and tame nature. Domination becomes the necessary way of life, and we create hierarchies— with humans above nature, men above women, owners above labour, and some races and ethnicities above others. Social ecology traces both ecological and social problems—pollution, destruction of ecosystems, poverty, inequality—to the concept of domination that we have read in nature.

To counter this entrenched domination, Bookchin follows a long line of anarchist thinkers and naturalists, starting with Peter Kropotkin, who argue that nature is not the blind, cruel, stingy, competitive, hostile environment that we are often taught. Rather, nature is a participatory realm of interactive life forms: creative, cooperative, symbiotic, and productive. If nature is a realm of freedom, participation, and mutual aid, human society can be the same. Bookchin believes that with a radicalized sense of the way nature really works, the human potential for cooperation can be tapped and released. Once we see that hierarchy and domination in human society is institutional, rather than biological, we can work more symbiotically both amongst ourselves and with the rest of the natural world. The selection from Bookchin here first differentiates social ecology from what he sees as the less critical and more misanthropic deep ecology; he then goes on to describe his vision of a more cooperative co-development of human and natural societies.

Ynestra King, having worked for years with Bookchin at the Institute for Social Ecology in Vermont, approaches ecofeminism from the perspective of social ecology. Her argument, as for many ecofeminists, is that there is a relationship between the despoliation of nature and the domination of women. The central reason for women's oppression is their association with nature. In this selection, King addresses the basic question of whether this women/nature association is potentially emancipatory, or whether it provides a rationale for further and continued domination. Some ecofeminists celebrate women's supposed connection with nature, and see it as a source of female freedom outside the destructive world of men. Other feminists, suspicious of the notion of ecofeminism, insist on being liberated from the association with nature, which they see as an imprisoning female ghetto. King argues for a move beyond this dualism, insisting that human culture is itself an inherent part of nature.

We have selected James O'Connor and Rudolf Bahro to represent eco-Marxism and socialist ecology. From O'Connor we include the founding document of the red/green journal *Capitalism, Nature, Socialism*. In this essay, O'Connor lays out what he sees as the second crisis of capitalism. The first crisis focused on the commodification of labour and associated relationships of class conflict causing disparities in wealth and overproduction. The second crisis of capitalism is found on the supply side rather than the demand side of the economy. Here, capitalism is destroying its conditions of production—both land, which it uses up, despoils, or poisons, and labour, which it weakens with production-induced illnesses. As capitalism refuses to take the costs of this destruction into account, its practices lead to an ecological crisis, which leads to an economic crisis. Ecological movements, including those that focus on toxics and health, respond to this second crisis. These movements (and so not just Marx's proletariat) will be the ultimate agents of social change and societal democratization.

Rudolf Bahro was one of the most well-known 'fundamentalists' in the West German Green Party, at least until his resignation in 1985 over what he saw as a watered-down animal rights resolution. Bahro eventually came to see parliamentary politics as hopelessly compromised. In this piece from 1982 Bahro lays out the basic economic positions of the Greens. It is a scathing critique of capitalist industrial civilization (the 'megamachine') that calls for the minimization of work, a reorganization into small, self-sufficient communities, disarmament, and the extension of the political role of social movements. Bahro's vision of a green economy is a long way from either a reformed capitalism or a state-centred socialism, and this is why (elsewhere) he argues vehemently against coalitions with social democrats. His call for a 'fundamental reorientation' in the direction of interlinked ecological communities also involves a reorientation of socialism.

Further Reading

In social ecology, the required reading is Bookchin, Bookchin, and more Bookchin. His works include *Toward an Ecological Society* (1980), *The Ecology of Freedom* (1982), *The Modern Crisis* (1986), *The Philosophy of Social Ecology* (1990), and *Remaking Society* (1990). Broadly sympathetic is Brian Tokar's *The Green Alternative* (1987) and various essays in a book edited by John Clark that honours Bookchin, *Renewing the Earth* (1990). For more on a social (and socialist) ecology-oriented ecofeminism, see *The Death of Nature* (1980) and *Ecological Revolutions* (1989) by Carolyn Merchant, *Ecofeminism* (1993), edited by Maria Mies and Vandana Shiva, and Val Plumwood's *Feminism and the Mastery of Nature* (1993).

Along more socialist or eco-Marxist lines, the journal *Capitalism, Nature, Socialism* is a constant source. Classics of eco-socialism include Hugh Stretton's *Capitalism, Socialism, and the Environment* (1976), Allan Schnaiberg's *The Environment* (1980), and Andre Gorz's *Ecology as Politics* (1980). For a recent attempt at a socialist history of environmentalism, see John Bellamy Foster's *The Vulnerable Planet* (1994).

29 Society and Ecology

Murray Bookchin

....

The problems which many people face today in "defining" themselves, in knowing "who they are"—problems that feed a vast psychotherapy industry—are by no means personal ones. These problems exist not only for private individuals; they exist for modern society as a whole. Socially, we live in desperate uncertainty about how people relate to each other. We suffer not only as individuals from alienation and confusion over our identities and goals; our entire society, conceived as a single entity, seems unclear about its own nature and sense of direction. If earlier societies tried to foster a belief in the virtues of cooperation and care, thereby giving an ethical meaning to social life, modern society fosters a belief in the virtues of competition and egotism, thereby divesting human association of all meaning—except, perhaps, as an instrument for gain and mindless consumption.

We tend to believe that men and women of earlier times were guided by firm beliefs and hopes—values that defined them as human beings and gave purpose to their social lives. We speak of the Middle Ages as an "Age of Faith" or the Enlightenment as an "Age of Reason." Even the pre-World War II era and the years that followed it seem like an alluring time of innocence and hope, despite the Great Depression and the terrible conflicts that stained it. As an elderly character in a recent, rather sophisticated, espionage movie put it: what he missed about his younger years during World War II were their "clarity"—a sense of purpose and idealism that guided his behaviour.

That "clarity," today, is gone. It has been replaced by ambiguity. The certainty that technology and science would improve the human condition is mocked by the proliferation of nuclear weapons, by massive hunger in the Third World, and by poverty in the First World. The fervent belief that liberty would triumph over tyranny is belied by the growing centralization of states everywhere and by the disempowerment of people by bureaucracies, police forces, and sophisticated surveillance techniques—in our "democracies" no less than in visibly authoritarian countries. The hope that we would form "one world," a vast community of disparate ethnic groups that would share their resources to improve life everywhere, has been shattered by a rising tide of nationalism, racism, and an unfeeling parochialism that fosters indifference to the plight of millions.

We believe that our values are worse than those held by people of only two or three generations ago. The present generation seems more self-centred, privatized, and mean-spirited by comparison with earlier ones. It lacks the support systems provided by the extended family,

From Murray Bookchin, *Remaking Society: Pathways to a Green Future* (Boston: South End Press, 1990), 19–39. Reprinted with permission.

community, and a commitment to mutual aid. The encounter of the individual with society seems to occur through cold bureaucratic agencies rather than warm, caring people.

This lack of social identity and meaning is all the more stark in the face of the mounting problems that confront us. War is a chronic condition of our time; economic uncertainty, an all-pervasive presence; human solidarity, a vaporous myth. Not least of the problems we encounter are nightmares of an ecological apocalypse—a catastrophic breakdown of the systems that maintain the stability of the planet. We live under the constant threat that the world of life will be irrevocably undermined by a society gone mad in its need to grow—replacing the organic by the inorganic, soil by concrete, forest by barren earth, and the diversity of life-forms by simplified ecosystems; in short, a turning back of the evolutionary clock to an earlier, more inorganic, mineralized world that was incapable of supporting complex life-forms of any kind, including the human species.

Ambiguity about our fate, meaning, and purpose thus raises a rather startling question: is society itself a curse, a blight on life generally? Are we any better for this new phenomenon called "civilization" that seems to be on the point of destroying the natural world produced over millions of years of organic evolution?

An entire literature has emerged which has gained the attention of millions of readers: a literature that fosters a new pessimism toward civilization as such. This literature pits technology against a presumably "virginal" organic nature; cities against countryside; countryside against "wilderness"; science against a "reverence" for life; reason against the "innocence" of intuition; and, indeed, humanity against the entire biosphere.

We show signs of losing faith in all our uniquely human abilities—our ability to live in peace with each other, our ability to care for our fellow beings and other life-forms. This pessimism is fed daily by sociobiologists who locate our failings in our genes, by antihumanists who deplore our "antinatural" sensibilities, and by "biocentrists" who downgrade our rational qualities with notions that we are no different in our "intrinsic worth" than ants. In short, we are witnessing a widespread assault against the ability of reason, science, and technology to improve the world for ourselves and life generally.

The historic theme that civilization must inevitably be pitted against nature, indeed, that it is corruptive of human nature, has re-surfaced in our midst from the days that reach back to Rousseau—this, precisely at a time when our need for a truly human and ecological civilization has never been greater if we are to rescue our planet and ourselves. Civilization, with its hallmarks of reason and technics, is viewed increasingly as a new blight. Even more basically, society as a phenomenon in its own right is being questioned so much so that its role as integral to the formation of humanity is seen as something harmfully "unnatural" and inherently destructive.

Humanity, in effect, is being defamed by human beings themselves, ironically, as an accursed form of life that all but destroys the world of life and threatens its integrity. To the confusion that we have about our own muddled time and our personal identities, we now have the added confusion that the human condition is seen as a form of chaos produced by our proclivity for wanton destruction and our ability to exercise this proclivity all the more effectively because we possess reason, science, and technology.

Admittedly, few antihumanists, "biocentrists," and misanthropes, who theorize about the human condition, are prepared to follow the logic of their premises to such an absurd point. What is vitally important about this medley of moods and unfinished ideas is that the various forms, institutions, and relationships that make up what we should call "society" are largely ignored. Instead, just as we use vague words like "humanity" or zoological terms like *homo sapiens* that conceal vast differences, often bitter antagonisms, that exist between privileged whites and people of colour, men and women, rich and poor, oppressor and oppressed; so do we, by the same token, use vague words like "society" or "civilization" that conceal vast differences between free, nonhierarchical, class, and stateless societies on the one hand, and others that are, in varying degrees, hierarchical, class-ridden, statist, and authoritarian. Zoology, in effect, replaces socially oriented ecology. Sweeping "natural laws" based on population swings among animals replace conflicting economic and social interests among people.

Simply to pit "society" against "nature," "humanity" against the "biosphere," and "reason," "technology," and "science" against less developed, often primitive forms of human interaction with the natural world, prevents us from examining the highly complex differences and divisions within society so necessary to define our problems and their solutions.

Ancient Egypt, for example, had a significantly different attitude toward nature than ancient Babylonia. Egypt assumed a reverential attitude toward a host of essentially animistic nature deities, many of which were physically part human and part animal, while Babylonians created a pantheon of very human political deities. But Egypt was no less hierarchical than Babylonia in its treatment of people and was equally, if not more, oppressive in its view of human individuality. Certain hunting peoples may have been as destructive of wildlife, despite their strong animistic beliefs, as urban cultures which staked out an over-arching claim to reason. When these many differences are simply swallowed up together with a vast variety of social forms by a word called "society," we do severe violence to thought and even simple intelligence. Society *per se* becomes something "unnatural." "Reason," "technology," and "science" become things that are "destructive" without any regard to the social factors that condition their use. Human attempts to alter the environment are seen as threats—as though our "species" can do little or nothing to improve the planet for life generally.

Of course, we are not any less animals than other mammals, but we are more than herds that browse on the African plains. The way in which we are more—namely, the *kinds* of societies that we form and how we are divided against each other into hierarchies and classes—profoundly affects our behaviour and our effects on the natural world.

Finally, by so radically separating humanity and society from nature or naïvely reducing them to mere zoological entities, we can no longer see how human nature is *derived* from nonhuman nature and social evolution from natural evolution. Humanity becomes estranged or alienated not only from itself in our "age of alienation," but from the natural world in which it has always been rooted as a complex and thinking life-form.

Accordingly, we are fed a steady diet of reproaches by liberal and misanthropic environmentalists alike about how "we" as a species are responsible for the breakdown of the environment. One does not have to go to enclaves of mystics and gurus in San Francisco to find this species-centred, asocial view of ecological problems and their sources. New York City will do just as well.

I shall not easily forget an "environmental" presentation staged by the New York Museum of Natural History in the 1970s in which the public was exposed to a long series of exhibits, each depicting examples of pollution and ecological disruption. The exhibit which closed the presentation carried a startling sign, "The Most Dangerous Animal on Earth," and it consisted simply of a huge mirror which reflected back the human viewer who stood before it. I clearly recall a black child standing before the mirror while a white school teacher tried to explain the message which this arrogant exhibit tried to convey. There were no exhibits of corporate boards or directors planning to deforest a mountainside or government officials acting in collusion with them. The exhibit primarily conveyed one, basically misanthropic, message: people *as such*, not a rapacious society and its wealthy beneficiaries, are responsible for environmental dislocations—the poor no less than the personally wealthy, people of colour no less than privileged whites, women no less than men, the oppressed no less than the oppressor. A mythical human "species" had replaced classes; individuals had replaced hierarchies; personal tastes (many of which are shaped by a predatory media) had replaced social relationships; and the disempowered who live meagre, isolated lives had replaced giant corporations, self-serving bureaucracies, and the violent paraphernalia of the State.

The Relationship of Society to Nature

Leaving aside such outrageous "environmental" exhibitions that mirror privileged and under-privileged people in the same frame, it seems appropriate at this point to raise a highly relevant need: the need to bring society back into the ecological picture. More than ever, strong emphases must be placed on the fact that nearly *all ecological problems are social problems*, not simply or primarily the result of religious, spiritual, or political ideologies. That these ideologies may foster an anti-ecological outlook in people of all strata hardly requires emphasis. But rather than simply take ideologies at their face value, it is crucial for us to ask from whence these ideologies develop.

Quite frequently, economic needs may compel people to act against their best impulses, even strongly felt natural values. Lumberjacks who are employed to clear-cut a magnificent forest normally have no "hatred" of trees. They have little or no choice but to cut trees just as stockyard workers have little or no choice but to slaughter domestic animals. Every community or occupation has its fair share of destructive and sadistic individuals, to be sure, including misanthropic environmentalists who would like to see humanity exterminated. But among the vast majority of people, this kind of work, including such onerous tasks as mining, are not freely chosen occupations. They stem from need and, above all, they are the product of social arrangements over which ordinary people have no control.

To understand present-day problems—ecological as well as economic and political—we must examine their social causes and remedy them through social methods. "Deep," "spiritual," anti-humanist, and misanthropic ecologies gravely mislead us when they refocus our attention on social symptoms rather than social causes. If our obligation is to look at changes in social relationships in order to understand our most significant ecological changes, these ecologies steer us away from society to "spiritual," "cultural," or vaguely defined "traditional" sources. The Bible did not create European antinaturalism; it served to justify an antinaturalism that already existed on the continent from pagan times, despite the animistic traits of pre-Christian religions. Christianity's antinaturalistic influence became especially marked with the emergence of capitalism. Society must not only be brought into the ecological picture to understand why people tend to choose competing sensibilities—some, strongly naturalistic; others, strongly antinaturalistic—but we must probe more deeply into society itself. We must search out the *relationship of society to nature*, the *reasons* why it can destroy the natural world, and, alternatively, the reasons why it has and still can *enhance*, *foster*, and *richly contribute* to natural evolution.

Insofar as we can speak of "society" in any abstract and general sense—and let us remember that every society is highly unique and different from others in the long perspective of history—we are obliged to examine what we can best call "socialization," not merely "society." Society is a given arrangement of relationships which we often take for granted and view in a very fixed way. To many people today, it would seem that a market society based on trade and competition has existed "forever," although we may be vaguely mindful that there were pre-market societies based on gifts and cooperation. Socialization, on the other hand, is a *process*, just as individual living is a process. Historically, the *process* of socializing people can be viewed as a sort of social infancy that involves a painful rearing of humanity to social maturity.

When we begin to consider socialization from an in-depth viewpoint, what strikes us is that society itself in its most primal form stems very much *from* nature. Every social evolution, in fact, is virtually an extension of natural evolution into a distinctly human realm. As the Roman orator and philosopher, Cicero, declared some two thousand years ago: "by the use of our hands, we bring into being within the realm of Nature, a second nature for ourselves." Cicero's observation, to be sure, is very incomplete: the primeval, presumably untouched "realm of Nature" or "first nature," as it has been called, is reworked in whole or part into "second nature" not only by the "use of our hands." Thought, language, and complex, very important biological changes also play a crucial and, at times, a decisive role in developing a "second nature" within "first nature."

I use the term "reworking" advisedly to focus on the fact that "second nature" is not simply a phenomenon that develops outside of "first nature"—hence the special value that should be attached to Cicero's use of the expression "*within* the realm of Nature". To emphasize that "second nature" or, more precisely, society (to use this word in its broadest possible sense) emerges from *within* primeval "first nature' is to re-establish the fact that social life always has a naturalistic dimension, however much society is pitted against nature in our thinking. *Social* ecology clearly expresses the fact that society is not a sudden "eruption" in the world. Social life does not necessarily face nature as a combatant in an unrelenting war. The emergence of society is a *natural* fact that has its origins in the biology of human socialization.

The human socialization process from which society emerges—be it in the form of families, bands, tribes, or more complex types of human intercourse—has its source in parental relationships, particularly mother and child bonding. The biological mother, to be sure, can be replaced in this process by many surrogates, including fathers, relatives, or, for that matter, all members of a community. It is when *social* parents and *social* siblings—that is, the human community that surrounds the young—begin to participate in a system of care, that is ordinarily undertaken by biological parents, that society begins to truly come into its own.

Society thereupon advances beyond a mere reproductive group toward institutionalized human relationships, and from a relatively formless animal community into a clearly structured social *order*. But at the very inception of society, it seems more than likely that human beings were socialized into "second nature" by means of deeply ingrained blood ties, specifically maternal ties. We shall see that in time the structures or institutions that mark the advance of humanity from a mere animal community into an authentic society began to undergo far-reaching changes and these changes become issues of paramount importance in social ecology. For better or worse, societies develop around status groups, hierarchies, classes, and state formations. But reproduction and family care remain the abiding biological bases for every form of social life as well as the originating factor in the socialization of the young and the formation of a society. As Robert Briffault observed in the early half of this century, the "one known factor which establishes a profound distinction between the constitution of the most rudimentary human group and all other animal groups [is the] association of mothers and offspring which is the sole form of true social solidarity among animals. Throughout the class of mammals, there is a continuous increase in the duration of that association, which is the consequence of the prolongation of the period of infantile dependence,"[1] a prolongation which Briffault correlates with increases in the period of fetal gestation and advances in intelligence.

The biological dimension that Briffault adds to what we call society and socialization cannot be stressed too strongly. It is a decisive presence, not only in the origins of society over ages of animal evolution, but in the daily recreation of society in our everyday lives. The appearance of a newly born infant and the highly extended care it receives for many years reminds us that it is not only a human being that is being reproduced, but society itself. By comparison with the young of other species, children develop slowly and over a long period of time. Living in close association with parents, siblings, kin groups, and an ever-widening community of people, they retain a plasticity of mind that makes for creative individuals and ever-formative social groups. Although nonhuman animals may approximate human forms of association in many ways, they do not create a "second nature" that embodies a cultural tradition, nor do they possess a complex language, elaborate conceptual powers, or an impressive capacity to restructure their environment purposefully according to their own needs.

A chimpanzee, for example, remains an infant for only three years and a juvenile for seven. By the age of ten, it is a full-grown adult. Children, by contrast, are regarded as infants for approximately six years and juveniles for fourteen. A chimpanzee, in short, grows mentally and physically in about half the time required by a human being, and its capacity to learn or, at least to think, is already fixed by comparison with a human being, whose mental abilities may expand for decades. By the same token, chimpanzee associations are often idiosyncratic and fairly limited. Human associations, on the other hand, are basically stable, highly institutionalized, and they are marked by a degree of solidarity, indeed, by a degree of creativity that has no equal in nonhuman species as far as we know.

This prolonged degree of human mental plasticity, dependency, and social creativity yields two results that are of decisive importance. First, early human association must have fostered a strong predisposition for *interdependence* among members of a group—not the "rugged individualism" we associate with independence. The overwhelming mass of anthropological evidence suggests that participation, mutual aid, solidarity, and empathy were the social virtues early human groups emphasized within their communities. The idea that people are dependent upon each other for the good life, indeed, for survival, followed from the prolonged dependence of the young upon adults. Independence, not to mention competition, would have seemed utterly alien, if not bizarre, to a creature reared over many years in a largely dependent condition. Care for others would have been seen as the perfectly natural outcome of a highly acculturated being that was, in turn, clearly in need of extended care. Our modern version of individualism, more precisely, of egotism, would have cut across the grain of early solidarity and mutual aid—traits, I may add, without which such a physically fragile animal like a human being could hardly have survived as an adult, much less as a child.

Second, human interdependence must have assumed a highly structured form. There is no evidence that human beings normally relate to each other through the fairly loose systems of bonding we find among our closest primate cousins. That human social bonds can be dissolved or de-institutionalized in periods of radical change or cultural breakdown is too obvious to argue here. But during relatively stable conditions, human society was never the "horde" that anthropologists of the last century presupposed as a basis for rudimentary social life. On the contrary, the evidence we have at hand points to the fact that all humans, perhaps even our distant hominid ancestors, lived in some kind of structured family groups, and, later, in bands, tribes, villages, and other forms. In short, they bonded together (as they still do), not only emotionally and morally, but also structurally in contrived, clearly definable, and fairly permanent institutions.

Nonhuman animals may form loose communities and even take collective protective postures to defend their young from predators. But such communities can hardly be called structured, except in a broad, often ephemeral, sense. Humans, by contrast, create highly formal communities that tend to become increasingly structured over the course of time. In effect, they form not only communities, but a new phenomenon called *societies*.

If we fail to distinguish animal communities from human societies, we risk the danger of ignoring the unique features that distinguish human social life from animal communities—notably, the ability of society to *change* for better or worse and the factors that produce these changes. By reducing a complex society to a mere community, we can easily ignore how societies differed from each other over the course of history. We can also fail to understand how they elaborated simple differences in status into firmly established hierarchies, or hierarchies into economic classes. Indeed, we risk the possibility of totally misunderstanding the very meaning of terms like "hierarchy" as highly organized systems of command and obedience—these, as distinguished from personal, individual, and often short-lived differences in status that may, in all too many cases, involve no acts of compulsion. We tend, in effect, to confuse the strictly institutional creations of human will, purpose, conflicting interests, and traditions, with community life in its most fixed forms, as though we were dealing with inherent, seemingly unalterable, features of society rather than fabricated structures that can be modified, improved, worsened—or simply abandoned. The trick of every ruling elite from the beginnings of history to modern times has been to identify its own socially created hierarchical systems of domination with community life *as such*, with the result being that human-made institutions acquire divine or biological sanction.

A given society and its institutions thus tend to become reified into permanent and unchangeable entities that acquire a mysterious life of their own apart from nature—namely, the products of a seemingly fixed "human nature" that is the result of genetic programming at the very inception of social life. Alternatively, a given society and its institutions may be dissolved into nature as merely another form of animal community with its "alpha males," "guardians," "leaders," and "horde"-like forms of existence. When annoying issues like war and social conflict are raised, they are ascribed to the activity of "genes" that presumably give rise to war and even "greed."

In either case, be it the notion of an abstract society that exists apart from nature or an equally abstract natural community that is indistinguishable from nature, a dualism appears that sharply separates society *from* nature, or a crude reductionism appears that dissolves society *into* nature. These apparently contrasting, but closely related, notions are all the more seductive because they are so simplistic. Although they are often presented by their more sophisticated supporters in a fairly nuanced form, such notions are easily reduced to bumper-sticker slogans that are frozen into hard, popular dogmas.

Social Ecology

The approach to society and nature advanced by social ecology may seem more intellectually demanding, but it avoids the simplicities of dualism and the crudities of reductionism. Social ecology tries to show how nature slowly *phases* into society without ignoring the differences between society and nature on the one hand, as well as the extent to which they merge with each other on the other. The everyday socialization of the young by the family is no less rooted in biology than the everyday care of the old by the medical establishment is rooted in the hard facts of society. By the same token, we never cease to be mammals who still have primal natural urges, but we institutionalize these urges and their satisfaction in a wide variety of social forms. Hence, the social and the natural continually permeate each other in the most ordinary activities of daily life without losing their identity in a shared process of interaction, indeed, of interactivity.

Obvious as this may seem at first in such day-to-day problems as caretaking, social ecology raises questions that have far-reaching importance for the different ways society and nature have interacted over time and the problems these interactions have produced. How did a divisive, indeed, seemingly combative, relationship between humanity and nature emerge? What were the institutional forms and ideologies that rendered this conflict possible? Given the growth of human needs and technology, was such a conflict really unavoidable? And can it be overcome in a future, ecologically oriented society?

How does a rational, ecologically oriented society fit into the processes of natural evolution? Even more broadly, is there any reason to believe that the human mind—itself a product of natural evolution as well as culture—represents a decisive highpoint in natural development, notably, in the long development of subjectivity from the sensitivity and self-maintenance of the simplest life-forms to the remarkable intellectuality and self-consciousness of the most complex?

In asking these highly provocative questions, I am not trying to justify a strutting arrogance toward nonhuman life-forms. Clearly, we must bring humanity's uniqueness as a species, marked by rich conceptual, social, imaginative, and constructive attributes, into synchronicity with nature's fecundity, diversity, and creativity. I have argued that this synchronicity will not be achieved by opposing nature to society, nonhuman to human life-forms, natural fecundity to technology, or a natural subjectivity to the human mind. Indeed, an important result that emerges from a discussion of the interrelationship of nature to society is the fact that human intellectuality, although distinct, also has a far-reaching natural basis. Our brains and nervous systems did not suddenly spring into existence without a long antecedent natural history. That which we most prize as integral to our humanity—our extraordinary capacity to think on complex conceptual levels—can be traced back to the nerve network of primitive invertebrates, the ganglia of a mollusk, the spinal cord of a fish, the brain of an amphibian, and the cerebral cortex of a primate.

Here, too, in the most intimate of our human attributes, we are no less products of natural evolution than we are of social evolution. As human beings we incorporate within ourselves aeons of organic differentiation and elaboration. Like all complex life-forms, we are not only part of natural evolution; we are also its heirs and the products of natural fecundity.

In trying to show how society slowly grows out of nature, however, social ecology is also obliged to show how society, too, undergoes differentiation and elaboration. In doing so, social ecology must examine those junctures in social evolution where splits occurred which slowly brought society into opposition to the natural world, and explain how this opposition emerged from its inception in prehistoric times to our own era. Indeed, if the human species is a life-form that can consciously and richly enhance the natural world, rather than simply damage it, it is important for social ecology to reveal the factors that have rendered many human beings into parasites on the world of life rather than active partners in organic evolution. This project must be undertaken not in a haphazard way, but with a serious attempt to render natural and social development coherent in terms of each other, and relevant to our times and the construction of an ecological society.

Perhaps one of social ecology's most important contributions to the current ecological discussion is the view that the basic problems which pit society against nature emerge from *within* social development itself—not *between* society and nature. That is to say, the divisions between society and nature have their deepest roots in divisions within the social realm, namely, deep-seated conflicts between human and human that are often obscured by our broad use of the word "humanity."

This crucial view cuts across the grain of nearly all current ecological thinking and even social theorizing. One of the most fixed notions that present-day ecological thinking shares with liberalism, Marxism, and conservatism is the historic belief that the "domination of nature" requires the domination of human by human. This is most obvious in social theory. Nearly all of our contemporary social ideologies have placed the notion of human domination at the centre of their theorizing. It remains one of the most widely accepted notions, from classical times to the present, that human freedom from the "domination of man by nature" entails the domination of human by human as the earliest means of production and the use of human beings as instruments for harnessing the natural world. Hence, in order to harness the natural world, it has been argued for ages, it is necessary to harness human beings as well, in the form of slaves, serfs, and workers.

That this instrumental notion pervades the ideology of nearly all ruling elites and has provided both liberal and conservative movements with a justification for their accommodation to the status quo, requires little, if any, elaboration. The myth of a "stingy" nature has always been used to justify the "stinginess" of exploiters in their harsh treatment of the exploited—and it has provided the excuse for the political opportunism of liberal, as well as conservative, causes. To "work within the system" has always implied an acceptance of domination as a way of "organizing" social life and, in the best of cases, a way of freeing humans from their presumed domination by nature.

What is perhaps less known, however, is that Marx, too, justified the emergence of class society and the State as stepping stones toward the domination of nature and, presumably, the liberation of humanity. It was on the strength of this historical vision that Marx formulated his materialist conception of history and his belief in the need for class society as a stepping stone in the historic road to communism.

Ironically, much that now passes for antihumantistic, mystical ecology involves exactly the same kind of thinking—but in an inverted form. Like their instrumental opponents, these ecologists, too, assume that humanity is dominated by nature, be it in the form of "natural laws" or an ineffable "earth wisdom" that must guide human behaviour. But while their instrumental opponents argue the need to achieve nature's "surrender" to a "conquering" active-aggressive humanity, antihumanist and mystical ecologists argue the case for achieving humanity's passive-receptive "surrender" to an "all-conquering" nature. However much the two views may differ in their verbiage and pieties, *domination* remains the underlying notion of both: a natural world conceived as a taskmaster—either to be controlled or obeyed.

Social ecology springs this trap dramatically by re-examining the entire concept of domination, be it in nature and society or in the form of "natural law" and "social law." What we normally call domination in nature is a human projection of highly organized systems of *social* command and obedience onto highly idiosyncratic, individual, and asymmetrical forms of often mildly coercive behaviour in animal communities. Put simply, animals do not "dominate" each other in the same way that a human elite dominates, and often exploits, an oppressed social group. Nor do they "rule" through institutional forms of systematic violence as social elites do. Among apes, for example, there is little or no coercion, but only erratic forms of dominant behaviour. Gibbons and orangutans are notable for their peaceable behaviour toward members of their own kind. Gorillas are often equally pacific, although one can single out "high status," mature, and physically strong males among "lower status," younger and physically weaker ones. The "alpha males" celebrated among chimpanzees do not occupy very fixed "status" positions within what are fairly fluid groups. Any "status" that they do achieve may be due to very diverse causes.

One can merrily skip from one animal species to another, to be sure, falling back on very different, asymmetrical reasons for searching out "high" versus "low status" individuals. The procedure becomes rather silly, however, when words like "status" are used so flexibly that they are allowed to include mere differences in group behaviour and functions, rather than coercive actions.

The same is true for the word "hierarchy." Both in its origins and its strict meaning, this term is highly social, not zoological. A Greek term, initially used to denote different levels of deities and, later, of clergy (characteristically, Hierapolis was an ancient Phrygian city in Asia Minor that was a centre for mother goddess worship), the word has been mindlessly expanded to encompass everything from beehive relationships to the erosive effects of running water in which a stream is seen to wear down and "dominate" its bedrock. Caring female elephants are called "matriarchs" and attentive male apes who exhibit a great deal of courage in defense of their community, while acquiring very few "privileges," are often designated as "patriarchs." The absence of an organized system of rule—so common in hierarchical human communities and subject to radical institutional changes, including popular revolutions—is largely ignored.

Again, the different functions that the presumed animal hierarchies are said to perform, that is, the asymmetrical causes that place one individual in an "alpha status" and others in a lesser one, is understated where it is noted at all. One might, with much the same aplomb, place all tall sequoias in a "superior" status over smaller ones, or, more annoyingly, regard them as an "elite" in a mixed forest "hierarchy" over "submissive" oaks, which, to complicate matters, are more advanced on the evolutionary scale. The tendency to mechanically project social categories onto the natural world is as preposterous as an attempt to project biological concepts onto geology. Minerals do not "reproduce" the way life-forms do. Stalagmites and stalactites in caves certainly do increase in size over time. But in no sense do they grow in a manner that even remotely corresponds to growth in living beings. To take superficial resemblances, often achieved in alien ways, and group them into shared identities, is like speaking of the "metabolism" of rocks and the "morality" of genes.

This raises the issue of repeated attempts to read ethical, as well as social, traits into a natural world that is only *potentially* ethical insofar as it forms a basis for an objective social ethics. Yes, coercion does exist in nature; so does pain and suffering. However, *cruelty* does not. Animal intention and will are too limited to produce an ethics of good and evil or kindness and cruelty. Evidence of inferential and conceptual thought is very limited among animals, except for primates, cetaceans, elephants, and possibly a few other mammals. Even among the most intelligent animals, the limits to thought are immense in comparison with the extraordinary capacities of socialized human beings. Admittedly, we are substantially less than human today in view of our still unknown potential to be creative, caring, and rational. Our prevailing society serves to inhibit, rather than realize, our human potential. We still lack the imagination to know how much our finest human traits could expand with an ethical, ecological, and rational dispensation of human affairs.

By contrast, the known nonhuman world seems to have reached visibly fixed limits in its capacity to survive environmental changes. If mere *adaptation* to environmental changes is seen as the criterion for evolutionary success (as many biologists believe), then insects would have to be placed on a higher plane of development than any mammalian life-form. However, they would be no more capable of making so lofty an intellectual evaluation of themselves than a "queen bee" would be even remotely aware of her "regal" status—a status, I may add, that only humans (who have suffered the social domination of stupid, inept, and cruel kings and queens) would be able to impute to a largely mindless insect.

None of these remarks are meant to metaphysically oppose nature to society or society to nature. On the contrary, they are meant to argue that what unites society with nature in a graded evolutionary continuum is the remarkable extent to which human beings, living in a rational, ecologically oriented society, could *embody* the *creativity* of nature—this, as distinguished from a purely *adaptive* criterion of evolutionary success. The great achievements of human thought, art, science, and technology serve not only to monumentalize culture, *they serve also to monumentalize natural evolution itself*. They provide heroic evidence that the human species is a warm-blooded, excitingly versatile, and keenly intelligent life-form—not a cold-blooded, genetically programmed, and mindless insect—that expresses *nature's* greatest powers of creativity.

Life-forms that create and consciously alter their environment, hopefully in ways that make it more rational and ecological, represent a vast and indefinite extension of nature into fascinating, perhaps unbounded, lines of evolution which no branch of insects could ever achieve—notably, the evolution of a fully *self-conscious* nature. If this be humanism—more precisely, ecological humanism—the current crop of antihumanists and misanthropes are welcome to make the most of it.

Nature, in turn, is not a scenic view we admire through a picture window—a view that is frozen into a landscape or a static panorama. Such "landscape" images of nature may be spiritually elevating but they are ecologically deceptive. Fixed in time and place, this imagery makes it easy for us to forget that nature is not a static vision of the natural world but the long, indeed cumulative, *history* of natural development. This history involves the evolution of the inorganic, as well as the organic, realms of phenomena. Wherever we stand in an open field, forest, or on a mountain top, our feet rest on ages of development, be they geological strata, fossils of long-extinct life-forms, the decaying remains of the newly dead, or the quiet stirring of newly emerging life. Nature is not a "person," a "caring Mother," or, in the crude materialist language of the last century, "matter and motion." Nor is it a mere "process" that involves repetitive cycles like seasonal changes and the building-up and breaking-down process of metabolic activity—some "process philosophies" to the contrary notwithstanding. Rather, natural history is a *cumulative* evolution toward ever more varied, differentiated, and complex forms and relationships.

This *evolutionary* development of increasingly variegated entities, most notably, of life-forms, is also an evolutionary development which contains exciting, latent possibilities. With variety, differentiation, and complexity, nature, in the course of its own unfolding, opens new directions for still further development along alternative lines of natural evolution. To the degree that animals become complex, self-aware, and increasingly intelligent, they begin to make those elementary choices that influence their own evolution. They are less and less the passive objects of "natural selection" and more and more the active subjects of their own development.

A brown hare that mutates into a white one and sees a snow-covered terrain in which to camouflage itself is *acting* on behalf of its own survival, not simply "adapting" in order to survive. It is not merely being "selected" by its environment; it is selecting its own environment and making a *choice* that expresses a small measure of subjectivity and judgement.

The greater the variety of habitats that emerge in the evolutionary process, the more a given life-form, particularly a neurologically complex one, is likely to play an active and judgemental role in preserving itself. To the extent that natural evolution follows this path of neurological development, it gives rise to life-forms that exercise an ever-wider latitude of choice and a nascent form of freedom in developing themselves.

Given this conception of nature as the cumulative history of more differentiated levels of material organization (especially of life-forms) and of increasing subjectivity, social ecology establishes a basis for a meaningful understanding of humanity and society's place in natural evolution. Natural history is not a "catch-as-catch-can" phenomenon. It is marked by tendency, by direction, and, as far as human beings are concerned, by conscious purpose. Human beings and the social worlds they create can open a remarkably expansive horizon for development of the natural world—a horizon marked by consciousness, reflection, and an unprecedented freedom of choice and capacity for conscious creativity. The factors that reduce many life-forms to largely adaptive roles in changing environments are replaced by a capacity for consciously adapting environments *to* existing and new life-forms.

Adaptation, in effect, increasingly gives way to creativity and the seemingly ruthless action of "natural law" to greater freedom. What earlier generations called "blind nature" to denote nature's lack of any moral direction, turns into "free nature," a nature that slowly finds a voice and the means to relieve the needless tribulations of life for all species in a highly conscious humanity and an ecological society. The "Noah Principle" of preserving every existing life-form simply for its own sake—a principle advanced by the antihumanist, David Ehrenfeld—has little meaning without the presupposition, at the very least, of the existence of a "Noah"—that is, a conscious life-form called humanity that might well rescue life-forms that nature itself would extinguish in ice ages, land desiccation, or cosmic collisions with asteroids.[2] Grizzly bears, wolves, pumas, and the like, are not safer from extinction because they are exclusively in the "caring" hands of a putative "Mother Nature." If there is any truth to the theory that the great Mesozoic reptiles were extinguished by climatic changes that presumably followed the collision of an asteroid with the earth, the survival of existing mammals might well be just as precarious in the face of an equally meaningless natural catastrophe unless there is a conscious, ecologically oriented life-form that has the technological means to rescue them.

The issue, then, is not whether social evolution stands opposed to natural evolution. The issue is *how* social evolution can be situated *in* natural evolution and *why* it has been thrown—needlessly, as I will argue—against natural evolution to the detriment of life as a whole. The capacity to be rational and free does not assure us that this capacity will be realized. If social evolution is seen as the potentiality for expanding the horizon of natural evolution along unprecedented creative lines, and human beings are seen as the potentiality for nature to become self-conscious and free, the issue we face is *why* these potentialities have been warped and *how* they can be realized.

It is part of social ecology's commitment to natural evolution that these potentialities are indeed real and that they can be fulfilled. This commitment stands flatly at odds with a "scenic" image of nature as a static view to awe mountain men or a romantic view for conjuring up mystical images of a personified deity that is so much in vogue today. The splits between natural and social evolution, nonhuman and human life, an intractable "stingy" nature and a grasping, devouring humanity, have all been specious and misleading when they are seen as inevitabilities. No less specious and misleading have been reductionist attempts to absorb social into natural evolution, to collapse culture into nature in an orgy of irrationalism, theism, and mysticism, to equate the human with mere animality, or to impose a contrived "natural law" on an obedient human society.

Whatever has turned human beings into "aliens" in nature are social changes that have made many human beings "aliens" in their own social world: the domination of the young by the old, of women by men, and of men by men. Today, as for many centuries in the past, there are still oppressive human beings who literally own society and others who are owned by it. Until society can be reclaimed by an undivided humanity that will use its collective wisdom, cultural achievements, technological innovations, scientific knowledge, and innate creativity for its own benefit and for that of the natural world, all ecological problems will have their roots in social problems.

Notes

1. Robert Briffault, "The Evolution of the Human Species," in V. F. Calverton (ed.), *The Making of Man* (New York: Modern Library, 1931), 765–6.

2. David Ehrenfeld, *The Arrogance of Humanism* (New York: Oxford University Press, 1978), 207.

30 Toward an Ecological Feminism and a Feminist Ecology

Ynestra King

[Woman] became the embodiment of the biological function, the image of nature, the subjugation of which constituted that civilization's title to fame. For millennia men dreamed of acquiring absolute mastery over nature, of converting the cosmos into one immense hunting ground. It was to this that the idea of man was geared in a male-dominated society. This was the significance of reason, his proudest boast.

(Horkheimer and Adorno 1972: 248)

All human beings are natural beings. That may seem like an obvious statement, yet we live in a culture which is founded on repudiation and domination of nature. This has a special significance for women because, in patriarchal thought, women are believed to be closer to nature than men. That gives women a particular stake in ending the domination of nature—in healing the alienation between human and nonhuman nature. That is the ultimate goal of the ecology movement, but the ecology movement is not necessarily feminist. For the most part, ecologists, with their concern for nonhuman nature, have yet to understand that they have a particular stake in ending the domination of women because a central reason for woman's oppression is her association with the despised nature they are so concerned about. The hatred of women and the hatred of nature are intimately connected and mutually reinforcing. Starting with this premise, this chapter explores why feminism and ecology need each other and suggests the very beginnings of a theory of ecological feminism—ecofeminism.

What is ecology? Ecological science concerns itself with the interrelationships of all forms of life. It aims to harmonize nature, human and nonhuman. It is an integrative science in an age of fragmentation and specialization of knowledge. It is also a critical science, which grounds and necessitates a critique of our existing society. It is a reconstructive science in that it suggests directions for reconstructing human society in harmony with the natural environment.

Ecologists are asking the pressing questions of how we might survive on the planet and develop systems of food and energy production, architecture, and ways of life which will allow human beings to fulfill our material needs and live in harmony with nonhuman nature. This work has led to a social critique by biologists and an exploration of biology and ecology by social thinkers. The perspective that self-consciously attempts to integrate both biological and social

From *Machina Ex Dea: Feminist Perspectives on Technology* (New York: Pergamon Press, 1983), 118–28. Reprinted by permission of the author.

aspects of the relationship between human beings and their environment is known as "social ecology." This perspective, developed primarily by Murray Bookchin (1982), has embodied the anarchist critique which links domination and hierarchy in human society to the despoliation of nonhuman nature.[1] While this analysis is useful, social ecology without feminism is incomplete.

Feminism grounds this critique of domination by identifying the prototype of other forms of domination, that of man over woman. Potentially, feminism creates a concrete global community of interests among particularly life-oriented peoples of the world: women. Feminist analysis supplies theory, program, and process without which the radical potential of social ecology remains blunted. The theory and movement known as ecofeminism pushes social ecology to understand the necessary connections between ecology and feminism so that social ecology can reach its own avowed goal of creating a free and ecological way of life.

What are these connections? Social ecology challenges the dualistic belief that nature and culture are separate and opposed. Ecofeminism finds misogyny at the root of that opposition. Ecofeminist principles are based on the following beliefs:

1. The building of Western industrial civilization in opposition to nature interacts dialectically with and reinforces the subjugation of women because women are believed to be closer to nature in this culture against nature.

2. Life on earth is an interconnected web, not a hierarchy. There is not a natural hierarchy, but a multitiered human hierarchy projected onto nature and then used to justify social domination. Therefore ecofeminist movement politics and culture must show the connections between all forms of domination, including the domination of nonhuman nature, and be itself antihierarchical.

3. A healthy, balanced ecosystem, including human and nonhuman inhabitants, must maintain diversity. Ecologically, environmental simplification is as significant a problem as environmental pollution. Biological simplification, i.e. wiping out of whole species, corresponds to reducing human diversity into faceless workers, or to the homogenization of taste and culture through mass consumer markets. Social life and natural life are literally simplified to the inorganic for the convenience of market society. Therefore, we need a decentralized global movement founded on common interests but celebrating diversity and opposing all forms of domination and violence. Potentially, ecofeminism is such a movement.

4. The survival of the species necessitates a renewed understanding of our relationship to nature, of our own bodily nature and nonhuman nature around us; it necessitates a challenging of the nature–culture dualism and a corresponding radical restructuring of human society according to feminist and ecological principles.

When we speak of transformation we speak more accurately out of the vision of a process which will leave neither surfaces nor depths unchanged, which enters society at the most essential level of the subjugation of women and nature by men. (Rich 1979: 248)

The ecology movement, in theory and practice, attempts to speak for nature, the "other" which has no voice and is not conceived of subjectively in our civilization. Feminism represents the refusal of the original "other" in patriarchal human society to remain silent or to be the "other" any longer. Its challenge of social domination extends beyond sex to social domination of all kinds because the domination of sex, race, class, and nature are mutually reinforcing. Women are the "others" in human society who have been silent in public, and who now speak through the feminist movement.

Women, Nature, and Culture: The Ecofeminist Position

In the process of building Western industrial civilization, nature became something to be dominated, overcome, made to serve the needs of men. She was stripped of her magical powers and properties as these beliefs were relegated to the trashbin of superstition. Nature was reduced to "natural resources" to be exploited by human beings to fulfill human needs and purposes which were defined in opposition to nature (see Merchant 1980).[2] A dualistic Christianity had become ascendant with the earlier demise of old Goddess religions, paganism, and animistic belief systems (Reuther 1975). With the disenchantment of nature came the conditions for unchecked scientific exploration and technological exploitation (Merchant 1980). We bear the consequences today of beliefs in unlimited control over nature and in science's ability to solve any problem, as nuclear power plants are built without provisions for waste disposal, or satellites sent into space without provision for retrieval.

In this way, nature became "other," something essentially different from the dominant to be objectified and thus subordinated. Women, who are identified with nature, have been similarly objectified and subordinated in patriarchal society. Women and nature, in this sense, are the original "others." Simone de Beauvoir (1968) has clarified this connection. For de Beauvoir, "transcendence" is the work of culture, it is the work of men. It is the process of overcoming immanence, a process of culture-building which is opposed to nature and which is based on the increasing domination of nature. It is enterprise. Immanence, symbolized by woman, is that which calls man back, that which reminds man of what he wants to forget. It is his own links to nature that he must forget and overcome to achieve manhood and transcendence:

Man seeks in woman the Other as Nature and as his fellow being. But we know what ambivalent feelings Nature inspires in man. He exploits her, but she crushes him, he is born of her and dies in her; she is the source of his being and the realm that he subjugates to his will; Nature is a vein of gross material in which the soul is imprisoned, and she is the supreme reality; she is contingence and Idea, the finite and the whole; she is what opposes the Spirit, and the Spirit itself. Now ally, now enemy, she appears as the dark chaos from whence life wells up, as this life itself, and as the over-yonder toward which life tends. Woman sums up Nature as Mother, Wife, and Idea; these forms now mingle and now conflict, and each of them wears a double visage. (de Beauvoir 1968: 144)

For de Beauvoir, patriarchal civilization is almost the denial of men's mortality—of which women and nature are incessant reminders. Women's powers of procreation are distinguished from the powers of creation, the accomplishments through the vehicle of culture by which men achieve immortality. And yet, this transcendence over women and nature can never be total. Hence, the ambivalence, the lack of self without other, the dependence of the self on the other both materially and emotionally. Thus develops a love–hate fetishization of women's bodies, which finds its ultimate manifestation in the sadomasochistic, pornographic displays of women as objects to be subdued, humiliated, and raped—the visual enactment of these fears and desires.[3]

An important contribution of de Beauvoir's work is to show that men seek to dominate women and nature for reasons which are not simply economic. They do so as well for psychological reasons which involve a denial of a part of themselves, as do other male culture-making activities. The process begins with beating the tenderness and empathy out of small boys and directing their natural human curiosity and joy in affecting the world around them into arrogant attitudes and destructive paths.

For men raised in woman-hating cultures, the fact that they are born of women and dependent upon nonhuman nature for existence is frightening. The process of objectification, of the making of women and nature into "others" to be appropriated and dominated, is based on a profound forgetting by men. They forget that they are born of women, dependent on women in their early helpless years, and dependent on nonhuman nature all their lives, which allows first for objectification and then for domination. "The loss of memory is a transcendental condition for science. All objectification is a forgetting" (Horkheimer and Adorno 1972: 230).

But the denied part of men is never fully obliterated. The memory remains in the knowledge of mortality and the fear of women's power. A basic fragility of gender identity therefore exists that surfaces when received truths about women and men are challenged and the sexes depart from the "natural" roles. Opposition to the not-very-radical US Equal Rights Amendment can be partially explained on these grounds. More threatening are homosexuality and the gay liberation movement because they name a more radical truth—that sexual orientation is not indelible, nor is it naturally heterosexual. Lesbianism, particularly, which suggests that women, who possess this bottled up, repudiated primordial power, can be self-sufficient, reminds men that they may not be needed. Men are forced into remembering their own need for women to enable them to support and mediate the construction of their private reality and their public civilization. Again, there is the need to repress memory and suppress women.

The recognition of the connections between woman and nature or of women's bridge-like position poses three possible directions for feminism. One direction is the integration of women into the world of culture and production by severing the woman/nature connection. Writes anthropologist Sherry Ortner, "Ultimately both men and women can and must be equally involved in projects of creativity and transcendence. Only then will women be seen as aligned with culture, in culture's ongoing dialectic with nature" (1974: 87). This position does not necessarily question nature/culture dualism itself, and it is the position taken by most socialist-feminists (see King 1981) and by de Beauvoir and Ortner despite their insights into the connections between women and nature. They seek the severance of the woman/nature connection as a condition of women's liberation. Other feminists have built on the woman/nature connection by reinforcing this connection: woman and nature, the spiritual and intuitive versus men and the culture of patriarchal rationality.[4] This position also does not neccessarily question nature/culture dualism itself or recognize that women's ecological sensitivity and life orientation is a socialized perspective which could be socialized right out of us depending on our day-to-day lives. There is no reason to believe that women placed in positions of patriarchal power will act any differently from men or that we can bring about feminist revolution without a conscious understanding of history and a challenge to economic and political power structures.

Ecofeminism suggests a third direction: that feminism recognize that although the nature/culture opposition is a product of culture, we can, nonetheless, *consciously choose* not to sever the woman nature connections by joining male culture. Rather, we can use it as a vantage point for creating a different kind of culture and politics that would integrate intuitive/spiritual and rational forms of knowledge, embracing both science and magic insofar as they enable us to transform the nature/culture distinction itself and to envision and create a free, ecological society.

Ecofeminism and the Intersections of Feminism and Ecology

The implications of a culture based on the devaluation of life-giving (both biological and social) and the celebration of life-taking are profound for ecology and for women. This fact about our culture links the theories and the politics of the ecology and the feminist movements. Adrienne Rich has written,

We have been perceived for too many centuries as pure Nature, exploited and raped like the earth and solar system; small wonder if we now long to become Culture; pure spirit, mind. Yet it is precisely this culture and its political institutions which have split us off from itself. In so doing it has also split itself off from life, becoming the death culture of quantification, abstraction, and the will to power which has reached its most refined destructiveness in this century. It is this culture and politics of abstraction which women are talking of changing, of bringing into accountability in human terms. (1976: 285)

The way to ground a feminist critique of "this culture and politics of abstraction" is with a self-conscious ecological perspective that we apply to all theories and strategies, in the way that we are learning to apply race and class factors to every phase of feminist analysis.

Similarly, ecology requires a feminist perspective. Without a thorough feminist analysis of social domination that reveals the interconnected roots of misogyny and a hatred of nature, ecology remains an abstraction: it is incomplete. If male ecological scientists and social ecologists fail to deal with misogyny, the deepest manifestation of nature-hating in their own lives, they are not living the ecological lives or creating the ecological society they claim.

The goals of harmonizing humanity and nonhuman nature, at both the experiential and theoretical levels, cannot be attained without the radical vision and understanding available from feminism. The ecofeminist perspective thus affects our technology. Including everything from the digging stick to nuclear bombs, technology signifies the tools that human beings use to interact with nature. The twin concerns of ecofeminism with human liberation and with our relationship to nonhuman nature open the way to developing a set of technological ethics required for decision making about technology.

Ecofeminism also contributes an understanding of the connections between the domination of persons and the domination of nonhuman nature. Ecological science tells us that there is no hierarchy in nature itself, but rather a hierarchy in human society. Building on this unmasking of the ideology of natural hierarchy of persons, ecofeminism uses its ecological perspective to develop the position that there is no hierarchy in nature: among persons, between persons and the rest of the natural world, or among the many forms of nonhuman nature. We live on the earth with millions of species, only one of which is the human species. Yet, the human species, in its patriarchal form, is the only species which holds a conscious belief that it is entitled to dominion over the other species, and the planet. Paradoxically, the human species is utterly dependent on nonhuman nature. We could not live without the rest of nature: it could live without us.

Ecofeminism draws on another basic principle of ecological science, unity in diversity, and develops it politically. Diversity in nature is necessary, and enriching. One of the major effects of industrial technology—capitalist or socialist—is environmental simplification. Many species are being simply wiped out, never to be seen on the earth again. In human society, commodity capitalism is intentionally simplifying human community and culture so that the same products can be marketed anywhere to anyone. The prospect is for all of us to be alike, with identical needs and desires, around the globe: Coca Cola in China, blue jeans in Russia, and American rock music virtually everywhere. Few peoples of the earth have not had their lives touched and changed to some degree by the technology of industrialization. Ecofeminism as a social movement resists this social simplification through supporting the rich diversity of women the world over, and finding a oneness in that diversity. Politically, ecofeminism opposes the ways that differences can separate women from each other through the oppressions of class, privilege, sexuality, race, and nationality.

The special message of ecofeminism is that, when women suffer through both social domination and the domination of nature, most of life on this planet suffers and is threatened as well. For the brutalization and oppression of women is connected with the hatred of nature and with other forms of domination, and with threatened ecological catastrophe. It is significant that feminism and ecology as social movements have emerged now, as nature's revolt against domination plays itself out in human history and nonhuman nature at the same time. As we face slow environmental poisoning and the resulting environmental simplification, or the possible unleashing of our nuclear arsenals, we can hope that the prospect of the extinction of life on the planet will provide a universal impetus to social change. Ecofeminism supports utopian visions of harmonious, diverse, decentralized communities, using only those technologies based on ecological principles, as the only practical solution for the continuation of life on earth.

Visions and politics are joined as an ecofeminist culture and politic begin to emerge. Central to this development is ecofeminist praxis: taking direct action to effect changes that are immediate and personal as well as long term and structural. Direct actions include learning holistic health and alternate ecological technologies, living in communities which explore old and new forms of spirituality that celebrate all life as diverse expressions of nature, considering the ecological consequences of our lifestyles and personal habits, and participating in creative public forms of resistance. This sometimes involves engaging in nonviolent civil disobedience to physically stop the machines which are arrayed against life.

Toward an Ecofeminist Praxis: Feminist Antimilitarism

Theory never converts simply or easily into practice; in fact, theory often lags behind practice, attempting to articulate the understanding behind things people are already doing. Praxis is the unity of thought and action, or theory and practice. Many of the women who founded the feminist antimilitarist movement in Europe and the United States share the ecofeminist perspective

I have articulated. I believe that the movement as I will briefly describe it here grows out of such an understanding. For the last three years, I have been personally involved in the feminist antimilitarist movement, so the following is a firsthand account of this example of ecofeminist praxis.

The connections between violence against women, a militarized culture, and the development and deployment of nuclear weapons have long been evident to pacifist feminists (Deming 1974). Ecofeminists like myself, whose concerns with all of life stem from an understanding of the connections between misogyny and the destruction of nature, began to see militarism and the death-courting weapons industry as the most immediate threat to continued life on the planet, while the ecological effects of other modern technologies pose a more long-term threat. In this manner, militarism has become a central issue for most ecofeminists. Along with this development, many of us accepted the analysis of violence made by pacifist feminists and, therefore, began to see nonviolent direct action and resistance as the basis of our political practice.

The ecofeminist analysis of militarism is concerned with the militarization of culture and the economic priorities reflected by our enormous "defense" budgets and dwindling social services budgets. Together, these pose threats to our freedom and threaten our lives, even if there is no war and none of the nuclear weapons are ever used. We have tried to make clear the particular ways that women suffer from war-making—as spoils to victorious armies, as refugees, as disabled and older women and single mothers who are dependent on dwindling social services. We connect the fear of nuclear annihilation with women's fear of male violence in our everyday lives. The level of weaponry as well as the militaristic economic priorities are products of patriarchal culture that speaks violence at every level. For ecofeminists, military technology reflects a pervasive cultural political situation. It is connected with rape, genocide, and imperialism; with starvation and homelessness; the poisoning of the environment; and the fearful lives of the world's peoples—especially those of women. Military and state power hierarchies join and reinforce each other through military technology.

Particularly as shaped by ecofeminism, the feminist antimilitarist movement in the United States and Europe is a movement against a monstrously destructive technology and set of power relationships embodied in militarism.

Actions have been organized at the Pentagon in the United States and at military installations in Europe. The Women's Pentagon Action was conceived at an ecofeminist conference I initiated and organized with several other women in spring 1980.[5] It has taken place at the Pentagon twice so far, on November 16 and 17, 1980, and November 15 and 16, 1981. It included about 2,000 women the first year, and more than twice that the second. We took care to make the actions reflect all our politics. Intentionally, there were no speakers, no leaders; the action sought to emphasize the connections between the military issue and other ecofeminist issues. The action was planned in four stages, reflecting the depth and range of the emotions felt and the interconnection of issues, and culminating in direct resistance. A Unity Statement, describing the group's origins and concerns was drafted collectively. In the first stage, "mourning," we walked among the graves at Arlington National Cemetery and placed tombstones symbolically for all the victims of war and other forms of violence against women, beginning with a marker for "the unknown woman." The second stage was "rage," a venting of our anger. Next, the group circled the Pentagon, reaching all the way around, and singing for the stage of "empowerment." The final stage, "defiance," included a civil disobedience action in which women blocked entrances and were arrested in an act of nonviolent direct resistance. The choice to commit civil disobedience was made individually, without pressure from the group.[6]

The themes of the Women's Pentagon Action have carried over into other actions our group has participated in, including those organized by others. At the June 12–14, 1982, disarmament demonstrations in New York City, the group's march contingent proclaimed the theme: "A feminist world is a nuclear free zone," the slogan hanging beneath a huge globe held aloft. Other banners told of visions for a feminist future and members wore bibs that read "War is manmade," "Stop the violence in our lives," and "Disarm the patriarchy." There have been similar actions, drawing inspiration from the original Women's Pentagon Actions elsewhere in the United States and in Europe. In California, the Bohemian Club—a male-only playground for corporate, government, and military elite—was the site of a demonstration by women who surrounded the club in protest (Starhawk 1982: 168). In England, on December 12, 1982, 30,000 women surrounded a US military installation, weaving into the fence baby clothes, scarves, and other objects which meant something to them. At one point, spontaneously, the word "FREEDOM" rose from the lips of the women and was heard round and round the base. Three thousand women nonviolently blocked the entrances to the base on December 13 (see Fisher 1983).

The politics being created by these actions draw on women's culture: embodying what is best in women's life-oriented socialization, building on women's differences, organizing antihierarchically in small groups in visually and emotionally imaginative ways, and seeking an integration of issues. There actions exemplify ecofeminism. While technocratic experts (including feminists) argue the merits and demerits of weapons systems, ecofeminism approaches the disarmament issue on an intimate and moral level. Ecofeminism holds that a personalized, decentralized, life-affirming culture and politics of direct action are crucially needed to stop the arms race and transform the world's priorities. Because such weaponary does not exist apart from a contempt for women and all of life, the issue of disarmament and threat of nuclear war is a feminist issue. It is the ultimate human issue and the ultimate ecological issue. And so ecology, feminism, and liberation for all of nature, including ourselves, are joined.

Notes

1. I am indebted to Bookchin for my own theoretical understanding of social ecology which is basic to this chapter.

2. Merchant interprets the Scientific Revolution as the death of nature, and argues that it had a particularly detrimental effect on women.

3. See Susan Griffin (1981) for a full development of the relationship between nature-hating, woman-hating, and pornography.

4. Many such feminists call themselves ecofeminists. Some of them cite Susan Griffin's *Woman and Nature* (1978) as the source of their understanding of the deep connections between women and nature, and their politics. *Woman and Nature* is an inspirational poetic work with political implications. It explores the terrain of our deepest naturalness, but I do not read it as a delineation of a set of politics. To use Griffin's work in this way is to make it into something it was not intended to be. In personal conversation and in her more politically explicit works such as *Pornography*

and Silence (1981), Griffin is antidualistic, struggling to bridge the false oppositions of nature and culture, passion and reason. Both science and poetry are deeply intuitive processes. Another work often cited by ecofeminists is Mary Daly's *Gyn/ecology* (1978). Daly, a theologian/philosopher, is also an inspirational thinker, but she is a genuinely dualistic thinker, reversing the "truths" of patriarchal theology. While I have learned a great deal from Daly, my perspective differs from hers in that I believe that any truly ecological politics including ecological feminism must be ultimately antidualistic.

5. "Women and Life on Earth: Ecofeminism in the 80s," Amherst, Mass., March 21–23, 1980. Each of my sister founders of Women and Life on Earth contributed to the theory of ecofeminism I have articulated here, and gave me faith in the political potential of an ecofeminist movement. All of them would probably disagree with parts of this chapter. Nonetheless, I thank Christine Di Stefano, Deborah Gaventa, Anna Gyorgy, Amy Hines, Sue Hoffman, Carol Iverson, Grace Paley, Christina Rawley, Nancy Jack Todd, and Celeste Wesson.

6. See Ynestra King (1983) for my personal account and evaluation of the action.

References

Bookchin, Murray (1982), *The Ecology of Freedom: The Emergence and Dissolution of Hierarchy* (Palo Alto, Calif.: Cheshire Books).

Daly, Mary (1978), *Gyn/ecology: The Metaethics of Radical Feminism* (Boston: Beacon Press).

de Beauvoir, Simone (1968), *The Second Sex* (New York: Modern Library, Random House).

Deming, Barbara (1974), *We Cannot Live Without our Lives* (New York: Grossman).

Fisher, Berenice (1983), "Woman Ignite English Movement," *Womanews* (February).

Griffin, Susan (1978), *Woman and Nature: The Roaring Inside Her* (New York: Harper & Row).

—— (1981), *Pornography and Silence: Culture's Revenge against Nature* (New York: Harper & Row).

Horkheimer, Max, and Adorno, Theodor W. (1972), *Dialectic of Enlightenment* (New York: Seabury Press).

King, Ynestra (1981), "Feminism and the Revolt of Nature," *Heresies*, 13 (Fall), 12–16.

—— (1983), "All is Connectedness: Scenes from the Women's Pentagon Action USA," in Lynne Johnes (ed.), *Keeping the Peace: A Women's Peace Handbook* (London: The Women's Press).

Merchant, Carolyn (1980), *The Death of Nature: Women, Ecology, and the Scientific Revolution* (New York: Harper & Row).

Ortner, Sherry B. (1974), "Is Female to Male as Nature is to Culture?", in Michelle Zimbalist Rosaldo and Louise Lamphere (eds), *Women, Culture and Society* (Stanford, Calif.: Stanford University Press), 67–87.

Reuther, Rosemary (1975), *New Woman/New Earth: Sexist Ideologies and Human Liberation* (New York: Seabury Press).

Rich, Adrienne (1976), *Of Woman Born* (New York: W. W. Norton).

—— (1979), *On Lies, Secrets, and Silence: Selected Prose* (New York: W. W. Norton).

Starhawk (1982), *Dreaming the Dark: Magic, Sex and Politics* (Boston: Beacon Press).

31 Capitalism, Nature, Socialism: A Theoretical Introduction

James O'Connor

Those who insist that [environmental destruction] has nothing to do with Marxism merely ensure that what they choose to call Marxism will have nothing to do with what happens in the world.

(Aiden Foster-Carter)

Summary

This article expounds the traditional Marxist theory of the contradiction between forces and relations of production, over-production of capital and economic crisis, and the process of crisis-induced restructuring of productive forces and production relations into more transparently social, hence potentially socialist, forms. This exposition provides a point of departure for an "ecological Marxist" theory of the contradiction between capitalist production relations and forces and the *conditions of production*, under-production of capital and economic crisis, and the process of crisis-induced restructuring of production conditions and the social relations thereof also into more transparently social, hence potentially socialist, forms. In short, there may be not one but two paths to socialism in late capitalist society.

While the two processes of capital over-production and under-production are by no means mutually exclusive, they may offset or compensate for one another in ways which create the *appearance* of relatively stable processes of capitalist development. Study of the combination of the two processes in the contemporary world may throw light on the decline of traditional labor and socialist movements and the rise of "new social movements" as agencies of social transformation. In similar ways that traditional Marxism illuminates the practises of traditional labor movements, it may be that "ecological Marxism" throws light on the practices of new social movements. Although ecology and nature; the politics of the body, feminism, and the family; and urban movements and related topics are usually discussed in post-Marxist terms, the rhetoric deployed in this article is self-consciously Marxist and designed to appeal to Marxist theorists and fellow travelers whose work remains within a "scientific" discourse hence those who are least likely to be convinced by post-Marxist discussions of the problem of capital's use and abuse of nature (including human nature) in the modern world. However, the emphasis in this article on a political economic "scientific" discourse is tactical, not strategic. In reality, more

From *Capitalism, Nature, Socialism*, 1 (1986), 11–38. Reprinted with permission.

or less autonomous social relationships, often non-capitalist or anti-capitalist, constitute "civil society," which needs to be addressed on its own practical and theoretical terms. In other words, social and collective action is not meant to be construed merely as derivative of systemic forces, as the last section of the article hopefully will make clear.

1. Introduction

In 1944, Karl Polanyi published his masterpiece, *The Great Transformation*, which discussed the ways in which the growth of the capitalist market impaired or destroyed its own social and environmental conditions.[1] Despite the fact that this book is alive with insights into the problem of economic development and the social and natural environment, it was widely forgotten. The subject of the ecological limits to economic growth and the interrelationships between development and environment was reintroduced into Western bourgeois thought in the late 1960s and early 1970s. The results have been mixed and highly dubious. Polanyi's work remains a shining light in a heaven filled with dying stars and black holes of bourgeois naturalism, neo-Malthusianism, Club of Rome technocratism, romantic deep ecologyism, and United Nations one-worldism.[2] Class exploitation, capitalist crisis, uneven and combined capitalist development, national independence struggles, and so on are missing from these kinds of accounts. The results of these and most other modern efforts to discuss the problem of capitalism, nature, and socialism wither on the vine because they fail to focus on the nature of specifically capitalist scarcity, that is, the process whereby capital is its own barrier or limit because of its self-destructive forms of proletarianization of human nature and appropriation of labor and capitalization of external nature.[3] The usual approaches to the problem—the identification of "limits to growth" in terms of "resource scarcity," "ecological fragility," "harmful industrial technology," "destructive cultural values," "tragedy of the commons," "over-population," "wasteful consumption," "production treadmill," etc., either ignore or mangle Marx's theories of historically produced forms of nature and capitalist accumulation and development.

This should not be surprising since Marx wrote little pertaining to the ways that capital limits itself by impairing its own social and environmental conditions hence increasing the costs and expenses of capital, thereby threatening capital's ability to produce profits, i.e. threatening economic crisis. More, he wrote little or nothing about the effects of social struggles organized around the provision of the conditions of production on the costs and expenses and variability of capital. Nor did he theorize the relationship between social and material dimensions of production conditions, excepting his extended discussion of ground rent (i.e. social relation between landed and industrial capital and material and economic relation between raw materials and industrial production). Marx was, however, convinced of at least three things. The first was that deficiencies of production conditions or "natural conditions" ("bad harvests") may take the form of economic crisis.[4] Second, he was convinced of the more general proposition that some barriers to production are truly external to the mode of production ("the productiveness of labour is fettered by physical conditions")[5] but that in capitalism these barriers assume the form of economic crisis.[6] Put another way, some barriers are "general" not "specific" to capitalism. What is specific is the way these barriers assume the form of crisis. Third, Marx believed that capitalist agriculture and silviculture are harmful to nature, as well as that capitalist exploitation is harmful to human laborpower.

In sum, Marx believed that capitalist farming (for example) ruined soil quality. He was also clear that bad harvests take the form of economic crisis. However, (although he did state that a rational agriculture is incompatible with capitalism)[7] he never considered the possibility that ecologically destructive methods of agriculture might raise the costs of the elements of capital, which, in turn, might threaten economic crisis of a particular type, namely, underproduction of capital.[8] Put another way, Marx never put two and two together to argue that "natural barriers" may be capitalistically produced barriers, i.e. a "second" capitalized nature.[9] In other words, there may exist a contradiction of capitalism which leads to an "ecological" theory of crisis and social transformation.

2. Two Kinds of Crisis Theory

The point of departure of the traditional Marxist theory of economic crisis and the transition to socialism is the contradiction between capitalist productive forces and production relations.[10] The specific form of this contradiction is between the production and realization of value and surplus value, or between the production and circulation of capital. The agency of socialist revolution is the working class. Capitalist production relations constitute the immediate object of social transformation. The site of transformation is politics and the state and the process of production and exchange.

By contrast, the point of departure of an "ecological Marxist"[11] theory of economic crisis and transition to socialism is the contradiction between capitalist production relations (and productive forces) and the *conditions* of capitalist production, or "capitalist relations and forces of social reproduction."[12]

Marx defined three kinds of production conditions. The first is "external physical conditions"[13] or the natural elements entering into constant and variable capital. Second, the "laborpower" of workers was defined as the "personal conditions of production." Third, Marx referred to "*the communal, general conditions of social production*, e.g. "means of communication."[14]

Today "external physical conditions" are discussed in terms of the viability of eco-systems, the adequacy of atmospheric ozone levels, the stability of coastlines and watersheds; soil, air and water quality; and so on. "Laborpower" is discussed in terms of the physical and mental well-being of workers; the kind and degree of socialization; toxicity of work relations and the workers' ability to cope; and human beings as social productive forces and biological organisms generally. "Communal conditions" are discussed in terms of "social capital," "infrastructure," and so on. Implied in the concepts of "external physical conditions," "laborpower," and "communal conditions" are the concepts of space and "social environment." We include as a production condition, therefore, "urban space" ("urban capitalized nature") and other forms of space which structures and is structured by the relationship between people and "environment,"[15] which in turn helps to produce social environments. In short, production conditions include commodified or capitalized materiality and sociality excluding commodity production, distribution, and exchange themselves.

The specific form of the contradiction between capitalist production relations (and forces) and production conditions is also between the production and realization of value and surplus value. The agency of social transformation is "new social movements" or new social struggles including struggles within production over workplace health and safety, toxic waste production and disposal, and so on. The social relationships of reproduction of the conditions of production (e.g. state and family as structures of social relations and also the relations of production themselves insofar as "new struggles" occur within capitalist production) constitute the immediate object of social transformation. The immediate site of transformation is the material process of reproduction of production conditions (e.g. division of labor within the family, land-use patterns, education, etc.) and the production process itself, again insofar as new struggles occur within the capitalist workplace.

In traditional Marxist theory, the contradiction between production and realization of value and economic crisis takes the form of a "realization crisis," or over-production of capital. In ecological Marxist theory, economic crisis assumes the form of a "liquidity crisis," or under-production of capital. In traditional theory, economic crisis is the cauldron in which capital restructures productive forces and production relations in ways which make both more transparently social in form and content, e.g. indicative planning, nationalization, profit-sharing, etc. In ecological Marxism, economic crisis is the cauldron in which capital restructures the conditions of production also in ways which make them more transparently social in form and content, e.g. permanent yield forests, land reclamation, regional land use and/or resource planning, population policy, health policy, labor market regulation, toxic waste disposal planning, etc.

In traditional theory, the development of more social forms of productive forces and production relations is regarded as a necessary but not sufficient condition for the transition to socialism. In ecological Marxism, the development of more social forms of the provision of the conditions of production also may be regarded as a necessary but not sufficient condition for socialism. It should be quickly added that an "ecological socialism" would be different than that imagined by traditional Marxism, first, because from the perspective of the "conditions of production" most struggles have strong, particularistic "romantic anti-capitalist" dimensions, i.e. are "defensive" rather than "offensive," and, second, because it has become obvious that much capitalist technology, forms of work, etc., including the ideology of material progress, have become part of the problem not the solution. In sum, there may be not one but two paths to socialism, or, to be more accurate, two tendencies which together lead to increased (albeit historically reversible) socialization of productive forces, production relations, conditions of production and social relations of reproduction of these conditions.

3. The Traditional Marxist Account of Capitalism as a Crisis-Ridden System

In traditional Marxism, the contradiction between the production and circulation of capital is "internal" to capitalism because capitalist production is not only commodity production but also production of surplus value (i.e. exploitation of labor). It is a valorization process in which capitalists extract not only socially necessary labor (labor required to reproduce constant and variable capital) but also surplus labor from the working class. Everything else being the same,[16] any given amount of surplus value produced and/or any given rate of exploitation will have the effect of creating a particular shortfall of commodity demand at market prices. Or, put the opposite way, any particular shortage of commodity demand presupposes a given amount of surplus value produced and/or a given rate of exploitation. Further, the greater the amount of surplus value produced and/or the higher the rate of exploitation, the greater the difficulty of realizing value and surplus value in the market. Thus, the basic problem of capitalism is, where does the extra commodity demand which is required to buy the product of surplus labor originate? Time-honored answers include capitalist class consumption; capital investment which is made independently of changes in wage advances and consumer demand; markets created by these new investments; new investment, consumption, or government spending financed by expanded business, consumer or government credit; the theft of markets of other capitals and/or capitals in other countries; and so on. However, these "solutions" to the problem of value realization (that of maintaining a level of aggregate demand for commodities which is sufficient to maintain a given rate of profit without threatening economic crisis and the devaluation of fixed capital) turn into other kinds of potential "problems" of capitalism. Capitalist consumption constitutes an unproductive use of surplus value, as does the utilization of capital in the sphere of circulation with the aim of selling commodities faster. New capital investment may expand faster than, or independently of, new consumer demand with the result of increasing chances of a more severe realization crisis in the future. While a well-developed credit system can provide the wherewithal to expand commodity demand independent of increases in wages and salaries, the expansion of consumer demand based on increases in consumer or mortgage credit greater than increases in wages and salaries threatens to transform a potential crisis of capital over-production into a crisis of capital under-production. Moreover, any expansion of credit creates debt (as well as assets) and financial speculation, instabilities in financial structures, thus threatens a crisis in the financial system. The theft of markets from other capitals implies the concentration and/or centralization of capital hence a worsening of the problem of realization of value in the future and/or social unrest arising from the destruction of weaker capitals, political instability, bitter international rivalries, protectionism, even war. And so on. In sum, economic crisis can assume varied forms besides the traditional "realization crisis," including liquidity crisis, financial crisis or collapse, fiscal crisis of the state, and social and political crisis tendencies. However, whatever the specific forms of historical crises (the list above is meant to be suggestive not exhaustive), and whatever the specific course of their development and resolution, most if not all Marxists accept the premise based on the real conditions of capitalist exploitation that capitalism is a crisis-ridden system.

4. The Traditional Marxist Account of Capitalism as a Crisis-Dependent System and the Transition to Socialism

In traditional Marxism, capitalism is not only crisis-ridden but also crisis-dependent. Capital accumulates through crisis, which functions as an economic disciplinary mechanism. Crisis is the occasion which capital seizes to restructure and rationalize itself in order to restore its capacity to exploit labor and accumulate. There are two general, interdependent ways in which capital changes itself to weather the crisis and resolve it in capital's own favor. One is changes in the productive forces, the second is changes in the production relations. Changes in either typically presuppose or require new forms of direct and indirect cooperation within and between individual capitals and/or within the state and/or between capital and the state. More cooperation or planning has the effect of making production more transparently social, meanwhile subverting commodity and capital fetishism, or the apparent "naturalness" of capitalist economy. The telos of crisis is thus to create the possibility of imagining a transition to socialism.

Crisis-induced changes in productive forces by capital seeking to defend or restore profits (and exemplified by technological changes which lower unit costs, increase flexibility in production, and so on) have the systematic effect of lowering the costs of reproducing the work force; making raw materials available more cheaply or their utilization more efficient; reducing the period of production and/or circulation, etc. Whatever the immediate sources of the crisis, restructuring productive forces with the aim of raising profits is a foregone conclusion. More, crisis-induced changes in productive forces imply or presuppose more social forms of production relationships, e.g. more direct forms of cooperation within production.[17] Examples of changes in productive forces today, and associated changes in production relationships, include computerized, flexible manufacturing systems and robotics, which are associated with the development of "creative team play" and other forms of cooperation in the work place, profit sharing, etc. And, of course, the greatest productive force is human cooperation, and science or the social production of practical knowledge has become an almost completely cooperative enterprise[18] partly as a result of cumulative historical economic, social, and political crises.

The second way that capital restructures itself is crisis-induced changes in production relations within and between capital, within the state, and/or between the state and capital which are introduced with the aim of exercising more control of production, markets, and so on, i.e. more planning. Historically, planning has taken many forms, e.g. nationalization, fiscal policy, indicative planning, etc., including, at the political level, fascism, new dealism, and social democracy. Whatever the immediate sources of crisis, the restructuring of production relations with the aim of developing more control of labor, raw material supplies, etc. is a foregone conclusion. More, crisis-induced changes in production relations imply or presuppose more social forms of productive forces, e.g. more direct forms of cooperation. Examples of changes in production relations today are "strategic agreements" between high-tech capitals; massive state intervention in financial markets; and centralization of capital via take-overs and mergers. These changes imply sharing or socialization of high-tech secrets and technical personnel; new forms of financial controls; and restructuring of management and production systems, respectively.

To sum up, crisis forcibly causes capital to lower costs and increase flexibility *and* to exercise more control or planning over production and circulation. Crisis causes new forms of flexible planning and planned flexibility (even at the level of state-organized production), which increases the tensions between a more flexible capitalism (usually market-created) and a more planned capitalism (usually state-created). Crisis forcibly makes capital confront its own basic contradiction which is subsequently displaced to the spheres of the state, corporate management, etc. when there is introduced more social forms of productive forces and production relations, which imply or presuppose one another meanwhile developing independently of one another. In this way, capital itself creates some of the technical and social preconditions for the transition to socialism. However, whether we start from the productive force or production relation side, it is clear that technology and power embody one another hence that new forms of cooperation hold out only tenuous and ambiguous promises for the possibilities of socialism. For example, state capitalism, political capitalism, and so on contain within them socialist forms, but highly distorted ones, which in the course of the class struggle may be politically appropriated to develop less distorted social forms of material and social life. But this is a highly charged political and ideological question. Only in a limited sense can it be said that socialism is imminent in crisis-induced changes in productive forces and production relations. Whether or not these new social forms are imminently socialist forms depends on the ideological and political terrain, degree of popular mobilization and organization, national traditions, etc., including and especially the particular world conjuncture. The same cautionary warning applies to the specific forms of cooperation in the workplace which emerge from the crisis, which may or may not preclude other forms which would lend themselves better to socialist practice, which cannot be regarded as some fixed trajectory but itself an object of struggle, and defined only through struggle.

Nothing can be said *a priori* about "socialist imminence" except at the highest levels of abstraction. The key point is that capitalism tends to self-destruct or subvert itself when it switches to more social forms of production relations and forces. The premise of this argument is that *any given set of capitalist technologies, work relations, etc. is consistent with more than one set of production relations and that any given set of production relations is consistent with more than one set of technologies, etc.* The "fit" between relations and forces is thus assumed to be quite loose and flexible. In the *crisis*, there is a kind of two-sided struggle to fit new productive forces into new production relations and vice versa in more social forms without, however, any "natural" tendency for capitalism to transform itself to socialism. Nationalization of industry, for example, may or may not be a step toward socialism. It is certainly a step toward more social forms of production and a more specifically political form of appropriation and utilization of surplus value. On the other side, quality circles, work teams, technology sharing, etc. may or may not be a step toward socialism. They are certainly steps toward more social forms of productive forces.

5. Toward an Ecological Marxist Account of Capitalism as a Crisis-Ridden System

The point of departure of "ecological Marxism" is the contradiction between capitalist production relations and productive forces and conditions of production. Neither human laborpower nor external nature nor infrastructures including their space/time dimensions are produced capitalistically, although capital treats these conditions of production *as if* they are commodities or commodity capital. Precisely because they are not produced and reproduced capitalistically, yet are bought and sold and utilized as if they were commodities, the conditions of supply (quantity and quality, place and time) must be regulated by the state or capitals acting as if they are the state. Although the capitalization of nature implies the increased penetration of capital into the conditions of production (e.g. trees produced on plantations, genetically altered species, private postal services, voucher education, etc.), the state places itself between capital and nature, or mediates capital and nature, with the immediate result that the conditions of capitalist production are politicized. This means that whether or not raw materials and labor force and useful spatial and infrastructural configurations are available to capital in requisite quantities and qualities and at the right time and place depends on the political power of capital, the power of social movements which challenge particular capitalist forms of production conditions (e.g. struggles over land as means of production versus means of consumption), state structures which mediate or screen struggles over the definition and use of production conditions (e.g. zoning boards), and so on.[19] Excepting the branches of the state regulating money and certain aspects of foreign relations (those which do not have any obvious relation to accessing foreign sources of raw materials, laborpower, etc.), every state agency and political party agenda may be regarded as a kind of interface between capital and nature (including human beings and space). In sum, whether or not capital faces "external barriers" to accumulation, including external barriers in the form of new social struggles over the definition and use of production conditions (i.e. "social barriers" which mediate between internal or specific and external or general barriers);[20] whether or not these "external barriers" take the form of economic crisis; and whether or not economic crisis is resolved in favor of or against capital are political and ideological questions first and foremost, economic questions only secondarily. This is so because production conditions are by definition politicized (unlike production itself) and also because the whole corpus of Marx's work privileges laborpower as a production condition; access to nature is mediated by struggles while external nature has no subjectivity of its own.[21] Laborpower alone struggles around the conditions of its own well-being and social environment broadly defined.

An ecological Marxist account of capitalism as a crisis-ridden system focuses on the way that the combined power of capitalist production relations and productive forces self-destruct by impairing or destroying rather than reproducing their own conditions ("conditions" defined in terms of both their social and material dimensions). Such an account stresses the process of exploitation of labor and self-expanding capital; state regulation of the provision of production conditions; and social struggles organized around capital's use and abuse of these conditions. The main question—does capital create its own barriers or limits by destroying its own production conditions?—needs to be asked in terms of specific use values, as well as exchange value. This is so because conditions of production are not produced as commodities, hence problems pertaining to them are "site specific," including the individual body as a unique "site." The question—why does capital impair its own conditions?—needs to be asked in terms of the theory of self-expanding capital, its universalizing tendencies which tend to negate principles of site specificity, its lack of ownership of laborpower, external nature, and space, hence (without state or monopolistic capitalist planning) capital's inability to prevent itself from impairing its own conditions. The question—why do social struggles against the destruction of production conditions (which resist the capitalization of nature, for example, environmental, public health, occupational health and safety, urban, and other movements) potentially impair capital flexibility and variability?—needs to be asked in terms of conflicts over conditions defined both as use values and exchange values.

Examples of capitalist accumulation impairing or destroying capital's own conditions hence threatening its own profits and capacity to produce and accumulate more capital are well-known. The warming of the atmosphere will inevitably destroy people, places, and profits, not to speak of other species life. Acid rain destroys forests and lakes and buildings and profits alike. Salinization of water tables, toxic wastes, soil erosion, etc. impair nature and profitability. The pesticide treadmill destroys profits as well as nature. Urban capital running on an "urban renewal treadmill" impairs its own conditions hence profits, e.g. congestion costs, high rents, etc.[22] The decrepit state of the physical infrastructure in this country may be mentioned in this connection. There is also an "education treadmill," "welfare treadmill," "technological fix tread-mill," "health care treadmill," etc.[23] This line of thinking also applies to the "personal conditions of production . . . laborpower" in connection with capital's destruction of traditionalist family life as well as the introduction of work relations which impair coping skills, and the presently toxic social environment generally. In these ways, we can safely introduce "scarcity" into the theory of economic crisis in a Marxist, not neo-Malthusian, way. We can also introduce the possibility of capital *underproduction* once we add up the rising costs of reproducing the conditions of production. Examples include the health bill necessitated by capitalist work and family relations; the drug and drug rehabilitation bill; the vast sums expended as a result of the deterioration of the social environment (e.g. police and divorce bill); the enormous revenues expended to prevent further environmental destruction and clean-up or repair the legacy of ecological destruction from the past; monies required to invent and develop and produce synthetics and "natural" substitutes as means and objects of production and consumption; the huge sums required to pay off oil sheiks and energy companies, e.g. ground rent, monopoly profit, etc.; the garbage disposal bill; the extra costs of congested urban space; the costs falling on governments and peasants and workers in the Third World as a result of the twin crises of ecology and development. And so on. No one has estimated the total revenues required to compensate for impaired or lost production conditions and/or to restore these conditions and develop substitutes. It is conceivable that total revenues allocated to protecting or restoring production conditions may amount to one-half or more of the total social product—all unproductive expenses from the standpoint of self-expanding capital. Is it possible to link these unproductive expenditures (and those anticipated in the future) to the vast credit and debt system in the world today? To the growth of fictitious capital? To the fiscal crisis of the state? To the internationalization of production? The traditional Marxist theory of crisis interprets credit/debt structures as the result of capital overproduction. Ecological Marxism would interpret the same phenomena as the result of capital underproduction and unproductive use of capital produced. Do these tendencies reinforce or offset one another? Without prejudging the answer, the question clearly needs to be on the agenda of Marxist theory.

6. Towards an Ecological Marxist Account of Capitalism as a Crisis-Ridden System and the Transition to Socialism

Neither Marx nor any Marxists have developed a theory of the relationship between crisis-induced changes in the conditions of production and the establishment of the conditions of socialism. In traditional Marxism, crisis-induced changes in productive forces and relations are determined by the need to cut costs, restructure capital, etc. Forces and relations are transformed into more transparently social forms. In ecological Marxism, like traditional Marxism, capitalism is also not only crisis-ridden but also crisis-dependent. Crisis-induced changes in production conditions (whether crisis itself originates in capital overproduction or underproduction) are also determined by the need to cut costs, reduce ground rent, increase flexibility, etc. and to restructure conditions themselves, e.g. expand preventive health, reforestation, reorganization of urban space, etc.

There are two general, interdependent ways in which capital (helped by the state) changes its own conditions to weather the crisis and to resolve it in capital's favor. One is changes in conditions defined as productive forces. The other is changes in the social relations of reproduction of conditions. Changes in either typically presuppose or require new forms of cooperation between and within capitals and/or between capital and the state and/or within the state, or more social forms of the "regulation of the metabolism between humankind and nature" as well as the "metabolism" between the individual and the physical and social environment. More cooperation has the effect of making production conditions (already politicized) more transparently political, thereby subverting further the apparent "naturalness" of capital existence. The telos of crisis is thus to create the possibility of imagining more clearly a transition to socialism.

Crisis-induced changes in conditions as productive forces with the purpose of defending or restoring profit (exemplified by technological changes which lower congestion costs, increase flexibility in the utilization of raw materials, etc.) have the systemic effect of lowering the costs of reproducing the work force; making raw materials available more cheaply, etc. Whatever the immediate sources of the crisis, restructuring production conditions with the aim of raising profits is a foregone conclusion. More, crisis-induced changes in production conditions imply or presuppose more social forms of the social relations of reproduction of production conditions, e.g. more direct forms of cooperation within the sphere of production conditions. An example of a change in production conditions today, and the associated change in the social relations of reproduction of production conditions, is integrated pest management which presupposes not only more coordination of farmers' efforts but also more coordination of training and education programs.[24] Another example is preventative health technology in relation to AIDS and associated changes in community relations in a more cooperative direction.

The second form of restructuring is crisis-induced changes in the social relations of reproduction of production conditions introduced with the aim of exercising more control of production conditions, i.e. more planning. Historically, planning has taken many forms, e.g. urban and regional transportation and health planning, natural resource planning, etc.[25] Whatever the immediate sources of crisis, the restructuring of these social relations with the aim of developing more control of production conditions is also a foregone conclusion. More, crisis-induced changes in the social relations of reproduction of production conditions imply or presuppose more social forms of production conditions defined as productive forces. An example of such a change today is "planning" to deal with urban smog which presupposes coalitions of associations and groups, i.e. political cooperation, to legitimate tough yet cooperative smog-reduction measures.[26] Another example is the proposed restructuring of the US Bureau of Reclamation which new technical changes in water policy presuppose.[27]

To sum up, crisis forcibly causes capital and state to exercise more control or planning over production conditions (as well as over production and circulation of capital itself). Crisis brings into being new forms of flexible planning and planned flexibility, which increases tensions between a more flexible capitalism and a more planned capitalism—more so than in the traditional Marxist account of the restructuring of production and circulation because of the key role of the state bureaucracy in the provision of production conditions. Crisis forcibly makes capital and state confront their own basic contradictions which are subsequently displaced to the political and ideological spheres (twice removed from direct production and circulation) where there is introduced more social forms of production conditions defined both materially and socially, e.g. the dominance of political bipartisanship in relation to urban redevelopment, educational reform, environmental planning, and other forms of provision of production conditions which exemplify new and significant forms of class compromise. However, it is clear that technology and power embody one another at the level of conditions as well as production itself hence that new forms of political cooperation hold out only tenuous promises of socialism. Again, nothing can be said *a priori* about "socialist imminence" excepting at a high level of abstraction. The key point is that capitalism tends to self-destruct or subvert itself when it switches to more social forms of the provision of production conditions via politics and ideology. The premise of this argument (like the argument of the present interpretation of traditional Marxism) is that any given set of production condition technologies, work relations, etc. is consistent with more than one set of social relations of reproduction of these conditions and that any given set of these social relations is consistent with more than one set of production condition technologies, work relations, etc. The "fit" between social relations and forces of reproduction of production conditions is thus assumed to be quite loose and flexible. In the *crisis* (in which the future is unknowable), there is a kind of two-sided struggle to fit new production conditions defined as forces into new production conditions defined as relations, and vice versa, into more social forms without, however, any "natural" tendency for capitalism to transform itself into socialism. Urban and regional planning mechanisms, for example, may or may not be a step toward socialism. They are certainly a step toward more social forms of the provision of production conditions hence making socialism at least more imaginable. On the other side, regional transportation networks and health-care services and bioregional water distribution (for example) may or may not be a step towards socialism. They are certainly a step toward more social forms of the provision of production conditions.

In the modern world, the list of new social and political forms of reproduction of production conditions is endless. It seems highly significant, and also theoretically understated within Marxism, that the world crisis today appears to result in more, and require many additional, social forms not only of productive forces and relations but also production conditions, although the institutional and ideological aspects of these forms are confusing and often contradictory, and although these forms should not be regarded as irreversible (e.g. reprivatization, deregulation, etc.). Yet it is conceivable that we are engaging in a long process in which there occurs different yet *parallel* paths to socialism, hence that Marx was not so much wrong as he was half-right. It may be that the traditional process of "socialist construction" is giving way to a new process of "socialist reconstruction," or the reconstruction of the relationship between human beings and production conditions including the social environment. It is at least plausible that in the "first world" socialist reconstruction will be seen as, first, desirable, and second, necessary; in the "second world" as equally desirable and necessary; and in the "third world" as, first, necessary, and second, desirable. It is more plausible that atmospheric warming, acid rain, the pollution of the seas will make highly social forms of reconstruction of material and social life absolutely indispensable.

To elaborate somewhat, we know that the labor movement "pushed" capitalism into more social forms of productive forces and relations, e.g. collective bargaining. Perhaps we can surmise that feminism, environmental movements, etc. are "pushing" capital and state into more social forms of the reproduction of production conditions. As labor exploitation (the basis of Marxist crisis theory, traditionally defined) engendered a labor movement which during particular times and places turned itself into a "social barrier" to capital, nature exploitation (including exploitation of human biology) engenders an environmental movement (e.g. environmentalism, public health movement, occupational health and safety movements, women's movement organized around the politics of the body, etc.) which may also constitute a "social barrier" to capital. In a country such as Nicaragua, the combination of economic and ecological crisis and political dictatorship in the old regime has engendered a national liberation movement and eco-development planning.

Concrete analysis of concrete situations is required before anything sensible can be said about environmentalism defined in the broadest sense and capital's short- and long-term prospects. For example, acid rain causes ecological and economic damage. The environmental movement demands clean-up and restoration of environment and protection of nature. This may restore profits in the long run or reduce government clean-up expenses, which may or may not be congruent with short- and middle-term needs of capital. Implied in a systematic program of politically regulated social environment are kinds of planning which protect capital against its worst excesses, yet which may or may not be congruent with capital's needs in particular conjunctures. One scenario is that "the destruction of the environment can lead to vast new industries designed to restore it. Imagine, lake dredging equipment, forest cleaning machines, land revitalizers, air restorers, acid rain combatants."[28] These kinds of super-tech solutions would be a huge drain on surplus value, unless they lowered the reproduction cost of laborpower, yet at the same time help to "solve" any realization problems arising from traditional capital over-production. Vast sums of credit money would be required to restore or rebuild the social environment, however, which would displace the contradiction into the financial and fiscal spheres in more or less the same ways that the traditional contradiction between production and circulation of capital is displaced into the financial and fiscal spheres today.

This kind of technology-led restructuring of production conditions (including technique-led restructuring of the conditions of supply of laborpower) may or may not be functional for capital as a whole, individual capitals, in the short-or-long-run. The results would depend on other crisis prevention and resolution measures, their exact conjuncture, and the way in which they articulate with the crisis of nature broadly defined. In the last analysis, the results would depend on the degree of unity and diversity in labor movements, environmental movements, solidarity movements, etc. And this is a political, ideological, and organizational question.

In any event, crisis-induced changes in production conditions necessarily lead to more state controls, more planning within the bloc of large-scale capital, a more socially and politically administered or regulated capitalism, hence a less nature-like capitalism, one in which changes in production conditions would need to be legitimated because they would be more politicized, and one in which capitalist reification would be less opaque. The combination of crisis-stricken capitals externalizing more costs, the reckless use of technology and nature for value realization in the sphere of circulation, and the like, must sooner or later lead to a "rebellion of nature," i.e. powerful social movements demanding an end to ecological exploitation. Especially in today's crisis, whatever its source, capital attempts to reduce production and circulation time, which typically has the effect of making environmental practices, health and safety practices, etc. worse. Hence capital restructuring may deepen not resolve ecological problems. Just as capital ruins its own markets, i.e. realized profits, the greater is the production of surplus value, so does capital ruin its own produced profits, i.e. raise costs and reduce capital flexibility, the greater is the production of surplus value based on the destructive appropriation of nature broadly defined. And just as over-production crises imply a restructuring of both productive forces and relations, so do under-production crises imply a restructuring of production conditions. And just as restructuring of productive forces imply more social forms of production relations and vice versa, so does restructuring of production conditions imply a twofold effect—more social forms of production conditions defined as productive forces and more social forms of the social relationships in which production conditions are reproduced. In sum, more social forms of production relations, productive forces, and conditions of production together contain with them possibilities of socialist forms. These are, in effect, crisis-induced not only by the traditional contradiction between forces and relations, but also by the contradiction between forces/relations and their conditions. Two, not one, crises are thus inherent in capitalism; two, not one, sets of crisis-induced reorganizations and restructurings in the direction of more social forms are also inherent in capitalism.

7. Conclusion

Some reference needs to be made to post-Marxist thought and its objects of study, "post-industrial society," "alternative movements" or "new social movements," and "radical democracy."[29] This is so because post-Marxism has practically monopolized discussions of what Marx called "conditions of production." No longer is the working class seen as the privileged agent of historical transformation nor is the struggle for socialism first on the historical agenda. Instead, there is the fight for "radical democracy" by "new social movements" in a "post-industrial society."

These basic post-Marxist postulates deserve close scrutiny, especially given post-Marxist readings of Marx and Marxism, and the political implications therein.[30] So does the declaration by radical bourgeois feminists, eco-feminists, deep ecologists, libertarian ecologists, communitarians, etc. that Marxism is dead. In the present discussion, however, it is possible only to point out that in ecological Marxist theory, the struggle over production conditions has redefined and broadened the class struggle beyond any self-recognition as such, at least until now. This means that capitalist threats to the reproduction of production conditions are not only threats to profits and accumulation, but also to the viability of the social and "natural" environment as a means of life. The struggle between capital and "new social movements" in which the most basic concepts of "cost" and "efficiency" are contended, has two basic "moments." The first is the popular and nearly universal struggle to *protect* the conditions of production, or means of life, from further destruction resulting from capital's own inherent recklessness and excesses. This includes needs and demands for the reduction of risks in all forms. This struggle pertains to the form in which "nature" is appropriated, as means of reproduction of capital versus means of reproduction of civil and human society. The second is the struggle over the programs and policies of capital and state to *restructure* the production conditions, i.e. struggles over the forms and contents of changes in conditions. Put another way, new social struggles are confronted with both the impairment and also crisis-induced restructuring of production conditions at the same time. Both "moments" of struggle occur both outside the state and also within and against the state, i.e. they pertain to "public administration" (in Carlo Carboni's words). Seen this way, the demand for radical democracy is the demand to democratize the provision and reconstruction of production conditions, which in the last analysis is the demand to democratize the state, i.e. the administration of the division of social labor.[31] In truth, in the absence of struggles to democratize the state, it is difficult to take the demand for "radical democracy" seriously.

In post-Marxist thought, great stress is placed on "site specificity" and the "integrity" of the individual's body, a particular meadow or species life, a specific urban place, etc.[32] The word "difference" has become post-Marxism's mantra, which, it is thought, expels the word "unity," which in the post-Marxist mind is often another way to spell "totalitarian." In the well-thought-out versions of post-Marxist thought, the "site specificity" which new social movements base themselves on are considered to make any *universal* demands impossible,[33] at least any universal demand beyond the demand for the universal recognition of site specificity. This is contrasted with the bourgeois revolution which universalized the demand for rights against privilege and the old working-class struggle which universalized the demand for public property in the means of production against capitalist property. However, our discussion of production conditions and the contradictions therein reveals clearly that there is a universal demand implicit or latent in new social struggles, namely, the demand to democratize the state (which regulates the provision of production conditions), as well as the family, local community, etc. In fact, no way exists for diverse social struggles defending the integrity of particular sites to universalize themselves, hence win, and, at the same time, retain their diversity excepting through struggles for the democratic state and also by uniting with the labor movement, recognizing what we have in common, cooperative labor, thereby theorizing the unity of social labor.[34]

Moreover, post-Marxism, influenced by the "free rider problem" and problems of "rational choice" and "social choice" (all problems which presuppose bourgeois individualism), states or implies that struggles over production conditions are different than traditional wage, hours, and working conditions struggles because conditions of production are to a large degree "commons," clean air being an obvious example, urban space and educational facilities being somewhat less obvious ones. The argument is that struggles against air pollution (or capitalist urban renewal or racist tracking in the schools) do not have an immediate "pay off" for the individual involved; hence (in Offe's account) the phenomenon of cycles of social passivity and outrage owing to the impossibility of combining individual and collective action around goals which "pay off" for both the individual and group. Again, this is not the place for a developed critique of this view, one which would begin with an account of how the process of social struggle itself changes self-definitions of "individuality." It needs to be said, however, that labor unions, if they are anything, are disciplinary mechanisms against "free riders" (e.g. individual workers who try to offer their laborpower at less than the union wage are the object of discipline and punishment by the union). Further, it should be said that the "free rider" problem exists in struggles to protect the "commons" only insofar as these struggles are only ends in and of themselves, not also means to the specifically political hence universal end of establishing a democratic state.

Also in relation to the problem of the "commons," and beyond the problem of the relation *between* the individual and the group, there is the problem of the relationship between groups and classes. Specifically, the struggles of "new social movements" over conditions of production are generally regarded in the self-defined post-Marxist universe as non-class issues or multiclass issues. "Transformative processes that no doubt go on in our societies are very likely not class conflicts . . . but non-class issues."[35] Especially in struggles over production conditions (compared with production itself), it is understandable that these appear as non-class issues, and that agents define themselves as non-class actors. This is so not only because the issues cut across class lines (e.g. urban renewal, clean air, etc.), but also because of the site specificity and "people" specificity of the struggles, i.e. because the fight is to determine what kind of use values production conditions will in fact be. But, of course, there is a class dimension to all struggles over conditions, e.g. tracking in the schools, urban renewal as "people removal," toxic waste dumps in low income or poor districts and communities, the worker as the "canary" in the workplace, the inability of most unemployed and many workers to access "wilderness areas," etc. Most problems of the natural and social environments are bigger problems from the standpoint of the poor, including the working poor, than for the salariat and the well-to-do. In other words, issues pertaining to production conditions are class issues, even though they are also *more* than class issues, which becomes immediately obvious when we ask who opposes popular struggles around conditions? The answer is, typically, capital, which fights against massive public health programs, emancipatory education, controls on investments to protect nature, even adequate expenditures on child care, certainly demands for autonomy or substantive participation in the planning and organization of social life. What "new social movements" and their demands does capital support? Few, if any. What "new social movements" does labor oppose? Certainly, those which threaten ideologies of male supremacy and/or white race supremacy, in many instances, as well as those which threaten wages and jobs, even some which benefit labor, e.g. clean air. Hence, the struggle over conditions is not only a class struggle, but a struggle against such ideologies and their practices. This is why it can be said that struggles over conditions are not less but more than class issues. And that to the degree that this is true, the struggle for "radical democracy" is that much more a struggle to democratize the state, a struggle for democracy within state agencies charged with regulating the provision of production conditions. In the absence of this perspective and vision, "new social movements" will remain at the level of anarchocommunalist and related struggles which are bound to self-destruct themselves in the course of their attempts to "deconstruct" Marxism.

Notes

I am grateful to Carlo Carboni, John Ely, Danny Faber, Bob Marotto, and David Peerla for their encouragement and helpful criticisms and comments.

1. Karl Polanyi, *The Great Transformation* (Boston, 1967). Polanyi's focus was altogether on capitalist markets, not exploitation of labor.

2. World Commission on Environment and Development, *Our Common Future* (New York, 1987).

3. The closest anyone has come to a "Marxist" account of the problem is: Alan Schnaiberg, *The Environment: From Surplus to Scarcity* (New York, 1980). This is a path-breaking and useful work.

    The relation between the capitalization of nature and political conflict between states is another, albeit closely related, question (Lloyd Timberlake and Jon Tinker, "The Environmental Origin of Political Conflict," *Socialist Review*, 84: 15, 6 (November–December 1985)).

4. In the case of bad harvests, "*the value of the raw material . . . rises*; its *volume* decreases. . . . More must be expended on *raw material*, less remains for *labour*, and it is not possible to absorb the same quantity of labour as before. Firstly, this is *physically impossible*. . . . Secondly, it is impossible because a greater *portion of the value of the product* has to be converted into raw material. . . . Reproduction cannot be *repeated* on the same scale. A part of *fixed capital* stands idle and a part of the workers is thrown out into the streets. The *rate of profit* falls because the value of constant capital has risen as against that of variable capital. . . . The fixed charges—interest, rent—which were based on the anticipation of a *constant* rate of profit and exploitation of labour, remain the same and in part *cannot be paid*. Hence *crisis*. . . . More, although the *rate of profit* is decreasing, there is a *rise in the price of the product*. If this product enters into the other spheres of reproduction as a means of production, the rise in its price will result in the same disturbance in *reproduction* in these spheres" (Karl Marx, *Theories of Surplus Value*, Part Two (Moscow, 1968), 515–16).

5. "Apart from the degree of development, greater or less, in the form of social production, the productiveness of labour is fettered by physical conditions" (*Capital I*). In *Theories of Surplus Value* (Part Three, 449), Marx states that the precondition for the existence of absolute surplus value is the "natural fertility of the land."

6. Michael Lebowitz, "The General and the Specific in Marx's Theory of Crisis," *Studies in Political Economy*, 7 (Winter 1982). Lebowitz includes as "general" barriers the supply of labor and the availability of land and natural resources. However, he does not distinguish between the supply of labor per se and the supply of disciplined wage labor. As for natural resources, he does not distinguish between "natural" shortages and shortages capital creates for itself in the process of capitalizing nature nor those created politically by ecology movements.

7. *Capital III*, Chapter 6, 215.

8. We can therefore distinguish two kinds of scarcity: first, scarcity arising from economic crisis based on traditional capital overproduction, i.e. a purely social scarcity; second, scarcity arising from economic crisis based on capitalistically produced scarcity of nature or production conditions generally. Both types of scarcity are ultimately attributable to capitalist production relations. The second type, however, is not due to "bad harvests," for example, but to capitalistically produced "bad harvests" as a result of mining, not farming, land; polluting water tables; etc.

9. There are two reasons why Marx ran from any theory of capitalism and socialism which privileged any aspect of social reproduction besides the contradiction between production and circulation of capital. One is his opposition to any theory which might "naturalize" hence reify the economic contradictions of capital. His polemics against Malthus and especially his rejection of any and all naturalistic explanations of social phenomena led him away from "putting two and two together." Second, it would have been difficult in the third quarter of the 19th century to argue plausibly that the impairment of the conditions of production and social struggles therein are self-imposed barriers of capital because historical nature was not capitalized to the degree that it is today, i.e. the historical conditions of the reproduction of the conditions of production today make an "ecological Marxism" possible.

10. State of the art accounts of the problematic categories of productive forces and production relations are: Derek Sayer, *The Violence of Abstraction: The Analytical Foundations of Historical Materialism* (Oxford, 1987) and Robert Marotto, "Forces and Relations of Production," Ph.D. diss. (University of California, Santa Cruz, 1984).

11. Murray Bookchin deserves most credit for developing the theory of "social ecology" in the USA. The basic impulse of his method and theory is libertarian not Marxist, "social ecology" not "socialist ecology."
To my knowledge, "ecological Marxism" was coined by Ben Agger (*Western Marxism: An Introduction: Classical and Contemporary Sources* (Santa Monica, Calif., 1987), 316–39). Agger's focus is "consumption" not "production." His thesis is that ever-expanding consumption required to maintain economic and social stability impairs the environment, and that ecological crisis has replaced economic crisis as the main problem of capitalism. This article may be regarded as, among other things, a critique of Agger's often insightful views.

12. According to Carlo Carboni, who also uses the expression "social reproductive conditions." I use "conditions of production" because I want to reconstruct the problem using Marx's own terminology and also because I want to limit my discussion mainly to crisis tendencies in the process of the production and circulation of capital, rather than to the process of social reproduction, i.e. reproduction of the social formation as a whole. This means that I will follow Marx's lead and interpret "production conditions" in "objective" terms, excepting in the last section which suggests that these conditions are increasingly grasped as "subjective" today.

13. External physical conditions include "natural wealth in means of subsistence" and "natural wealth in the instruments of labour" (*Capital I*, Modern Library Edition, 562).

14. *Marx and Engels Selected Works in Two Volumes*, ii (Moscow, 1962), 25; *Grundrisse* (Harmondsworth, 1973), 533. See also Marino Folin, "Public Enterprise, Public Works, Social Fixed Capital: Capitalist Production of the 'Communal, General Conditions of Social Production,'" *International Journal of Urban and Regional Research*, 3:3 (September 1979).

15. In a conversation with David Harvey, who pioneered the theory of the spatial configurations and barriers to capital (*Limits to Capital* (Basil Blackwell, 1982)), tentative "permission" was granted the author to interpret urban and other forms of space as a "production condition."

16. The following is a deliberate "Smithian" simplification of the traditionally defined economic contradiction of capitalism which altogether neglects Marx's critique of Smith, namely, that it is the rising organic composition of capital, not a falling rate of exploitation, which causes the profit rate to fall, even though capitalism "presents itself" otherwise. To be absolutely clear, the following account is not meant to review Marx's critique of capital fetishism or Adam Smith, et al. I put the contradiction of capitalism in its simplest terms with the twofold aim of (*a*) preparing a discussion of crisis-induced restructuring of the productive forces and production relations and (*b*) setting up a standard by which we can

compare the "traditional" with the "non-traditional" or "second" contradiction of capitalism based on the process of capitalist-created scarcities of external and human nature.

17. "Cooperation" (e.g. "work relations") is both a productive force and production relationship, i.e. ambiguously determined by both "technological necessity" and "power."

18. David Knight, *The Age of Science* (Oxford, 1987).

19. This kind of formulation of the problem avoids the functionalism of the "state derivation school" of Marxism as well as political sociological or Weberian theories of the state which are not grounded in material existence.

20. So-called external barriers may be interpreted as internal barriers, in fact, if we assume that (a) external nature being considered is commodified or capitalized nature and (b) new social struggles organized under the sign of "ecology" or "environmentalism" have their roots in the class structure and relations of modern capitalism, e.g. the rise of the new middle class or salariat, which is the backbone of environmentalism in the USA.

21. "External and universal nature can be considered to be differences within a unity from the standpoint of capital accumulation and state actions necessary to assure that capital can accumulate. Yet the difference is no less significant than the unity from the standpoint of social and ecological action and political conflict. The reason is that laborpower is a subject which struggles over health and the (natural) conditions of social health broadly defined, whereas the 'natural elements entering into constant and variable capital' are objects of struggle" (Robert Marotto, Correspondence).

22. "Economists and business leaders say that urban areas in California are facing such serious traffic congestion that the state's economic vitality is in jeopardy" (*The New York Times*, 5 April 1988).

23. "If schools cannot figure out how to do a better job of educating these growing populations and turn them into productive workers and citizens, then the stability of the economy could be threatened" (Edward B. Fiske, "US Business Turns Attention to Workers of the Future," *International Herald Tribune*, 20–21 February 1988). Fisk is referring to minorities which today make up 17 percent of the population, a figure expected to jump to one-third by 2020.

In the USA, health-care costs as a percentage of GNP were about 6 percent in 1965; in 2000 they are expected to be 15 percent. "Health care has become an economic cancer in this country," screams a *San Francisco Chronicle* headline writer (14 March 1988).

24. The well-known IPM program in Indonesia reportedly increases profits by reducing costs and also increasing yields. It depends on new training and education programs, coordination of farm planning, etc. (Sandra Postel, "Indonesia Steps Off the Pesticide Treadmill," *World Watch*, January–February 1988, 4).

25. For example, West German organized industry and industry–state coordination successfully internalizes many externalities or social costs. This occurs without serious harm to profits because the FRG produces such high quality and desirable goods for the world market that costs of protecting or restoring production conditions can be absorbed while industry remains competitive (Conversation, Claus Offe).

26. Christopher J. Daggett, "Smog, More Smog, and Still More Smog," *The New York Times*, 23 January 1988.

27. The idea that crisis induced by inadequate conditions of production results in more social forms of production and production relations is not new in non-Marxist circles. Schnaiberg linked rapid economic expansion to increased exploitation of resources and growing environmental problems, which in turn posed restrictions on economic growth, hence making some kind of planning of resource use, pollution levels, etc. essential. He interpreted environmental legislation and control policies of the 1970s as the start of

environmental planning (*The Environment*, op. cit.).

More, the idea that crisis induced by unfavorable production conditions results in more social productive forces, as well as production relationships (which is also Schnaiberg's thesis, since planning is a form of cooperation, hence both a force and relation of production), can be found in embryonic form in works such as: R. G. Wilkinson, *Poverty and Progress: An Ecological Perspective on Economic Development* (New York, 1973) which argues that epoch-making technological changes have often resulted from ecological scarcities; O. Sunkel and J. Leal, "Economics and Environment in a Developmental Perspective" (*International Social Science Journal*, 109 (1986), 413) which argues that depletion of resources and scarcity increases the costs of economic growth because of declines in natural productivity of resources hence that new energy resources and technological subsidies (implying more planning) are needed.

28. Correspondence, Saul Landau.

29. The most sophisticated post-Marxist text is: Ernesto Laclau and Chantal Mouffe, *Hegemony and Socialist Strategy: Towards a Radical Democratic Politics* (London, 1985). A home-grown version is Michael Albert et al., *Liberating Theory* (Boston, 1986).

30. For example, Laclau and Mouffe's discussion of what they call Marxist "essentialism" violates both the spirit and substance of Marx's theory of capital.

31. James O'Connor, "The Democratic Movement in the United States," *Kapitalistate*, 7 (1978). It should be noted that in the entire post-Marxist literature it is impossible for me to find any reference to the division of social labor, so obsessed are the "theorists" with the division of industrial labor, division of labor within the family, etc. This absence or silence permits us to grasp post-Marxism as recycled anarchism, populist-anarchism, communitarianism, libertarianism, etc.

32. According to Carboni, "the challenge of specificity is propelled by all new social actors in advanced capitalist societies. It is an outcome of the complex network of policies, planning, and so on which are implemented by both capital and the state in order to integrate people while changing production conditions. On the one hand, this specificity (difference) represents the breakage of collective and class solidarity. On the other hand, it reveals both new micro-webs of social solidarity and the universalistic network of solidarity based on social citizenship" (Communication to the author).

33. This and the following point were made by Claus Offe in conversation with the author, who is grateful for the chance to discuss these issues with someone who gracefully and in a spirit of scientific collaboration presents a post-Marxist point of view.

34. "The issue in dispute is the post-Marxist claim that we have multiple social identities against the present claim that there exists a theoretical unity in these identities in the unity of the conditions of production and capital production and realization. On the level of appearances, it is true that we have multiple identities, but in essence the unity of our identity stems from capitalism as a mode of production. The trick is to make the theoretical unity a reality. An environmental struggle may be an unintentional barrier to capital in the realm of accumulation while not being ideologically anti-capitalist. The question is how to make environmentalists conscious of the fact that they are making the reproduction of the conditions of production more social. The post-Marxists do not want to find a unity in the fragmented social identities we have. But even to build alliances between social movements some unity must be constructed. In the absence of an agreed upon telos of struggle, or any common definitions, dialogue cannot take place. If we are unable to agree on any terms and objects of struggle in what sense can we say new social movements are reconstructing the public realm as a realm of dialogue? It is agreed that we have to struggle over what socialism means but in some sense we are required to struggle for a common language which will necessarily

obscure particular differences. As capitalism abstracts out the social nature of labor in the exchange of commodities, it obscures what we have in common, cooperative labor, thereby fragmenting our identity. What is disturbing is the lack of any move on the part of the post-Marxists to theorize the unity of social labor" (Communication, David Peerla).

35. Claus Offe, "Panel Discussion," *Scandanavian Political Studies*, 10: 3 (1987), 234.

32 Basic Positions of the Greens: For an Ecological Answer to the Economic Crisis

Rudolf Bahro

I. The Greens and the Economy

In the richest, industrially over-developed countries of the West a fundamental opposition is growing—above all in the diverse form of the new social movements. It is reacting to the now clearly and markedly self-destructive, outwardly murderous and inwardly suicidal character of our industrial civilization, and to its institutional system which is geared to continuing in the same old way. What makes this opposition fundamental is above all the fact that it throws into question both the material foundation and its counterpart in our basic attitudes which are oriented towards possessions and having. It gives expression to the ever more obvious truth that we shall only survive if we equip ourselves to live differently than we have up till now. The Greens see themselves as the parliamentary political arm of this fundamental opposition movement.

The development that has proceeded from Europe in the past two hundred years and more has been decisively characterized by the simultaneously most expansive (aggressive) and most effective (productive) economic system in world history, the capitalist mode of production. The merciless struggle to remove competitors—first between private individuals, then between firms, and finally between multinational and state corporations—has proved to be the mightiest economic impetus of all times. The East and the South are only emulating it; they are doing so under different political systems and socio-economic conditions, resulting from a weaker and more or less dependent position, and often with even worse direct consequences for the people affected.

Whilst the independent, alienated Megamachine is preparing to collide against the bounds of the Earth, pressing us—its original creators—up against the wall and crushing us, it is already destroying untold millions of human lives in the Third World each year, where we have for a while diverted war, unemployment, hunger and misery of all kinds. To stop the industrial system—and first of all the military machine it has created—in its tracks, here in the metropolises where it started, is just as much the first command of solidarity with the most wretched of this Earth as it is the requirement of a reasonable self-interest. For we shall not be able to bear the

From Rudolf Bahro, *Building the Green Movement* (Philadelphia: New Society, 1986), 11–22. Reprinted with permission.

backlash of either the social crises or the ecological catastrophes which our way of work and life leads to on a world scale.

The global industrialization process not only devours and destroys its own preconditions, the resources which it soaks up in ever greater quantities, but also the natural foundations of human life, of the very biosphere which sustains us. The completion of this process on a world scale would be the ultimate natural catastrophe. It cannot be continued for a further 200 years and it must be braked and stopped much earlier. The work which made us into human beings, the specific ability of our species comprehensively to change nature, has developed in such a way that it can become the cause of our downfall. Our planet can be transformed by the nuclear bomb and other direct means of annihilation into a desert largely devoid of human beings. Seen as a whole, industrialized labour of the kind which has dominated up till now—notwithstanding its numerous individual blessings—has proved to be fatal. Production for war is only the tip of the iceberg.

This industrial system must not be further extended. On the contrary, we must begin to dismantle the Tower of Babel before it collapses on top of us. We want to gain the assent of the majority so that a restructuring of our civilization, which is necessary for survival, can be decided, planned and executed step by step. For this we need a Great Moratorium on any kind of expansionist investments of the old type and a critique of all products and conditions of labour. Even so-called "investments in the future" must be examined to determine whether they too do not only serve to facilitate the breakthrough to a new thrust of industrialization and to build a new storey onto the industrial system—for example, in the form of expanded large-scale production for environmental protection. Too many "alternative" investment ideas reinforce the existing structures, as for example the installation of district heating networks reinforces the concentration of the population in industrial conurbations.

II. The Greens and Unemployment

When those interested in an investment breakthrough reproach us that environmental protection costs jobs, the Greens don't immediately respond with a zealous attempt to prove—correct though it often is—that on the contrary our policies would create jobs, but rather with an unambiguous explanation that we want to combat the approaching total ecological catastrophe even at the cost of the loss of jobs. Industries in which products are produced on a mass scale to compete for profits on the world market, and with a material- and energy-intensive division of labour, must shrink in size.

We still regard the ecological crisis as the overriding and broader challenge. The economic crisis and the capitalist response of mass unemployment and dismantling of the welfare state may well change the conditions for the ecology and peace movement. But it would simply be a further victory for the existing order if we let ourselves be pushed into giving priority to the fight against unemployment and social decline in the wake of the old trade-union and left socialist defence strategies. We are not here to defend or create jobs in the industrial system.

In our view the present crisis, which we see not least as a crisis of industrial society, a society of labour and achievement, must be used to detach the question of an income, a secure basis of life for everybody, from the compulsion to wage-labour for the world market. It is not our aim to give everybody back "wages and bread". It is rather a case of reducing the expenditure of labour—wage-labour for the anonymous market—far beyond the extent of the present restructuring which is taking place in the interest of profit. There is not too little work but still to much.

The creation of new jobs is not our actual goal even where the restructuring of the economy will in fact lead to that. For us the main point is to withdraw investments and the deployment of human energies from all large-scale projects whatsoever. If we decentralize the work process and make the units smaller, what will come about in the first place are not new jobs but new conditions of life. Though decentralization as a rule creates jobs and working conditions more worthy of human beings than those in large-scale production.

With regard to our policy on working hours, we will support everything which:

(a) minimizes the amount of work as a whole, i.e. cuts down relatively on work;
(b) above all relaxes time structures in every respect so as to increase the freedom of individuals to do what they want with their own time.

Minimization of working hours presupposes first of all a critique of production and of needs. It is actually aimed at the total structure of conditions of reproduction of life, because only thus can certain needs—as for example the need for private cars—become superfluous.

III. Where are the Greens Going?

We consider the complexity of industrial society based on the worldwide division of labour as the cause of multiplied consumption and the tendency to anonymous bureaucratic rule or administration to death. There is no salvation without dismantling this complexity, which in itself means an intolerable susceptibility to sudden breakdown and is thus one of the most important sources of anxiety.

A fundamental reorientation of the economy such as we are striving for can only succeed hand in hand with the spread of a new ("post-modern, post-industrial") way of life. Only a different society will found a different technology and organization out of the arsenal of sciences and skills that have been handed down.

In this respect lasting new solutions presuppose the existence of a network of interlinked base communities. The social weight and political influence of this new social formation must be sufficient to increasingly subordinate the remaining industrial sector and the other institutions and organizations necessary for overall social functions to the requirements of the base community network. The present social and economic crisis goes so deep that it favours steps towards this by making them urgently necessary, while the old remedies no longer help. Now is the very time to take our fundamental ecological attitude onto the offensive in the attempts at a solution.

As yet the numerous beginnings of alternative ways of life do not represent a complete context. In most cases they do not have their own economic cycle but exist on the margins, more or less dependent on the general market, relying on the one hand on the welfare state, and on the other on gaps in supply. The real alternative, which at the same time would begin to reconcile us with the peoples of the Third World, can only be the building of base communities (of—it is suggested—a maximum of 3,000 people), which agree on a mode of simple, non-expanded reproduction of their material basis.

These would produce their basic needs in the way of food, clothing, housing, education and health care to a large extent by their own labour, decide on some specialized production mainly for exchange in the immediate locality, and contribute to the upkeep of general communications (transport and exchange of information) and conditions of production either by the manufacture of parts designed for this or by contributing labour-power.

Instead of the communities being unilaterally dependent on the more or less centralized functions, these functions will on the contrary be dependent on the needs of a society which realizes its basic functions in a decentralized fashion. Above all, this will not be an economic society in the sense of a society geared towards economic success and economic development. Material production and reproduction are only undertaken as the basis, which has to be kept relatively constant, for a learning process geared to people's psychological capabilities and for personal communication.

Having regard to the scarcity of resources, we must develop an expenditure norm for basic supplies which tends to minimal consumption of materials and energy. Ending material expansion will prove not only necessary for survival but also desirable and useful for the higher development of human beings in relation to their "non-material" needs (though these needs are still bound to material realities, endogenous and social). The new culture will once more have a spiritual dimension, if only because it will otherwise be impossible to break through the vicious circle of material expansion. Without a system of values which from the start is set above the purely economic, this ecological cyclical economy we are striving for cannot come about.

And here too is the real place for intermediate steps leading towards the radical, ecological, and pacifist alternative. It is not a case of making something palatable to people, of seducing them to a certain degree to the new perspective, but of providing them with an opportunity for active experience in dealing with the concrete contradictions of their everyday existence. Above all, it is a question of opening up for them a minimum of space that affords them security, into which they can step when they want to risk withdrawal from the industrial system.

This involves on the one hand material possibilities for a new beginning beyond the "formal" structures, and on the other hand a social cohesion for the project, which is perhaps even more important. Since the new structures have first to be founded, small groups or individual personalities must seize the initiative in order to create an active nucleus for the project in question and in order to be able to face the rest of society, or the state, as initiators.

Within the remaining industrial sector (which at first will by no means function in dependence on the society of base communities which is anticipated as the ideal) we will support everything which favours the power of disposal, the free space, the creative activity of those active in it. (In this we are to some extent following the concept of the dissident trade-union group at Daimler-Benz; what interests us above all in the experience of Lucas Aerospace are the ideas about a technology subordinated once more to human beings and at the disposal of their creativity.)[1] In principle, the criteria for technology and organization must not be primarily cost efficiency and competitiveness, but providing the conditions for the workers to develop.

The Greens do not deny that in the long term our overall policy runs counter to the predominant trade-union efforts to secure jobs in the industrial system. And the contradiction between environmental protection and jobs is not merely an apparent one. At least in the short term, a rigorous implementation of ecological priorities would raise the cost of production in the Federal Republic and thus worsen our chances of selling on the world market. We are faced with the question as to whether we are prepared consciously to run this risk in the country of Western Europe with the greatest economic reserves. It would be a shabby kind of politics if the Greens were to try to conceal from the public and our potential voters the consequences that our political influence can have. The sincerity of our position is our greatest capital. As on the question of unilateral disarmament, we must not hide the risks, but rather try to motivate people so that they obtain the psychological bonus of the courage of their decision. The point we must really use to enlist support is the long-term advantage of a timely change. Precisely in this sense fundamental opposition is constructive.

Above all, in this the richest industrial country of Europe we must not just try to carry out repairs and shift our problems elsewhere. Those involved must unite their strength in order to force a restructuring different from that which is likely to result from the new international division of labour and the shift towards a new phase of super-industrialization. Then it can even become a gain to abandon the old advantages of the strong economic position by making use of them to start along a completely new course. In any case the Federal Republic is of all European countries the one where the impoverishment of the population in the old industrial locations is least likely. More is needed than just a conventional slogan of "protection against danger levels". The workforce must demand power of disposal over production plants which no longer have any market, they must win the right to use the capacities and resources for any purposes they consider worthwhile—including dismantling them in favour of completely new, decentralized enterprises.

As experience shows, the German trade unions as currently constituted are only to a very limited extent an institution for such struggles, so that new structures must be created at the grassroots. The Greens will support every step towards concrete appropriation by the workforce, at the same time asserting our particular standpoint that the means available should be used by those sections of the workforce involved and by the unemployed for a new social beginning beyond large-scale industrial production.

IV. Ecological Economic Policy—Baselines

1. INDUSTRIAL DISARMAMENT AND ADAPTATION

The Greens start from the realistic assumption that the new social forces which we rest on and our influence in the realm of politics are still nowhere near sufficient to achieve such a fundamental reorientation of the economy. Therefore we see our first and most important task as being to continue and to extend into the political realm precisely that practice which has defined the conduct of the new social movements: to put up resistance against continuing in the same old way.

It is not only the economy, which wants to make its profits in the customary way, but also the entire institutional system—the state, the legal system, the political parties, the trade unions and the other traditional interest groups—which taken as a whole is committed by its history and constitution to continuing along the same path and can aim at nothing more than at best adjusting externally to the new demands. We shall oppose this force of inertia, which rests upon a multitude of habits in the general consciousness, is preserved and strengthened by the media, and also has a share in our own personal interests.

Our parliamentary practice, following the example of the extra-parliamentary practice (the peace movement, the citizens' initiatives, the alternative movement, the women's movement and so on), must concentrate on preventing any steps which continue in the same dangerous direction. This means in particular all investments in the expansion of the Big Machine, i.e. any military installations, any installations of the nuclear industry, any projects to extend the heavy transport infrastructure (airports, motorways, trunk roads, canals, river straightening, ports), all large industrial projects, as well as all large projects in the school and university system, in the health service, and in public administration, the police, computerized control of society, etc.

Investments in the formal sector are only permissible at all if they do not require a single square metre of land not previously built on. If however there has to be new building, then at least the equivalent area must be balanced against it for recultivation. The Greens will pursue locally a consistent policy of environmental and nature protection, aimed at the restoration of varied landscapes and the elimination of buildings that ruin the natural habitat. Everywhere that we have influence we will oppose expansion, prevent industrial subsidies, combat construction with all conceivable counter-measures, stimulate and support the extra-parliamentary resistance.

Even where, as it is now fashionable, projects claim to be "investments in the future", the Greens will examine whether these are not in fact steps which simply create for the industrial system an outlet into new directions, which presuppose the continuation of the existing structure and indirectly help it to continue. We are—for example—not in favour of a new industry to manufacture filters for the chimneys of power stations; we want to save the forests from acid rain by replacing large power stations with small, locally controllable and responsible units of energy production. We are in general against the concentration of plant and capital, against mergers, in favour of breaking up and decentralization, right down to technology.

Taken as a whole, this first point primarily involves a strategy of prevention, an anti-investment and a deconcentration strategy, an emergency brake against any further "progress" in the fateful direction which the accumulation of capital, driven by the world market, is taking. According to all previous experience capital needs expanded reproduction and concentration in ever greater conglomerations. Our practice is aimed at the encirclement and restriction of capital in terms of investment opportunities, material and energy supplies and marketing. We shall attack both the products and the technology, the motivation to work and the motivation to buy, and do everything to encourage inside the market-orientated enterprises the growth of scepticism as to whether one should research, develop, produce, advertise and sell at all in the present context.

People will then ask us how our economy is to maintain its position against international competition, where it is after all dependent to the highest degree on imports and exports. Our reply is that we want to withdraw from the world market and believe that as a result our standard of living will not quantitatively deteriorate but will be qualitatively changed. We have in mind an economic order of the greatest possible self-sufficiency at a local, regional, provincial and national level. We envisage markets for the exchange of activities between base communities and cooperation at levels above this, complementing each other to form a market-free economy for basic needs and built from the bottom up.

The international division of labour—as it affects the flow of materials and energy across state frontiers and oceans, as opposed to the flow of information—we conceive as strictly limited. Our question, which we shall examine more thoroughly, is: how can the population—in a situation where the supplies for our gluttonous Big Machine will in any case fail to materialize and the war-mongering struggle for resources will increase—reproduce its life on the given territory with the resources still available?

In contrast to the merely reformist strategy of the Social-Democrats and the old left, this is also the truly anti-capitalist and anti-colonialist answer to the challenges of our time.

2. DEFEND AND EXTEND THE SPACE FOR THE DEVELOPMENT OF THE NEW SOCIAL MOVEMENTS

The Greens believe we will represent in Parliament not only heads (the number of our voters) but also growing parts of the consciousness of those people who still vote for the traditional parties. What we regard as decisive is that the scope for each individual to make new decisions should increase, right down to a new fundamental decision about his or her life. That includes the extension of the political space, where citizens must not be limited to voting and the expression of individual opinions but must have the opportunity of expressing themselves in demonstrative actions right through to non-violent civil disobedience.

The basic tendency of established politics (already visible at the end of the SPD-FDP coalition) is to allow the polarization of society between a tied, pacified core and a growing number of fringe existences, if not actually promoting this in order to keep those excluded as socially and politically weak and atomized as possible. The CDU's cuts in the welfare state have as their main objective to weaken the social base of the ecology and peace movement, which is rightly regarded by Franz-Josef Strauss as a danger to the stability of government insofar as it is dissolving the previous consensus.

In the most fundamental interest of our constituency we oppose any deterioration in social services. We absolutely refuse to be deflected back to discussions about financeability within the framework of the usual budget procedures, and instead challenge the monstrous sums spent on all the deadly and harmful investments which we want to prevent.

Every mark that is withdrawn from investment in large-scale industry or from expenditure on the expansion of the state machine, and flows instead to the alternative movement, is already in itself a contribution to the protection of life, quite independent of whether we use it for subsistence purposes or for the construction of "lifeboats" (which is what it primarily comes down to). Since the alternative movement in the metropolises is near enough to the centre of power to disturb significant parts of the established forces and their social following, it has a chance of keeping the issue open.

If the decisive point here is not to sever the link between the wage-earners in the factories and offices and those who have opted out, this question must not be settled in such a way that the new forces subordinate themselves to the traditional patterns of trade-union politics. On the contrary, the release of the potential in the factories and offices depends upon the union bureaucrats losing their ideological influence and organizational control. In any case the new social movements will not stop at the gates of the factories and institutions, precisely because they are not proceeding via the old structures. The question of organizing working conditions in accordance with human rights and the wholesomeness of the products can today only be effectively posed from the ecological perspective.

The Greens will support organized alternatives to the German Trade-Union Federation and its constituent unions, wherever these appear on the scene. It is in this way and not through adjustment and subordination to the traditional rules of the game that the new forces can have the strongest influence on the debates inside the trade unions. Here too it will be a case of how consistently we can articulate the new contexts and link actions to them. Only in conflict will the unsuitability of the old structures and their role as a constant hindrance become apparent in the general experience. Our arguments must consciously appeal to needs which go far beyond the wage-earning interest as monopolized by the trade unions, and play for maximum stakes.

3. BEGIN WITHDRAWAL FROM THE INDUSTRIAL SYSTEM

The specific response of the Greens to the challenge of mass unemployment is the use of our political influence to facilitate departure from the industrial system into a positive new way of life. Only if there is a genuine provision of start-up assistance will we be able seriously to test, not only how many of the unemployed, but also how many people who are still employed and perhaps even relatively successful functionaries, are already prepared or inclined to change their general perspective.

The Greens set themselves the goal of diverting one thousand million marks into the alternative sector, to make possible there a kind of primary accumulation for the new social formation. On this foundation a comprehensive network of autonomous base communities can emerge, which will subsequently support and reproduce themselves. This objective also includes support for all those alternative undertakings of the most diverse type and level which are only (or as yet) halfway between the old and new ways of production and life. We consider it our main task to provide political cover for this long-term transitional process and to help secure the material foundation for it.

For this end, we basically want to bring into existence, against the present *de facto* Grand Coalition of the established parties and at right angles to the traditional political and social division, a Grand Coalition of our own (which should not be envisaged in the form of a new party system). To build this up, we shall pick up on the uncertainties and the new attitudes which the ecological crisis has already aroused in almost everybody in our society. There will soon be two souls dwelling in almost every breast, and the process is leading slowly but surely to the general upheaval which will enable us to start out on a new overall course. Psychologically the exodus from the capitalist industrial system has already begun, and the same process is already beginning to reach across to our Eastern counterpart.

4. CORRECTIONS AND REPAIRS WITHIN THE PRESENT SYSTEM—LEARNING PROCESSES

This basically involves critical and selective cooperation in all projects which make up the catalogue of ecological reformism (and which have in common above all that they appeal to the existing state, the existing institutional system, and taken in themselves do not point beyond it). In this the focal point is not a compromise with the old parties, which are pursuing a different basic direction, but an appropriate appeal beyond them to their supporters, designed in each case to expose their half-measures and demagogic subterfuges and to promote a change in thinking.

In all factory initiatives for alternative production plans, the Greens support those tendencies which press for the achievement of self-determination by those concerned against the power of disposal held by capital, the management hierarchy and the trade-union bureaucracy. Here more and more battles are being decided on the field of manufacturing technology and data processing. Our position is to spread the experience that large-scale industrial production for the world market has become altogether questionable, continuously comes up against the limits of toleration of both external nature and human nature, here and abroad, and inevitably frustrates hopes for self-management and humane working conditions.

Decisive in all developments inside the so-called "formal" sector are the social learning processes which transcend the horizon of the labour-divided and bureaucratic industrial society of both Western and Eastern types and in which the subjective preconditions of a new culture are maturing.

November 1982, for the Hagen Congress[2]

Notes

1. Mike Cooley, director of technology at the Greater London Enterprise Board under the Labour GLC, was the leading figure in the Lucas Aerospace workers' campaign for an alternative (i.e. non-military) corporate plan, and author of *Architect or Bee* (Langley Technical Services, 1980).

2. The national congress of the Greens met in Hagen in November 1982, and placed eight conditions for the "toleration" of an SPD Government in the event of that party's victory in the Federal elections to be held in March 1983. The prime condition was the rejection of the Euromissiles.

Section X: Environmental Justice

The basic claim, and organizing principle, of the North American environmental justice movement is that the poor, people of colour, and indigenous peoples are disproportionately at risk from environmental hazards. The movement asserts an inequity in the siting of toxic waste sites, hazardous materials landfills, incinerators, municipal landfills, and polluting industry. It has addressed issues as diverse as occupational illnesses borne by the poor and people of colour (such as those linked to dioxin, pesticide, or solvent exposure) and the displacement and poisoning of indigenous populations faced with uranium mining or hydroelectric dams.

While there is substantial diversity in the movement (which some might argue is actually a number of distinct, yet related, movements), its political focus is generally centred on both distributive and procedural equity. Not only do community groups argue for more equity (and overall reduction) in exposure to environmental risks and hazards, but they also often demand recognition of their position and participation in the development of environmental policy. In this, the movement challenges both mainstream environmental organizing and reformist efforts on the part of government. Large mainstream environmental groups are seen as too distant, paternalistic, and unrepresentative; and governmental reforms are often criticized for not only failing to address questions of the distribution of hazards, but also for not involving communities in the policy process. In response to the political shortcomings of these organizing strategies, the environmental justice movement has eschewed traditional, centralized organizations and has instead relied on the networking of local groups in regions or around particular issues. These networks not only lobby government agencies, but often take their case, and their collective power, directly to targeted industries, corporations, and/or communities.

Our first selection is a statement of the 'Principles of Environmental Justice' adopted at the First National People of Color Environmental Summit in October 1991 in Washington, DC. This statement identifies the environmental problems targeted by the movement and the politics needed to address them. The selection by Robert Bullard, one of the leading academic observers of the movement, lays out some of the motivations for environmental justice, describes a few of the key early battles of the movement, and argues that the environmental justice movement will and should remain distinct from the mainstream movement in the United States. While the Bullard essay focuses on the inequity in the distribution of environmental risks and community responses, the piece by Celene Krauss examines the politicization of women in the movement. From their common experience and perspective as mothers, and their particular cultural identities, Krauss argues that women in the movement have become keenly aware of the gender, class, and ethnic dimensions of environmental inequities. Along the way, they have learned much about the biases of the political process and the limitations of mainstream environmental organizing.

Further Reading

There are a number of good anthologies on environmental justice. Robert Bullard has edited two volumes which focus on communities of colour: *Confronting Environmental Racism: Voices from the Grassroots* (1993) and *Unequal Protection: Environmental Justice and Communities of Color* (1994). Bunyan Bryant has also edited two volumes: *Race and the Incidence of Environmental Hazards* (1992), which focuses on the analysis of racial inequities in environmental risk, and *Environmental Justice: Issues, Policies, and Solutions* (1995), which develops policy suggestions. *Toxic Struggles: The Theory and Practice of Environmental Justice* (1993), edited by Richard Hofrichter, addresses issues of race, class, and the internationalization of environmental inequities. A fine analysis of the development of environmental justice generally is offered by Andrew Szasz in his *Ecopopulism: Toxic Waste and the Movement for Environmental Justice* (1994). For an examination of the environmental justice movement as an example of a new form of pluralist politics, see David Schlosberg, *Environmental Justice and the New Pluralism: The Challenge of Difference for Environmentalism (1999)*. Environmental justice resources abound on-line; information, along with links to various issues and groups, can be found at Econet's Ecojustice Network (http://www.igc.apc.org/envjustice/) and Clark Atlanta University's Environmental Justice Resource Center, headed by Robert Bullard (http://www.ejrc.cau.edu/).

33 Principles of Environmental Justice
First National People of Color Environmental Leadership Summit

Preamble

We the people of color, gathered together at this multi-national People of Color Environmental Leadership Summit, to begin to build a national and international movement of all peoples of color to fight the destruction and taking of our lands and communities, do hereby re-establish our spiritual interdependence to the sacredness of our Mother Earth; to respect and celebrate each of our culture's languages and beliefs about the natural world and our roles in healing ourselves; to insure environmental justice; to promote economic alternatives which would contribute to the development of environmentally safe livelihoods; and, to secure our political, economic and cultural liberation that has been denied for over 500 years of colonization and oppression, resulting in the poisoning of our communities and land and the genocide of our peoples, do affirm and adopt these Principles of Environmental Justice:

1. **Environmental justice** affirms the sacredness of Mother Earth, ecological unity and the interdependence of all species, and the right to be free from ecological destruction. *En*

2. **Environmental justice** demands that public policy be based on mutual respect and justice for all peoples, free from any form of discrimination or bias. *Soc.*

3. **Environmental justice** mandates the right to ethical, balanced and responsible uses of land and renewable resources in the interest of a sustainable planet for humans and other living things. *En.*

4. **Environmental justice** calls for universal protection from nuclear testing, extraction, production and disposal of toxic/hazardous wastes and poisons and nuclear testing that threaten the fundamental right to clean air, land, water, and food. *En.*

5. **Environmental justice** affirms the fundamental right to political, economic, cultural and environmental self-determination of all peoples.

6. **Environmental justice** demands the cessation of the production of all toxins, hazardous wastes, and radioactive materials, and that all past and current producers be held strictly accountable to the people for detoxification and the containment at the point of production.

7. **Environmental justice** demands the right to participate as equal partners at every level of decision-making including needs assessment, planning, implementation, enforcement and evaluation.

From 'Principles of Environmental Justice'. Adopted at the First National People of Color Environmental Leadership Summit, Washington DC, October 1991.

8. Environmental justice affirms the right of all workers to a safe and healthy work environment, without being forced to choose between an unsafe livelihood and unemployment. It also affirms the right of those who work at home to be free from environmental hazards.

9. Environmental justice protects the right of victims of environmental injustice to receive full compensation and reparations for damages as well as quality health care.

10. Environmental justice considers governmental acts of environmental injustice a violation of international law, the Universal Declaration on Human Rights, and the United Nations Convention on Genocide.

11. Environmental justice must recognize a special legal and natural relationship of Native Peoples to the US government through treaties, agreements, compacts, and covenants affirming sovereignty and self-determination.

12. Environmental justice affirms the need for urban and rural ecological policies to clean up and rebuild our cities and rural areas in balance with nature, honoring the cultural integrity of all our communities, and providing fair access for all to the full range of resources.

13. Environmental justice calls for the strict enforcement of principles of informed consent, and a halt to the testing of experimental reproductive and medical procedures and vaccinations on people of color.

14. Environmental justice opposes the destructive operations of multi-national corporations.

15. Environmental justice opposes military occupation, repression and exploitation of lands, peoples and cultures, and other life forms.

16. Environmental justice calls for the education of present and future generations which emphasizes social and environmental issues, based on our experience and an appreciation of our diverse cultural perspectives.

17. Environmental justice requires that we, as individuals, make personal and consumer choices to consume as little of Mother Earth's resources and to produce as little waste as possible; and make the conscious decision to challenge and reprioritize our lifestyles to insure the health of the natural world for present and future generations.

Adopted October 7, 1991, Washington, DC.

34 Anatomy of Environmental Racism and the Environmental Justice Movement

Robert D. Bullard

Communities are not all created equal. In the United States, for example, some communities are routinely poisoned while the government looks the other way. Environmental regulations have not uniformly benefited all segments of society. People of color (African Americans, Latinos, Asians, Pacific Islanders, and Native Americans) are disproportionately harmed by industrial toxins on their jobs and in their neighborhoods. These groups must contend with dirty air and drinking water—the byproducts of municipal landfills, incinerators, polluting industries, and hazardous waste treatment, storage, and disposal facilities.

Why do some communities get "dumped on" while others escape? Why are environmental regulations vigorously enforced in some communities and not in others? Why are some workers protected from environmental threats to their health while others (such as migrant farmworkers) are still being poisoned? How can environmental justice be incorporated into the campaign for environmental protection? What institutional changes would enable the United States to become a just and sustainable society? What community organizing strategies are effective against environmental racism? These are some of the many questions addressed in my book.

This chapter sketches out the basic environmental problems communities of color face, discusses how the mainstream environmental movement does not provide an adequate organizational base, analysis, vision, or strategy to address these problems, and, finally, provides a glimpse of several representative struggles within the grassroots environmental justice movement. For these purposes, the pervasive reality of racism is placed at the very center of the analysis.

Internal Colonialism and White Racism

The history of the United States has long been grounded in white racism. The nation was founded on the principles of "free land" (stolen from Native Americans and Mexicans), "free labor" (cruelly extracted from African slaves), and "free men" (white men with property). From the outset, institutional racism shaped the economic, political, and ecological landscape, and

From Robert D. Bullard (ed.), *Confronting Environmental Racism: Voices from the Grassroots* (Boston: South End Press, 1993), 15–39. Reprinted with permission.

buttressed the exploitation of both land and people. Indeed, it has allowed communities of color to exist as internal colonies characterized by dependent (and unequal) relationships with the dominant white society or "Mother Country." In their 1967 book, *Black Power*, Carmichael and Hamilton were among the first to explore the "internal" colonial model as a way to explain the racial inequality, political exploitation, and social isolation of African Americans. As Carmichael and Hamilton write:

The economic relationship of America's black communities [to white society] . . . reflects their colonial status. The political power exercised over those communities goes hand in glove with the economic deprivation experienced by the black citizens.

Historically, colonies have existed for the sole purpose of enriching, in one form or another, the "colonizer"; the consequence is to maintain the economic dependency of the "colonized." (1967: 16–17)

Generally, people of color in the United States—like their counterparts in formerly colonized lands of Africa, Asia, and Latin America—have not had the same opportunities as whites. The social forces that have organized oppressed colonies internationally still operate in the "heart of the colonizer's mother country" (Blauner 1972: 26). For Blauner, people of color are subjected to five principal colonizing processes: they enter the "host" society and economy involuntarily; their native culture is destroyed; white-dominated bureaucracies impose restrictions from which whites are exempt; the dominant group uses institutionalized racism to justify its actions; and a dual or "split labor market" emerges based on ethnicity and race. Such domination is also buttressed by state institutions. Social scientists Omi and Winant (1986: 76–8) go so far as to insist that "every state institution is a racial institution." Clearly, whites receive benefits from racism, while people of color bear most of the cost.

Environmental Racism

Racism plays a key factor in environmental planning and decisionmaking. Indeed, environmental racism is reinforced by government, legal, economic, political, and military institutions. It is a fact of life in the United States that the mainstream environmental movement is only beginning to wake up to. Yet, without a doubt, racism influences the likelihood of exposure to environmental and health risks and the accessibility to health care. Racism provides whites of all class levels with an "edge" in gaining access to a healthy physical environment. This has been documented again and again.

Whether by conscious design or institutional neglect, communities of color in urban ghettos, in rural "poverty pockets," or on economically impoverished Native-American reservations face some of the worst environmental devastation in the nation. Clearly, racial discrimination was not legislated out of existence in the 1960s. While some significant progress was made during this decade, people of color continue to struggle for equal treatment in many areas, including environmental justice. Agencies at all levels of government, including the federal EPA, have done a poor job protecting people of color from the ravages of pollution and industrial encroachment. It has thus been an up-hill battle convincing white judges, juries, government officials, and policymakers that racism exists in environmental protection, enforcement, and policy formulation.

The most polluted urban communities are those with crumbling infrastructure, ongoing economic disinvestment, deteriorating housing, inadequate schools, chronic unemployment, a high poverty rate, and an overloaded health-care system. Riot-torn South Central Los Angeles typifies this urban neglect. It is not surprising that the "dirtiest" zip code in California belongs to the mostly African-American and Latino neighborhood in that part of the city (Kay 1991a). In the Los Angeles basin, over 71 percent of the African Americans and 50 percent of the Latinos live in areas with the most polluted air, while only 34 percent of the white population does (Ong and Blumenberg 1990; Mann 1991). This pattern exists nationally as well. As researchers Wernette and Nieves note:

In 1990, 437 of the 3,109 counties and independent cities failed to meet at least one of the EPA ambient air quality standards . . . 57 percent of whites, 65 percent of African Americans, and 80 percent of Hispanics live in 437 counties with substandard air quality. Out of the whole population, a total of 33 percent of whites, 50 percent of African Americans, and 60 percent of Hispanics live in the 136 counties in which two or more air pollutants exceed standards. The percentage living in the 29 counties designated as nonattainment areas for three or more pollutants are 12 percent of whites, 20 percent of African Americans, and 31 percent of Hispanics. (1992: 16–17)

Income alone does not account for these above-average percentages. Housing segregation and development patterns play a key role in determining where people live. Moreover, urban development and the "spatial configuration" of communities flow from the forces and relationships of industrial production which, in turn, are influenced and subsidized by government policy (Feagin 1988; Gottdiener 1988). There is widespread agreement that vestiges of race-based decisionmaking still influence housing, education, employment, and criminal justice. The same is true for municipal services such as garbage pickup and disposal, neighborhood sanitation, fire and police protection, and library services. Institutional racism influences decisions on local land use, enforcement of environmental regulations, industrial facility siting, management of economic vulnerability, and the paths of freeways and highways.

People skeptical of the assertion that poor people and people of color are targeted for waste-disposal sites should consider the report the Cerrell Associates provided the California Waste Management Board. In their 1984 report, *Political Difficulties Facing Waste-to-Energy Conversion Plant Siting*, they offered a detailed profile of those neighborhoods most likely to organize effective resistance against incinerators. The policy conclusion based on this analysis is clear. As the report states:

All socioeconomic groupings tend to resent the nearby siting of major facilities, but middle and upper socioeconomic strata possess better resources to effectuate their opposition. Middle and higher socioeconomic strata neighborhoods should not fall within the one-mile and five-mile radius of the proposed site. (1984: 43)

Where then will incinerators or other polluting facilities be sited? For Cerrell Associates, the answer is low-income, disempowered neighborhoods with a high concentration of nonvoters. The ideal site, according their report, has nothing to do with environmental soundness but everything to do with lack of social power. Communities of color in California are far more likely to fit this profile than are their white counterparts.

Those still skeptical of the existence of environmental racism should also consider the fact that zoning boards and planning commissions are typically stacked with white developers. Generally, the decisions of these bodies reflect the special interests of the individuals who sit on these boards. People of color have been systematically excluded from these decisionmaking boards, commissions, and governmental agencies (or allowed only token representation). Grassroots leaders are now demanding a shared role in all the decisions that shape their communities. They are challenging the intended or unintended racist assumptions underlying environmental and industrial policies.

Toxic Colonialism Abroad

To understand the global ecological crisis, it is important to understand that the poisoning of African Americans in South Central Los Angeles and of Mexicans in border *maquiladoras* have their roots in the same system of economic exploitation, racial oppression, and devaluation of human life. The quest for solutions to environmental problems and for ways to acheive sustainable development in the United States has considerable implications for the global environmental movement.

Today, more than 1,900 *maquiladoras*, assembly plants operated by American, Japanese, and other foreign countries, are located along the 2,000-mile US–Mexico border (Center for Investigative Reporting 1990; Sanchez 1990; Zuniga 1992: 22A). These plants use cheap Mexican labor to assemble products from imported components and raw materials, and then ship them back to the United States (Witt 1991). Nearly half a million Mexicans work in the *maquiladoras*. They earn an average of $3.75 a day. While these plants bring jobs, albeit low-paying ones, they exacerbate local pollution by overcrowding the border towns, straining sewage and water systems, and reducing air quality. All this compromises the health of workers and nearby community residents. The Mexican environmental regulatory agency is understaffed and ill-equipped to adequately enforce the country's laws (Working Group on Canada-Mexico Free Trade 1991).

The practice of targeting poor communities of color in the Third World for waste disposal and the introduction of risky technologies from industrialized countries are forms of "toxic colonialism," what some activists have dubbed the "subjugation of people to an ecologically-destructive economic order by entities over which the people have no control" (Greenpeace 1992: 3). The industrialized world's controversial Third World dumping policy was made public by the release of an internal, 12 December 1991, memorandum authored by Lawrence Summers, chief economist of the World Bank. It shocked the world and touched off a global scandal. Here are the highlights:

"Dirty" Industries: Just between you and me, shouldn't the World Bank be encouraging MORE migration of the dirty industries to the LDCs [Less Developed Countries]? I can think of three reasons:

(1) The measurement of the costs of health impairing pollution depends on the foregone earnings from increased morbidity and mortality. From this point of view a given amount of health impairing pollution should be done in the country with the lowest cost, which will be the country with the lowest wages. I think the economic logic behind dumping a load of toxic waste in the lowest wage country is impeccable and we should face up to that.

(2) The costs of pollution are likely to be non-linear as the initial increments of pollution probably have very low cost. I've always thought that under-polluted areas in Africa are vastly UNDER-polluted; their air quality is probably vastly inefficiently low compared to Los Angeles or Mexico City. Only the lamentable facts that so much pollution is generated by non-tradable industries (transport, electrical generation) and that the unit transport costs of solid waste are so high prevent world welfare-enhancing trade in air pollution and waste.

(3) The demand for a clean environment for aesthetic and health reasons is likely to have very high income elasticity. The concern over an agent that causes a one in a million change in the odds of prostate cancer is obviously going to be much higher in a country where people survive to get prostate cancer than in a country where under 5 [year-old] mortality is 200 per thousand. Also, much of the concern over industrial atmosphere discharge is about visibility impairing particulates. These discharges may have very little direct health impact. Clearly trade in goods that embody aesthetic pollution concerns could be welfare enhancing. While production is mobile the consumption of pretty air is a non-tradable.

The problem with the arguments against all of these proposals for more pollution in LDCs (intrinsic rights to certain goods, moral reasons, social concerns, lack of adequate markets, etc.) could be turned around and used more or less effectively against every Bank proposal . . .

Beyond the Race vs. Class Trap

Whether at home or abroad, the question of who *pays* and who *benefits* from current industrial and development policies is central to any analysis of environmental racism. In the United States, race interacts with class to create special environmental and health vulnerabilities. People of color, however, face elevated toxic exposure levels even when social class variables (income, education, and occupational status) are held constant (Bryant and Mohai 1992). Race has been found to be an independent factor, not reducible to class, in predicting the distribution of (1) air pollution in our society (Freeman 1972; Gianessi, Peskin, and Wolff 1979; Gelobter 1988; Wernette and Nieves 1992); (2) contaminated fish consumption (West, Fly, and Marans 1990); (3) the location of municipal landfills and incinerators (Bullard 1983, 1987, 1990, 1991a); (4) the location of abandoned toxic waste dumps (United Church of Christ Commission for Racial Justice 1987); and (5) lead poisoning in children (Agency for Toxic Substances and Disease Registry 1988).

Lead poisoning is a classic case in which race, not just class, determines exposure. It affects between three and four million children in the United States—most of whom are African Americans and Latinos living in urban areas. Among children 5 years old and younger, the percentage of African Americans who have excessive levels of lead in their blood far exceeds the percentage of whites at all income levels (Agency for Toxic Substances and Disease Registry 1988: I–12).

The federal Agency for Toxic Substances and Disease Registry found that for families earning less than $6,000 annually an estimated 68 percent of African-American children had lead poisoning, compared with 36 percent for white children. For families with incomes exceeding $15,000, more than 38 percent of African-American children have been poisoned, compared with 12 percent of white children. African-American children are two to three times more likely than their white counterparts to suffer from lead poisoning independent of class factors.

One reason for this is that African Americans and whites do not have the same opportunities to "vote with their feet" by leaving unhealthy physical environments. The ability of an individual

to escape a health-threatening environment is usually correlated with income. However, racial barriers make it even harder for millions of African Americans, Latinos, Asians, Pacific Islanders, and Native Americans to relocate. Housing discrimination, redlining, and other market forces make it difficult for millions of households to buy their way out of polluted environments. For example, an affluent African-American family (with an income of $50,000 or more) is as segregated as an African-American family with an annual income of $5,000 (Denton and Massey 1988; Jaynes and Williams 1989). Thus, lead poisoning of African-American children is not just a "poverty thing."

White racism helped create our current separate and unequal communities. It defines the boundaries of the urban ghetto, *barrio*, and reservation, and influences the provision of environmental protection and other public services. Apartheid-type housing and development policies reduce neighborhood options, limit mobility, diminish job opportunities, and decrease environmental choices for millions of Americans. It is unlikely that this nation will ever achieve lasting solutions to its environmental problems unless it also addresses the system of racial injustice that helps sustain the existence of powerless communities forced to bear disproportionate environmental costs.

The Limits of Mainstream Environmentalism

Historically, the mainstream environmental movement in the United States has developed agendas that focus on such goals as wilderness and wildlife preservation, wise resource management, pollution abatement, and population control. It has been primarily supported by middle- and upper-middle-class whites. Although concern for the environment cuts across class and racial lines, ecology activists have traditionally been individuals with above-average education, greater access to economic resources, and a greater sense of personal power (Buttel and Flinn 1978; Morrison 1980, 1986; Dunlap 1987; Bullard 1990; Bullard and Wright 1987; Bachrach and Zautra 1985; Mohai 1985, 1990).

Not surprisingly, mainstream groups were slow in broadening their base to include poor and working-class whites, let alone African-Americans and other people of color. Moreover, they were ill-equipped to deal with the environmental, economic, and social concerns of these communities. During the 1960s and 1970s, while the "Big Ten" environmental groups focused on wilderness preservation and conservation through litigation, political lobbying, and technical evaluation, activists of color were engaged in mass direct action mobilizations for basic civil rights in the areas of employment, housing, education, and health care. Thus, two parallel and sometimes conflicting movements emerged, and it has taken nearly two decades for any significant convergence to occur between these two efforts. In fact, conflicts still remain over how the two groups should balance economic development, social justice, and environmental protection.

In their desperate attempt to improve the economic conditions of their constituents, many African-American civil rights and political leaders have directed their energies toward bringing jobs to their communities. In many instances, this has been achieved at great risk to the health of workers and the surrounding communities. The promise of jobs (even low-paying and hazardous ones) and of a broadened tax base has enticed several economically impoverished, polit-ically powerless communities of color both in the United States and around the world (Center for Investigative Reporting and Bill Moyers 1990; Bullard 1990; Bryant and Mohai 1992). Environmental job blackmail is a fact of life. You can get a job, but only if you are willing to do work that will harm you, your families, and your neighbors.

Workers of color are especially vulnerable to job blackmail because of the greater threat of unemployment they face compared to whites and because of their concentration in low-paying, unskilled, nonunionized occupations. For example, they make up a large share of the nonunion contract workers in the oil, chemical, and nuclear industries. Similarly, over 95 percent of migrant farmworkers in the United States are Latino, African-American, Afro-Caribbean, or Asian, and African-Americans are overrepresented in high-risk, blue-collar, and service occupations for which a large pool of replacement labor exists. Thus, they are twice as likely to be unemployed as their white counterparts. Fear of unemployment acts as a potent incentive for many African-American workers to accept and keep jobs they know are health threatening. Workers will tell you that "unemployment and poverty are also hazardous to one's health." An inherent conflict exists between the interests of capital and that of labor. Employers have the power to move jobs (and industrial hazards) from the Northeast and Midwest to the South and Sunbelt, or they may move the jobs offshore to Third World countries where labor is even cheaper and where there are even fewer health and safety regulations. Yet, unless an environmental movement emerges that is capable of addressing these economic concerns, people of color and poor white workers are likely to end up siding with corporate managers in key conflicts concerning the environment.

Indeed, many labor unions already moderate their demands for improved work-safety and pollution control whenever the economy is depressed. They are afraid of layoffs, plant closings, and the relocation of industries. These fears and anxieties of labor are usually built on the false but understandable assumption that environmental regulations inevitably lead to job loss (Brown 1980, 1987).

The crux of the problem is that the mainstream environmental movement has not sufficiently addressed the fact that social inequality and imbalances of social power are at the heart of environmental degradation, resource depletion, pollution, and even overpopulation. The environmental crisis can simply not be solved effectively without social justice. As one academic human ecologist notes, "Whenever [an] in-group directly and exclusively benefits from its own overuse of a shared resource but the costs of that overuse are 'shared' by out-groups, then in-group motivation toward a policy of resource conservation (or sustained yields of harvesting) is undermined" (Catton 1982).

The Movement for Environmental Justice

As this book testifies, activists of color have begun to challenge both the industrial polluters and the often indifferent mainstream environmental movement by actively fighting environmental threats in their communities and raising the call for environmental justice. This groundswell of environmental activism in African-American, Latino, Asian, Pacific Islander, and Native-

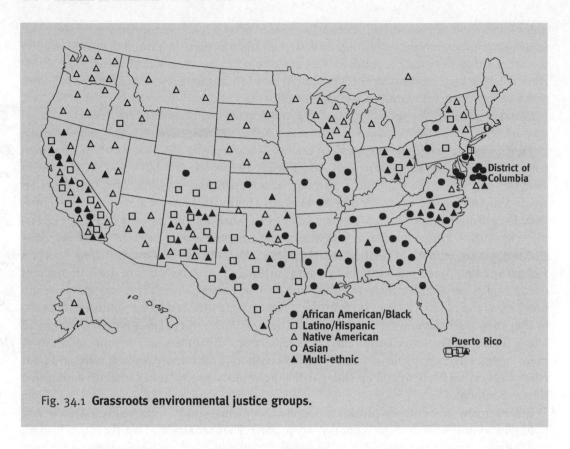

District of
Columbia

● African American/Black
□ Latino/Hispanic
△ Native American
○ Asian
▲ Multi-ethnic

Puerto Rico

Fig. 34.1 **Grassroots environmental justice groups.**

American communities is emerging all across the country. While rarely listed in the standard environmental and conservation directories, grassroots environmental justice groups have sprung up from Maine to Louisiana and Alaska (see map in Fig. 34.1).

These grassroots groups have organized themselves around waste-facility siting, lead contamination, pesticides, water and air pollution, Native self-government, nuclear testing, and workplace safety (Alston 1990; Bullard 1990, 1992a; Bryant and Mohai 1992). People of color have invented and, in other cases, adapted existing organizations to meet the disproportionate environmental challenges they face. A growing number of grassroots groups and their leaders have adopted confrontational direct action strategies similar to those used in earlier civil rights conflicts. Moreover, the increasing documentation of environmental racism has strengthened the demand for a safe and healthy environment as a basic right of all individuals and communities (United Church of Christ Commission for Racial Justice 1987; Bullard and Wright 1987, 1990; Bryant and Mohai 1992).

Drawing together the insights of *both* the civil rights and the environmental movements, these grassroots groups are fighting hard to improve the quality of life for their residents. As a result of their efforts, the environmental justice movement is increasingly influencing and winning support from more conventional environmental and civil rights organizations. For example, the National Urban League's *1992 State of Black America* included—for the first time in the seventeen years the report has been published—a chapter on the environmental threats to the African-American community (Bullard 1992*b*). In addition, the NAACP, ACLU, and NRDC led the fight to have poor children tested for lead poisoning under Medicaid provisions in California. The class-action lawsuit *Matthews* v. *Coye*, settled in 1991, called for the state of California to screen an estimated 500,000 poor children for lead poisoning at a cost of $15 to $20 million (Lee 1992). The screening represents a big step forward in efforts to identify children suffering from what federal authorities admit is the number one environmental health problem of children in the United States. For their part, mainstream environmental organizations are also beginning to understand the need for environmental justice and are increasingly supporting grassroots groups in the form of technical advice, expert testimony, direct financial assistance, fundraising, research, and legal assistance. Even the Los Angeles chapter of the wilderness-focused Earth First! movement worked with community groups to help block the incinerator project in South Central Los Angeles.

Case Studies from the Grassroots

For all of their current and potential significance, however, little research has yet been done on these African-American, Latino, Asian, Pacific Islander, and Native American organizations which make up the grassroots environmental justice movement. The research discussed here focuses on environmentally threatened communities of color in Houston (TX), Dallas (TX), Los Angeles (CA), Richmond (CA), Kettleman City (CA), Alsen (LA), and Rosebud (SD). Each of these communities is embroiled in a wide range of environmental disputes against both government and private industry.

We had three major objectives in looking at these nine communities: (1) to examine the organizations and the dispute mechanisms people of color use in resolving environmental conflicts, (2) to explore the conditions and circumstances under which communities of color mobilize against an environmental threat, and (3) to assess the level of external support that grassroots groups of color receive from environmental, social justice, and other groups. To gather this information, in-depth interviews were conducted with opinion leaders, who were identified through a "reputational" approach. We started out with a small number of local informants. The informants were asked to "identify the *most* influential person or persons who had played a role in resolving the local dispute." These influential leaders were later asked the same question, and this second group of leaders was also interviewed.

The interviews focused on a number of key issue areas, including the nature of the dispute, leadership and external support, opposition tactics, and dispute outcomes. The questions included: Were the environmental problems caused by the government and/or corporations? Did the dispute involve a proposed or existing facility? Was the community group started as an environmental group? Do its leaders and members see themselves as environmentalists? Were equity and social justice concerns dominant organizing themes? Who led the local citizen opposition in the disputes? What kind of support did the local groups receive from environmental and other organizations? What tactics did the groups use? Which were most effective? How was the dispute resolved?

A summary of the various communities, grassroots groups, and types of environmental disputes included in this study are presented in Table 34.1. Here is a more detailed overview of each community's situation.

Houston: In the 1970s, Houston was dubbed the "golden buckle" of the Sunbelt (Bullard 1987, 1990). In 1982, it became the nation's fourth largest city with 1.7 million inhabitants. Its black community of some 450,000 is the largest in the South. For decades, Houston boasted that it was the only major city without zoning. During the "boom" years of the 1970s, this no-zoning policy contributed to haphazard and irrational land-use planning and infrastructure chaos (Bullard 1983). A mostly African-American suburban neighborhood was selected as the site for a municipal landfill. The Northeast Community Action Group (NECAG) formed to block the construction of the landfill.

Dallas: Dallas is the seventh largest city in the nation with a population of just under one million. The 265,594 African-Americans who live in Dallas represent 29.4 percent of the city's population. West Dallas is one of many segregated black enclaves in the city. It has a population of 13,161, of which 85 percent is black. The neighborhood has lived with a polluting lead smelter for five decades (Nauss 1983; Bullard 1990). Early on, West Dallas residents formed the Neighborhood Coalition on Lead Pollution to get the smelter closed and the area cleaned up. Another group, West Dallas Coalition for Environmental Justice, continued the fight after the Neighborhood Coalition for Lead Pollution was disbanded.

Alsen (LA): Alsen is an unincorporated community on the Mississippi River several miles north of Baton Rouge, Louisiana's state capital. It had a population of 1,104 individuals in 1980, of which 98.9 percent were African-Americans. Alsen lies at the beginning of "Cancer Alley," the 85-mile stretch of land from Baton Rouge to New Orleans, an area that accounts for one-fourth of the nation's petro-chemical production (See Maraniss and Weisskopf 1987; Anderson, Dunn, and Alabarado 1985; Bullard 1990; Bullard and Wright 1990). Much of Louisiana's hazardous waste is disposed of in the Rollins Environmental Services incinerators located near Alsen. The

Table 34.1 **Summary of community disputes**

Group (year founded), location	Type of dispute	Facility
Northeast Community Action Group (1979), Houston, TX	Solid waste landfill	Existing
Neighborhood Committee on Lead Pollution (1981), Dallas, TX	Lead smelter	Existing
West Dallas Coalition for Environmental and Economic Justice (1989), Dallas, TX	Lead smelter	Existing
Coalition for Community Action (1979), Alsen, LA	Hazardous waste incinerator	Existing
Concerned Citizens of South Central Los Angeles (1985), Los Anglees, CA	Solid waste incinerator	Proposed
Mothers of East Los Angeles (1985), Los Angeles, CA	Hazardous waste incinerator	Proposed
People for Clean Air and Water (1990), Kettleman City, CA	Hazardous waste incinerator	Proposed
West County Toxics Coalition (1989), Richmond, CA	Petrochemical refinery	Existing
Good Road Coalition (1991), Rosebud, SD	Solid waste landfill	Proposed

residents formed Coalition for Community Action to challenge the Rollins hazardous waste incinerator operation.

Los Angeles: Los Angeles is the nation's second largest city with a population of 3.5 million. It is one of the nation's most culturally and ethnically diverse big cities. People of color (Latinos, Asians, Pacific Islanders, African-Americans, and Native Americans) now constitute 63 percent of the city's population. Residents of South Central Los Angeles, a neighborhood that is over 52 percent African-American and about 44 percent Latino, was slated to host the city's first state-of-the-art municipal solid waste incinerator. Local residents organized Concerned Citizens of South Central Los Angeles to fight the incinerator (Sanchez 1988; Russell 1989; Blumberg and Gottlieb 1989; Hamilton 1990).

Just as Los Angeles's largest African-American community was selected as a site for a city-sponsored municipal incinerator, East Los Angeles, the city's largest Latino community, was chosen as a site for a hazardous waste incinerator (Russell 1989). Officially, the incinerator was planned for Vernon, an industrial suburb that has only 96 people. But, several East Los Angeles neighborhoods (made up of mostly Latino residents) are located only a mile away and down-wind from the proposed site. The group Mothers of East Los Angeles (MELA) took the lead in fighting the proposed hazardous waste site (Pardo 1990).

Richmond (CA): Richmond has a population of 80,000. Over half are African-Americans and about 10 percent are Latinos. Most of the African-American population live next to the city's petrochemical corridor—a cluster of 350 facilities that handle hazardous waste (Citizens for a Better Environment 1989). The five largest industrial polluters in the city are the Chevron oil refinery, Chevron Ortho pesticide plant, Witco Chemical, Airco Industrial Gases, and an ICI pesticide plant (formerly Stauffer Chemical). Chevron Ortho generates over 40 percent of the hazardous waste in Richmond. The bulk of it is incinerated on the plant's grounds. Local citizens founded the West County Toxics Coalition to address the problem of toxic emissions.

Kettleman City (CA): Kettleman City is a small farmworker community of approximately 1,200. Over 95 percent of the residents are Latino. It is home to a hazardous waste landfill operated by the world's largest waste-disposal company, Chemical Waste Management (see Corwin 1991; Siler 1991). The company proposed that a new incinerator be built in Kettleman City. Residents organized an opposition group called El Pueblo para el Aire y Agua Limpio (People for Clean Air and Water).

Rosebud Reservation (SD): As state environmental regulations have become more stringent in recent years, Native-American reservations have become prime targets of waste disposal firms (Beasley 1990; Tomsho 1990; Kay 1991*b*). Many waste-disposal companies have attempted to skirt state regulations (which are often tougher than the federal regulations) by targeting Native lands (Angel 1992). Because of their quasi-independent status, Native-American reservations are not covered by state environmental regulations. The threat to Native lands exists for the Mohawk Indians in New York to the Mission Indians (i.e. Campo, La Posta, Los Coyotes, Morongo, Pala, and Soboda) in southern California to the Gwichin people in Alaska (Kay 1991*b*). The problem is typified in the case of the Rosebud Reservation in South Dakota. RSW, a Connecticut-based company, proposed in 1991 to build a 6,000-acre municipal landfill on Sioux lands (Daschle 1991). Local residents founded the Good Road Coalition to block the landfill.

who controls Indian lands?

What We Learned

Eight of the nine community opposition groups were started as environmental groups. Mothers of East Los Angeles was the only exception. It grew out of a six-year dispute involving a proposed 1,450-bed state prison in East Los Angeles (Pardo 1991). MELA also fought a proposed underground pipeline through their neighborhood. Its fight against the incinerator is an extension of this earlier battle.

All of the groups have multi-issue agendas and incorporate social justice and equity as their major organizing themes. The leaders see their communities as "victims" and are quick to make the connection between other forms of discrimination, the quality of their physical environment, and the current dispute. Some of the leaders have worked in other organizations that fought discrimination in housing, employment, and education.

It is clear that the local grassroots activists in the impacted communities provided the essential leadership in dealing with the disputes. The typical grassroots leader was a woman. For example, women led the fight in seven of the nine cases examined. Only the West Dallas Coalition for Environmental Justice and Richmond's West County Toxics Coalition were headed by men.

Women activists were quick to express their concern about the threat to their family, home, and community. The typical organizer found leadership thrust upon her by immediate circumstances with little warning or prior training for the job. Lack of experience, however, did not prove an insurmountable barrier to successful organizing.

The manner in which the local issue was framed appears to have influenced the type of leadership that emerged. Local activists immediately turned their energies to what they defined as environmental discrimination, for discrimination is a fact of life in all of these communities. Most people of color face it daily.

The quest for environmental justice thus extends the quest for basic civil rights. Actions taken by grassroots activists to reduce environmental inequities are consistent with the struggle to end the other forms of social injustice found throughout our society—in housing, education, employment, health care, criminal justice, and politics.

The mainstream environmental groups do not have a long history of working with African-American, Latino, Asian, Pacific Islander, and Native-American groups. For the most part, they have failed to adequately address environmental problems that disproportionately impact people of color. Despite some exceptions, the national groups have failed to sufficiently make the connection between key environmental and social justice issues.

The experience of the organizations discussed here suggests that the situation is beginning to change for the better. While still too little, the mainstream environmental movement's support of environmental justice struggles has visibly increased between the first Earth Day in 1970 and Earth Day 1990. Certainly, the early environmental struggles by communities of color were less likely than more recent ones to attract significant support from the mainstream groups.

Because of the redefinition of "environmentalism" spurred on by grassroots challenges to the elitism and environmental racism of the mainstream groups, more mainstream groups now acknowledge and try to address the widespread inequities throughout our society. Many of these groups are beginning to understand and embrace the cause of social justice activists mobilizing to protect their neighborhoods from garbage dumps or lead smelters. These first steps have been a long time in coming, however. For many conservationists, the struggle for social justice is still seen as separate from environmental activism. Because of this, environmental activists of color have usually had better luck winning support for their cause by appealing to more justice-oriented groups. For example, Houston's Northeast Community Action Group (NECAG) was able to enlist support from a number of local social justice activists in their dispute with Browning-Ferris Industries. The anti-discrimination theme was a major tool in enlisting the Houston Black United Front (an African-American self-help group), the Harris County Council of Organizations (an African-American voter education and political group), and a Houston chapter of ACORN (Association of Community Organizations for Reform Now).

The situation in Dallas somewhat resembled that found in Houston. Leaders of West Dallas's Neighborhood Committee on Lead Pollution received no assistance from any outside environmental group in resolving their dispute. Instead, they relied exclusively on a grassroots self-help group, the Common Ground Community Economic Development Corporation, to get their grievances publicly aired. Common Ground not surprisingly has a long history of working on equity issues in the city's African-American community.

The Neighborhood Committee on Lead Pollution disbanded after the lead-smelter dispute was resolved. In 1989, the West Dallas Coalition for Environmental Justice, a multiracial group, formed to fill the leadership vacuum. It pressed for cleanup of the RSR site in West Dallas, closure of the Dixie Metals lead smelter in Dallas's East Oak Cliff neighborhood, and pollution prevention measures for the remaining industries in the neighborhood. The multiracial coalition has about 700 members and 20 volunteers. It has worked closely with Common Ground and Texas United, a grassroots environmental group affiliated with the Boston-based National Toxics Campaign. The local Sierra Club also wrote several letters endorsing the actions taken by the West Dallas group to get their neighborhood cleaned up.

Leaders in Alsen, on the other hand, did receive support (although late in their struggle) from several environmental groups. Rollins's proposal to burn PCBs in the Alsen incinerator had gotten the attention of several national environmental groups, including Greenpeace, Citizens' Clearinghouse for Hazardous Waste, and the National Toxics Campaign.

Alsen residents also enlisted the support of the Louisiana Environmental Action Network (a mostly white group) and Gulf Coast Tenants Organization (a mostly African-American group). Gulf Coast has, for example, led Earth Day "toxics marches" from New Orleans to Baton Rouge.

The four California community groups examined in this study all had great success in getting support from and forming alliances with both grassroots and national environmental groups. Again, the level of outside support was greatest for the groups fighting new facilities proposals.

The African-American leaders of Concerned Citizens of South Central Los Angeles found allies and built strong working relationships with a diverse set of international, national, and grassroots environmental groups. Greenpeace was the first national group to join Concerned Citizens in their fight to kill LANCER 1 (Russell 1989; Blumberg and Gottlieb 1989). Others joined later, including Citizens for a Better Environment (CBE), National Health Law Program, and the Center for Law in the Public Interest. Concerned Citizens also forged alliances with two white Westside "slow-growth" groups: Not Yet New York (a coalition of environmental and homeowner groups) and the anti-incineration group California Alliance in Defense of Residential Environments (CADRE).

Mothers of East Los Angeles lined up the support of groups such as Greenpeace, the Natural Resources Defense Council, the Environmental Policy Institute, the Citizens' Clearinghouse on Hazardous Waste, the National Toxics Campaign, and the Western Center on Law and Poverty. These allies provided valuable technical advice, expert testimony, lobbying, research, and legal assistance.

The Kettleman City dispute attracted widespread attention and became a topic on prime-time newscasts. The local group, El Pueblo para el Aire y Agua Limpio (People for Clean Air and Water), got a lot of support from both national and grassroots environmental and social justice groups. The dispute brought together environmental leaders of color from inside and outside California. The decision to site a hazardous waste incinerator in Kettleman City also acted as a rallying point for many environmental justice groups ranging from Greenpeace to the Albuquerque-based Southwest Network for Environmental and Economic Justice (a coalition of environmental activists of color from eight states in the Southwest).

The Richmond-based West County Toxics Coalition was founded with assistance from the National Toxics Campaign. It then got the Sierra Club (headquartered just across the Bay in San Francisco) involved in their struggle. The San Francisco-based Citizens for a Better Environment (CBE) furnished the group with technical assistance and documentation of the local environmental problem (see the 1989 report *Richmond at Risk*). The report offers graphic evidence of the threat posed by polluting industries in the city's African-American and Latino communities.

Disputes involving Native lands present special problems to conventional environmental movements. Given the long history of exploitation and genocide directed at Native Americans by whites, environmental disputes take on larger historical and cultural meanings. However, the Good Road Coalition was able to enlist the support of Greenpeace activists and two Native-American groups (the Indigenous Environmental Network and the Natural Resource Coalition).

Organizing Tactics

The grassroots environmental groups and their allies have used a wide range of tactics to fend off what they see as a threat to family, home, and community. The leaders have borrowed many of their tactics from the earlier civil rights movement. All of the groups have used public protest, demonstrations, petitions, lobbying, reports and fact-finding, and hearings to educate the community and intensify public debate on the dispute. In addition, leaders organized community workshops and neighborhood forums to keep local residents informed on the disputes and new developments.

All of the grassroots groups targeted local, state, and federal governments for their direct or indirect influence in siting and enforcement decisions. For example, the leaders of Houston's Northeast Community Action Group directed their actions toward both the local and state government bodies responsible for permitting the facility.

A number of tangible results emerged from the Houston dispute. First, the Houston City Council, acting under intense political pressure from local residents, passed a resolution in 1980 that prohibited city-owned garbage trucks from dumping at the controversial landfill in the Northwood Manor subdivision. Second, the council also passed an ordinance restricting the construction of solid-waste sites near public facilities such as schools and parks. (This action was nothing less than a form of protective zoning.) And, third, the Texas Department of Health updated its requirements for landfill permit applicants. Applications now must include detailed land-use, economic impact, and sociodemographic data on areas where proposed municipal solid-waste landfills are to be sited.

The Neighborhood Committee on Lead Pollution challenged the Dallas Health Department for its lax enforcement of the city's lead ordinance and the repeated violations by the nearby smelter. Grassroots leaders in West Dallas extended their influence beyond the neighborhood by pressuring the Dallas mayor to appoint a government-sanctioned city-wide task force (the Dallas Alliance Environmental Task Force) to address lead contamination. The impetus for the task force came from the local West Dallas group.

The two Los Angeles neighborhood groups also sought to have the city intervene in their dispute. The LANCER dispute was injected into local city politics and became a contributing factor in both the defeat of the pro-LANCER City Council President Pat Russell and the election of environmental advocate Ruth Galanter. Concerned Citizens of South Central Los Angeles and its allies proved that local citizens can fight city hall and win. Opponents of the city-initiated incinerator project applied pressure on key elected officials, including Mayor Tom Bradley. Bradley reversed his position and asked the city council to kill the project, which had been in the planning stage since 1969 and included a commitment to contribute $12 million (Russell 1989).

Mothers of East Los Angeles, in its struggle, targeted the South Coast Air Quality Management District (AQMD), the California Department of Health Services (DHS), and the US Environmental Protection Agency (EPA)—the agencies responsible for awarding a permit for the Vernon hazardous waste incinerator project. The facility was to be California's first "state-of-the-art" toxic waste incinerator.

To block the project, Mothers of East Los Angeles and its allies arranged for more than 500 residents to attend a 1987 DHS hearing on it. They pressed their demands in other public forums as well. The alliance questioned DHS's 1988 decision that allowed California Thermal Treatment Services (CTTS) to move the project forward without preparing an environmental impact report (EIR). The City of Los Angeles, MELA, and others joined in a lawsuit to review the decision. The federal EPA, however, approved the permit without an EIR.

This prompted California Assemblywoman Lucille Roybal-Allard to lead a successful fight to change the California law and require EIRs for all toxic waste incinerators. In December 1988, as CTTS was about to start construction, the AQMD decided that the company should do the environmental studies and redesign its original standards to meet the new, more stringent clean air regulations. CTTS legally challenged the AQMD's decision all the way up to the State Supreme Court and lost.

The Coalition for Community Action (Alsen, LA) focused its attack on the Louisiana Department of Environmental Quality and its less-than-enthusiastic enforcement of air quality standards in North Baton Rouge and the African-American communities affected by emissions from the nearby polluting industries. The group also worked on getting the federal EPA more actively involved in pollution prevention efforts in "Cancer Alley."

Richmond's West County Toxics Coalition worked to get both state and federal government agencies involved in reducing emissions from the nearby polluting industries. On the other hand, Kettleman City's People for Clean Air and Water focused its attention on the Kings County Board of Supervisors, the California Department of Health Services, and the federal EPA.

The Native Americans who founded the Good Road Coalition appealed to their Tribal Council (the government of the sovereign Sioux Nation on the Rosebud Reservation) to rescind the contract signed with RSW to build the 6,000-acre landfill on the reservation. Tribal Chairman Ralph Moran had supported the construction. It is interesting that six of the nine grassroots groups used litigation as a tactic. The three groups that did not were the West Dallas Coalition for Environmental Justice (its predecessor had already filed a lawsuit), Richmond's West County Toxics Coalition, and Rosebud's Good Road Coalition. All of the groups that filed lawsuits used their own lawyers. Three of them (Concerned Citizens of South Central Los Angeles, Mothers of East Los Angeles, and People for Clean Air and Water) applied to public interest law centers to file their lawsuits.

The West Dallas and East Los Angeles groups were joined in their lawsuits by the local government: both the city of Dallas and the Texas Attorney General joined the West Dallas plaintiffs, while the city of Los Angeles joined MELA.

Three of the neighborhood groups (the two in West Dallas and the one in Richmond) used negotiations as a dispute resolution tactic. The West Dallas groups were able to negotiate two different cleanup plans—the first in 1984, the second in 1992.

Richmond's West County Toxics Campaign brought in the Reverend Jesse Jackson of the National Rainbow Coalition to negotiate with Chevron, the major polluter in the community. Richmond's Mayor George Livingston helped arrange the 7 May 1990 meeting with Chevron that included representatives from the West County Toxics Coalition, the National Rainbow Coalition, and the Sierra Club. Jackson described the negotiations as a "test case, a test example, both with dangers and possibilities." He and the West County Toxics Coalition presented Chevron with a six-point plan (Reed 1990: A1):

- Annually set aside 1 percent of the cost of Chevron's proposed $1 billion modernization for a cleanup fund. The fund should employ Richmond's unemployed to help clean up the environment, and should also be used to finance health care and new pollution-reduction technology;
- Establish a 24-hour, fully funded clinic to provide medical attention to those harmed by the dozens of polluting industries in Richmond;
- Reduce the tons of toxic waste destroyed in Chevron's Ortho Chemical plant incinerator. (Chevron, which currently burns about 75,000 tons annually in the furnace, is seeking state permits to double the incinerator's capacity);
- Bring together representatives of other polluting industries and pressure them to reduce their companies' toxic emissions;

- Divest from South Africa; and
- Negotiate a timetable for accomplishing the above goals.

Nobody knows what these negotiations will yield or how long it will take to get tangible results. Nevertheless, both sides appear willing to talk. Of course, talking about emission reduction is different from actual emission reduction. But the Coalition and its allies did get Chevron to agree not to bring in outside waste to burn at the Richmond site.

The other concrete result of the negotiations was an agreement to meet again to negotiate specifics. Nevertheless, the meeting itself represented a major community victory in that the West County Toxics Coalition finally won the right to bargain with Chevron, something local leaders had unsuccessfully attempted to do since 1987.

Resolutions and Outcomes

These case studies demonstrate that African-Americans, Latino Americans, and Native Americans are actively pursuing strategies to improve the overall quality of life in their neighborhoods. The grassroots leaders have not waited for "outsiders" or "elites" to rush to their rescue; they have taken the initiative themselves.

As expected, the groups had more success in blocking proposed facilities than closing those already operating. The West Dallas residents were successful in shutting down the lead smelter and in winning an out-of-court settlement worth over $45 million—one of the largest awards ever in a lead pollution case in the country. It was made on behalf of 370 children—almost all of whom were poor, black residents of the West Dallas public housing project—and 40 property owners.

The lawsuit was finally settled in June 1983 when RSR agreed to a soil cleanup program in West Dallas, a blood-testing program for the children and pregnant women, and the installation of new antipollution equipment. The equipment, however, was never installed. In May 1984 the Dallas Board of Adjustments, a city agency responsible for monitoring land-use violations, requested that the city attorney order the smelter permanently closed for violating the zoning code. It had operated in the neighborhood for some 50 years without the necessary use permits.

The 1984 lead cleanup proved inadequate. A more comprehensive cleanup of West Dallas was begun in December 1991–20 years after the first government study of lead smelters. Some 30,000 to 40,000 cubic yards (roughly 1,800 truckloads) of lead-tainted soil are to be removed from several West Dallas sites, including schoolyards and about 140 private homes (Loftis 1992). The project will cost between $3 to $4 million. The contaminated soil was originally planned to be shipped to a landfill in Monroe, Louisiana—a city that is 60 percent African-American.

The municipal landfill in Houston, the hazardous waste incinerator in Alsen, and the petrochemical plant (and on-site hazardous waste incinerator) in Richmond are still operating. Although the three groups and their allies fell short of completely eliminating the threat by bringing about actual plant closures, they were able to extract concessions from the polluting industries in the form of capacity reduction and emission controls. In Alsen, after more than six years, a 1987 out-of-court settlement was reached between Rollins and the residents. It was reported to be worth an average of $3,000 per resident. The company was also required to reduce emissions from its facilities.

Construction of four proposed facilities were prevented: the two waste facilities in Los Angeles (South Central and East Los Angeles), the one on Rosebud Reservation in South Dakota, and the one in Kettleman City. The two lawsuits filed on behalf of South Central and East Los Angeles residents never reached the trial or settlement stage, for the two construction proposals were withdrawn. The city-sponsored LANCER project was killed by the mayor and city council. In May 1991, CTTS decided to "throw in the towel" because the lawsuits threatened to drive up costs beyond the $4 million the company had already spent on the project (Dolan 1991). The Vernon hazardous waste incinerator became a dead issue.

On the other hand, the Good Road Coalition blocked plans to build the 6,000-acre landfill on the Rosebud Reservation through the electoral process. A majority of the residents voted the proposal down. In 1991, former tribal chairman Ralph Moran, who had favored the landfill proposal, was defeated in the tribal primary election and residents convinced the tribal council to cancel the agreement to build the facility. The proposal was resurrected in 1992 in yet another offer to the tribal council by RSW. Again, the plan was rejected by the council.

Although part of the lawsuit involving the Kettleman City incinerator dispute is still pending, People for Clean Air and Water won a major victory in delaying construction. A superior court judge in January 1992 overturned the Kings. County Board of Supervisors' approval of the Kettleman City incinerator, citing its detrimental impact on air quality in the agriculture-rich Central Valley of California.

The judge ruled that Kings County's environmental impact report was inadequate and that county leaders had failed to involve the local residents in the decision by not providing Spanish translations of material about the project. This court ruling represents a victory since the waste-disposal company must now begin the permit process all over again if it is still interested in siting the facility.

Conclusion

The mainstream environmental movement has proven that it can help enhance the quality of life in this country. The national membership organizations that make up the mainstream movement have clearly played an important role in shaping the nation's environmental policy. Yet, few of these groups have actively involved themselves in environmental conflicts involving communities of color. Because of this, it's unlikely that we will see a mass influx of people of color into the national environmental groups any time soon. A continuing growth in their own grassroots organizations is more likely. Indeed, the fastest growing segment of the environmental movement is made up by the grassroots groups in communities of color which are increasingly linking up with one another and with other community-based groups. As long as US society remains divided into separate and unequal communities, such groups will continue to serve a positive function.

It is not surprising that indigenous leaders are organizing the most effective resistance within communities of color. They have the advantage of being close to the population immediately affected by the disputes they are attempting to resolve. They are also completely wedded to social and economic justice agendas and familiar with the tactics of the civil rights movement. This makes effective community organizing possible. People of color have a long track record in challenging government and corporations that discriminate. Groups that emphasize civil rights and social justice can be found in almost every major city in the country.

Cooperation between the two major wings of the environmental movement is both possible and beneficial, however. Many environmental activists of color are now getting support from mainstream organizations in the form of technical advice, expert testimony, direct financial assistance, fundraising, research, and legal assistance. In return, increasing numbers of people of color are assisting mainstream organizations to redefine their limited environmental agendas and expand their outreach by serving on boards, staffs, and advisory councils. Grassroots activists have thus been the most influential activists in placing equity and social justice issues onto the larger environmental agenda and democratizing and diversifying the movement as a whole. Such changes are necessary if the environmental movement is to successfully help spearhead a truly global movement for a just, sustainable, and healthy society and effectively resolve pressing environmental disputes. Environmentalists and civil rights activists of all stripes should welcome the growing movement of African-Americans, Latinos, Asians, Pacific Islanders, and Native Americans who are taking up the struggle for environmental justice.

References

Agency for Toxic Substances and Disease Registry (1988), *The Nature and Extent of Lead Poisoning in Children in the United States: A Reprint to Congress* (Atlanta: US Department of Health and Human Services).

Alston, Dana (1990), *We Speak for Ourselves: Social Justice, Race, and Environment* (Washington, DC: Panos Institute).

Anderson, Bob (1992), "Plant Sites: Is Racism an Issue?," *Baton Rouge Morning Advocate*, 12 May: A1, A5.

——Dunn, Mike, and Alabarado, Sonny (1985), "Prosperity in Paradise: Louisiana's Chemical Legacy," *Morning Advocate*, 25 April.

Angel, Bradley (1992), *The Toxic Threat to Indian Lands: A Greenpeace Report* (San Francisco: Greenpeace).

Bachrach, Kenneth M., and Zautra, Alex J. (1985), "Coping with Community Stress: The Threat of a Hazardous Waste Landfill," *Journal of Health and Social Behavior*, 26 (June): 127–41.

Beasley, Conger, Jr. (1990), "Of Poverty and Pollution: Deadly Threat on Native Lands," *Buzzworm*, 2 (September/October): 39–45.

Blauner, Robert (1972), *Racial Oppression in America* (New York: Harper and Row).

Blumberg, Michael, and Gottlieb, Robert (1989), *War on Waste: Can America Win Its Battle with Garbage?* (Washington, DC: Island Press).

Brown, Michael H. (1980), *Laying Waste: The Poisoning of America by Toxic Chemicals* (New York: Pantheon Books).

——(1987), *The Toxic Cloud: The Poisoning of America's Air* (New York: Harper and Row).

Bryant, Bunyan, and Mohai, Paul (1992), *Race and the Incidence of Environmental Hazards* (Boulder, Colo.: Westview Press).

Bullard, Robert D. (1983), "Solid Waste Sites and the Black Houston Community," *Sociological Inquiry*, 53 (Spring): 273–88.

——(1984), "Endangered Environs: The Price of Unplanned Growth in Boomtown Houston," *California Sociologist*, 7 (Summer): 84–102.

——(1987), *Invisible Houston: The Black*

Experience in Boom and Bust (College Station, Tex.: Texas A & M University Press).

Bullard, Robert D. (1990), *Dumping in Dixie: Race, Class, and Environmental Quality* (Boulder, Colo.: Westview Press).

—— (1991*a*), "Environmental Justice for All," *EnviroAction*, Environmental News Digest for the National Wildlife Federation (November).

—— (1991*b*), "Environmental Racism," *Environmental Protection*, 2 (June): 25–6.

—— (1992*a*), *Directory of People of Color Environmental Groups 1992* (Riverside, Calif.: University of California, Riverside, Department of Sociology).

—— (1992*b*), "Urban Infrastructure: Social, Environmental, and Health Risks to African Americans," in Billy J. Tidwell (ed.), *The State of Black America 1992* (New York: National Urban League), 183–96.

—— and Wright, Beverly H. (1987), "Blacks and the Environment," *Humboldt Journal of Social Relations*, 14: 165–84.

—— —— (1990), "The Quest for Environmental Equity: Mobilizing the African American Community for Social Change," *Society and Natural Resources*, 3: 301–11.

Buttel, Frederick, and Flinn, William L. (1978), "Social Class and Mass Environmental Beliefs: A Reconsideration," *Environment and Behavior*, 10 (September): 433–50.

Carmichael, S., and Hamilton, C. V. (1967), *Black Power* (New York: Vintage).

Catton, William (1982), *Overshoot: The Ecological Basis of Revolutionary Change* (Chicago: University of Illinois Press).

Center for Investigative Reporting and Bill Moyers (1990), *Global Dumping Grounds: The International Trade in Hazardous Waste* (Washington, DC: Seven Locks Press).

Cerrell Associates, Inc. (1984), *Political Difficulties Facing Waste-to-Energy Conversion Plant Siting* (California Waste Management Board, Technical Information Series; prepared by Cerrell Associates, Inc. for the California Waste Management Board, Los Angeles, Calif.: Cerrell Associates, Inc.).

Citizens for a Better Environment (1989), *Richmond at Risk: Community Demographics and Toxic Hazards from Industrial Polluters* (San Francisco: CBE).

Corwin, Miles (1991), "Unusual Allies Fight Waste Incinerator," *Los Angeles Times*, 24 February: A1, A36.

Daschle, Thomas (1991), "Dances with Garbage," *Christian Science Monitor*, 14 February.

Denton, Nancy A., and Massey, Douglas S. (1988), "Residential Segregation of Blacks, Hispanics, and Asians by Socioeconomic Class and Generation," *Social Science Quarterly*, 69: 797–817.

Dolan, Maura (1991), "Toxic Waste Incinerator Bid Abandoned," *Los Angeles Times*, 24 May.

Dunlap, Riley E. (1987), "Public Opinion on the Environment in the Reagan Era: Polls, Pollution, and Politics," *Environment*, 29: 6–11, 31–7.

Feagin, Joe R. (1988), *Free Enterprise City: Houston in Political and Economic Perspective* (Englewood Cliffs, NJ: Prentice Hall).

Freeman, Myrick A. (1972), "The Distribution of Environmental Quality," in Allen V. Kneese and Blair T. Bower (eds), *Environmental Quality Analysis* (Baltimore: Johns Hopkins University Press for Resources for the Future).

Gelobter, Michel (1988), "The Distribution of Air Pollution by Income and Race," paper presented at the Second Symposium on Social Science in Resource Management, Urbana, Illinois, June.

Gianessi, Leonard, Peskin, H. M., and Wolff, E. (1979), "The Distributional Effects of Uniform Air Pollution Policy in the U.S.," *Quarterly Journal of Economics*, May: 281–301.

Gottdiener, Mark (1988), *The Social Production of Space* (Austin: University of Texas Press).

Greenpeace (1992), "The 'Logic' Behind Hazardous Waste Export," *Greenpeace Waste Trade Update*, First Quarter: 1–2.

Hamilton, Cynthia (1990), "Women, Home, Community," *Race, Poverty, and the Environment Newsletter*, 1 (April).

Jaynes, Gerald D., and Williams, Robin M., Jr. (1989), *A Common Destiny: Blacks and American Society* (Washington, DC: National Academy Press).

Kay, Jane (1991*a*), "Fighting Toxic Racism: L.A.'s

Minority Neighborhood is the "Dirtiest' in the State," *San Francisco Examiner*, 7 April: A1.

—— (1991*b*), "Indian Lands Targeted for Waste Disposal Sites," *San Francisco Examiner*, 10 April: A10.

Lee, Bill Lann (1992), "Environmental Litigation on Behalf of Poor, Minority Children: *Matthews v. Coye:* A Case Study," paper presented at the Annual Meeting of the American Association for the Advancement of Science, Chicago, April.

Loftis, Randy Lee (1992), "Louisiana OKs Dumping of Tainted Soil," *Dallas Morning News*, 12 May: A1, A30.

Mann, Eric (1991), *L.A.'s Lethal Air: New Perspectives for Policy, Organizing, and Action* (Los Angeles: Labor/Community Strategy Center).

Maraniss, David, and Weisskopf, Michael (1987), "Jobs and Illness in Petrochemical Corridor," *Washington Post*, 22 December.

Mohai, Paul (1985), "Public Concern and Elite Involvement in Environmental Conservation," *Social Science Quarterly*, 66 (December): 820–38.

—— (1990), "Black Environmentalism," *Social Science Quarterly*, 71 (April): 744–65.

Morrison, Denton E. (1980), "The Soft Cutting Edge of Environmentalism and How the Appropriate Technology Notion is Changing the Movement," *Natural Resources Journal*, 20 (April): 275–98.

—— (1986), "How and Why Environmental Consciousness has Trickled Down," in Allan Schnaiberg, Nicholas Watts, and Klaus Zimmerman (eds), *Distributional Conflict in Environmental Resource Policy* (New York: St Martin's Press), 187–220.

Nauss, D. W. (1973), "The People vs. the Lead Smelter," *Dallas Times Herald*, 17 July.

Omi, Michael, and Winant, Howard (1986), *Racial Formation in the United States: From the 1960's to the 1980's* (New York: Routledge, Kegan and Paul).

Ong, Paul, and Blumenberg, Evelyn (1990), "Race and Environmentalism," paper read at Graduate School of Architecture and Urban Planning, 14 March, at UCLA.

Pardo, Mary (1990), "Mexican American Women Grassroots Community Activists: Mothers of East Los Angeles," *Frontiers: A Journal of Women's Studies*, 11 (January): 1–6.

Reed, Dan (1990), "Jackson to Chevron: Clean Up," *West County Times*, 8 May: A1.

Russell, Dick (1989), "Environmental Racism: Minority Communities and their Battle against Toxics," *Amicus Journal*, 11 (Spring): 22–32.

Sanchez, Jesus (1988), "The Environment: Whose Movement?," *California Tomorrow*, 3: 10–17.

Sanchez, Roberto (1990), "Health and Environmental Risks of the Maquiladora in Mexicali," *Natural Resources Journal*, 30 (Winter): 163–86.

Siler, Julia Flynn (1991), "Environmental Racism? It Could Be a Messy Fight," *Business Week*, 20 May: 116.

Tomsho, Robert (1990), "Dumping Grounds: Indian Tribes Contend with Some of the Worst of America's Pollution," *Wall Street Journal*, 29 November.

United Church of Christ Commission for Racial Justice (1987), *Toxic Wastes and Race in the United States: A National Report on the Racial and Socio-Economic Characteristics of Communities with Hazardous Waste Sites* (New York: United Church of Christ).

—— (1992), *The First National People of Color Environmental Leadership Summit: Program Guide* (New York: United Church of Christ).

Wernette, D. R., and Nieves, L. A. (1992), "Breathing Polluted Air," *EPA Journal*, 18 (March/April): 16–17.

West, Pat C., Fly, F., and Marans, R. (1990) "Minority Anglers and Toxic Fish Consumption: Evidence from a State-Wide Survey of Michigan," in B. Bryant, and P. Mohai (eds), *The Proceedings of the Michigan Conference on Race and the Incidence of Environmental Hazards* (Ann Arbor: University of Michigan School of Natural Resources), 108–122.

Witt, Matthew (1991), "An Injury to One is an Gravio A Todo: The Need for a Mexico–U.S. Health and Safety Movement," *New Solutions: A*

Journal of Environmental and Occupational Health Policy, 1 (March): 28–33.

Working Group on Canada–Mexico Free Trade (1991), "Que Pasa? A Canada–Mexico 'Free' Trade Deal," *New Solutions: A Journal of Environmental and Occupational Health Policy*, 2 (January): 10–25.

Zuniga, Jo Ann (1992), "Watchdog Keeps Tabs on Politics of Environment along Border," *Houston Chronicle*, 24 May: 22A.

35 Women of Color on the Front Line

Celene Krauss

Toxic waste disposal is a central focus of women's grass-roots environmental activism.[1] Toxic waste facilities are predominantly sited in working-class and low-income communities and communities of color, reflecting the disproportionate burden placed on these communities by a political economy of growth that distributes the costs of economic growth unequally.[2] Spurred by the threat that toxic wastes pose to family health and community survival, female grass-roots activists have assumed the leadership of community environmental struggles. As part of a larger movement for environmental justice, they constitute a diverse constituency, including working-class housewives and secretaries, rural African American farmers, urban residents, Mexican American farm workers, and Native Americans.

These activists attempt to differentiate themselves from what they see as the white, male, middle-class leadership of many national environmental organizations. Unlike the more abstract, issue-oriented focus of national groups, women's focus is on environmental issues that grow out of their concrete, immediate experiences.[3] Female blue-collar activists often share a loosely defined ideology of environmental justice and a critique of dominant social institutions and mainstream environmental organizations, which they believe do not address the broader issues of inequality underlying environmental hazards. At the same time, these activists exhibit significant diversity in their conceptualization of toxic waste issues, reflecting different experiences of class, race, and ethnicity.

This chapter looks at the ways in which different working-class women formulate ideologies of resistance around toxic waste issues and the process by which they arrive at a concept of environmental justice. Through an analysis of interviews, newsletters, and conference presentations, I show the voices of white, African American, and Native American female activists and the resources that inform and support their protests. What emerges is an environmental discourse that is mediated by subjective experiences and interpretations and rooted in the political truths women construct out of their identities as housewives, mothers, and members of communities and racial and ethnic groups.

The Subjective Dimension of Grass-Roots Activism

Grass-roots protest activities have often been trivialized, ignored, and viewed as self-interested actions that are particularistic and parochial, failing to go beyond a single-issue focus. This view

From Robert D. Bullard (ed.), *Unequal Protection: Environmental Justice and Communities of Color* (San Francisco: Sierra Club Books, 1994), 256–71. Reprinted with permission.

of community grass-roots protests is held by most policymakers as well as by many analysts of movements for progressive social change.[4]

In contrast, the voices of blue-collar women engaged in protests regarding toxic waste issues tell us that single-issue protests are about more than the single issue. They reveal a larger world of power and resistance, which in some measure ends up challenging the social relations of power. This challenge becomes visible when we shift the analysis of environmental activism to the experiences of working-class women and the subjective meanings they create around toxic waste issues.

In traditional sociological analysis, this subjective dimension of protest has often been ignored or viewed as private and individualistic. Feminist theory, however, helps us to see its importance. For feminists, the critical reflection on the everyday world of experience is an important subjective dimension of social change.[5] Feminists show us that experience is not merely a personal, individualistic concept. It is social. People's experiences reflect where they fit in the social hierarchy. Thus, blue-collar women of differing backgrounds interpret their experiences of toxic waste problems within the context of their particular cultural histories, starting from different assumptions and arriving at concepts of environmental justice that reflect broader experiences of class and race.

Feminist theorists also challenge a dominant ideology that separates the "public" world of policy and power from the "private" and personal world of everyday experience. By definition, this ideology relegates the lives and concerns of women relating to home and family to the private, nonpolitical arena, leading to invisibility of their grass-roots protests about issues such as toxic wastes.[6] As Ann Bookman has noted in her important study of working-class women's community struggles, women's political activism in general, and working-class political life at the community level in particular, remain "peripheral to the historical record . . . where there is a tendency to privilege male political activity and labor activism."[7] The women's movement took as its central task the reconceptualization of the political itself, critiquing this dominant ideology and constructing a new definition of the political, located in the everyday world of ordinary women rather than in the world of public policy. Feminists provide a perspective for making visible the importance of particular, single-issue protests regarding toxic wastes by showing how ordinary women subjectively link the particulars of their private lives with a broader analysis of power in the public sphere.

Social historians such as George Rudé have pointed out that it is often difficult to understand the experience and ideologies of resistance because ordinary working people appropriate and reshape traditional beliefs embedded within working-class culture, such as family and community.[8] This point is also relevant for understanding the environmental protests of working-class women. Their protests are framed in terms of the traditions of motherhood and family; as a result, they often appear parochial or even conservative. As we shall see, however, for working-class women, these traditions become the levers that set in motion a political process, shaping the language and oppositional meanings that emerge and providing resources for social change.

Shifting the analysis of toxic waste issues to the subjective experience of ordinary women makes visible a complex relationship between everyday life and the larger structures of public power. It reveals the potential for human agency that is hidden in a more traditional sociological approach and provides us with a means of seeing "the sources of power which subordinated groups have created."[9]

The analysis presented in this chapter is based on the oral and written voices of women involved in toxic waste protests. Interviews were conducted at environmental conferences such as the First National People of Color Environmental Leadership Summit, Washington, DC, 1991, and the World Women's Congress for a Healthy Planet, Miami, Florida, 1991, and by telephone. Additional sources include conference presentations, pamphlets, books, and other written materials that have emerged from this movement. This research is part of an ongoing comparative study that will examine the ways in which experiences of race, class, and ethnicity mediate women's environmental activism. Future research includes an analysis of the environmental activism of Mexican American women in addition to that of the women discussed here.

Toxic Waste Protests and the Resource of Motherhood

Blue-collar women do not use the language of the bureaucrat to talk about environmental issues. They do not spout data or marshal statistics in support of their positions. In fact, interviews with these women rarely generate a lot of discussion about the environmental problem per se. But in telling their stories about their protest against a landfill or incinerator, they ultimately tell larger stories about their discovery or analysis of oppression. Theirs is a political, not a technical, analysis.

Working-class women of diverse racial and ethnic backgrounds identify the toxic waste movement as a women's movement, composed primarily of mothers. Says one woman who fought against an incinerator in Arizona and subsequently worked on other anti-incinerator campaigns throughout the state, "Women are the backbone of the grass-roots groups; they are the ones who stick with it, the ones who won't back off." By and large, it is women, in their traditional role as mothers, who make the link between toxic wastes and their children's ill health. They discover the hazards of toxic contamination: multiple miscarriages, birth defects, cancer deaths, and so on. This is not surprising, as the gender-based division of labor in a capitalist society gives working-class women the responsibility for the health of their children.

These women define their environmental protests as part of the work that mothers do. Cora Tucker, an African American activist who fought against uranium mining in Virginia and who now organizes nationally, says:

It's not that I don't think that women are smarter, [she laughs] but I think that we are with the kids all day long. . . . If Johnny gets a cough and Mary gets a cough, we try to discover the problem.

Another activist from California sums up this view: "If we don't oppose an incinerator, we're not doing our work as mothers."

For these women, family serves as a spur to action, contradicting popular notions of family as conservative and parochial. Family has a very different meaning for these women than it does for the middle-class nuclear family. Theirs is a less privatized, extended family that is open, permeable, and attached to community. This more extended family creates the networks and resources that enable working-class communities to survive materially given few economic resources.[10] The destruction of working-class neighborhoods by economic growth deprives blue-collar communities of the basic resources of survival; hence the resistance engendered by toxic waste issues. Working-class women's struggles over toxic waste issues are, at root, issues about survival. Ideologies of motherhood, traditionally relegated to the private sphere, become political resources that working-class women use to initiate and justify their resistance. In the process of protest, working-class women come to reject the dominant ideology, which separates the public and private arenas.

Working-class women's extended network of family and community serves as the vehicle for spreading information and concern about toxic waste issues. Extended networks of kinship and friendship become political resources of opposition. For example, in one community in Detroit, women discovered patterns of health problems while attending Tupperware parties. Frequently, a mother may read about a hazard in a newspaper, make a tentative connection between her own child's ill health and the pollutant, and start telephoning friends and family, developing an informal health survey. Such a discovery process is rooted in what Sarah Ruddick has called the everyday practice of mothering.[11] Through their informal networks, they compare notes and experiences and develop an oppositional knowledge used to resist the dominant knowledge of experts and the decisions of government and corporate officials.

These women separate themselves from "mainstream" environmental organizations, which are seen as dominated by white, middle-class men and concerned with remote issues. Says one woman from Rahway, New Jersey: "The mainstream groups deal with safe issues. They want to stop incinerators to save the eagle, or they protect trees for the owl. But we say, what about the people?"

Another activist implicitly criticizes the mainstream environmental groups when she says of the grass-roots Citizens' Clearinghouse for Hazardous Wastes:

Rather than oceans and lakes, they're concerned about kids dying. Once you've had someone in your family who has been attacked by the environment—I mean who has had cancer or some other disease—you get a keen sense of what's going on.

It is the traditional, "private" women's concerns about home, children, and family that provide the initial impetus for blue-collar women's involvement in issues of toxic waste. The political analyses they develop break down the public–private distinction of dominant ideology and frame a particular toxic waste issue within broader contexts of power relationships.

The Role of Race, Ethnicity, and Class

Interviews with white, African American, and Native American women show that the starting places for and subsequent development of their analyses of toxic waste protests are mediated by issues of class, race, and ethnicity.

White working-class women come from a culture in which traditional women's roles center on the private arena of family. They often marry young; although they may work out of financial necessity, the primary roles from which they derive meaning and satisfaction are those of mothering and taking care of family. They are revered and supported for fulfilling the ideology of a patriarchal family.[12] And these families often reflect a strong belief in the existing political system. The narratives of white working-class women involved in toxic waste issues are filled with the process by which they discover the injustice of their government, their own insecurity about entering the public sphere of politics, and the constraints of the patriarchal family, which ironically prevent them from becoming fully active in the defense of their family, especially in their protest. Their narratives are marked by a strong initial faith in "their" government, as well as a remarkable transformation as they become disillusioned with the system. They discover "that they never knew what they were capable of doing in defense of their children."

For white working-class women, whose views on public issues are generally expressed only within family or among friends, entering a more public arena to confront toxic waste issues is often extremely stressful. "Even when I went to the PTA," says one activist, "I rarely spoke. I was so nervous." Says another: "My views have always been strong, but I expressed them only in the family. They were not for the public." A strong belief in the existing political system is characteristic of these women's initial response to toxic waste issues. Lois Gibbs, whose involvement in toxic waste issues started at Love Canal, tells us, "I believed if I had a problem I just had to go to the right person in government and he would take care of it."

Initially, white working-class women believe that all they have to do is give the government the facts and their problem will be taken care of. They become progressively disenchanted with what they view as the violation of their rights and the injustice of a system that allows their children and family to die. In the process, they develop a perspective of environmental justice rooted in issues of class, the attempt to make democracy real, and a critique of the corporate state. Says one activist who fought the siting of an incinerator in Sumter County, Alabama: "We need to stop letting economic development be the true God and religion of this country. We have to prevent big money from influencing our government."

A recurring theme in the narratives of these women is the transformation of their beliefs about government and power. Their politicization is rooted in the deep sense of violation, betrayal, and hurt they feel when they find that their government will not protect their families. Lois Gibbs sums up this feeling well:

I grew up in a blue-collar community. We were very into democracy. There is something about discovering that democracy isn't democracy as we know it. When you lose faith in your government, it's like finding out your mother was fooling around on your father. I was very upset. It almost broke my heart because I really believed in the system. I still believe in the system, only now I believe that democracy is of the people and by the people, the people have to move it, it ain't gonna move by itself.

Echoes of this disillusionment are heard from white blue-collar women throughout the country. One activist relates:

We decided to tell our elected officials about the problems of incineration because we didn't think they knew. Surely if they knew that there was a toxic waste dump in our county they would stop it. I was politically naive. I was real surprised because I live in an area that's like the Bible Belt of the South. Now I think the God of the United States is really economic development, and that has got to change.

Ultimately, these women become aware of the inequities of power as it is shaped by issues of class and gender. Highly traditional values of democracy and motherhood remain central to their lives. But in the process of politicization through their work on toxic waste issues, these values become transformed into resources of opposition that enable women to enter the public arena and challenge its legitimacy. They justify their resistance as a way to make democracy real and to protect their children.

White blue-collar women's stories are stories of transformations: transformations into more self-confident and assertive women; into political activists who challenge the existing system and feel powerful in that challenge; into wives and mothers who establish new relationships with their spouses (or get divorced) and new, empowering relationships with their children as they provide role models of women capable of fighting for what they believe in.

 African American working-class women begin their involvement in toxic waste protests from a different place. They bring to their protests a political awareness that is grounded in race and that shares none of the white blue-collar women's initial trust in democratic institutions. These women view government with mistrust, having been victims of racist policies throughout their lives. Individual toxic waste issues are immediately framed within a broader political context and viewed as environmental racism. Says an African American activist from Rahway, New Jersey:

When they sited the incinerator for Rahway, I wasn't surprised. All you have to do is look around my community to know that we are a dumping ground for all kinds of urban industrial projects that no one else wants. I knew this was about environmental racism the moment that they proposed the incinerator.

An African American woman who fought the siting of a landfill on the South Side of Chicago reiterates this view: "My community is an all-black community isolated from everyone. They don't care what happens to us." She describes her community as a "toxic doughnut":

We have seven landfills. We have a sewer treatment plant. We have the Ford Motor Company. We have a paint factory. We have numerous chemical companies and steel mills. The river is just a few blocks away from us and is carrying water so highly contaminated that they say it would take seventy-five years or more before they can clean it up.

This activist sees her involvement in toxic waste issues as a challenge to traditional stereotypes of African American women. She says, "I'm here to tell the story that all people in the projects are not lazy and dumb!"

Some of these women share experiences of personal empowerment through their involvement in toxic waste issues. Says one African American activist:

Twenty years ago I couldn't do this because I was so shy. . . . I had to really know you to talk with you. Now I talk. Sometimes I think I talk too much. I waited until my fifties to go to jail. But it was well worth it. I never went to no university or college, but I'm going in there and making speeches.

However, this is not a major theme in the narratives of female African American activists, as it is in those of white blue-collar women. African American women's private work as mothers has traditionally extended to a more public role in the local community as protectors of the race. As a decade of African American feminist history has shown, African American women have historically played a central role in community activism and in dealing with issues of race and economic injustice.[13] They receive tremendous status and recognition from their community. Many women participating in toxic waste protests have come out of a history of civil rights activism, and their environmental protests, especially in the South, develop through community organizations born during the civil rights movement.[14] And while the visible leaders are often male, the base of the organizing has been led by African American women, who, as Cheryl Townsend Gilkes has written, have often been called "race women," responsible for the "racial uplift" of their communities.[15]

African American women perceive that traditional environmental groups only peripherally relate to their concerns. As Cora Tucker relates:

This white woman from an environmental group asked me to come down to save a park. She said that they had been trying to get black folks involved and that they won't come. I said, "Honey, it's not that they aren't concerned, but when their babies are dying in their arms they don't give a damn about a park." I said, "They want to save their babies. If you can help them save their babies, then in turn they can help you save your park." And she said, "But this is a real immediate problem." And I said, "Well, these people's kids dying is immediate."

Tucker says that white environmental groups often call her or the head of the NAACP at the last minute to participate in an environmental rally because they want to "include" African Americans. But they exclude African Americans from the process of defining the issues in the first place. What African American communities are doing is changing the agenda.

Because the concrete experience of African Americans' lives is the experience and analysis of racism, social issues are interpreted and struggled with within this context. Cora Tucker's story of attending a town board meeting shows that the issue she deals with is not merely the environment but also the disempowerment she experiences as an African American woman. At the meeting, white women were addressed as Mrs. So-and-So by the all-white, male board. When Ms. Tucker stood up, however, she was addressed as "Cora":

One morning I got up and I got pissed off and I said, "What did you call me?" He said, "Cora," and I said, "The name is Mrs. Tucker." And I had the floor until he said. "Mrs. Tucker." He waited five minutes before he said "Mrs. Tucker." And I held the floor. I said, "I'm not gonna let you call me Cora!" And when he said, "Yes, Mrs. Tucker," I said, "Mr. Chairman, I don't call you by your first name and I don't want you to call me by mine. My name is Mrs. Tucker. And when you want me, you call me Mrs. Tucker." It's not that—I mean it's not like you gotta call me Mrs. Tucker, but it was the respect.

In discussing this small act of resistance as an African American woman, Cora Tucker is showing how environmental issues may be about corporate and state power, but they are also about race. For female African American activists, environmental issues are seen as reflecting environmental racism and linked to other social justice issues, such as jobs, housing, and crime. They are viewed as part of a broader picture of social inequity based on race. Hence, the solution articulated in a vision of environmental justice is a civil rights vision—rooted in the everyday experience of racism. Environmental justice comes to mean the need to resolve the broad social inequities of race.

The narratives of Native American women are also filled with the theme of environmental racism. However, their analysis is laced with different images. It is a genocidal analysis rooted in the Native American cultural identification, the experience of colonialism, and the imminent endangerment of their culture. A Native American woman from North Dakota, who opposed a landfill, says:

Ever since the white man came here, they keep pushing us back, taking our lands, pushing us onto reservations. We are down to 3 percent now, and I see this as just another way for them to take our lands, to completely annihilate our races. We see that as racism.

Like that of the African American women, these women's involvement in toxic waste protests is grounded from the start in race and shares none of the white blue-collar women's initial belief in the state. A Native American woman from southern California who opposed a landfill on the Rosebud Reservation in South Dakota tells us:

Government did pretty much what we expected them to do. They supported the dump. People here fear the government. They control so many aspects of our life. When I became involved in opposing the garbage landfill, my people told me to be careful. They said they annihilate people like me.

Another woman involved in the protest in South Dakota describes a government official's derision of the tribe's resistance to the siting of a landfill:

If we wanted to live the life of Mother Earth, we should get a tepee and live on the Great Plains and hunt buffalo.

Native American women come from a culture in which women have had more empowered and public roles than is the case in white working-class culture. Within the Native American community, women are revered as nurturers. From childhood, boys and girls learn that men depend on women for their survival. Women also play a central role in the decision-making process within the tribe. Tribal council membership is often equally divided between men and women; many women are tribal leaders and medicine women. Native American religions embody a respect for women as well as an ecological ethic based on values such as reciprocity and sustainable development: Native Americans pray to Mother Earth, as opposed to the dominant culture's belief in a white, male, Anglicized representation of divinity.[16]

In describing the ways in which their culture integrates notions of environmentalism and womanhood, one woman from New Mexico says:

We deal with the whole of life and community; we're not separated, we're born into it—you are it. Our connection as women is to the Mother Earth, from the time of our consciousness. We're not environmentalists. We're born into the struggle of protecting and preserving our communities. We don't separate ourselves. Our lifeblood automatically makes us responsible; we are born with it. Our teaching comes from a spiritual base. This is foreign to our culture. There isn't even a word for dioxin in Navajo.

In recent years, Native American lands have become common sites for commercial garbage dumping. Garbage and waste companies have exploited the poverty and lack of jobs in Native

American communities and the fact that Native American lands, as sovereign nation territories, are often exempt from local environmental regulations. In discussing their opposition to dumping, Native American women ground their narratives in values about land that are inherent in the Native American community. They see these projects as violating tribal sovereignty and the deep meaning of land, the last resource they have. The issue, says a Native American woman from California, is

protection of the land for future generations, not really as a mother, but for the health of the people, for survival. Our tribe bases its sovereignty on our land base, and if we lose our land base, then we will be a lost people. We can't afford to take this trash and jeopardize our tribe.

If you don't take care of the land, then the land isn't going to take care of you. Because everything we have around us involves Mother Earth. If we don't take care of the land, what's going to happen to us?

In the process of protest, these women tell us, they are forced to articulate more clearly their cultural values, which become resources of resistance in helping the tribe organize against a landfill. While many tribal members may not articulate an "environmental" critique, they well understand the meaning of land and their religion of Mother Earth, on which their society is built.

Conclusion

The narratives of white, African American, and Native American women involved in toxic waste protests reveal the ways in which their subjective, particular experiences lead them to analyses of toxic waste issues that extend beyond the particularistic issue to wider worlds of power. Traditional beliefs about home, family, and community provide the impetus for women's involvement in these issues and become a rich source of empowerment as women reshape traditional language and meanings into an ideology of resistance. These stories challenge traditional views of toxic waste protests as parochial, self-interested, and failing to go beyond a single-issue focus. They show that single-issue protests are ultimately about far more and reveal the experiences of daily life and resources that different groups use to resist. Through environmental protests, these women challenge, in some measure, the social relations of race, class, and gender.

These women's protests have different beginning places, and their analyses of environmental justice are mediated by issues of class and race. For white blue-collar women, the critique of the corporate state and the realization of a more genuine democracy are central to a vision of environmental justice. The definition of environmental justice that they develop becomes rooted in the issue of class. For women of color, it is the link between race and environment, rather than between class and environment, that characterizes definitions of environmental justice. African American women's narratives strongly link environmental justice to other social justice concerns, such as jobs, housing, and crime. Environmental justice comes to mean the need to resolve the broad social inequities of race. For Native American women, environmental justice is bound up with the sovereignty of the indigenous peoples.

In these women's stories, their responses to particular toxic waste issues are inextricably tied to the injustice they feel as mothers, as working-class women, as African Americans, and as

Native Americans. They do not talk about their protests in terms of single issues. Thus, their political activism has implications far beyond the visible, particularistic concern of a toxic waste dump site or the siting of a hazardous waste incinerator.

Notes

1. This chapter is a revised version of an article written by Celene Krauss, "Women and Toxic Waste Protests," *Qualitative Sociology*, 16: 3 (1993), 247–62. For additional reading on women and toxic waste protests, see e.g. Lawrence C. Hamilton, "Concern about Toxic Wastes: Three Demographic Predictors," *Sociological Perspectives*, 28 (1985), 463–86; Celene Krauss, "Blue-Collar Women and Toxic Waste Protests," in Richard Hofrichter (ed.), *Toxic Struggles* (Philadelphia: New Society, 1993); Mary Pardo, "Mexican American Women Grassroots Community Activists: 'Mothers of East Los Angeles,'" *Frontier*, 11 (1990), 1–7; Cynthia Hamilton, "Women, Home, and Community," *Woman of Power*, 20 (1991), 42–5; Sherry Cable, "Women's Social Movement Involvement: The Role of Structural Availability in Recruitment and Participation Processes," *Sociological Quarterly*, 33 (1992).

2. Writings on the relationship of race, class, and inequities in the siting of environmental facilities include Allan Schnaiberg, *The Environment: From Surplus to Scarcity* (New York: Oxford University Press, 1980); Robert D. Bullard, *Dumping in Dixie: Race, Class, and Environmental Quality* (Boulder, Colo: Westview Press, 1990); Robert D. Bullard and Beverly H. Wright, "Dumping Grounds in a Sunbelt City," *Urban Resources*, 2 (1985), 37–9; United Church of Christ Commission for Racial Justice, *Toxic Wastes and Race in the United States: A National Study of the Racial and Socioeconomic Characteristics of Communities with Hazardous Waste Sites* (New York: United Church of Christ Commission for Racial Justice, 1987); Phil Brown and Edwin J. Mikkelsen, *No Safe Place: Toxic Waste, Leukemia, and Community Action* (Berkeley: University of California Press, 1990); Bunyan Bryant and Paul Mohai (eds),

Race and Incidence of Environmental Hazards (Boulder, Colo: Westview Press, 1992).

3. The relationship between environmental grass-roots activism and concrete experience is developed in Krauss, "Blue-Collar Women and Toxic Waste Protests"; Celene Krauss, "Community Struggles and the Shaping of Democratic Consciousness," *Sociological Forum*, 4 (1989), 227–38; Vandana Shiva *Staying Alive: Women, Ecology and Development* (London: Zed, 1989); Dorceta Taylor, "Can the Environmental Movement Attract and Maintain the Support of Minorities?," in Bunyan Bryant and Paul Mohai (eds), *Proceedings of the Michigan Conference on Race and the Incidence of Environmental Hazards* (Ann Arbor: University of Michigan, School of Natural Resources, 1990), 28–59.

4. For a complex analysis of single-issue community protests, see Joseph M. Kling and Prudence S. Posner (eds), *Dilemmas of Activism: Class, Community, and the Politics of Local Mobilization* (Philadelphia: Temple University Press, 1990). Also see Robert Bellah, "Populism and Individualism," *Social Polity*, Fall 1985.

5. For illustrations of feminist theories and methodologies that develop this perspective, read Patricia Hill Collins, *Black Feminist Thought: Knowledge, Consciousness, and the Politics of Empowerment* (Boston: Unwin Hyman, 1990); Nancy Hartsock, *Money, Sex and Power* (Boston: Northeastern University Press, 1984); Dorothy Smith, *The Everyday World as Problematic: A Feminist Sociology* (Boston: Northeastern University Press, 1987).

6. For an analysis of the private–public split in feminist political theory, see Susan Okin, *Women in Western Political Thought* (Princeton: Princeton University Press, 1979); Jean Bethke Elshtain, *Public Man, Private*

Woman (Princeton: Princeton University Press, 1981); Martha A. Ackelsberg, "Communities, Resistance, and Women's Activism: Some Implications for a Democratic Polity," in Ann Bookman and Sandra Morgen (eds), *Women and the Politics of Empowerment* (Philadelphia: Temple University Press, 1988), 53–76.

7. Sandra Morgen, "'It's the Whole Power of the City Against Us!': The Development of Political Consciousness in a Women's Health Care Coalition," in Bookman and Morgen (eds), *Women and the Politics of Empowerment*, 97.

8. See George Rudé, *Ideology and Popular Protest* (New York: Pantheon, 1980). Others include Herbert Gutman, *Work, Culture and Society in Industrializing America* (New York: Vintage, 1977); Sheila Rowbotham, *Women, Resistance and Revolution* (New York: Vintage, 1974); E. P. Thompson, *The Making of the English Working Class* (New York: Vintage, 1966).

9. Sheila Rowbotham, *Women's Consciousness, Man's World* (New York: Penguin, 1973).

10. The relationship of extended families, friendship networks, and the community activism of working-class women is explored by numerous writers. See e.g. Terry Haywoode, "Working Class Feminism: Creating a Politics of Community, Connection, and Concern," Ph.D. diss. (The Graduate School and University Center of the City University of New York, 1990). For the importance of this relationship in African American communities, read Nancy Naples, "Activist Mothering: Cross-Generational Continuity in the Community Work of Women from Low-Income Urban Neighborhoods," *Gender and Society*, May 1992; Patricia Hill Collins, *Black Feminist Thought: Knowledge, Consciousness, and the Politics of Empowerment* (Boston: Unwin Hyman, 1990); Karen Sacks, "Generations of Working-Class Families," in Karen Sacks (ed.), *My Troubles are Going to Have Trouble with Me: Everyday Trials and Triumphs of Women*

Workers (New Brunswick, NJ: Rutgers University Press, 1984) 15–38; Carol Stack, *All Our Kin: Strategies for Survival in a Black Community* (New York: Harper Colophon, 1974). Family networks also play an important role in Native American communities. See e.g. Rayna Greene, "American Indian Women: Diverse leadership for Social Change," in Lisa Albrect and Rose Brewer (eds), *Bridges of Power: Women's Multicultural Alliances* (Philadelphia: New Society, 1990).

11. See Sara Ruddick, *Maternal Thinking: Towards a Politics of Peace* (New York: Ballantine, 1989).

12. Terry Haywoode, "Working Class Feminism: Creating a Politics of Community, Connection, and Concern," paper presented at the annual meeting of the American Sociological Association, Pittsburgh, Pennsylvania, August 1992; Ida Susser, *Norman Street: Poverty and Politics in an Urban neighborhood* (New York: Oxford University Press, 1982).

13. Paula Giddings, *When and Where I Enter: The Impact of Black Women on Race and Sex in America* (New York: Morrow, 1984). Also, in *Black Feminist Thought*, Patricia Hill Collins develops the history of African American women as "othermothers" in her discussion of community activism.

14. Bullard, *Dumping in Dixie*.

15. Cheryl Townsend Gilkes, "Building in Many Places: Multiple Commitments and Ideologies in Black Women's Community Work," in Bookman and Morgen (eds), *Women and the Politics of Empowerment*.

16. See Teresa Amott and Julie Mathaei, *Race, Gender & Work: A Multicultural Economic History of Women in the United States* (Boston: South End Press, 1991); Rayna Greene, "American Indian Women: Diverse Leadership for Social Change"; Annette M. Jaimes and Theresa Halsey, "American Indian Women at the Center of Indigenous Resistance in North America," in Annette M. Jaimes (ed.), *The State of Native America* (Boston: South End Press, 1992).

SOCIETY, THE STATE, AND THE ENVIRONMENT

How might green critiques of the sort canvassed in Part Four be put into political practice? In Part Five we look at the prospects for different sorts of political change, and how they might be brought about through the efforts of environmental movements. These sections look forward to a green politics that moves beyond the conventional forms presently entrenched in the liberal democratic states, to new kinds of democracy.

Section XI: The Green Movement

Environmental politics often comes to life in social movements. These movements involve a diverse array of individuals, groups, and coalitions organizing in order to bring about changes in environmental policies and practices. While numerous political and economic reforms have been achieved at local, national, and international levels, it is arguable that these would not be possible without the pressure of the environmental movement, which is the focus of this section.

Our first two selections emphasize the importance of political activity outside of conventional political structures. Paul Wapner claims that continued action in civil society can often get things done without state assistance—or even in the face of state recalcitrance. Wapner argues that environmental non-governmental organizations (NGOs) and what he calls "transnational environmental activist organizations" (TEAGs) occupy a space outside of traditional politics. The organizations he writes about are not simply interest groups that have formed to influence the state, as they work both with and, importantly, against states. In addition, environmental groups in 'world civic politics' focus on influencing the ecological sensibility of citizens and directly pressuring corporations to change environmentally destructive practices.

The piece by Jeremy Brecher and Tim Costello argues that this type of action is the only possible form of organizing that can counter the practices of global neoliberal economics. Brecher and Costello use the metaphor of Jonathan Swift's Lilliputians to describe a strategy of networking among community groups. They assert that a variety of local actions, woven together, can create a network strong enough to harness problems larger than any of the localities might be able to attack on their own.

Greens have long debated whether or not to shun the state in favour of oppositional politics. This tension is illustrated by the long-running split between the *Fundi* and *Realo* factions of the German Greens (now resolved in favour of the *Realos*), paralleled in many other green organizations. The basic question is whether the green movement should emphasize movement-building, cultural transformation, and oppositional politics, or participation in (and so compromise with) the existing political process. Andrew Dobson suggests that these two strategies are not incompatible, and surveys a number of tactics necessary for green change, including action both through the state and in civil society.

Further Reading

For further development of their themes, see Wapner's *Environmental Activism and World Civic Politics* (1996) and Brecher and Costello's *Global Village or Global Pillage* (1994). Like Wapner, Ronnie Lipschutz in *Global Civil Society and Global Environmental Governance* (1995) discusses the move away from state-centred environmental action in the international realm. For specific examples of grassroots and coordinated ecological movements worldwide, see *Ecological Resistance Movements* (1995), edited by Bron Taylor.

Following the theme of Brecher and Costello, much in the recent literature on environmental movements has focused more thoroughly on the role of corporations in social and environmental degradation, and on the importance of building global movements from the grassroots in response. Kevin Danaher's edited volume, *Corporations are Gonna Get Your Mama* (1997), and Josh Karliner's *Corporate Planet* (1997) examine (and promote) this development. Gould, Schnaiberg, and Weinberg argue in *Local Environmental Struggles: Citizen Activism in the Treadmill of Production* (1996) that local struggles that do not take capital and corporate power seriously will fail.

A celebration of the significance of the environmental movement in North America can be found in Robert Paehlke's *Environmentalism and the Future of Progressive Politics* (1989). Mark Dowie's *Losing Ground: American Environmentalism at the Close of the 20th Century* (1995) is more sceptical, an environmentalist's critique of the movement's mainstream.

Green groups in Europe are well covered in Dick Richardson and Chris Rootes (eds.), *The Green Challenge: The Development of Green Politics in Europe* (1995). The more general literature on new social movements is also instructive (because the greens constitute one of the most important such movements). Good sources include Russell J. Dalton and Manfred Kuechler (eds.), *Challenging the Political Order: New Social and Political Movements in Western Democracies* (1990) and Alberto Melucci, *Nomads of the Present: Social Movements and Individual Needs in Contemporary Society* (1989). Anna Bramwell chastises the greens in *The Fading of the Greens: The Decline of Environmental Politics in the West* (1994).

36 Politics Beyond the State: Environmental Activism and World Civic Politics

Paul Wapner

....

Interest in transnational activist groups such as Greenpeace, European Nuclear Disarmament (END), and Amnesty International has been surging. Much of this new attention on the part of students of international relations is directed at showing that transnational activists make a difference in world affairs, that they shape conditions which influence how their particular cause is addressed. Recent scholarship demonstrates, for example, that Amnesty International and Human Rights Watch have changed state human rights practices in particular countries.[1] Other studies have shown that environmental groups have influenced negotiations over environmental protection of the oceans, the ozone layer, and Antarctica and that they have helped enforce national compliance with international mandates.[2] Still others have shown that peace groups helped shape nuclear policy regarding deployments in Europe during the cold war and influenced Soviet perceptions in a way that allowed for eventual superpower accommodation.[3] This work is important, especially insofar as it establishes the increasing influence of transnational nongovernmental organization (NGOs) on states. Nonetheless, for all its insight, it misses a different but related dimension of activist work—the attempt by activists to shape public affairs by working within and across societies themselves.

Recent studies neglect the societal dimension of activists' efforts in part because they subscribe to a narrow understanding of politics. They see politics as a practice associated solely with government and thus understand activist efforts exclusively in terms of their influence upon government. Seen from this perspective, transnational activists are solely global pressure groups seeking to change states' policies or create conditions in the international system that enhance or diminish interstate cooperation. Other efforts directed toward societies at large are ignored or devalued because they are not considered to be genuinely political in character.

Such a narrow view of politics in turn limits research because it suggests that the conception and meaning of transnational activist groups is fixed and that scholarship therefore need only measure activist influence on states. This article asserts, by contrast, that the meaning of activist groups in a global context is not settled and will remain problematic as long as the strictly societal dimension of their work is left out of the analysis. Activist efforts within and across societies are a proper object of study and only by including them in transnational activist research can one render an accurate understanding of transnational activist groups and, by extension, of world politics.

This article focuses on activist society-oriented activities and demonstrates that activist organizations are not simply transnational pressure groups, but rather are political actors in their own right. The main argument is that the best way to think about transnational activist societal efforts is through the concept of "world civic politics." When activists work to change conditions without directly pressuring states, their activities take place in the civil dimension of world collective life or what is sometimes called global civil society.[4] Civil society is that arena of social engagement which exists above the individual yet below the state.[5] It is a complex network of economic, social, and cultural practices based on friendship, family, the market, and voluntary affiliation.[6] Although the concept arose in the analysis of domestic societies, it is beginning to make sense on a global level. The interpenetration of markets, the intermeshing of symbolic meaning systems, and the proliferation of transnational collective endeavors signal the formation of a thin, but nevertheless present, public sphere where private individuals and groups interact for common purposes. Global civil society as such is that slice of associational life which exists above the individual and below the state, but also across national boundaries. When transnational activists direct their efforts beyond the state, they are politicizing global civil society.

Like its domestic counterpart, global civil society consists of structures that define and shape public affairs. For example, market forces shape the way vast numbers of people in various countries act with reference to issues of public concern. Additionally, voluntary associations affiliated with trade, cultural expression, religion, science, and production have widespread influence. In targeting these processes and institutions, activists use the realms of transnational social, cultural, and economic life to influence world public affairs.

One can appreciate the idea of world civic politics by drawing an analogy between activist efforts at the domestic and international levels. According to Melucci, Habermas, Offe, and others, the host of contemporary domestic peace, human rights, women's, and human potential movements in the developed world both lobby their respective governments and work through their societies to effect change. In this latter regard, movements identify and manipulate non-state levers of power, institutions, and modes of action to alter the dynamics of domestic collective life.[7] The French antinuclear movement, the German Green Party in its early years, and the feminist movement in the United Kingdom represent significant attempts to politicize various arenas and thereby bring about change.[8] Likewise, present-day grassroots organizations—from new populism in the United States to Christian-based communities in Latin America and alternative development organizations in India—are both targeting their governments and nurturing modes of political expression outside state control.[9] Finally, the early years of Solidarity in Poland and Charter 77 in Czechoslovakia illustrate the multifaceted character of activist politics. Recognizing the limits of influencing their respective states, Solidarity and Charter 77 created and utilized horizontal societal associations involving churches, savings associations, literary ventures, and so forth to bring about widespread change. As with the other organizations, this does not mean that they ignored the state but rather that they made a strategic decision to explore the political potential of unofficial realms of collective action.[10] In each instance groups target government officials when it seems likely to be efficacious. If this approach fails or proves too dangerous, however, they seek other means of affecting widespread conditions and practices.[11] Analytically, these other means are found in civil society.

Moved up a political notch, this form of politics helps explain the efforts of transnational activist groups. Amnesty International, Friends of the Earth, Oxfam, and Greenpeace target governments and try to change state behavior to further their aims. When this route fails or proves less efficacious, they work through transnational economic, social, and cultural networks to achieve their ends. The emphasis on world civic politics stresses that while these latter efforts may not translate easily into state action, they should not be viewed as simply matters of cultural or social interest. Rather, they involve identifying and manipulating instruments of power for shaping collective life. Unfortunately, the conventional wisdom has taken them to be politically irrelevant.

In the following I analyze the character of world civic politics by focusing on one relatively new sector of this activity, transnational environmental activist groups (TEAGs). As environmental dangers have become part of the public consciousness and a matter of scholarly concern in recent years, much attention has been directed toward the transboundary and global dimensions of environmental degradation. Ozone depletion, global warming, and species extinction, for instance, have consequences that cross state boundaries and in the extreme threaten to change the organic infrastructure of life on earth. Responding in part to increased knowledge about these problems, transnational activist groups have emerged whose members are dedicated to "saving the planet." World Wildlife Fund, Friends of the Earth, Greenpeace, Conservation International, and Earth Island Institute are voluntary associations organized across state boundaries that work toward environmental protection at the global level. TEAGs have grown tremendously since the 1970s, with the budgets of the largest organizations greater than the amount spent by most countries on environmental issues and equal to, if not double, the annual expenditure of the United Nations Environment Program (UNEP).[12] Furthermore, membership in these groups has grown throughout the 1980s and 1990s to a point where millions of people are currently members of TEAGs.[13] This article demonstrates that, while TEAGs direct much effort toward state policies, their political activity does not stop there but extends into global civil society. In the following, I describe and analyze this type of activity and, in doing so, make explicit the dynamics and significance of world civic politics.

This article is divided into five sections. The first places my argument within theoretical literature of international relations to highlight where my thesis is similar to and yet different from earlier efforts to underscore the role of nongovernmental organizations. The second is an empirical presentation of the way TEAGs specifically practice world civic politics. It describes how they foster an ecological sensibility and explicates the significance of this form of politics. The third section outlines how environmental groups pressure corporations and explores the political dimension of this strategy. The fourth section describes how TEAGs empower local communities and considers the ramifications for world politics. In each of these instances activists operate outside the province of state-to-state interaction yet engage in genuine political activity. The final section evaluates the concept of world civic politics from a theoretical perspective.

Two caveats are in order before proceeding. First, although I refer to transnational environmental activist groups in general, the focus here is on so-called northern organizations. These are groups that originated in advanced industrial societies and, although they have offices throughout both the developed and the developing worlds, maintain their central headquarters in the North. An implicit assumption is that an understanding of northern organizations will shed light upon transnational activist groups in general; this premise, however, may turn out to be false.[14] Second, I do not mean to suggest that transnational environmental organizations have a monopoly on ecological wisdom, are the harbingers of an ecologically sound future, or are beyond criticism. Like all other political actors, activists have their own problems. One must question, for example, their use and at times misuse of scientific evidence; their accountability (they are not elected officials); and the complex and often antagonistic relations among different transnational groups. I do not address these aspects of activist groups in detail here, although in a number of places I refer to particular instances when they become relevant. This is not to overlook the problems associated with transnational activist groups so much as to maintain a focus on the type of politics they employ to further their goals. In other words, one need not necessarily support the work of transnational environmental groups to understand how they operate in the international arena.

Beyond the Transnationalist Debate

Throughout the 1960s and early 1970s NGOs were the objects of tremendous scholarly attention. At the time the statecentric model of world politics was undergoing one of its many attacks and NGOs were enlisted in the assault. Many scholars argued that since nonstate actors were growing in number and power, students of world politics would be better served by paying attention to these as well as, if not instead of, nation-states. For example, a substantial number of multinational corporations (MNCs) had assets in excess of the gross national product (GNP) of certain states and had projects in numerous countries,[15] leading many scholars to argue that MNCs were curtailing state action and represented an independent variable for explaining world events.[16] Likewise, advances in communications technology opened the way for nonstate actors such as revolutionary groups, the Catholic church, and political parties to play a greater role in world politics. Innovations in overseas travel, international wire services, computer networks, and telecommunications were enabling these actors to influence the ideas, values, and political persuasions of people around the globe. Scholars argued that they were having a significant impact on questions of peace, international morality, and the salience of political issues.[17] In short, the surge in transnational activity suggested that the state might not be the most important variable for explaining world events.[18]

The debate over the relative importance of the state in world affairs had an impact in the field insofar as it convinced realists—those who most explicitly privileged the state in the 1960s and 1970s—that NGOs matter.[19] To be sure, this took some effort. Defenders of the strictly statecentric model argued, for example, that the proliferation of NGOs was a function of hegemonic stability and thus derivative of interstate behavior.[20] Others challenged the contention that transnationalism was increasing interdependence between states and hence restricting states' ability to control events, and argued instead that the amount of interdependence had actually been on the decrease.[21] Furthermore, many claimed that despite the rise in the number of nonstate actors, NGOs were not a factor in the most consequential world events at the time and that, indeed, compared with nation-states, nonstate actors were of only marginal political importance.[22] Notwithstanding these arguments, by the 1980s NGOs had made their presence felt and scholars began to take them seriously as a legitimate object of study.

The debate about NGOs, while important, suffered premature closure, because scholars ultimately saw NGO significance in terms of state power. That is, NGOs assumed prominence in subsequent studies only to the extent that they affected state policies; their influence on world affairs apart from this role was neglected.[23] One of the reasons for this is that the debate itself was framed in a way that could have had only this result. Scholars saw the controversy as a "unit of analysis" problem. They argued over which variable was the proper object of research in world politics. In order to understand world affairs, should one study, for instance, MNCs, the state, revolutionary groups, or transnational political parties? With the problem formulated in this way, transnationalists were associated with a "sovereignty at bay" model of world politics, which claimed that NGOs were eclipsing states as the key independent actors in world affairs.[24] Unfortunately, this set up the debate as an either/or proposition: either the state was the primary mover and shaker of world affairs or it was not. As a result, critics had only to demonstrate the superior causal agency of the state to dismiss or greatly deflate the transnationalist challenge—which is exactly what occurred.[25]

More recently, a resurgence of interest in NGOs has led to efforts to conceptualize them outside the unit-of-analysis problem. Most of this work is part of a broader set of concerns loosely associated with the so-called third debate, the argument over the proper paradigm for studying international relations. The origins of the third debate lie in the questioning of the statecentric model of the 1970s and 1980s, but it has since expanded to include epistemological, ontological, and axiological concerns.[26] Interest in NGOs has emerged under the rubric of the third debate insofar as scholars have advanced a number of propositions regarding how, why, and to what extent NGOs matter in world affairs based on sophisticated understandings of power, knowledge, and agency. Notable here is Rosenau's notion of sovereignty-free actors and the influence of microprocesses on macrophenomena,[27] Walker's insights concerning the critical component of social movements,[28] and Falk's understanding of the antistatist logic of activist groups.[29] My work takes these propositions as a point of departure but seeks to situate them within a broader frame of reference. In my view the analytic significance of these and similar efforts can be advanced by encompassing them within a larger investigation into the nature of world politics.

Throughout the earlier transnationalist debate, scholars never questioned the essential quality of world political activity. Having lost part of the argument, after being forced to acknowledge the centrality of the state, they failed to ask what constitutes relevant political behavior, what power is, and which dimensions of collective life are most significant for bringing about changes in human practices. Students of international relations fell back on the traditional notion that genuine political activity is the interaction of nation-states, that power consists in the means available to states, and that the state system is *the* arena for affecting human behavior throughout the world. Thus, NGOs became important, but only because they influenced state behavior. They did not affect world affairs in their own right.[30] Current research can fall into this same trap if not understood to be part of a more fundamental type of examination.[31]

This article studies NGOs with a particular focus on the meaning of world politics. It eschews an understanding in which the multifarious activities of actors gain relevance only insofar as they affect states, and concentrates instead on identifying NGO activity that orders, directs, and manages widespread behavior throughout the world. One can get a sense of this through a study of transnational environmental activist groups. In doing so, however, one must focus on the political action per se of these organizations and trace its world significance and interpret its meaning independent of the argument about relative causal weight. That is, one must be more interested in understanding the nature of certain types of political action than in ranking different agents that engage in politics. By doing so, scholars will be able to recognize that NGOs are significant in world affairs not only because they influence states but also because they affect the behavior of larger collectivities throughout the world. They do so by manipulating governing structures of global civil society.

Disseminating an Ecological Sensibility

Few images capture the environmental age as well as the sight of Greenpeace activists positioning themselves between harpoons and whales in an effort to stop the slaughter of endangered sea mammals. Since 1972, with the formal organization of Greenpeace into a transnational environmental activist group, Greenpeace has emblazoned a host of such images onto the minds of people around the world. Greenpeace activists have climbed aboard whaling ships, parachuted from the top of smokestacks, plugged up industrial discharge pipes, and floated a hot air balloon into a nuclear test site. These direct actions are media stunts, exciting images orchestrated to convey a critical perspective toward environmental issues. Numerous other organizations, including the Sea Shepherds Conservation Society, Earth-First! and Rainforest Action Network, engage in similar efforts. The dramatic aspect attracts journalists and television crews to specific actions and makes it possible for the groups themselves to distribute their own media presentations. Greenpeace, for example, has its own media facilities; within hours it can provide photographs to newspapers and circulate scripted video news spots to television stations in eighty-eight countries.[32] The overall intent is to use international mass communications to expose antiecological practices and thereby inspire audiences to change their views and behavior vis-à-vis the environment.[33]

Direct action is based on two strategies. The first is simply to bring what are often hidden instances of environmental abuse to the attention of a wide audience: harpooners kill whales on the high seas; researchers abuse Antarctica; significant species extinction takes place in the heart of the rain forest; and nuclear weapons are tested in the most deserted areas of the planet. Through television, radio, newspapers, and magazines transnational activist groups bring these hidden spots of the globe into people's everyday lives, thus enabling vast numbers of people to "bear witness" to environmental abuse.[34] Second, TEAGs engage in dangerous and dramatic actions that underline how serious they consider certain environmental threats to be. That activists take personal risks to draw attention to environmental issues highlights their indignation and the degree of their commitment to protecting the planet. Taken together, these two strategies aim to change the way vast numbers of people see the world—by dislodging traditional understandings of environmental degradation and substituting new interpretive frames. This was put particularly well by Robert Hunter, a founding member of Greenpeace, who participated in the group's early antiwhaling expeditions. For Hunter, the purpose of the effort was to overturn fundamental images about whaling: where the predominant view was of brave men battling vicious and numerous monsters of the deep, Greenpeace documented something different. As Hunter put it:

Soon, images would be going out into hundred of millions of minds around the world, a completely new set of basic images about whaling. Instead of small boats and giant whales, giant boats and small whales; instead of courage killing whales, courage saving whales; David had become Goliath, Goliath was now David; if the mythology of Moby Dick and Captain Ahab had dominated human consciousness about Leviathan for over a century, a whole new age was in the making.[35]

Raising awareness through media stunts is not primarily about changing governmental policies, although this may of course happen as state officials bear witness or are pressured by constituents to codify into law shifts in public opinion or widespread sentiment. But this is only one dimension of TEAG direct action efforts. The new age envisioned by Hunter is more than passing environmental legislation or adopting new environmental policies. Additionally, it involves convincing all actors—from governments to corporations, private organizations, and ordinary citizens—to make decisions and act in deference to environmental awareness. Smitten with such ideas, governments will, activists hope, take measures to protect the environment. When the ideas have more resonance outside government, they will shift the standards of good conduct and persuade people to act differently even though governments are not requiring them to do so. In short, TEAGs work to disseminate an ecological sensibility to shift the governing ideas that animate societies, whether institutionalized within government or not, and count on this to reverberate throughout various institutions and collectivities.

The challenge for students of international relations is to apprehend the effects of these efforts and their political significance. As already mentioned, scholars have traditionally focused on state policy and used this as the criterion for endowing NGOs with political significance. Such a focus, however, misses the broader changes initiated by NGOs beyond state behavior. To get at this dimension of change requires a more sociological orientation toward world affairs.[36] One such orientation is a so-called fluid approach.

The fluid approach has been used in the study of domestic social movements but can be adopted to analyze TEAGs.[37] It gauges the significance of activist groups by attending to cultural expressions that signal cognitive, affective, and evaluative shifts in societies. Observers are attuned to the quickening of actions and to changes in meaning and perceive that something new is happening in a wide variety of places. When analyzing the peace movement, for instance, a fluid approach recognizes that activists aim not only to convince governments to cease making war but also to create more peaceful societies. This entails propagating expressions of nonviolence, processes of conflict resolution, and, according to some, practices that are more cooperative than competitive. A fluid approach looks throughout society and interprets shifts in such expressions as a measure of the success of the peace movement.[31] Similarly, a fluid approach acknowledges that feminist groups aim at more than simply enacting legislation to protect women against gender discrimination. Additionally, they work to change patriarchal practices and degrading representations of women throughout society. Thus, as Joseph Gusfield notes, the successes of the feminist movement can be seen "where the housewife finds a new label for discontents, secretaries decide not to serve coffee and husbands are warier about using past habits of dominance."[39] A fluid approach, in other words, interprets activist efforts by noticing and analyzing, in the words of Herbert Blumer, a "cultural drift," "societal mood," or "public orientation" felt and expressed by people in diverse ways.[40] It focuses on changes in lifestyle, art, consumer habits, fashion, and so forth and sees these, as well as shifts in laws and policies, as consequences of activist efforts.

Applied to the international arena, a fluid approach enables one to appreciate, however imperfectly, changes initiated by transnational activists that occur independently of state policies. With regard to TEAGs, it allows one to observe how an environmental sensibility infiltrates deliberations at the individual, organizational, corporate, governmental, and interstate levels to shape world collective life.

Consider the following. In 1970 one in ten Canadians said the environment was worthy of being on the national agenda; twenty years later one in three felt not only that it should be on the agenda but that it was the most pressing issue facing Canada.[41] In 1981, 45 percent of those polled in a US survey said that protecting the environment was so important that "requirements and standards cannot be too high and continuing environmental improvements must be made regardless of cost"; in 1990, 74 percent supported the statement.[42] This general trend is supported around the world. In a recent Gallup poll majorities in twenty countries gave priority to safeguarding the environment even at the cost of slowing economic growth; additionally, 71 percent of the people in sixteen countries, including India, Mexico, South Korea, and Brazil, said they were willing to pay higher prices for products if it would help to protect the environment.[43]

These figures suggest a significant shift in awareness and concern about the environment over the past two decades. It is also worth noting that people have translated this sentiment into changes in behavior. In the 1960s the US Navy and Air Force used whales for target practice. Twenty-five years later an international effort costing $5 million was mounted to save three whales trapped in the ice in Alaska.[44] Two decades ago corporations produced products with little regard for their environmental impact. Today it is incumbent upon corporations to reduce negative environmental impact at the production, packaging, and distribution phases of industry.[45] When multilateral development banks and other aid institutions were established after the Second World War, environmental impact assessments were unheard of; today they are commonplace.[46] Finally, twenty years ago recycling as a concept barely existed. Today recycling is mandatory in many municipalities around the world, and in some areas voluntary recycling is a profit-making industry. (Between 1960 and 1990 the amount of municipal solid waste recovered by recycling in the United States more than quintupled.)[47] In each of these instances people are voluntarily modifying their behavior in part because of the messages publicized by activists. If one looked solely at state behavior to account for this change, one would miss a tremendous amount of significant world political action.

A final, if controversial, example of the dissemination of an ecological sensibility is the now greatly reduced practice of killing harp seal pups in northern Canada. Throughout the 1960s the annual Canadian seal hunt took place without attracting much public attention or concern. In the late 1960s and throughout the 1970s and 1980s the International Fund for Animals, Greenpeace, the Sea Shepherds. Conservation Society, and a host of smaller preservation groups saw this—in hindsight inaccurately, according to many—as a threat to the continued existence of harp seals in Canada. They brought the practice to the attention of the world, using, among other means, direct action. As a result, people around the globe, but especially in Europe, changed their buying habits and stopped purchasing products made out of the pelts. As a consequence, the market for such merchandise all but dried up with the price per skin plummeting.[48] Then, in 1983, the European Economic Community (EEC) actually banned the importation of seal pelts.[49] It is significant that the EEC did so only after consumer demand had already dropped dramatically.[50] Governmental policy, that is, may have simply been an afterthought and ultimately unnecessary. People acted in response to the messages propagated by activist groups.[51]

When Greenpeace and other TEAGs undertake direct action or follow other strategies to promote an ecological sensibility, these are the types of changes they are seeking. At times, governments respond with policy measures and changed behavior with respect to environmental issues. The failure of governments to respond, however, does not necessarily mean that the efforts of activists have been in vain. Rather, they influence understandings of good conduct throughout societies at large. They help set the boundaries of what is considered acceptable behavior.[52]

When people change their buying habits, voluntarily recycle garbage, boycott certain products, and work to preserve species, it is not necessarily because governments are breathing down their necks. Rather, they are acting out of a belief that the environmental problems involved are severe, and they wish to contribute to alleviating them. They are being "stung," as it were, by an ecological sensibility. This sting is a type of governance. It represents a mechanism of authority that can shape widespread human behavior.

Multinational Corporate Politics

In 1991 the multinational McDonald's Corporation decided to stop producing its traditional clamshell hamburger box and switch to paper packaging in an attempt to cut back on the use of disposable foam and plastic. In 1990 Uniroyal Chemical Company, the sole manufacturer of the apple-ripening agent Alar, ceased to produce and market the chemical both in the United States and abroad. Alar, the trade name for daminozide, was used on most kinds of red apples and, according to some, found to cause cancer in laboratory animals. Finally, in 1990 Starkist and

Chicken of the Sea, the two largest tuna companies, announced that they would cease purchasing tuna caught by setting nets on dolphins or by any use of drift nets; a year later Bumble Bee Tuna followed suit. Such action has contributed to protecting dolphin populations around the world.

In each of these instances environmental activist groups—both domestic and transnational—played an important role in convincing corporations to alter their practices. To be sure, each case raises controversial issues concerning the ecological wisdom of activist pressures, but it also nevertheless demonstrates the effects of TEAG efforts. In the case of McDonald's, the corporation decided to abandon its foam and plastic containers in response to prodding by a host of environmental groups. These organizations, which included the Citizens Clearinghouse for Hazardous Waste, Earth Action Network, and Kids against Pollution, organized a "send-back" campaign in which people mailed McDonald's packaging to the national headquarters. Additionally, Earth Action Network actually broke windows and scattered supplies at a McDonald's restaurant in San Francisco to protest the company's environmental policies. The Environmental Defense Fund (EDF) played a mediating role by organizing a six-month, joint task force to study ways to reduce solid waste in McDonald's eleven thousand restaurants worldwide. The task force provided McDonald's with feasible responses to activist demands.[53] What is clear from most reports on the change is that officials at McDonalds did not believe it necessarily made ecological or economic sense to stop using clamshell packaging but that they bent to activist pressure.[54]

Uniroyal Chemical Company ceased producing Alar after groups such as Ralph Nader's Public Interest Research Group (PIRG) and the Natural Resources Defense Council (NRDC) organized a massive public outcry about the use of the product on apples in the USA and abroad. In 1989 NRDC produced a study that found that Alar created cancer risks 240 times greater than those declared safe by the US Environmental Protection Agency (EPA).[55] This was publicized on CBS's *60 Minutes* and led to critical stories in numerous newspapers and magazines. Moreover, activists pressured supermarket chains to stop selling apples grown with Alar and pressured schools to stop serving Alar-sprayed apples. The effects were dramatic. The demand for apples in general shrank significantly because of the scare, lowering prices well below the break-even level.[56] This led to a loss of $135 million for Washington State apple growers alone.[57] Effects such as these and continued pressure by activist groups convinced Uniroyal to cease production of the substance not only in the USA but overseas as well. Like McDonalds, Uniroyal changed its practices not for economic reasons nor to increase business nor because it genuinely felt Alar was harmful. Rather, it capitulated to activist pressure. In fact, there is evidence from nonindustry sources suggesting that Alar did not pose the level of threat publicized by activists.[58]

Finally, in the case of dolphin-free tuna, Earth Island Institute (EII) and other organizations launched an international campaign in 1985 to stop all drift-net and purse seine fishing by tuna fleets. For unknown reasons, tuna in the Eastern Tropical Pacific Ocean swim under schools of dolphins. For years tuna fleets have set their nets on dolphins or entangled dolphins in drift nets as a way to catch tuna. While some fleets still use these strategies, the three largest tuna companies have ceased doing so. TEAGs were at the heart of this change. Activists waged a boycott against all canned tuna, demonstrated at stockholders' meetings, and rallied on the docks of the Tuna Boat Association in San Diego. Furthermore, EII assisted in the production of the film *Where Have All the Dolphins Gone?* which was shown throughout the United States and abroad; it promoted the idea of "dolphin-safe" tuna labels to market environmentally sensitive brands; and it enlisted Heinz, the parent company of Starkist, to take an active role in stopping the slaughter of dolphins by all tuna companies. Its efforts, along with those of Greenpeace, Friends of the Earth, and others, were crucial to promoting dolphin-safe tuna fishing.[59] One result of these efforts is that dolphin kills associated with tuna fishing in 1993 numbered fewer than 5,000. This represents one-third the mortality rate of 1992, when 15,470 dolphins died in nets, and less than one-twentieth of the number in 1989, when over 100,000 dolphins died at the hands of tuna fleets.[60] These numbers represent the effects of activist efforts. Although governments did eventually adopt domestic dolphin conservation policies and negotiated partial international standards to reduce dolphin kills, the first such actions came into force only in late 1992 with the United Nations moratorium on drift nets. Moreover, the first significant actions against purse seine fishing, which more directly affects dolphins, came in June 1994 with the United States International Dolphin Conservation Act.[61] As with the Canadian seal pup hunt, government action in the case of tuna fisheries largely codified changes that were already taking place.

In each instance, activist groups did not direct their efforts at governments. They did not target politicians; nor did they organize constituent pressuring. Rather, they focused on corporations themselves. Through protest, research, exposés, orchestrating public outcry, and organizing joint consultations, activists won corporate promises to bring their practices in line with environmental concerns. The levers of power in these instances were found in the economic realm of collective life rather than in the strictly governmental realm. Activists understand that the economic realm, while not the center of traditional notions of politics, nevertheless furnishes channels for effecting widespread changes in behavior; they recognize that the economic realm is a form of governance and can be manipulated to alter collective practices.

Perhaps the best example of how activist groups, especially transnational ones, enlist the economic dimensions of governance into their enterprises is the effort to establish environmental oversight of corporations. In September 1989 a coalition of environmental, investor, and church interests, known as the Coalition for Environmentally Responsible Economies (CERES), met in New York City to introduce a ten-point environmental code of conduct for corporations. One month later CERES, along with the Green Alliance, launched a similar effort in the United Kingdom. The aim was to establish criteria for auditing the environmental performance of large domestic and multinational industries. The code called on companies to, among other things, minimize the release of pollutants, conserve nonrenewable resources through efficient use and planning, utilize environmentally safe and sustainable energy sources, and consider demonstrated environmental commitment as a factor in appointing members to the board of directors. Fourteen environmental organizations, including TEAGs such as Friends of the Earth and the International Alliance for Sustainable Agriculture, publicize the CERES Principles (formerly known as the Valdez Principles, inspired by the Exxon *Valdez* oil spill) and enlist corporations to pledge compliance. What is significant from an international perspective is that signatories include at least one Fortune 500 company and a number of multinational corporations. Sun Company, General Motors, Polaroid, and a host of other multinational corporations have pledged compliance or are at least seriously considering doing so. Because these companies operate in numerous countries, their actions have transnational effects.

The CERES Principles are valuable for a number of reasons. In the case of pension funds, the code is being used to build shareholder pressure on companies to improve their environmental performance. Investors can use it as a guide to determine which companies practice socially responsible investment. Environmentalists use the code as a measuring device to praise or criticize corporate behavior. Finally, the Principles are used to alert college graduates on the job market about corporate compliance with the code and thus attempt to make environmental issues a factor in one's choice of a career. Taken together, these measures force some degree of corporate accountability by establishing mechanisms of governance to shape corporate behavior. To be sure, they have not turned businesses into champions of environmentalism, nor are they as effectual as mechanisms available to governments. At work, however, is activist discovery and manipulation of economic means of power.[62]

Via the CERES Principles and other forms of pressure, activists thus influence corporate behavior.[63] McDonald's, Uniroyal, and others have not been changing their behavior because governments are breathing down their necks. Rather, they are voluntarily adopting different ways of producing and distributing products. This is not to say that their actions are more environmentally sound than before they responded to activists or that their attempt to minimize environmental dangers is sincerely motivated. As mentioned, environmental activist groups do not have a monopoly on ecological wisdom, nor is corporate "greening" necessarily well intentioned.[64] Nonetheless, the multinational corporate politics of transnational groups are having an effect on the way industries do business. And to the degree that these enterprises are involved in issues of widespread public concern that cross state boundaries, activist pressure must be understood as a form of world politics.

Empowering Local Communities

For decades TEAGs have worked to conserve wildlife in the developing world. Typically, this has involved people in the First World working in the Third World to restore and guard the environment. First World TEAGs—ones headquartered in the North—believed that Third World people could not appreciate the value of wildlife or were simply too strapped by economic pressures to conserve nature. Consequently, environmental organizations developed, financed, and operated programs in the field with little local participation or input.

While such efforts saved a number of species from extinction and set in motion greater concern for Third World environmental protection, on the whole they were unsuccessful at actually preserving species and their habitats from degradation and destruction.[65] A key reason for this was that they attended more to the needs of plants and especially animals than to those of the nearby human communities. Many of the earth's most diverse and biologically rich areas are found in parts of the world where the poorest peoples draw their livelihood from the land. As demographic and economic constraints grow tighter, these people exploit otherwise renewable resources in an attempt merely to survive.[66] Ecological sustainability in these regions, then, must involve improving the quality of life of the rural poor through projects that integrate the management of natural resources with grassroots economic development.

Often after having supported numerous failed projects, a number of TEAGs have come to subscribe to this understanding and undertake appropriate actions. World Wildlife Fund (WWF) or World Wide Fund for Nature, as it is known outside English-speaking countries, is an example of such an organization. WWF is a conservation group dedicated to protecting endangered wildlife and wildlands worldwide. It originated in 1961 as a small organization in Switzerland, making grants to finance conservation efforts in various countries. Over the past thirty years it has grown into a full-scale global environmental organization with offices in over twenty countries. Within the past decade, WWF has established a wildlands and human needs program, a method of conservation to be applied to all WWF projects linking human economic well-being with environmental protection. It structures a game management system in Zambia, for example, which involves local residents in antipoaching and conservation efforts, and the channeling of revenues from tourism and safaris back into the neighboring communities that surround the preserves.[67] It informs a WWF-initiated Kilum Mountain project in the Cameroon that is developing nurseries for reforestation, reintroducing indigenous crops, and disseminating information about the long-term effects of environmentally harmful practices.[68] Finally, it is operative in a project in St Lucia, where WWF has lent technical assistance to set up sanitary communal waste disposal sites, improved marketing of fish to reduce overfishing, and protected mangroves from being used for fuel by planting fast-growing fuel-wood trees.[69] WWF is not alone in these efforts. The New Forests Project, the Association for Research and Environmental Aid (AREA), the Ladakh Project, and others undertake similar actions.

In these kinds of efforts, TEAGs are not trying to galvanize public pressure aimed at changing governmental policy or directly lobbying state officials; indeed, their activity takes place far from the halls of congresses, parliaments, and executive offices. Rather, TEAGs work with ordinary people in diverse regions of the world to try to enhance local capability to carry out sustainable development projects. The guiding logic is that local people must be enlisted in protecting their own environments and that their efforts will then reverberate through wider circles of social interaction to affect broader aspects of world environmental affairs.[70]

Independent of the content of specific projects, the efforts of TEAGs almost always bring local people together.[71] They organize people into new forms of social interaction, and this makes for a more tightly woven web of associational life. To the degree that this is attentive to ecological issues, it partially fashions communities into ecologically sensitive social agents. This enables them more effectively to resist outside forces that press them to exploit their environments, and it helps them assume a more powerful role in determining affairs when interacting with outside institutions and processes. To paraphrase Michael Bratton, hands-on eco-development projects stimulate and release popular energies in support of community goals.[72] This strengthens a community's ability to determine its own affairs and influence events outside its immediate domain.

The dynamics of environmental destruction often do not originate at the local or state level.

Poor people who wreck their environments are generally driven to do so by multiple external pressures. Embedded within regional, national, and ultimately global markets, living under political regimes riven by rivalries and controlled by leadership that is not popularly based, penetrated by MNCs, and often at the mercy of multilateral development banks, local people respond to the consumptive practices and development strategies of those living in distant cities or countries.[73] Once empowered, however, communities can respond to these pressures more successfully. For example, since 1985 tens of thousands of peasants, landless laborers, and tribal people have demonstrated against a series of dams in the Narmada Valley that critics believe will cause severe environmental and social damage. The Sardar Sarovar projects are intended to produce hydroelectric energy for the states of Gujarat, Madhya Pradesh, and Maharashtra and have been supported by the governments of these states, the Indian government, and until recently the World Bank. Resistance started locally, but since 1985 it has spread with the formation by local and transnational groups of an activist network that operates both inside India and abroad to thwart the project. While the final outcome has yet to be determined, local communities have already redefined the debate about the environmental efficacy of large dam projects, as well as those having to do with displacement and rehabitation. As a result, the Indian government, the World Bank, and other aid agencies now find themselves profoundly hesitant about future dam projects; indeed, in 1993 the Indian government withdrew its request for World Bank funding to support the Sardar Sarovar project.[74] Finally, local communities have served notice, through their insistence that they will drown before they let themselves be displaced, that they are better organized to resist other large-scale, external environmental and developmental designs.[75]

Local empowerment affects wider arenas of social life in a positive, less reactive fashion when communities reach out to actors in other regions, countries, and continents. Indeed, the solidification of connections between TEAGs and local communities itself elicits responses from regional, national, and international institutions and actors. This connection is initially facilitated when TEAGs that have offices in the developed world transfer money and resources to Third World communities. In 1989, for example, northern NGOs distributed $6.4 billion to developing countries, which is roughly 12 percent of all public and private development aid.[76] Much of this aid went to local NGOs and helped to empower local communities.[77]

This pattern is part of a broader shift in funding from First World governments. As local NGOs become better able to chart the economic and environmental destinies of local communities, First World donors look to them for expertise and capability. For instance, in 1975 donor governments channeled $100 million through local NGOs; in 1985 the figure had risen to $1.1 billion.[78] This represents a shift on the part of Official Development Assistance (ODA) countries. In 1975 they donated only 0.7 percent of their funding through Third World NGOs; in 1985 the figure rose to 3.6 percent.[79] This pattern is further accentuated when First World governments turn to transnational NGOs in the North for similar expertise. According to a 1989 OECD report, by the early 1980s virtually all First World countries adopted a system of co-financing projects implemented by their national NGOs. "Official contributions to NGOs' activities over the decades have been on an upward trend, amounting to $2.2 billion in 1987 and representing 5 percent of total ODA," according to the report.[80] While much of this was funneled through voluntary relief organizations such as Catholic Relief Services, overall there has been an upgrading in the status of NGOs concerned with development and environmental issues.[81]

Increased aid to local NGOs has obvious effects on local capability. It enhances the ability of communities to take a more active and effectual role in their economic and environmental destinies. The effects are not limited, however, to a more robust civil society. Many of the activities and certainly the funding directly challenge or at least intersect with state policies; thus, governments are concerned about who controls any foreign resources that come into the country. When funds go to NGOs, state activity can be frustrated. This is most clear in places like Kenya and Malaysia, where environmental NGOs are part of broader opposition groups. In these instances outside aid to local groups may be perceived as foreign intervention trying to diminish state power. At a lesser degree of challenge, outside support may simply minimize the control government exercises over its territory. Empowering local communities diminishes state authority by reinforcing local loyalties at the expense of national identity. At a minimum, this threatens government attempts at nation building. Put most broadly, TEAGs pose a challenge to state sovereignty and more generally redefine the realm of the state itself. Thus, while TEAGs may see themselves working outside the domain of the state and focusing on civil society per se, their actions in fact have a broader impact and interfere with state politics.

Nevertheless, it would be misleading to think about TEAGs as traditional interest groups. Rather, with their hands-on development/environmental efforts TEAGs attempt to work independent of governmental activity at the level of communities themselves. That their activities end up involving them in the political universe of the state is indicative of the porous boundary between local communities and the state or, more broadly, between the state and civil society. It does not mean that activist efforts in civil society gain political relevance only when they intersect state activities.[82]

The grassroots efforts of transnational environmental activists aim to engage people at the level at which they feel the most immediate effects—their own local environmental and economic conditions. At this level, TEAGs try to use activism itself, rooted in the actual experience of ordinary people, as a form of governance. It can alter the way people interact with each other and their environment, literally to change the way they live their lives. To the degree that such efforts have ramifications for wider arenas of social interaction—including states and other actors—they have world political significance.

World Civic Politics

The predominant way to think about NGOs in world affairs is as transnational interest groups. They are politically relevant insofar as they affect state policies and interstate behavior. In this article I have argued that TEAGs, a particular type of NGO, have political relevance beyond this. They work to shape the way vast numbers of people throughout the world act toward the environment using modes of governance that are part of global civil society.

Greenpeace, Sea Shepherds Conservation Society, and Earth First!, for example, work to disseminate an ecological sensibility. It is a sensibility not restricted to governments nor exclusively within their domain of control. Rather, it circulates throughout all areas of collective life. To the degree this sensibility sways people, it acts as a form of governance. It defines the boundaries of good conduct and thus animates how a host of actors—from governments to voluntary associations and ordinary citizens—think about and act in reference to the environment.

A similar dynamic is at work when TEAGs pressure multinational corporations. These business enterprises interact with states, to be sure, and state governments can restrict their activities to a significant degree. They are not monopolized by states, however, and thus their realm of operation is considerably beyond state control. Due to the reach of multinational corporations into environmental processes, encouraging them to become "green" is another instance of using the governing capacities outside formal government to shape widespread activities.

Finally, when TEAGs empower local communities, they are likewise not focused primarily on states. Rather, by working to improve people's day-to-day economic lives in ecologically sustainable ways, they bypass state apparatuses and activate governance that operates at the community level. As numerous communities procure sustainable development practices, the efforts of TEAGs take effect. Moreover, as changed practices at this level translate up through processes and mechanisms that are regional, national, and global in scope, the efforts by TEAGs influence the activities of larger collectivities, which in turn shape the character of public life.

I suggested that the best way to think about these activities is through the category of "world civic politics." When TEAGs work through transnational networks associated with cultural, social, and economic life, they are enlisting forms of governance that are civil as opposed to official or state constituted in character. Civil, in this regard, refers to the quality of interaction that takes place above the individual and below the state yet across national boundaries. The concept of world civic politics clarifies how the forms of governance in global civil society are distinct from the instrumentalities of state rule.

At the most foundational level, states govern through legal means that are supported by the threat or use of force. To be sure, all states enjoy a minimum of loyalty from their citizens and administrate through a variety of nonlegal and noncoercive means. Ultimately, however, the authority to govern per se rests on the claim to a monopoly over legitimate coercive power. By contrast, civic power has no legally sanctioned status and cannot be enforced through the legitimate use of violence. It rests on persuasion and more constitutive employment of power in which people change their practices because they have come to understand the world in a way that promotes certain actions over others or because they operate in an environment that induces them to do so. Put differently, civic power is the forging of voluntary and customary practices into mechanisms that govern public affairs. When TEAGs disseminate an ecological sensibility, pressure corporations, or empower local communities, they are exercising civic power across national boundaries. They are turning formerly nonpolitical practices into instruments of governance; they are, that is, politicizing global civil society.

The distinction between state and civic power rests on the more fundamental differentiation between the state and civil society as spheres of collective life. According to Hegel, the thinker most associated with contrasting the two, civil society is a sphere or "moment" of political order in which individuals engage in free association. Although it is an arena of particular needs, private interests, and divisiveness, it is also one in which citizens can come together to realize joint aims.[83] As it is more generally understood, civil society is the arena beyond the individual.[84]

It is there that people engage in spontaneous, customary, and nonlegalistic forms of association with the intention of pursuing "great aims in common," as Tocqueville put it.[85] The state, on the other hand, is a complex network of governmental institutions—including the military, the bureaucracy, and executive offices—that together constitute a legal or constitutional order. This order is undergirded by formal, official authority and aims to administer and control a given territory.[86]

While distinct analytically, civil society is never wholly autonomous or completely separate from the activities of states. As Gramsci and others have argued, state rule often permeates civil society to consolidate power. In these instances, the state and civil society are practically indistinguishable as schools, councils, universities, churches, and even activist groups are regulated, monitored, or run by the state itself.[87] At other times, societies are less saturated by the presence of the state and a robust civil society enjoys a significant degree of independence. But even here, it is inaccurate to assume a sharp distinction. The boundaries of the state are always ill defined and essentially amorphous, overlapping with civil society itself.[88] Because the boundaries between the state and civil society are elusive, porous, and mobile, when actions take place in one realm—although they have a distinct quality of efficacy about them—they have consequences for the other.

The same is true at the global level, and the notion of world civic politics is not meant to obscure this. While global civil society is analytically a distinct sphere of activity, it is shaped by, and in turn shapes, the state system. States' actions greatly influence the content and significance of economic, social, and cultural practices throughout the world and vice versa. While not emphasized above, when TEAGs disseminate an ecological sensibility, pressure corporations, or work to empower local communities, their efforts are neither immune from nor wholly independent of state activity. In each instance, activist efforts intersect with the domain of the state even if this is not the initial intention.[89] What is absolutely essential to recognize, however, is that it is not the entanglements and overlaps with states and the state system that make efforts in global civil society "political." Transnational activism does not simply become politically relevant when it intersects with state behavior. Rather, its political character consists in the ability to use diverse mechanisms of governance to alter and shape widespread behavior. That these networks happen to imbricate the domain of states reveals more about the contours and texture of the playing field within which activists and others operate than about the character of politics itself.

At stake in this analysis, then, is the concept of world politics. Implicit is the understanding that politics in its most general sense concerns the interface of power and what Cicero called *res publico*, the public domain.[90] It is the employment of means to order, direct, and manage human behavior in matters of common concern and involvement. Generically, at least, this activity has nothing to do with government or the state. Government, on the one hand, is an institution that coordinates and shapes public life, by virtue of its authority to make decisions binding on the whole community. The state, on the other hand, is a particular modality of government that emerged in the modern period and came to be associated with political rule itself.[91] Possessing as it does military, administrative, legislative, and juridical bodies, the state has become the most able mechanism to reach into and affect the lives of vast numbers of people. Notwithstanding the extensive governing capability of government and the state, however, neither exhausts the realm of the political. Other actors govern public affairs; other actors shape, direct, and order widespread practices regarding issues of public involvement.[92] The concept of world civic politics aims to clarify conceptually the political character of governing efforts not associated with the state. It specifies the quality of governance activists employ and distinguishes it from the instrumentalities of state rule.

A final note on the conceptual boundaries of world civic politics: a focus on the civil dimension of world collective life is not meant to obscure the central importance of interstate relations in world affairs. States are the main actors in the international system and will remain so for the indefinite future. In this regard, the concept of world civic politics is not meant to replace or subsume interstate relations. Rather, it is offered as a way of augmenting scholarly understanding. It must be considered alongside state-centered analyses. For this reason, it is still worthwhile measuring and interpreting the lobbying efforts of TEAGs and refining scholarly comprehension of NGO influence on states. Nonetheless, a sensitivity to world civic politics makes clear that this cannot be done to the exclusion of the more general societal efforts employed by TEAGs and NGOs—a failure to take note of the world civic efforts of nonstate actors leaves one with only a partial picture of world affairs and thus presents an incomplete understanding of world politics itself.

Notes

The author wishes to thank the John D. and Catherine T. MacArthur Foundation and the School of International Service at the American University for generous financial support for this project. The author also wishes to thank Daniel Deudney, Richard Falk, Nicholas Onuf, Leslie Thiele, and Michael Walzer for helpful comments on earlier drafts.

1. See e.g. David Forsythe, *Human Rights and World Politics*, 2nd edn. (Lincoln: University of Nebraska Press, 1989); Kathryn Sikkink, "Human Rights Issue-Networks in Latin America," *International Organization*, 47 (Summer 1993); Robert Goldman, "International Humanitarian Law: Americas Watch's Experience in Monitoring Internal Armed Conflict," *American University Journal of International Law and Policy*, 9 (Fall 1993).

2. See e.g. Kevin Stairs and Peter Taylor, "Non-Governmental Organizations and the Legal Protection of the Oceans: A Case Study," and Barbara Bramble and Gareth Porter, "Non-Governmental Organizations and the Making of US International Environmental Policy," both in Andrew Hurrell and Benedict Kingsbury (eds.), *The International Politics of the Environment* (Oxford: Clarendon Press, 1992); Lee Kimble, "The Role of Non-Governmental Organizations in Antarctic Affairs," in Christopher Joyner and Sudhir Chopra (eds), *The Antarctica Legal Regime* (Dordrecht, Netherlands: Martinus Nijhoff, 1988); Gareth Porter and Janet Brown, *Global Environmental Politics* (Boulder, Colo.: Westview Press, 1991); P. J. Sands, "The Role of Non-Governmental Organizations in Enforcing International Environmental Law," in W. E. Butler (ed.), *Control over Compliance with International Law* (Dordrecht, Netherlands: Martinus Nijhoff, 1991).

3. See e.g. Thomas Rochon, *Mobilizing for Peace: The Antinuclear Movements in Western Europe* (Princeton: Princeton University Press, 1988); David Cortright, *Peace Works: The Citizen's Role in Ending the Cold War* (Boulder, Colo.: Westview Press, 1993).

4. On the concept of "global civil society," see Richard Falk, *Explorations at the Edge of Time* (Philadelphia: Temple University Press, 1992); and Ronnie Lipschultz, "Restructuring World

Politics: The Emergence of Global Civil Society," *Millennium*, 21 (Winter 1992).

5. There is no single, static definition of civil society. The term has a long and continually evolving, if not contestable, conceptual history. For an appreciation of the historical roots of the term and its usage in various contexts, see Jean Cohen and Andrew Arato, *Civil Society and Political Theory* (Cambridge, Mass.: MIT Press, 1992); John Keane, "Despotism and Democracy: The Origins and Development of the Distinction between Civil Society and the State, 1750–1850," in Keane (ed.), *Civil Society and the State: New European Perspectives* (London: Verso, 1988).

6. I follow a Hegelian understanding of civil society, which includes the economy within its domain. Later formulations, most notably those offered by Gramsci and Parsons, introduce a three-part model that differentiates civil society from both the state and the economy. See Talcott Parsons, *The System of Modern Societies* (Englewood Cliffs, NJ: Prentice-Hall, 1971); Antonio Gramsci, *Prison Notebooks* (New York: International Publishers, 1971). For an extensive argument to exclude the economy from civil society, see Cohen and Arato (n. 5).

7. Alberto Melucci, "The Symbolic Challenge of Contemporary Movements," *Social Research*, 52 (Winter 1985); Jurgen Habermas, "Introduction," in Habermas (ed.), *Observations of "The Spiritual Situation of the Age*," trans. Andrew Buchwalter (Cambridge, Mass.: MIT Press, 1985); idem, "Social Movements," *Telos*, no. 49 (Fall 1981); Claus Offe, "Challenging the Boundaries of Institutional Politics: Social Movements since the 1960s," in Charles Maier (ed.), *Changing Boundaries of the Political* (Cambridge: Cambridge University Press, 1987). See generally Russell Dalton and Manfred Kuechler (eds), *Challenging the Political Order: New Social and Political Movements in Western Democracies* (New York: Oxford University Press, 1990).

8. Alain Touraine, *Anti-Nuclear Protest* (Cambridge: Cambridge University Press, 1983); Fritjof Capra and Charlene Spretnak, *Green Politics* (London: Hutchinson, 1984); Joyce Gelb, "Feminism and Political Action," in Dalton and Kuechler (n. 7).

9. Harry Boyte, "The Pragmatic Ends of Popular Politics," in Craig Calhoun (ed.), *Habermas and the Public Sphere* (Cambridge, Mass.: MIT Press, 1992); Richard Shaull, *Heralds of a New Reformation: The Poor of South and North America* (New York: Orbis Books, 1984); Anil Agarwal, "Ecological Destruction and the Emerging Patterns of Poverty and People's Protests in Rural India," *Social Action*, 35 (January–March 1985). See generally Alan During, "Action at the Grassroots: Fighting Poverty and Environmental Decline," *Worldwatch Paper 88* (Washington, DC: Worldwatch Institute, 1989).

10. In these cases, groups could not politicize existing civil societies but actually had to create them. See Adam Michnik, *Letters from Prison and Other Essays*, trans. Maya Latynski (Berkeley: University of California Press, 1985); Václav Haval, *Open Letters: Selected Writings, 1965–1990*, ed. Paul Wilson (New York: Alfred Knopf, 1991).

11. The danger of engaging the state in places like Poland provided the impetus to create horizontal associations. This was the central idea behind the Polish "self-limiting revolution," which recognized the power of the state with its Soviet support and hence the improbability of toppling it. See Michnik (n. 10).

12. In 1992 the budgets of Greenpeace International and World Wildlife Fund were roughly $100 million and $200 million, respectively. UNEP's budget was roughly $75 million.

13. In 1994 both Greenpeace and World Wildlife Fund each had over six million members.

14. For a comprehensive study of environmental NGOs in the developing world, with important references to transnational ones, see Julie Fisher, *The Road from Rio: Sustainable Development and the Nongovernmental Movement in the Third World* (Westport, Conn.: Praeger 1993).

15. In 1967, for example, General Motors had production facilities in 24 countries and total

sales of $20 billion. This total was greater than the GNP of all but 14 of the 124 members of the UN at the time. Also in 1967 Standard Oil of New Jersey had facilities in 45 countries and total sales of $13.3 billion. See Gerald Sumida, "Transnational Movements and Economic Structures," in Cyril Black and Richard Falk (eds), *The Future of the International Legal Order* (Princeton: Princeton University Press, 1972), iv. 553.

16. See e.g. George Modelski, "The Corporation in World Society," *Year Book of World Affairs 1968* (New York: Praeger, 1968); Werner Feld, *Nongovernmental Forces and World Politics: A Study of Business, Labor and Political Groups* (New York: Praeger, 1972); Abdul A. Said and Luiz Simmons (eds), *The New Sovereigns: Multinational Corporations as World Powers* (Englewood Cliffs, NJ: Prentice-Hall, 1975).

17. Robert Angell, *Peace on the March: Transnational Participation* (New York: Van Nostrand Reinhold, 1969); Robert Keohane and Joseph Nye (eds), *Transnational Relations and World Politics* (Cambridge, Mass.: Harvard University Press, 1972), esp. essays by J. Bowyer Bell, Ivan Vallier, and Donald Warwock; Seyom Brown, *New Forces in World Politics* (Washington, DC: Brookings Institution, 1974); Richard Mansbach, Yale Ferguson, and Donald Lampert, *The Web of World Politics: Nonstate Actors in the Global System* (Englewood Cliffs, NJ: Prentice-Hall, 1976).

18. For discussions of the world political system with special emphasis on transnational activity, see Johan Galtung, *The True Worlds: A Transnational Perspective* (New York: Free Press, 1980).

19. For an overview of the debate, see Ray Maghroori and Bennett Ramberg (eds), *Globalism versus Realism: International Relations' Third Debate* (Boulder, Colo.: Westview Press, 1982); and Kalevi J. Holsti, *The Dividing Discipline: Hegemony and Diversity in International Theory* (Boston: Allen and Unwin, 1985).

20. Robert Gilpin, "The Politics of Transnational Economic Relations," in Keohane and Nye (n. 17).

21. Kenneth N. Waltz, *Theory of International Politics* (New York: Random House, 1979).

22. Michael Sullivan, "Transnationalism, Power Politics and the Realities of the Present System," in Maghroori and Ramberg (n. 19).

23. See e.g. Werner Feld and Robert Jordan, *International Organizations: A Comparative Approach* (New York: Praeger, 1983); and Harold Jacobson, *Networks of Interdependence: International Organizations and the Global Political System* (New York: Alfred Knopf, 1984).

24. The term "sovereignty at bay" comes from the title of the 1971 book by Raymond Vernon (New York: Basic Books). It is important to note that Vernon was not a proponent of the transnationalist challenge, even though the title of his book provided a catchphrase to encapsulate the host of arguments advanced by its proponents. See Raymond Vernon, "*Sovereignty at Bay*: Ten Years After," *International Organization*, 35 (Summer 1981).

25. In the words of John Ruggie, it could be said that the debate died down because scholars studied NGOs with an eye toward "institutional substitutability." If NGOs cannot substitute for the state as an institutional entity, they become politically irrelevant. Ruggie argues that such a mind-set bleaches out much of the phenomena responsible for long-term political change. See John Gerard Ruggie, "Territoriality and Beyond: Problematizing Modernity in International Relations," *International Organization*, 47 (Winter 1993), 143.

26. See K. J. Holsti, "Mirror, Mirror on the Wall, Which Are the Fairest Theories of All," *International Studies Quarterly*, 37 (September 1987); and Yosef Lapid, "The Third Debate: On the Prospects of International Theory in a Post-Positivist Era," *International Studies Quarterly*, 33 (September 1989). For one of the more provocative books to emerge from reflection on the third debate, see R. B. J. Walker, *Inside/Outside: International Relations as Political Theory* (Cambridge: Cambridge University Press, 1993).

27. James Rosenau, *Turbulence in World Politics* (Princeton: Princeton University Press, 1990).

28. R. B. J. Walker, *One World/Many Worlds* (Boulder, Colo.: Lynne Rienner, 1988).

29. Falk (n. 4).

30. The very term "nongovernmental organization" betrays a statecentric understanding of politics.

31. This is not to imply that studies of the influence of NGOs on states are unnecessary. There is still much to understand regarding the extent to which NGOs influence governments and the quality of their lobbying efforts. A focus on world civic politics, then, is not meant to supplant a statecentric notion of international politics so much as to augment it.

32. Michael Harwood, "Daredevils for the Environment," *New York Times Magazine*, 2 October 1988, 7. Also confirmed in private interviews at the time. See also Clive Davidson, "How Greenpeace Squeezed onto Satellite Link," *New Scientist*, 135 (July 1992), 20.

33. For discussions on the media-directed dimension of ecological political action, see Rik Scarce, *Eco-Warriors: Understanding the Radical Environmental Movement* (Chicago: Noble Press, 1990); David Day, *The Environmental Wars* (New York: Ballantine Books, 1989); Robert Hunter, *Warriors of the Rainbow: A Chronicle of the Greenpeace Movement* (New York: Holt, Rinehart and Winston, 1979); Walter Truett Anderson, *Reality Isn't What It Used to Be* (San Francisco: Harper and Row, 1990), chap. 7.

34. Bearing witness is a type of political action that originated with the Quakers. It requires that one who has observed a morally objectionable act (in this case an ecologically destructive one) must either take action to prevent further injustice or stand by and attest to its occurrence; one may not turn away in ignorance. For bearing witness as used by Greenpeace, see Hunter (n. 33); Michael Brown and John May, *The Greenpeace Story* (Ontario: Prentice-Hall Canada, 1989); Greenpeace, "Fifteen Years at the Front Lines," *Greenpeace Examiner*, 11 (October–December 1986).

35. Hunter (n. 33), 229.

36. Sociological perspectives on world politics have proliferated over the past few years. See e.g. Leslie Sklair, *Sociology of the Global System* (Baltimore: Johns Hopkins University Press, 1991); and David Jacobson, "The States System in the Age of Rights," Ph.D. diss. (Princeton University, 1991).

37. Joseph Gusfield, "Social Movements and Social Change: Perspectives on Linearity and Fluidity," in Louis Kriesberg (ed.), *Research in Social Movements, Conflicts and Change* (Greenwich, Conn.: JAI Press, 1981), iv. 326.

38. Paul Joseph, *Peace Politics* (Philadelphia: Temple University Press, 1993), 147–51; Johan Galtung, "The Peace Movement: An Exercise in Micro-Macro Linkages," *International Social Science Journal*, 40 (August 1989), 377–82.

39. Gusfield (n. 37), 326.

40. Blumer, "Social Movements," in Barry McLaughlin (ed.), *Studies in Social Movements: A Social Psychological Perspective* (New York: Free Press, 1969).

41. Linda Starke, *Signs of Hope: Working toward Our Common Future* (New York: Oxford University Press, 1990), 2, 105.

42. Mathew Wald, "Guarding the Environment: A World of Challenges," *New York Times*, 22 April 1990, A1.

43. George Gallup International Institute, "The Health of the Planet Survey," quoted in "Bush Out of Step, Poll Finds," *Terra Viva: The Independent Daily of the Earth Summit* (Rio de Janiero), 3 June 1992, 5. See generally Riley Dunlap, George Gallup, Jr., and Alec Gallup, "Of Global Concern: Results of the Health of the Planet Survey," *Environment*, 53 (November 1993).

44. David Day, *The Whale War* (San Francisco: Sierra Club Books, 1987), 157. For a critical view of Operation Breakout, see Tom Rose, *Freeing the Whales: How the Media Created the World's Greatest Non-Event* (New York: Birch Lane Press, 1989).

45. See Council on Economic Priorities, *Shopping for a Better World* (New York: Council on Economic Priorities, 1988); Cynthia Pollock Shea, "Doing Well by Doing Good," *World-Watch*, 2 (November–December 1989).

According to a 1991 Gallup poll, 28 percent of the US public claimed to have "boycotted a company's products because of its record on the environment," and, according to Cambridge Reports, in 1990, 50 percent of respondents said that they were "avoiding the purchase of products by a company that pollutes the environment"—an increase of 18 percent since 1987. Quoted in Riley Dunlap, "Public Opinion in the 1980s: Clear Consensus, Ambiguous Commitment," *Environment*, 33 (October 1991), 36. See more generally Bruce Smart, *Beyond Compliance: A New Industry View of the Environment* (Washington, DC: World Resources Institute, 1992).

46. Jeremy Warford and Zeinab Partow, "Evolution of the World Bank's Environmental Policy," *Finance and Development*, no. 26 (December 1989).

47. US Bureau of the Census, *Statistical Abstract of the United States, 1993* (Washington, DC: Bureau of the Census, 1993), 227, table 372.

48. The average price per seal pup skin dropped from $23.09 in 1979 to $10.15 in 1983. See George Wenzel, *Animal Rights, Human Rights* (Toronto: University of Toronto Press, 1991), 124, table 6.12.

49. This led to a further drop in price. By 1985 the price per skin had dropped to $6.99. See n. 48.

50. Wenzel (n. 48), 52–3; idem, 'Baby Harp Seals Spared," *Oceans*, 21 (March–April 1988); see generally Day (n. 33), 60–4.

51. This example also demonstrates that environmental activists are not always accurate in assessing environmental threats and guaranteeing the ecological soundness of the sensibility they wish to impart. There is no evidence that harp seals were ever an endangered species. This is particularly troubling because the activities of Greenpeace, IFAW, and others produced severe social dislocation and hardship for communities as far away as Greenland, Iceland, and the Faroe Islands, as well as in the coastal communities of Newfoundland and Baffin Island. See Oran Young, *Arctic Politics: Conflict and Cooperation in the Circumpolar*

North (Hanover, NH: University Press of New England, 1992), 128; J. Allen, "Anti-Sealing as an Industry," *Journal of Political Economy*, 87 (April 1979); Leslie Spence et al., "The Not So Peaceful World of Greenpeace," *Forbes*, 11 November 1991; Wenzel (n. 46).

52. On the issue of good conduct, see Gary Orren, "Beyond Self-Interest," in Robert Reich (ed.), *The Power of Public Ideas* (Cambridge, Mass.: Harvard University Press, 1988).

53. Bramble and Porter (n. 2), 238; Porter and Brown (n. 2), 61; Michael Parrish, "McDonald's to Do Away with Foam Packages," *Los Angeles Times*, 2 November 1990, A1.

54. "McDonalds Admits to Bowing to Ill-Informed Opinion on Polystyrene," *British Plastics and Rubber* (January 1991), 35; Phyllis Berman, "McDonald's Caves In," *Forbes*, 4 February 1991; Brian Quinton, "The Greening of McDonalds," *Restaurants and Institutions*, 100 (December 1990), 28; John Holusha, "Packaging and Public Image: McDonald's Fills a Big Order," *New York Times*, 2 November 1990.

55. Natural Resources Defense Council, "Intolerable Risk: Pesticides in Our Children's Food: Summary," *A Report by the Natural Resources Defense Council* (New York, 27 February 1989).

56. Timothy Egan, "Apple Growers Bruised and Bitter after Alar Scare," *New York Times*, 9 July 1991, A1.

57. Michael Fumento, *Science under Seige: Balancing Technology and the Environment* (New York: William Morrow, 1993), 20.

58. "Revenge of the Apples," *Wall Street Journal*, 17 December 1990, A8. See generally Allan Gold, "Company Ends Use of Apple Chemical," *New York Times*, 17 October 1990; Adrian de Wind, "Alar's Gone, Little Thanks to the Government," *New York Times*, 30 July 1991; Leslie Roberts, "Alar: The Numbers Game," *Science*, 24 March 1989, 1430. For criticisms of the Alar campaign, see Fumento (n. 57), 19–44; Bruce Ames, "Too Much Fuss about Pesticides," *Consumer's Research Magazine* (April 1990); and more generally idem, "Misconceptions about Pollution and

Cancer," *National Review*, 42 (December 1990).

59. Dave Phillips, "Breakthrough for Dolphins: How We Did It," *Earth Island Journal*, 5 (Summer 1990); idem, "Taking Off the Gloves with Bumble Bee," *Earth Island Journal*, 6 (Winter 1991); "Three Companies to Stop Selling Tuna Netted with Dolphins," *New York Times*, 13 April 1990, A1, A14.

60. "Dolphin Dilemmas," *Environment*, 35 (November 1993), 21.

61. "US Law Bans Sale of Dolphin-UnSafe Tuna," *Earth Island Journal*, 9 (Summer 1994), 7.

62. See CERES Coalition, *The 1990 Ceres Guide to the Valdez Principles* (Boston: CERES, 1990); Valerie Ann-Zondorak, "A New Face in Corporate Environmental Responsibility: The Valdez Principles," *Boston College Environmental Affairs Law Review*, 18 (Spring 1991); Jack Doyle, "Valdez Principles: Corporate Code of Conduct," *Social Policy*, 20 (Winter 1990); Joan Bavaria, "Dispatches from the Front Lines of Corporate Social Responsibility," *Business and Society Review*, no. 81 (Spring 1992).

63. For an extended discussion of NGO corporate politics that provides additional examples, see Starke (n. 41), 89 ff.

64. See e.g. Jack Doyle, "Hold the Applause: A Case Study of Corporate Environmentalism," *Ecologist*, 22 (May–June 1992); David Beers and Catherine Capellaro, "Greenwash!", *Mother Jones*, March–April 1991. For sympathetic views, see Stephan Schmidheiny, *Changing Course: A Global Business Perspective on Development and the Environment* (Cambridge, Mass.: MIT Press, 1992); Smart (n. 45).

65. See e.g. Philip Hurst, *Rainforest Politics: Ecological Destruction in South East Asia* (Atlantic Highlands, NJ: Zed Books, 1990); H. Jeffrey Leonard (ed.), *Environment and the Poor: Development Strategies for a Common Agenda* (New Brunswick, NJ: Transaction Books, 1989).

66. The relationship between the world's poor and environmental destruction is a complicated one. See e.g. Robin Broad, "The Poor and the Environment: Friends or Foes?," *World Development*, 22 (June 1994); and Robert W. Kates and Viola Haarmann, "Where the Poor Live: Are the Assumptions Correct?," *Environment*, 34 (May 1992).

67. See World Wildlife Fund, *The African Madagascar Program* (pamphlet) (April 1994); Nyamaluma Conservation Camp Lupande Development Project, *Zambian Wildlands and Human Needs Newsletter* (Mfuwe) (March 1990); Gabrielle Walters, "Zambia's Game Plan," *Topic Magazine* (US Information Agency), no. 187 (1989); Roger Stone, "Zambia's Innovative Approach to Conservation," *World Wildlife Fund Letter*, no. 7 (1989); *WWF Project Folder #1652*.

68. Proceedings of the workshop on Community Forest/Protected Area Management, Maumi Hotel, Yaounde, Cameroon, 12–13 October 1993, sponsored by the Cameroon Ministry of Environment and Forests; Roger Stone, "The View from Kilum Mountain," *World Wildlife Fund Letter*, no. 4 (1989); Michael Wright, "People-Centered Conservation: An Introduction," *Wildlands and Human Needs: A Program of World Wildlife Fund* (pamphlet) (Washington, DC: WWF, 1989); World Wildlife Fund, *1988–1989 Annual Report on the Matching Grant for a Program in Wildlands and Human Needs*, US AID Grant #OTR-0158-A-00-8160-00 (Washington, DC: WWF, 1989).

69. Roger Stone, "Conservation and Development in St. Lucia," *World Wildlife Fund Letter*, no. 3 (1988).

70. See Vandana Shiva, "North–South Conflicts in Global Ecology," *Third World Network Features*, 11 December 1991; John Hough and Mingma Norbu Sherpa, "Bottom Up vs. Basic Needs: Integrating Conservation and Development in the Annapurna and Michiru Mountain Conservation Areas of Nepal and Malawi," *Ambio*, 18: 8 (1989); Robin Broad, John Cavanaugh, and Walden Bellow, "Development: The Market Is Not Enough," *Foreign Policy*, no. 81 (Winter 1990); Hurst (n. 65).

71. Outside contact may also splinter traditional associations causing economic and social dislocation. See e.g. James Mittelman, *Out*

from Underdevelopment: Prospects for the Third World (New York: St Martin's Press, 1988), 43–4.

72. Bratton, "The Politics of Government–NGO Relations in Africa," *World Development*, 17: 4 (1989), 574.

73. See "Whose Common Future," *Ecologist* (special issue), 22: 4 (July–August 1992); Robert McC. Adams, "Foreword: The Relativity of Time and Transformation," in B. L. Turner et al. (eds.), *The Earth as Transformed by Human Action* (New York: Columbia University Press with Clark University, 1990). For how these pressures work in one particular area, see Susanna Hecht and Alexander Cockburn, *The Fate of the Forest: Developers, Destroyers and Defenders of the Amazon* (New York: Harper Perennial, 1990).

74. Hilary French, "Rebuilding the World Bank," in Lester Brown et al., *State of the World, 1994* (New York: W. W. Norton, 1994), 163.

75. See Bramble and Porter (n. 2); "Withdraw from Sardar Sarovar, Now: An Open Letter to Mr. Lewis T. Preston, President of the World Bank," *Ecologist*, 22 (September–October 1992); James Rush, *The Last Tree: Reclaiming the Environment in Tropical Asia* (New York: Asia Society, distributed by Boulder, Colo.: Westview Press, 1991).

76. Robert Livernash, "The Growing Influence of NGOs in the Developing World," *Environment*, 34 (June 1992), 15.

77. Such funding was evident in the preparatory meetings organized for the United Nations Conference on Environment and Development (UNCED). Organizations such as WWF spent thousands of dollars to bring Third World NGOs to Geneva, New York, and eventually to Brazil to attend the proceedings.

78. Michael Cernea, "Nongovernmental Organizations and Local Development," *Regional Development Dialogue*, 10 (Summer 1989), 117. One should note that although the overall trend is to fund local NGOs, the amount of money going to local NGOs decreased in 1987. It increased the following year, however.

79. Gernea (n. 78), 118, table 1. One should note that the reason for this shift in funding is a combination of the perceived failure of governments to promote development, the proved effectiveness of NGO responses to recent famines throughout Africa, and donors' preference for private sector development. See Anne Drabek, "Editor's Preface," *World Development*, 15, supplement (Autumn 1987).

80. Organization for Economic Cooperation and Development (OECD), *Development Cooperation in the 1990s: Efforts and Policies of the Members of the Development Assistance Committee* (Paris: OECD, 1989), 82.

81. See Fisher (n. 14).

82. For a discussion of the interface at the local level, see Philip Hirsch, "The State in the Village: The Case of Ban Mai," *Ecologist*, 23 (November–December 1993).

83. As a moment of social organization, civil society sits at an intermediate stage of collective development that finds its apex at the state. The state, however, does not supersede civil society but rather contains and preserves it in order to transform it into a higher level of social expression. The state's job, as it were, is to enable universal interest— in contrast to private interest—to prevail. In Hegelian terminology, it allows for the realization of ethical life in contrast to the abstract morality available in civil society. See *Hegel's "Philosophy of Right*," trans. T. M. Knox (London: Oxford University Press, 1967).

84. More recent formulations of civil society, informed by new understandings of the public/private distinction, include the family as part of civil society. See Cohen and Arato (n. 5).

85. Alexis de Tocqueville, *Democracy in America*, ed. Jacob P. Mayer (Garden City, NY: Doubleday, 1969), 520.

86. David Held, "Introduction: Central Perspectives on the Modern State," in Held et al. (eds.), *States and Societies* (New York: New York University Press, 1983).

87. Gramsci (n. 6), 238 ff.

88. Timothy Mitchell, "The Limits of the State: Beyond Statist Approaches and Their Critics,"

American Political Science Review, 85 (March 1991).

89. There are, of course, many instances when activists *do* target the state, in which the interface of global civil society and the state system is critical to strategies pursued by TEAGs. For an extended discussion of this type of action, see Paul Wapner, *Environmental Activism and World Civic Politics* (Albany, NY: SUNY Press, forthcoming).

90. Cited in Sheldon Wolin, *Politics and Vision: Continuity and Innovation in Western Political Thought* (Boston: Little, Brown, 1960), 2.

91. Machiavelli was one of the first to recognize this conflation. It led to his "lowering the sights" of politics—that is, removing such matters as salvation and morality from the domain of political life—insofar as he recognized the limited capacities of state apparatuses. See Niccolò Machiavelli, *The Prince* (Middlesex: Penguin Books, 1988); idem, *The Discourses* (New York: Cambridge University Press, 1988).

92. This point rests on the distinction between government and governance. See James Rosenau, "Governance, Order and Change in World Politics," in James Rosenau and Ernst-Otto Czempiel (ed.), *Governance without Government: Order and Change in World Politics* (Cambridge: Cambridge University Press, 1992); Oran Young, George Demko, and Kilaparti Ramakrishma, "Global Environmental Change and International Governance" (Summary and recommendations of a conference held at Dartmouth College, Hanover, NH, June 1991).

37 The Lilliput Strategy: Taking on the Multinationals

Jeremy Brecher and Tim Costello

Today, opposition to the revised General Agreement on Tariffs and Trade (GATT) may seem like the last quixotic battle in a futile war against globalizing capital. But the efforts of labor, consumer, environmental and other popular constituencies will be remembered tomorrow as one of the opening shots of an epochal worldwide struggle to reverse the catastrophic effects of globalization. That struggle needs a strategy.

Global corporations are using established international institutions like GATT, the World Bank and the International Monetary Fund, plus newly minted ones like NAFTA and the Asia-Pacific Economic Cooperation, to create a new, highly undemocratic governing structure for the global economy. These institutions are imposing a global corporate agenda designed to extract wealth and resources from poorer countries and communities and concentrate them among the global elite.

These new institutions of global governance—whether GATT with its "dispute resolution panels" or the IMF and World Bank with their "structural adjustment" and "shock therapy" programs—restrict democratic self-government in the interest of this corporate agenda. Globalization has largely outflanked the efforts of local and national governments, political parties, trade unions and grass-roots organizations to protect popular interests. Corporations force workers, communities, and countries to compete to attract investment, bringing about a worldwide downward leveling: Each tries to reduce labor, environmental and social costs below the others, leading to a disastrous "race to the bottom" in which the conditions of all tend to fall toward those of the poorest and most desperate (see Brecher, "Global Village or Global Pillage?", *The Nation*, 6 December 1993).

The outflanking of national governments and movements can make the new corporate order appear unassailable. But in fact downward leveling is being challenged all over the world. A few recent examples:

- In Rome last month, 1.5 million people joined the largest demonstration since the end of World War II to protest social welfare cuts whose goal, according to *The New York Times*, is "to restore international confidence in the Italian economy."
- In the city of Bangalore, India, a half-million farmers—joined by supporters from ten other countries—marched in a "seed satyagraha" to protest proposed GATT provisions they believed would allow global corporations to destroy their livelihood.

- When the Zapatista National Liberation Army seized the principal cities of Chiapas, Mexico, it stated: "The North American Free Trade Agreement is the death certificate for the indigenous people of Mexico. We rose up in arms to respond to [President] Salinas's death sentence against our people."

Such occurrences may seem unconnected. But while each has its local causes and character, they are part of a little-recognized worldwide resistance to the effects of globalization. Similar resistance can be found in formerly Communist countries like Poland and Hungary and newly industrialized countries like South Korea and Brazil, as well as throughout the First and Third Worlds. And as global institutions have become more powerful, resistance has also begun to globalize, for example in the recent transnational campaigns against the World Bank and GATT.

Downward leveling is producing a common interest among people in different countries and regions of the world. According to the logic of global competition, they should compete with each other to attract global capital by providing the cheapest environmental, social and labor conditions. But downward leveling is opening the way for a different logic—a common interest in forestalling the race to the bottom.

The key to reversing the race to the bottom lies in "upward leveling"—raising the standards of those at the bottom and thereby reducing their downward pull on everybody else. That requires a cumulative increase in both power and well-being for the poorest and least powerful—working people, women, marginalized groups and their communities. The vehicles to achieve upward leveling can include, among others, corporate codes of conduct, international labor and environmental-rights campaigns, social charters in international trade agreements and grass-roots economic initiatives.

Resistance to the global corporate agenda is ubiquitous but fragmented. For those outflanked by global capital we propose what we call the Lilliput Strategy.

In Jonathan Swift's satiric fable *Gulliver's Travels*, the tiny Lilliputians, only a few inches tall, captured the marauding Gulliver, many times their height, by tying him down with hundreds of threads while he slept. Gulliver could have crushed any Lilliputian under the heel of his boot, but the dense network of threads tied around him held him immobile and powerless. Similarly, facing powerful global forces and institutions, people need to combine their relatively modest sources of power with often very different sources of power available to participants in other movements and locations. Just as the tiny Lilliputians captured Gulliver by tying him with many small pieces of thread, the Lilliput Strategy weaves many particular actions designed to prevent downward leveling into a system of rules and practices that together force upward leveling.

Guidelines for Lilliputian Linking

At the core of the Lilliput Strategy lies the work of linking often-divided groups and interests. Free-market ideology may debunk the idea of common or social interests across such boundaries, in effect maintaining—to paraphrase Margaret Thatcher—that only the interests of individuals are real. But in fact the linking of self-interest and common interest is the starting point for all collective action, including resistance to downward leveling.

To link self-interest with common *global* interests, the first step is to clarify the connections between the immediate conditions people face and the global processes that are affecting them. A good example is the Sierra Club study *GATT Double Jeopardy: State Environmental Laws at Risk*, which provides state-by-state information on how GATT could undermine recycling, packaging, fuel efficiency and food safety laws. Similarly, in the long and bitter struggle of workers at the Caterpillar tractor company, the United Auto Workers stressed the international dimension; as one union official explained, "CAT would like to force workers in different countries to compete with one another to see who will work for the lowest wage." In both these instances, the link between local problems and the global forces promoting downward leveling were made clear.

The second step is to link local struggles with global support. A classic example is the international network of indigenous peoples, environmental activists and trade unionists that supported the struggles of Chico Mendes and the indigenous Amazonian rubber tappers, ultimately forcing the World Bank to shift its development policies in the Amazon rain forest. In the case of Caterpillar, the International Metalworkers Federation convened a world conference of metalworkers in Peoria, Illinois. UAW secretary-treasurer Bill Casstevens declared, "While the company is hard at work trying to divide people, we're going to unite workers from different countries to discuss common problems, plan common strategies and work toward common solutions." Fifty unionists from eight countries set up a network to exchange information about Caterpillar's anti-union activities and to challenge its violation of internationally accepted labor rights in the International Labor Organization. In sum, resist downward leveling where you are and help others resist it where they are.

The third step is to link local problems to global solutions. For example, the United States has refused to ratify most of the 175 ILO conventions establishing basic worldwide labor rights and standards, such as freedom of association, elimination of discrimination, minimum wages and protection of worker health and safety. A serious international labor rights system would forbid many of the worst US abuses, such as sweatshop child labor and the firing of workers who try to organize. In a case brought by the AFL-CIO, the ILO in 1993 held that US laws do not "meet the requirements of the principle of voluntary collective bargaining" because of their restrictions on bargaining rights for public employees. This decision shows the potential of an international labor rights system to provide a court of appeals for abuses here at home. Thus the campaign initiated by the Oil, Chemical and Atomic Workers and other unions for US ratification of ILO conventions links the protection of rights for US workers with protection of those same rights in Brazil, China and other countries with which US workers must compete.

Many social groups already cut across national boundaries, providing important forms of transnational linkage. The women's movement provides many valuable examples. International efforts have challenged sex tourism. An internationally coordinated effort forced the 1993 UN World Conference on Human Rights in Vienna to integrate the concerns of women with internationally recognized rights standards. The transnational network Mujer a Mujer has linked women in the United States, Canada and Mexico to develop common approaches to the exploitation of women through transborder workshops, publications and computer conferencing.

Linking Constituencies North and South

Downward leveling hurts countries at every level of development, generating a common interest among the majority in both rich and poor countries. Yet globalization itself creates barriers to cooperation between First and Third World countries and movements. First World attempts to limit job loss can easily take a form that hurts Third World workers—for example, excluding products made in developing countries from First World markets. Conversely, Third World countries are portrayed as "stealing" jobs from the industrialized nations.

Latin American political scientist Jorge Castañeda has proposed a "Grand Bargain" between North and South. Such a bargain requires that people in industrial countries actively support imports from poor countries as long as they maintain appropriate social, labor and environmental standards. This approach was embodied in a joint position paper prepared by textile and garment unions from all over the Americas who met under the auspices of the International Textile, Garment and Leather Workers' Federation. The paper proposed an alternative to the running battle over the admission of Third World exports into the United States: Unions of the hemisphere should agree that such imports would be allowed if and only if basic human and labor rights, like the right to organize and bargain collectively, are protected.

Linking Economic Issues and Democratization

The centerpiece of the corporate agenda has been the elimination of all forms of popular democratic control of the economy. It has done this by dismantling pro-people, pro-environment regulation; creating institutions of economic regulation outside the reach of democratic control, such as the proposed international tribunals of the World Trade Organization; and marginalizing popular representatives in the political process. To force economic change it will be necessary to challenge these political realities—to make a virtual democratic revolution. Conversely, the movement to expand democracy will mean little to most people unless democracy gives them the opportunity to reshape the economic, social and environmental conditions of their daily lives. The key to moving people from political apathy to political participation is to make that participation a vehicle for improving daily life. The Zapatista movement provides a brilliant example of this approach. The Zapatistas made very specific demands regarding land distribution, economic development, social services and cultural rights for the indigenous peoples of Chiapas. But they maintained that even if the Mexican government made concessions, there was no way that it could be held accountable for implementing them as long as it was fundamentally undemocratic. For that reason the Zapatistas made democratic reform of the Mexican political system a basic objective, one they saw as necessary to achieving their economic and social goals.

No single tactic, campaign, law or institution is likely to counter successfully downward leveling and the corporate agenda. The Lilliput Strategy assumes that multiple threads of grass-roots action around the world are needed. It envisions the construction of a transnational social movement composed of those who resist downward leveling, participate in efforts for upward leveling and connect with others pursuing the same goals.

The Lilliput Strategy requires grass-roots rebellions against downward leveling; local coalition-building; transnational networking; and the creation or reformation of international institutions. Only by combining their efforts can those resisting the effects of globalization in Chicago and Warsaw, Chiapas and Bangalore begin to bring the New World Economy under control.

38 Strategies for Green Change

Andrew Dobson

How do we start? By what imaginable transition can we move from here to a green future? Can the immense gap at least be narrowed, between the Green-thinking dreamers and the present reality?

(Schwarz and Schwarz 1987: 253)

Ecologism provides us with a critique of current patterns of production and consumption, and the Schwarzes' 'Green-thinking dreamers' referred to in the quotation above have painted pictures of the sustainable society that they would like us to inhabit. Two of the classic requirements of a functional definition of 'ideology' are thus far fulfilled by ecologism: it has a description (which is already an interpretation) of 'political reality', and it has a prescription for the future, which amounts to a description of the Good Life. In the light of the space between the former and the latter, the primary question addressed in this chapter is: 'What is ecologism's strategy for social change?' The subsidiary question posed is: 'Will this strategy (or these strategies) do the job required of them?'

The first point to note about ecologism and social change is that very little serious thinking has been done about it. Boris Frankel has rightly observed that: 'one reads very little about how to get there from here' (1987: 227), and it is noticeable how many conversations about green politics very soon dry up when the issue of change is broached. Several reasons for the lack of material might be advanced.

In the first place there is the belief that the changes required are so far-reaching that nothing short of an environmental catastrophe could produce the political will needed to bring them about: 'it is quite "unrealistic" to believe that we shall choose simplicity and frugality except under ecological duress' (Daly 1977a: 170).

Second, amongst more optimistic observers there has been a tendency to believe that the delivery of the message of impending catastrophe would be enough to generate social change. After all, how could a humanity aware of the threat to its existence fail to act in its own best interests? This certainly seems to have been the line taken in the original *Limits to Growth* report: 'We believe that an unexpectedly large number of men and women of all ages and conditions will readily respond to the challenge and will be eager to discuss not if but how we can create this new future' (Meadows et al., 1974: 196). Contrary to its authors' expectations, however, the publication of their report has not of itself produced the changes for which they argue.

It is often the immaturity of the ideology that is held responsible for its not having got to grips

Reprinted with permission from Andrew Dobson, *Green Political Thought: An Introduction*, 2nd edn. (London: Routledge, 1995), 124–65. The version printed here has been edited with the cooperation of the author.

with the issue of social change: green thinkers have had their work cut out simply describing our environmental malaise and convincing us of their arguments. It follows, from this perspective, that the very newness of the ideology is the reason for its current lack of a strategy that might be productive in the light of the ends it proposes. Now that the foundations are more or less in place, it is held, the strategy will follow.

This argument would be more persuasive if ecologism really did have no strategy for social change. The point is, rather, that it does have various strategies, but there is a suspicion that they have been found wanting—it is not as though its strategies are correct and that they just need more time to work. Jonathon Porritt sets the agenda for this chapter:

> Though the environmental movement has indeed been growing in strength over the past few years, so that its influence is now greater than it has been since the early 1970s, this has not brought about the kind of fundamental shift that one might have anticipated. (in Goldsmith and Hildyard 1986: 343)

Porritt goes on to argue that this is because the green movement has founded its project on reform of the system rather than its 'radical overhaul'. This might be true, but it simply pushes the problem back one space and the problem still remains. How is the radical overhaul to be brought about? It must be stressed, though, that 'radical overhaul' is what we are talking about in the context of ecologism. No one would dispute that significant improvements to the environment can be brought about by parliamentary party and pressure group activity—it would be a mistake to underestimate the achievements of groups like Friends of the Earth, brought about by high levels of commitment and undeniable expertise. Similarly, many governments are now (to a greater or lesser degree) committed to environmental policies. However, Porritt's concern at the lack of change is based on his desire for a 'fundamental shift' and it is this objective that provides the backdrop for this chapter.

The distinction around which I intend to organize the discussion is that between parliamentary and extra-parliamentary political activity. There is evidently nothing particularly novel about this, although the very fact that this turns out to be the most fruitful way of approaching the issue is symptomatic of the general theme of ecologism and social change: that liberal democratic politics and the spaces in which it allows one to act constitute the parameters for the majority of ecological political action.

Action Through and Around the Legislature

Green movements in most countries are attached to recognizably green parties which seek election to national legislatures. Green movements in all countries that have one see it as at least part of their role to try to influence the legislative process, either while policy is being drawn up, while bills are being debated, or during their execution. The principal assumption behind both kinds of activity (broadly speaking, party political activity and pressure group activity) is that the liberal-democratic decision-making process and the economic structures with which it is engaged are sufficiently open to allow the green agenda to be fulfilled through them. It seems to be accepted that even if a green party is not elected to government then sufficient pressure can be brought to bear on the incumbents to bring about a sustainable society:

> The Government . . . must intervene, using the full range of sticks and carrots at its disposal, to address the root causes of our current crisis, not the symptoms. Through legislation, direct regulation, changes in the taxation system, subsidies, grants, loans, efficiency standards, the Government has it in its power to effect the sort of transition I am talking about. (Porritt 1984a: 133)

The great majority of green literature on the issue of strategies for political change is written in the same vein. Peter Bunyard and Fern Morgan-Grenville's *The Green Alternative* (1987) is typical, and the following constitutes a representative sample of the advice given (my emphasis added in each case): 'If we act immediately, through *lobbying local councils* and rallying support amongst the community, we may be able to save areas of beauty for ourselves and the rest of humanity' (p. 1); 'We should *lobby Parliament* and voice concern that our money, via taxes, is being used to perpetuate policies that are ultimately destructive' (p. 30); 'We must make our own voices heard through, for instance, *informing our MPs*' (p. 4); '*write to your MPs*' (pp. 58, 89). It is important to understand that these are not isolated examples of the kind of strategy advanced by the green movement. On the contrary, at this level the movement's prescriptions rely extremely heavily on operation within the liberal-democratic framework. The question is: 'Is such reliance advisable given the radical political and social change that ecologism proposes?'

   The first problem for any green party (in some countries, and certainly in Britain) is that of getting elected in the first place—by which I mean not necessarily being elected to government but garnering sufficient votes to gain even minimal representation in the legislature. In Britain, the first-past-the-post system; in which the candidate in a given constituency with the most number of votes takes the seat, militates notoriously against small parties. The results of such a system were most obviously on view in the 1989 European Elections when the British Green Party gained 15 per cent of the popular vote and yet won no seats in the Strasbourg Parliament. It is extremely hard to imagine the British Parliament with even one green representative, let alone with sufficient members to be able to enter into coalition with one of the major parties. Of course, most members of the Green Party in Britain are aware of this, and the parliamentary candidates I have talked to are evidently serious about political power, but see their role principally in educative terms. The platform provided by elections is used to 'get the message across'. Of course, not all countries make it so difficult for small parties to taste electoral success, and shortly I shall consider the situation where a green party does have representation in a national legislature.

   In any case, a green party's political problems clearly do not end with getting elected. It would be faced with confronting and overcoming the constraints imposed by powerful interests intent on preventing the radical political and social change that a radical green government would seek. Even at the level of relatively minor changes, opposition would most likely be intense. Werner Hülsberg, for example, discusses the notion of a green government taxing resource-intensive industries and observes that 'the question of power is largely ignored in this approach' (Hülsberg 1988: 182), and that '[it is] clear that attempt at structural reform would be met with an investment strike and flight of capital' (ibid. 183). The central question in this context is whether a sustainable society can be brought about through the use of existing state institutions.

It has been argued that from two points of view the answer would seem to be 'No'. In the first place, political institutions are not best seen as neutral instruments that can be used by just any operator to achieve just any political ends. Political institutions are always already tainted by precisely those strategies and practices that the green movement, in its radical pretensions, seeks to replace. An instance of this would be the way in which political institutions (in the Western world at least) have come to embody the principles of representative forms of democracy. These institutions represent the formal abandonment of notions of mass participation in political life; they are indeed 'designed' to preclude the possibility of massive regular participation.

The exclusive nature of these institutions, which is constitutive of them, makes it impossible for them to be used for inclusive ends. If they were to be inclusive, in the sense of participatory, then they would be something other than they are. On this reading, participatory politics demands the radical restructuring (if not the abolition) of present institutions rather than their use in the service of participation. Attempts to press them into such service will necessarily result in the progressive dilution of the original project. Jonathon Porritt has argued that 'the taking of power from below, by this process of self-empowerment, must be combined with the passing down of power from above' (1984a: 167), or as the 1994 *Green Party (EWNI) Manifesto* puts it: 'Parliament's role in the first five years of a green government will be . . . to devolve functions to more local bodies' (p. 44). It has been suggested that this is a Utopian strategy, not because greens are as likely to be corrupted by power as anyone else (although this is a respectable argument), but because the institutions Porritt proposes to use already have centralization built into them.

Second, we have to take into account Hülsberg's point that political change is a matter of political and economic power. Even if we assume a green party in government, we are still left with the problem of powerful sources of resistance in other institutions such as the bureaucracy, the financial centres and so on. The *Die Grünen* Sindelfingen programme of January 1983 expressed the hopeful belief that

the desire for a different kind of life and work will grip the majority, and that this majority will be strong enough to demonstrate clearly to the opposing minority the superiority of an economic system whose goal is not itself but ecological and social need. (Hülsberg 1988: 127)

Hülsberg himself cogently observes that, in this formulation, 'The question as to what would happen if the "opposing minority" could not be convinced is simply avoided' (ibid.).

The question is: How far can radical green politics be achieved through the parliamentary context if its 'structural imperatives' demand the progressive abandonment of the principles of such politics?

In 1985 Rudolf Bahro, the most famous 'fundamentalist' in *Die Grünen*, left the party. He argued that by then the party had 'no basic ecological position' because 'what people are trying to do . . . is to save a party—no matter what kind of party, and no matter for what purpose. The main thing is for it to get re-elected to parliament in 1987' (1986: 210). Bahro is here articulating the experience of a fundamentalist green who has seen the party colonized by the demands of the very system that it originally sought to overcome. His conclusion ran as follows:

At last I have understood that a party is a counterproductive tool, that the given political space is a trap into which life energy disappears, indeed, where it is rededicated to the spiral of death. This is not a general but a quite concrete type of despair. It is directed not at the original project which is today called 'fundamental', but at the party. I've finished with it now. (Bahro 1986: 211)

The problem that has informed this discussion of the possibility of bringing about green change through the parliamentary process centres on the difficulty of bringing about a decolonized society through structures that are already colonized—structures that are deeply (perhaps irremediably) implicated in the *status quo* that green politics seeks to shift. This is not a new problem: socialists have been debating the issue for over 150 years. I think it important to reiterate it in this context, though, because it points up the tension between the radical nature of the green project and the piecemeal strategy that has often been advanced to bring it about. Indeed, if one focused solely on the parliamentary strategy one could be forgiven for thinking that the green movement had no radical project beyond environmentalism at all, so far is this strategy removed from any radical pretensions. Raymond Williams has pointed out the dangers of the 'practical surrender of the real agenda of issues to just that version of politics which the critique has shown to be defective and is offering to supersede' (1986: 252–3). This is the point of the general critique of the parliamentary road to the sustainable society.

Most people in the green movement who argue for change through liberal-democratic political structures will also support other forms of action. The rest of this chapter will be taken up with discussing these other options, under the four headings of lifestyle, communities, direct action and class.

Lifestyle

The general principle behind both lifestyle and community strategies is that changes of consciousness and changes in behaviour are mutually reinforcing. Lifestyle change concerns changes in the patterns of individual behaviour in daily life. Typical examples of this would be: care with the things you buy, the things you say, where you invest your money, the way you treat people, the transport you use, and so on.

During the late 1980s there was a veritable explosion in the popularity of green lifestyle changes in Britain. Home ecology, among certain sections of the community at least, was all the rage. Retailers picked up and reinforced this trend and the major supermarket chains fell over themselves to stock their shelves with environmentally friendly goods. Products in green packets sold significantly better than similar products packaged in any other colour. In this context, green rapidly becomes the colour of capitalist energy and enterprise. From the point of view of lifestyle changes, the spaces for political action are in principle infinite—even the toilet is a potential locus for radical politics, for as John Seymour and Herbert Girardet inform us: 'A quarter of all domestic water in most countries goes straight down the toilet. Every time somebody flushes the toilet about 20 litres of water are instantly changed from being pure to being polluted' (Seymour and Girardet 1987: 27). They offer concise advice: 'If it's brown wash it down. If it's yellow let it mellow' (ibid.). I suppose that's one way to start a revolution. Although the recession has taken its toll on the green consumer somewhat, as people buy the cheapest rather than the greenest washing-up liquid, green consumption still exists. If anything, its relative invisibility is due to its success rather than its failure—it is now so much a normal part of the product parade that we don't notice it as much as we used to.

The lifestyle strategy has been around for a long time in the green movement and it has spawned an enormous number of books and pamphlets on practical action to avert environmental decay. Back in 1973 Fritz Schumacher wrote, 'Everywhere people ask: 'What can I actually *do*?" the answer is as simple as it is disconcerting: we can, each of us, work to put our own inner house in order' (1976: 249–50). The theme is consistent: that personal transformation leads to altered behaviour, which in turn can be translated into sustainable community living: 'The only possible building blocks of a Greener future are individuals moving towards a Greener way of life *themselves* and joining together with others who are doing the same' (Bunyard and Morgan-Grenville 1987: 336).

The positive aspect of this strategy is that some individuals do indeed end up living sounder, more ecological lives. More bottles and newspapers are recycled, more lead-free petrol is bought, and less harmful detergents are washed down the plughole. The disadvantage, though, is that the world around goes on much as before, ungreened and unsustainable—certainly in terms of Porritt's desire for a 'radical overhaul', which I took as my rubric for this chapter. In the first place, one has the problem of persuading sufficient numbers of people to lead sustainable lives for it to make a difference to the integrity of the environment. It is evidently hard to predict just how far the message will spread, and how many people will act on it, but it seems unlikely that a massive number of individuals will experience the conversion that will lead to the necessary changes in their daily behaviour.

At the same time, many of the proposals for change of this sort ask us to alter our behaviour at particular points in our daily life and then allow us back on the unsustainable rampage. There is nothing inherently green, for example, in green consumerism, briefly referred to above. It is true that consumer pressure helped bring about a reduction in the use of CFCs in aerosol sprays. It is true that the Body Shop will supply you with exotic perfumes and shampoos in reusable bottles and that have not been tested on animals. It is true that we can help extend the life of tropical rainforests by resisting the temptation to buy mahogany toilet seats. None of these activities should be belittled as actions to help save the environment, and they are particularly important in that they show it is possible to do something. However, the consumer strategy is arguably counter-productive at a deeper level of green analysis.

First, it does nothing to confront the central green point that unlimited production and consumption—no matter how environmentally friendly—is impossible to sustain in a limited system. The problem here is not so much to get people to consume soundly but to get them—or at least those living in profligate societies—to consume less. The Body Shop strategy is a hymn to consumption: in their contribution to the Friends of the Earth Green Consumer Week leaflet (12–18 September 1988) they urge people to 'wield their purchasing power responsibly' rather than to wield it less often. It is this that makes green consumerism environmental rather than radically green.

Second, it has been pointed out that 'there are masses of people who are disenfranchised from this exercise of power by virtue of not having the money to spend in the first place' (*Green Line*, no. 60, March 1988: 12). Third, parts of the green movement feel consumerism to be too grubby and materialistic a means to lead us reliably to the stated end of a society of 'voluntary simplicity'. This is the point behind Porritt and Winner's observation that 'A crude, consumer-driven culture prevails, in which the spirit is denied and the arts are rejected or reduced to a privileged enclave for the few' (Porritt and Winner 1988: 247) and, more generally, that 'it is . . . worth stressing that the underlying aim of this green consumerism is to reform rather than fundamentally restructure our patterns of consumption' (ibid. 199). Once more we are forced to recognize the difference between environmentalism and ecologism: the strategy of green consumerism, in its call for change substantially in line with present strategies based on unlimited production and consumption, is a child of the former rather than the latter.

The strategy of change in individual habits leading to long-term social change takes no account, either, of the problem of political power and resistance to which I referred in the previous section. It is perhaps unrealistic to assume that those forces that would be positively hostile to sustainability will allow present forms of production and consumption to wither away. Of course, this is much less of a problem if the green movement has in mind only some form of attenuated environmentalism, but if (once again) it is serious about the desire to usher in a radically ecocentric society, then it will eventually be forced to confront the issue of massive resistance to change.

What seems common to these lifestyle strategies as I have treated them is that they mostly reject the idea that bringing about change is a properly 'political' affair—they do not hold that green change is principally a matter of occupying positions of political power and shifting the levers in the right direction. Spirituality is of much greater importance to the green perspective than is probably publicly realized, and this has made a significant impression on some activists in the movement with regard to how change might come about. Rudolf Bahro's writings from the period of his increasing disillusionment with *die Grünen* and the parliamentary strategy are the locus classicus of what we might tentatively call the 'religious' approach to green change.

The general point behind the religious approach is that the changes that need to take place are too profound to be dealt with in the political arena, and that the proper territory for action is the psyche rather than the parliamentary chamber. This approach takes seriously the point made above—namely, that political opposition to radical green change would be massive—and side-steps it.

Communities

A general problem with the strategy of lifestyle change is that it is ultimately divorced from where it wants to go, in that it is not obvious how the individualism on which it is based will convert into the communitarianism that is central to most descriptions of the sustainable society. It would appear more sensible to subscribe to forms of political action that are already communitarian, and that are therefore both a practice and anticipation of the advertised goal. In this sense the future is built into the present and the programme is more intellectually convincing and practically coherent.

In this context Robyn Eckersley has argued that 'The revolutionary subject is . . . the active, responsible person-in-community, *homo communitas*, if you like' (1987: 19). She goes on to suggest, in a vein referred to above, that this is because 'Perhaps the ultimate principle of ecopraxis is the need to maintain consistency between means and ends' (ibid. 21). Consequently, 'The most revolutionary structures are seen to be those that foster the development of self-help, community responsibility and free activity and are consistent with the ecotopian ideal of a loose federation of regions and communes' (ibid. 22).

Community strategies might be an improvement on lifestyle strategies, then, because they are already a practice of the future in a more complete sense than that allowed by changes in individual behaviour patterns. They are more clearly an alternative to existing norms and practices, and, to the extent that they work, they show that it is possible to live differently—even sustainably. Rudolf Bahro has expressed it as follows:

To bring it down to the basic concept, we must build up areas liberated from the industrial system. That means, liberated from nuclear weapons and from supermarkets. What we are talking about is a new social formation and a different civilisation. (Bahro 1986: 29)

Obviously not just any communities will do. It is not enough to say that 'a major priority for both reds and greens is the campaign to win for communities, greater control over their environment' (Weston 1986: 160), without those communities having a clear idea of how they might operate sustainably. In this context, the kinds of communities that advertise for ecological lifestyles are rural self-sufficiency farms, city farms, some workers' co-operatives, some kinds of squat throughout the cities of Europe, and, more concretely (in Britain), the Centre for Alternative Technology (CAT) at Machynlleth in Wales and the Findhorn community in Scotland. In 1991, David Pepper published the results of a series of interviews with more than eighty commune members from twelve communes in England, Scotland and Wales (Pepper 1991). Using a measure of 'greenness' revolving around ecologically sound practices such as the sharing of resource, recycling, cutting energy use and so on, Pepper comes to the conclusion that

communards [those studied, at least] have a world view that is indeed radically and overwhelmingly green. This view translates rather patchily into individual and group practice, but it is probably true that communes can provide an institutional context which encourages ecologically sound practices. (Pepper 1991: 156)

The Schwarzes have observed that 'these ventures operate outside and potentially in opposition to, the prevailing culture' (1987: 73), and with that they may have put their finger on the necessary defining characteristic of any strategy that hopes to bring about radical change. In the section on parliamentary change, it was suggested that initiatives in and around the legislature were too easily absorbed, and thus neutralized, by their context. Initiatives that live 'outside' the prevailing culture and its diversionary channels have a much brighter chance of remaining oppositional and therefore of bringing about radical change.

However, even this needs to be qualified because 'to be outside' and 'to be oppositional' are not the same thing, and the difference is crucial in terms of understanding the options for green political strategy. This is because it can be argued that the dominant set of modes and practices needs an opposition against which to define itself and with respect to which to judge itself. In this sense the polarity that opposition sets up helps to sustain and reproduce that which it opposes. One can see this phenomenon in operation at the Centre for Alternative Technology in Wales. At the outset the community at the Centre intended to be 'outside' the prevailing culture, independent of the National Electricity Grid and living a daily life organized around radically democratic and sustainable principles: 'low-tech methods, reduced or simplified methods of consumption, job-rotation, personal growth, priority to collective resources, blurring the distinction of work/non-work, a strong emphasis on community life, and "living the technology"' (Harper n.d.: 4). But, as the same member of the community put it, 'Gradually the bloom faded. I watched it happen in myself. A combination of hard experience, exhaustion, human frailty, pressures of family life, a desire to be acceptable to ordinary humanity, ageing . . . turned me into a reluctant moderate' (ibid. 2). One CAT member in Pepper's commune study argued that the Quarry (the Centre is built around an old slate quarry) was now a way for people 'already into social change to renew their batteries. But it's not a way to change society. I'd like the green movement to promote communes, but it's more important for it to get political power' (Pepper 1991: 181).

This journey towards moderation must be the story of a thousand alternative communities that have found that opposition ends up at incorporation. Now the CAT processes thousands of visitors a year who come from all over the world and pay money to look in on an experiment that, by virtue of the visitors themselves, is shown to have lapsed.

Of course it might be argued that the respectability produced by becoming part of the system is precisely the Centre's strongest card in the context of persuading visitors to go home and practise the kind of lifestyle change described above. The CAT's success will lie in raising an environmental consciousness rather than in providing a 'liberated zone' (in Rudolf Bahro's evocative phrase) of sustainable living, and this is the distinction Harper was pointing to in describing the Centre as a 'successful institution' rather than a 'community'.

Most community initiatives, then, oppose the prevailing culture rather than live outside it. Just what 'living outside' means, and how far it is even possible, will be discussed shortly, but it seems clear that part of the reason why community initiatives have not brought about the 'fundamental shift' that Jonathon Porritt mentioned at the beginning of the chapter is because their opposition is easily neutralized and, indeed, turns out to be necessary for the very survival and reproduction of that which it opposes. What I have called community strategies are arguably an improvement on lifestyle change because they make more ready connections between present practice and future aspirations. However, besides easy neutralization, such strategies depend too heavily (like their lifestyle counterparts) on change by example. They may indeed show us that sustainable styles of life are possible, but as agents for political change they rely entirely on their seductive capacity. The problem is that people refuse to be seduced: rather than producing radical changes in consciousness, sustainable communities perform the role of the surrogate good conscience, and we can go at the weekend to see it operating.

Direct Action

As far as individual actors in the green movement are concerned, of course, all the approaches to green change discussed above can be combined. Any one person could be (and most likely will be) a member of a green party as well as a buyer of Ecover washing-up liquid. S/he might also live in a community which was trying to turn the world green by example. More recently, in Britain at least, s/he might also have been one of the many thousands of people battling it out—sometimes violently, sometimes not—with building contractors intent on carrying out the government's road-building programme. Direct action to halt what protestors see as environmental degradation has become an increasingly prominent feature of the political scene in recent years, and it is carried out by an apparently disparate collection of people, ranging from middle-class 'Nimbys' through to New Age travellers. Disillusionment with mainstream political parties and the agendas they promote has given rise to a form of do-it-yourself politics: groups of (mostly) young people organize around a squat, a sound system, a drug, a piece of land, and try to live a self-reliant life:

Perhaps because of the very feeling of isolation a growing number of what can only be described as 'tribes' have been popping up quietly all over the country . . . Although they all have different identities and aims, when it comes to their motivation, these groups all speak with one voice. They talk about a resurgence of the free-spirit movement . . . a quiet dignity that refuses to be caught up in the fast-track of winners and losers, fashions and fads . . . Who knows when this spirit began to speed up from a tricklet to a wave but certainly in the past few recession-hit years, a network of the skint but proud has slowly been falling into place. (*Pod*, 1994, p. 7)

The politics of these groups varies, but a number are moved by concerns that motivate the wider green movement—such as opposition to the road-building programme. Rather than (or sometimes, in the case of more traditional protestors, as well as) lobbying their Members of Parliament or joining a mainstream pressure group, activists choose to oppose the roads through direct action. This usually takes the form of a continuing presence at the site in question (if possible) and non-violent (normally) resistance to contractors when they appear for work. Some celebrated battles between contractors and protestors took place in this context in the South of England in the summer of 1994, and opposition to one motorway in particular gave rise to perhaps the best-known 'tribe' of all—the Dongas. One member of the Dongas explains how her opposition to the motorway constitutes part of a world-view which is recognizably green: 'we've gone back to the essence of what life is all about, living with the land rather than destroying it. We've learned to appreciate the basic things like the warmth of a fire and the natural world around us' (*Pod*, 1994, p. 20). She also shares the decentralist impulse that informs much green political design: 'Looking on the outside, I think everything has become too centralised. A few bods in London controlling areas they've never seen. Local areas should be controlled by local communities' (ibid. 20).

In international terms the best-known direct action environmental group is undoubtedly Earth First!. Earth First! was founded in 1980 by a group of activists in the United States of America concerned that timid campaigning was doing too little too late to save the planet. From the outset, Earth First! recommended direct action (or what they call 'monkeywrenching', after their techniques for disabling bulldozers and other heavy machinery) as a strategy for opposing industrialism and preserving wilderness. Their activities have drawn criticism from both inside and outside the green movement, and they are variously accused of valuing animals and trees above human beings, of endangering human life, and of getting the rest of the movement a bad name.

Monkeywrenching is not unprincipled, however. Dave Foreman—an erstwhile central figure in Earth First!—and Bill Haywood compiled a *Field Guide to Monkeywrenching* (1989), in which the principles of sabotage and its political effectiveness are explained and discussed. Above all, Foreman writes that monkeywrenching is non-violent in respect of persons. Earth First! received adverse publicity during its campaign to spike trees with long nails to prevent them being cut down, because of the possibility of injury to loggers from their own saws. The 'Field Guide' consequently carefully explains that nails should be driven in high enough up the tree to prevent loggers' access. The intention is to damage industrial saws in the mill rather than injure the loggers themselves (Foreman and Haywood 1989: 14–17).

The political intentions of Earth First! sabotage are to increase the operating costs of environmentally destructive businesses, to raise public awareness regarding environmental despoliation, and (interestingly) to increase the respectability of more mainstream environmentalists (pp. 21–3). Judging the effectiveness of direct action is a hazardous business: it is extremely difficult to trace effect back to cause with any degree of certainty. Earth First!'s intentions, outlined above, might be taken as the yardstick by which any direct action group's success should be measured, and I think it would be hard to deny success in these terms to the various groups engaged in the road-building opposition described earlier.

Yet the motorway was still completed, even if a little behind schedule. Direct action supporters would no doubt see this as a case of 'lose a battle, win the war', and they could now point to the government's apparent intention of cutting back its road-building programme as evidence of their longer term success. Cynics, though, will say that this has more to do with pressure from Conservative Members of Parliament in the South of England worried about losing their seats in the next general election than with protestors risking their lives by lying down in front of bulldozers.

Class

Sometimes greens speak as though a simple 'change of consciousness' is enough to bring about radical shifts in social and political life. Generally speaking, this kind of sentiment is accompanied by an exhortation to education as a necessary preface to conversion. However, as David

Pepper has rightly observed, 'people will not change their values just through being "taught" different ones' (Pepper 1984: 224). Pepper goes on: 'What, then, is the real way forward, if it is not to be solely or even largely through education? It must be through seeking *reform at the material base of society, concurrent with educational change*' (ibid., emphasis in the original). Quite—but how?

The answer to this question might just turn on initially side-stepping it and asking instead: '*Who* is best placed to bring about social change?' A central characteristic of green political theory is that it has never consistently asked that question, principally because the answer is held to be obvious: everyone. The general political-ecological position that the environmental crisis will eventually be suffered by everybody on the planet, and that therefore the ideology's appeal is universal, has been perceived as a source of strength for the green movement. What could be better, from the point of view of advertising an idea, than to be able to claim that failure to embrace it might result in a global catastrophe that would leave no one untouched? From the present point of view this may be the movement's basic strategic political error because the universalist appeal is, properly speaking, Utopian. It is simply untrue to say that, given present conditions, it is in everybody's interest to bring about a sustainable and egalitarian society. A significant and influential proportion of society, for example, has a material interest in prolonging the environmental crisis because there is money to be made from managing it. It is Utopian to consider these people to be a part of the engine for profound social change.

Perhaps the most sophisticated expression of the universalist approach comes from Rudolf Bahro:

> If proceeding from these assumptions we are seeking a hegemonic project and want to keep to the level of the overall interest of humanity—which is what Marx had in mind with the world-historic mission of the proletariat—we must go beyond Marx's own concept and direct ourselves to a more general subject than the western working-class of today. Like the utopian socialists and communists who Marx sought to dispense with, we must once again take the species interest as our fundamental point of reference. (Bahro 1982: 65)

Bahro's point here, couched in language expressive of his Marxist background, is that the social subject to which we must look in order to bring about change is not this or that social class but the whole human race. Again, he writes that 'From all appearances . . . the organizing factors which can bring the alternative forces together and give then a social co-ordination (as must be desired) will in future not be any particular class interest, but rather a long-term human interest' (ibid. 115). As I pointed out earlier, he can argue this because it appears transparent that the threatened environmental crisis will not discriminate between classes—the catastrophe, if it is to come, will be visited upon everybody. While this may be true in the long run, it is not necessarily the best point from which to plan immediate political strategy.

Generally, it is simply not in the immediate interests of everybody to usher in sustainable society. *The Limits to Growth* report remarks that,

> The majority of the world's people are concerned with matters that affect only family or friends over a short period of time. Others look farther ahead in time or over a larger area—a city or a nation. Only a very few people have a global perspective that extends far into the future. (Meadows et al. 1974: 19)

This captures the problem of persuasion with which the green movement is confronted. Somehow people are required to begin to think in global terms and with respect to events that might or might not occur generations hence. 'Only a very few people' think like that and they are precisely the people who already live in sustainable communities, refuse to use chemical pesticides in the garden, and flush the toilet only when they really have to. If these people constitute a vanguard, it is hard at present to see how they are going to drag large numbers of people with them. In the light of this, class theory has it that radical greens must abandon their Utopian, universalistic strategy, and instead identify and organize a group of people in society whose immediate interests lie in living the dark-green life, with all that that implies.

With respect to everything that has been said so far about green strategies for political change, it is interesting to look at the critique that Marx made of the Utopian socialists of the early nineteenth century (without jumping to the conclusion that this endorses everything Marx had to say, or comprises an embryonic Marxist critique of ecologism as a whole). This is what he said of them:

They want to improve the condition of every member of society, even that of the most favoured. Hence they habitually appeal to society at large, without distinction of class; nay, by preference, to the ruling class. For how can people, when once they understand their system, fail to see in it the best possible plan of the best possible state of society? Hence they reject all political, and especially revolutionary, action; they wish to attain their ends by peaceful means, and endeavour, by small experiments, necessarily doomed to failure, and by the force of example, to pave the way for the new social gospel. (From *The Manifesto of the Communist Party* (1848), in Feuer, 1976: 79)

Word for word, these comments literally describe most present green, as well as Utopian socialist, approaches to political change. Marx makes two principal criticisms here, each of which contributes to his characterization of the type of socialism to which he refers as 'Utopian'. First, that Utopian socialism's appeal was counter-productive: it was objectively impossible to expect all classes to usher in socialism. Second, that its strategy of change through 'small experiments' and 'force of example' was an unfounded attempt to change *people* without changing the *conditions* in which they lived and worked. Both of these criticisms of Utopian political strategy are relevant to the contemporary green movement.

It is well known that Marx's solution to the problem posed by the false universal appeal of the Utopian socialists was to recommend the identification and formation of a class in society (given the right historical conditions) whose prime interest lay in changing that society. This is how he put it in his *Toward a Critique of Hegel's Philosophy of Right* of 1844:

Where is there, then, a *real* possibility of emancipation in Germany? This is our reply. A class must be formed which has *radical chains*, a class in civil society which is not a class of civil society, a class which is the dissolution of all classes, a sphere of society which has a universal character because its sufferings are universal, and which does not claim a *particular redress* because the wrong which is done to it is not a *particular wrong*, but *wrong in general*. There must be formed a sphere of society which claims no traditional status but only a human status, a sphere which is not opposed to particular consequences but is totally opposed to the assumptions of the German political system, a sphere which finally cannot emancipate itself without therefore emancipating all those other spheres, which is, in short, a *total loss* of humanity and which can only redeem itself by a *total redemption of humanity*. (in Bottomore and Rubel 1984: 190; emphasis in original)

According to Marx, then, the basic characteristics of the 'sphere of society' (or 'class') capable of bringing about profound social change were as follows: first, it had to have 'radical chains', such that, second, its emancipation would involve the general emancipation of humanity; and third, it had to be opposed not just to the 'particular consequences' of a political system but to its general 'assumptions'. For Marx, of course, this class with a universal historical mission was the proletariat. It is not novel to point out that the proletariat has not proved to be the class that Marx thought it was: its claims were not so radical that it questioned the assumptions of the political system, and its emancipation (while anyway only partial and material) has not led to the emancipation of humanity.

We are left, then, with a critique of Utopian (in Marx's rather specialized sense) political strategies, and how he considers it possible to transcend them.

We have already established that green ideologues are typically averse to class theories of politics because they believe them divisively to undermine the green universal appeal. There has, though, been some discussion of the general issue of agents for change in green literature. Two suggestions can briefly be followed up: that of the middle class as the instigators of change, and the potentially central role of the 'new social movements', such as feminism, the peace movement, gays and so on.

Jonathon Porritt presents a classic formulation of the first position:

one must of course acknowledge that the post-industrial revolution is likely to be pioneered by middle-class people. The reasons are simple: such people not only have more chance of working out where their own genuine self-interest lies, but they also have the flexibility and security to act upon such insights. (Porritt 1984a: 116)

Much depends here on just what one understands by 'pioneer'. If Porritt means simply the questioning of current social and political practices and the presentation of alternatives, then the middle class clearly has a central role to play. Indeed, there is plenty of sociological evidence to show that the environmental movement is preponderantly a middle-class affair. Just why this is the case is hotly disputed, but the debate suggests that throwing one's eggs prematurely in the middle-class basket could be a mistake. The general position combines two suggestions: first, that rises in post-war living standards have shifted political goals (for some) away from material concerns and towards 'quality of life' issues (Inglehart 1977); and second, that a 'new' middle class of non-marketized professionals (educationalists, health workers, etc.) have occupations that are conducive to the generation and pursuing of green values.

Luke Martell, though (for example) has doubts regarding the long-term position of this middle class in radical green politics on the grounds that 'it is difficult to see a basis for economic interest in middle-class concern for the environment' (1994: 130). He points out that

[R]adical environmentalism argues for slowing down growth and rates of consumption. A comfortable group, but which sees itself to be materially disadvantaged relative to otherwise comparable groups, would not be likely to perceive cuts in growth as in its interest. (Martell 1994: 130)

This kind of observation renders Porritt's faith in the middle class somewhat problematic.

Beyond the middle class, one sometimes reads that the 'new social movements' represent new forms of political activity that anticipate new forms of society. Fritjof Capra, for example, writes of a 'winning majority' of 'environmentalists, feminists, ethnic minorities etc.', and then that 'the new coalitions should be able to turn the paradigm shift into political reality' (1983: 465). More explicitly, Murray Bookchin refers to 'the new classes' and argues that they are 'united more by cultural ties than economic ones: ethnics, women, counter-cultural people, environmentalists, the aged, the déclassé, unemployables or unemployed, the "ghetto" people' (1986: 152).

Similarly Jurgen Habermas, who is of course not a representative of the green movement itself, has theorized a 'new politics' centring on 'the peace movement, the anti-nuclear and environmental movement, minority liberation movements, the movement for alliterative lifestyles, the tax protest movement, religious fundamentalist protest groups and, finally, the women's movement' (Roderick 1986: 136). Habermas goes on to make an important distinction that helps us to make some sense of the social pot-pourri offered up by himself, Capra and Bookchin. He argues that not all of these groups have the same emancipatory potential, and suggests that we distinguish between those that seek 'particularistic' change and 'those that seek fundamental change from a universalistic viewpoint' (ibid.). This ought to remind us of the quotation from Marx cited earlier in which he argued that the source of social change must be found in 'a sphere which is not opposed to particular consequences but is totally opposed to the assumptions of the German political system'. 'For Habermas,' continues Roderick, 'at the present time only the women's movement belongs to this latter category to the extent that it seeks not only a formal equality, but also a fundamental change in the social structure and in real concrete life situation' (ibid.).

This is a very important observation, particularly in the context of the most typical critique of social movements as agents for social change: i.e. that they have no common interest and therefore cannot act coherently. As Boris Frankel has written, for example, 'women, environmentalists, peace activists, gays, etc., do not have a ready-formed identity as a social movement' (1987: 235). This is undoubtedly true, but with reference to Habermas's distinction it is hardly important. The crucial project would be not to manufacture an identity between heterogeneous groups, but to identify that group (or those groups) whose project most profoundly questions the presuppositions on which present social practices depend. Only such a group can already be in a sufficiently 'disengaged' position to resist the attempts at colonization by the system that it seeks to overcome, and even then, of course, success is by no means guaranteed.

The point of all this is to suggest that a possible strategy for the green movement would be to identify and foment a group in society that is not only relatively 'disengaged' from it, but that also is already inclined towards the foundations of sustainable living. This will be the agent for radical green change.[1]

Central difficulties with the class-based strategy for green change remain, however. Even assuming that the class has been formed, one is left with the problem of how it is going to act. Is it, for example, envisaged as some sort of revolutionary political subject? If so, then the class is confronted with a series of classic problems: the stability of current political systems (in the West at least), the issue of revolutionary organization, and (particularly difficult for non-violent greens) waging the revolutionary struggle.

If, on the other hand, reformist strategies are chosen and the class operates through pressure groups or a parliamentary party, then all of the dilemmas and difficulties referred to in the first part of this chapter resurface: 'How far should compromise be taken?', 'How should elections be contested?', 'Is election a realistic possibility anyway?' Intermediate strategies do present themselves, such as building up green communities through local money schemes (perhaps focused on unemployment centres), but all thoughts of green class action seem vitiated by the fact that no unified sense of such a class is presently in sight.

Conclusion

Discussion of any aspect of green politics is always dogged by the necessity to distinguish between its dark-green and light-green, or environmental, manifestations. The issue of green social change is no exception. From a light-green point of view, for instance, the reflections which took place under the heading 'class' will probably seem superfluous. It appears self-evident that a parliamentary presence, or pressure through the lobby system can bring about a cleaner, more sustainably environment. It appears self-evident that we can lead more environment-friendly lives by buying the right things and refusing to buy the wrong ones. It also appears self-evident that sustainable communities are vital as sources of inspiration for the rest of us to live more lightly on the earth.

But from ecologism's point of view all of these strategies must be measured in terms of a radical green critique of present practices, and the kind of life it is suggested we need to lead to overcome them. Bringing about that kind of sustainable society is an infinitely more difficult task than simply putting environmentalism on the political agenda. So far, that is what the strategies adopted have done, and taking radical green politics seriously—rather than some attenuated environmentalist version of it—might involve a move beyond those strategies.

Notes

1. Some progress is being made in this respect, and the connections between poverty and environmental degradation are powerfully expressed by the environmental justice movement in the United States. As Andrew Szasz has written, 'Toxic victims are, typically, poor or working people of modest means. Their environmental problems are inseparable from their economic condition. People are more likely to live near polluted industrial sites if they live in financially strapped communities' (Szasz 1994: 151). In the context for the search for a group coalescing around an issue which has broad social and political implications, it is interesting to read that the hazardous waste movement 'increasingly defines its environmental mission in terms of a larger critique of society . . . [I]t even envisions a future in which grass-roots environmentalism spearheads the reconstitution of a broad social justice movement' (ibid. 166). See the section in this collection on Environmental Justice.

References

Bahro, R. (1982), *Socialism and Survival* (London: Heretic Books).

—— (1986), *Building the Green Movement* (London: GMP).

Bookchin, M. (1986), *The Modern Crisis* (Philadelphia: New Society).

Bottomore, T., and Rubel, M. (1984), *Karl Marx: Selected Writings in Sociology and Social Philosophy* (Harmondsworth: Penguin).

Bunyard, P., and Morgan-Grenville, F. (1987) (eds), *The Green Alternative* (London: Methuen).

Capra, F. (1983), *The Turning Point* (London: Flamingo).

Daly, H. (1977a), 'The Politics of the Sustainable Society', in Pirages (ed.), *The Sustainable Society*.

Eckersley, R. (1987), 'Green Politics: A Practice in Search of a Theory', paper delivered at the Ecopolitics II Conference, University of Tasmania, 22–5 May 1987.

EWNI (1994), *Green Party Manifesto*, http://www.gn.apc.org/greenparty/

Feuer, L. (1976), *Marx and Engels: Basic Writings on Politics and Philosophy* (Glasgow: Fontana).

Foreman, D., and Haywood, B. (1989) (eds), *Ecodefense: A Field Guide to Monkeywrenching*, 2nd edn. (Tucson: Ned Ludd Books).

Frankel, B. (1987), *The Post-Industrial Utopians* (Oxford: Polity Press).

Goldsmith, E., and Hildyard, N. (1986). *Green Britain or Industrial Wasteland?* (Oxford: Polity Press).

Harper, P. (n.d.), 'Life at the Quarry', unpublished.

Hülsberg, W. (1988), *The German Greens* (London and New York: Verso).

Inglehart, R. (1977), *The Silent Revolution: Changing Values and Political Style among Western Publics* (Princeton: Princeton University Press).

Martell, L. (1994), *Ecology and Society: An Introduction* (Cambridge: Polity Press).

Meadows, D., Meadows, D., Randers, J., and Behrens III, W. (1974), *The Limits to Growth* (London: Pan).

Pepper, D. (1984), *The Roots of Modern Environmentalism* (Beckenham: Croom Helm).

—— (1991), *Communes and the Green Vision: Counterculture, Lifestyle and the New Age* (London: Green Print).

Porritt, J. (1984a), *Seeing Green* (Oxford: Blackwell).

—— and Winner, D. (1988), *The Coming of the Greens* (London: Fontana).

Roderick, R. (1986), *Habermas and the Foundations of Critical Theory* (London: Macmillan).

Schumacher, E. (1976), *Small is Beautiful* (London: Sphere).

Schwarz, W., and Schwarz, D. (1987), *Breaking Through* (Bideford: Green Books).

Seymour, J., and Girardet, H. (1987), *Blueprint for a Green Planet* (London: Doring Kindersley).

Szasz, A. (1994), *Ecopopulism: Toxic Waste and the Movement for Environmental Justice* (London and Minneapolis: Minnesota University Press).

Weston, J. (1986) (ed.), *Red and Green* (London: Pluto).

Williams, Raymond (1986), *Towards 2000* (Harmondsworth: Pelican).

World Resources Institute (1992), *World Resources 1992–93: A Guide to the Global Environment* (New York and Oxford: Oxford University Press).

Section XII: Ecological Democracy

Green movements press the liberal state in new and often uncomfortable directions. While liberal states are today almost all democratic, the kind of democracy they embody is limited. It is always constrained by the need above all to maintain the confidence of actual and potential investors in the economy; if environmental concerns clash with economic ones, then environmental concerns are compromised. While ecological modernization as dealt with in Section VII tries to get around this problem, that very attempt may stretch the liberal state into new kinds of post-liberal democracy, as the selection by Ulrich Beck argued. A further constraint on the capacity of the liberal democratic state in environmental affairs is its philosophical grounding in liberalism, which is an unremittingly individualistic and anthropocentric doctrine. Many greens believe that environmental issues demand holistic and ecocentric thinking. Finally, the liberal democratic state is a national state; given that many environmental issues and problems transcend state boundaries, we need to think about transnational democratic action that transcends these boundaries. Global civil society made an appearance in Section XI, but what does this mean for democratic institutions and practices more generally?

These sorts of concerns have led to an explosion in thinking and writing on democracy and the environment in recent years. This literature covers a spectrum from those who believe that modest reforms to liberal democracy are quite capable of producing effective solutions to environmental problems to those who believe that a more radical overhaul is necessary (though only a few advocate transformation through revolution). Particular authors can be found at many points on this spectrum. The more moderate have already put in appearances in earlier sections; here we take a look at more radical proposals.

If liberal democracy is currently not performing to an acceptable environmental standard, then the fault, according to our selection from leading ecofeminist Val Plumwood, is to be found in its liberalism rather than its democracy. Plumwood argues that liberalism is pervaded by mechanisms that suppress environmental concern: notably, dualism between reason and nature, celebration of the property-owning individual and associated denial of collective life, and consignment of many key environmental values to a private realm beyond the reach of politics. She argues for the cultivation of an alternative democratic culture informed by both ecological and feminist principles.

Building on notions that the essence of democracy is effective communication rather than voting or the representation of interests, the selection by John Dryzek anticipates democratic structures that embrace communication with the natural world. The kind of democracy without boundaries which he envisages does not fit well with existing liberal democratic states; but it is congruent with the kind of emerging order found in connection with transnational civil society. This conception of ecological democracy can inspire a search for institutions beyond the capitalist state.

Further Reading

Three recent edited books contain an exploration of connections between environmentalism and democracy. Freya Mathews (ed.), *Ecology and Democracy* (1996) is a set of philosophically oriented essays on this theme. William Lafferty and James Meadowcroft (eds.), *Democracy and the Environment* (1996) ranges widely over the performance of existing democratic institutions to more radical alternatives. Brian Doherty and Marius de Geus (eds.), *Democracy and Green Political Thought: Sustainability, Rights and Citizenship* (1996) deals with issues of democracy as they arise in green politics and philosophy, with a view to movement beyond liberal democracy. Robert E. Goodin in 'Enfranchising the Earth, and its Alternatives', *Political Studies*, 44 (1996), 835–49 provides a justification for greens' emphasis on participatory, discursive democracy that is a useful corrective to his earlier criticisms of such an emphasis in his *Green Political Theory* (1992).

39 Inequality, Ecojustice, and Ecological Rationality

Val Plumwood

The Rationality of the EcoRepublic

I invite you to join me in imagining a future ecological and global version of Plato's great rationalist utopia, the EcoRepublic. A global scientist leader, notable for his rationality and brilliant scientific knowledge, establishes a major decision-making discipline of EcoGuardianship (called THE WAY) designed to generate a global bureaucratic-military class of rational decision-makers. Their skills, like those of Roman consuls, will be employed in the various national provinces, coordinating across world society to deal with the massive ecological problems a global capitalist economy has fathered on an injured and captive nature. The leader chooses the initial group of EcoGuardians, who go on to specify a perfectly objective, recursive process which will select their replacements and train them from infancy in every field of relevant knowledge, to become finally decision-makers in THE WAY. For this reproductive purpose they employ, not the Platonic method of selecting promising young rationalists from among the subordinated and devalued non-Guardian population, but the more rationally-appealing method of cloning themselves. This method, which they believe offers a higher degree of control over the chaotic and troublesome sphere of nature and the body, eliminates the need for any immediate affective community other than the EcoGuardians themselves. The EcoGuardians don't mix with the rest of the population, so as not to compromise by attachment their judgement, which often has to be harsh and punitive. They take a pledge to lead austere, Spartan lives, and always to put species survival and planetary health before every human desire.

We can further imagine that the EcoRepublic has come into existence because a working party of scientists and economists in 2099, faced with a severe global ecological crisis, have identified the conditions of compliance and flexibility as the two major political requirements needed to enable the human race to make the necessary sacrifices to survive into the next millenium.[1] Scientific reason must now be left to save the earth, and in the EcoRepublic, they reason, scientific reason will be in charge—perfect, objective, and uncontaminated by ridiculous prejudices and emotions, and constantly improving itself. Rational rulers must have a compliant world community, and lots of flexibility for dealing with environmental problems. They will require maximum freedom and speed, without cumbersome constituency or time-consuming debate. A topdown, military style autocratic decision-making chain will be maximally flexible and allow

From Yeager Hudson (ed.), *Technology, Morality and Social Policy* (Lewiston: Edwin Mellen Press, 1998). Reprinted with permission.

lightning changes in policy and direction to be sent down from the hyper-rational Scientist Commander and his team. In the perfectly eco-rationalist society this thinking gives rise to the EcoGuardians, a quasi-military as well as scientific order, who acquire total power to force compliance from the global population with the rules and quotas the EcoGuardians specify for every human community on earth.

At first, there is an improvement in some of the world's ecological problems, although mainly around THE WAY'S headquarters where most EcoGuardians live, and at a horrendous price in human lives (by now very little non-human life remains). Many people hate THE WAY for its policies of random hostage taking and extermination of citizens from nations which do not meet their standards, the number executed being in exact rational proportion to their nation's degree of offence. Initially, the EcoGuardians stick to their mission of global coordination and of enforcing the global population's compliance with their eco-rational edicts. But after a time, things begin to get worse again after dissension begins to make itself felt among the EcoGuardians themselves. Many of the EcoGuardians seem to lose touch with THE WAY and the GREAT CRISIS it was their order's purpose to resolve. There are several attempts at reform by still committed Guardians, but a time eventually comes when it is clear that despite the austerity pledges, some of the EcoGuardians have become more interested in hedonism than in performing their guardian role. This group has taken to interpreting their pledges to mean spending most of their time supervising THE WAY's eugenic breeding festivals. This group is purged as heretics and replaced, but the remaining EcoGuardians increasingly merge religion and science. Their science was claimed to be the best available at the time THE WAY was set up, but now it seems to be turning out some seriously wrong predictions and is becoming increasingly ossified.

As ecological and human problems proliferate over time in what remains of the global market economy, the EcoGuardians increasingly turn inwards and confine themselves to their own protected planetary places. They avoid the degraded places, which increasingly join up to make large decaying patches on the face of the planet occupied by diseased, forgotten people. Those who are more in contact with what is happening in these places know things have gone badly wrong, and those who have not been too disabled by their situation have some ideas about what might be done. But these people have been cut off from theoretical knowledge and education, as well as decision-making competences, all of which have been monopolised by the remote elite of EcoGuardians. Despite this, some of these people have important knowledge, but they can't get any messages through to or motivate the decision-makers, because the society's formal structures are so one-way and authoritarian the arteries of communication and change from below are thoroughly blocked. "Complaining" carries a long prison term, and questioning an EcoGuardian's orders is punishable by death. The EcoGuardians themselves are well taken care of, and they lead such remote lives they don't seem to know or care about what is happening any more outside their specially protected, elite enclaves. Since there is no way for anyone to tell or engage them, their society proceeds towards alternatives of ecological collapse or major structural change.

The EcoRepublic is an extreme case, but the poor correctiveness and failure of ecological reflexivity and responsiveness to ecological deterioration it displays may be something it increasingly shares with contemporary forms of global capitalist society. The EcoRepublic illustrates what can happen when crucial reflexive and communicative feedback is undeveloped, disabled, or discounted. In a highly centralised society like the EcoRepublic it would be relatively easy to lose ecological correctiveness, since this is not linked across social spheres to other forms of social correctiveness, for example that of justice. Failure could be the consequence of the isolation of a ruling elite together with the silencing and disabling of other human groups who have key roles in providing ecological communication. It could result from communicative failure, or from the failure of decision-makers' motivation, even in the presence of good information networks, to use their power to maintain ecological relationships. We may imagine that, for the EcoRepublic, privilege and remoteness progressively erode the political and scientific elite's capacity to hear and to care about what is happening to degraded natural communities or their human inhabitants.

The initial EcoRepublic scenario represents a social structure not unlike that proposed by ecological oligarchs such as Garret Hardin and William Ophuls, and secretly dreamed of by many scientists. The EcoRepublic's privileging of groups seen as pre-eminent in rationality may be a dream of rationalism, but we can nevertheless imagine this society dying of a kind of rationalist arteriosclerosis. The EcoRepublic may have lots of rationalism, but rationalist solutions of this kind have very little ecological rationality. Institutions that encourage and express self-critical rationality are poorly developed in the EcoRepublic, which could reflect its generation from the least self-critical forms of current knowledge, dominant economics, and establishment science. As Beck, Giddens, and Lash (1994) argue, self-critical rationality, institutions and dispositions of knowledge are necessary conditions for dealing with postmodern and ecological crises. I shall argue that much more is required, including institutions which encourage speech from below and deep forms of democracy where communicativeness and redistributive equality are found across a range of social spheres.

Rationalism and the Crisis of Ecological Rationality

Several writers, especially John Dryzek (1987) have elaborated a concept of ecological rationality, initially defined as "the capacity of a system to maintain or increase the life supporting capability of ecosystems consistently" (Bartlett 1986; Dryzek 1987, 1990; Hayward 1994). In the context of the sorts of capacities for ecological damage now available to most human cultures, self-reflective and organised social capacities to correct human-induced ecological deterioration are required for human ecological survival. For modernist societies capable of very major and rapid ecological impacts, to lack adequate ecological correctiveness is rather like having a vehicle which is capable of going very fast but has a faulty or poorly developed brake and steering system. In the case of an organism, we could expect a similar imbalance between functions to lead to rapid death or extinction. For these high-impact contexts, ecological rationality must therefore be defined in more active terms than Bartlett's, as the capacity to correct tendencies to damage or reduce life-support systems. An ecologically rational society would be sustainable to the extent that its corrective capacities enable it to make consistently good ecological decisions that maintain its ecological relationships.

Ecological rationality under this conception is a species of critical rationality, operating across a range of human spheres and relating them to the ecological communities in which human societies are embedded. The EcoRepublic demonstrates a failure of ecological rationality through the more general failure of critical rationality in the social and epistemological spheres. The EcoGuardians believe that their rational knowledge must save the world, and pour resources into knowledge, but resist adequate development of its self-critical functions. One reason for this failure is that the EcoGuardians are unable to recognise their own knowledge as politically situated knowledge, hence fail to recognise the need to make it socially inclusive, sensitive to its limitations, and actively engaged with its boundaries and others (Haraway 1991; Harding 1991). Relying on claims to objectivity to create a hegemonic 'we' whose truth claims dominion over all others, the EcoGuardians construct a form of knowledge that is insensitive in the very area in which the main ecological threats present themselves, the area given news of by marginal voices, in speech from below.

How does ecological rationality relate to rationalism and to other forms of rationality? As there are different forms of rationality, so there are different failures of rationality. Ecological rationality includes that higher-order form of prudential,[2] self-critical reason which scrutinises the match or fit between an agent's choices, actions, and effects and that agent's overall desires, interests, and objectives as they require certain ecological conditions for their fulfilment. Initially such an inquiry might aim at developing a balance between ecologically destructive capacities and corrective capacities, although a more sensible and ambitious objective would aim at phasing out destructive capacities and evolving a sympathetic partnership or communicative relationship with nature. A civilisation which lacks or underdevelops ecological rationality, which sets in motion massive processes of biospheric and ecological degradation which it cannot respond to or correct, does not match its actions to the survival aims it may be assumed it to have. Unless it has for good reasons chosen a path of self-extinction, its actions display a rationality failure in the ecological area in the same way that the actions of someone in the grip of a terminal addiction may be thought of as displaying a rationality failure, as contrary to their overall wishes and well-being.

The questions raised here under the rubric of rationality are those of the match between means and ends, the organisation and consistency of ends, whether some ends presuppose others, and whether subsidiary ends are overwhelming major ones, for example. In these terms there is a strong case for conceding a certain kind of priority (which I shall call basic priority) to ecological rationality; a certain level of ecological health, like individual health, is ultimately an essential precondition for most other projects. But also like individual health, it does not have to be expressed in a single specific form, but can be realised in relation to other projects and in terms of many different possible healthily organised lives. Conceding this kind of priority to ecological rationality is not however to assume any form of ecological reductionism, nor is it to assume a Malthusian approach giving automatic privilege to ecological factors in explanation and discounting or occluding social ones. Indeed I shall be arguing in this paper for a strong link between ecological rationality and social equality.

We had better not understand ecological rationality or, as I shall show, any of its main supporting concepts, in a rationalist way that links it to the doctrine of the separateness and supremacy of reason in human life. As the example of the EcoRepublic illlustrates, the form of rationality involved in ecological rationality is in opposition to the form involved in rationalism, which elevates reason to Promethean status[3] and treats it as the ultimate value. A concept of ecological rationality should not repeat these mistakes by tying itself to traditional dualistic concepts of reason or by assuming that rationality has a monopoly of the capacities we need to mobilise for survival. Converging perspectives from feminist, postmodernist, and critical theory see the ecological crisis as an aspect and symptom of a more general crisis of the Western master concept of reason, whose project of rational colonisation of the inferiorised sphere of nature, rooted in antiquity, has come to flower in modernity in the domination of scientific reason and of impersonal rational mechanisms such as the global market. In the crises of limits which characterise postmodernity, we harvest the fruits of this limited and distorted form of rationality, whose bitterness gives the new era its characteristic rueful and self-critical stance which indicates a further, more fully reflexive stage of reason. The ecological wing of this new form critiques the ecological rationality of those rationalist and dualistic forms of reason that deny the social and ecological ground which supports our lives, and are unable to acknowledge their own insufficiency or the material and ecological conditions of their own production or continuation. If these over-elevated and dependency-denying forms of rationality can be traced to the historical alignment of dominant forms of reason with elite social formations (Plumwood 1993), ecological reason as a new and more fully self-critical form of reason must forge different political alliances (Harding 1991, 1993).

In these terms we can see the ecological crises of limits pressing us on multiple fronts—the oceans, the atmosphere, the forests, biodiversity loss, pollution, and human health—as indicators of rationality failures that bring up for question also our dominant systems of knowledge and decision-making. These questions about dominant forms of rationality are raised when, despite what we think of as sophisticated systems of ecology, information, and observation, few ecological limits have been anticipated sufficiently far in advance to avoid damage from human over-exploitation, when despite major existing levels of damage, more resources are poured into developing further exploitative capacities while corrective capacities remain seriously underdeveloped or are curtailed. If even where limit problems are identifiable in advance, as in the case of world fisheries, dominant forms of science have tended systematically to underestimate their seriousness and imminence, and to overestimate the resilience of the ecological systems in which we are embedded, questions must be raised about scientific rationality. In the sphere of global politics, the failures of the First Earth Summit and recent reversals in environmental regulation raise disturbing questions about the rationality of our present systems of national and global governance and their ability to stem escalating processes of ecological injury or to match constraining to destructive capacities. Ecological rationality then brings into question ordinary forms of rationality.

As a resting point for explanation, the concept of ecological rationality would have dubious strategic value. The tensions the concept flags rather invite further questions, especially about what kinds of societies would consistently make good ecological decisions.[4] As we increasingly press ecological limits, these are perhaps the most important questions of our time. As Dryzek's work shows, criteria of ecological rationality provide much political discriminatory power. They can help us critique the ecological irrationality of the EcoRepublic. It is clear that authoritarian political systems, especially the military systems organised around protecting privilege which still control so much of the planet, provide very few means or motivations for correctiveness and ecological feedback, especially those important kinds which come from below and register advanced ecological and social damage. This remains so where such systems are combined with the global market, which also provides a poor mechanism for registering such damage. Both political argument (Dryzek 1987) and general observation make a case for ruling out military and oligarchical systems as possible routes to solving environmental problems, contrary to the arguments of the authoritarian school of environmental thinkers who pin their hopes on ecological and scientific oligarchy.

Remoteness and Decision

Such oligarchies are said to be flexible, but as the EcoRepublic shows, care is needed in defining flexibility here: in the EcoRepublic, as increasingly in contemporary concepts of work flexibility (Martin 1995), the concept of flexibility is misleadingly one-way, going down but not up.[5] And even if we grant regimes of ecological oligarchy possession of both flexibility and powerful means to enforce compliance with environmental regulation (Thompson 1996), what is unexplained is how they can develop or maintain the political conditions for knowledge[6] or communication of this damage or for guaranteeing the rulers' motivation to use these powerful means for the purpose of protecting nature or ecological relationships. A major reason why the EcoGuardian structure is unsatisfactory for ecological decision-making is that their position as a privileged elite gives them a high level of remoteness from the consequences of their decisions, since the EcoGuardians themselves can largely escape being affected by ecological damage, and they have poor communicative and other motivating links to those who are affected. In oligarchical and authoritarian regimes there is a fatal lack of ecological correctiveness in part because the quality of decision-making suffers from forms of remoteness which dissociate decision-makers very strongly from consequent ecological damage and which can distort decision-makers' knowledge of and motivation to correct that damage.

Dryzek argues that an ecologically rational polity should meet various conditions which he believes point towards discursive democracy. It should be robust (capable of performing in different conditions), flexible (capable of adjusting to new situations), resilient (capable of correcting severe disequilibrium), and allow negative feedback ("react against human-induced shortfalls in life support capability"), coordinate responses and actions across different circumstances and boundaries, and match the scale of decision-making systems to the scale of ecological problems (Dryzek 1987, 1996). The EcoRepublic may fail on all these counts, but it fails perhaps most significantly in another important axis with major implications for democratic and ecological polities, which I shall term remoteness. Remoteness reduction is a good decision-making principle, because remoteness disturbs feedback and disrupts connections and balances between decisions and their consequences that are important for learning and for maintaining motivation, responsibility, and correctiveness. I will argue that Dryzek's conditions can usefully be supplemented by a further range of considerations about the effect of remoteness on the correctiveness of ecological decision-making and explore some of their implications for liberal democracy.

An understanding of the effect of remoteness may hold the key to making ecological rationality compatible with democracy and avoiding authoritarian or highly centralised approaches to securing it. There is a convergence between minimising remoteness in a decision-making system and maximising democracy in Mill and Dewey's sense that those who bear consequences in a democratic system must have a proportionate share in the relevant decision-making.[7] The concept of remoteness provides a way to focus on the kinds of political patterns that make some places better at the price of making other more distant places ecologically worse. Remoteness covers not only those direct consequential forms in which those who make decisions are enabled to avoid their adverse ecological consequences, but also communicative and epistemological forms of remoteness, in which they are remote from news or knowledge of these consequences. This kind of remoteness can involve communicative barriers or compartmentalisation both between decision-makers and damage to non-human nature, and also between decision-makers and those human beings associated with damaged nature. Remoteness principles thus confirm what the ecological behaviour of stratified and authoritarian systems also suggests, that an ecologically rational society is unlikely to be found where the kinds of political structures and culture necessary for human justice and communicativeness are also lacking. The same point applies to nature itself. As Hayward observes "only in a culture where humans are accustomed to listen to one another will there be any real prospect of heeding nature's protestations too" (Hayward 1994: 209).

The link between a society's incapacity to heed speech—warning or distress signals—from below in human society and ecological warning signals from non-human nature is especially significant in those cultural nodes of global capitalism whose culture is rationalist in flavour, drawn by a deep and strong-flowing historical current associating devalued humans and devalued forms or spheres of non human nature (Plumwood 1993). Global market-based distributive systems augment these cultural systems in making a close association between vulnerable and abused places and vulnerable and abused people. Remoteness is a decision-making feature which links ecojustice and ecological rationality. The concepts of ecojustice and remoteness point to cyclical, positive feedback processes which enable the transfer of inequalities and harms from the social to the ecological sphere and back again, in much the same way that inegalitarian societies foster the transfer of harms across social spheres (Walzer 1983). When the remoteness from ecological harms of privileged groups most influential in decision-making systems meets a parallel silencing in the same decision-making systems of those most vulnerable to ecological harms, the social stage is set for major failures of ecological rationality. I will argue that remoteness is a rationality feature preventing contemporary liberal-capitalist societies, apparently the most promising candidates for ecologically rational societies, from dealing effectively with ecological problems, and that it has major implications for ecologically rational social structure. But first, I will look at the identification of remoteness with spatial remoteness characteristic of bioregionalism.

Remoteness, Autarchy and Spatial Scale

Bioregionalists have argued that small-scale autarchic communities which are designed specifically around recognition of their ecological relationships can best counter the adverse contemporary effects of remoteness on correctiveness and ecological decision-making (Sale 1980). In these types of communities, advocates think, a community's ecological relationships will be more clearly visible. People who are less epistemically remote from these relationships will be sensitive both to signals from nature and to the ecological harm done by their consumption and production decisions. Second, in autarchic bioregional communities, decision-makers will not be remote from decisions made about distant places and other peoples' lives, as centralised decision-making must be. Instead, when participatory decisions are made in a local community, decision-makers have to live with the ecological consequences of their decisions, including the ecological effects on themselves, their community, neighbours and direct descendents. And third, because democracy can only be truly participatory at the level of the small, face-to-face community, people will be in a position to have the knowledge and motivation as well as the democratic and communicative means to make good ecological decisions, decisions that reflect their own extended long-term and familiar interests as well as those of their local ecologically-defined communities. Indeed under such conditions these apparently divergent interests can be thought of as convergent and harmonious, if not identical. The democratic participation that societies on a human scale supposedly make possible would guarantee maximum feedback and correctiveness, exactly what is missing in the EcoRepublic.

These sorts of bioregional arguments seem to have succeeded in identifying an important set of decision parameters concerned with different kinds of remoteness, defining the boundaries of the ideal social community in terms of spatial remoteness conditions for good ecological decision-making. But remoteness is more than just spatial remoteness, and if we generalise these insights, we can see other relevant kinds of remoteness. They include consequential remoteness (where the consequences fall systematically on some other person or group leaving the originator unaffected), communicative and epistemic remoteness (where there is poor or blocked communication with those affected which weakens knowledge and motivation about ecological relationships), and temporal remoteness (from the effect of decisions on the future). One principle suggested by this implicit appeal to remoteness principles in bioregionalist thought might for example state that, other things being equal, an ecologically rational form of agency would minimise the remoteness of agents from the ecological consequences of their decisions (actions).[8] The principle aims to provide agents with the maximum motivation to reach responsible ecological decision, to correct bad ecological decisions, and to minimise the possibilities for ecojustice violations which systematically redistribute rather than eliminate adverse ecological consequences. Bioregionalism then proposes a participatory political structure which will empower those who bear the consequences,[9] or at least one which does not silence and disempower them.

Although the appeal of bioregionalism is often put down to nostalgia for the past, the remoteness conditions suggested by bioregionalism are in fact ways to maximise relevant ecological feedback and obtain the best conditions for ecologically benign decisions. The conditions that decision-makers should live in ways that make transparent the relevance to their own lives of the ecological relationships of their communities, and that they are minimally consequentially and epistemically remote from the ecological consequences of their consumption and production decisions, conduce to decision-making based on maximum relevant knowledge and motivation. Decision-makers who have little or no opportunity for remoteness from the ecological consequences of their decisions should, other things being equal, be well motivated to make decisions that are ecologically benign. But although bioregionalism is right to draw attention to the importance of spatial remoteness and points towards an important set of remoteness principles for good ecological decision-making, there are several problematic assumptions in its proposals. First, it tends to assume a reductionist rather than a basic form of ecological priority that privileges ecological relationships automatically over other kinds of relationships. Thus decision-making communities are to be formed to coincide exactly with important ecological boundaries, although there must on a non-reductionist view be other important components to community formation than ecological ones. Second, bioregionalism fails to consider adequately other causes and kinds of remoteness relevant to decision-making communities than spatial remoteness, and is mistaken, in my view, in identifying these remoteness principles as closely as it does with autarchy and smallness of scale.

A closer look suggests that the conditions of small-scale self-sufficiency assumed by bioregionalists to be the leading feature of ecological communities are neither necessary nor sufficient to guarantee that other important forms of remoteness are avoided. Observable small-scale communities (like the one I live in) suggest that proximity to local nature does little to guarantee the first condition of the bioregionalist, the transparency to inhabitants of ecological relationships and dependencies. The need to respect and maintain these relationships can still be obscured or overridden by other cultural factors, for example by the distorting and backgrounding force of anthropocentric cultural traditions, by the conditions of both general and ecological education, or by the intractability of local economic and social relationships. Many ecological impacts may still not be evident at the level of the local community, for example, the contribution of local animal waste to the global store of biospheric methane, and this would remain true for small self-sufficient communities. "Living close to the land" may under the right conditions help knowledge of and concern for ecological effects in a local community, but neither this closeness nor the local ecological literacy it might help generate is sufficient to guarantee knowledge of ecological effects and relationships in the larger global community or even a larger regional one; this requires a larger network, whose formation seems unlikely to be assisted by economic autarchy. Given that contemporary ecological effects are rarely likely to be contained within a single political community, autarchy is in general in conflict with the participatory principle that those most affected by decisions should have a proportionate share in making them. Similarly, small-scale communities, including self-sufficient ones, may have difficulty in meeting Dryzek's conditions of coordination across boundaries, flexibility, and matching scale (Dryzek 1996). Autarchy is not likely to be the best way of matching the scale of decision-making with the scale of impact to take responsibility for those wider ecological effects that are inevitably generated even by small-scale autarchic communities.

Nor does smallness of scale guarantee the absence of politically-based kinds of remoteness. Even face-to-face autarchic communities can make themselves epistemically and consequentially remote from ecological consequences through opportunities to redistribute ecological harms onto marginalised citizens, onto the future, and onto other less powerful communities. The extent to which this is possible within any given small-scale community depends on its political organisation, among other things, and especially on what sorts of opportunities for redistribution of ecological consequences these structures offer them. This would also be true of an economically self-sufficient community, unless we again make the question-begging and highly improbable assumption that it could be self-sufficient in its ecological impacts. The match between small scale and remoteness reduction is not as good as autarchy advocates have thought both because remoteness is more plural than they allow and because both human-scale and autarchy as such are much too politically and structurally underdetermined. This means that only under special conditions of political and cultural structure that are usually left unspecified would such a face-to-face community be likely meet optimum overall conditions for remoteness reduction.[10]

If remoteness has political as well as spatial conditions and expressions, this allows us to consider other crucial areas and ways to reduce remoteness than minimising the spatial scale of communities, ways that might bear on improving the ecological rationality of larger-scale societies (for example, by making ecological relationships more transparent in their economic and cultural systems). It is important to increase the range of options relating to size because, although smaller-scale communities certainly can reduce epistemic and responsive remoteness, and in some areas such as energy use can greatly reduce consequential remoteness, they can often also offer people fewer alternatives to damaging forms of economic activity, so that their benefits of reducing remoteness can be offset or cancelled out. This suggests that we should investigate remoteness reduction as a political and not only a spatial organising principle for ecological rationality.

Remoteness principles are consistently, blatantly and almost maximally violated by the dominant global order, but this is perhaps as much due to its political and other forms of organisation as it is to its global scale. Since laissez-faire market forms permit extreme levels of consequential, communicative and epistemic remoteness, and crusading neoliberalism is increasingly successful in maximising the social areas where this kind of market is used for decision-making, global neoliberalism may be close to maximising ecological remoteness. The present form of the global market economy creates very high levels of dissociation between consumption acts and production acts and their ecological consequences, actually encouraging remoteness as a form of comparative advantage, and so scores at a very high level on ecological irrationality. But social inequality is perhaps just as much of a factor here as geography. Inequality, whether inside the nation or out of it, is a major sponsor of remoteness, especially where it creates systematic opportunities and motivations to shift ecological ills onto others rather than to prevent their generation in the first place.

Inequality combines with geographical remoteness to generate excellent conditions for epistemic remoteness, creating major barriers to knowledge and offering massive opportunities for redistributing ecoharms onto others in ways that elude the knowledge and responsibility of consumers and producers along with concern for ecological consequences. Under conditions which allow both remoteness and rational egoism to flourish, such actions even emerge as mandatory for the rational self-maximiser, since the logic of the global market treats the least privileged as the most expendable, defining them as having "the least to lose" in terms of the low value of their health, land, and assets, and, by implication, of their lives.[11] This logic helps ensure that the least privileged are likely to feel the first and worst impacts of environmental degradation, as in the case of much global deforestation, pollution, waste dumping in poor and coloured communities, and environmentally hazardous working and living conditions for the poor. As it comes increasingly to dominate over other spheres, the global market systematically violates complex equality, enabling "one good or one set of goods [to be] dominant and determinative of value in all the spheres of distribution" (Walzer 1983), facilitating the positive feedback patterns adding ecological ills to social ills which are the mark of ecojustice violations. The next section draws out some implications of dominant forms of globalisation for an ecologically irrational distributive politics which permits those most influential in decision systems high levels of remoteness from ecological consequences and gives them a corresponding capacity to distribute ecoharms onto others.

Liberal Democracy and Ecological Rationality

Theoretically, it seems, a democracy where all have input into decisions should have a low level of remoteness and a maximum of ecological rationality. It should have a high level of correctiveness because it should maximise the informational base relevant to environmental degradation and should enable all affected citizens to be heard and have their problems addressed by responsive decision-makers.[12] But in actually existing liberal democracy, it doesn't seem to work quite like that, and it is commonly observed that liberal democracies are not performing well either in remedying ecological crises or in listening to disadvantaged citizens (Dowie 1995; Plumwood 1996b). Shallow forms of democratic politics provide only weak forms of ecological rationality, not well correlated with correctiveness on ecological or social matters, and their inequalities allow privileged groups many opportunities for remoteness. But we can draw few conclusions from this observation about the ecological rationality of deeper forms of democracy that may enable systematic reductions in remoteness.

Identifying the structural features that account for these rationality failures of liberal democracy is more difficult than noting the failures. Dryzek (1992) argues persuasively that the political and administrative spheres of liberal capitalism are unable to respond adequately to the complexity of the ecological problems generated by its imprisoning capitalist production systems. The interest group interpretation of liberal democracy is another feature which is highly problematic from the perspective of ecological rationality. It is increasingly apparent that the form of 'interest group' politics that flourishes in liberal democracy is unable to create stable measures for the protection of nature, or to recognise basic ecological priority,[13] that ecological well-being is not just another interest-group concern but ultimately a condition for most other interests. The conception of democracy and decision-making in terms of a central state mediating a multiplicity of competing (private) interest groups takes egoism, inequality and domination for granted, provides poorly for collective goods, and allows systematic redistribution of ecological ills to weaker groups.

The liberal-individualist model, as is well known, stresses a view of politics as the aggregation of self-interested individual preferences—increasingly market-weighted individual preferences. As Nancy Fraser notes, this means that "political discourse consists of registering individual preferences and bargaining, looking for formulas that satisfy as many private interests as possible. It is assumed that there is no such thing as the common good over and above the sum of all the various individual goods, and so private interests are the legitimate stuff of political discourse" (1989: 80). The upshot of treating environmental interests this way is, at best, the process of progressive compromise between environmentalist interest groups and exploitative interests, and in this process, as it is easy to show in the case of forests and biodiversity, it is very difficult to maintain environmental values over the long haul.

For other ecological issues too, the liberal interest group model is highly problematic. Collective goods, which cover a major range of environmental cases, are not well treated. For many generalisable interests, the liberal interest group model faces the collective action problem in which an unquantifiable, highly diffused, generalisable, and perhaps not easily detectable ecological harm is pitted in a political contest against a quantifiable economic benefit accruing to a small (often very small) but highly concentrated and influential group. Interest group models tend to give poor results in this situation, while generating much community polarisation around environmental issues. (Both fisheries and forest issues exemplify this pattern.) Models stressing compromise between interest groups have a poor track record on many environmental problems, rarely stopping ecologically destructive activities as opposed to introducing ameliorative modifications which allow major damage to persist while also "giving something" to ecological interests.[14] These modifications sometimes represent worthwhile ecological gains in limited areas but rarely halt the overall progress of ecological damage.

However, a further major set of reasons for liberal capitalism's failures of ecological rationality derive from the structural features that generate both inequality and remoteness in systematic, large-scale, and connected ways. Liberal democracy as an interest group model, produces, not as a matter of accident, radical economic inequality, often in association with ethnic, gender, and other kinds of marginality and cultural subordination, which feed liberal capitalism's structural potential and need for the differential distribution of ecoharms, and generate failures of environmental justice. Environmental theory has mostly tended to assume that ecoharms are generalisable, affecting all people within an abstract national community more or less equally, and that ecological rationality should be approached therefore through a politics of the "common good". The appeal to many environmentalists of the small-scale communitarian ideal also tends to support the framing of ecological rationality issues in terms of the politics of the common good. While adherents of this approach are right to note that liberal democracy deals poorly with the politics of the common good, these perspectives also collude with the power-masking tendencies of liberal politics to create a widespread perception of ecoharms as innocent and accidental distributions of damage affecting everyone more or less equally. As a result many green theorists have been reluctant to take seriously questions of distribution of ecoharms.

Thus according to Ulrich Beck (1995), the politics of class conflict is mainly concerned with the distribution of social rewards, which is inequitable in class-differentiated societies. In contrast, he claims, in risk society ecological ills tend to be distributed more evenly, cutting across boundaries of class and power. This view is summed up in his aphorism: "Poverty is hierarchical, while smog is democratic" (1995: 60), a memorable and widely quoted statement. But unfortunately for Beck's theory, many ecological harms, including smog, are distributed just as unevenly as most commodities. A smog map of Sydney, for example, correlates the heaviest air pollution areas very closely with low socio-economic status. The veil of uncertainty Beck tries to throw over ecological harms is already thoroughly rent, by class, race, and gender as well as other forms of inequality.

The assumption of equality and generalisability in ecoharms holds good only for a certain range of ecoharms—those forms of degradation which have highly diffused or unpredictable effects not amenable to redistribution—and it holds even for many of those only very partially. It is hard to think of anything more likely to be generalisable than global warming, with its predictable outcome of increasingly extreme climatic events from which we all suffer in unpredictable ways. Events like the 1995 Chicago heatwave, where the 500 or more who died were mainly poor elderly people unable to afford air-conditioners, show that even these generalisable kinds of ecoharms tend to affect disproportionately those who already suffer from a social distribution deficit. So even in such apparently generalisable cases, what may mean discomfort for someone higher up the social scale may mean death to someone more marginal. For those kinds of degradation that are more localised and particularised in their impacts, such as exposure to toxins through residential and occupational area, much the same kind of politics of distribution can be played out as in the case of other societal goods.

For a range of environmental ills resulting from the institutions of accumulation, then, some considerable degree of redistribution and remoteness from consequences is possible along lines of social privilege. This is the basis of the ecojustice phenomenon known as "environmental racism" (which should often be termed, in my view, "environmental classism"). The socially privileged groups in a society can most readily make themselves remote from these easily perceived and particularised forms of environmental degradation; if their suburb, region or territory becomes degraded or polluted, they can buy a place in a more salubrious one. When local resources become depleted, they will be best placed to make themselves remote from local scarcities by taking advantage of wider supply sources and markets that continue to deplete distant communities in ways that elude knowledge and responsibility. They can buy expert help and remedies for environmental health and for other problems, and they are better able to mobilise in the public sphere for action on the ecological and other problems which concern them. Their working life is likely to involve a minimum of environmental pollution and disease compared to marginalised groups—for example compared to the US farm workers whose immediate life-expectancy is estimated to be twenty years below the national average (Jennings and Jennings 1993). At the same time, privileged groups are those who consume (both directly for their own use and indirectly for income generation) the greatest proportion of resources, and who have the strongest economic stake in the forms of accumulation which generate environmental harms. That is, the most socially privileged groups can make themselves relatively spatially, consequentially and epistemically remote from redistributable ecoharms, will usually have the most to gain and the least to lose from the processes that produce ecoharms, and their interests will often be better satisfied if ecoharms are redistributed rather than prevented. Some parallel conclusions can be drawn for ecological goods.

The situation is not much better for generalisable harms and damage to collective goods. Because socially privileged groups can most easily purchase alternative private resources (clean water for example), they have the least interest in maintaining in generally good condition collective goods and services of the sort typically provided by undamaged nature. In terms of their own experience, privileged groups are also likely to be more epistemically remote and distanced from awareness of both their own and nature's vulnerability and limits. For some very general forms of environmental degradation (such as nuclear radiation or biospheric degradation),[15] the ability of privileged groups to buy relief from vulnerability to environmental ills is ultimately an illusion. But for the key groups who are active in political decision-making it may still be the master illusion, fostered by their remoteness in other areas and sustained by their social privilege and influential in their choices and attitudes. The socially privileged also have a political opportunity to redistribute collective goods in their favour, via privatisation, which guarantees them superior access, and insulates them from many kinds of limits and scarcity. In short, the inequalities which thrive in liberal democracy provide systematic opportunities for consequential and epistemic remoteness in the case of both non-collective and collective goods.[16] Liberal capitalism thus provides a set of impersonal NIMBY mechanisms which guarantee that an important range of ecoharms, from both redistributable and collective sources, are redistributed to marginalised groups.

In a polity like this where the socially privileged have the main or central role in social decision-making, decisions are likely to reflect their relatively high level of consequential, epistemic, and communicative remoteness from ecological harms. From the perspective of ecological rationality then, these are among the worst groups therefore, to be allocated the role of decision-making. Yet in liberal democracies they are precisely the ones who have that role. The finding that it is socially privileged groups who are selected as politically active and effective in the liberal political structure is so well supported by empirical studies that Carole Pateman describes it as "one of the best attested findings in political science" (Pateman 1989: 163). That there is a complementary silencing of those marginalised citizens on whom most ecoharm falls is attested by the unresponsiveness of liberal systems to their redistributive deprivation and cultural subordination. Several indirect sources are available to provide information about the ecoharms of the marginalised and about prevalent ecological ills, including, in liberalism, the discourse of the public sphere and the market. If the market, considered as an information system about needs, registers information not equally but according to "market power" (income), information about the needs of those without "market power" registers very little. Bad news from below is not registered well by any of liberal democracy's information systems, hardly at all by the market, and often poorly by liberal democratic, electoral and administrative systems. Yet it is precisely this bad news from below that has to be heard if many crucial forms of ecological damage are to be socially registered and opened to political action.[17]

The epistemic remoteness of privileged groups from the kinds of ecoharms that fall on the marginal others impacts strongly on information and on the public sphere to the extent that privileged experience is hegemonic. This can create a general level of silence and epistemic distancing from these submerged kinds of ecoharms which can affect even those who suffer most from them. The consequential and epistemic remoteness of privileged groups from certain kinds of harms is reflected in what counts as ecological issue in the dominant public spheres.[18] The occupational health hazards of minority workers, the systematic poisoning of millions of migrant agricultural workers, and the dumping of toxic wastes on poor communities can pass unremarked while environmental attention is focused on consumer issues which impact on more privileged groups (Jennings and Jennings 1993) or on issues concerning "good nature". Again, socially privileged groups often aim to set themselves apart from otherised groups (in the process of hyperseparation (Plumwood 1993)) through overconsumption, and develop a culture celebrating consumption. Cultural and social values may be distorted in ways which inferiorise low consumers or "losers", for example in the West, those associated with bodily labour, materiality, and nature, and which give little attention to their ills. Cultural ideals will often tend to idealise the rich and successful and reflect their styles and standards of resource overconsumption, while portraying low consumption, satisficing lifestyles in negative or contemptuous terms (hooks 1994). If these consumerist values come to dominate in the public sphere, the cultural hegemony of social privilege can contribute to ecological damage as much as its economic domination.

There is clearly a serious problem about the ecological rationality of any system that allows those who have most access to political voice and decision-making power to be also those most relatively remote from the ecological degradation it fosters, and those who tend to be least remote from ecological degradation and who bear the worst ecological consequences to have the least access to voice and decision power. My argument implies not only that the inegalitarian power structure of liberalism is ecologically irrational, but also that the political and communicative empowerment of those least remote from ecological harms must form an important part of strategies for ecological rationality. There are many specific contextual forms this empowerment might take, such as access for community action groups to resources like public funding, but its general conditions surely require institutions which encourage speech and action from below and deep forms of democracy where communicative and redistributive equality flourish across a range of social spheres.

Beyond Liberal Democracy: Deliberative Modifications

The discussion above has suggested principles about who must be able to speak and participate effectively in the political process if the sorts of ecoharms suffered to a disproportionate degree by marginalised groups are to be subject to effective political action. As advocates of deliberative democracy note, the liberal interest group model which treats people as private political consumers provides little encouragement for the development of any public ecological morality, for collective responsibility or problem solving, or for people to transform their conception of their interests, their convictions or sympathies in response to social dialogue with affected groups (Young 1995; Dean 1996). To resolve conflicts over ecological harms through such means of reducing remoteness, we may need to create contexts in which both harming and harmed parties can communicate,[19] in which the harmed group is not disadvantaged as communicators and the harming group is neither remote (consequentially or epistemically), nor privileged in some other way in the decision-making process.[20] We can extend these conditions for equal dialogue and consensus to other matters. Ideally, to enable such transformation of interests to occur more readily, those who depend on producing the harms to earn a living should have a sufficient degree of confidence and social responsibility, overall access to economic flexibility, to social support and work reconstruction to be able make occupational and technological changes without incurring significant life penalties, that is, such penalties would need to be as far as possible socially borne. None of these conditions can be well realised in liberal forms of democracy; rather they point towards deliberative, participatory, or radical forms of democracy.

To some however the problems I have outlined suggest not that any major or general transformation of liberalism is required but rather that the problems can be resolved by adding minor and highly localised deliberative modifications to liberal democracy, such as stakeholder panels designed to address specifically ecological issues. Thus Denis Collins and John Barkdull (1995) argue that classical liberalism is the most ecologically rational system (although they consider only one source of comparison, the Soviet bloc), and that a solution to the kinds of ecological difficulties of liberal capitalism I have outlined can be found in the form of stakeholder panels that can operate within it to create dispute resolution dialogue between harming and harmed groups. Not only does this not involve any major repudiation of liberal thought, they argue, but this kind of intervention has a respectable pedigree in the thought of that father of liberal capitalist theory, Adam Smith.

As in the case of bioregionalism, the extent to which stakeholder panels can provide a solution depends upon many factors which are not specified in the model, which is radically underdetermined and ambiguous. It seems likely that the outcome will be partly dependent on how stakeholders are selected and how judicial functionaries are chosen, for example. But there is also a radical ambiguity in stakeholder panels as Barkdull and Collins describe them as between a judicial model (with an impartial judge), a voluntary interest group bargaining model, and a deliberative model attempting to arrive at a consensus about the common good. The first two return us to the liberal problems I have discussed above. To the extent that the third deliberative interpretation is intended, stakeholder panels may really represent a major modification and suspension of the interest group model, but they also provide an implicit admission that the classical liberal model Collins and Barkdull have set themselves the task of defending is inadequate for ecological rationality. My own experience of stakeholder panels suggests that, while there can be useful elements of social deliberation and consensus-seeking in the negotiation phase of the discussions, the interest group model which is so problematic for environmental issues tends to remain the basis upon which final political decisions are made. On such an interpretation, stakeholder panels will not only inherit the problems of liberal interest group bargaining, but will also inherit its difficulties in the ecojustice area and in representing adequately collective goods and public interests. Negotiation between harmed and harming parties must include advocates for and ways of representing more-than-human nature and also for the "public interest" or collective good. Both of these are among the potentially harmed parties, but they are omitted in many versions of the stakeholder panel and in Collins and Barkdull's discussion.

Collins and Barkdull concede that business is responsible for most ecoharms and that the poor or racially marginalised are the recipients of most ecoharms. But first, we are entitled to be puzzled as to why, if judicial panel-bargaining is so easily able to solve the kinds of ecological injuries Collins and Barkdull concede to be closely connected to social privilege, they are unable to solve the originating problems of social inequality they implicitly identify as at the source of the problem. Second, Collins and Barkdull do not explain how, in the situation of major, systematically produced, and strongly embedded inequalities they concede between the parties to the negotiation, stakeholder panels that bring them together to negotiate will overcome the problem that the harmed parties will often be in the same unequal position as they are in these other kinds of negotiations and contracts, such as the labour contract, and other kinds of speech contexts such as the liberal public sphere and the courts. The appearance of a solution here depends upon the assumption that such panels will be able successfully to bracket—set aside as irrelevant—social inequality. Third, they leave unexplained how the negotiation model will overcome the acute problems for the marginalised of silencing and political participation many theorists have identified as the failure of the liberal public sphere (Walzer 1983; Young 1990, 1995; Dean 1996). Unless stakeholder panels can somehow overcome pervasive social inequality to provide more than formal and assumed equality of voice, there is a danger that the panels would function in hegemonic ways to secure the appearance of consent from affected parties to solutions which may not truly represent their voice or interest in stopping the injury. In the context of "the wider failure in liberal democratic theory to distinguish free commitment and agreement from domination, subordination and inequality" (Pateman 1989: 83), it seems more likely that the panels would function to manufacture consent, by generating the hegemonic "we" which subsumes the marginal "I". In short, it is hard to see how stakeholder panels can meet the conditions for transformation of interests and deliberative process I have suggested above without a larger context of equality between the negotiating parties.

The same point holds for attempts to introduce veils of uncertainty. We might try to reinterpret Beck's thesis of risk society as a higher-order normative rather than a descriptive thesis, prescribing that effective political action to stem ecological harms is most likely if ecological risks are equally born and no group can be confident of escaping them. Beck's thesis is certainly more plausible in this form, which suggests a veil of uncertainty approach to involving those groups most influential in decision-making in reducing ecological harms (Young 1997). There is some apparent convergence between this strategy and the strategy of empowering the least remote, to the extent that a more equal society is likely to distribute ecological risks more equally, to have a thicker veil of uncertainty. But the converse does not hold, a veil of uncertainty strategy does not necessarily imply greater equality, since veils of uncertainty as limited devices for specific institutional uses are quite compatible with highly unequal and unjust social arrangements in the larger society. We can imagine the EcoRepublic simulating the uncertainty produced by equality by introducing some kind of stochastic ecological ordeal for decision-makers, for example assignment by lot to a highly polluted area, as a device to counter some of the dangers of remoteness. Yet it is hard to see what could motivate or maintain such measures in the context of the EcoRepublic. Similarly it is hard to see how such indirect strategies emphasising uncertainty could be made thorough or effective as general ways to deal with ecological damage without a larger context of equality which cannot be provided without major transformations of liberal capitalism.

Beyond Deliberative Democracy: The Public Sphere and the Ecological Rationality of Procedural and Participatory Democracy

We have seen that the radical inequality generated in liberal capitalism is a major remoteness factor that hinders the ability to respond both to collective forms of ecological degradation and also to those forms which impact differentially in terms mediated by privilege (ecojustice issues). Radical inequality acts as an incentive to redistribute rather than eliminate ecological harms, and to substitute private ecological goods for collective ecological goods. Inequality creates barriers to communication about ecoharms, both in the form of information and feedback on ecological degradation and its human impacts, and to responsiveness to this information as articulated need, as well as distorting information flows, public sphere knowledge and culture. Inequality is both itself a hindrance to ecological rationality and an indicator of other hindrances. The kind of society whose democratic forms open communication and spread decision-making processes as equally as possible should, other things being equal, offer the best chance of effective action on these significant kinds of ecoharms. Thus systems which are able to articulate and respond to the needs of the least privileged should be better than less democratic systems which reserve effective participation in decision-making for privileged groups.

In an ecologically rational society, ecoharms to marginalised groups as well as to other groups would be able to emerge as important issues in the public sphere, and those most subject to (potential) ecological harms would have an understanding of them and an effective political and public sphere voice. A strong and diverse public sphere not dominated by privileged groups and able to hear the bad news from below is essential to remoteness reduction. If the ability of all those who are injured as and with nature to have their needs considered is linked to their ability to participate in the political structure,[21] this suggests again that the elements of an ecologically rational and responsive democracy will have to be sought within the tradition which interprets democracy as widespread popular participation, choice, and involvement in decision-making, or which draws on the communicative or deliberative concepts of democracy which emphasise the public sphere.

Many of those dissatisfied with shallow interest group democracy have turned to the idea of a deliberative or communicative process to obtain a stronger account of democracy. In this model, democracy is envisaged variously as a process of participation, of deliberation, or of communication: the last two, it should be noted, somewhat narrowing the concept of participation in a potentially rationalist and inegalitarian direction. In my view, remoteness reduction requires us to go beyond these conceptions to a deep form of democracy that involves a justice dimension as redistributive equality (Fraser 1997), equality and plurality of communicative process (Young 1995), and complex equality (Walzer 1983). It requires not only a strong public sphere but perhaps more: communicative and participatory ideals and institutions that not only permit but actively solicit the voice from below. A strong case can also be made, I think, for solidarity and social citizenship, as well as robust collective life, as likely to reduce remoteness and increase ecological responsibility (Plumwood 1996b). And as I've argued elsewhere, it is also crucial to develop a democratic and non-anthropocentric culture which displaces reason/nature dualism in its various contemporary expressions (Plumwood 1993, 1996a,b), as a condition not only of greater human equality, but as the basis of more ecologically sensitive and communicative relationships with the natural world.

The notion that an ecologically rational society would need to take a participatory form derives some of its appeal from the idea that ecological harms are generalisable, so that, once these harms are recognised, general participation should be able to solve the problem of correcting them through consensus formation. If all are equally affected, and all are equally decision-makers in a participatory Rousseauian exercise of the general will, participatory democracy should be the obvious choice for a political framework to satisfy remoteness principles. But since, as we have seen, many ecological harms in modern large-scale societies have strong redistributive aspects based on various kinds of privilege, political structures, and ecological strategies premised on a "common good" framework will be insufficient to deal with them, since major parties are left out. As Iris Young notes "where some groups have greater symbolic or material privilege than others, appeals to a 'common good' are likely to perpetuate such privilege" (Young 1995: 141). Participatory projects that aim to form a "general will" through face-to-face decision-making are open to the objection that they assume simplistic, mystifying, or oppressive projects of unity (Young 1995). Thus too, communitarian and civic republican frameworks which posit a common good but lack any orientation towards recognising either difference or social equality will be correspondingly lacking in conceptual resources for tackling these redistributive features and will not foster ecological rationality in this area.

There are several more plausible recent refinements of the participation concept which replace the instrumental liberal concept of interest group bargaining by the concept of a participatory, communicative, or deliberative procedure which is not valued only instrumentally, in terms of the results it produces, but itself carries intrinsic value as democratic process: John Dryzek's discursive democracy and Iris Young's "communicative democracy" are two such refinements (both of Habermas's original communicative process idea). Dryzek describes discursive democracy as an attempt to "rescue communicative rationality from Habermas" (Dryzek 1990: 20). According to Habermas the liberal public sphere approximates the ideal speech situation of communicative rationality, constituting "a warning system with sensors that, though unspecialised, are sensitive to the entire gamut of society".[22] That is, the liberal public sphere is taken to represent a deliberative arena where everyone, despite other inequalities, has an equal opportunity to speak. This is just what we seem to need for ecological rationality.

Could such a strong public sphere come to the rescue and sufficiently counter the effects of remoteness elsewhere in a system? Not, I shall suggest, without larger transformative changes that are necessary to give a more adequate representation of the bad news from below. Once the formation of the public sphere in ways which reflect the cultural hegemony of privileged groups is recognised, its rescue potential appears much more contingent. Iris Young (1990, 1995) points up the exclusions produced by a model of critical deliberation which fails to recognise cultural specificity and other hegemonic baggage in the assumption of disengaged reason as the basis of deliberative process in the public sphere. Young's discussion shows how rationalist conceptions of speech distort and narrow both what is counted as legitimate speech and who is thought of as qualified to be a speaker. Since Western deliberative norms, Young argues, are hegemonic and agonistic, different "voices" and styles of communication need to be recognised and accorded equal legitimacy in any discussion-based process which aims to be open to all. Gendered and class or race-based norms of assertiveness and gendered speaking styles are signs and expressions of social privilege which exclude and silence. Dominant Western norms of deliberation follow the strongly entrenched cultural pattern of reason/nature dualism, privileging speech which is dispassionate and disembodied.

Young's analysis of cultural hegemony provides some illuminating philosophical confirmation for the empirical work confirming the domination of the public sphere by privileged groups (Pateman 1989). A communicative arrangement which aims to be non-exclusionary must be one which "attends to social difference, to the way power sometimes enters speech itself". But although Young's communicative democracy represents perhaps the most inclusive process account to date in terms of allowing for a multiplicity of voices, there are several remaining problems in her approach to communicative inequality as difference and the exclusive orientation to process. Young's account of silencing is based on a multicultural or ethnic recognition paradigm which aims at the expression of difference: "communicative democracy" she writes, "is better conceived as speaking across differences of culture, social position and need, which are preserved in the process" (p. 143). There are several problems here. First, this model is not appropriate for certain kinds of differences. If some differences are injuries, ways of incapacitating speech or expression even in the most favourable cultural paradigm, should our orientation be so exclusively to representing, expressing, and preserving difference, or do these kinds of differences demand also an orientation to healing action, to actively working for their elimination?[23] Should class differences and other disabling differences directly attributable to subordination be "preserved in the process" and viewed simply as a positive resource to be affirmed or represented? Those who are disabled by or in their difference cannot be empowered by affirming or preserving such differences. In the absence of distinctions between kinds of differences,[24] this formula disappears class differences and discounts the role of redistributive inequality in closing the public sphere to certain kinds of voices.

The hidden assumption here that social or redistributive inequality is irrelevant to political equality (a liberal version of mind/body dualism) and has no bearing on the ability to participate in the public sphere has been justly criticised by Carole Pateman and Nancy Fraser, among others. As Fraser (1997) states, to declare social inequalities, hierarchies, and status differentials bracketed or irrelevant to deliberation is not to make it so. If participatory or discursive democracy proliferates formal structures for participation and deliberation without considering and creating the material conditions necessary for equal participation, the result can only be what Carole Pateman calls "mini-liberalism". One source of the neglect of redistributive equality in liberal concepts of political equality are concepts of justice and equality defined in terms of reason and the state (Fraser 1997). These inherit the distortions of rationalist conceptions of reason which deny the conditions of reason's own production. To guarantee genuine equality of speech, discursive democracy has to attend to the conditions of social and cultural equality which will make equal participation in the public sphere more than a formal possibility. A discursive form of democracy which permits the silencing of those groups most likely to bear ecological harms and continues to select privileged groups as major participants in the same way as liberal forms will have no obviously better claim to reduce remoteness or to be ecologically rational.

The second problem is related to the first but is more general, and turns on difficulties of adopting an exclusively procedural approach to hearing the bad news from below (whether the procedure is based on Habermas or Rawls). The idea that equality of access to social goods is entirely a matter of getting the right process for political communication has come to be widely accepted in the last twenty years. But an exclusive orientation to process neglects the other half of the process/product relationship, the redistributive outcome of the communicative process, and the relations of reciprocal corrigibility that must hold between process and product. For many activities, we may need to decide if a process is working well by seeing if it is turning out the right sort of product; the quality of a product can act as a test for the adequacy of the process, as the quality of the process can for the product in the democratic context. We can recognise this reciprocity of process and product even where the process is conceived as valuable in itself. A process of artistic expression, for example, may have value in its own right as an expressive process, but both we and the artist will still often want to assess that process, at least in part, in terms of the kinds of products it turns out. Although an artistic process, unlike an instrumental one, is not judged entirely in relation to its product, an artist will often attempt to keep a balance between attention to the process and attention to the product, modifying each in the light of the other. Where process and product are reciprocally corrigible, a choice between a concept of democracy driven exclusively by process and a concept which treats process in exclusively instrumental terms, as purely a means to some predetermined outcome, is a false one. If communicative processes are themselves, as Young suggests, imbued with power, communicative processes and democratic products must be among this "reciprocal" group, and we must seek ways to check and modify allegedly equal communicative processes, for example in terms of the kinds of distributive product which emerges from them.

To the extent that voices excluded by a flawed communicative process cannot proclaim or contest their own exclusion within the framework it offers (a version of the liar paradox), an illusion of adequacy and completeness of the process may be produced which cannot be corrected on a purely procedural level. To that extent also, external checks of fairness, such as that provided by the product, are required. Where the process of equal communication is revealed as politically problematic, as subject to all kinds of hegemonic modification, inflection, and interference (as Young's arguments do so reveal it), checking and modifying the communicative process by reference to the redistributive outcome is clearly essential. If a process of political communication is working well, if it is inclusive and open in a real and not just formal way to all, it should be producing a certain kind of distributive product. That product is substantive social and redistributive equality. Can we imagine a situation where a process whereby everyone has an equal opportunity to communicate needs and goals will result in a distributive outcome of serious social deprivation for some, and of substantial over-affluence for others? I believe that we would be entitled to conclude from the redistributive product that such a process is seriously flawed as a process of equal communication, and that the process has not yielded an adequate form of communicative democracy.

I want to draw out several points in conclusion. Ecologically rational societies would attend to various kinds of remoteness, including especially those consequential kinds based on social inequality. A society which aimed to reduce consequential remoteness and open ecojustice issues to effective political action would need, among other things, to be participatory and communicative, and it would need to be a society of substantial equality and democratic culture. Where we have good reason to believe that a hegemonic "we" has subsumed an excluded "I", and that existing inequalities will skew processes of communication and public sphere activity for a long time to come, we can't just hope that sufficient redistributive equality will emerge in the course of an apparently open communication process. A political structure that aimed to hear the bad news from below could not rely on somehow representing "below" in apparently fair communicative processes which were open to wide expressions of cultural difference, but would also need to adopt substantial social equality as a major redistributive and transformative objective (Fraser 1997). My argument has suggested that an ecologically rational society would need to be more ambitious in this direction than any society we now know, but that this may ultimately be the condition of our survival.

Notes

1. These conditions of compliance and flexibility are suggested in Thompson 1996.

2. Which is not to be identified with instrumental reason. See Plumwood 1996a. Indeed, since anthropocentric culture contributes in a major way to remoteness, such a prudential inquiry must go beyond concern with the arrangement of existing ends and extend to questioning the instrumental treatment of ecology and nature itself.

3. On Prometheanism, see Hayward 1994. For a feminist critique of rationalist interpretations of reason, see esp. Lloyd 1984.

4. Although culture, epistemology, ethics, and rationality itself are all implicated in questions of ecological rationality, and not only questions of political structure (contra Pepper 1993).

5. The interpretation of flexibility is plainly highly politically inflected and defined relative to larger political choices and parameters: thus an alternative interpretation of flexibility suitable for a democratic polity might see it as best realised in conjunction with features such as basic income security and democratic workplace responsibility.

6. An appeal to science will not solve the problem raised by ecological rationality. Unless we make the assumptions that the initial knowledge and judgement of the Scientist King is perfect, and that there is a method for perfectly reproducing and perfectly applying this body of knowledge, science itself cannot escape the need for epistemic, political, and social structures which enable good ecological correctiveness. To the extent that environmental oligarchy

assumes that "objective science" can itself provide a reliable source of correctiveness, its proponents depend on ignoring the substantial body of work showing how power distorts conceptual frameworks and knowledges, and how science produces for the needs of the powerful. Recent work on the way such distortions in science are generated by forms of power and oppression includes Harding 1991.

7. Dewey 1961.

8. This formulation aims to avoid the ecological reductionism that haunts bioregionalism, and the implication that ecological consequences are automatically privileged or are the only ones that must be considered.

9. It cannot without endorsing strong ecological priority empower those who bear the ecological consequences over those who bear other consequences, since ecological consequences are not the only kinds of consequences that will flow from a community's decisions. Not silencing and disempowering those who bear the consequences is a minimum condition, although some way might be found to supplement it by reflecting weak ecological priority.

10. Some theorists, for example, libertarian municipalists like Murray Bookchin, recognise that certain political conditions must be specified before we can decide whether or not a given small-scale autarchy is ecologically viable. But the question of how far the larger political networks they propose, such as federations, preserve remoteness principles remains to be considered.

11. This was the argument recently employed by World Bank officials to justify Third World waste dumping.

12. This is a bit narrow, of course, since not all ecological issues and areas of degradation or concern can be reduced to "ecoharms".

13. This is at least in part because it prioritises interests according to a completely different political logic than that involved in ranking ends according to whether they are pre-conditions for other ends.

14. This is the normal form of the lobbying contest between powerful economic interests and vocal green organisations the interest group model generates.

15. Many of these forms also impact on future people, who, in terms of exclusion from decisions which impact on their welfare, have to be considered highly disadvantaged.

16. So although we have the term "environmental racism" established to cover such issues of redistribution, these points provide reasons for thinking that, contra Beck, we still need concepts of class if we wish to understand them, and that we cannot work exclusively with the racialised "difference" discourses which are often used now as surrogates for suppressed concepts of class. Perhaps we can even regard class privilege as partly constituted by access to such forms of remoteness, and as having multiple determinants depending on the form at work.

17. Of course not all environmental issues have this association with marginality. Theorists of ecojustice have noted that those that have associations with more privileged groups, such as wilderness and biodiversity, tend to have a better public profile (Jennings and Jennings 1993). I do not intend to suggest that these more prestigious forms are less important or are negligible, but rather that the consequential remoteness of privileged groups is often reflected in what counts as an ecological issue in the public sphere. The divide coincides roughly with the difference between a concern about damage to 'good' nature versus a concern with repairing or avoiding further damage to 'bad' (already damaged) nature.

18. This is one among a number of reasons why the privileged may appear in opinion polls and the like as more environmentally concerned, a result which should clearly not be taken at face value.

19. I assume here neither that all ecoharms can be dealt with via party negotiation nor that these should take the form of "bargaining sessions," judicial or otherwise. Although consensus-oriented deliberation might deal better than liberalism with cases where there is agreement about what constitutes a collective ecological

good, it will face problems in situations where there is no consensus about different conceptions of the ecological good, as in the case of different cultural conceptions of "the best state" of nature.

20. This condition seems to me to rule out individualist forms of capitalism and to point to community control of investment decisions, since the power to control these decisions so crucial to community well-being would tend to make entrepeneurial interests sponsoring a polluting or damaging process highly privileged in any dispute resolution or communicative process.

21. See "The Civic Culture: A Philosophic Critique," in Pateman 1989.

22. Habermas, quoted in Dean 1996.

23. See also Phillips 1991, who argues that class differences require better parliamentary representation, but does not discuss the paradox of making an allegedly equal political form complicit in representing differences of subordination.

24. Nancy Fraser has written insightfully of the need to discriminate among differences, only some of which are to be affirmed (Fraser 1995, 1997).

References

Bartlett, Robert (1986), "Ecological Rationality: Reason and Environmental Policy," *Environmental Ethics*, 8 (3): 221–39.

Beck, Ulrich (1995), *Ecological Enlightenment* (Atlantic Highlands, NJ: Humanities Press).

——Giddens, Anthony, and Lash, Scott (1994), *Reflexive Modernisation* (Cambridge: Polity).

Collins, Denis, and Barkdull, John (1995), "Capitalism, Environmentalism, and Mediating Structures: From Adam Smith to Stakeholder Panels," *Environmental Ethics*, Fall: 227–324.

Dean, Jodi (1996), "Civil Society: Beyond the Public Sphere," in David M. Rasmussen (ed.), *Handbook of Critical Theory* (Cambridge, Mass.: Blackwell), 422–43.

Dewey, John (1961), *Democracy and Education* (London: Macmillan).

Dowie, Mark (1995), *Losing Ground* (Cambridge, Mass.: MIT Press).

Dryzek, John (1987), *Rational Ecology: Environment and Political Economy* (Oxford: Blackwell).

——(1990), *Discursive Democracy: Politics, Policy and Political Science* (Cambridge: Cambridge University Press).

——(1992), "Ecology and Discursive Democracy: Beyond Liberal Capitalism and the Administrative State," *Capitalism, Nature, Socialism*, 3 (2): 18–42.

——(1996), "Political and Ecological Communication," in Freya Mathews (ed.), *Ecology and Democracy* (Portland, Ore: Frank Cass), 3–30.

Fraser, Nancy (1989), *Unruly Practices* (Cambridge: Polity Press).

——(1995), "From Redistribution to Recognition? Dilemmas of Justice in a 'PostSocialist'Age," *New Left Review*, Sept./Oct., 68–95.

——(1997), *Justus Interruptus* (Routledge: London).

Haraway, Donna (1991), "Situated Knowledges," in *Simians, Cyborgs and Women* (London: Free Association Books), 183–202.

Harding, Sandra (1991), *Whose Science, Whose Knowledge?* (Milton Keynes: Open University Press).

——(1993) (ed.), *The Racial Economy of Science: Toward a Democratic Future* (Bloomington: Indiana University Press).

Hayward, Tim (1994), *Ecological Thought*, (Cambridge: Polity).

hooks, bell (1994), *Outlaw Culture* (London: Routledge).

Jennings, Cheri Lucas, and Jennings, H. Bruce (1993), "Green Fields/Brown Skin: Posting as a Sign of Recognition," in Jane Bennett and William Chaloupka (eds), *In the Nature of Things* (London: University of Minnesota Press), 173–96.

Lloyd, Genevieve (1984), *The Man of Reason* (London: Methuen).

Martin, Emily (1995), "Flexible Bodies: Health and Work in an Age of Systems," *Ecologist* 25 (6): 221–226.

Pateman, Carole (1989), *The Disorder of Women* (Cambridge: Polity).

Pepper, David (1993), *Eco-Socialism: From Deep Ecology to Social Justice* (London: Routledge).

Phillips, Anne (1991), *Engendering Democracy* (Cambridge: Polity).

Plumwood, Val (1993), *Feminism and the Mastery of Nature* (London: Routledge).

—— (1996a), "Anthrocentrism and Androcentrism: Parallels and Politics," *Ethics and the Environment*, 1 (2): 119–52.

—— (1996b), "Has Democracy Failed Ecology?," in Freya Mathews (ed.), *Ecology and Democracy* (Portland, Ore.: Frank Cass), 134–68.

Sale, Kirkpatrick (1980), *Human Scale* (London: Secker and Warburg).

Thompson, Janna (1996), "Towards a Green World Order: Environment and World Politics," in Freya Mathews (ed.), *Ecology and Democracy* (Portland, Ore.: Frank Cass), 32–48.

Walzer, Michael L. (1983), *Spheres of Justice* (New York: Basic Books).

Young, Iris (1990), *Justice and the Politics of Difference* (Princeton: Princeton University Press).

—— (1995), "Communication and the Other: Beyond Deliberative Democracy," in Margaret Wilson and Anna Yeatman (eds), *Justice and Identity* (Wellington: Allen and Unwin), 134–52.

Young, Oran (1997), "Fairness Matters: The Role of Equity in International Regimes," "Environmental Justice: Global Ethics for the 21st Century," Conference Melbourne, 1–3 October.

40 Political and Ecological Communication

John S. Dryzek

We can, I believe, best explore the prospects for an effective green democracy by working with a political model whose essence is authentic communication rather than, say, preference aggregation, representation, or partisan competition. The ecological context means that the kind of communicative democracy that ensues ought to take a particular shape or shapes. This shape depends not on the set of values through reference to which democrats have always justified their projects, though such values have an important place in any contemplation of appropriate political structure. It is, more importantly, a question of some political forms being better able to enter into fruitful engagement with natural systems than others, and so more effectively cope with the ecological challenge.

Why we Need Green Structures, not just Green Values

Inasmuch as there is a conventional wisdom on the matter of ecology and democracy, it would draw a sharp distinction between procedure and substance. As Robert Goodin (1992: 168) puts it, 'To advocate democracy is to advocate procedures, to advocate environmentalism is to advocate substantive outcomes'. And there can never be any guarantee that democratic procedure will produce ecologically benign substance. This distinction between procedure and substance forms the core of Goodin's (1992) treatment of green political theory. To Goodin, the green theory of value represents a coherent set of ends related to the protection and preservation of nature, whereas the green theory of agency addresses where and how these values might be promoted. Goodin argues that a green theory of agency cannot be derived from the green theory of value. Greens may still want to advocate, say, grassroots participatory democracy; but they should recognise that any such advocacy has to be on grounds separate from basic green values. This procedure/substance divide arises most graphically in the context of green advocacy of decentralisation and community self-control. Such decentralisation of political authority would have decidedly anti-ecological substantive consequences in many places with natural-resource-based local economies. Many counties in the Western United States are currently trying to assert their authority against federal environmental legislation (so far with little success in the courts) in order that mining, grazing on federal lands, and forest clearcutting can proceed unchecked.

Decentralisation will only work to the extent that local recipients of authority subscribe to ecological values or, alternatively, the degree to which they must stay put and depend for their livelihoods solely on what can be produced locally.

On this kind of account, political structure obviously matters far less than the adoption of green values on the part of denizens in that structure, or the occupancy of key positions (such as membership in Parliament) in that structure by greens. Along these lines, Eckersley (1992) concludes that the key to green political transformation is the dissemination and adoption of ecocentric culture. In fairness, she also addresses the issue of political structure, though the kind of structure she advocates is quite close to what already exists in federal liberal democracies. Similarly, to Goodin the key to green politics is participation in electoral politics and coalition with other parties in an effort to ensure that governments in liberal democracies adopt, if only partially and incrementally, those parts of the green political agenda inspired by the green theory of value. As he puts it, 'we can, and probably should, accept green political prescriptions without necessarily adopting green ideas about how to reform political structures and processes' (Goodin 1992: 5).

The trouble with Goodin's position here is that it regards political agency as essentially unproblematical. In other words, all that has to be done is to convince people in positions of political authority that X should be pursued, and X will be pursued. Goodin's 'X' is in fact a rather large one: he considers (and I agree) that the green programme merits adoption on an all-or-nothing basis. But there are good reasons why dominant political mechanisms cannot adopt and implement that programme, or even substantial chunks of it, irrespective of the degree to which green values are adopted by participants in these mechanisms. For any complex system, be it economic, political, ecological, or social, embodies imperatives or emergent properties that take effect regardless of the intentions of the denizens of the system. Such imperatives constitute values that the system will seek. Other values will be downplayed or ignored.

To begin with the currently dominant order of capitalist democracy, all liberal democracies currently operate in the context of a capitalist market system. Any state operating in the context of such a system is greatly constrained in terms of the kinds of policies it can pursue. Policies that damage business profitability—or are even perceived as likely to damage that profitability—are automatically punished by the recoil of the market. Disinvestment here means economic downturn. And such downturn is bad for governments because it both reduces the tax revenue for the schemes those governments want to pursue (such as environmental restoration), and reduces the popularity of the government in the eyes of the voters. This effect is not a matter of conspiracy or direct corporate influence on government; it happens automatically, irrespective of anyone's intentions.

The constraints upon governments here are intensified by the increasing mobility of capital across national boundaries. So, for example, anti-pollution regulation in the United States stimulates an exodus of polluting industry across the Rio Grande to Mexico's *maquiladora* sector. Thus irrespective of the ideology of government—and irrespective of the number of green lobbyists, coalition members, or parliamentarians—the first task of any liberal democratic state must always be to secure and maintain profitable conditions for business.

Environmental policy is possible in such states, but only if its damage to business profitability is marginal, or if it can be shown to be good for business. Along these lines, Albert Weale (1992: 66–92) discusses the ideology of 'ecological modernisation', which he believes has gained a toe-hold in German policy-making. More recently, United States Vice-President Albert Gore has pointed to the degree to which environmental protection can actually enhance business profitability. Yet it remains to be demonstrated that a systemic reconciliation of economic and ecological values is achievable here, as opposed to isolated successes on the part of green capital-ists. If green demands are more radical, or 'all or nothing' in Goodin's terms, then 'nothing' remains the likely consequence in any clash with economic imperatives.

Even setting aside the economic context of policy determination under capitalist democracy, there remain reasons why the structure of liberal democracy itself is ultimately incapable of responding effectively to ecological problems. To cut a long story short, these problems often feature high degrees of complexity and uncertainty, and substantial collective action problems. Thus any adequate political mechanism for dealing with them must incorporate negative feed-back (the ability to generate corrective movement when a natural system's equilibrium is dis-turbed), coordination across different problems (so that solving a problem in one place does not simply create greater problems elsewhere), coordination across actors (to supply public goods or prevent the tragedy of the commons), robustness (an ability to perform well across different conditions and contexts), flexibility (an ability to adjust internal structure in response to chang-ing conditions), and resilience (an ability to correct for severe disequilibrium, or environmental crisis).[1]

One can debate the degree to which these criteria are met by different political-economic mechanisms, such as markets, administrative hierarchies, and international negotiations, as well as liberal democracies. My own judgment is that liberal democracy does not perform particu-larly well across these criteria. Negative feedback under liberal democracy is mostly achieved as a result of particular actors whose interests are aggrieved giving political vent to their annoy-ance, be it in voting for green candidates, lobbying, contributing money to environmentalist interest groups, or demonstrating. But such feedback devices are typically dominated by the rep-resentation of economic interests, businesses and (perhaps) labour. Coordination is often prob-lematical because the currency of liberal democracy consists of tangible rewards to particular interests. Such particular interests do not add up to the general ecological interest. Further, com-plex problems are generally disaggregated on the basis of these same particular interests, and piecemeal responses crafted in each of the remaining subsets. The ensuing 'partisan mutual adjustment', to use Lindblom's (1965) term, may produce a politically rational resultant. But there is no reason to expect this resultant to be ecologically rational. In other words, interests may be placated in proportion to their material political influence, and compromises may be achieved across them, but wholesale ecological destruction can still result. Resilience in liberal democracy is inhibited by short time horizons (resulting from electoral cycles) and a general addiction to the 'political solvent' of economic growth (politics is much happier, and choices easier, when the size of the available financial 'pie' is growing).

Despite its inadequacies, I would argue that among the political mechanisms that have been tried by nations from time to time, liberal democracy is the most ecologically rationally system (Dryzek 1987: ch. 9). But even setting aside the issue of the ecological adequacy of liberal democracy, and its relative merits compared to other systems, the fact remains that the way political systems are structured can make an enormous difference when it comes to the likelihood or otherwise of realising green values. And if this is true, then (to use Goodin's distinction) we should be able to derive a model of politics from the green theory of value, not just the green theory of agency. Let me now attempt such a derivation.

Biocentric and Anthropocentric Models, and their Inadequacies

What, then, might such a model look like? Would it be democratic? If so, in what sense of democracy? Presumably, what we are looking for is some kind of polity that could embed something more than short-term human material interests, and achieve more sustainable equilibria encompassing natural and human systems. Along these lines, Eckersley (1992) uses the term 'ecocentric' to describe her preferred kind of system. The term 'ecocentric' or 'biocentric' implies that intrinsic value is located in nature, and can connote an absence of regard for human interests, essentially shedding one 'centrism' in favour of another. But Eckersley herself is careful to say that she also wants the variety of human interests in nature to be sheltered under her ecocentric umbrella.

Does it make sense for us to speak in terms of ecocentric or biocentric democracy? In perhaps its most widely-used sense, 'ecocentric politics' refers only to a human political system that would give priority to ecological values. To advocate ecocentric politics in such terms is unremarkable, reducing as it does to advocacy of a biocentric ethic—one that accords intrinsic value to natural entities, irrespective of human interest in those entities. Beyond this ethical imperative politics is unchanged, and does not need to stand in any particular *structural* relation to nature. The problem with such a minimalist approach to ecocentric democracy is that it returns us directly to the position that was rejected in the previous section, where I tried to establish that we need green political structures as well as green values.

What more can ecocentric politics mean, beyond advocacy of biocentric values? A maximalist view here might emphasise the 'politics' created by and in nature, to which humans could adjust *their* politics. Now, Aristotle suggested long ago that what sets humans apart is that man is *zoon politikon*, the political animal. Primate ethology now suggests that there is something like politics that occurs in animal societies involving, for example, bargaining and trickery in the establishment of dominance hierarchies among males, though even here, one should be wary of anthropomorphising observed behaviour. Yet even if a quasi-politics can be found among primates or other animals, that kind of politics is one in which we humans cannot participate, just as animals cannot participate in our politics. Moreover, most of what goes on in the natural world (outside animal societies) would still be extremely hard to assimilate to any definition of politics.

The last century or so has seen the ascription of all kinds of political and social models to nature. Social Darwinists saw in nature a reflection of naked capitalism. Marx and Engels saw evolutionary justification for dialectical materialism. In 1915 the US political scientist Henry Jones Ford saw collectivist justification for an organic state. Nazis saw justification for genocide. Microeconomists see something like market transactions in the maximisation of inclusive fitness. Eco-anarchists from Kropotkin to Murray Bookchin see in nature models only of co-operation and mutualism. Roger Masters (1989) has recently suggested that liberal democracy is 'natural' in its flexibility in responding to changing environments. Ecofeminists see caring and nurturing, at least in female nature. And so forth. In short, just about every human political ideology and political-economic system has at one time or another been justified as consistent with nature, especially nature as revealed by Darwinism.

But this sheer variety should suggest that in nature we will find no single blueprint for human politics. And even if we did, that model would only prove *ecologically* benign to the extent that it could demonstrate that cross-species interactions were universally mutualistic and benign, rather than often hostile and competitive. Following Kropotkin, Murray Bookchin (1982) propounds exactly such a mutualistic, co-operative view of nature, to which he suggests human social, economic, and political life should be assimilated. But Bookchin's position here is, to say the least, selective in its interpretation of nature, and no more persuasive than all the other selective interpretations which have been used to justify all manner of human political arrangements. So a maximalist notion of ecocentric politics of the sort advocated by Bookchin should be rejected.

Yet nature is not devoid of political lessons. What we *will* find in nature, or at least in our interactions with it, is a variety of levels and kinds of communication to which we might try to adapt. The key here is to downplay 'centrism' of any kind, and focus instead on the kinds of interactions that might occur across the boundaries between humanity and nature. In this spirit, the search for green democracy can indeed involve looking for progressively less anthropocentric political forms. For democracy can exist not only among humans, but also in human dealings with the natural world—though not *in* that natural world, or in any simple *model* which nature provides for humanity. So the key here is seeking more egalitarian interchange at the human/natural boundary; an interchange that involves progressively less in the way of human autism. In short, ecological democratisation here is a matter of more effective integration of political and ecological communication.

On the face of it, this requirement might suggest that the whole history of democratic theory—and democratic practice—should be jettisoned, and that a truly green programme of institutional innovation should be sought under a different rubric than 'democracy'. For democracy, however contested a concept, and in however many varieties it has appeared in the last two and a half thousand years, is, if nothing else, anthropocentric. One way to substantiate this point would be to go through all the major models of democracy (for example, as presented in Held (1987)), and test them for anthropocentrism. Obviously I have not the space to do that. But let me just note that inasmuch as democratic theory has been taken under the wing of liberalism in the last few hundred years (and most of it has been), then its anthropocentrism has been guaranteed. As Freya Mathews (1991b: 158) notes, 'liberalism as it stands is of course anthropocentric: it takes human interest as the measure of all value'. Liberalism does so because only reasoning entities are accorded political standing. The members of a liberal democracy might, of course, choose to enact positive measures for environmental protection, for example by granting legal rights to natural objects. Guardians for those objects might then make claims on political and legal systems. But any such representation might simply *down*grade nature to another set of interests, disaggregating and isolating these interests by assigning them to identifiable natural objects, thus ignoring their intrinsically ecological (interconnected) character.

If we take the major alternative to liberalism, we find that Marxism (and so its associated models of democracy) is equally materialistic and anthropocentric, seeking human liberation in part through more effective domination and control of nature (Eckersley 1992: 75–95).[2]

The Communicative Rationality of Ecological Democracy

To attempt to move in a different direction here, let me return to the issue of the connection between democracy and reason, as highlighted in Mathews's mention of liberalism. Without wishing to get too involved in the various debates surrounding democracy and rationality (Spragens 1990; Dryzek 1990a), let me suggest that the best or most fruitful approach to the issue of how we might rescue rationality and perhaps democracy from anthropocentrism begins with Jürgen Habermas's analysis of the dialectics of rationalisation attendant upon modernity. To Habermas (notably, 1984, 1987), modernisation connotes two kinds of rationalisation. The first is instrumental: instrumental rationality may be defined in terms of the capacity to devise, select, and effect good means to clarified and consistent ends. The second is communicative: communicative action involves understanding across subjects, the coordination of their actions through discussion, and socialisation. Communicative rationality is the degree to which these processes are uncoerced, undistorted, and engaged by competent individuals. On Habermas's account, instrumental rationalisation has so far come out ahead, and with it the domination of money and power in political and social life, especially through bureaucracy and capitalism. One can imagine a democracy of instrumental or strategically rational individuals, and this kind of democracy is modelled in great detail by public choice analysis but, as public choice has itself shown, such a democracy is an incoherent mess, producing unstable and arbitrary outcomes (Dryzek 1992). Thus some degree of communicative rationality is crucial to *any* democracy. More important for present purposes, communicative rationality constitutes the model for a democracy that is deliberative rather than strategic in character; or at least one where strategic action is kept firmly in its place.

But could such a democracy be green? Eckersley (1992: 109–17) for one argues that it cannot. And in the terms in which she argues, she is entirely correct. She points out that for Habermas (just as for most liberals) the only entities that matter are ones capable of engaging as subjects in dialogue—in other words, human beings. In a belief carried over from his earlier work on the philosophy of science, Habermas considers that the only fruitful human attitude toward the natural world is one of instrumental manipulation and control. Indeed, the whole point of communicative rationalisation is to *prevent* human interactions with one another becoming like human interactions with the natural world (Alford 1985: 77). Human liberation is bought at the expense of the domination of nature, and so Habermas is as anthropocentric as orthodox Marxists here. And for this reason Eckersley dismisses Habermas as having any possible relevance to the search for an ecocentric politics.

Let me suggest that it would be more appropriate here to try to rescue communicative rationality from Habermas. The key would be to treat communication, and so communicative rationality, as extending to entities that can act as agents, even though they lack the self-awareness that connotes subjectivity. Agency is not the same as subjectivity, and only the former need be sought in nature. Habermas treats nature as though it were brute matter. But nature is not passive, inert, and plastic. Instead, this world is truly alive, and pervaded with meanings.[3]

Minimally, a recognition of agency in nature would underwrite respect for natural objects and ecological processes. Just as democrats should condemn humans who would silence other humans, so should they condemn humans who would silence nature by destroying it. But there are implications here for politics, as well as morality. For this recognition of agency in nature means that we should treat signals emanating from the natural world with the same respect we accord signals emanating from human subjects, and as requiring equally careful interpretation. In other words, our relation to the natural world should not be one of instrumental intervention and observation of results oriented to control. Thus communicative interaction with the natural world can and should be an eminently rational affair (Dryzek 1990b). Of course, human *verbal* communication cannot extend into the natural world.[4] But greater continuity is evident in non-verbal communication—body language, facial displays, pheromones, and so forth (Dryzek 1990b: 207). And a lot goes on in human conversation beyond the words, which is why a telephone discussion is not the same as a face-to-face meeting. More important than such continuities here are the ecological processes which transcend the boundaries of species, such as the creation, modification, or destruction of niches; or cycles involving oxygen, nitrogen, carbon, and water. Disruptions in such processes occasionally capture our attention, in the form, for example, of climate change, desertification, deforestation, and species extinction.

The idea that there may be agency in nature might seem to fly in the face of several hundred years of Western natural science, social science, and political theory. But perhaps the suggestion is not so far-fetched. Accounts of the actual practice of biological science often emphasise not manipulation and control, but rather understanding and communication. Examples here are especially prominent in work on animal thinking (notably by Donald Griffin), ethology (as in the work of Jane Goodall on chimpanzees), ecology (Worster 1985), and even genetics (see Keller's (1983) discussion of the 'feeling for the organism' in the work of Barbara Mclintock).

Agency in nature on a grand scale is proposed in James Lovelock's Gaia hypothesis, which suggests that the biosphere as a whole acts so as to maintain the conditions for life. Lovelock does not suggest that Gaia has awareness, and so it cannot be described as a subject (still less a goddess). Rather, Gaia consists of a complex, self-regulating intelligence. But taking the hypothesis to heart 'implies that the stable state of our planet includes man as a part of, or partner in, a very democratic entity' (Lovelock 1979: 145). Let me suggest that Lovelock's words here may be taken more literally than perhaps he intends, and that his hypothesis can indeed help us conceptualise a non-anthropocentric democracy.[5]

All of these suggestions of agency in nature have their critics, especially among philosophers, probably less frequently among natural scientists. And it may often be hard to prove these positions scientifically. But that may not be the point. No democratic theory has ever been founded on scientific *proof* of anything, and there is no reason to seek an exception here. When it comes to the essence of *human* nature, political theorists can only disagree among themselves. To some, a utility-maximising *homo economicus* captures the essence of human nature; to others (mostly sociologists), it is a plastic, socialised conception of humanity in which there are no choices to be made, let alone utilities to be maximised; to others (such as critical theorists) a communicative and creative self; to others (such as civic republicans) a public-spirited and reflective self. In the present context, the idea of an ecological self (Mathews 1991*a*) is perhaps more appropriate than these established paradigms of personhood. My general point here is that when it comes to an ecological democracy that opens itself toward non-human nature, we should not apply standards of proof which no other democratic theory could possibly meet.

I have tried to show that it is conceivable that processes of communicative reason can be extended to cover non-human entities. Communicative reason can underwrite a particular kind of democracy in purely human affairs—one that is discursive or deliberative in character, whose essence is talk and scrutiny of the interests common to a group of people, or of particular interests of some subset of that group. But of course non-human entities cannot talk, and nor should they be anthropomorphised by giving them rights against us or preferences to be incorporated in utilitarian calculation, still less votes. However, as I have suggested, there are senses in which nature can communicate. So what kind of politics or democracy can be at issue here?

Democracy Without Boundaries

To approach an answer, we first need to clear away some of the underbrush that has accumulated with the pervasiveness of liberal discourse in the last few centuries. In a liberal conception of democracy, the essence of democracy is preference aggregation (Miller 1992: 54–5). Liberals themselves might disagree as to what mechanisms for preference aggregation work best, or whose preferences should be aggregated, or to what extent aggregated preferences should be restrained by other considerations (such as basic human rights). But on one thing they all agree: preferences need to be aggregated, and if so, then a basic task is to define the population (society, or citizenry) whose preferences are to be taken into account. In practice, this can be done very precisely, with electoral registers and so forth. The liberal model of democracy requires a hard-and-fast boundary between the human and non-human world (not to mention a boundary between public and private realms, now challenged by feminists). For non-human entities cannot have preferences that we could easily recognise, or be at all confident in attributing to them. Thus ecological democracy cannot be sought in the image of preference aggregation in liberal democracy.

This liberal ideal of democracy as preference aggregation also presupposes the notion of a self-contained, self-governing community. But in today's world, that notion is becoming increasingly fictional, as political, social, and especially economic transactions transcend national boundaries. In which case, it might be productive to start thinking about models of democracy in which the boundaries of communities are indeterminate. Burnheim's proposals for demarchy can be interpreted as interesting moves in this direction. To Burnheim (1985), democracy and democratic legitimacy are not to be sought in geographically-bounded entities like nation states, but rather in functional authorities of varying geographical scope, run by individuals selected by lot from among those with a material interest in the issue in question. Now,

Burnheim's functional authorities arguably establish different boundaries: between functional issue areas, rather than geographical territories. But the trouble here is that there are of course major interactions across issue areas. So interactions across issue areas, no less than interactions across state boundaries, force us to look for the essence of democracy not in the mechanical aggregation of the preferences of a well-defined and well-bounded group of people (such as a nation-state, or set of persons with a material interest in an issue), but rather in the content and style of interactions. Some styles may be judged anti-democratic (for example, the imposition of a decision without possibility for debate or criticism), some relatively democratic (for example, wide dissemination of information about an issue, the holding of hearings open to any interested parties, and so on).

A focus on the style and content of interactions fits well with the communicative rationality grounding for democracy to which I have already alluded. Now, some critics of deliberative democracy and its grounding in communicative rationality argue that it privileges rational argument, and effectively excludes other kinds of voices. But the solution to any such exclusion is obvious: the deliberative model should be extended so as to make provision for such alternative voices.[6] A similar extension may be in order to accommodate non-human communication.

Along with a recognition of the indefinite nature of boundaries of the political community, such extension means that we are now well-placed (or at least better-placed than liberal democrats) to think about dismantling what is perhaps the biggest political boundary of them all: that between the human and the non-human world. This is indeed a big step, and no doubt some people would still believe that it takes us out of the realm of politics and democracy altogether, at least as those terms are conventionally defined. Yet there is a sense in which human relationships with nature are *already* political. As Val Plumwood points out in her contribution to this collection, politicisation is a concomitant of the human colonization of nature. Such colonization connotes an authoritarian politics; democratisation would imply a more egalitarian politics here.

Democracy is, if nothing else, both an open-ended project and an essentially contested concept; indeed, if debates about the meaning of democracy did not occur in a society, we would hesitate to describe that society as truly democratic. All I am trying to do here is introduce another—major—dimension of contestation.

At one level, it is possible to propose ecological democracy as a regulative ideal. This is, after all, how the basic principles of both liberal and deliberative democracy can be advanced (Miller 1992: 55–6). For liberals, the regulative ideal is fairness and efficiency in preference aggregation: the various institutional forms under which preference aggregation might proceed are then a matter for investigation, comparison, and debate. Similarly, for deliberative democrats, the regulative ideal is free discourse about issues and interests; again, various institutional forms might then be scrutinised in the light of this ideal. For ecological democrats, the regulative ideal is effectiveness in communication that transcends the boundary of the human world. As it enters human systems, then obviously ecological communication needs to be interpreted. However, unlike the situation in liberal democracy (or for that matter in Burnheim's demarchy), this communication does not have to be mediated by the material interests of particular actors.

The content of such communication might involve attention to feedback signals emanating from natural systems; in which case, the practical challenge when it comes to institutional design becomes one of dismantling barriers to such communication. With this principle in mind, it is a straightforward matter to criticise institutions that try to subordinate nature on a large scale. Think, for example, of the development projects sponsored by the World Bank, which until recently did not even pretend to take local environmental factors into account (now they at least pretend to). Yet it is also possible to criticise approaches to our dealings with the environment that do exactly the reverse, and seek only the removal of human agency. On one of his own interpretations, Lovelock's Gaia can do quite well without people. And a misanthrope such as David Ehrenfeld (1978) would prefer to rely on natural processes left well alone by humans.

With this regulative ideal of ecological democracy in mind we are, then, in a position both to criticise existing political-economic arrangements and to think about what might work better. I am not going to offer a blueprint for the institutions of such a democracy. The design of such a democracy should itself be discursive, democratic, and sensitive to ecological signals. Moreover, idealist political prescription insensitive to real-world constraints and possibilities for innovation is often of limited value. And variation in the social and natural contexts within which political systems operate means that we should be open to institutional expermentation and variety across these contexts (though, as I noted earlier, an ability to operate in different contexts may itself be a highly desirable quality for any political-economic mechanism).

When it comes to criticism of existing political (and economic) mechanisms, it is reasonably easy to use the ecological communicative ideal to expose some gross failings. Perhaps most obviously, to the degree that any such mechanism allows internal communication to dominate and distort signals from the outside, it merits condemnation. So, for example, a bureaucracy with a well-developed internal culture may prove highly inattentive to its environment. And bureaucratic hierarchy pretty much ensures distortion and loss of information across the levels of hierarchy. Indeed, these are standard criticisms of bureaucracy as a problem-solving device, though such criticisms are usually couched in terms of a human environment, not a natural one. Markets can be just as autistic, if in different ways. Obviously, they respond only to *human, consumer* preferences that can be couched in *monetary* terms. Any market actor trying to take non-pecuniary factors into account is going to have its profitability, and so survival chances, damaged (this is not to gainsay the possibility of green consumerism). Conversely, the positive feedback of business growth (and the growth of the capitalist market in general) is guided by processes entirely internal to markets.

Above all, existing mechanisms merit condemnation to the extent that their size and scope do not match the size and scope of ecosystems and/or ecological problems. Under such circumstances, communications from or about particular ecological problems or disequilibria will be swamped by communications from other parts of the world. Here, markets that transcend ecological boundaries, which they increasingly do, merit special condemnation. The internationalisation and globalisation of markets make it that much easier to engage in local despoliation. It may be quite obvious that a local ecosystem is being degraded and destroyed, but 'international competitiveness' is a good stick with which to beat environmentalist critics of an operation. For example, they can be told that old growth forests must be clearcut, rather than logged selectively.

Obviously, some ecological problems are global, as are some markets. This does not of course mean that effective response mechanisms to global ecological problems can be found in global markets. Market autism guarantees that they cannot.

Turning to the desirable scope and shape of institutions suggested by the ideal of ecological democracy, the watchword here is 'appropriate scale'. In other words, the size and scope of institutions should match the size and scope of problems. There may be good reasons for the predispositions toward small scale in ecoanarchism and 'small is beautiful' green political thought. Most notably, feedback processes in natural systems are diffuse and internal (Patten and Odum 1981), and do not pass through any central control point. Highly centralised human collective choice mechanisms are not well-placed to attend to such diffuse feedback. Moreover, the autonomy and self-sufficiency advocated by green decentralisers can force improved perception of the natural world. To the degree that a community must rely on local ecological resources, it will have to take care of them. It does not follow that local self-reliance should be taken to an extreme of autarky. Rather, it is a matter of degree: the more the community is politically and economically self-reliant, then the more it must take care of its local ecosystems. Presumably the degree of self-reliance necessary to secure adequate care here depends a great deal on the level of environmental consciousness in the community in question. To the extent that environmental consciousness is lacking, then economic consciousness has to do all the work, so there are many places (such as resource-dependent local economies in the American West) where only autarky would do the trick.

But obviously not all ecological problems and feedback signals reside at the local level. Some of them are global, and hence demand global institutional response. There is no need in this scheme of things to privilege the nation-state, and every reason not to; few, if any, ecological problems coincide with state boundaries. There is only slightly greater reason to privilege bioregions. Bioregions are notoriously hard to define, and again many problems transcend their boundaries. For example, an airshed will not necessarily correspond with a watershed, and a single watershed may contain several radically different types of ecosystems. (I lived in the Columbia river basin, which contains both mid-continent deserts and coastal forests.)

Coordination through Spontaneous Order

An ecological democracy would, then, contain numerous and cross-cutting *loci* of political authority. The obvious question here is: how does one coordinate them, given that one cannot (for example) resolve air pollution problems while completely ignoring the issue of water pollution, or deal with local sulphur dioxide pollution while ignoring the long-distance diffusion of sulphur dioxide in acid rain? The way this coordination is currently accomplished is by privileging one level of political organisation. In unitary political systems, this will normally be the national state, though matters can be a bit more complicated in federal systems. The state (national or sub-national) will of course often contain an anti-pollution agency which (nominally, if rarely in practice) coordinates policy in regard to different kinds of pollutants. But, as I have already noted, this is an entirely artificial solution, and no more defensible than privileging the local community, or for that matter the global community.

The main conceivable alternative to privileging the state is to rely on the emergence of some spontaneous order that would somehow coordinate the actions of large numbers of bodies. One example of such an order is the market, especially as celebrated by von Hayek (Goodin 1992: 154). But markets, as noted, are not exactly an ecological success story. Nor are they much good at coordinating the activities of *political* authorities. Within decentralised political systems, coordination is achieved largely through the spontaneous order of partisan mutual adjustment, which to Lindblom (1965) is at the core of collective decision in liberal democracies. Such regimes may contain more formal and consciously-designed constitutions, but partisan mutual adjustment proceeds regardless of the content of such formalisms. This adjustment involves a complex mix of talk, strategy, commitment, and individual action devised in response to the context created by the actions of others. As I noted earlier, this kind of spontaneous order under liberal democracy leaves much to be desired when scrutinised in an ecological light.

Ecosystems, including the global ecosystem, are also examples of spontaneous order, so one might try to devise an imitation which included humans. Along these lines, Murray Bookchin (1982) attempts to develop a naturalistic justification for human political organisation. His eco-anarchist prescriptions might make some sense at the local level. But he can develop no *naturalistic* justification for the kinds of political order that would be needed to transcend localities, beyond relying on the spontaneous generation of structures whose specification is completely indeterminate (which is really no answer at all).

Let me suggest that there is a kind of spontaneous order which might perform the requisite coordinating functions quite well. Discussions in democratic theory are normally directed toward how the state, or state-analogues such as local governments and intergovernmental authorities, shall be constructed. What this focus misses is the possibility of democratisation *apart from* and *against* established authority (Dryzek 1996). This latter kind of democratisation is associated with the idea of a public sphere or civil society. Public spheres are political bodies that do not exist as part of formal political authority, but rather in confrontation with that authority. Normally, they find their identity in confrontation with the state (think, for example, of Solidarity in Poland in the early 1980s), though authority constituted at levels both higher and lower than the state can also be the object of their ire. Resistance here is often 'local' in the sense of being issue-specific. Such local resistance is celebrated by Michel Foucault, though he would not be interested in the constructive role for public spheres intimated here. The internal politics of public spheres is usually defined by relatively egalitarian debate, and consensual modes of decision making. Contemporary examples are afforded by new social movements, especially on behalf of feminism, ecology, and peace. Indeed, the green movement may be conceptualised in these terms—at least the parts of that movement that do not seek entry into the state through electoral politics.

Such public spheres fit well with communicative and deliberative models of democracy. But what do they have to do with coordination across geographical jurisdictions or functional issue area boundaries? The answer is that scope in these terms is unbounded and variable, possibly responding to the scope of the issue in question. To take a simple example, the environmental movement is now international, and organisations such as Greenpeace or Friends of the Earth International can bring home to particular governments the international dimension of issues, such as the consequences to Third World countries of toxic wastes exported by industrialised countries. Along these lines, Goodin (1992: 176–7) notes that green parties can assist in the 'coordination of international environmental policies', though as a green 'Realo' he appears to have only conventional party political participation in state politics in mind, rather than public spheres. To take another example, international public spheres constituted by indigenous peoples and their advocates can bring home to boycotters of furs in London or Paris the resulting economic devastation such boycotts imply for indigenous communities in the Arctic, which rely for cash income on trapping. A public sphere on a fairly grand scale was constituted by the unofficial Global Forum which proceeded in parallel with the United Nations Conference on Environment and Development in Rio in 1992. The point is that the reach of public spheres is entirely variable and not limited by formal boundaries on jurisdictions, or obsolete notions of national sovereignty. And they can come into existence, grow, and die along with the importance of particular issues. So, for example, it is entirely appropriate that the West European peace movement declined as cold war tensions eased in the 1980s.

Conclusion

In contemplating the kinds of communication that might ensure more harmonious coordination across political and ecological systems, there is an ever-present danger of lapsing into ungrounded idealism and wishful thinking. Yet green democracy is not an all-or-nothing affair, and it can constitute a process as well as a goal. As a goal, any such green democracy might appear very distant, given the seeming global hegemony of profoundly anti-environmental liberal democratic and capitalist ideas, celebrated by Francis Fukuyama (1992) as the end of history. But if the 'grow or die' system of capitalist democracy is ultimately unsustainable in the light of ecological limits, green democrats are well-placed to both hasten its demise and intimate political alternatives. This might not be a bad way to see history moving again.

Notes

For helpful comments. the author would like to thank the other participants in the Melbourne *Democracy and the Environment* Working Group, especially Robyn Eckersley, Freya Mathews, and Val Plumwood; Robert Goodin; David Schlosberg; and audiences at Griffith University's School of Australian Environmental Studies, Australian National University's Research School of Social Sciences, and the Ecopolitics VII conference.

1. Greater detail on these requirements may be found in Dryzek (1987).
2. Curiously enough, Fascism may do better than either liberalism or Marxism in the anti-anthropocentrism stakes; as Anna Bramwell (1989: 195–208) notes, the first green 'party' in Europe was actually a strand in Hitler's Nazi Party. But Fascism obviously takes us quite a long way from democracy, and the arguments of eco-authoritarians such as Robert Heilbroner and Garrett Hardin have been too thoroughly discredited to warrant any attention here.
3. This point should not be confused with the green spirituality advocated by deep ecologists, goddess worshippers, and others who see divinity in nature. The choice here is not between an inert nature on the one hand and a nature populated by wood nymphs, sprites, and goddesses on the other. Nor does a recognition of agency in the natural world

imply that its entities should be treated like human subjects.

4. Prince Charles may talk to his rhododendrons, but they do not talk back.

5. The Gaia hypothesis bears some resemblance to superorganismic and teleological treatments of ecosystem development, which have long been abandoned by most academic ecologists (except Eugene Odum), who are committed to more reductionist and stochastic models. But the superorganismic view lives on in the pages of *The Ecologist*.

6. Iris Marion Young points to the equal validity of greeting, rhetoric, and storytelling.

References

Alford, C. Fred (1985), *Science and the Revenge of Nature: Marcuse and Habermas* (Gainesville, FL: University Press of Florida).

Bookchin, Murray (1982), *The Ecology of Freedom: The Emergence and Dissolution of Hierarchy* (Palo Alto, Calif.: Cheshire).

Bramwell, Anna (1989), *Ecology in the 20th Century: A History* (New Haven: Yale University Press).

Burnheim, John (1985), *Is Democracy Possible?* (Cambridge: Cambridge University Press).

Dryzek, John S. (1987), *Rational Ecology: Environment and Political Economy* (Oxford: Basil Blackwell).

——(1990*a*), *Discursive Democracy: Politics, Policy, and Political Science* (Cambridge: Cambridge University Press).

——(1990*b*), 'Green Reason: Communicative Ethics for the Biosphere', *Environmental Ethics*, 12: 195–210.

——(1992), 'How Far Is It from Virginia and Rochester to Frankfurt? Public Choice as Critical Theory', *British Journal of Political Science*, 22: 397–417.

——(1996), *Democracy in Capitalist Times: Ideals, Limits, and Struggles* (Oxford: Oxford University Press).

Eckersley, Robyn (1992), *Environmentalism and Political Theory: Toward an Ecocentric Approach* (Albany, NY: State University of New York Press).

Ehrenfeld, David (1978), *The Arrogance of Humanism* (New York: Oxford University Press).

Fukuyama, Francis (1992), *The End of History and the Last Man* (New York: Free Press).

Goodin, Robert E. (1992), *Green Political Theory* (Cambridge: Polity).

Habermas, Jürgen (1984), *The Theory of Communicative Action*, i. *Reason and the Rationalization of Society* (Boston: Beacon).

——(1987), *The Theory of Communicative Action*, ii. *Lifeworld and System* (Boston: Beacon).

Held, David (1987), *Models of Democracy* (Cambridge: Polity).

Keller, Evelyn Fox (1983), *A Feeling for the Organism: The Life and Work of Barbara McClintock* (San Francisco: W. H. Freeman).

Lindblom, Charles E. (1965), *The Intelligence of Democracy: Decision Making Through Mutual Adjustment* (New York: Free Press).

Lovelock, James (1979), *Gaia: A New Look at Life on Earth* (Oxford: Oxford University Press).

Masters, Roger D. (1989), *The Nature of Politics* (New Haven: Yale University Press).

Mathews, Freya (1991*a*), *The Ecological Self* (Savage, Md.: Barnes & Noble).

——(1991*b*), 'Democracy and the Ecological Crisis', *Legal Service Bulletin*, 16 (4): 157–9.

Miller, David (1992), 'Deliberative Democracy and Social Choice', *Political Studies*, 40 (special issue): 54–67.

Patten, Bernard C., and Odum, Eugene P. (1981), 'The Cybernetic Nature of Ecosystems', *American Naturalist*, 118: 886–95.

Spragens, Thomas A., Jr. (1990), *Reason and Democracy* (Durham, NC: Duke University Press).

Weale, Albert (1992), *The New Politics of Pollution* (Manchester: Manchester University Press).

Worster, Donald (1985), *Nature's Economy: A History of Ecological Ideas* (Cambridge: Cambridge University Press).

Bibliography

Abbey, Edward (1975), *The Monkey Wrench Gang* (Philadelphia: J. B. Lippincott).

Ackerman, Bruce A., and Hassler, William T. (1981), *Clean Coal, Dirty Air: or How the Clean Air Act became a Multibillion-Dollar Bail-Out for High-Sulfur Coal Producers and What Should Be Done About It* (New Haven: Yale University Press).

Amy, Douglas J. (1987), *The Politics of Environmental Mediation* (New York: Columbia University Press).

Anderson, Terry L., and Leal, Donald R. (1991), *Free Market Environmentalism* (Boulder, Colo.: Westview).

Andruss, V., Plant, C., Plant, J., and Wright, E. (1990) (eds.), *Home! A Bioregional Reader* (Philadelphia: New Society).

Barnett, Harold J., and Morse, Chandler (1963), *Scarcity and Growth: The Economics of Natural Resource Availability* (Baltimore: Johns Hopkins University Press for Resources for the Future).

Beck, Ulrich (1992), *Risk Society: Towards a New Modernity* (London: Sage).

Beckerman, Wilfred (1974), *In Defence of Economic Growth* (London: Cape).

—— (1995), *Small is Stupid: Blowing the Whistle on the Greens* (London: Duckworth).

Bookchin, Murray (1980), *Toward an Ecological Society* (Montreal: Black Rose).

—— (1982), *The Ecology of Freedom: The Emergence and Dissolution of Hierarchy* (Palo Alto, Calif.: Cheshire).

—— (1986), *The Modern Crisis* (Philadelphia: New Society).

—— (1988), 'Social Ecology Versus Deep Ecology', *Socialist Review*, 18(3): 9–29.

—— (1990*a*), *The Philosophy of Social Ecology* (Montreal: Black Rose).

—— (1990*b*), *Remaking Society: Pathways to a Green Future* (Boston: South End Press).

—— and Foreman, Dave (1991), *Defending the Earth* (Boston: South End Press).

Bramwell, Anna (1994), *The Fading of the Greens: The Decline of Environmental Politics in the West* (New Haven: Yale University Press).

Brecher, Jeremy, and Costello, Tim (1994), *Global Village or Global Pillage: Economic Reconstruction from the Bottom Up* (Boston: South End Press).

Brown, George E. (1996), *Environmental Science Under Siege: Fringe Science and the 104th Congress* (Washington, DC: Office of Representative George E. Brown).

Bryant, Bunyan (1995) (ed.), *Environmental Justice: Issues, Policies, and Solutions* (Covelo, Calif.: Island Press).

—— and Mohai, Paul (1992) (eds), *Race and the Incidence of Environmental Hazards: A Time for Discourse* (Boulder, Colo.: Westview Press).

Bullard, Robert D. (1993) (ed.), *Confronting Environmental Racism: Voices from the Grassroots* (Boston: South End Press).

—— (1994) (ed.), *Unequal Protection: Environmental Justice and Communities of Color* (San Francisco: Sierra Club Books).

Catton, William R. (1980), *Overshoot: The Ecological Basis of Revolutionary Change* (Urbana: University of Illinois Press).

Christoff, Peter (1996), 'Ecological Modernisation, Ecological Modernities', *Environmental Politics*, 5: 476–500.

Clark, John (1990), *Renewing the Earth: The Promise of Social Ecology: A Celebration of the Work of Murray Bookchin* (London: Green Print).

Cole, H. S. D. (1973), *Models of Doom: A Critique of the Limits to Growth* (New York: Universe Books).

Dalton, Russell J., and Kuechler, Manfred (1990), *Challenging the Political Order: New Social and Political Movements in Western Democracies* (Cambridge: Polity).

Daly, Herman E. (1973) (ed.), *Toward a Steady-State Economy* (San Francisco: W. H. Freeman).

——(1992), 'Free Market Environmentalism: Turning a Good Servant into a Bad Master', *Critical Review*, 6: 171–83.

——and Townsend, Kenneth E. (1993) (eds.), *Valuing the Earth: Economics, Ecology, Ethics* (Cambridge, Mass.: MIT Press).

Danaher, Kevin (1997) (ed.), *Corporations Are Gonna Get Your Mama: Globalization and the Downsizing of the American Dream* (Monroe, Me.: Common Courage Press).

Devall, Bill, and Sessions, George (1985), *Deep Ecology: Living as if Nature Mattered* (Salt Lake City: Peregrine Smith).

Diamond, Irene, and Orenstein, Gloria Feman (1990) (eds), *Reweaving the World: The Emergence of Ecofeminism* (San Francisco: Sierra Club Books).

DiZerega, Gus (1993), 'Unexpected Harmonies: Self-Organization in Liberal Modernity and Ecology', *The Trumpeter*, 10: 25–32.

Doherty, Brian, and de Geus, Marius (1996) (eds.), *Democracy and Green Political Thought: Sustainability, Rights, and Citizenship* (London: Routledge).

Dowie, Mark (1995), *Losing Ground: American Environmentalism at the Close of the Twentieth Century* (Cambridge, Mass.: MIT Press).

Doyle, Timothy, and Kellow, Aynsley (1995), *Environmental Politics and Policy Making in Australia* (South Melbourne: Macmillan).

Eckersley, Robyn (1995) (ed.), *Markets, the State and the Environment: Towards Integration* (Melbourne: Macmillan).

Ehrlich, Paul (1968), *The Population Bomb* (New York: Ballantine).

Fischer, Frank, and Black, Michael (1995) (eds.), *Greening Environmental Policy: The Politics of a Sustainable Future* (New York: St Martin's Press).

Foreman, Dave, and Davis, John (1991), *The Earth First Reader: Ten Years of Radical Environmentalism* (Salt Lake City: Peregrine Smith).

Foster, John Bellamy (1994), *The Vulnerable Planet: A Short Economic History of the Environment* (New York: Monthly Review Press).

Fox, Warwick (1990), *Toward a Transpersonal Ecology: Developing New Foundations for Environmentalism* (Boston: Shambhala).

Georgescu-Roegen, Nicholas (1976), *Energy and Economic Myths: Institutional and Analytical Economic Essays* (New York: Pergamon Press).

Goldsmith, Edward, and the editors of *The Ecologist* (1972), *Blueprint for Survival* (Boston: Houghton-Mifflin).

Goodin, Robert E. (1992), *Green Political Theory* (Cambridge: Polity).

——(1996), 'Enfranchising the Earth, and its Alternatives', *Political Studies*, 44: 835–49.

Gorz, Andre (1980), *Ecology as Politics* (Boston: South End).

Gould, Kenneth A., Schnaiberg, Allan, and Weinberg, Adam S. (1996), *Local Environmental Struggles: Citizen Activism in the Treadmill of Production* (Cambridge: Cambridge University Press).

Gundersen, Adolf (1995), *The Environmental Promise of Democratic Deliberation* (Madison: University of Wisconsin Press).

Hajer, Maarten A. (1995), *The Politics of Environmental Discourse: Ecological Modernization and the Policy Process* (Oxford: Oxford University Press).

Hardin, Garrett (1993), *Living Within Limits: Ecology, Economics, and Population Taboos* (New York: Oxford University Press).

Hays, Samuel P. (1987), *Beauty, Health, and Permanence: Environmental Politics in the United States, 1955–1985* (Cambridge: Cambridge University Press).

Heilbroner, Robert (1991), *An Inquiry into the Human Prospect: Looked at Again for the 1990s* (New York: Norton).

Hofrichter, Richard (1993) (ed.), *Toxic Struggles: The Theory and Practice of Environmental Justice* (Philadelphia: New Society).

Jacobs, Michael (1991), *The Green Economy: Environment, Sustainable Development and the Politics of the Future* (London: Pluto).

Karliner, Joshua (1997), *Corporate Planet: Ecology and Politics in an Age of Globalization* (San Francisco: Sierra Club).

Kaufman, Herbert (1960), *The Forest Ranger: A Study in Administrative Behavior* (Baltimore: Johns Hopkins).

Kelman, Steven (1981), *What Price Incentives? Economists and the Environment* (Boston: Auburn House).

Lafferty, William, and Meadowcroft, James (1996) (eds.), *Democracy and the Environment: Problems and Prospects* (Cheltenham, UK: Edward Elgar).

Lappé, Frances Moore, and Collins, Joseph (1977), *Food First: Beyond the Myth of Scarcity* (Boston: Houghton-Mifflin).

Lee, Kai N. (1993), *Compass and Gyroscope: Integrating Science and Politics for the Environment* (Washington, DC: Island Press).

Lester, James P. (1995) (ed.), *Environmental Politics and Policy: Theories and Evidence*, 2nd edn. (Durham, NC: Duke University Press).

Lipschutz, Ronnie D. (1995), *Global Civil Society and Global Environmental Governance: The Politics of Nature from Place to Planet* (Albany: State University of New York Press).

Luke, Timothy (1995), 'Sustainable Development as a Power/Knowledge System: The Problem of Governmentality', in Frank Fischer and Michael Black (eds), *Greening Environmental Policy: The Politics of a Sustainable Future* (New York: St Martin's Press).

Mathews, Freya (1996) (ed.), *Ecology and Democracy* (Portland, Ore.: Frank Cass).

McGinnis, Michael (1998) (ed.), *Bioregionalism* (London: Routledge).

Meiners, Roger E., and Yandle, Bruce (1993) (eds.), *Taking the Environment Seriously* (Lanham, Md.: Rowman and Littlefield).

Melucci, Alberto (1989), *Nomads of the Present* (Philadelphia: Temple University Press).

Merchant, Carolyn (1980), *The Death of Nature: Women, Ecology, and the Scientific Revolution* (San Francisco: Harper and Row).

——(1989), *Ecological Revolutions: Nature, Gender, and Science in New England* (Chapel Hill: University of North Carolina Press).

Mies, Maria, and Shiva, Vandana (1993), *Ecofeminism* (London: Zed).

Mol, Arthur P. J. (1996), 'Ecological Modernisation and Institutional Reflexivity: Environmental Reform in the Late Modern Age', *Environmental Politics*, 5: 302–23.

Myers, Norman, and Simon, Julian L. (1994), *Scarcity or Abundance: A Debate on the Environment* (New York: Norton).

Naess, Arne (1989), *Ecology, Community and Lifestyle* (Cambridge: Cambridge University Press).

Ostrom, Elinor (1990), *Governing the Commons* (Cambridge: Cambridge University Press).

Paehlke, Robert (1989), *Environmentalism and the Future of Progressive Politics* (New Haven: Yale University Press).

——and Torgerson, Douglas (1990) (eds.), *Managing Leviathan: Environmental Politics and the Administrative State* (Peterborough, Ontario: Broadview).

Pearce, David, Markandya, Anil, and Barbier, Edward R. (1989), *Blueprint for a Green Economy* (London: Earthscan).

Plumwood, Val (1993), *Feminism and the Mastery of Nature* (London: Routledge).

Press, Daniel (1994), *Democratic Dilemmas in the Age of Ecology: Trees and Toxics in the American West* (Durham, NC: Duke University Press).

Ray, Dixy Lee (1993), *Environmental Overkill: Whatever Happened to Common Sense?* (Washington, DC: Regnery Gateway).

Redclift, Michael (1987), *Sustainable Development: Exploring the Contradictions* (London: Methuen).

Richardson, Dick, and Rootes, Chris (1995) (eds.), *The Green Challenge: The Development of Green Parties in Europe* (London: Routledge).

Rosenbaum, Walter A. (1985), *Environmental Politics and Policy* (Washington, DC: Congressional Quarterly Press).

Sagoff, Mark (1988), *The Economy of the Earth* (Cambridge: Cambridge University Press).

Sale, Kirkpatrick (1985), *Dwellers in the Land: The Bioregional Vision* (San Francisco: Sierra Club Books).

Scarce, Rik (1990), *Eco-Warriors: Understanding the Radical Environmental Movement* (Chicago: Noble).

Schlosberg, David (forthcoming), *Environmental Justice and the New Pluralism: The Challenge of Difference for Environmentalism* (Oxford: Oxford University Press).

Schmidheiny, Stephan (1992), *Changing Course: A Global Business Perspective on Development and the Environment* (Cambridge, Mass.: MIT Press).

Schnaiberg, Allan (1980), *The Environment: From Surplus to Scarcity* (Oxford: Oxford University Press).

Seed, J., Macy, J., Fleming, P., and Naess, A. (1988), *Thinking Like a Mountain: Towards a Council of All Beings* (Philadelphia: New Society).

Simon, Julian (1981), *The Ultimate Resource* (Princeton: Princeton University Press).

——(1995) (ed.), *The State of Humanity* (Oxford: Blackwell).

——and Kahn, Herman (1984) (eds.), *The Resourceful Earth: A Response to Global 2000* (New York: Basil Blackwell).

Snyder, Gary (1974), *Turtle Island* (New York: New Directions).

Stretton, Hugh (1976), *Capitalism, Socialism, and the Environment* (Cambridge: Cambridge University Press).

Szasz, Andrew (1994), *EcoPopulism: Toxic Waste and the Movement for Environmental Justice* (Minneapolis: University of Minnesota Press).

Taylor, Bron (1995) (ed.), *Ecological Resistance Movements* (Albany: State University of New York Press).

Tokar, Brian (1987), *The Green Alternative* (San Pedro, Calif.: R. & E. Miles).

United States Council on Environmental Quality and the Department of State (1981), *The Global 2000 Report to the President, Entering the 21st Century* (Charlottesville, Va.: Blue Angel, Inc.).

Vogel, David (1986), *National Styles of Regulation: Environmental Policy in Great Britain and the United States* (Ithaca, NY: Cornell University Press).

Wapner, Paul (1996), *Environmental Activism and World Civic Politics* (Albany: State University of New York Press).

Weale, Albert (1992), *The New Politics of Pollution* (Manchester: Manchester University Press).

Wildavsky, Aaron (1995), *But Is It True? A Citizen's Guide to Environmental Health and Safety Issues* (Cambridge, Mass.: Harvard University Press).

Williams, Bruce A., and Matheny, Albert R. (1995), *Democracy, Dialogue, and Environmental Disputes: The Contested Languages of Social Regulation* (New Haven: Yale University Press).

Yaffee, Steven Lewis (1994), *The Wisdom of the Spotted Owl: Policy Lessons for a New Century* (Washington, DC: Island Press).

Name Index